Public Law and Economics

Public Law and Economics

ROBERT D. COOTER
University of California, Berkeley

MICHAEL D. GILBERT
University of Virginia

OXFORD
UNIVERSITY PRESS

OXFORD
UNIVERSITY PRESS

Oxford University Press is a department of the University of Oxford. It furthers the University's objective of excellence in research, scholarship, and education by publishing worldwide. Oxford is a registered trade mark of Oxford University Press in the UK and certain other countries.

Published in the United States of America by Oxford University Press
198 Madison Avenue, New York, NY 10016, United States of America.

Library of Congress Cataloging-in-Publication Data
Names: Cooter, Robert D. author. | Gilbert, Michael D. (Law teacher), author.
Title: Public law and economics / Robert D. Cooter, Michael D. Gilbert.
Description: New York : Oxford University Press, [2022?] | Includes index.
Identifiers: LCCN 2022006743 (print) | LCCN 2022006744 (ebook) |
ISBN 9780197655887 (paperback) | ISBN 9780197655870 (hardback) |
ISBN 9780197655900 (epub) | ISBN 9780197655894 (updf) | ISBN 9780197655917 (online)
Subjects: LCSH: Law and economics. | Public law—Economic aspects—United States
Classification: LCC K487.E3 C6657 2022 (print) | LCC K487.E3 (ebook) |
DDC 343.07—dc23/eng/20220630
LC record available at https://lccn.loc.gov/2022006743
LC ebook record available at https://lccn.loc.gov/2022006744

DOI: 10.1093/oso/9780197655870.001.0001

Note to Readers

This publication is designed to provide accurate and authoritative information in regard to the subject matter covered. It is based upon sources believed to be accurate and reliable and is intended to be current as of the time it was written. It is sold with the understanding that the publisher is not engaged in rendering legal, accounting, or other professional services. If legal advice or other expert assistance is required, the services of a competent professional person should be sought. Also, to confirm that the information has not been affected or changed by recent developments, traditional legal research techniques should be used, including checking primary sources where appropriate.

(Based on the Declaration of Principles jointly adopted by a Committee of the American Bar Association and a Committee of Publishers and Associations.)

To Peter Hacker, my teacher and friend.
RDC

To Lisa, my mother, and the warm memory of my father.
MDG

Contents

Detailed Contents

List of Figures

List of Tables

List of Boxes by Chapter

Chapter 2. Theory of Bargaining

Chapter 3. Bargaining Applications

Chapter 4. Theory of Voting

Chapter 5. Voting Applications

Chapter 6. Theory of Entrenchment

Chapter 7. Entrenchment Applications

Chapter 8. Theory of Delegation

Chapter 9. Delegation Applications

Chapter 10. Theory of Adjudication

Chapter 11. Adjudication Applications

Chapter 12: Theory of Enforcement

Chapter 13: Enforcement Applications

Acknowledgments

This project germinated during a walk in Berkeley, California. Cooter expressed disappointment that *The Strategic Constitution*, a book he published in 2000, had not penetrated mainstream legal scholarship. Gilbert, a student of Cooter's and devotee of that book, suggested a follow-up focused less on economic theory and more on legal doctrine. Many years later, we are proud to present this work, which attempts to provide a comprehensive picture of public law and economics. We hope that readers will experience some of the delight (and none of the frustration) that we had in writing the book.

We have presented materials from the book to our students and colleagues at the University of California, Berkeley, and the University of Virginia. We have discussed ideas from the book at many conferences, including meetings of the American Law & Economics Association, Latin American and Caribbean Law and Economics Association, Law and Society Association, Midwest Law & Economics Association, and Midwest Political Science Association. We have presented some of this material at Duke Law School, Florida State University, Georgetown Law Center, the ICON-S Conference, the Maryland Carey Law Constitutional Law and Economics Workshop, the Political Economy and Public Law Conference, Pontificia Universidad Católica del Ecuador, Tel Aviv University School of Law, Universidad Científica del Sur, Universidad Espiritu Santo, Universidad San Francisco, Universidad Torcuato di Tella, the University of Chicago Law School, the University of Illinois at Champaign-Urbana, the University of Michigan Law School, and the University of San Diego Law School. In every setting we have received valuable feedback.

We owe special thanks to many scholars and friends who have improved our ideas by listening, discussing, and commenting on drafts of the manuscript: Charles Barzun, Josh Bowers, Álvaro Bustos, Kevin Cope, Quinn Curtis, Josh Fischman, Ivo Gico, Tom Ginsburg, John Harrison, Andrew Hayashi, Rich Hynes, Leslie Kendrick, Doug Laycock, Mike Livermore, Paul Mahoney, Richard McAdams, Greg Mitchell, Caleb Nelson, Dan Ortiz, Fred Schauer, Rich Schragger, Micah Schwartzman, Doug Spencer, Paul Stephan, Matthew Stephenson, Eduardo Stordeur, Pierre Verdier, and Mila Versteeg.

We could not have completed this project without exceptional research assistance from Jameil Brown, Alexandra Butler, Daniel Graulich, Connor James, Maya Kammourieh, Kevin Krotz, Lauren Lipsyc, Wilson Parker, and Yehonatan Shiman. Mauricio Guim did triple duty as research assistant, scholarly critic, and cheerleader. The librarians at the University of Virginia School of Law went above and beyond the call of duty to help with countless queries and requests. Gilbert gratefully acknowledges support from two research chairs at UVA Law, the Sullivan and Cromwell Professorship and the Martha Lubin Karsh and Bruce A. Karsh Bicentennial Professorship.

Our book builds on foundations laid by others. We draw on the pioneering work of Kenneth Arrow, Duncan Black, James Buchanan, Ronald Coase, Anthony Downs, Mathew McCubbins, Roger Noll, Mancur Olson, William Riker, Amartya Sen, Ken

Shepsle, Gordon Tullock, and Barry Weingast, among many others. We have learned much from the following works and are delighted to join them on the library shelf: *Law and Public Choice: A Critical Introduction* (1991) by Daniel Farber and Philip Frickey; *Constitutional Democracy* (1996) by Dennis Mueller; *Greed, Chaos, and Governance* (1997) by Jerry Mashaw; *Law and Economics: Private and Public* (2018) by Maxwell Stearns, Thomas Miceli, and Todd Zywicki; *Constitutional Economics: A Primer* (2020) by Stefan Voigt; and *An Economic Analysis of Public Law: Demos and Agora* (2021) by George Dellis.

1
Introduction to Public Law and Economics

King John and the barons negotiated the Magna Carta in 1215. Three thousand years earlier, Hammurabi enacted his famous code. Law is an ancient discipline. By comparison, economics is young. Adam Smith laid its foundation in 1776 with his masterpiece, *An Inquiry into the Nature and Causes of the Wealth of Nations*. Since then, economists have studied and influenced policy on many topics. During most of that time, however, economists have not studied or influenced law, at least not in the sense that lawyers use the term.

For lawyers, "law" means more than policy. Law encompasses constitutions, statutes, regulations, treaties, customs, and prior cases. Law involves certain forms of reasoning. To decide if a prior case governs the present case, lawyers reason by analogy. To determine rights and obligations, lawyers interpret law. Through interpretation, judges determine the meaning of law. Interpretation can lead to monumental decisions, as when the U.S. Supreme Court held that the Constitution prohibits racial segregation in public schools.[1] According to Alexander Hamilton, one of the Founders of the U.S. Constitution, "Laws are a dead letter without courts to expound and define their true meaning and operation."[2]

To resolve cases, judges apply law to facts. Prior to the 1960s, economists supplied the facts on some market-related topics. For example, economists might have estimated a company's market share for a case about antitrust law, or they might have calculated the wages lost by a worker injured in an accident. In cases like these, economists provided the inputs necessary for the operation of law, but little more.

Beginning in the 1960s, the relationship between economics and law changed dramatically.[3] Economics expanded into traditional areas of law, especially criminal law, property law, contract law, and torts (the law of accidents). Economists began asking questions like these: Which party to an accident should pay its costs? What is the efficient remedy for a breach of contract? Will harsher punishments deter more crime?

Economics changed the study and practice of law. Today the top law schools in many countries have economists on their faculties; joint degree programs (a Ph.D. in

[1] Brown v. Bd. of Ed. of Topeka, Shawnee Cnty., Kan., 347 U.S. 483 (1954). We use the Bluebook style of citation with minor exceptions, the main one being that we don't use short forms. This saves readers from hunting for complete citation information. For cases, the citation begins with the name of the case, followed by the volume of the reporter in which the case was published, the abbreviated name of the reporter, the page on which the case begins, and the year of decision. For articles, the citation begins with the author(s), followed by the name of the article, the volume number of the journal in which it appears, the abbreviated name of the journal, the first page of the article, and the year of publication. Citations for other kinds of work are self-explanatory.

[2] THE FEDERALIST NO. 22, at 112 (Alexander Hamilton) (Ian Shapiro ed., 2009).

[3] The birth of modern law and economics is usually traced to two articles: Ronald H. Coase, *The Problem of Social Cost*, 3 J.L. ECON. 1 (1960) and Guido Calabresi, *Some Thoughts on Risk Distribution and the Law of Torts*, 70 YALE L.J. 499 (1961).

Public Law and Economics. Robert D. Cooter and Michael D. Gilbert, Oxford University Press. © Oxford University Press 2022.
DOI: 10.1093/oso/9780197655870.003.0001

economics and a degree in law) exist at many prominent universities; law reviews routinely publish articles using economics; and several journals devote themselves exclusively to the field. Many areas of law, such as corporate law and bankruptcy, are taught from a law-and-economics perspective. In the United States, prominent law-and-economics scholars have become judges. Professional organizations on law and economics exist in Asia, Europe, North America, South America, and elsewhere. Two economists who helped found the field, Ronald Coase and Gary Becker, received the Nobel Prize in Economics.

Economic analysis has enjoyed remarkable success in law. However, it still has room to grow. Lawyers divide law into two parts, private and public. Private law involves private relationships among individuals. When a homeowner hires a painter, private law governs their agreement. When a driver injures a pedestrian, private law resolves their dispute. Public law involves the state. Public law establishes the powers of government and fundamental rights like speech and religion. Public law regulates war, pollution, immigration, elections, discrimination, education, and health.

Most work in law and economics addresses private law. The economic analysis of private law has exerted enormous influence on legal scholarship and teaching. By comparison, the economic analysis of public law has not. We do not mean that scholars have not written in this area. Many important works apply economics to topics in public law. We will discuss many of those works in this book. Outside of criminal law, however, economics has had limited influence on public law scholarship and pedagogy. When teaching constitutional law, legal scholars do not usually think of economic analysis. When arguing cases about elections, lawyers do not ask, "What do economists say about voting?" When interpreting statutes, judges do not use economic models.

We believe that economics can illuminate public law in the same way that it has illuminated private law. This book attempts to show how and why. Our ambition is to make public law and economics as influential as its private law counterpart.

To explain the potential of economics in public law, we begin by discussing its roots. Economic analysis of law proceeds in three modes: positive, normative, and interpretive. Positive theory predicts when laws arise and how people respond to them. Normative theory evaluates laws using different conceptions of efficiency. Interpretive theory ascertains the meaning of law. We will elaborate briefly on each mode.[4] Although we have strived for clarity, some readers might find this discussion a little daunting. Beginning in the next chapter and continuing throughout the book, we will work through the ideas step by step.

I. Positive Law and Economics

Lawmakers make laws to achieve certain objectives. To illustrate, legislators lower the speed limit to slow traffic, and regulators cap emissions to reduce pollution. To achieve these objectives, law usually must influence the behavior of people.

[4] Our discussion draws on Robert D. Cooter & Michael D. Gilbert, *Constitutional Law and Economics*, *in* Research Methods in Constitutional Law: A Handbook (Malcolm Langford & David S. Law eds., Forthcoming).

Thus, the behavior of people is usually relevant to making, revising, repealing, and interpreting law. Economics provides a theory of behavior. The theory relies on three concepts: preferences, maximization, and equilibrium. We will briefly explain each.[5]

Economists assume that people can rank the benefit or "payoff" to themselves from different outcomes. Thus, a consumer can rank goods—gourmet coffee, leather shoes, smartphones, electric cars, and chocolate cake. A politician can rank offices—town council, governor, member of Congress, and President. A college student can rank careers—business that promises wealth, or art that gives pleasure. "Utility function" is the technical name that economists give to a preference ranking. Sometimes utility functions involve complicated math. However, the idea behind utility functions is simple. As a person better satisfies her preferences, her payoff or "utility" increases.

Preference rankings must fulfill some formal conditions.[6] However, economics does not assume anything about the reasons for a preference ranking. The values underlying a person's preferences might include pleasure, love, status, happiness, wealth, power, altruism, or justice. People's actual preferences are complicated and difficult to measure. To simplify the analysis, economists make assumptions. In business, economists often assume that people care only about money. Economic models of material self-interest are often simple and compelling. However, the analysis need not end there. Immaterial values—political philosophies, moral commitments, religious beliefs—influence people too.

Having discussed preferences, we consider their satisfaction. Each person wishes to satisfy her preferences to the greatest extent. When alternatives are ranked, a rational person chooses the highest-ranking alternative. Given boundless opportunities, everyone would fully satisfy their preferences. In reality, opportunities are limited. People have imperfect information, and we face many constraints, including time and money. Economists assume that people satisfy their preferences as best they can given their beliefs and constraints. To make specific predictions, economists use the mathematics of maximization.

Utility maximization often provides a good model for predicting how people will behave. However, the model is imperfect. Real people are psychological, not purely logical. Many people err when making choices, especially when facing novel situations and time pressure. Whereas traditional economics anticipates "full rationality," real people exhibit "diminished rationality." Cognitive psychologists and behavioral economists study diminished rationality. Incorporating diminished rationality into economic models improves their predictions.

So far, we have concentrated on individuals' behavior. Next, we consider how individuals interact. A social interaction tends to persist when no individual can increase her satisfaction by changing behavior, given that others do not change their behavior. Everyone maximizes simultaneously. This characteristic defines an "equilibrium." If others drive on the right side of the road, I cannot increase my satisfaction by driving on the left side of the road. Driving on the left would cause an accident, decreasing my

[5] Readers can find fuller introductions to microeconomic analysis in many sources, including Robert Cooter & Thomas Ulen, Law and Economics (6th ed. 2016).

[6] The usual list has three conditions: reflexivity, completeness, and transitivity.

satisfaction. Everyone reasons this way, so everyone drives on the right side of the road. Driving on the right is an equilibrium.

Law creates incentives, and people respond to them. Positive incentives create opportunities to increase preference satisfaction, as when a constitution protects political expression. Negative incentives create opportunities to avoid preference frustration, as when a law punishes discrimination. Economics specializes in predicting incentive effects. It predicts these effects by combining utility maximization for individuals and equilibria for groups.

Economics cannot model human behavior perfectly. However, its models are accurate enough to be useful when predicting the causes and effects of many laws.

II. Normative Law and Economics

"Positive" economics makes predictions without evaluating. To illustrate, when economists predict the amount of coal burned, the number of cars produced, and the pounds of potatoes eaten, they conduct positive analysis. In contrast, "normative" economics evaluates. Should we increase the minimum wage, subsidize solar energy, or forbid high-interest loans? To answer questions like these, economists conduct normative analysis. Normative analysis involves values.

Economists usually focus on one value: efficiency. Most people prefer efficiency to inefficiency. The fact that one law achieves a goal more efficiently than another is usually an argument in its favor, regardless of the law's topic. Economists rely on three standards of efficiency: Pareto efficiency, cost-benefit efficiency, and social welfare.

A change in law is Pareto efficient if someone supports it and no one opposes it. This standard of efficiency does not cause much controversy. If someone prefers the new law and no one opposes it, most people would agree that we should enact the new law. Unfortunately, Pareto efficiency is not very useful. Nearly every law has at least one supporter. How else could a law get enacted in the first place? If a law has even one supporter, then changing it is not Pareto efficient. If we only make Pareto-efficient changes to law, then we will not make many changes. Laws that nearly everyone hates will remain in place.

To move beyond Pareto efficiency, we can inquire into magnitudes. We can assess whether a change in law helps beneficiaries more than it harms others. To illustrate, consider a ban on high-interest loans. The ban will benefit consumers who get tricked by predatory lenders. However, it will harm some consumers who lose access to credit. The ban is not Pareto efficient because one or more people oppose it (consumers who lose access to credit). However, the ban might be cost-benefit efficient. Cost-benefit analysis might compare the money saved by the first group of consumers to the money lost by the second. Specifically, it might compare the first group's willingness to pay to enact the law and the second group's willingness to pay not to enact the law. The ban is cost-benefit efficient if the first group is willing to pay more.

Cost-benefit efficiency helps economists evaluate many laws. However, it has shortcomings. Among other features, it often gives equal weight to rich and poor. A law that creates a one-dollar loss for the poor and a two-dollar gain for the rich is cost-benefit efficient. Sometimes equal weighting of dollars makes sense. Other times, however, equal weighting does not make sense.

Public law often makes equality a goal. When equality is a goal, we might set aside cost-benefit efficiency and concentrate on social welfare. Social welfare aggregates the utility functions of all individuals in society.[7] We achieve "social welfare efficiency" by maximizing aggregate utility.

Social welfare can account for inequalities. A poor person uses money to satisfy urgent needs, such as food, shelter, and clothing. A rich person uses money to satisfy wants, such as entertainment and leisure. When he gets even more money, he buys luxuries—fine food in restaurants, designer clothing, and international vacations. According to a long tradition in philosophy, the utility that a person gets from an additional dollar decreases as he gets more money. Receiving $1,000 increases the utility of a poor person by more than it increases the utility of a rich person. Social welfare accounts for this. Moving money from rich to poor does not increase the total amount of money in society. However, it might increase social welfare.

Social welfare provides a powerful framework for assessing many laws. It can accommodate a variety of commitments that people hold, including commitments to equality.

III. Interpretive Law and Economics

Positive theory predicts law's effects, and normative theory evaluates them. These modes of analysis are familiar to all economists, including those who do not study law. Together these activities constitute much of law and economics. However, they do not constitute all of it. Sometimes scholars deploy a third mode of analysis that we consider especially interesting and that we develop throughout the book: interpretive law and economics. This mode of analysis does not predict or evaluate law's effects. It identifies law's meaning.

Laws impose obligations on people. Clients pay lawyers to advise them on their obligations. Lawyers tell people what the law requires them to do. What the law requires people to do is the law's content, or the law's meaning, or an account of the law itself.

Sometimes a lawyer can tell a person what the law requires by reciting a statute, regulation, or other official document. However, most legal documents require more than recitation. They require interpretation. To interpret law, jurists draw on various sources including the text of the law, the intent of lawmakers, and the history of the law, including prior cases about it. Jurists find law's meaning by reasoning about diverse sources. The practice of law requires mastering legal reasoning, not just remembering rules. Legal reasoning is a humanistic discipline expressed in legal practice and theory and learned by legal education and experience.

Interpretive law and economics merges the humanistic discipline of law and the social science of economics. Combining different methodologies can seem confusing. Economic reasoning does not always resemble legal reasoning. Proof in law does not resemble proof in an economics journal. However, combining the two disciplines is rewarding. Economics can increase rigor in legal reasoning, and legal reasoning can increase the relevance of economics to public life.

[7] In its simplest formulation, social welfare is the sum of the utility of all individuals. In more complicated formulations, social welfare is some other function of the utility of all individuals.

Economics can aid interpretation in different ways that we will elaborate throughout the book. Here we sketch one way. The purpose of a law often provides an important source in interpretation. Laws have various purposes, such as preserving liberty, increasing equality, reducing discrimination, and protecting endangered species. Sometimes the correct interpretation of a law is the one that best fulfills its purpose. Whether an interpretation fulfills the law's purpose depends in part on the incentives it creates. Economics specializes in incentives. By identifying the incentives that will best fulfill a law's purposes, economics can help with interpretation.

To illustrate, consider tort law. If a person behaves negligently and causes an accident, she is often liable for the harm. What does it mean to behave "negligently"? According to a common account, the purpose of tort law is to protect people from unreasonable risks imposed by others. Thus, a person is negligent when she imposes unreasonable risks. What constitutes an unreasonable risk? Economists help answer by comparing costs and benefits. Specifically, they compare the marginal costs of additional precautions against accidents and the marginal benefits of reduced risk. If a person fails to take a precaution for which the marginal benefit exceeds the marginal cost, he acts negligently. This is not a normative argument about what negligence ought to be. It's an interpretive argument about what negligence *is*. Interpreting negligence this way incentivizes people to take cost-justified precautions.

The purpose of some laws is efficiency. For such laws, the normative and interpretive modes of analysis generally yield the same conclusions. The efficient reading of the law (normative) is the legally correct reading of the law (interpretive). This overlap makes interpretive law and economics easy to overlook. However, many laws have purposes other than efficiency. For such laws, the normative and interpretive modes of analysis diverge. Economists might be tempted to follow the normative road. Lawyers and judges care about the interpretive road, so we will try throughout the book to follow it. One of our main objectives is to develop interpretive law and economics.

IV. Making Economics Relevant to Public Law

We have summarized the three modes of analysis used in law and economics. Scholars have successfully deployed these modes (especially the positive and normative modes) in private law. However, these modes have not enjoyed the same success in public law. Why? We offer three hypotheses.

First, as described earlier, economics emphasizes efficiency as the proper measure of social value. Efficiency seems like a natural value to prioritize in many areas of private law. Parties to a contract do not want to leave value on the table. No one wants to waste money on unnecessary precautions against accidents. The connection between efficiency and contract law, property law, and torts helps explain the success of economics in those subjects. In public law, the connection is weaker. Many public laws do not seem to involve efficiency. People doubt the relevance of economics to topics such as human rights, discrimination, and constitutional interpretation.

Second, scholarship on public law and economics tends to be technical. Economics journals overflow with game theory, calculus, statistics, and specialized language.

Economists study abstract models, and they usually write for other economists, not for nonexperts. For many jurists, the work is impenetrable.

Third, much research on public law and economics focuses on institutions. Scholars study the design of courts, agencies, and legislatures. They contrast presidential, parliamentary, and autocratic regimes. They measure the effect of property rights on economic growth. These topics are very interesting and important. However, they're mostly irrelevant to legal practice. Most legal practice does not involve institutional design. In court, judges do not ask the lawyers, "How many chambers should the legislature have?", "Should the agency be independent of politics?", or "Are federal states more corrupt than unitary states?" In sum, much economic research on public law does not address the concerns of jurists.

In this book, we attempt to remedy these problems. Regarding efficiency, we consider Pareto and cost-benefit efficiency, but we also consider social welfare. Social welfare provides a measure of social value that does not focus exclusively on wealth and that can accommodate commitments like equality. Furthermore, we do not assume that public law aims to maximize efficiency in any sense. We allow for the possibility that law can have other objectives such as justice. Whatever a law's objective, lawmakers usually must change people's behavior to achieve it. Changing behavior requires good incentives. By studying incentives, economists can make valuable contributions to law, whatever its purpose.

Regarding technicality, we strive throughout the book to provide clear and straightforward explanations of ideas. We use many graphs, but we mostly avoid math (and we avoid calculus entirely). We rely on only simple game theory. Our aim is to make public law and economics accessible to nonexperts. The book should be suitable for teaching advanced undergraduates, law students, and perhaps graduate students in political science, public policy, and related disciplines. We hope the book will provide a resource for scholars as well.

Regarding relevance, we devote attention in every chapter to concrete questions in law. For example, we consider cases about federalism, voter fraud, free speech, racial discrimination, and police searches. We study constitutions, statutes, and judicial precedents. We compare methods of interpretation like textualism and intentionalism. Throughout the book, we try to show the applicability of economics to the questions of lawyers. Like the existing literature, we also discuss questions of institutional design. The economic analysis of legal institutions can inform the work of jurists, as we will try to show.

V. Organization of the Book

Public law encompasses everything from the separation of government powers to seat belts. Given the range, we cannot organize the book around substantive legal subjects. Instead, we organize the book around processes. Public law relates to six fundamental processes of government: bargaining, voting, entrenching, delegating, adjudicating, and enforcing. These processes make, sustain, amend, and implement public law. We devote two chapters to each process. The first chapter in each pair presents economic theory. We divide the theory chapters into three parts: positive, normative, and interpretive.

The second chapter in each pair presents applications. Here we briefly summarize the chapters.

Chapter 2 addresses bargaining. Bargaining pervades government, so it comes first in our analysis. We present the positive theory of bargaining, explaining concepts like efficiency and distribution. We develop the Private Coase Theorem, which is familiar from private law, and the Public Coase Theorem, which applies to actors like legislators, administrators, and judges. Turning to normative theory, we explain when bargaining by public law actors is likely to benefit or harm the public. We also explain concepts like utility and social welfare. In our interpretive analysis, we apply economics to questions about the "intentions" of lawmakers. Chapter 3 applies the theory of bargaining to topics in public law including regulations, the separation of powers, and Article I, Section 8, of the U.S. Constitution, which divides power between the federal government and the states.

Chapter 4 addresses voting, which is ubiquitous in public law. This chapter begins with the positive theory of voting. We consider why people vote and when abstention is rational. Then we present the median voter theorem. Turning to normative theory, we explain the relationship between the median voter theorem, efficiency, and social welfare. Our interpretive analysis introduces the "median theory of interpretation." This theory provides a way to interpret laws enacted by casting separate votes on separate issues, as when voting on ballot initiatives. Chapter 5 applies the theory of voting to issues in public law. Among other topics, we address the right to vote, political communities, campaign finance, and gerrymandering.

Chapter 6 presents the theory of entrenchment. Many laws are "entrenched," meaning they are especially difficult to change. We show how entrenchment creates an "equilibrium set" within which law remains fixed. We explore the conditions under which entrenched law can change and how small or large such changes are likely to be. Turning to normative analysis, we consider justifications for entrenchment. The conventional justifications involve protecting minority rights and promoting stability. We conclude with interpretive analysis, relating the economic theory of entrenchment to judicial precedent and the doctrine of stare decisis. Chapter 7 applies these ideas to topics in public law, especially constitutional law. Our topics include equality, the freedom of speech, and conflicts among rights. This chapter concludes by contrasting two methods for modernizing rights, constitutional amendments and judicial "updating."

Chapter 8 addresses delegation. The delegation of power—from the President to administrators, from citizens to legislators, and so on—is central to public law. This chapter begins with the positive theory of delegation. We analyze the trade-offs principals face when deciding whether to delegate authority, and we consider whether principals should guide their agents using "rules" or "standards." Turning to normative theory, we consider the circumstances under which delegation benefits principals, agents, and the general public. Finally, we consider interpretive theory. Lawyers and judges routinely ask whether a statute grants an agency the power to take a particular action. We develop the "delegation canon," which helps answer that question. Chapter 9 applies the theory of delegation to legal topics like judicial review of agency action, the nondelegation doctrine, void for vagueness, and bribery laws.

Chapter 10 presents the theory of adjudication. Courts sit at the heart of public law, and economists have analyzed many aspects of the judicial process. We start with the positive theory of adjudication. We examine how litigants determine the value of their claims and whether they settle or litigate. We discuss trials and appeals, and we relate these processes to economic tools like Bayesian updating and the Condorcet Jury Theorem. Then we turn to judicial behavior. We consider the legal, attitudinal, and strategic models of judging. Turning to normative theory, we analyze the trade-off between accuracy in adjudication and the costs of fact-finding and interpretation. Finally, we present an incentive principle of interpretation. According to this principle, a law's correct interpretation creates incentives that best fulfill its purpose. Chapter 11 applies these ideas to legal topics. We address theories of interpretation, prophylactic rules, scrivener's errors, and the development of precedent.

Chapter 12 presents the theory of enforcement. We begin with a positive theory of enforcement by the state. We discuss deterrence, the probability of enforcement, and the severity of punishment. We also discuss fines, imprisonment, and enforcement costs. Turning to normative theory, we consider the circumstances under which enforcement benefits the public. Finally, we consider interpretive theory. We analyze the doctrine of "coercive contempt," which empowers courts to enforce their orders. Chapter 13 applies these ideas to topics in public law. We address police searches, the exclusionary rule, qualified immunity, and standards of proof. We also show how law can change people's behavior without threatening punishment, as when it supplies information and coordinates action. We conclude with a venerable question: When will the state comply with its own laws?

People advise writers to "write what you know." We know law in the United States better than law elsewhere, so our chapters mostly concentrate on law in the United States. However, the six fundamental processes of government are universal, as is the economic analysis of those processes. Many of the U.S. laws that we address resemble laws elsewhere. We hope that our book will have value for students and scholars worldwide.

* * *

In 1973, Richard Posner published the first edition of *The Economic Analysis of Law*. His book sketched the contours of the burgeoning field. Since then, many other books have provided a comprehensive picture of law and economics with a focus on private law.[8] These books serve as teaching tools. Every year they introduce thousands of students, lawyers, and judges to the economic analysis of law. These books also serve as resources for scholars. Thousands of scholarly works cite and build upon them. These books unify and organize private law and economics. We hope our book will unify and organize public law and economics.

[8] *See, e.g.*, A. Mitchell Polinsky, An Introduction to Law and Economics (5th ed. 2018); Maxwell L. Stearns, Todd Z. Zywicki, & Thomas J. Miceli, Law and Economics: Private and Public (2018); Robert Cooter & Thomas Ulen, Law and Economics (6th ed. 2016); Steven Shavell, Foundations of Economic Analysis of Law (2004).

2
Theory of Bargaining

Bargaining pervades government—warring nations negotiate peace, rival parties amend the constitution, two houses of Congress reconcile different bills, judges haggle over a decision, and so on. Because bargaining pervades government, it comes first in our analysis. We apply to public law the same theory of bargaining that economists apply to goods. We show that lawmakers bargain with each other because successful bargains can benefit them, just as trading stamps can benefit collectors. A successful bargain among officials concludes in lawmaking or other acts to create mutual benefit. This logic applies to legislators, regulators, and even judges.

Besides explaining the creation or "supply" of public law, bargaining can explain "demand" for public law. Successful private bargaining reduces the pressure to make law. If a nightclub agrees to abate noise, its neighbors do not seek noise ordinances. Conversely, *unsuccessful* private bargaining *increases* pressure to make law. If the nightclub and its neighbors fail to agree, the neighbors seek noise ordinances. Whether private parties agree among themselves or officials make new law depends on which group can strike a deal. To strike a deal, parties must overcome obstacles to bargaining.

These ideas illuminate fundamental questions in public law, including the following:

Example 1: When and why do legislators trade votes to enact laws?

Example 2: Most legislators cut deals—you vote for my bill, and I will vote for yours. In contrast, professional norms prohibit judges from trading votes across cases. When should people bargain across issues like most legislators, and when should they vote their conscience like most judges?

Example 3: Congress sues the President, regulators sue manufacturers, and citizens sue police. Most legal disputes settle out of court, but some go to trial. Why do some disputes settle and others litigate?

Example 4: At the U.S. Constitutional Convention, populous states wanted *people* represented in Congress (states with more citizens get more representatives). In contrast, small states wanted *states* represented (equal number of representatives per state). The "Great Compromise" resulted in representation of people in the House of Representatives and representation of states in the Senate. It has endured for over 200 years. Meanwhile, Congress rewrites the budget every year. Why do some political bargains persist and others change?

To answer these questions, this chapter begins with the positive theory of bargaining, turns to normative consequences, and concludes by showing how bargaining can aid in the interpretation of laws.

Public Law and Economics. Robert D. Cooter and Michael D. Gilbert, Oxford University Press. © Oxford University Press 2022.
DOI: 10.1093/oso/9780197655870.003.0002

I. Positive Theory of Bargaining

Bargaining usually mixes two activities: production and distribution. *Production* refers to the creation of value. *Distribution* refers to the allocation of value among people. To distinguish production and distribution, we consider two pure bargaining situations: games of pure distribution, and games of pure production.

A. Conflict versus Cooperation

George Washington wrote, "[W]e must consult our means rather than our wishes."[1] Lawmakers confront this reality every time they engage in a fundamental activity of government: budgeting. Consider bargaining by legislators over how to spend the state's budget. If the total budget is fixed, then each dollar spent on one project is a dollar that cannot be spent on another. Allocating expenditures on projects is a zero-sum game, like poker. For one player to win, another must lose; wins and losses sum to zero. Since value gets distributed but not produced, allocating items in a fixed budget is a game of *pure distribution*.

Games of pure distribution are often unstable, as players make and unmake coalitions to secure more for themselves. Imagine three legislators bargaining over how to spend $100 on three projects (A, B, C). The first legislator would prefer to spend everything on project A ($100, $0, $0). The second legislator would prefer to spend everything on project B ($0, $100, $0). The third legislator would prefer to spend everything on project C ($0, $0, $100).[2] The legislature operates under majority rule, meaning any coalition of two legislators can determine how to spend the money. They begin bargaining with a proposal to divide the money equally among the projects ($33, $33, $33). Then the first legislator proposes spending equally on the first two projects and none on the third project ($50, $50, $0). This proposal commands a majority of votes—2 to 1—over the original proposal. As another alternative, the third legislator proposes cutting out the first project and spending on the second and third projects ($0, $75, $25). This proposal commands a majority of votes—2 to 1—over the preceding proposal. Among the three proposals, each one beats one and loses to one.

For every proposal, a counterproposal exists that two legislators prefer.[3] Consequently, there is no stable majority. The legislators run in circles as they haggle, and they may never reach agreement. The problem lies in the distributive nature of the game, not the specific proposals. Pure distribution games risk indefinite squabbling. To make sure that squabbling eventually ends, law restricts it. For example, some state constitutions impose deadlines on legislators to agree on a budget.[4]

[1] Letter from George Washington to the Marquis de Lafayette (Oct. 30, 1780), *in* 20 The Writings of George Washington 266–67 (John C. Fitzpatrick ed., 1937).

[2] Here is a fuller statement of the legislators' preferences: each would prefer to spend more money on his or her own project and less on the others.

[3] We assume the legislators are symmetrical: they each have the same number of votes (one), none has more control over the agenda than others, and so forth. Under these assumptions, the contest for distribution destabilizes every possible coalition. We return to this kind of instability in later chapters.

[4] *E.g.*, Cal. Const. art. IV, § 12(c)(3) ("The Legislature shall pass the budget bill by midnight on June 15 of each year.").

Opposite from games of pure distribution are games of pure production, or *coordination games*. A coordination game produces value without creating any conflict over its distribution. The interests of all players converge.[5] The best plan for anyone is best for everyone. To illustrate, imagine a group of motorists deciding whether to drive on the left or right side of the road. The drivers do not care which side they drive on as long as they all make the same choice. Moving from a noncooperative solution (they drive on different sides) to a cooperative one (they drive on the same side) produces value for all drivers (more safety and speed). Pure coordination games help to explain compliance with some laws. For example, the "Treaty of the Metre" establishes uniform methods of measurement that many countries follow, even though the treaty lacks an enforcement mechanism.

In games of pure production, coordination succeeds if the parties can communicate. If drivers approaching one another on a dirt road can exchange text messages, they will agree to swerve right or left to avoid an accident. With obstacles to communication, however, coordination may fail. Consider the width of railroad tracks. To connect railway lines, all tracks should have the same width. However, coordination is sometimes difficult. Countries in South America did not coordinate when building railroads, leading to tracks of different width in different places. In contrast, railroad tracks in the U.S. state of Utah connect seamlessly to tracks in the state of Nevada, thanks in part to the Pacific Railroad Acts. Coordination over tracks in the United States avoids the problem of some tracks in South America. Tracks connect in the United States because one central government can coordinate more easily than many separate governments.

Questions

2.1. Driving in Haiti can be chaotic and dangerous. Levy Azor, "a freelancer with a passion for order" but no legal authority, successfully directed traffic at a major intersection. He worked for tips. Suppose Azor favored drivers who tip. Why might non-tipping drivers still follow his signals?[6]

2.2. Three legislators begin with the following payoffs: (20, 20, 60). After bargaining, their payoffs will be either (50, 50, 0) or (45, 35, 20). Are the legislators playing a game of production or distribution?

2.3. Medicaid is a congressional program that gives money to the states to spend on medical care for the poor. Spending on Medicaid is "mandatory," not "discretionary," meaning that the allocation of money to the states follows set formulas.[7] What problems does Congress avoid by making Medicaid spending mandatory instead of discretionary?

2.4. The Uniform Law Commission (ULC) is a nonprofit organization in the United States that drafts model statutes on topics where uniformity across the states is

[5] *See* Thomas C. Schelling, The Strategy of Conflict (1960).

[6] *See* Damien Cave, *The Rhapsody of Port-au-Prince's Streets*, N.Y. Times, June 3, 2010; Richard McAdams, The Expressive Powers of Law 23–24 (2015).

[7] 42 U.S.C. § 1396b(a).

desirable. States can enact the model statutes, or modified versions of them, if they choose. What kind of game among states does the ULC help solve?

B. Mixed Bargains

Instead of being pure, most bargaining games are mixed: they involve production and distribution. The parties can cooperate and produce, provided they can agree on distribution. We explain these elements in public law by using an example. Criminals who violate federal law in the United States go to federal prison, and criminals who violate state law go to state prison. Sometimes one system becomes overcrowded, as when federal officials arrest more drug suspects than their prisons can hold. In that event, the federal government pays states a "jail-day rate" to house detainees. The jail-day rate expresses the value of a jail cell in money, just like market prices for automobiles, toothpaste, or insurance.

Adam is the warden of a state prison with extra cells, and he has authority to house federal prisoners. For safety, he prefers to keep his prison below capacity. Translating into money, the value he places on keeping some cells empty equals $3,000. Blair works for the U.S. Marshals Service. She would prefer to transfer some federal detainees to Adam's prison rather than overcrowd the federal facility. She has a budget of $5,000 and authority to negotiate the jail-day rate. Let's assume the value she places on transferring the detainees equals $4,000. Since Adam values the cells less than Blair, there is scope for a bargain. Adam will not accept less than $3,000, and Blair will not pay more than $4,000. The jail-day rate will have to be somewhere in between.[8]

Some technical language clarifies the logic of this example. The parties have engaged in a *bargaining game*, which means communication that may yield an agreement. The *noncooperative solution* occurs if the parties cannot agree. In that case, Adam's prison remains below capacity, which is worth $3,000 to him. Also, if the parties cannot agree, then Blair retains the $5,000 in her budget to spend on something other than Adam's extra cells. The *noncooperative payoffs* equal $3,000 to Adam and $5,000 to Blair.[9]

The players' noncooperative payoffs are called *threat values*. Here's why. In the course of bargaining, Adam and Blair may assert facts ("The detainees are violent"), appeal to norms ("$3,700 is an unfair price"), and make threats ("I won't take less than $3,500"). The economic theory of bargaining focuses on the credibility of threats.

Adam and Blair both can make credible threats. Without Blair's cooperation, Adam's prison remains below capacity, which he values at $3,000. He can credibly threaten not to cooperate unless the price equals $3,000 or more, so his threat value is $3,000. Similarly, Blair starts with $5,000, so she can credibly threaten to walk away unless she gets more than that from the deal. Her threat value is $5,000. If the parties fail to cooperate, Adam keeps his value from the empty cells of $3,000, and Blair keeps her budget of $5,000.

To generalize, a credible threat demands no more than the actor can obtain without the other's cooperation. The payoff that the first actor can obtain without the second

[8] This game draws on ROBERT COOTER & THOMAS ULEN, LAW AND ECONOMICS 74–76 (6th ed. 2016).

[9] We assume that the value to Blair of the money equals its face value.

actor's cooperation is the first actor's noncooperative payoff. Thus, a credible threat asks for no more than the threatener's noncooperative payoff. The sum of the threat values is the *noncooperative value of the game*. In the case of Adam and Blair, the noncooperative value equals $8,000.

By bargaining successfully, Adam and Blair can reallocate a resource (empty prison cells) from someone who values it less (Adam) to someone who values it more (Blair). With cooperation, Blair receives her use-value of the cells, which is $4,000. To use the cells, Blair pays some of her $5,000 to Adam. For the sake of example, let's assume she pays him $3,600. Adam's *cooperative payoff* equals $3,600. Blair's cooperative payoff equals her use-value of the cells ($4,000) plus her remaining money ($1,400), so $5,400. Thus, $9,000 equals the sum of the cooperative payoffs and the *cooperative value* of the bargaining game.

Notice that the cooperative value of the game is $9,000 and the noncooperative value is $8,000. The *cooperative surplus* equals the amount by which the game's cooperative value exceeds its noncooperative value. In this example, cooperation produces a surplus of $1,000.

In addition to producing a surplus, bargaining determines its distribution between the parties. The price distributes the surplus from cooperation, but it usually does not affect the total amount of the surplus. For example, if Adam and Blair agree on a price of $3,600 as described earlier, then Adam gets $600 of the surplus and Blair gets $400 of the surplus. Alternatively, if the price is $3,800, Adam gets $800 of the surplus and Blair gets $200. In both cases the surplus equals $1,000.

Neither party will accept a bargain with a smaller payoff than his or her threat value. Rationality requires the parties to agree to a price between $3,000 and $4,000, as any price in that range will benefit both parties relative to noncooperation. However, the exact price on which the parties will agree is unpredictable. If Blair offers $3,100, Adam may storm away, even though accepting would leave him better off than not cooperating. Similarly, if Adam demands $3,900, Blair may refuse, even though accepting would make her better off than not cooperating.

The distribution of the cooperative surplus is unpredictable because it depends partly on psychology, not purely on rationality. Although the exact bargain is unpredictable, bargaining theory provides a useful rule of thumb. A *reasonable distribution* gives each player an equal share of the cooperative surplus. Applied to this case, the cooperative surplus equals $1,000, so Adam and Blair should each get $500. To divide the surplus in this way, Blair must pay Adam $3,500 for the cells. To generalize, the reasonable distribution requires each party to receive his or her threat value plus half of the cooperative surplus.[10]

In game theory, an equal division of the surplus is called the "Nash bargaining solution."[11] The Nash bargaining solution combines the economic concept of rationality and the legal concept of reasonableness.

[10] If Blair pays Adam $3,500, Adam receives his threat value of $3,000 plus $500, half of the surplus. Blair gets the cells, which she values at $4,000, and she has $1,500 left over, for a total payoff of $5,500. This equals her threat value of $5,000 plus $500, half of the surplus.

[11] The idea traces to John F. Nash Jr., *Equilibrium Points in N-Person Games*, 36 PROC. NAT'L ACAD. SCI. 48 (1950).

In sum, when the player who owns a resource values it less than another player, the difference in value creates scope for a bargain. Moving resources from one person to another produces value when the person who receives the resource values it more than the person who gives it up. They can create a surplus if they can agree on its distribution. Bargaining has three elements: establish threat values, determine the cooperative surplus, and distribute the surplus. The threat values and cooperative surplus depend on rationality alone. Distribution of the surplus depends on psychology and other factors. A distribution is "reasonable" in our sense if each player receives his threat value plus an equal share of the surplus. The reasonable distribution predicts the price, although not perfectly.

Questions

2.5. In the example of Adam and Blair, how is the surplus distributed if the price equals $3,700?

2.6. In the example of Adam and Blair, explain why the price cannot fall to $2,500.

2.7. Like Blair, suppose that a third party wants empty cells. Adam receives a bid of $3,200 from the third party. How does the third-party's bid change the threat values, the surplus from cooperation, and the Nash bargaining solution in negotiations between Adam and Blair?

Settle or Litigate?

Bargaining theory illuminates many aspects of law, including the choice to settle or litigate.[12] Consider this example. The state alleges that the Contamination Corporation illegally discharged toxic chemicals into a river, harming fish. The fine for doing so equals $300,000. The facts are confusing. The corporation contends that it did not discharge chemicals; even if it did discharge chemicals, they were not toxic; and even if the chemicals were toxic, they did not kill the fish.

Because of the confusing facts, neither side is confident about its prospects in court. Instead, each party believes that it has a 50 percent chance of winning (and therefore a 50 percent chance of losing). Litigating will cost each party $50,000, while settling out of court will cost nothing. Cooperation in this case means settling out of court and saving the cost of litigation. Noncooperation means going to court and spending money on litigation.

Assume that the state, like the corporation, wants more money rather than less. The state's threat value equals its expected payoff from noncooperation. We can calculate this with math: if the state goes to court, it has a 50 percent chance of winning $300,000 and a 50 percent chance of winning nothing, and it will pay $50,000

[12] For an early analysis, see John P. Gould, *The Economics of Legal Conflicts*, 2 J. LEGAL STUD. 279 (1973). *See also* Robert H. Mnookin & Lewis Kornhauser, *Bargaining in the Shadow of the Law: The Case of Divorce*, 88 YALE L.J. 950 (1979).

in litigation costs. Hence, its threat value equals $100,000. By the same logic, the corporation's threat value equals –$200,000.[13]

Already, we see how bargaining theory provides guidance in settlement negotiations. The state gains by accepting any settlement offer greater than $100,000, and the corporation gains by offering a settlement up to $200,000. If the parties cooperate, they will save $100,000 in litigation costs, so the cooperative surplus equals $100,000. The reasonable settlement would give each party its threat value plus half the surplus, meaning the corporation would settle with the state for $150,000.

C. Vote Trading

The value produced by successful bargaining is often expressed in money, as in the example of Adam and Blair. Instead of money, however, bargaining in public law often involves a different currency: votes.[14] Turn on the video cameras and the legislature might resemble a high-minded debating society. Turn off the cameras and the legislature resembles Istanbul's Grand Bazaar, with politicians trading votes the way merchants trade rugs.

Here is an example of bargaining over votes involving two members of a city council, Caleb and Dee. Caleb proposes spending more money on public schools. Dee will cast the tie-breaking vote on Caleb's proposal, so he needs her vote to pass it. Similarly, Dee proposes spending more money on police. Caleb will cast the tie-breaking vote on Dee's proposal, so she needs his vote to pass it. Each one would prefer for his or her proposal to pass and for the other's proposal to fail. Will they make a deal and pass both measures? Or will they fail to agree and pass neither measure, thus maintaining the status quo?

Let's formulate the problem in terms of the city council's budget. Caleb proposes to raise taxes by $100,000 and to spend it on a school gym. Dee proposes to raise taxes by $50,000 and to spend it on hiring another policeman. If Caleb and Dee agree, expenditures on schools will rise by $100,000, expenditures on police will rise by $50,000, and taxes will rise by $150,000. In order to agree, Caleb and Dee must each prefer the full package of expenditures and taxes to the status quo.

Unlike the previous example, this one has a constraint: the choices are "lumpy," not smooth. The parties cannot build a fraction of a gym for, say, $80,000. Nor can they hire a police officer and a half for, say, $75,000. With lumpy choices, an agreement may give one party a disproportionate share of the surplus, without the possibility of transferring some of it to the other party. Consequently, the parties cannot split the surplus from cooperation equally as required by the Nash bargaining solution. Even so, reasonable parties will cooperate and divide the surplus unequally among themselves.

[13] Here is the calculation for the state's threat value: 0.5(300,000) + 0.5(0) – 50,000 = 100,000. Here is the calculation for the corporation's threat value: 0.5(–300,000) + 0.5(0) – 50,000 = –200,000.

[14] The germinal analysis of vote trading is JAMES M. BUCHANAN & GORDON TULLOCK, THE CALCULUS OF CONSENT: LOGICAL FOUNDATIONS OF CONSTITUTIONAL DEMOCRACY (1962).

Questions

2.8. Is there scope for a bargain if Caleb gains less from a school gym than he loses from hiring an extra policeman?

2.9. If Caleb does not get his school gym, his career will not suffer. If Dee does not get her extra policeman, her constituents will vote her out of office. Who has the upper hand in negotiations, Caleb or Dee? Can you express this idea using the language of threat values?

2.10. For Caleb and Dee to split the surplus equally, one must make a *side payment* to the other. Here are examples of side payments: Dee gets Caleb's parking spot at city hall, Caleb gets Dee's vote on a future issue, or Dee gives Caleb a bag of cash. Should law allow side payments like these?

2.11. Wisconsin law prohibits legislators from trading votes, but it permits "agreements to compromise conflicting provisions of different measures."[15] If one measure funds schools but not police, and if the other measure funds police but not schools, does a compromise that funds both violate Wisconsin's law?

D. Sphere of Cooperation

Vote trading pervades the institutions of public law—international bodies, legislative committees, regulatory agencies, citizen commissions, and even courts. Sometimes the law extends the sphere of trading, as when states create an international body like the United Nations and allow delegates to trade votes. Conversely, sometimes the law prohibits vote trading, as with judges on a panel deciding a case. Next, we discuss the advantages and disadvantages of extending or reducing the sphere of vote trading.

Consider the extension of the sphere of trade in private goods. Moving a resource from someone who values it less to someone who values it more increases total value. Value is maximized when the resource goes to the person who values it most. To maximize value, sellers must have access to many buyers, and vice versa. The widest sphere of cooperation encompasses all buyers and sellers, maximizing the potential gains from bargaining and trade.

To illustrate, before the Second World War, the countries of Europe imposed tariffs on the flow of goods among them. Each tariff benefited some industries in the country that imposed it, but taken as a whole tariffs prevented resources from going to their highest-value users, which harmed European economies. After the Second World War, the tariffs were gradually abolished to create a common market. Wider trading benefited all European economies (but not every individual in every country).[16]

[15] Here is the complete text of the statute: "Nothing in ss. 13.05 and 13.06 shall be construed as prohibiting free discussion and deliberation upon any question pending before the legislature by members thereof, privately or publicly, nor as prohibiting agreements by members to support any single measure pending, on condition that certain changes be made in such measure, nor as prohibiting agreements to compromise conflicting provisions of different measures." Wis. Stat. Ann. § 13.07 (West 2022).

[16] Behind this assertion rests a theorem stating that narrow trading groups are Pareto inefficient compared to wider trading groups. *See* Kenneth J. Arrow & Frank Hahn, General Competitive Analysis (1st ed. 1971).

The advantage of wide trading in markets for goods and services presumably applies to politics. For centuries, the countries of Europe pursued national policies. Many of these policies benefited the enacting country and harmed other countries. The conflicts escalated out of control, resulting in devastating wars. After the Second World War, Europeans formed a political union to widen the sphere of political bargaining, just as the common market widened the sphere of economic bargaining. The European Union brought political benefits, notably peace, just as the common market brought an economic benefit, prosperity.

Like increasing the number of parties, increasing the number of issues widens the sphere of cooperation. To illustrate by a preceding example, instead of making independent decisions about schools and police, Caleb and Dee bargained across them and created a surplus. Likewise, members of Congress can create a surplus by bargaining across issues such as highways, fighter jets, food stamps, school funding, and health care. The advantages of wide scale and scope in bargaining argue in favor of global trade and government.

Another consideration, however, argues against global trade and government. An advantage of smaller states is that bargaining is easier within each one. As the sphere of bargaining gets smaller, fewer people participate, making it easier to reach an agreement. Thus, bargaining is easier in a town council than in Congress, and bargaining is easier in Congress than in the United Nations. Recently, proponents of Britain's exit from the European Union ("Brexit") asserted that a smaller, more homogeneous polity would be more agile in regulating business.

We will often compare the gains from wider cooperation against the costs of reaching wider agreement.

Questions

2.12. In 2002, the United States created the Department of Homeland Security, a federal agency comprising over 20 smaller agencies that used to be separate, like the Immigration and Naturalization Service and the U.S. Coast Guard. From the viewpoint of bargaining, what is the advantage of combining those smaller agencies?

2.13. The U.S. House of Representatives, which has 435 members, has a "germaneness" rule. The rule requires amendments to address the same subject as the underlying bill. The U.S. Senate, which has 100 members, has no such rule. Why?

E. Private Coase Theorem

Bargaining has *transaction costs*, such as renting a conference room, spending time in negotiations, and drafting an agreement. As transaction costs fall, the probability of a successful bargain usually increases. Conversely, as transaction costs rise, the probability of a successful bargain usually decreases.

To illustrate, assume that a nightclub cannot operate after midnight unless a neighbor waives her right to quiet. By operating after midnight, the nightclub would earn $500, and the neighbor would suffer a loss from noise that she values at $100. If the neighbor and the nightclub owner cannot bargain—perhaps they speak different languages, or perhaps they are engaged in a bitter divorce—then the nightclub will close at midnight. If they can bargain, the nightclub could pay the neighbor for permission to operate, say, $300. Consequently, the neighbor would net $200 ($300 in cash less $100 in harm from noise), and the nightclub would net $200 ($500 in earnings less $300 paid to the neighbor). Both parties prefer this deal to no deal.

In this example, the nightclub and the neighbor reach a private agreement in which one pays the other to waive her right to quiet. Bargaining achieves mutual gain by allocating the legal entitlement—control over noise after midnight—to the party who values it more, the nightclub. If the transaction costs of bargaining are zero, we expect parties like the nightclub and the neighbor to reach such agreements.

In one of the most famous law articles of all time, Ronald Coase discussed examples like this one.[17] Commentators formulated his arguments as the *Coase Theorem*.[18] The theorem asserts that *bargains will allocate legal entitlements to the parties who value them most, provided that transaction costs do not impede the bargaining process*. The theorem is positive, meaning it makes predictions about how people behave.

The Coase Theorem deserves much thought and discussion. Consider one of Coase's examples. Imagine two neighbors, a farmer who grows corn and a rancher who keeps cows. Without a fence, the cows will trample the corn, causing $50 in damage. A fence will prevent trampling. The farmer can fence the cows out of the crops, or the rancher can fence the cows inside the pasture. It costs the farmer $10 to fence the cows out, and it costs the rancher $20 to fence the cows in. The difference in fencing cost is due to the shorter perimeter of the farm and the longer perimeter of the ranch.

Who will build the fence? If the legal rule is "open range," meaning the rancher is not responsible for damage caused by the cows, then the farmer will build the fence. The farmer would rather pay $10 for a fence than lose $50 in trampled corn.

What if the rule is "closed range," meaning the rancher is liable for damage caused by the cows? One might expect the rancher to build the fence, which costs him $20. But Coase showed that this behavior is irrational, so the prediction may be wrong. The farmer can build the fence for $10. If the transaction costs of bargaining are zero, the farmer and rancher will strike a deal under which the rancher pays the farmer to build the fence. For example, the rancher might pay the farmer $15. After building the fence, the farmer would gain $5 ($15 from the rancher, minus $10 to build the fence), and the rancher would spend $15, which is better than spending $20 to build the fence himself—and much better than paying $50 in damages for trampled corn.

Bargaining theory makes this reasoning precise. If the rule is closed range, and if the parties do not cooperate, the rancher pays $20 for the fence and the farmer pays $0. The noncooperative value of the game is the sum of these threat values, −$20. If the parties cooperate, the rancher pays some amount to the farmer, call it x, and $0 for the fence. The farmer receives x from the rancher and pays $10 for the fence. The cooperative value of the game is the sum of the parties' payoffs when they cooperate: $-x + x - \$10 = -\$10$. The cooperative surplus is the difference between −$10 and −$20, which

[17] Ronald H. Coase, *The Problem of Social Cost*, 3 J.L. ECON 1 (1960).
[18] *See, e.g.*, Robert Cooter, *The Cost of Coase*, 11 J. LEGAL STUD. 1 (1982).

is \$10.[19] If the parties agree to a reasonable division of the surplus, the rancher pays the farmer \$15, and the farmer builds the fence.[20]

In this example, the farmer can build at lower cost and bargaining leads him to do so, regardless of the legal rule. If transaction costs are zero, the farmer builds whether the legal rule is open range or closed range. What happens when high transaction costs prevent bargaining? Without exchange, the law's initial allocation of rights is the final allocation. If the rule is open range, the farmer will build the fence at a cost of \$10. But if the rule is closed range and high transaction costs preclude a bargain, the rancher will build the fence at a cost of \$20.

Similarly, consider the nightclub example when bargaining fails. Given failed bargaining, the club owner and the neighbor enforce their rights rather than exchanging them. The law could give the nightclub the right to play music, in which case it will earn \$500 and the neighbor will lose \$100. Or the law could give the neighbor the right to quiet. In that case, assuming no bargaining, the nightclub owner will forego earning \$500 and the neighbor will avoid harm of \$100.

Examples like these illustrate an important generalization. *When transaction costs are zero, law affects distribution but not production.* If the nightclub and the neighbor can bargain easily, the law does not affect whether the nightclub operates and creates net \$400 in value (it does). The rule only affects the parties' payoffs. Conversely, *when transaction costs are high, law determines distribution and production.*[21] If the nightclub and the neighbor cannot bargain, the law determines whether the nightclub operates, and it determines the parties' payoffs.

Questions

2.14. In the preceding example, suppose the legal rule is "open range," meaning the rancher is not liable for harm caused by the cows. Will the parties bargain over who builds the fence? Why or why not?

2.15. Suppose building the fence would cost the farmer \$18 instead of \$10 and the legal rule is "closed range." Everything else in the example remains the same. In negotiations between the farmer and the rancher, what is the Nash bargaining solution?

2.16. In the nightclub example, what are the payoffs to the club owner and the neighbor if the transaction costs are high and the club has a right to play music? What are the payoffs if the transaction costs are high and the neighbor has a right to quiet?

[19] To be clear, –\$10 – (–\$20) = \$10.

[20] The reasonable solution requires each party to get his or her threat value plus half the surplus. The rancher gets –\$20 + \$5, or –\$15, and the farmer gets \$0 + \$5, or \$5. Both prefer this to noncooperation.

[21] The italicized generalizations refer to the efficiency of production, not the quantity of production. The difference is usually unimportant. To illustrate, the law on whether the range is open or closed affects the relative wealth of the farmer and rancher. Consequently, the law might affect the demand for goods, in terms of prices and quantities. Suppose the rancher prefers to eat beef and the farmer prefers to eat corn. A rule of open range might result in more wealth for the rancher and thus more demand for beef, whereas a rule of closed range may result in the opposite. Differences in demand for beef and corn might imply different placement of fences. The law affects where fences are placed but not the efficiency of their placement.

2.17. Apartment owners in New York City discovered plans to build a tower next door. The tower would block their views of the Empire State Building. The owners paid $11 million to buy the "air rights" to the neighboring lot, preventing the construction of the tower.[22] Who had the law on their side, the owner of the lot or the owners of the apartment? Was building the tower efficient?

Bargaining and Norms

Do parties actually bargain as the Coase Theorem implies? Robert Ellickson studied interactions between farmers and ranchers in Shasta County, California.[23] The legal rule varied between open and closed range. Ellickson found that changes in the law did not affect fencing decisions, just as the Coase Theorem would predict when transaction costs are low. However, the parties did not explicitly bargain around the law. Instead, they obeyed social norms, according to which ranchers kept their cows under control to avoid negative gossip and injury to their animals.

This research led to a vigorous inquiry by economists into the evolution of social norms. In general, informal social norms and formal legal rules can increase production and solve distribution problems. When the transaction costs of social interactions are low, social norms may produce good results with little help from formal law. For example, family firms whose members are in close social relationships may not need much help from formal law to coordinate their behavior. However, when transaction costs of social interactions are high, social norms may produce bad results unless helped by formal law. For example, real estate transactions involve such large sums of money that informal mechanisms like reputation and boycott cannot prevent wrongdoing. Buying a house involves a complicated ritual. In general, failures in social norms require legal remedies, just as failures in markets require regulatory remedies.[24]

F. Public Coase Theorem

The Private Coase Theorem concerns bargains over private goods—fences, insurance, computers, cars, and so on. What about bargains over public laws? Bargaining over laws occurs among executives, legislators, regulators, administrators, committee members, commissioners, lobbyists, interest groups, and even some judges. Like collectors trading stamps, lawmakers trade support to benefit themselves. Consequently, we can reformulate the Coase Theorem for application to public laws. *The Public Coase Theorem asserts that as the transaction costs of bargaining among lawmakers approach zero, they will cooperate with each other and allocate public entitlements to the lawmakers who value*

[22] J. David Goodman, *How Much Is a View Worth in Manhattan? Try $11 Million*, N.Y. Times, July 22, 2019.
[23] Robert C. Ellickson, Order Without Law (1991).
[24] Robert Cooter, *The Normative Failure Theory of Law*, 82 Cornell L. Rev. 947, 949 (1997).

them the most. To illustrate by the example of Caleb and Dee, if transaction costs are sufficiently low, they will trade votes and provide greater funding for their preferred programs, schools and police.

To clarify the theorem, consider one more example. Caleb and Dee gain by pushing their legislation on schools and police through the city council. Expressed in money, Caleb gains $100,000 and Dee gains $50,000. In contrast, Graham, a third member of the city council, opposes the proposals. Expressed in money, Graham will lose $250,000 if the proposals get enacted. Thus, enacting the proposals would create a net loss of $100,000. If the transaction costs of bargaining are zero, Graham will pay Caleb and Dee *not* to enact their legislation. For example, he could do a favor for Caleb (e.g., vote for a future bill) valued at $140,000 and a favor for Dee (e.g., appoint her to a powerful committee) valued at $60,000. Caleb and Dee prefer Graham's offers to enacting their proposals. And Graham prefers his offers, which cost him $200,000, to enacting the proposals, which would cost him $250,000.[25] All parties are better off. Instead of enacting the proposals and destroying $100,000 in value, the parties bargain to a mutually beneficial outcome.

In this example, three officials bargain to benefit themselves, but what about their constituents? Do citizens benefit when their leaders cut deals? We will return to this question later in the chapter.

Taken together, the private and public forms of the Coase Theorem have an implication for lawmaking: private bargains and public laws often substitute as solutions to problems of cooperation. Consider the example of the noisy nightclub and the neighbor. If they can bargain privately, they will cooperate by making a private agreement—say, the nightclub pays the neighbor, and the neighbor does not complain about noise. If they cannot bargain privately, the neighbor may demand noise restrictions from the city council.

Here is another example. Emily owns a cement factory, and Frank owns an adjacent farm. Dust from Emily's factory contaminates Frank's crops, and Frank's tractors congest the road, impeding Emily's trucks. If the transaction costs of private bargaining are low, Emily and Frank may strike a deal under which Emily reduces dust and Frank reduces congestion. If the transaction costs of private bargaining are high and the parties fail to reach an agreement, Frank may demand pollution regulations and Emily may demand congestion regulations.

These examples yield a generalization: *successful private bargaining decreases the pressure for new laws, and failed private bargaining increases the pressure for new laws*. To illustrate, consider a Supreme Court case called *Masterpiece Cakeshop, Ltd. v. Colorado Civil Rights Commission*.[26] A gay couple asked a baker to make a cake for their wedding. The baker refused because of his religion. Does the couple's right to equal treatment trump the baker's right to (discriminatory) religious beliefs? The answer depends on the meaning of the Constitution, which is contested. If the couple and the baker had resolved their disagreement privately, the Supreme Court would not have gotten the case.

[25] To simplify, we assume that the cost to Graham of doing the favors equals the benefits to Caleb and Dee of receiving the favors.

[26] 138 S. Ct. 1719 (2018).

In fact, the parties failed to resolve their disagreement, so the Supreme Court got the case. The baker won. We will say more about this case later in the book.

Questions

2.18. Beginning in 2018, the U.S. government "shut down" for 35 days because Congress and the President could not agree on immigration policy. After the President relented, a bill to reopen the government passed in Congress within hours.[27] Use the Public Coase Theorem to analyze the shutdown.

2.19. During his first term, President Barack Obama threatened to veto bills containing "earmarks," spending measures tacked onto other legislation, like a $500,000 grant to the Teapot Museum.[28] Throughout Obama's presidency, Congress found it difficult to compromise.[29] Can you relate the President's threat to compromising in Congress?

2.20. In a monetary economy, people trade with money, as when the nightclub pays the neighbor in cash. In a barter economy, people trade with goods and services, as when the nightclub pays the neighbor by giving her free admission to concerts. Does bargaining among legislators resemble a monetary or barter economy? Which economy has higher transaction costs?

Everyday Politics?

Rod Blagojevich, the former governor of Illinois, was convicted of 18 crimes. His most sensational crime involved the U.S. Senate. When Barack Obama left the Senate to become President of the United States, Blagojevich had the power to name his replacement (Obama was a Senator from Illinois). Blagojevich offered the Senate seat to an Obama ally in exchange for money or a position in Obama's Cabinet, like Secretary of Labor. Obama refused, and Blagojevich was convicted of extortion and corruption.

Blagojevich appealed his convictions, and he succeeded on one count. The instructions to the jury did not distinguish Blagojevich's demand for money from his demand for a Cabinet appointment. Jurors were told that both demands were prohibited. However, a federal court disagreed, holding that the two demands were "legally different: a proposal to trade one public act for another, a form of logrolling, is fundamentally unlike the swap of an official act for a private payment."[30] The court continued:

[27] Jacob Pramuk, *Trump Signs Bill to Temporarily Reopen Government After Longest Shutdown in History*, CNBC, Jan. 25, 2019, https://www.cnbc.com/2019/01/25/senate-votes-to-reopen-government-and-end-shutdown-without-border-wall.html.

[28] Bill Marsh, *Pork Under Glass? Small Museums and Their Patrons on Capitol Hill*, N.Y. Times, Apr. 30, 2006.

[29] Niki Papadogiannakis, *Laws Plummet in Post-Earmark Era*, The Hill, Oct. 15, 2014.

[30] United States v. Blagojevich, 794 F.3d 729, 734 (7th Cir. 2015).

> [A] quid pro quo [occurs when] a public official performs an official act (or promises to do so) in exchange for a private benefit, such as money. . . . A political logroll, by contrast, is the swap of one official act for another. Representative A agrees with Representative B to vote for milk price supports, if B agrees to vote for tighter controls on air pollution. A President appoints C as an ambassador, which Senator D asked the President to do, in exchange for D's promise to vote to confirm E as a member of the National Labor Relations Board. Governance would hardly be possible without these accommodations, which allow each public official to achieve more of his principal objective while surrendering something about which he cares less, but the other politician cares more strongly.
>
> A proposal to appoint a particular person to one office (say, the Cabinet) in exchange for someone else's promise to appoint a different person to a different office (say, the Senate), is a common exercise in logrolling. We asked the prosecutor at oral argument if, before this case, logrolling had been the basis of a criminal conviction in the history of the United States. Counsel was unaware of any earlier conviction for an exchange of political favors. Our own research did not turn one up. It would be more than a little surprising to Members of Congress if the judiciary found in [federal criminal law] a rule making everyday politics criminal.[31]

Blagojevich spent many years in prison, but not for demanding a position in Obama's Cabinet. That conviction was overturned. Did the court make the right decision? Is logrolling just "everyday politics?"

G. Coase Theorem as a Rule of Thumb versus Law of Nature

To put our discussion of the Coase Theorem in perspective, we contrast rules of thumb and laws of nature. To make a simple generalization, the Coase Theorem extends the meaning of "transaction costs" to encompass all obstacles that cause bargaining to fail. By this definition, bargaining *must* succeed as transaction costs approach zero, so the theorem becomes true by definition. A proposition that is true by definition of its words is a tautology, like "all husbands are married." Regarded as a tautology, the Coase Theorem is a truth about language.[32]

Alternatively, regarded as a factual proposition, the Coase Theorem is a rule of thumb about behavior. As transaction costs fall, more extensive bargaining is easier and agreement is more likely. However, some obstacles to bargaining are persistent and agreement is never certain.

What obstacles to bargaining are persistent? Strategy is one. The best move by one player in a bargaining game often depends on another player's strategy, and vice versa.[33] Strategy is the essence of games among people. Instead of having simple solutions,

[31] *Id.* at 735.

[32] A long literature addresses whether the Coase Theorem is tautological. *See, e.g.*, Douglas W. Allen, *The Coase Theorem: Coherent, Logical, and Not Disproved*, 11 J. Inst. Econ. 379 (2015).

[33] Sometimes the best strategies involve randomizing, and sometimes the best strategies have multiple equilibria without a rational way to choose among them. A *Nash equilibrium* exists if no player wants to

strategic games are usually complicated, as everyone who watches sports or chess knows. By treating strategy as a transaction cost, the Coase Theorem reduces complicated game theory to what economists call "price theory," which is much simpler. This simplification makes the Coase Theorem useful.

To illustrate, contrast price taking and price making.[34] Shoppers who purchase milk at the listed price in a grocery store are price takers. Price taking is relatively simple and determinate. In contrast, a buyer of a used car makes a price by negotiating with the seller. Price making involves strategic behavior, which is hard to model and predict.

The Coase Theorem is a rule of thumb because its assumptions eliminate strategy, which simplifies the analysis while remaining approximately accurate. Bargaining usually succeeds as transaction costs approach zero, but not always. The Coase Theorem is not a law of nature like Newton's law of universal gravitation.

II. Normative Theory of Bargaining

Like collectors trading coins, lawmakers trade votes for mutual gain. Throughout the institutions of public law—international bodies, legislative committees, regulatory agencies, citizen commissions, and even courts—bargaining benefits the participants. However, parties to bargains in public law are mostly officials, not citizens. Is political bargaining good or bad for the public? Earlier we explained that bargaining produces and distributes value. Efficiency and distribution are two policy values that influence politics and dominate economics. We can use them to assess political bargaining.

A. Efficiency

As formulated earlier, the Coase Theorem makes a positive prediction: bargains will allocate legal entitlements to the parties who value them the most, provided that transaction costs do not impede the exchange. Now consider this prediction's normative significance. When entitlements belong to the people who value them the most, their allocation is *efficient*. Consequently, the Coase Theorem can be restated in terms of efficiency: bargaining allocates legal entitlements efficiently among the bargainers when transaction costs are zero.

To illustrate by the jail example, bargaining moves entitlement to the empty cells from Adam, who values them less, to Blair, who values them more. After movement stops, Adam and Blair have the entitlements that they value most. Consequently, the allocation is efficient with respect to Adam and Blair.[35]

change his strategy, given the strategy of other players. *See* John Nash, *Non-Cooperative Games*, 54 ANNALS OF MATHEMATICS 286 (1951). Multiple Nash equilibria are common in bargaining games.

[34] In a perfectly competitive market, there is no room to bargain. Participants are price takers, accepting market prices as given. Price taking eliminates strategic behavior. Conversely, in imperfectly competitive markets there is room to bargain. Participants try to get a larger share of the surplus from cooperation by getting the best price from others. Participants are price makers.

[35] Efficiency comes in different forms. *Pareto efficiency* is achieved when no change to the existing allocation of entitlements would make someone better off without also making someone else worse off. *Cost-benefit efficiency* is achieved when any reallocation of an entitlement would impose more costs than benefits

Earlier we explained that public laws and private bargains are substitutes. We can restate this fact as a matter of efficiency. A change from inefficient to efficient allocation of legal entitlements creates a surplus. Public laws or private deals are alternative means to achieve that surplus. The efficient approach depends on transaction costs. If transaction costs of public bargaining are lower than private bargaining, new law is the efficient means of achieving the surplus. Conversely, if transaction costs of public bargaining are higher than private bargaining, private agreements are the efficient means of achieving the surplus.

Most people agree that efficiency is better than inefficiency. Politicians coo about the need for efficiency like pigeons around a slice of bread. State officials never publicly advocate wasting money. In contrast to efficiency, there is disagreement about distribution among politicians, as well as among lawyers, economists, and the general public. Later we will say more about distribution.

B. Representation

Bargains in public law promote efficiency among the officials who make them. What about everyone else? Is political bargaining good or bad for the public? To answer this question, we extend the scope of the Public Coase Theorem. If political bargaining were costless, then everyone could join the bargain. If everyone joins the bargain, then everyone can share in its benefits. Every law creating more benefits than costs will get enacted. When every law creating more benefits than costs gets enacted, political outcomes are "socially efficient." We can restate the Public Coase Theorem in terms of social efficiency. *As the transaction costs of political bargaining approach zero, laws will become socially efficient.*

To illustrate, assume again that Caleb and Dee gain by pushing their legislation on schools and police through the city council. In contrast, Graham, the third member of the city council, loses. Assume that legislating requires a majority among the three of them. Consider two possible consequences. First, if Caleb and Dee gain more from the legislation than Graham loses, then Graham cannot pay Caleb and Dee enough to withdraw their legislation. They will enact the legislation, as social efficiency among the three of them requires. Second, if Caleb and Dee gain less from the legislation than Graham loses, then Graham can pay Caleb and Dee enough to withdraw their legislation. They will withdraw the legislation, as social efficiency among the three of them requires.

Suppose Graham is not a member of the city council but a private citizen. The logic works the same way. If bargaining is costless and the legislation is socially efficient for the three of them, Caleb and Dee can offer Graham something of value in exchange for his agreement not to impede their proposals. For example, they can offer to hold a hearing on legislation Graham favors in exchange for his agreement not to disrupt city

overall. When Adam and Blair trade money for cells, they achieve Pareto efficiency and cost-benefit efficiency. Suppose instead that Adam started with all of the money and the cells. That allocation would be Pareto efficient because changing it—moving money, the cells, or both to Blair—would make Adam worse off. However, that allocation would not be cost-benefit efficient. Moving the cells from Adam to Blair would create $1,000 in value. When we refer to "efficiency" in this book, we usually mean cost-benefit efficiency.

council meetings. If the legislation is inefficient, Graham can offer Caleb and Dee something in exchange for withdrawing their proposals.

Legislation usually affects many citizens, not just one like Graham. Costless bargaining implies that all lawmakers and all citizens can negotiate, and they will agree to the socially efficient package of laws. No law gets enacted unless its benefits exceed the costs.

In reality, the transaction costs of bargaining among large groups are usually high, not low. Consequently, citizens cannot bargain with one another over public laws. Instead, officials bargain on their behalf. In a democracy, lawmakers should represent the citizens. Representative lawmakers ideally strike the same bargains that citizens would strike if the transaction costs among citizens were not prohibitive. This leads to another restatement of the Public Coase Theorem: *As the transaction costs of political bargaining among representative lawmakers approach zero, laws will become socially efficient.* Representation is an important and complicated topic that we will return to in later chapters.

Questions

2.21. If the transaction costs of bargaining were zero, would we need city councils? Can you relate your answer to the Massachusetts law according to which small towns hold open meetings at which private citizens make laws?[36]

2.22. Lawmakers sometimes want to enact proposals that would benefit them (e.g., higher salaries, more vacation) but hurt private citizens more. In a democracy, what can private citizens offer legislators in exchange for their agreement to withdraw such proposals?

2.23. If bargaining between citizens and lawmakers promotes efficiency, why do bribery laws prohibit citizens from paying lawmakers to vote a particular way?

Majority Rule and Minority Rights

The Voting Rights Act of 1965 is a landmark in American law. By removing racist barriers to voting, it vastly improved the ability of African Americans to elect their preferred candidates to office.[37] But did electing preferred candidates actually empower racial minorities? Consider the U.S. Congress, which has 535 members and operates under majority rule. One might wonder if adding a few representatives of a minority group, or even a few dozen representatives, will change legislative outcomes in Congress. James Madison, one of the Framers of the Constitution, wrote, "If a majority be united by a common interest, the rights of the minority will be insecure."[38]

[36] These are called Town Meetings. Authorization for them springs from the state constitution. *See* Mass. Const. art. LXXXIX.
[37] 52 U.S.C. §10101.
[38] The Federalist No. 51, 265 (James Madison) (Ian Shapiro ed., 2009).

Bargaining theory shows how even a small minority can exercise power in a majoritarian system. Legislators can trade their votes on issues they do not care about in exchange for votes on issues they do care about. In this way, a few legislators might ensure passage of a bill that their constituents value highly. As the transaction costs of bargaining approach zero, this will happen every time the value to those constituents (even if they are few in number) exceeds the costs to others (even if they are many in number).

By making it possible for minorities to win seats in Congress, the Voting Rights Act facilitated bargaining between them and the majority. Furthermore, as more seats were won by minorities, they gained more bargaining power. Of course, transaction costs always exceed zero, and minority groups may still exercise too little power. But they exercise more power than they would if bargaining among members of Congress were prohibited.

C. Distribution and Social Welfare

People mostly agree on the value of efficiency but disagree on distribution. Some argue that more equal distribution of society's wealth is better than less, and others argue the opposite. In the nightclub example, operating after midnight generates $400 in surplus. Some would argue that sum should go to the neighbor, others would argue it belongs to the nightclub. People who stand to gain from redistribution especially disagree with people who stand to lose from it. Thus, the neighbor who stands to gain from a right to quiet is likely to favor that right, whereas the nightclub that stands to gain from a right to make noise is likely to favor that right.

Since people disagree about distribution, they also disagree over how much efficiency they would sacrifice for more equality. In the nightclub example, suppose the neighbor is poor and the nightclub is rich. Assuming no bargaining between them, the right to quiet will save the poor neighbor $100 at a cost of $500 to the rich club. Is this worthwhile? People will disagree.

Many clashes in public law trace to two questions: How much equality should we seek, and how much efficiency should we sacrifice to achieve it? Disagreements about efficiency and distribution relate to how they are valued. Economists often discuss their value in terms of *utility*. Utility refers to an individual's well-being, which depends on the things that matter to her, like health, family, social standing, and the fit between her preferred laws and actual laws. As a person's well-being grows, her utility increases.

Like health, money increases utility. However, most economists believe it does so at a declining rate. A check for $100,000 grows the utility of a homeless person by more than it grows the utility of a billionaire. Thus, transferring money from one person to another does not change the total wealth, but it might change the total utility.

To illustrate, add some details to the nightclub example. Suppose the neighbor is a struggling writer, and the club's noise distracts her. Operating earns the club $500 and costs the neighbor $100 from late work. If the nightclub operates, value equal to $400 gets produced. How that money gets distributed does not affect the sum—the surplus always equals $400—but it might affect utility. Transferring more of the cooperative surplus to the poor neighbor may increase her utility by more than it decreases the utility of the nightclub's rich owner.

To transfer utility, the law can change the rights underlying the bargain. By granting the neighbor a right to quiet, the law forces the nightclub to pay the neighbor for the right to make noise. Given our assumptions, a payment from the club costs the owner less utility than the neighbor gains. Thus, granting the neighbor a right to quiet generates more utility than granting the nightclub a right to operate.

This conclusion, however, depends on measuring the utility of different people and adding them. There is no generally agreed upon or accepted way to measure and compare the utility of different people. Many agree that social welfare increases with individual utility, but most disagree about the rate of increase. These disagreements reflect political and moral philosophy more than social science.[39]

Efficient Redistribution

In California, limousines pass homeless camps, and private jets fly over impoverished neighborhoods. In Brazil, the six wealthiest people have as much money as the 100 million poorest people.[40] The world features profound inequalities in wealth. Many people believe that we could increase social welfare by moving money from the rich to the poor. How should we move the money?

We could reallocate rights. To explain this idea, recall the rich nightclub and the poor neighbor. Suppose we grant neighbors a right to quiet. This forces the club to pay the neighbor for permission to play music, transferring money from rich to poor.

In this example, giving the neighbor a right to quiet redistributes money from rich to poor. But what about down the block, where another nightclub is poor and its neighbor is rich? Here the right to quiet transfers money from poor to rich. To generalize, redistributing wealth through the legal system often requires relying on crude averages, like the typical wealth of nightclubs and the typical wealth of their neighbors.[41]

Reallocating rights can cause another problem. Suppose an entrepreneur chooses between two activities, opening a nightclub and opening a doughnut shop. The nightclub would create $500 in value for the entrepreneur and $100 in losses for the neighbor. The doughnut shop would create $250 in value for the entrepreneur and no losses for anyone. Efficiency requires the entrepreneur to open the nightclub (net value of $400 instead of $250). If the government grants the neighbor a right to quiet, the entrepreneur will have to pay the neighbor for permission to operate. This might cost say, $300, meaning the club's profit shrinks to $200. The entrepreneur prefers $250 to $200, so she opens the doughnut shop. The doughnut shop is the best choice for the entrepreneur but not for society. To generalize, reallocating rights causes inefficiency by distorting people's choices.

[39] For sophisticated discussions, see MATTHEW ADLER, WELL BEING AND FAIR DISTRIBUTION: BEYOND COST-BENEFIT ANALYSIS (2012); MATTHEW ADLER, MEASURING SOCIAL WELFARE: AN INTRODUCTION (2019).

[40] This remarkable statistic comes from a report by Oxfam International titled Brazil: extreme inequality in numbers, which is available at this link: https://www.oxfam.org/en/brazil-extreme-inequality-numbers.

[41] *See* ROBERT COOTER & THOMAS ULEN, LAW AND ECONOMICS 107 (6th ed. 2016).

Instead of reallocating rights, we could tax the rich and transfer the revenue to the poor. A tax-and-transfer system avoids the problem of crude averages. We can tax rich nightclub owners, not all nightclub owners. Likewise, taxes cause fewer distortions.[42] To see why, suppose that instead of reallocating rights to the neighbor we require the entrepreneur to pay a 10 percent tax. If the entrepreneur opens the nightclub, her after-tax profit equals \$450. If she opens the doughnut shop, her after-tax profit equals \$225. So she opens the club. The tax leads to the efficient choice (open the nightclub), whereas reallocating the right leads to the inefficient choice (open the doughnut shop).

This discussion makes taxes sound better. However, running a tax system is not cheap. We must identify the rich, assess tax bills, collect the money, identify the poor, and transfer the money. Every step requires people (accountants, lawyers, tax collectors) and resources. The Internal Revenue Service, which collects federal taxes in the United States, employs over 70,000 people and has an annual budget of about \$12 billion. According to one study, about one-third of each marginal dollar of taxes goes to waste.[43]

Most law-and-economics scholars prefer to redistribute money through the tax system, not through legal entitlements. They believe that taxes cost less and create fewer distortions all things considered. Of course, not everyone agrees.[44]

III. Bargaining Failures

We have explained the positive and normative theory of bargaining. The underlying generalization is that low transaction costs facilitate private and public bargains for mutual gain. As discussed, bargaining sometimes succeeds and sometimes fails. A good theory of bargaining diagnoses the cause and cure of failures, like a good doctor diagnoses the cause and cure of a disease. We will sketch theories of bargaining failure based on economic theories of market failure. These theories connect the cause of bargaining failure to its cure.

Economists often divide market failures into three categories: externalities, asymmetrical information, and monopoly. These labels capture problems that public law

[42] Both taxes and the reallocation of rights can cause inefficiency by discouraging work or wealth accumulation. In our example, if taxes are too high, or if the neighbors have too many rights, the entrepreneur will not earn enough to justify working. Compared to taxes, however, reallocating rights can cause a second source of inefficiency by changing behavior connected to those rights. In our example, granting the neighbor a right to quiet causes the entrepreneur to open a doughnut shop instead of a club, which is the inefficient choice. On the "double distortion" from reallocating rights, see Steven Shavell, *A Note on Efficiency vs. Distributional Equity in Legal Rulemaking: Should Distributional Equity Matter Given Optimal Income Taxation?*, 71 Am. Econ. Rev. 414 (1981); Louis Kaplow & Steven Shavell, *Why the Legal System Is Less Efficient Than the Income Tax in Redistributing Income*, 23 J. Legal Stud. 667 (1994).

[43] *See* Charles L. Ballard, John B. Shoven, & John Whalley, *General Equilibrium Computations of the Marginal Welfare Costs of Taxes in the United States*, 75 Am. Econ. Rev. 128 (1985).

[44] *See, e.g.*, Zachary Liscow, *Reducing Inequality on the Cheap: When Legal Rule Design Should Incorporate Equity as Well as Efficiency*, 123 Yale L.J. 2478 (2014); Chris William Sanchirico, *Taxes Versus Legal Rules as Instruments for Equity: A More Equitable View*, 29 J. Legal Stud. 797 (2000).

aims to overcome. Economists have spent decades studying these impediments to cooperation. We will discuss each briefly.

A. Externalities, Public Goods, and Free Riding

In 1948, a toxic fog descended on the town of Donora, Pennsylvania, killing 20 residents and sickening thousands.[45] Emissions from industrial plants contributed to the disaster. In economic terms, the smog was a *negative externality*. A negative externality exists whenever an actor's decision excludes a cost that he imposes on others. In the case of Donora, plant owners apparently did not consider the harm their pollution caused to nearby residents. If plant owners had considered those costs when making decisions, they would have polluted less. Negative externalities lead to inefficiently high levels of pollution.

To see the logic clearly, attach some numbers to Donora. Suppose a plant owner earns money by operating. Expressed in utility, the money is worth 10. Expressed in utility, the cost to the owner of breathing the dirty air equals 4, and the cost to everyone else equals 12. If the owner takes all costs into account, he will not operate. He would prefer not operating and getting zero to operating and getting −6 (10 from profit, −4 from his breathing dirty air, −12 from others breathing dirty air). If the owner externalizes the costs to others, he will operate. He prefers operating and getting 6 (10 from profit, −4 from his breathing dirty air) to not operating and getting zero. Negative externalities lead people to engage in inefficient activities.

Negative externalities relate to the problem of *free riding*. To understand free riding, consider how a polluter might reason: "If many factories reduce pollution, the air will be clean whether or not I reduce my pollution. If few factories reduce pollution, the air will be dirty whether or not I reduce my pollution. My abatement matters little to air quality, so I will not spend money reducing my pollution." Each polluter reasons this way. Thus, each polluter waits for others to abate, no one reduces pollution, and the air gets dirtier. Negative externalities cause free riding on abatement by others.

Unlike polluting, some activities have a *positive externality*. Positive externalities are the opposite of negative externalities. Imagine a stateless village preyed upon by bandits. For protection, the community could ask hundreds of volunteers to build a stone wall around the village. Anyone who volunteers creates a benefit for himself and others in the village. The benefit to others is the positive externality.

Like negative externalities, positive externalities can lead to free riding. A villager might reason, "If many people volunteer, the wall will get built whether I haul stones or not. If few people volunteer, the wall will not get built whether I haul stones or not. My participation does not matter to my safety, so I will stay home and relax." A villager who reasons this way free rides on others' efforts. If most people reason in this way, everyone stays home. The wall does not get built even though its benefits exceed its costs. When a decision maker is not paid for the positive externalities of his activity, there is usually too little of the activity.

[45] Lorraine Boissoneault, *The Deadly Donora Smog of 1948 Spurred Environmental Protection—But Have We Forgotten the Lesson?*, SMITHSONIAN MAGAZINE, Oct. 26, 2018.

Specific characteristics cause free riding. If you take a bite from a sandwich, there is less for me. If you drive the car, then I cannot drive it at the same time. Sandwiches and cars are *rivalrous*. Consumption uses up rivalrous goods, preempting their use by others. In contrast, we can breathe air simultaneously without exhausting the supply. Similarly, architects have used the Pythagorean Theorem for two millennia, and just as much remains as before. Air and geometry are *non-rivalrous*.

Besides rivalry, consider excludability. I can exclude you from driving my car by locking it, whereas I cannot easily exclude you from breathing air. Similarly, preventing someone from using your idea is harder than preventing someone from biting your sandwich. Cars and sandwiches are *excludable* while air and ideas are *non-excludable*.

We can apply these concepts to our village wall. The security it provides is non-rivalrous because everyone in the village can enjoy it at once, and it is non-excludable because no one in the village can be omitted from its protection. Non-rivalry and non-excludability are the characteristics that define a *public good* in economics.[46] Radio broadcasts and national security are standard examples of pure public goods. In contrast, rivalry and excludability characterize *private goods*. Pure private goods include bananas, bicycles, and bedrooms. In fact, many goods have characteristics of both public and private goods. Examples of mixed goods include roads and schools.

The public characteristics of a good cause free riding. For the villager, non-rivalry means there is plenty of protection to go around, and non-excludability means he can enjoy that protection whether he hauls stones or not. So he stays home and relaxes. If the wall did not have positive externalities—if the villager did not benefit when others haul stones—he could not free ride on others' efforts.

Like positive externalities, negative externalities cause free riding. To see why, return to Donora. The smog harmed thousands of residents. The dirty air was non-rivalrous (all could breathe it simultaneously) and non-excludable (no one in Donora could avoid it). Residents might have proposed this deal with the industrialists: "Rather than polluting and earning $1 million, stop polluting and we will pay you $2 million." This bargain would benefit residents and industrialists alike. However, all residents would benefit, and this would lead to free riding. Residents would wait for others to contribute to the $2 million payment just like villagers would wait for others to haul stones. Free riding by nonpaying residents would prevent the bargain from taking place.

Generalizing from events like Donora, some economists connect free riding to the origins of the state. Protection and defense provide opportunities to free ride, and free riding prevents private individuals from cooperating over security and other public goods. The state arises as a solution. Thus, we can interpret many public laws and the legal institutions (legislatures, courts) that produce them as solutions to free riding.

[46] The economic theory of public goods, and the associated concepts of rivalry and excludability, are usually traced to a remarkable, three-page paper: Paul A. Samuelson, *The Pure Theory of Public Expenditure*, 36 Rev. Econ. & Stat. 387 (1954).

The Prisoner's Dilemma

The *prisoner's dilemma* is a paradigm in social science for situations where individual rationality causes mutually destructive behavior. Police arrest Mr. Byrne and Mr. Char for jointly setting a building on fire. After being placed in separate interrogation rooms, each suspect faces a choice: confess to the crime or remain silent. If both confess, both will spend five years in prison. If neither confesses, both will spend one year in prison. If one confesses and the other does not, the confessor will spend only six months in prison—a reward for helping the police—and the non-confessor will spend seven years in prison. Figure 2.1 summarizes the facts.

		Mr. Char	
		Confess	Stay silent
Mr. Byrne	Confess	−5, −5	−0.5, −7
	Stay silent	−7, −0.5	−1, −1

Figure 2.1. The Prisoner's Dilemma

What should each suspect do? If Mr. Char confesses, then Mr. Byrne can either confess and face five years in prison or stay silent and face seven years in prison. So he prefers to confess. Alternatively, if Mr. Char stays silent, then Mr. Byrne can either confess and spend six months in prison or stay silent and spend one year in prison. So he prefers to confess. Regardless of Mr. Char's choice, Mr. Byrne is better off if he confesses. The same logic applies to Mr. Char, so he will also confess. The best strategy for each individual leads to a bad outcome for both of them.

In the payoff matrix, "confess" means "don't cooperate" and "stay silent" means "cooperate." Can you use the prisoner's dilemma to analyze the failure of the villagers to build a stone wall?

Informal enforcement mechanisms such as social pressure can prevent a little free riding. If pollution harms only a few people (law calls this a private nuisance), each of them may chip in and pay the industrialist to abate. Each one chips in to avoid being ostracized by the group.

Alternatively, if pollution harms thousands of people (law calls this a public nuisance), private bargaining seldom succeeds. Correcting a public nuisance usually requires public law. In the example involving a stone wall, law could prevent free riding by taxing villagers who do not help build. In Donora, the Clean Air Acts could have prevented the toxic fog.

For the state to correct free riding among citizens, lawmakers must overcome free riding themselves.[47] This can be difficult. To illustrate, assume that Helen and Ike are congressional representatives from Michigan where cars get made, and they care intensely about an automobile bill in Congress. Assume that votes on the bill are equipoised, with the same number in favor and against. To enact the bill, the Michigan representatives need to trade a vote with a representative from New York, who cares intensely about a banking bill. Helen may hold back in the hope that Ike will shoulder the burden of trading for the needed vote. Ike may do the same. If both of them hold back, the bargain will never take place. Free riding by private actors causes inefficiency, and free riding by public actors may prevent the state from correcting it.

Since free riding impedes bargaining, it can be described as a transaction cost. Thus, the Public Coase Theorem can be restated: bargaining can overcome externalities if low transaction costs mitigate free riding. With private nuisances (small numbers of people), social norms may mitigate free riding. With public nuisances (large numbers of people), legislation is usually necessary to mitigate free riding by the citizens. However, legislating may require overcoming free riding by the officials who make laws.

Questions

2.24. A factory in Northfield, Minnesota, makes the town smell like popcorn and chocolate. The smell is a positive externality. Explain how this positive externality can lead to inefficiency. Does the factory operate too much or too little?

2.25. Imagine a two-by-two matrix with columns labeled "rivalrous" and "non-rivalrous" and rows labeled "excludable" and "non-excludable." In which box would the following goods fit: parking spaces, fish stocks in international waters, broadband internet access, FM radio, satellite radio?[48]

2.26. Some kinds of information are public goods. For example, music is non-rivalrous and, given the ease of copying and sharing, largely non-excludable. Explain how free riding could affect music sales and music production. Can you think of any laws that mitigate free riding in music?

2.27. The theory of public goods justifies many state actions, but some doubt that it explains the genesis of the state. Under what circumstances will private individuals fail to cooperate in providing a public good but succeed in cooperating to form a state?[49]

[47] *See* W.M. Crain & R.D. Tollison, *Team Production in Political Majorities*, 2 MICROPOLITICS 111 (1982). The connection between team production and free riding is developed in Armen A. Alchian & Harold Demsetz, *Production, Information Costs, and Economic Organization*, 62 AM. ECON. REV. 777 (1972).

[48] As discussed, rivalrous, excludable goods are "private" goods, while non-rivalrous, non-excludable goods are "public" goods. Rivalrous, non-excludable goods are "common" goods or "common-pool resources." Non-rivalrous, excludable goods are "club" goods. As resources like pastures get crowded, they switch from public goods to common goods.

[49] *See* Russell Hardin, *Economic Theories of the State*, *in* PERSPECTIVES ON PUBLIC CHOICE: A HANDBOOK 24 (Dennis C. Mueller ed., 1996) ("[W]e resolve the problem of failure to supply public goods by supplying a super-public good, the state, so that it can supply lesser public goods.").

The Articles of Confederation

The Articles of Confederation established a central government for the United States after the colonies declared their independence from Great Britain. But the Articles only lasted for a few years, in part because of money. Under the Articles, the central government could request funding from the states, but the Articles provided no mechanism to force the states to pay their assigned shares. Some states did not pay, apparently hoping that payments from other states would keep the central government afloat. The nonpaying states were free riding.

Without income, the central government could not finance a military to protect the states from foreign aggressors. This failure convinced people that the central government needed more authority. In 1787, the Philadelphia Convention drafted the U.S. Constitution, adoption of which required support from nine of the 13 states. A year later the Constitution took effect, replacing the Articles of Confederation. The Constitution made important changes that get attention, like creating the presidency and protecting individual rights. Critically, it also empowered the federal government to raise money, first through tariffs and later through the income tax. This mitigated the problem of free riding. When war erupted in 1812, the United States had a powerful navy.

B. Information Asymmetry

On September 11, 2001, Al Qaeda terrorists destroyed the World Trade Center in New York City and killed almost 3,000 people. The United States accused Iraq of aiding Al Qaeda and stockpiling chemical, biological, and nuclear weapons. Iraq denied terrorism and permitted only limited inspections of its military facilities. Diplomacy failed and the United States invaded Iraq in 2003, overthrowing a dictatorial government but finding no ties to Al Qaeda or weapons of mass destruction. If the United States had known the facts, it might not have threatened war, and if Iraq had known the United States would invade, it might have allowed inspections. Misinformation causes miscalculations, and miscalculations cause bargaining to fail. The following pages explain why.

In our opening example, we considered the case of Adam and Blair trading money for jail cells. We assumed that each knew his or her own threat value ($3,000 in the case of Adam, $5,000 for Blair). In fact, parties often have incomplete information about their own threat values. Misinformation causes mistakes in bargaining. To demonstrate, most scientists agree that global temperatures will rise over time, but they disagree on the rate, cost, and amount attributable to human activity. This makes legislators uncertain about the value of regulating greenhouse gases. Without good information, legislators may deregulate greenhouse gases and then find the effects are worse than expected.

Aside from imperfect science, bills are often so complicated that legislators cannot comprehend their full effects. In 2014, Congress passed a single bill exceeding 1,500 pages in length that authorized $1 trillion in spending on child immigrants, disease in Africa, drought, gun control, sales taxes, campaign finance, museums, the transfer of detainees from an American military base in Guantanamo Bay, Cuba, and so forth. When bargaining, each legislator understood some of the bill's details, and no legislator understood all of them.

In these examples, parties must gather costly information to determine their own threat values. A different problem arises for determining the threat values of other people. Suppose the President negotiates with Congress over an immigration bill. If the President and Congress agree, they can change the number of immigrants allowed by law. Congress would prefer to admit, say, up to 500,000 additional immigrants, whereas the President would prefer to admit, say, up to 200,000 additional immigrants. Since both prefer additional immigrants, there is scope for cooperation. Suppose the President offers to admit up to 200,000 additional immigrants, but Congress thinks the President is actually willing to accept up to 300,000 additional immigrants. Thus, Congress holds out for admitting more immigrants, and bargaining with the President fails.

If Congress knew that the President would only accept 200,000 additional immigrants, it would accept the President's offer. In the example, the President knows his own preferences, but Congress does not. *Information asymmetry* means one player knows something the other does not know. In this example, information asymmetry blocks bargaining.

Players withhold information about their threat values to gain a strategic advantage. To see this clearly, consider Adam and Blair. Adam values the jail cells at $3,000 and Blair values them at $4,000, meaning a successful bargain will create $1,000 in surplus. Price determines the distribution of that surplus. If Adam reveals his threat value, Blair may offer him $3,001, meaning he gets just $1 of the surplus. If he withholds the information—if he bluffs and says he values the cells at $3,900—she may offer him a lot more. Adam has an incentive to exaggerate his threat value. Blair has a similar incentive. Asymmetrical information persists partly because of strategic behavior. However, it can cause miscalculation and failure to agree.[50]

The problem of verification exacerbates information asymmetry. Suppose that the President truthfully declares that he prefers to admit up to 200,000 additional immigrants, but no more. Recognizing the powerful incentive to bluff, the Congress may not believe him. How could the President verify his statement and make Congress believe him? That would be as hard as Adam proving to Blair that he values the empty jail cells at $3,000. Choices are observable but preferences are unobservable. Because they are unobservable, preferences are unverifiable.

Suppose Congress and the President agree on an immigration deal. Another problem looms: Will they follow through? Will Congress pass the bill as promised or renege and embarrass the President? Will the President sign as promised or veto? If either party expects the other to back out, they will not bother bargaining in the first place. The parties can make promises to one another, but talk is cheap.[51] To facilitate bargaining, making false promises must be costly.

[50] Roger B. Myerson & Mark A. Satterthwaite, *Efficient Mechanisms for Bilateral Trading*, 29 J. ECON. THEORY 265 (1983) (proving that individually rational, strategic behavior can prevent efficient bargaining).

[51] For groundbreaking work on cheap talk, see Vincent P. Crawford & Joel Sobel, *Strategic Information Transmission*, 50 ECONOMETRICA 1431 (1982).

The costliness of a false promise can be understood through the idea of *credible commitments*. A credible commitment forecloses an opportunity. In a classical book on the art of war, the Chinese philosopher Sun Tzu wrote, "When your army has crossed the border, you should burn your boats and bridges, in order to make it clear to everybody that you have no hankering after home."[52] Before the boats burn, the cost of retreat is low. After the boats burn, the cost of retreat is high. The burning of the boats commits the army to advance. Realizing that the invading army cannot turn back, the defenders are prone to negotiate peace. "To subdue the enemy without fighting," Sun Tzu wrote, "is the acme of skill."[53]

We can connect these ideas more closely to bargaining theory. Recall that "threat value" refers to the payoff a player can get on his own without the other's cooperation. A commitment often consists in a player reducing his own threat value. By making noncooperation less appealing, one commits to cooperating. For example, if the President publicly commits to signing the immigration bill, he makes noncooperation—vetoing the bill at the last minute—politically costly to himself. Foreseeing that the President will not veto, Congress passes the bill.

As another example, consider private parties bargaining over a house. The seller promises not to damage the house before transferring ownership, but the buyer doubts the seller's promise. Fearful of damage, the buyer might walk away from the deal, leaving both parties worse off. Now suppose the seller can do more than make a promise; she can sign a contract requiring her to maintain the house or pay for its repair. Unlike a bare promise, the contract is enforceable. If the home is damaged, the buyer can use the legal system to force the seller to pay. No longer fearful of damages, the buyer will proceed with the deal. The contract lets the seller make a credible commitment not to damage the house, facilitating its sale.

Good law facilitates bargaining, and bad law obstructs it. In places with good legal systems, parties can use contracts to make credible commitments. A good legal system enforces contracts and prompts deals. Bad legal systems fail to enforce contracts and impede deals. Thus, farmers in Ohio can contract to buy and sell land, while farmers in South Sudan, a new country embroiled in conflict, cannot settle land disputes with a piece of paper.

Public officials often resemble farmers in South Sudan: law does not enforce their bargains. Caleb and Dee cannot sign a contract, enforceable in court, committing each to vote for the other's proposal. Legal contracts usually do not exist for bargains in public law. Credible commitments in public law often require legal institutions other than contracts. Consider the long struggle for power between the British Parliament and the King.[54] The King often borrowed money, especially in time of war, but failed to repay the loans. Creditors became reluctant to lend the King more money. In 1688, Parliament removed and replaced the King in an event called the Glorious Revolution. The new monarch was forbidden to alter the terms of loans except by the lender's consent. One might think this restriction weakened the Crown, but the opposite is true.

[52] Sun Tzu, On the Art of War 115 (Lionel Giles trans., 1910).
[53] Sun Tzu, On the Art of War 77 (Samuel B. Griffith trans., 1963).
[54] Douglas C. North & Barry R. Weingast, *Constitutions and Commitment: The Evolution of Institutions Governing Public Choice in Seventeenth-Century England*, 49 J. Econ. Hist. 803 (1989).

The Crown strengthened itself by making a credible commitment to repay its lenders. Afterward the Crown could borrow more money, and at lower interest rates, than before. The money funded successful wars with France that established England's dominance for world power.

Bluffing, verifiability, commitment, credibility, trust—these are problems of asymmetrical information in bargaining. They arise in private and public bargaining alike. The vast literature on asymmetrical information encompasses many other problems, some of which we will discuss later.

Questions

2.28. In the United States, Supreme Court Justices are independent of Congress and the President. However, nominees need Senate approval to join the Court. If you were a Senator, would you trust a nominee who promises to interpret the law objectively?

2.29. There are few international courts and no international executives. This makes international law hard to enforce. Some countries have incorporated international law into their domestic systems. This gives international law the same status as (or even higher status than) national law. Does incorporation as we have described it make a country's commitment to international law stronger? Why might the promise to incorporate international law make bargaining over the substance of that international law easier?[55]

2.30. Wars waste lives and money in disputes that diplomacy could resolve. Why can't nations agree to reduce their armies by 50 percent?[56] Why are civil wars within countries harder to end than wars between countries?[57] (Hint: in civil wars, the losing side usually must lay down its arms.)

2.31. Imagine a dictatorial society with two types of people. The few rich are organized politically. The numerous poor are disorganized politically. Random events like economic recessions briefly unite the poor. While united, they demand from the rich a greater share of the nation's wealth. The rich would prefer to pay the poor to go away, but they might have to implement democracy instead. Why?[58]

[55] Tom Ginsburg, Svitlana Chernykh, & Zachary Elkins, *Commitment and Diffusion: How and Why National Constitutions Incorporate International Law*, 2008 U. Ill. L. Rev. 201, 210–13 (2008); Pierre-Hugues Verdier & Mila Versteeg, *International Law in National Legal Systems: An Empirical Investigation*, *in* Comparative International Law 525–26 (Anthea Roberts, Paul B. Stephan, Pierre-Hugues Verdier, & Mila Versteeg eds., 2018).

[56] *See* James D. Fearon, *Bargaining, Enforcement, and International Cooperation*, 52 Int'l Org. 269 (1998); Robert Powell, *Absolute and Relative Gains in International Relations Theory*, 85 Am. Pol. Sci. Rev. 1303 (1991).

[57] Barbara F. Walter, *The Critical Barrier to Civil War Settlement*, 51 Int'l Org. 335 (1997).

[58] Daron Acemoglu & James A. Robinson, Why Nations Fail (2012).

Optimism: A Menace in Court

The state accuses the Contamination Corporation of dumping toxic chemicals into a river. The corporation can pay a $300,000 fine or go to court. Consider the expected costs to the corporation. Litigating costs the corporation $50,000. The corporation believes (incorrectly) that it has a 10 percent chance of losing in court and paying $300,000, and a 90 percent chance of winning in court and paying no fine. The corporation's perceived threat value equals −$50,000 + 0.1(−$300,000) + 0.9($0) = −$80,000. Now consider the expected costs of the state. Litigating costs the state $50,000. The state believes (correctly) that it has a 50 percent chance of winning in court and gaining $300,000 and a 50 percent chance of losing and gaining nothing. The state's perceived threat value equals −$50,000 + 0.5($300,000) + 0.5($0) = $100,000.

Under these assumptions, the most the corporation would be willing to pay in a settlement equals $80,000, and the least the state would be willing to accept in a settlement equals $100,000. Thus, the parties will litigate rather than settle. Litigating wastes $100,000 in time and money. The corporation's false optimism precludes a bargain.[59]

Asymmetrical information often contributes to false optimism. To illustrate, suppose a state official recorded a video of the Contamination Corporation dumping the chemicals in the river. One side knows something the other does not know. To encourage settlement, the state may show the recording to the corporation. Alternatively, to secure victory by surprising the corporation at trial, the state may not show the recording to the corporation. Without information about the recording, the corporation is too optimistic, and its optimism precludes a deal.

In reality, the legal process would probably require the state to share the recording with the corporation. Can you use bargaining theory to explain why?

C. Monopoly

In 1882, the industrialist John D. Rockefeller and his associates formed a secret trust, combining their companies into Standard Oil, which dominated the petroleum market. *Monopoly* occurs when a market has one seller like Standard Oil and many potential buyers. The monopolist restrains trade by setting prices at high levels, as with Standard Oil. As another example, AT&T once controlled telephone service in the United States. A ten-minute distance call cost about $20 in today's money.[60]

Monopoly does more than enrich companies at the expense of consumers; it causes inefficiency. To see why, consider the Junction Company, which owns a bridge and charges a toll to cross. Each crossing costs $1 in wear and tear on the bridge. Driver 1

[59] *See* John P. Gould, *The Economics of Legal Conflicts*, 2 J. LEGAL STUD. 279 (1973).

[60] Common Carrier Bureau of the Federal Communications Commission, The Industry Analysis Division's Reference Book of Rates, Price Indices, and Household Expenditures 62 (Tracy Waldon & James Lande eds., 1997).

is on a trip for pleasure, and he values crossing the bridge at $5. Driver 2 is delivering materials for a job, and she values crossing the bridge at $10. Because the Junction Company has a monopoly, it can choose the toll. If it sets the toll at $4, both drivers will pay to cross, and the company will earn $6 in profit (with two drivers, the company makes a total of $8 in tolls and pays a total of $2 to maintain the bridge). If the company sets the toll at $9, only Driver 2 will cross. The company will earn $8 in profit ($9 from the toll minus $1 in maintenance). The company prefers $8 to $6, so it will set the toll at $9.

As in this example, monopolists usually earn more when they charge a high price and have few customers than when they charge a low price and have many customers.[61] This is rational for the monopolist but inefficient. Efficiency demands that every driver cross when the benefit of crossing exceeds the cost. With a $9 toll, drivers who value crossing at $5 do not cross, even though crossing would create more benefits ($5 per driver) than costs ($1 in wear and tear). Monopoly creates inefficiency.[62]

In general, law can correct inefficient monopolies in private markets in two ways: by regulating prices and by promoting competition. Thus, law can regulate tolls on a single bridge, or law can establish competing governments to build multiple bridges. However, sometimes bargaining will solve the problem of monopoly without government intervention, as we will explain.

According to the Coase Theorem, bargaining among private actors tends toward efficiency as transaction costs approach zero. We can apply the theorem to our example. If the Junction Company's toll creates inefficiency, there must be a bargaining failure. To see the connection between monopoly and bargaining, consider two ways that monopolists can determine prices. First, the monopolist can name a firm price, as when the Junction Company sets the toll at $9. Drivers can take or leave the price. Inflexibility creates inefficiency by discouraging Driver 1, who is unwilling to pay $9 but whose benefit from crossing ($5) would exceed the cost ($1).

Second, the monopolist can name a flexible price, and each buyer can make a counteroffer. With price flexibility, the parties bargain to reach an exact price. To illustrate, the Junction Company might charge some drivers $4 to cross and others $9 to cross. Everyone who values crossing the bridge at an amount greater than the cost of crossing ($1) strikes a deal and crosses. The bargains are efficient. The inefficiency of monopoly disappears.

Price flexibility faces an obstacle: transaction costs. If the monopolist bargains successfully with buyers, each one pays a negotiated price,[63] but arriving at such a price takes time and effort. Given transaction costs, the monopolist may gain more from naming a firm price and not bargaining over a flexible price.

We have analyzed a classic monopoly in which one buyer faces many sellers. Now consider a *bilateral monopoly*. This occurs when there is only one seller and only

[61] In the standard economic model of monopoly, the monopolist maximizes profits by setting a firm price where the marginal revenue from a small increase in production equals the marginal cost.

[62] Besides raising prices, monopolies tend to suppress innovation. For example, members of the New York Stock Exchange collected fees for matching buyers and sellers of stock. When a new technology allowed computers to make matches electronically, the Exchange delayed its adoption. Jacob Goldstein, *Putting a Speed Limit on the Stock Market*, N.Y. TIMES MAGAZINE, Oct. 8, 2013.

[63] Economists call this perfect price discrimination. Perfect price discrimination is efficient, although all of the bargaining surplus goes to the monopolist and none goes to the buyer.

one buyer. If the Junction Company has the only bridge and the Krosswise Shipping Company is the only customer who uses it, there is a bilateral monopoly, and the two parties must deal with each other. Knowing that Junction needs its business, Krosswise demands a low toll. Knowing that Krosswise needs its bridge, Junction demands a high toll. Bilateral monopoly makes bargaining inevitable, and strategic behavior makes the outcome uncertain.

Instead of two-party bargaining, consider three-party bargaining. The U.S. House of Representatives, the Senate, and the President must bargain with one another to make law. Each of the three institutions can prevent a new law.[64] The familiar term for this power arrangement is *unanimity rule*. Unanimity rule requires all parties to agree. The UN Security Council cannot make certain decisions without the unanimous consent of the five permanent member states. Similarly, the state compact that created the Metro train system required the unanimous agreement of Maryland, Virginia, and Washington, DC. In general, increasing the number of actors who must agree on collective action decreases its probability.

Unlike unanimity rule that requires all three actors in our example to agree, majority rule only requires a majority to agree (two of the three actors in our example). Most state legislatures and appellate courts make decisions using majority rule. A switch from unanimity rule to majority rule reduces the number of actors who must agree on a collective action. The majority need only negotiate an agreement that creates value for them, not for everyone. Consequently, majority rule lowers the transaction costs of collective action.

Specifically, majority rule avoids the problem of *holdouts*. A holdout is a person whose cooperation is essential for collective action and who refuses to provide it, except under terms that greatly favor him or her. To illustrate, suppose the state wishes to build a road across three parcels of private property. The road will produce \$1 million in commerce. Construction of the road will cause \$100,000 in damage to each of the parcels. On balance, the road across the three parcels will produce \$700,000 in value. However, a road across less than three parcels—two, one, or zero parcels—will be incomplete and produce no value. After construction of the road on two parcels, the owner of the third parcel may hold out for a very high price. The sale of his land will allow completion of the road, increasing value from zero to \$700,000. So he may demand \$700,000. When the state begins to buy land for the road, each owner can make this same demand for \$700,000. If each holds out for \$700,000, the state would have to pay \$2.1 million for a road that generates \$700,000 in value. The state will probably refuse to pay such a high price. Holdouts prevent bargains that would create value.

Short of preventing bargains, holdouts slow bargaining and increase its costs. Holdouts encumber bargaining throughout public law. Thus, Congress cannot enact law without the President's signature.[65] Like the third parcel owner, the President can hold out, demanding favors from the Senate and the House in exchange for his or her support. With few actors, the problem of holdouts can be overcome; Congress and the President often cooperate and enact statutes. With many actors, holdouts become

[64] This is not quite correct. Congress can override a President's veto if two-thirds of the members of the House and the Senate agree, but this happens rarely.

[65] Again, Congress can override a President's veto if two-thirds of the members of the House and the Senate agree, but this happens rarely.

insurmountable. For over a century, Poland's legislature operated under unanimity rule. Holdouts paralyzed lawmaking, contributing to the failure of the state.[66]

As these facts suggest, public law can lower transaction costs by switching from unanimity to majority rule. Consistent with this prescription, as more countries have joined the European Union, the Council of Ministers has replaced unanimity rule with majority rule for its decisions.[67] Compared to unanimity rule, majority rule increases the pace of collective action, but it also has a downside. With unanimity rule, no agreement happens unless it makes all parties better off. With majority rule, any majority can cut out a minority. A majority of legislators, for example, can omit a minority from an expenditure program or impose disproportionate taxes on them. This is analogous to the example of Caleb and Dee, who agreed to pass proposals that helped them but hurt Graham, the third city councilman, by more. A switch from unanimity to majority rule exacerbates contests over distribution.

In conclusion, unanimity rule risks holdouts that majority rule prevents, and majority rule risks minority exploitation that unanimity rule prevents. This fundamental tradeoff animates the allocation of power in basic laws like the U.S. Constitution. Good public law finds the best balance.

Questions

2.32. Movie theaters charge high prices for popcorn and forbid customers from bringing their own. Should the state regulate this monopoly by setting popcorn prices?

2.33. In the example of holdouts, three landowners each demand $700,000 from the state in exchange for their property. The state is unlikely to pay $2.1 million for the land since the road it wants to build only creates value of $700,000. But suppose the state did pay the $2.1 million. Is this inefficient? Do the payments from the state to the landowners destroy money or transfer money?

2.34. The Takings Clause in the U.S. Constitution allows the government to expropriate private property for public use if it pays "just compensation."[68] In general, "just compensation" means the market price. Why does the government expropriate property instead of simply buying it at the market price?

2.35. As discussed, many states free rode on others under the Articles of Confederation. Providing the central government with taxing authority could have alleviated the problem, but amending the Articles required unanimous agreement among 13 states. Why did states fail to amend the Articles but succeed in adopting a new Constitution?

2.36. The process for amending the U.S. Constitution has never changed. Nevertheless, amendment has become more difficult over time. Why?

[66] Liberum Veto, Encyclopædia Britannica, Oct. 30, 2008, https://www.britannica.com/topic/liberum-veto.

[67] The European Council and the Council of the EU Through Time: Decision- and law-making in European Integration, Council of the European Union (2016), https://www.consilium.europa.eu/media/29975/qc0415219enn.pdf.

[68] U.S. Const. amend. V.

Madison and the Sphere of Democracy

In the 1780s, James Madison, along with Alexander Hamilton and John Jay, wrote a series of essays encouraging the states to ratify the new Constitution. Those essays, commonly called the *Federalist Papers*, are a landmark of American political theory and an important aid in constitutional interpretation. The *Federalist Papers* addressed important concerns, including this. In the eighteenth century, many people thought democracy could work in city-states like ancient Athens but not in large countries like the United States. Madison famously disagreed.

In *Federalist No. 10*, Madison addressed the danger of factions, "a number of citizens . . . united and actuated by some common impulse of passion, or of interest, adverse to the rights of other citizens."[69] In Madison's view, factions are inevitable because people disagree (the "latent causes of faction are thus sown" in our nature).[70] Since factions cannot be eliminated, Madison reasoned that they must be held in check. He argued that enlarging the country would prevent factions from achieving a majority and controlling government: "Extend the sphere, and you take in a greater variety of parties and interests; you make it less probable that a majority of the whole will have a common motive to invade the rights of other citizens."[71]

We can interpret and develop Madison's argument using bargaining theory. Extending the sphere reduces the chance of a faction attaining a majority. Without a majority, a faction cannot exploit others but must bargain and cooperate with them. If a faction does attain a majority, competing factions ensure it will be short lived: today's majority becomes tomorrow's minority, and vice versa. Any majority that enriches itself by exploiting today's minority must fear that the tables will turn tomorrow. The possibility of being exploited tomorrow tempers the urge to exploit others today. Thus, the solution to factions is more factions. This is Madison's central claim for extending the sphere of the country, and it demonstrates a powerful connection between bargaining and democracy.[72]

IV. Interpretive Theory of Bargaining

According to positive theory, low transaction costs facilitate bargains, and according to normative theory, bargains create mutual gain. Three persistent sources of transaction costs inhibit bargains: free riding, asymmetrical information, and monopoly. Bargaining theory illuminates how legislators enact laws. But it can do more; bargaining theory can help judges. To show how, we turn to interpretation, the third branch of law and economics.

[69] The Federalist No. 10, at 48 (James Madison) (Ian Shapiro ed., 2009).
[70] *Id.*
[71] *Id.* at 52.
[72] *See* Neil Siegel, Intransitivities Protect Minorities: Interpreting Madison's Theory of the Extended Republic (2001) (unpublished Ph.D. dissertation, University of California, Berkeley) (on file with UMI Dissertation Services).

A. The Problem of Legislative Intent

Sometimes the words of a statute seem to contradict the legislature's intent. Consider *United States v. Kirby*.[73] A federal statute prohibited "knowingly and willfully obstruct[ing] . . . the passage of the mail."[74] The Supreme Court had to decide if a sheriff violated the statute when he arrested a mail carrier. Arresting the mail carrier certainly obstructed the passage of the mail. But the sheriff had a good reason for the arrest: the mailman was wanted for murder. Even though the sheriff violated the plain language of the statute, the Court concluded that the statute did not apply to the sheriff's conduct. According to the Court, "the legislature intended exceptions to its language" to avoid "an absurd consequence."[75] Considering legislative intent allowed the Court to avoid an unreasonable outcome.

Judges often consider legislative intent when interpreting statutes. Sometimes legislative intent is inferred from common sense, as in *Kirby*. Surely Congress did not intend its statute to protect murderous mail carriers from arrest. Other times legislative intent is inferred from *legislative history*. While enacting a bill, many actors—sponsors, opponents, committee chairs, and other members of the legislature—make statements about it. In the United States, committees in the House of Representatives and Senate often write official reports about the bill. Together these materials constitute the legislative history. Sometimes legislative history offers clues about intent.

To demonstrate the use of legislative history, consider *Church of the Holy Trinity v. United States*.[76] A church in New York signed a contract with an alien ("alien" is a legal term for a noncitizen) named Warren. Under the terms of the contract, Warren moved to New York and worked as a pastor for the church. The question in the case was whether the church violated a federal statute, which stated:

> [I]t shall be unlawful for any person, company, partnership, or corporation, in any manner whatsoever, to prepay the transportation, or in any way assist or encourage the importation or migration of any alien . . . into the United States . . . under contract or agreement . . . to perform labor or service of any kind[.][77]

The church seemed to break the law according to its plain language. However, the Supreme Court reached the opposite conclusion. According to the Court, Congress did not *intend* the statute to prohibit churches from recruiting foreign pastors. The Court based its conclusion in part on legislative history. A committee in the House of Representatives had written a report about the statute before it passed. According to the report, the law targeted aliens "from the lowest social stratum" who "live upon the coarsest food, and in hovels of a character before unknown to American workmen."[78]

[73] 74 U.S. 482 (1868).
[74] *Id.* at 485. Here is the complete text of the statute: "That if any person shall knowingly and willfully obstruct or retard the passage of the mail or of any driver or carrier or of any horse or carriage carrying the same, he shall, upon conviction, for every such offense pay a fine not exceeding one hundred dollars." 4 Stat. 104 (1825).
[75] *Kirby*, 74 U.S. at 486–87.
[76] 143 U.S. 457 (1892).
[77] *Id.* at 458.
[78] *Id.* at 465. This is not the only language in the opinion that shocks modern sensibilities.

Pastors did not fit that description, the Court reasoned, so Congress did not intend the law to cover contracts with pastors.

Many judges use legislative history when searching for legislative intent. Nevertheless, the practice is controversial. Statements from legislators and committees often contradict one another. In anticipation of judges consulting legislative history, legislators might "salt" the record, strategically making statements that reflect their preferred interpretations rather than the proper interpretation. From this morass, the argument goes, judges can extract legislative history to support any interpretation they like. Judge Harold Leventhal quipped that citing legislative history is like "looking over a crowd and picking out your friends."[79]

The criticism runs deeper yet. Legislative history is supposed to clarify legislative intent. But legislative intent, some critics argue, is nonexistent. The legal scholar Max Radin wrote, "A legislature certainly has no intention whatever in connection with words which some two or three [people] drafted, which a considerable number rejected, and in regard to which many of the approving majority might have had, and often demonstrably did have, different ideas and beliefs."[80]

B. The Bargain Theory of Interpretation

Judges interpreting statutes have sought legislative intent for centuries. Have the critics proved them wrong? Should judges abandon the search for legislative intent? No, but it should be reformulated. Legislation is often the product of bargaining. Like Caleb and Dee, legislators compromise over the content of law. To understand a legislative bargain, do not try to aggregate the intentions of individual legislators. This is impossible, as a later chapter will show. Instead, look to the bargain the legislators intended to strike. This is the *bargain theory of interpretation*.[81]

How can one find the terms of a legislative bargain? The text of the statute is the natural place to start. Like buyers and sellers drafting contracts, legislators formalize their deals in the language of the law. According to the bargain theory, judges ordinarily should emphasize the text of statutes when interpreting them. This is consistent with modern judicial practice in many places.

When interpreting a statute, some judges refuse to look beyond the statute's text. Such judges are called "textualists."[82] A later chapter will say more about the textualist approach to interpretation. Here we focus on judges who are prepared to look beyond the statute's text. Many judges will consider a statute's legislative history. The bargain theory shows them where to look.

[79] *See* Patricia M. Wald, *Some Observations on the Use of Legislative History in the 1981 Supreme Court Term*, 68 Iowa L. Rev. 195, 214 (1983).

[80] Max Radin, *Statutory Interpretation*, 43 Harv. L. Rev. 863, 870 (1930).

[81] The theory is developed in McNollgast, *Legislative Intent: The Use of Positive Political Theory in Statutory Interpretation*, 57 Law & Contemp. Probs. 3 (1994); McNollgast, *Positive Canons: The Role of Legislative Bargains in Statutory Interpretation*, 80 Geo. L.J. 705 (1992). *See also* Frank H. Easterbrook, *Foreword: The Court and the Economic System*, 98 Harv. L. Rev. 4, 42–58 (1984); Victoria Nourse, Misreading Law, Misreading Democracy (2016).

[82] In fact, many textualist judges will consider legislative history in certain circumstances. *See, e.g.*, Frank H. Easterbrook, *What Does Legislative History Tell Us?*, 66 Chi.-Kent L. Rev. 441, 448 (1990) ("Intelligent, modest use of the background of American laws can do much to bring the execution into line with the plan.").

The legislative process features many decisive players. In the U.S. Congress, bills do not ordinarily become law unless the chairs of the relevant committees support them. Likewise, bills typically do not get a vote unless the leaders (the Speaker of the House and the Majority Leader in the Senate) agree. To make law, liberals and conservatives often need support from moderates. In exchange for their support, moderates often demand modifications to the proposals. Moderates, leaders, and committee chairs are pivotal: you cannot make law without them. Understanding the views of pivotal players helps us understand the bargain they struck. When interpreting legislation, the bargain theory of interpretation directs judges to focus on the deal struck by the pivotal players.

To demonstrate, consider one of the most important and inspiring statutes in American history: the Civil Rights Act of 1964. It prohibited discrimination based on race, color, sex, religion, or national origin. It opened job opportunities and public accommodations, like restaurants and hotels, to African Americans and other minorities who had long suffered from unequal treatment. This landmark of civil rights remade American society and sparked litigation.

Consider a famous case about the Act, *United Steelworkers of America v. Weber*.[83] A company had two kinds of workers: unskilled workers who earned low wages, and skilled workers who earned higher wages. At one of the company's plants, about 2 percent of skilled workers were African American, but 39 percent of the community's workforce was African American. The company started a training program to turn unskilled workers into skilled workers. Half of the positions in the program were reserved for African Americans. The question in the case was: Does the Civil Rights Act permit voluntary affirmative action programs by private employers?

To interpret a statute, lawyers begin with its language. In Section 703(a), the Civil Rights Act forbade employers from classifying employees "in any way which would deprive . . . any individual of employment opportunities . . . because of such individual's race[.]"[84] In Section 703(d), the statute forbade employers from discriminating against "any individual because of his race . . . in admission to, or employment in, any program established to provide apprenticeship or other training."[85] This language cast doubt on the legality of the company's training program. Reserving half the spots in the program for black workers made it harder for white workers to get in. Thus, white workers were denied opportunities because of their race.

Despite the language of the statute, the Supreme Court upheld the affirmative action program. The Court reached its conclusion by looking to legislative intent. What was Congress trying to achieve when it passed the Civil Rights Act? According to the Court, Congress intended the law to open employment opportunities for African Americans.

[83] 443 U.S. 193 (1979).

[84] Here is the complete, relevant text: "It shall be an unlawful employment practice for an employer . . . to limit, segregate, or classify his employees or applicants for employment in any way which would deprive or tend to deprive any individual of employment opportunities or otherwise adversely affect his status as an employee, because of such individual's race, color, religion, sex, or national origin."

[85] Here is the complete text: "It shall be an unlawful employment practice for any employer, labor organization, or joint labor-management committee controlling apprenticeship or other training or retraining, including on-the-job training programs, to discriminate against any individual because of his race, color, religion, sex, or national origin in admission to, or employment in, any program established to provide apprenticeship or other training."

The affirmative action program was consistent with that purpose, so the program did not violate the statute.

How did the Court identify the purpose of the statute? By looking at legislative history. Consider this statement from Senator Hubert Humphrey, a key supporter of the act, which appeared in the legislative record:

> What good does it do a Negro to be able to eat in a fine restaurant if he cannot afford to pay the bill? What good does it do him to be accepted in a hotel that is too expensive for his modest income? How can a Negro child be motivated to take full advantage of integrated educational facilities if he has no hope of getting a job where he can use that education?[86]

The legislative history of the Civil Rights Act has many statements like this, though few so eloquent. This history persuaded the Supreme Court that programs to benefit African American workers were consistent with the law.

Two scholars, Daniel Rodriguez and Barry Weingast, analyzed *Weber* using the bargain theory of interpretation.[87] Here is a brief version of their account. The Democrats in Congress were split. Northern Democrats supported the Civil Rights Act, but southern Democrats strongly opposed it. To pass the law, northern Democrats needed support from Republicans. Senator Everett Dirksen, the leader of Republicans in the Senate, negotiated with the northern Democrats. He and his bloc of Republicans were pivotal; the law could not pass without them.

In exchange for their support, the Republicans demanded that the statute include Section 703(j). Section 703(j) provides that the Civil Rights Act shall not:

> be interpreted to require any employer . . . to grant preferential treatment to any individual or to any group because of the race . . . of such individual or group on account of an imbalance which may exist with respect to the total number or percentage of persons of any race . . . employed by any employer.[88]

Focus on the language: Section 703(j) shall not "require" preferential treatment. The Supreme Court reasoned that although employers cannot be *required* to grant preferential treatment, they are *permitted* to grant preferential treatment. Thus, Section 703(j) did not prohibit the company's voluntary affirmative action program.

86 United Steelworkers of Am. v. Weber, 443 U.S. 193, 203 (1979). The term "Negro" was common in Senator Humphrey's day, but it has become uncommon and offensive over time.

87 *See* Daniel B. Rodriguez & Barry R. Weingast, *The Positive Political Theory of Legislative History: New Perspectives on the 1964 Civil Rights Act and Its Interpretation*, 151 U. Pa. L. Rev. 1417 (2003).

88 Here is the complete text: "Nothing contained in this subchapter shall be interpreted to require any employer, employment agency, labor organization, or joint labor-management committee subject to this subchapter to grant preferential treatment to any individual or to any group because of the race, color, religion, sex, or national origin of such individual or group on account of an imbalance which may exist with respect to the total number or percentage of persons of any race, color, religion, sex, or national origin employed by any employer, referred or classified for employment by any employment agency or labor organization, admitted to membership or classified by any labor organization, or admitted to, or employed in, any apprenticeship or other training program, in comparison with the total number or percentage of persons of such race, color, religion, sex, or national origin in any community, State, section, or other area, or in the available work force in any community, State, section, or other area."

Is this the proper interpretation? Rodriguez and Weingast argue that the answer is no. The Republicans seemed to oppose all discrimination based on race, whether voluntary or not.[89] The Republicans were pivotal and therefore in a position of strength. Given their strength, the proper interpretation of Section 703(j) is broad. That provision prohibits all discrimination at work. The Republicans made their support conditional on that interpretation. The Court erred by reading the provision narrowly, as if Republicans were not pivotal.

Do Rodriguez and Weingast have it right? Maybe yes, maybe no. Beachcombers use metal detectors to find buried jewelry. Sometimes they find trinkets, and sometimes they find treasures. The bargain theory of interpretation is like a metal detector. It tells searchers where to look in the legislative history, but it cannot guarantee a find. Still, the theory improves on traditional approaches to legislative intent.

Questions

2.37. In general, courts do not consult legislative history if the text of the statute is clear and does not yield absurd results. Is concentrating on the text of the statute consistent with the bargain theory of interpretation?[90]

2.38. Suppose the legislature enacts a statute with two parts, X and Y. A court reviews the statute and concludes that X is constitutional but Y is unconstitutional. According to the *severability doctrine*, the court should ask this question: Would the legislature have enacted X without Y? If so, the court should "sever" Y and uphold X. If not, the court should invalidate the entire statute.[91] Would the bargain theory of interpretation and the traditional approach to intentionalism give different answers to the question about X and Y?

2.39. Some statutes include severability clauses that explicitly direct courts to sever unconstitutional parts of the statute and leave the remaining parts intact. Do severability clauses increase or decrease the transaction costs of political bargaining?

2.40. Sumitomo Shoji America, Inc., was a New York corporation and wholly owned subsidiary of a Japanese corporation. The company only hired Japanese men for managerial positions. Female employees in New York sued the company for discrimination. The company claimed that a treaty between the United States and Japan exempted it from U.S. discrimination law. The governments of Japan and the United States disagreed with the company's interpretation of the treaty. The Supreme Court ruled against the company, stating, "When the

[89] *See* United Steelworkers of Am. v. Weber, 443 U.S. 193, 240 (1979) (quoting senators supporting the bill as saying, "There is no requirement in title VII that an employer maintain a racial balance in his work force. On the contrary, any deliberate attempt to maintain a racial balance, whatever such a balance may be, would involve a violation of title VII because maintaining such a balance would require an employer to hire or refuse to hire on the basis of race. . . . [I]f a business has been discriminating in the past and as a result has an all-white working force, when the title comes into effect the employer's obligation would be to simply fill future vacancies on a nondiscriminatory basis. He would not be obliged—or indeed permitted—to fire whites in order to hire Negroes.").

[90] *See* John F. Manning, *What Divides Textualists from Purposivists?*, 106 Colum. L. Rev. 70 (2006).

[91] For a discussion of severability, see Caleb Nelson, Statutory Interpretation 142–46 (2011).

parties to a treaty both agree as to the meaning of a treaty provision, and that interpretation follows from the clear treaty language, we must . . . defer to that interpretation."[92]

(a) Is the Court's decision consistent with the bargain theory of interpretation?

(b) Suppose Japan and the United States agreed that U.S. discrimination law *did not* apply to the company, but the language of the treaty stated that U.S. discrimination law *did* apply to the company. Would deciding that discrimination law did not apply to the company be consistent with the bargain theory of interpretation?

The Hierarchy of Legislative History

Legislative history comes in different forms. Sponsors, supporters, and opponents of bills make statements. Sometimes the President makes a "signing statement" when he signs a bill into law. To become law, bills usually travel through committees, and committees usually write reports explaining the bills. When the House and Senate pass different versions of the same bill, a conference committee is formed to reconcile them. The conference committee proposes a bill to both chambers under a *closed rule*, meaning the bill cannot be amended, and it usually attaches a report explaining the bill. Legislative history comes in other forms too.

Courts do not treat all forms of legislative history the same. In their search for legislative intent, they prioritize some forms over others. Here is a list of some legislative history types, organized from most to least influential on courts: conference reports, committee reports, sponsor statements, statements by other legislators, executive signing statements.[93]

What legislative history should courts credit, and what legislative history should they ignore? Economics has answers.[94] According to the bargain theory of interpretation, courts should search for the bargain legislators struck. The bargain theory implies that courts should credit statements by pivotal players. Courts do this in some respects. Like the Supreme Court in *Church of the Holy Trinity*, courts place weight on reports from committees whose support was necessary for a bill's passage. However, courts fail to do this in other respects. They systematically discount signing statements by the President, even though the President is decisive in most legislation.

These ideas have a converse. If courts should place more weight on statements by decisive players, they should place less weight on statements by nondecisive players. Consider the sponsors of a bill. They usually start by proposing major reforms and compromise to achieve minor reforms, which they prefer to nothing. Courts often

[92] Sumitomo Shoji America, Inc. v. Avagliano, 457 U.S. 176, 185 (1982).

[93] *See* Caleb Nelson, Statutory Interpretation 362–67 (2011); William N. Eskridge Jr. et al., Cases and Materials on Legislation and Regulation: Statutes and the Creation of Public Policy 93 (5th ed. 2014).

[94] *See* McNollgast, *Legislative Intent: The Use of Positive Political Theory in Statutory Interpretation*, 57 Law & Contemp. Probs. 3 (1994).

credit statements from sponsors and discredit statements from other legislators, including decisive players.

Separate from decisive players, economics provides broader perspective on legislative history. Some legislative statements are *cheap talk*, meaning legislators face no penalties for saying false or misleading things. Legislators who make statements about a bill after it passes, for example, are usually engaged in cheap talk. Judges should ignore cheap talk. In contrast, statements are credible when legislators face penalties for making false or misleading statements. Senator Humphrey was the Majority Whip in the Senate, and he organized support for the Civil Rights Act. Senators asked him for information about the bill, and he gave it. If Humphrey made false statements, he would endanger his leadership position and reputation. Consequently, Humphrey had a strong incentive not to mislead his colleagues. His statements about the meaning of the act were credible. Perhaps this justifies the weight accorded to his statements by the Court in *Weber*.

Conclusion

Galileo introduced the concept of a "frictionless plane," where objects move forever in the same direction at the same speed. Frictionless planes do not exist, but they provide a theoretical baseline for predicting movements of real objects. Similarly, a world with "zero transaction costs" does not exist, but the idea provides a baseline for making predictions about real bargains. When the transaction costs of bargaining are low, private parties allocate entitlements to the parties who value them the most, as required for efficiency. When the costs are high, private parties fail to reach efficient agreements.

To supply public laws, lawmakers must overcome the impediments to political bargaining, which resemble the impediments to private bargaining (externalities, information asymmetries, and monopoly). Lawmakers overcome these impediments through the governmental processes discussed in subsequent chapters—voting, entrenching, delegating, adjudicating, and enforcing. However, the same mechanisms used to correct inefficiencies can be used to aggravate them for political advantage. As subsequent chapters show, the processes of government resemble a drug that can cure or kill, depending on the circumstances and dosage.

3
Bargaining Applications

The germ theory of disease gave us antibiotics, and calculus gave us skyscrapers. As in medicine and math, good ideas in economics have useful applications. The previous chapter developed the bargaining theory of public law, and this chapter applies it. Bargaining theory provides insights into questions like these:

Example 1: To fix prices on their products, oil companies collude with other oil companies, and oystermen collude with other oystermen. Collusion creates inefficient monopolies. Why should law prevent oil monopolies but not necessarily oyster monopolies?

Example 2: Lawyers want to give people rights to protect them from the state. Many economists want to give people rights so they can exchange them with the state. Should rights be "unalienable" like the Declaration of Independence says, or should they be tradable like Pokémon cards?

Example 3: According to the Supreme Court, the Commerce Clause of the U.S. Constitution empowers Congress to regulate one farmer's wheat, which has a trivial effect on the economy, but not violence against women, which has a large effect on the economy. Does economic theory support the Supreme Court's interpretation?

To answer such questions, this chapter blends positive, normative, and interpretive analysis. We begin by examining laws regulating citizens, and then we turn to laws organizing government.

I. On Regulation

Food labels, prescription drugs, speed limits—regulations touch many aspects of our lives. Some regulations are simple (do not speed), while others are technical (use the Johnson Permeameter for soil infiltration tests of storm water). We focus on regulations whose purpose is correcting externalities, where one person's activity affects another person's well-being. Whether the topic is speeding or soil erosion, regulations present a fundamental choice: Should the state facilitate private solutions or impose public solutions?

Public Law and Economics. Robert D. Cooter and Michael D. Gilbert, Oxford University Press. © Oxford University Press 2022.
DOI: 10.1093/oso/9780197655870.003.0003

A. Congestion and Externalities

The public has access to "common" resources like air, oceans, and pastures. In the language of the previous chapter, common resources are non-excludable. When few people use these resources, they do not interfere with each other (the resource is non-rivalrous). When many people use these resources, however, they become congested, and they interfere with each other (the resource becomes rivalrous). With congestion, each additional user harms other users. Thus, with uncongested common pasture, ranchers in Montana can graze their cattle without affecting each other's livelihood. With congestion, each additional cow harms the livelihood of other ranchers. In the previous chapter, we explained that when an activity has negative externalities, there is usually too much of it. Left to their own devices, ranchers harm the land by overgrazing.

Barren pasture illustrates the *tragedy of the commons*.[1] The tragedy arises when everyone's individually rational decision to use a common resource depletes the resource for all. The tragedy of the commons explains why there is too much smog in Beijing, too many industrial pollutants in the Ganges River, and too few trees left in the Amazon. It explains why drivers in Los Angeles face gridlock (when you drive, you slow others down) and why radio stations interfere with each other (more on this later).

To understand the tragedy better, consider a numerical example. Five fishers have access to a lake (a "fisher" is a person who catches fish). Every fish caught has a market value of $1, so each fisher earns $1 for each fish he or she catches. Instead of fishing, each fisher can stay home and enjoy leisure (say, binge-watching television), which he or she values at $4 per day. To decide between work and leisure, each fisher weighs benefits and costs. Thus, if a fisher expects to catch six fish that day, he chooses between earning $6 by fishing or getting $4 of leisure, so he chooses to fish. Conversely, if a fisher expects to catch three fish that day, he chooses between earning $3 by fishing or getting $4 of leisure, so he chooses leisure.

Table 3.1 shows the long-run relationship between the number of fishers on the lake and the number of fish caught per day. The first row indicates that one fisher will catch 20 fish, two fishers will catch 32 fish, and three fishers will catch 39 fish. More fishers can catch more fish, but only up to a point. Increasing the number of fishers from three to four causes the catch to decline to 36 fish, and increasing from four fishers to five causes the catch to decline to 25 fish. With so many fishers, the fish cannot reproduce quickly enough. In the long run, this means fewer fish will be caught.

If fishers have open access to the lake, how many will fish? Consider the problem sequentially. If the lake is empty to start, the first fisher will think: "If I work, I will catch 20 fish and earn $20, and if I stay home I will get only $4 from leisure. I will fish." The second fisher arrives to find only one other person fishing on the lake. She reasons: "If I fish, I will earn $16, and if I stay home I will get only $4 from leisure. I will fish." Following the same logic, the third, fourth, and fifth fishers decide to fish, as row 3 of the table illustrates. Thus, individually rational decisions result in fishing by five people.

Is this result efficient? No. Efficiency maximizes the total net revenues. Total net revenues are maximized when three fishers fish on the lake, as row 4 of the table shows.

[1] Garrett Hardin, *The Tragedy of the Commons*, 162 Science 1243 (1968).

Table 3.1. Tragedy of the Commons

	Number of fishers on the lake				
	1	2	3	4	5
1. Total revenue from selling all fish (total number of fish caught * sale price of fish)	\$20	\$32	\$39	\$36	\$25
2. Revenue per fisher	\$20	\$16	\$13	\$9	\$5
3. Net revenue per fisher (revenue minus lost leisure)	\$16	\$12	\$9	\$5	\$1
4. Total net revenue (total revenue minus total loss of leisure for all fishers)	\$16	\$24	\$27	\$20	\$5
5. Marginal net revenue (change in total net revenue from an additional fisher)	\$16	\$8	\$3	−\$7	−\$15

What causes the inefficiency? Each fisher gets paid for the number of fish she catches, which includes fish that others would have caught if she had stayed home. Thus, each fisher internalizes only some of the costs of fishing. If the fourth fisher were paid his *marginal* contribution to the total catch as indicated by the table's row 5, he would not work and the lake would not be overfished. In sum, open access to the lake causes too many individuals to fish, congestion on the lake is a negative externality, and overfishing depletes the number of fish.

The lake is a common resource in the sense that different people share its use. Sometimes private actors successfully manage common resources. Fishermen in Port Lameron, a village in Nova Scotia, have informally divided territory in nearby fisheries.[2] For centuries, ranchers have managed communally the mountain pastures of Iceland.[3] But for each success, there are many failures. In the 1930s, California's annual sardine harvest exceeded 500,000 tons. Within 20 years, overfishing led to a collapse in the sardine stock and the failure of this industry.[4]

Questions

3.1. When the COVID-19 pandemic swept across the United States, many businesses shut down. The mayor of Las Vegas pushed for businesses in her city to reopen. When asked how they could reopen without spreading the disease, the mayor responded, "[W]e're in a crisis healthwise, and so for a restaurant to be open or a small boutique to be open, they better figure it out. That's their job.

[2] Elinor Ostrom, Governing the Commons 173–78 (2015) (citing Anthony Davis, *Property Rights and Access Management in the Small Boat Fishery: A Case Study from Southwest Nova Scotia*, *in* Atlantic Fisheries and Coastal Communities: Fisheries Decision-making Case Studies 133–64 (Cynthia Lamson & Arthur Hanson eds., 1984)).

[3] Thráinn Eggertsson, *Analyzing Institutional Successes and Failures: A Millennium of Common Mountain Pastures in Iceland*, 12 Int'l Rev. L. Econ. 423 (1992).

[4] Gary D. Libecap, Contracting for Property Rights 76 (1993).

That's not the mayor's job."[5] Do you agree? Relate your answer to the tragedy of the commons.

3.2. When people file lawsuits, they create a negative externality by slowing down other cases in the legal system. How does the law try to correct this externality?

3.3. Many people use Wikipedia, an online encyclopedia, but only a fraction pay for their use. Is Wikipedia a public good? How does it try to overcome free riding?

Marginal Costs and Benefits

In Table 3.1, the last row shows "marginal net revenue." Here is the intuition behind those numbers. Without any fishers the lake produces nothing, and with one fisher the lake produces net revenue of $16. Thus, the marginal net revenue associated with the first fisher is $16. The lake produces net revenue of $16 with one fisher and $24 with two fishers. Thus, the second fisher's marginal net revenue is $8, and so on. Marginal net revenue is positive for the third fisher but negative for the fourth and fifth. The fourth and fifth fishers do more harm than good.

This is *marginal analysis*, a hallmark of economics. According to marginal analysis, we should do more of an activity until the additional benefit of doing more equals the additional cost. Then we should stop. Efficiency is achieved when marginal benefits equal marginal costs.

To illustrate, consider an important question: How many hours should a student spend studying for an exam? The first hour of studying greatly improves comprehension, and it does not interrupt the student's social life. The marginal benefit greatly exceeds the marginal cost, so the student should study. By the time the student gets to, say, the eleventh hour, the calculation changes. Studying for 10 hours is sufficient to get an A. Studying for an eleventh hour does not improve comprehension, and it would require the student to skip a party. The marginal cost of that hour exceeds the marginal benefit. The student should stop studying after 10 hours.

Marginal analysis can be counterintuitive. To see why, suppose the student would gain 50 utility from getting an A on the exam. By studying for 20 hours at a cost of 20 utility, the student will get an A. Foreseeing a net gain of 30, the student decides to study for 20 hours. This is *not* efficient. The student is thinking in total rather than marginal terms. Ten hours of study are enough to get an A, so the marginal benefit of studying for the eleventh hour is zero. Meanwhile, the marginal cost of studying for the eleventh hour is high (remember the party). Instead of studying for 20 hours and receiving a payoff of 30, efficiency requires the student to study for 10 hours and receive a payoff greater than 30.

Marginal analysis is central to public law. Consider a case, *Corrosion Proof Fittings v. Environmental Protection Agency*.[6] Pursuant to the Toxic Substances Control Act (TSCA), the Environmental Protection Agency (EPA) regulated asbestos, a material that has many valuable uses but causes cancer. The EPA could have required labeling

[5] Justin Wise, *Las Vegas Mayor Doubles Down on Push to Reopen Casinos, Says It's Not Her Job to Do It Safely: "They Better Figure It Out"*, The Hill, Apr. 22, 2020.

[6] 947 F.2d 1201 (5th Cir. 1991).

of asbestos or limited its use. Instead, the EPA banned asbestos. The question in the case was whether the EPA had authority to issue such a strong regulation. The TSCA required the EPA to use the "least burdensome" regulation. According to the court, the EPA failed to prove that banning asbestos was least burdensome:

> While the EPA may have shown that a world with a complete ban of asbestos might be preferable to one in which there is only the current amount of regulation, the EPA has failed to show that there is not some intermediate state of regulation that would be superior to both. . . . [T]he proper course for the EPA to follow is to consider each regulatory option, beginning with the least burdensome, and the costs and benefits of regulation under each option. The EPA cannot simply skip several rungs, as it did in this case, for in doing so, it may skip a less-burdensome alternative mandated by TSCA. Here, although the EPA mentions the problems posed by intermediate levels of regulation, it takes no steps to calculate the costs and benefits of these intermediate levels.[7]

The court does not use the exact language of marginal analysis. However, the court understands the TSCA to require it. To see this clearly, make a comparison. The court refers to two "worlds," one with few regulations on asbestos and one with a complete ban on asbestos. The first world is analogous to the student not studying, and the second world is analogous to the student studying for 20 hours. Can you see why the EPA should have considered an alternative in between?

B. Regulation and Information

In the previous chapter, we explained that when private actors cannot cooperate, as in the tragedy of the commons, pressure for public law grows. Many citizens demand action on climate change, spotted owls, water management, and so forth. In the United States, the Clean Air Acts, the Endangered Species Act, and many other laws aim to correct externalities. Laws to correct externalities usually mandate certain behavior by private people. To clean the air, the state prohibits smoking in public and forbids power plants from emitting mercury above a certain threshold. To protect pasture on public land, the state limits grazing. To reduce radio static, the state confines each broadcaster to one frequency.

Much of the American administrative state involves regulations like these. They are sometimes called *command-and-control regulations* because they define permissible and impermissible behavior (the command) and they induce compliance by sanctions (the control). In practice, command-and-control regulations have shortcomings. Take our fishing example. How can the state reduce fishing on the lake by commands? It can limit the number of fishers, limit each fisher's catch, restrict fishing to certain days, regulate fishing technology (e.g., permit lines but not nets), or forbid taking fish below a

[7] *Id.* at 1217.

certain size. However, limiting fishers requires issuing permits and monitoring the lake, limiting the catch requires publicizing the limits and monitoring the scales at the dock, and so on. Each alternative command is costly to enforce.

Command-and-control regulations require state officials to have private information. To prevent overfishing, the state needs to know the relationship between profits and the number of fishers. Fishers know their profits from fishing, but the state does not, so the state easily makes regulatory errors. When Peru established no-catch periods for anchovies, fishers bought larger, faster boats with sonar technology, allowing them to catch the same number of fish in a shorter time.[8] Instead of reducing the catch, the regulation led fishers to spend more money on boats that spent less time at sea. The state did not anticipate how fishers would upgrade their fleets because officials did not know the profitability of fishing.

To illustrate by our numerical example, row 4 of Table 3.1 indicates that when three fishers fish on the lake, total net revenue (i.e., profit) equals $27. However, open access causes five fishers to fish on the lake, and total net revenue equals $5. Thus, open access causes a social loss of $22. Assume that the state regulates to correct the inefficiency by monitoring the number of fishers. The regulation causes a net gain if monitoring costs less than $22, and the regulation causes a net loss if monitoring costs more than $22. Sometimes enforcing commands is so costly that society is better off without regulation, or with an alternative kind of regulation.

Questions

3.4. Is it easier to enforce fishing regulations on Lake Tahoe, which is about 200 square miles in size, or Lake Michigan, which is over 20,000 square miles in size? Which lake do you think suffers more from overfishing?

3.5. Public utilities like gas companies are often monopolies. Government boards set the rates that public utilities can charge. The best rate depends on how much it costs the utilities to provide their product to consumers. Who has better information on the cost of the product, the utilities that supply gas or the state?

3.6. A *Pigouvian tax* is a tax equal to the negative externality that an actor causes.[9] To demonstrate, a polluter whose factory imposes harm of $10 on the community would pay a tax of $10. Carbon emissions harm the planet. Why can't nations agree on a Pigouvian tax for carbon?

Cost-Benefit Analysis in the Administrative State

In *Michigan v. Environmental Protection Agency*, the Supreme Court struck down an EPA regulation requiring power plants to reduce their emissions.[10] The problem

[8] Milena Arias Schreiber & Andrew Halliday, *Uncommon Among the Commons? Disentangling the Sustainability of the Peruvian Anchovy Fishery*, 18 ECOLOGY & SOC'Y 12 (2013).
[9] ARTHUR C. PIGOU, THE ECONOMICS OF WELFARE (4th ed. 1932).
[10] 135 S. Ct. 2699 (2015).

was not that the regulation had no benefit. According to the EPA, the quantifiable benefit would total between $4 million and $6 million. Rather, the problem was cost. Complying with the regulation would cost power plants about $10 *billion*. According to the Court, the EPA cannot "impose billions of dollars in economic costs in return for a few dollars in health or environmental benefits."[11]

In that case, one of the Clean Air Acts required the EPA to account for the costs of its regulation. Different laws in the United States impose a similar requirement. Executive Order 12866 requires federal agencies to "assess all costs and benefits of available regulatory alternatives, including the alternative of not regulating." The Administrative Procedures Act requires courts to set aside agency actions that are "arbitrary, capricious, an abuse of discretion, or otherwise not in accordance with law." In a case called *Business Roundtable v. Securities and Exchange Commission*, a court struck down a regulation requiring public companies to inform shareholders about candidates for the board of directors.[12] According to the court, the agency acted "arbitrarily and capriciously" because it failed to consider the regulation's costs.[13]

Cost-benefit analysis has become central to the regulatory process. Conceptually, the task is straightforward, as in our fishing example. In practice, cost-benefit analysis requires answering hard questions, like how much society benefits when fewer children get cancer. Many disputes in law and politics trace to disagreements about the costs and benefits of regulation.

C. The Market Mechanism

In the previous chapter, we explained how externalities cause free riding. Command-and-control regulations attempt to stop free riding by prohibiting it. A different approach aims to stop free riding by encouraging bargaining. With lower transaction costs, parties may reach a private agreement that eliminates the inefficiency. If private parties can bargain with one another, they can overcome free riding and achieve the efficient solution on their own.

To illustrate, consider the electromagnetic spectrum. Parts of the spectrum are used for communications like radio broadcasts and cellular phones. If two people send signals on the same frequency at the same time, interference results. In 1910, the Secretary of the Navy complained about "irresponsible operators" jamming the Navy's signals: "calls of distress from vessels in peril . . . are drowned out in the etheric bedlam."[14] To mitigate the externality, the federal government gave away licenses to broadcasters for free and required them to use only their assigned frequencies.

Who should get a valuable license for free? The Federal Communications Commission (FCC) held hearings, sometimes called "beauty contests," to decide which

[11] *Id.* at 2707.
[12] 647 F.3d 1144 (D.C. Cir. 2011).
[13] *Id.* at 1148.
[14] Ronald H. Coase, *The Federal Communications Commission*, 2 J.L. Econ 1, 2 (1959).

uses of the spectrum advanced the public interest. Ronald Coase offered a different solution.[15] Instead of giving away licenses and restricting their use, he proposed auctioning licenses and permitting their resale. Individuals would hold a property right to part of the spectrum like homeowners hold a property right to their houses. Private exchange would reallocate spectrum to the highest-value use. The federal government would not have to hold a beauty contest to assign the licenses. Instead of government allocation, there would be market allocation.

Moreover, a property right would empower a spectrum owner to exclude "irresponsible operators"—people transmitting unlawfully on the owner's frequency—in the way homeowners can exclude trespassers. The power to exclude prevents free riding (recall the connection between free riding and non-excludability). Influenced by Coase, the FCC has held dozens of spectrum auctions and raised tens of billions of dollars for the government.[16]

We can generalize from Coase's analysis of the spectrum: *clear rights ease bargaining*. Granting and clarifying rights lowers the transaction costs of bargaining by reducing the errors and miscalculations that obstruct people when they try to cooperate.[17] Clearer rights make threat points easier for the parties to determine. Agreement is achieved more easily when threat positions are known by everyone.

To illustrate this idea, consider land ownership in Peru.[18] Many poor people live on land that they cannot prove they own. Uncertainty over property rights hinders exclusion and trade (would you purchase land from someone who may not own it?). In recent decades, the Peruvian government has given many people formal titles to their land. Clear property rights permit people to exclude and make trades. With a title, farmers can use their property as collateral to secure loans. Clear rights ease bargaining. They offer a *market mechanism* for correcting inefficiencies.

Questions

3.7. Marijuana is legal under Colorado law but illegal under U.S. federal law. How would legalizing marijuana at the federal level affect the market for the drug in Colorado?

3.8. In 1952, steel mills and workers in the United States failed to agree on wages, leading to a nationwide strike during the Korean War.[19] Federal labor law structures bargaining between employers and unions by requiring them to meet

[15] *Id.*

[16] Federal Communications Commission, Auctions Summary (Nov. 26, 2019), https://www.fcc.gov/auctions-summary.

[17] For supporting evidence, see Elizabeth Hoffman & Mathew Spitzer, *The Coase Theorem: Some Experimental Tests*, 25 J.L. Econ. 73 (1982). *See also* Varouj A. Aivazian, Jeffrey L. Callen, & Susan McCracken, *Experimental Tests of Core Theory and the Coase Theorem: Inefficiency and Cycling*, 52 J.L. Econ. 745 (2009); Stewart Schwab, *A Coasean Experiment on Contract Presumptions*, 17 J. Legal Stud. 237 (1988).

[18] *See* Hernando De Soto, The Other Path: The Economic Answer to Terrorism (1986); Chris Arsenault, *Property Rights for World's Poor Could Unlock Trillions in "Dead Capital"*, Reuters, Aug. 1, 2016, https://www.reuters.com/article/us-global-landrights-desoto/property-rights-for-worlds-poor-could-unlock-trillions-in-dead-capital-economist-idUSKCN10C1C1.

[19] *See* A.H. Raskin, *600,000 Quit Steel Mills; Industry Offers to Bargain*, N.Y. Times, June 3, 1952.

at reasonable times, negotiate in good faith, and so on.[20] Does labor law impose command-and-control regulations, or does it lower transaction costs?

3.9. Privatizing a common pasture should prevent its depletion. If you own the pasture, then only you can use it, and you will internalize the costs of overgrazing. Did privatization work better before or after the invention of barbed wire fences?[21]

3.10. In our fishing example, efficiency requires three people to fish, but five people fish instead. If the transaction costs of bargaining were zero, the fishers could solve the tragedy of the commons and achieve efficiency on their own, without state intervention. Explain how.

Collusion and Conservation

In the 1930s, Frank Manaka caught fish off the California coast but could not sell them.[22] Canneries and a private association of fishermen had struck a deal under which the canneries only bought fish from the association's members, and the members sold their fish at a fixed price. Manaka was not a member of the association, so no one would buy his fish. He sued, and a federal court found the association guilty of conspiracy in restraint of trade under the Sherman Act.

Collusion between canneries and fishermen created a monopoly, just like the court held, and monopolies cause inefficiency. But the monopoly had another effect: it conserved fish stocks by limiting the harvest. A similar arrangement conserved shrimp off the coast of Mississippi. Shrimpers and packers colluded, creating a monopoly that encouraged harvesting few large shrimp instead of many small shrimp. Courts struck down this arrangement and dozens like it.

Courts used the Sherman Act to trade one inefficiency for another.[23] They prevented monopoly but accelerated the tragedy of the commons. Courts prohibited bargaining, rather than lowering its costs. Antitrust law does not necessarily require this result. The "rule of reason" in antitrust law permits anticompetitive arrangements to stand if they have offsetting efficiency benefits.[24] A court could find that conserving common resources is an offsetting benefit. Until courts adopt this approach, antitrust law will continue to promote the tragedy of the commons.

[20] *See, e.g.*, Kenneth G. Dau-Schmidt, *A Bargaining Analysis of American Labor Law and the Search for Bargaining Equity and Industrial Peace*, 91 MICH. L. REV. 419 (1992); Steward J. Schwab, *Collective Bargaining and the Coase Theorem*, 72 CORNELL L. REV. 245 (1987).

[21] Terry L. Anderson & P.J. Hill, *The Evolution of Property Rights: A Study of the American West*, 18 J.L. ECON. 163 (1975). *See also* Harold Demsetz, *Toward a Theory of Property Rights*, 57 AM. ECON. REV. 347 (1967).

[22] This discussion draws on GARY D. LIBECAP, CONTRACTING FOR PROPERTY RIGHTS (1989); Jonathan H. Adler, *Conservation Through Collusion: Antitrust as an Obstacle to Marine Resource Conservation*, 61 WASH. & LEE L. REV. 3 (2004).

[23] Policy interventions to correct one inefficiency often introduce other inefficiencies. *See generally* R.G. Lipsey & Kelvin Lancaster, *The General Theory of Second Best*, 24 REV. ECON. STUD. 11 (1956).

[24] The rule of reason is usually attributed to Justice Brandeis's opinion in *Chicago Board of Trade v. United States*, 246 U.S. 231 (1918).

D. Coase or Hobbes?

When bargaining fails, the state has two methods for correcting the inefficiency: give orders (command and control) or facilitate bargaining (market mechanism). Giving orders presupposes that people cannot resolve the inefficiency on their own. We call giving orders the *Hobbesian solution* after the philosopher Thomas Hobbes, who doubted people's capacity to cooperate. Facilitating bargaining presupposes that people can cooperate if transaction costs are low enough. We call facilitating bargaining the *Coasean solution*.[25]

The Hobbesian and Coasean solutions have distinctive costs, as an example illustrates. Much of San Francisco Bay's shoreline that was "soft" (sand, marsh, flood plain) is now "hard" (stone, concrete, docks). The environment benefits from soft shoreline, and commerce benefits from hard shoreline. A local authority that authorizes hardening part of the shoreline—say, building at Marina south of San Francisco—externalizes environmental costs and internalizes commercial benefits. To prevent too much hardening, the central authority could prohibit local governments from hardening some parts of the shore and permit hardening elsewhere. This is a Hobbesian solution. For it to work efficiently, the central authority must find out the relative worth of particular parcels of hard and soft shoreline. This is an information-gathering cost.

Alternatively, the central authority could forbid each local authority from hardening shore anywhere unless a specific amount is softened somewhere else. To implement this solution, local governments could be given hardening rights that they can trade with each other. Local governments would respond by bargaining with each other and trading their development rights. This is a Coasean solution. For it to work efficiently, the central authority does not need to know the relative worth of particular parcels of hard and soft shoreline. Information-gathering costs are reduced. However, the central authority needs to define the boundaries of the parcels and distribute them initially, which is costly.

The choice between Hobbesian and Coasean solutions illuminates much regulatory law. To correct externalities, the state can command by issuing non-tradable grazing permits, or it can facilitate bargaining by issuing tradable grazing permits that ranchers can exchange. To correct monopoly, the state can command by limiting a monopolist bridge's tolls, or it can facilitate bargaining by permitting price discrimination (the bridge can charge different users different amounts) or subsidizing construction of a competing bridge. To correct information asymmetry, the state can command by banning high-interest loans, or it can facilitate bargaining by permitting the loans and requiring banks to disclose their terms.

Economists take all costs into account. The best solution depends on which one has lower total costs. The costs of Hobbesian solutions include information-gathering (e.g., learning the relative worth of particular parcels on San Francisco Bay) and enforcing (e.g., inspecting for unlicensed development). Alternatively, the costs of Coasean solutions include defining development rights and initially distributing them. In practice, a regulatory program that combines Hobbes and Coase, rather than using just one or the other, might minimize total costs.

[25] On Hobbes and Coase, see Robert Cooter, *The Cost of Coase*, 11 J. LEGAL STUD. 1 (1982).

E. On Liability

We have analyzed regulation to correct externalities. Now we consider an alternative approach familiar to lawyers: *liability*.[26] To prevent drivers from harming pedestrians, the state can regulate them (e.g., speed limits, yield signs). Alternatively, the state can impose liability. If a negligent driver causes $100 in harm to a pedestrian, the pedestrian can sue. Paying $100 in damages makes the driver internalize his harm.

Like regulation, liability involves a command (do not drive negligently) and a control (if you drive negligently and cause harm, you will pay). However, regulation and liability differ in other ways. To begin, consider the informational demands of each approach. In general, parties with better information should make the decisions. A pedestrian struck by a car will usually understand her injuries—medical bills, missed work, emotional distress—better than state regulators. In contrast, when schoolchildren drink leaded water, the state might have better information about the consequences than the parents. Regulation tends to work best when the state has better information, and liability tends to work best when the victims have better information.

Now consider the identity of the enforcer. In general, the state enforces regulations, whereas private parties sue liable defendants. Private parties face many challenges when filing suit. Litigation takes time and money (lawyers, expert witnesses). Collective action problems can arise. If 100 victims each suffer $100 in harm (total $10,000), and if the cost of suit totals $200, no victim sues, meaning the injurer externalizes $10,000 in harm. Litigation causes many people stress. In the end, the plaintiff might lose, meaning the time, money, and stress are wasted. This possibility discourages plaintiffs from suing in the first place. The state does not suffer as much from these problems. Regulations work better as the litigation costs of private parties increase.

We have analyzed plaintiffs' ability to sue. Now consider injurers' ability to pay. Suppose a chemical company accidentally discharges toxic waste, causing $1 million in harm to a victim. If the company has $1 million on hand, the victim can sue and get a full recovery. Liability will force the company to internalize all of the harm it caused. However, if the company has only $500,000 on hand, the victim cannot get a full recovery, and the company will only internalize a fraction of its harm.

Injurers are *judgment proof* when they cannot pay for all of the harm they cause. A judgment-proof injurer externalizes costs, leading to inefficiency. Liability tends to worsen the problem of judgment proofness. Like the company in our example, many injurers cannot pay large damages awards. In contrast, regulation mitigates the problem of judgment proofness. Injurers who cannot pay large damages often can pay small fines. Regulations might require the chemical company to transport toxic waste using safe equipment or pay a $20,000 fine. As long as the company has $20,000, it will internalize the cost of violating the law. Internalization encourages the company to obey the regulation and transport waste safely. To generalize, regulations tend to work best when injurers' have a limited ability to pay.

Finally, consider administrative costs. Regulations require ongoing monitoring and enforcement by the state. To keep bacteria out of the food supply, dairy farms are subject

[26] This discussion draws on Steven Shavell, *Liability for Harm Versus Regulation of Safety*, 13 J. Legal Stud. 357 (1984).

to regulations on pasteurizing milk. The state might inspect many farms, including farms with responsible owners who protect against bacteria even without the threat of enforcement. Likewise, the state might test a lot of milk, even though only a tiny fraction is contaminated. This ongoing effort is costly. In comparison, liability tends to be cheap. No one inspects farms or tests milk unless someone gets sick and sues. The threat of a lawsuit makes farmers careful without ongoing inspections and tests. In general, liability has lower administrative costs than regulation.

We have compared regulations and liability, showing that each has advantages and disadvantages. To maximize advantages, the state can combine regulations and liability. In the United States, truck drivers are subject to many regulations—licensing, lighting requirements, weight limits—and they are liable for accidents. The optimal mix of regulations and liability depends on many factors, including those previously mentioned.

II. Federalism

We distinguished public laws that regulate private persons with Hobbesian and Coasean solutions. Now we apply this distinction to public officials. Laws can command officials, facilitate bargaining among them, or both. To illustrate, with tens of thousands of citizens, a nation's people cannot bargain with one another over lawmaking. The citizens can, however, elect representatives to bargain for them. The constitution stipulates how to create a legislature. The constitution commands the process for legislating, but not the substance. Thus, the constitution creates a legislative forum in which representatives can bargain over laws. This is a bargaining justification for representative democracy.

A constitution usually creates several legislative bodies and divides power among them. Power can be divided horizontally, as when school boards and water boards work independently. Neither legislative body is above the other. Dividing powers among several bodies of lawmakers increases the ease of bargaining within them. However, dividing powers diminishes the scope of bargaining across them. For example, earlier we discussed Caleb and Dee, city councilmembers who traded votes on police and schools. Striking a bargain between Caleb and Dee would be hard if Caleb belonged to the city council that controlled the police budget and Dee belonged to the school board that controlled the school's budget. However, striking a bargain within the city council on police, or striking a bargain within the school board on schools, might be easier.

Alternatively, power can be united horizontally, as when the town council has comprehensive power over police and schools. Uniting powers in one body of lawmakers extends the scope of bargaining by its members. For example, striking a bargain between Caleb and Dee would be easier if both of them belonged to the city council that controlled the budget for police and schools, as opposed to one of them belonging to the city council and the other belonging to the school board. In general, comprehensive power facilitates bargaining across issues.

The city council and the school board illustrate the horizontal division of power, where neither body of lawmakers is higher than the other. Power can also be divided vertically between the central government and the state governments. In the

United States, the vertical division is called federalism. Federalism is a core feature of American constitutionalism and the source of many legal and policy disputes. The U.S. Constitution enumerates the powers of the central government and reserves unenumerated powers to the states, as we explain later in detail. We use bargaining theory to analyze federalism.

A. Legal Externalities

Earlier we discussed free riding on the supply of public goods like clean air and the abatement of public "bads" like noise pollution. Without corrective laws, private actors supply too little clean air and too much noise. Similarly, free riding mars the making of corrective laws. Laws often come with externalities, as we saw in the previous chapter. Under the Articles of Confederation, states like Virginia failed to pay taxes to the central government, which harmed the security of all states.[27] As another illustration, suppose the state of Nebraska makes a law to reduce the number of feedlots within its borders. By cleaning the air, the law benefits Nebraska. It also benefits Iowa, which is downwind.

Legal externalities arise when law has effects beyond the enacting government's borders. Like market externalities, legal externalities cause inefficiency. If Virginia had accounted for Maryland's security, it might have paid up, making the confederation better off. Similarly, feedlots in Nebraska cause too much pollution in Iowa. If Nebraska accounted for the harm to Iowa, it might reduce pollution.

What can cure legal externalities? As usual, bargaining offers a solution. If transaction costs are low, Nebraska and Iowa can strike a deal under which Iowa pays Nebraska to reduce pollution from its feedlots. According to the Supreme Court's interpretation, the Constitution authorizes states to make interstate compacts like this without federal involvement.[28] Thus, the Compact Clause and the Court's interpretation of it facilitate bargaining between states. States have negotiated hundreds of interstate compacts. Some compacts solve coordination problems, like the Driver License Agreement, under which states honor driver's licenses issued by other states. All states benefit when their licenses are honored everywhere. Because interests align, coordination is relatively easy to achieve, and nearly all states have joined the Driver License Agreement. Other compacts involve distribution. Virginia and West Virginia have signed numerous compacts to settle their border.

States can choose to join or not join interstate compacts. Like a contract between a buyer and a seller, interstate compacts require all parties to agree. This process is a form of unanimity rule. As the previous chapter explained, unanimity rule provokes holdouts that make bargaining difficult. Recall that thirteen states could not agree to fund the central government under the Articles of Confederation.

[27] *See, e.g.*, Randolph E. Paul, Taxation in the United States (1954).

[28] The constitution requires congressional consent for interstate compacts. *See* U.S. Const. art. I, § 10 ("No State shall, without the Consent of Congress . . . enter into any Agreement or Compact with another State[.]"). In *Virginia v. Tennessee*, 148 U.S. 503 (1893), however, the Supreme Court held that not all agreements between states constitute "Agreements or Compacts" requiring congressional consent.

Questions

3.11. Is North Korea's decision to manufacture nuclear weapons a legal externality? How is the world trying to resolve this situation?

3.12. Is bargaining over the border between two states a game of production or distribution? Why are border disputes difficult to resolve?

3.13. In *Virginia v. Tennessee*, the Supreme Court held that interstate compacts require Congress's approval only if they threaten to increase the power of states at the expense of the federal government.[29] What negative externality does this decision prevent? What negative externalities does it permit?

B. The Internalization Principle

If bargaining cannot solve legal externalities, what can? Internalization. Expanding a government's borders makes external effects internal. Suppose Nebraska's law on feedlots affects Iowa. If Nebraska and Iowa cannot bargain, they can merge. If a single state encompasses both places, its laws have no externalities. The new state internalizes the effects of its law.

Larger governments imply fewer legal externalities. This suggests that governments should have broad reach. However, larger governments come with a disadvantage: they lack information about local matters. Consider the distinction between national and local public goods. National defense benefits everyone within the nation's borders, making it a national public good. In contrast, Central Park in New York City mostly benefits people who live or work nearby, making it a local public good. Similarly, congestion on the Golden Gate Bridge mostly harms commuters between San Francisco and Marin County, making it a local public "bad." An air-quality basin, a city park, and a congested street are standard examples of local public goods and bads.

People affected by a law have more reason to inform themselves about it and to influence it than those unaffected by it. Thus, affected people are more likely to cast informed votes, monitor politicians, impose taxes on themselves, design optimal regulations, and perform the acts of citizenship that make democracy work. Considerations of information and motivation imply a prescription for allocating government power called the *internalization principle: assign power to the smallest unit of government that internalizes the effects of its exercise.*[30]

The internalization principle provides a guide to fundamental laws. If a public good is national, or nearly so, the central government should provide it. The central government should raise revenues and use them to supply national public goods. Conversely, if a public good is local, like a small city park, the local government should supply it. Funding for the park should come from a local source, like a community tax, which primarily hits beneficiaries of the park and misses nonbeneficiaries.

[29] 148 U.S. 503 (1893).

[30] *See* Robert D. Cooter & Neil S. Siegel, *Collective Action Federalism: A General Theory of Article I, Section 8*, 63 STAN. L. REV. 115 (2010). For an early formulation of this approach that influenced economists, see WALLACE E. OATES, STUDIES IN FISCAL FEDERALISM (1972). For a later summary of this approach, see Wallace E. Oates, *Federalism and Government Finance*, *in* MODERN PUBLIC FINANCE 126 (John M. Quigley & Eugene Smolensky eds., 1994).

The internalization prescription for supplying public goods also applies to abating public bads. If a negative externality is national, or nearly so, the central government should control it. Likewise, if a negative externality is local, or nearly so, the local government should control it.

We have presented internalization as a normative principle. It provides an economic theory for how states *ought* to be organized. However, the principle is also positive. It helps explain how states *are* organized. To illustrate, suppose that establishing a large park in the mountains would attract visitors from all over the nation. If most financing must come from taxes and not entrance fees, financing the national park from a national tax burdens all potential visitors. The national government, not state or local government, represents all potential visitors. Thus, federal officials have better incentives than state or local officials to build a large park that would attract visitors nationally. Responsibility for parks benefitting the nation should fall upon officials who have a national perspective, which is mostly what we observe. The largest and finest parks in the United States are almost entirely the work of the federal government.

As another illustration, consider special government districts. Many externalities cross borders. Water and air circulate in regions formed by rivers and mountains, not political boundaries. Consequently, pollution spills over from one government jurisdiction to another. Sometimes special governments can be created to fit the boundaries of a natural region. A special district might provide clean water to several counties, or it might impose liability on local governments that pollute an air basin. According to the internalization principle, the jurisdiction of a special district should extend as far as the effects of the public goods that it supplies, or the public bad that it abates. The United States contains many special governments that approximately satisfy the principle. California alone has more than 5,000 special districts, including water, school, park, and transportation districts.[31] Similarly, the Washington Metropolitan Area Transit Authority operates the Metro train system for commuters in Washington, DC, and its neighboring jurisdictions.[32]

C. Introduction to Article I, Section 8

The internalization principle helps explain and justify general features of American federalism. However, you will not find the principle written in the Constitution. There is no "internalization clause." Instead, the Constitution contains Article I, Section 8, which enumerates the powers of the federal government. If a power is not listed in Article I, Section 8, the federal government cannot exercise it. According to the Tenth Amendment, powers not delegated to the federal government are reserved to the states. Thus, Article I, Section 8 allocates power between the federal and state governments. This section reviews Article I, Section 8, beginning with its text:

[31] *See* California Special Districts Association, Special Districts Mapping Project, https://mydashgis.com/CSDA/map.
[32] Washington Metropolitan Area Transit Authority, History, https://www.wmata.com/about/history.cfm.

The Congress shall have power to

1. lay and collect taxes, duties, imposts and excises, to pay the debts and provide for the common defense and general welfare of the United States; but all duties, imposts and excises shall be uniform throughout the United States;
2. To borrow money on the credit of the United States;
3. To regulate commerce with foreign nations, and among the several states, and with the Indian tribes;
4. To establish a uniform rule of naturalization, and uniform laws on the subject of bankruptcies throughout the United States;
5. To coin money, regulate the value thereof, and of foreign coin, and fix the standard of weights and measures;
6. To provide for the punishment of counterfeiting the securities and current coin of the United States;
7. To establish post offices and post roads;
8. To promote the progress of science and useful arts, by securing for limited times to authors and inventors the exclusive right to their respective writings and discoveries;
9. To constitute tribunals inferior to the Supreme Court;
10. To define and punish piracies and felonies committed on the high seas, and offenses against the law of nations;
11. To declare war, grant letters of marque and reprisal, and make rules concerning captures on land and water;
12. To raise and support armies, but no appropriation of money to that use shall be for a longer term than two years;
13. To provide and maintain a navy;
14. To make rules for the government and regulation of the land and naval forces;
15. To provide for calling forth the militia to execute the laws of the union, suppress insurrections and repel invasions;
16. To provide for organizing, arming, and disciplining, the militia, and for governing such part of them as may be employed in the service of the United States, reserving to the states respectively, the appointment of the officers, and the authority of training the militia according to the discipline prescribed by Congress;
17. To exercise exclusive legislation in all cases whatsoever, over such District (not exceeding ten miles square) as may, by cession of particular states, and the acceptance of Congress, become the seat of the government of the United States, and to exercise like authority over all places purchased by the consent of the legislature of the state in which the same shall be, for the erection of forts, magazines, arsenals, dockyards, and other needful buildings; —And
18. To make all laws which shall be necessary and proper for carrying into execution the foregoing powers, and all other powers vested by this Constitution in the government of the United States, or in any department or officer thereof.

The first clause gives Congress authority to "lay and collect taxes." This prevents the free riding that took place under the Articles of Confederation by empowering the central government to fund itself. To many people, the remaining powers look like a hodgepodge. Why does Congress have authority over things like bankruptcies (clause 4), post offices (clause 7), and the "useful arts" (clause 8)? Why does Congress not have authority over health care, education, and the police? And what do the clauses mean? Consider clause 17, which gives Congress power to erect certain "forts, magazines, arsenals, dockyards, and other needful buildings." Military hospitals are not on the list. Do they constitute "needful buildings"? What about hangars for military helicopters, which were invented 150 years after the Constitution was written?

To answer these questions, we must interpret the Constitution. Lawyers and judges have interpreted, and reinterpreted, many of the clauses in Article I, Section 8. We focus on interpreting two clauses critical to federalism: the General Welfare Clause and the Commerce Clause.

Clause 1 empowers Congress to "provide for the common defense and general welfare of the United States." Whereas the common defense seems relatively transparent, the general welfare seems relatively opaque. In the 1800s, lawmakers thought the clause was quite limited. As President, James Madison vetoed a bill to fund roads and canals because, in his view, Congress lacked constitutional authority to make such "internal improvements."[33] Many decades later, the Supreme Court in *United States v. Butler* disagreed.[34] The Court held that the General Welfare Clause gives Congress broad authority to spend the money it raises through taxation. Thus, Congress can tax citizens to pay for things like roads and canals, as well as social security, unemployment benefits, and education.[35]

The General Welfare Clause grants Congress broad spending power, but it does *not* grant regulatory power. Interpreting the clause to grant regulatory power would render the rest of Article I, Section 8 superfluous. Why bother granting power over bankruptcies in clause 4 and post offices in clause 7 if Congress already has that power (and much more) in clause 1? Interpreting clause 1 to grant general regulatory authority would seem to give the federal government *all* power, not *some* power. As the Court wrote in *Butler*, interpreting the clause this way would make the United States "a government of general and unlimited powers, notwithstanding the subsequent enumeration of specific powers."[36]

Now consider the Commerce Clause. Clause 3 empowers Congress to regulate "commerce with foreign nations, and among the several states, and with the Indian tribes." The question of what constitutes "commerce . . . among the several states" has preoccupied jurists since the eighteenth century. During the so-called Lochner era, the Supreme Court interpreted the clause narrowly. Thus, Congress could regulate "commerce" but not "manufacturing."[37] Commerce within a state was not "among the several states," and therefore outside of Congress's jurisdiction. Congress could regulate goods

[33] James Madison, Veto Message on the Internal Improvements Bill (Mar. 3, 1817) (transcript available at https://millercenter.org/the-presidency/presidential-speeches/march-3-1817-veto-message-internal-improvements-bill).

[34] 297 U.S. 1 (1936).

[35] Helvering v. Davis, 310 U.S. 619 (1937).

[36] *Butler*, 297 U.S. at 64 (quoting 1 Joseph Story, Commentaries on the Constitution of the United States § 907 (Melville M. Bigelow ed., 5th ed. 1905) (1833)).

[37] United States v. E.C. Knight Co., 156 U.S. 1, 12–13 (1895).

in the "flow" of commerce,[38] but not goods outside the flow that affect interstate commerce.[39] Also, it could regulate "harmful" but not "harmless" goods.[40]

The Supreme Court eventually abandoned these distinctions. During the Great Depression, President Roosevelt threatened to "pack" the Supreme Court with judges sympathetic to federal power. Under pressure, the Supreme Court Justices developed a new interpretation of the Commerce Clause that greatly expanded Congress's power,[41] as illustrated by *Wickard v. Filburn*.[42] A farmer grew more wheat than a federal law allowed, and he used the excess wheat to feed his family and livestock. The excess wheat was outside the flow of commerce. Even so, the Supreme Court allowed Congress to regulate the farmer's excess wheat. Growing wheat for oneself reduces demand for wheat at the store, which implies lower prices for wheat on interstate markets. Thus, in the Court's new view, wheat grown by one farmer in one state for home consumption involved "commerce . . . among the several states."

For decades, the Supreme Court seemed to allow Congress unlimited power to regulate under the Commerce Clause. That changed in 1995 when the Supreme Court decided *United States v. Lopez*, a case involving a federal statute that criminalized possession of a firearm within 1,000 feet of a school.[43] The challengers to the law argued that the federal government did not have authority under the Commerce Clause to regulate this activity. The Supreme Court agreed, concluding that gun possession near schools does not have a "substantial" effect on interstate commerce. Similarly, *United States v. Morrison* struck down part of the Federal Violence Against Women Act.[44] The Court reasoned that gender-motivated crimes of violence do not constitute economic activity, and therefore the Commerce Clause does not authorize Congress to regulate them. In *Gonzales v. Raich*, the Court held that Congress can regulate "economic" activity but not "noneconomic" activity.[45]

To summarize, Congress has power to tax and, under the General Welfare Clause, power to spend, but it lacks general power to regulate. The Commerce Clause grants Congress specific power to regulate, but only if the regulated activity is "economic."

Alexis de Tocqueville, a keen observer of the United States, said the federal system was designed to combine "the different advantages which result from the magnitude

[38] Carter v. Carter Coal Co., 298 U.S. 238, 305 (1936). *Compare* Swift & Co. v. United States, 196 U.S. 375, 398–99 (1905) (upholding application of the Sherman Act to price fixing by stockyard owners), *with* A.L.A. Schechter Poultry Corp. v. United States, 295 U.S. 495, 543 (1935) ("So far as the poultry here in question is concerned, the flow in interstate commerce had ceased. The poultry had come to a permanent rest within the state.").

[39] *A.L.A. Schechter Poultry Corp.*, 295 U.S. at 523–25, 527–28, 542–51 (1935) (invalidating the Federal Live Poultry Code for the New York City metropolitan area, which regulated the sale of diseased chickens and which included wage, hour, and child labor provisions, based on an "indirect" relationship to interstate commerce).

[40] *E.g.*, Hammer v. Dagenhart, 247 U.S. 251, 268–72, 276–77 (1918) (invalidating a federal ban on the shipment in interstate commerce of goods produced by child labor, and distinguishing cases in which the Court upheld federal regulation on the ground that in those cases "the use of interstate transportation was necessary to the accomplishment of harmful results," whereas in the case at bar "[t]he goods shipped [were] of themselves harmless").

[41] For evidence that law, and not political threats, caused the Court's reinterpretation of the Commerce Clause, see Barry Cushman, *Rethinking the New Deal Court*, 80 VA. L. REV. 201 (1994).

[42] 317 U.S. 111 (1942).

[43] 514 U.S. 549 (1995).

[44] 529 U.S. 598 (2000).

[45] 545 U.S. 1 (2005).

and the littleness of nations."[46] Do the Supreme Court's interpretations achieve this? We will use economics to provide an answer.

Questions

3.14. Congress has general power to tax but not regulate. Thus, Congress can tax people for failing to buy a house (the interest deduction on home mortgages is equivalent to an extra tax on people who rent instead of own). However, Congress cannot require people to buy houses and fine them for renting instead. What is the difference between a tax and fine?[47]

3.15. Is growing wheat for home consumption, which has a trivial effect on the market price, "economic" activity? Are gender-motivated crimes of violence, which have a large effect on the economy (doctors, lawyers, police, jailers, employers, courts), a "noneconomic" activity?

D. Collective Action Federalism

While cataloging the failures of the Articles of Confederation, Madison decried the "want of concert in matters where common interest requires it."[48] For common concerns like security, the states should act together, not individually. The Framers lacked the tools of modern economics, but they knew a collective action problem when they saw it. The Constitution's federalism reflects this. Table 3.2 summarizes and sorts the clauses of Article I, Section 8 into three categories that we will describe.[49]

The first category concerns interstate externalities. Most of the clauses listed there involve national defense. Defense is a public good that individual states will undersupply on their own. According to the internalization principle, the national government, not the states, should control defense, and under the Constitution it does.

Now consider clause 7. The post office is a network that becomes more valuable as it acquires more pickup and delivery points. If the postal industry consisted of private firms that cooperated, each firm's activity would expand the network and benefit the other firms. The post office in the eighteenth century resembles the railroad in the nineteenth century and the internet in the twentieth century in this respect: participation has positive externalities. Legal scholars who observed positive externalities on the internet called them "network effects."

[46] 1 ALEXIS DE TOCQUEVILLE, DEMOCRACY IN AMERICA 206 (Francis Bowen ed., Henry Reeve trans., 1898).

[47] *Cf.* Neil S. Siegel & Robert D. Cooter, *Not the Power to Destroy: An Effects Theory of the Tax Power*, 98 VA. L. REV. 1195 (2012).

[48] James Madison, *Vices of the Political System of the United States*, *in* JAMES MADISON: WRITINGS 69, 71 (Jack N. Rakove ed., 1999).

[49] This discussion is based on Robert D. Cooter & Neil S. Siegel, *Collective Action Federalism: A General Theory of Article I Section 8*, 63 STAN. L. REV. 115 (2010). *See also* Jack M. Balkin, *Commerce*, 109 MICH. L. REV. 1 (2010); Max Stearns, *The New Commerce Clause Doctrine in Game Theoretical Perspective*, 60 VAND. L. REV. 1 (2007); Adam Badawi, *Unceasing Animosities and the Public Tranquility: Political Market Failure and the Scope of the Commerce Power*, 91 CAL. L. REV. 1331 (2003).

Table 3.2. Collective Action in Article I

Category	Art. I, Sec. 8 Clause	Power
Interstate Externalities	1	Common defense
	10	Suppress piracy
	11	Declare war
	12	Raise armies
	13	Maintain navy
	14	Make military law
	15	Call militia
	16	Govern militia
Interstate Markets	7	Establish post offices
	8	Make intellectual property law
	3	Regulate interstate and foreign commerce
	4	Naturalization law
	4	Bankruptcy law
	5	Issue money
	5	Fix weights and measures
	6	Punish counterfeiting
Federal Administration	1	Taxes and duties
	2	Issue bonds
	9	Create lower federal courts
	17	Govern DC and federal buildings in states
	18	Make laws necessary and proper to execute these and other powers

Firms are reluctant to invest in a business that externalizes benefits. Given positive externalities, the initial problem of creating a network is to grow it to sufficient size so that it becomes profitable. The federal government's interest in promoting the post office resembles its subsequent interest in promoting the railroad and the internet. Once such an industry is viable, competition often propels the market toward a single provider or a small number of large providers, as with the railroads and Google. A large firm can internalize positive market externalities in the way that a large state can internalize positive legal externalities. Economists call this situation a "natural monopoly."[50] With a natural monopoly like the postal service at the national level, the federal government should have power to regulate it or to provide the service itself. Under the Constitution, it does.

[50] A natural monopoly arises when production has high fixed costs but low marginal costs. Electricity offers an example. Building an electricity distribution system costs a lot (high fixed costs). Once the system is built, however, serving each additional customer is cheap (low marginal costs). Extending service to an additional customer only requires, say, running one wire from the street to the house, or maybe just switching the power from off to on. If one company builds an electricity distribution system, other companies will find it hard to compete. They must incur the high fixed costs necessary to build a competing distribution system, but then they will attract only a fraction of all potential customers (many customers will remain with the initial company). The first company has a natural monopoly.

Turning to clause 8, an inventor without a patent cannot prevent someone from copying her invention. The benefit of the invention to a copier is a positive externality. External benefits discourage making inventions, novels, songs, and other creative works. Because the problem of unauthorized use extends across state lines, the problem is national, so Congress is better placed than states to solve it. Federal intellectual property laws enable creators to collect fees from users across the nation, which creates a unified national market for creative works. This is the economic justification for clause 8.

Now consider the second general category in Table 3.2: interstate markets. In the eighteenth century, America faced the problem of creating a unified market for goods, capital, and labor. Legal obstacles to the movement of resources inhibit national markets. In contrast, a uniform regulatory framework lubricates national markets. Recognizing the federal government's decisive advantage over state governments, the drafters of the Constitution gave Congress the power to create unified national markets in clauses 3 through 6.

Congress used this power. Labor mobility increased as a result of uniform federal laws enacted pursuant to clause 3, such as social security and civil rights, and as a consequence of naturalization laws passed pursuant to clause 4. Stability and trust in capital markets increased following federal statutes enacted pursuant to clause 3, such as federal deposit insurance, compulsory disclosure by issuers of stocks, registration of brokers, and uniform bankruptcy law passed pursuant to clause 4. Federal statutes enacted pursuant to clause 3 also provide the legal foundation for industries like radio and television, in which the Federal Communications Commission prevents broadcasters from interfering with one another. Congress created a common currency as authorized in clauses 5 and 6 and established national standards for weights and measures as authorized in clause 5. These actions solved coordination problems and lowered the transaction costs of interstate trade. Together these laws made the United States the world's largest zone of unrestricted mobility of goods, capital, and labor for more than 150 years, which helps explain the country's remarkable economic success.

Implementing the preceding powers requires federal administration. Clauses 1, 2, 9, 17, and 18 authorize robust means to achieve the ends specified in the other clauses.

With the help of economics, Article I, Section 8 looks like a rational response to collective action problems, not a hodgepodge. Earlier we wrote that the Constitution does not contain a general "internalization clause." Instead, it contains individual clauses that authorize Congress to internalize spillovers.

So far, our analysis of Article I, Section 8 is descriptive. Now we turn to interpretation. Recall clause 1: "Congress shall have power to . . . provide for the . . . general welfare of the United States."[51] The Supreme Court has interpreted the General Welfare Clause as empowering Congress to spend but not to regulate. Granting Congress power to regulate would, the Court wrote in *Butler*, give the federal government "unlimited powers."[52]

[51] U.S. Const. art. I, § 8, cl. 1.
[52] 297 U.S. at 64.

Can one interpret the General Welfare Clause to grant Congress some regulatory power but not all regulatory power? We think the answer is yes. Economics shows how.

When interpreting laws, courts often use a principle called "ejusdem generis," which is Latin for "of the same kind." Ejusdem generis clarifies the meaning of catch-all terms in a list. For example, consider a law forbidding "cars, trucks, motorcycles, and other vehicles" on a public path. Ejusdem generis directs courts to read "other vehicles" in a way consistent with the terms "cars," "trucks," and "motorcycles." Thus, tractors count as "other vehicles" forbidden on the path because they are heavy and motorized like the others. Skateboards and bicycles, however, are light and not motorized, so they may not count as "other vehicles."

Applied to Article I, Section 8, ejusdem generis directs courts to read the General Welfare Clause consistently with specific clauses that empower Congress to act in situations involving interstate externalities. The specific clauses arose in response to failures of states under the Articles of Confederation to solve interstate externalities through bargaining. Thus, the General Welfare Clause can be interpreted to authorize Congress to act on interstate externalities when the transaction costs of bargaining among states are high and congressional power is not authorized by another clause.[53]

To demonstrate, suppose a disease sweeps across the nation. Vaccine programs in one state have positive externalities on other states. Suppose the states cannot agree on the best vaccination program. Article I, Section 8 does not explicitly authorize Congress to regulate disease.[54] Under the interpretation offered here, however, the General Welfare Clause would authorize Congress to enact a vaccination program. Conversely, if the states could agree on the best program, then they could manage the issue themselves, and Congress would lack authority to intervene.

To give another example, suppose a composting facility converts food waste into rich soil for nearby farms. The facility attracts rodents and produces odors, so the neighbors complain. The facility has negative externalities. If the externalities do not cross state lines, then our interpretation of the General Welfare Clause does not authorize Congress to act. The externalities must be interstate.

In sum, we can read Article I, Section 8 as a unified whole, like a well-written paragraph. Clause 1 expresses the unifying principle of a federal government empowered to promote the general welfare, meaning to overcome collective action problems among the states. Clauses 2 through 17 provide instances of the principle that were most important at the time the Framers wrote the paragraph. Clause 18, the Necessary and Proper Clause, underscores the broad availability of means to promote the general welfare.

This understanding of Article I, Section 8 is called *collective action federalism*. Collective action federalism is a theory of interpretation rooted in economics. It demonstrates the usefulness of economics for the work of lawyers and judges.

[53] For an elaboration and defense of this interpretation, see Robert D. Cooter & Neil S. Siegel, *Collective Action Federalism: A General Theory of Article I Section 8*, 63 STAN. L. REV. 115 (2010).

[54] Under existing jurisprudence, the Commerce Clause and the Necessary and Proper Clause authorize Congress to act in this scenario. The General Welfare Clause might offer a more logical basis for that authorization.

Questions

3.16. Many states have enacted laws limiting where convicted sex offenders can live. A law like this in Minneapolis may cause sex offenders to move to the neighboring city of St. Paul. Should courts interpret the General Welfare Clause to empower Congress to make a national law on sex offenders?

3.17. According to collective action federalism, Congress can act on interstate externalities when states cannot bargain successfully among themselves. Suppose New Jersey prefers a federal solution to an interstate externality. What can New Jersey do to ensure that the federal government has constitutional authority to impose a solution?

E. Commerce Revisited

The Commerce Clause, as interpreted by courts, often determines the reach of federal power. Recall *Wickard v. Filburn*, in which the Supreme Court held that Congress can regulate one farmer's home production of wheat.[55] Does this holding address a collective action problem among the states that Congress needed to solve? Congress perceived overproduction of wheat as a national problem. (Put aside the question of whether Congress's perception was accurate, or whether production restrictions were a remedy for the Great Depression.) To solve this perceived problem, individual states could have ordered limits on production within their own borders. However, restrictions in one state disadvantage its producers relative to producers in other states with unrestricted production. Given this fact, each state has an incentive not to restrict production within its borders.

Lawyers call the problem we have described the "race to the bottom." In national markets, producers look for advantages over their competitors. This can cause them to adopt harmful practices, like destroying the environment. The "race" refers to the pressure among states to relax their laws to advantage their producers. The "bottom" refers to the bad outcome of the race—too much pollution.

In theory, interstate compacts can facilitate cooperation and prevent the race to the bottom. To prevent overproduction of wheat during the Great Depression, states could have agreed by compact to limit it. However, compacts require unanimous support, empowering states to hold out. Holding out is a classic collective problem in regulating interstate commerce. The power to hold out makes it hard for states to cooperate.

In contrast to compacts, national regulation can prevent the race to the bottom. In the 1930s, Congress could effectively reduce production of wheat. In *Wickard*, the Court concluded that the Commerce Clause gave Congress that power.[56] Holdouts make it hard for states to prevent the race to the bottom on their own, and the Commerce Clause permits Congress to act instead.

Here is another illustration of these ideas. In *Hodel v. Virginia Surface Mining & Reclamation Association*, the question was whether Congress had authority under

[55] 317 U.S. 111 (1942).
[56] *Id.*

the Commerce Clause to regulate mining, including its environmental impacts. The Court answered yes, stating that national standards "insure that competition in interstate commerce among sellers of coal produced in different States will not be used to undermine the ability of the several States to improve and maintain adequate standards on coal mining operations within their borders."[57] The Commerce Clause empowers Congress to prevent a race to the bottom in the national mining market.

In recent decades, the Supreme Court has pared back the Commerce Clause. Collective action federalism illuminates the Court's logic.[58] In *Lopez*, the Court held that Congress could not regulate guns near schools.[59] Failing to regulate guns near schools in one state probably does not affect such regulations in another state. There is no negative externality. (The same cannot be said of gun sales, where loose regulations in one state can undermine strict regulations in another state.[60])

Similarly, in *Morrison* the Supreme Court held that Congress could not regulate violence against women.[61] The regulation of violent crimes against people—women or men—is traditionally a power reserved for the states. States disagree with each other concerning criminal law and punishment, with some states punishing more severely than others. The Supreme Court apparently perceived some disagreement among states with respect to violent crimes against women, but not a holdout problem among the states or a race to the bottom. Less severe punishment in one state probably does not affect states with more severe punishments. This does not mean violence against women is not a serious problem (it is!). But it does not appear to be a collective action problem among states.

In another case, *Gonzales v. Raich*, California law permitted marijuana for medical use, but federal law prohibited it.[62] Did the Commerce Clause authorize Congress to preempt California law and forbid marijuana? The Court answered yes, and collective action federalism may explain why. Marijuana for medicinal purposes is indistinguishable from marijuana for other purposes. Furthermore, drugs do not respect political boundaries. California's authorization of marijuana could make it more difficult for other states to ban marijuana. If there is an externality—medical marijuana use in California makes it harder to police drugs at, say, the Arizona border—then Congress can intervene. (The legal principle that the federal government has authority to criminalize marijuana remains unchanged, but the federal government no longer has the will to enforce its prohibition, so legalization is proceeding in many state and local jurisdictions.)

In *Lopez*, *Morrison*, and *Raich*, the Supreme Court's reasoning is mostly consistent with collective action federalism, but it did not use this language. In explaining its

[57] 452 U.S. 264, 281–82 (1981) (citation omitted).

[58] This discussion draws on Robert D. Cooter & Neil S. Siegel, *Collective Action Federalism: A General Theory of Article I Section 8*, 63 Stan. L. Rev. 115 (2010).

[59] 514 U.S. 549 (1995).

[60] *See, e.g.*, Leo H. Kahane, *State Gun Laws and the Movement of Crime Guns Between States*, 61 Int'l Rev. L. Econ. 1 (2020) (presenting evidence that guns used for crime move from states with weak gun regulations to states with strong gun regulations).

[61] 529 U.S. 598 (2000).

[62] 545 U.S. 1 (2005).

decisions, the Court distinguished between "economic" and "noneconomic" activity. This distinction, however, is probably untenable. The main reason for dividing power between the federal and state governments is their comparative advantage in different government activities. However, the federal government is not especially able in economic matters, and state governments are not especially able in noneconomic matters. The economic/noneconomic distinction does not systematically relate to the reason for giving some powers to the federal government and other powers to the state governments. A better approach distinguishes individual and collective actions by the states.

The Dormant Commerce Clause

Under the Commerce Clause, Congress can regulate commerce "among the several states."[63] Courts have interpreted the clause to mean that *states* cannot regulate commerce among the several states. This prohibition operates even when state law does not conflict with federal statutes. The "dormant commerce clause" refers to the prohibition against the states regulating interstate commerce, whereas the "active commerce clause" refers to the empowerment of Congress to regulate interstate commerce.

In *H.P. Hood & Sons, Inc. v. Du Mond*, a Massachusetts company wanted to build a milk depot in New York.[64] New York farmers would deliver raw milk to the depot, where it would get weighed, tested, and shipped to Massachusetts for sale. New York law forbade construction of the depot, thus effectively retaining more milk for consumers in New York at the expense of consumers in Massachusetts. No federal statute conflicted with New York's law. Nevertheless, the Supreme Court struck down New York's law for violating the dormant Commerce Clause. The Court wrote:

> [T]he established interdependence of the states only emphasizes the necessity of protecting interstate movement of goods against local burdens and repressions.... Our system, fostered by the Commerce Clause, is that every farmer and every craftsman shall be encouraged to produce by the certainty that he will have free access to every market in the Nation.[65]

The dormant Commerce Clause is consistent with collective action federalism. Each state has an incentive to make laws benefitting their own producers or consumers at the expense of the rest of the nation. Such laws raise the transaction costs of interstate exchange. The dormant Commerce Clause prevents states from acting individually when they should act collectively.

63 U.S. Const. art I, § 8, cl. 3.
64 336 U.S. 525 (1949).
65 *Id.* at 538–39.

III. Separation of Powers

The U.S. Constitution divides the state vertically through federalism, and it divides the state horizontally through the separation of powers. Rather than concentrating authority in a monarch, we divide it among executive, legislative, and judicial branches. The separation of powers is a core feature of constitutions worldwide, and it has many legal and policy dimensions. We will return to the separation of powers throughout this book as we develop new tools for studying it. Here we focus on the relationship between the separation of powers and bargaining. Bargaining theory helps explain why separating powers is usually a good idea, and it helps predict the laws that separated powers will produce. Before analyzing the separation of powers, we sketch some examples of it.

A. Forms of Separated Powers

The executive, legislative, and judicial powers of government can be united or separated. A dictatorship unites all three powers in the executive, who governs by decree. In contrast, a state with the rule of law, such as Great Britain, Germany, or the United States, separates the judicial power from the others. Beyond judicial separation, the remaining powers are organized in different ways. A parliamentary system unites executive and legislative powers as in Great Britain, where the Parliament's lower chamber elects the prime minister. In contrast, a presidential system separates executive and legislative powers as in France and the United States, where citizens directly elect the president. A unicameral system unites legislative powers in a single house, as in Mali and New Zealand. In contrast, a bicameral system divides legislative powers between two houses, as in Canada and South Africa. The number of powers can range from 1 in a dictatorship to 4 in a presidential, bicameral democracy, as depicted in Table 3.3.

Table 3.3 simplifies reality. South Korea has a mixed system with a president and a prime minister. The president has much executive power, but the prime minister has some responsibilities day by day. Another complication occurs when the effective allocation of power in politics does not correspond to the legal allocation in the

Table 3.3. Separation of Powers

Type	Powers	Number	Example
Dictatorship	Executive holds all	1	North Korea
Rule of law + unicameral parliamentary	Courts + one legislative house with prime minister	2	Greece
Rule of law + bicameral parliamentary	Courts + upper house + lower house with prime minister	3	Japan
Rule of law + unicameral presidential	Courts + one legislative house + president	3	Costa Rica
Rule of law + bicameral presidential	Courts + upper house + lower house + president	4	United States

constitution. For example, a dominant political party can unite powers separated in the constitution, as illustrated by the Communist Party in the Soviet Union. Conversely, fragmented parties can separate powers united in the constitution. The effective separation of powers depends on law (the constitution) and politics (parties). We focus on law, and we focus on the separation of powers in the United States. Much of the analysis generalizes to other settings.

B. Separation and Competition

The English Crown oppressed the American colonies. Oppression caused the revolution and, later, opposition to a strong central state. The Articles of Confederation created a weak central state, preventing oppression but also collective action. After the Articles failed, the Framers of the new Constitution faced a challenge: How to design a powerful government that could facilitate collective action without oppressing like the Crown? In a famous passage, Madison captured the problem: "In framing a government . . . the great difficulty lies in this: you must first enable the government to control the governed; and in the next place oblige it to control itself."[66]

Elections help. The threat of removal from office should cause officials to respond more to voters and less to their own whims. But elections are insufficient.[67] The Framers also separated powers. Dividing the state, and making its parts compete and cooperate with one another, should prevent oppression. The division of the state is called separation of powers, and the competition and cooperation is called checks and balances.

Economic theory provides an analogy. Monopoly in business leads to high prices and inefficiency. One way to correct monopoly in business is to foster competition. To lower the price of telephone service, the U.S. government split AT&T into multiple companies. After the split, no company could monopolize the market alone. To form a monopoly, they would have to collude and fix prices, which was difficult. Not only was price fixing illegal but collusion required unanimous agreement by the companies. Each company had a strong incentive to violate the agreement by reducing its prices and capturing more of the market.

Monopoly in government leads to dictatorship. Like monopoly in business, dictatorship leads to inefficiency, though the stakes are much higher. The world's most vicious regimes—Nazi Germany, Stalinist Russia—had monopolies on government. To prevent government monopoly, the Framers split the state into three branches that would vie for power. No branch could control the government alone, and if one tried, the other branches would block it. Rather than concentrating power, the Framers fragmented it. Separating powers divided the state like antitrust laws divided AT&T. Division prevents the concentration of power.

Apart from preventing monopoly, separating powers changes the conduct of the state. Rather than proceeding through orders like a dictator, the state proceeds through bargaining. To govern, the branches of government must cooperate. In the United

[66] THE FEDERALIST No. 51, 264 (James Madison) (Ian Shapiro ed., 2009).

[67] According to Madison, "A dependence on the people is, no doubt, the primary control on the government; but experience has taught mankind the necessity of auxiliary precautions." *Id.*

States, federal legislation ordinarily requires support from the Senate, the House, the President, and the courts (courts "support" legislation by not striking it down). This structure is akin to unanimity rule, which empowers holdouts. Consider the New Deal. During the Great Depression, President Roosevelt and the Congress agreed on national legislation intended to improve the economy and citizens' lives. The Supreme Court struck down many laws—price controls, agriculture subsidies, a minimum wage—because they exceeded Congress's authority under the Commerce Clause. The Court effectively held out, preventing government action.

This example shows a link between bargaining and the division of the state. Separating powers raises the transaction costs of bargaining. Sometimes transaction costs are so high that they impede state action. Impeding state action benefits society when the state is rapacious but harms it when the state is benevolent. The Framers worried more about the former.[68]

Questions

3.18. To prevent monopoly and oppression, the Framers divided government. Why not divide government further by having three legislative chambers rather than two and two presidents rather than one?

3.19. In the United States, citizens elect presidents and legislators but not central bankers or police officers. If elections make officials accountable, why don't we elect all officials?

C. Checks and Balances

Separation of powers fragments the state, and checks and balances keep it fragmented. Without mechanisms for mutual influence, one branch can overpower the others, and monopoly may result. Consider an example. A state is divided into a legislature and an executive. Who decides how the state spends its budget? One option would permit either branch to spend the budget unilaterally. This leads to a tragedy of the commons. The legislature benefits from its spending but externalizes some of the costs (spending costs the legislature *and* the executive). The same goes for the executive, and together they spend too much.[69]

Another option would let the legislature spend the budget alone. This mitigates overspending but may unbalance power. Consider some numbers. The legislature would like to pass a budget bill that prioritizes spending on roads. The bill would

[68] Hamilton wrote: the "power of preventing bad laws includes that of preventing good ones," but the "injury that may possibly be done by defeating a few good laws" will be "amply compensated by the advantage of preventing a number of bad ones." The Federalist No. 73, 372 (Alexander Hamilton) (Ian Shapiro ed., 2009).

[69] Torsten Persson, Gérard Roland, & Guido Tabellini, *Separation of Powers and Political Accountability*, 112 Q.J. Econ. 1163, 1176–79 (1997) (treating unilateral spending as a "common pool problem"). *See also* Richard T. Boylan, *The Impact of Court-Ordered District Elections on City Finances*, 62 J.L. Econ. 633 (2019) (presenting evidence that replacing at-large municipal elections with district elections increases government spending).

provide a benefit to the legislature of 10. This could be a policy benefit if the legislators favor the substance of the bill, or a political benefit if legislators think the bill will get them reelected. The bill would cost the executive 2. Thus, the net gain from the bill among these actors equals 8.

Without a formal role in the budget, the executive cannot veto or modify the bill. But the executive can try to bargain. Suppose she favors a budget bill that prioritizes spending on health care. A budget that prioritizes spending on health care would provide a benefit to the executive of 10 and a loss to the legislature of 2. The executive can bargain with the legislature, proposing passage of a budget that prioritizes roads and health care rather than just roads.

If the parties do not make a deal, the roads-only budget will pass, yielding 10 for the legislature, −2 for the executive, and a net gain of 8. If the parties make a deal, the roads-and-health-care budget will pass. This yields 8 for the legislature (10 from roads and −2 from health care) and 8 for the executive (−2 from roads and 10 from health care) for a net gain of 16.[70] Cooperating creates a surplus of 8. If the parties agree on the reasonable distribution, they each get their threat value plus half the surplus. Thus, the legislature gets 14 and the executive gets 2. To achieve this distribution will require the executive to make a side payment to the legislature. Perhaps the executive will promise to support a future bill.

In this example, the combined budget is more efficient than the roads-only budget. If the transaction costs of bargaining are zero, the combined budget will pass, even though the executive has no formal role in budgeting. This is consistent with the Coase Theorem: given zero transaction costs, parties will bargain to the efficient outcome regardless of the legal rule. Recall, however, that the legal rule affects distribution. Without a role in budgeting, the executive gets a payoff of 2. With a role in budgeting, the executive's payoff grows. Suppose the legislature cannot pass a budget without the executive's support. Without an agreement, no one gains or loses anything. Thus, instead of 10, the legislature's threat value equals 0, as does the executive's. With an agreement, the combined budget passes and they split a surplus of 16. Now the reasonable distribution gives the parties 8 apiece instead of 14 and 2.

Empowering the executive in budgeting equalizes the branches. It stops one from making law at the other's expense, as with the legislature's roads-only budget. It prevents one branch from gaining a lot while the other gains little, as with the payoffs of 14 and 2. This inequality may seem trivial in a law on roads and health care. But suppose the law addressed immigration, diplomacy, control over the bureaucracy, or the executive's war powers. Unequal outcomes on such law could concentrate power in one branch. Checks and balances prevent this. In economic terms, checks and balances prevent one branch from worsening the threat point of other branches in bargaining.

Questions

3.20. Congress passed a law that sought to reduce the U.S. government's budget deficit. The law directed the Comptroller General, a legislative-branch official, to

[70] We assume these expenditures are separable.

make some decisions about government spending. In *Bowsher v. Synar*, the Supreme Court found a constitutional problem with this arrangement.[71] The law vested *executive* power in a *legislative* official. Use our analysis of checks and balances to defend the Court's decision.

3.21. The Court concluded that the Comptroller General was subservient to the legislative branch because Congress could fire him. However, to fire him, Congress would have to pass a veto-proof resolution. As Justice White argued in dissent, "Congress will have no independent power to coerce the Comptroller unless it can muster a two-thirds majority in both Houses," which is very difficult.[72] Is Justice White making an assumption about the transaction costs of bargaining?

The Line-Item Veto

In 1996, Congress passed and the President signed the Line-Item Veto Act, which aimed to reduce government spending. The act gave the President power to "cancel" individual items in spending bills. For example, suppose Congress passed a bill with two elements, a subsidy for potato farming and money to care for the indigent. Without the line-item veto, the President could either sign or veto the entire bill. With the line-item veto, the President could veto selectively. He could veto the money for indigents, or he could veto the potato subsidy, and then sign. Either way, only part of the original bill would become law.

In *Clinton v. City of New York*, the Supreme Court held that the Line-Item Veto Act violated the Constitution.[73] Specifically, the Court concluded that the act ran afoul of the Presentment Clause.[74] According to the Justices, that clause gives the President power to sign bills or to veto bills and nothing else. "The power to enact statutes," the Court wrote, "may only be exercised in accord with a single, finely wrought and exhaustively considered, procedure."[75] The line-item veto was not part of that procedure.

Bargaining theory illuminates the line-item veto.[76] It could raise the transaction costs of bargaining by blocking side payments. Suppose proponents of a bill need one more vote. They could approach a Congressman who opposes the bill and offer $500,000 for a bridge in his home district in exchange for his support. Without a line-item veto, those proponents only need to bargain with the Congressman. With the line-item veto, they need to bargain with the President too. The Congressman will not agree to the deal unless the President agrees not to veto the bridge.

[71] 478 U.S. 714 (1986).

[72] *Id.* at 771.

[73] 524 U.S. 417 (1998).

[74] The Presentment Clause appears in Article I, Section 7 of the Constitution: "Every Bill which shall have passed the House of Representatives and the Senate, shall, before it become a Law, be presented to the President of the United States: If he approve he shall sign it, but if not he shall return it, with his Objections to that House in which it shall have originated, who shall enter the Objections at large on their Journal, and proceed to reconsider it."

[75] *Clinton*, 524 U.S. at 419 (internal quotation marks and citation omitted).

[76] On connections between the line-item veto and bargaining in government, see Glen O. Robinson, *Public Choice Speculations on the Item Veto*, 74 VA. L. REV. 403 (1988); Maxwell L. Stearns, *The Public Choice Against the Item Veto*, 49 WASH. & LEE. L. REV. 385 (1992).

In some cases, the line-item veto could lower bargaining costs. Suppose the Congressman supports the bill. He nevertheless has an incentive to bluff and pretend he opposes it. He may say, "I will oppose the bill unless you give my district $500,000 for a bridge." Without a line-item veto, legislators may have to haggle with the Congressman over the bridge. With a line-item veto, they can simply agree and let the President veto the bridge. Foreseeing the veto, the Congressman will not bother bluffing.

Now consider the Coase Theorem. If the transaction costs of bargaining among lawmakers are zero, the line-item veto will not affect the efficiency of law. Legislators will agree to the efficient package of laws regardless of the nature of the President's veto power. However, the line-item veto affects distribution. By empowering the President to cancel parts of bills, the line-item veto raises his threat value and reduces Congress's. This could undermine the separation of powers. Justice Kennedy wrote, "Concentration of power in the hands of a single branch is a threat to liberty," and the Line-Item Veto Act "enhances the President's powers beyond what the Framers would have endorsed."[77]

These ideas lead to a rule of thumb: laws that significantly change the threat points of Congress or the President in negotiations violate the separation of powers.

D. Bargaining across Branches

Separating the legislative and executive branches requires them to agree to make new law. The example of spending on roads and health care provided a snapshot of interbranch bargaining. This section analyzes interbranch bargaining more generally. We explain the logic of bargaining between the legislature and executive with the help of Figure 3.1, which depicts a *spatial model*.[78] A later chapter discusses spatial models in detail. To simplify, we mostly ignore details like filibusters, committees, and agenda setters. We also treat the legislature as a unitary actor rather than a collection of individuals. We will return to some of these issues later.

The government considers spending money on a new program. Unless the legislature and executive agree, no bill will pass, meaning the status quo prevails and expenditures equal 0. The executive would be happiest spending 12 (point E in Figure 3.1). However, she prefers every expenditure level between 0 and 24 (point E_0) to the status quo. She is indifferent between spending 0 and spending 24. Thus, the executive is prepared to discuss every expenditure level in the set [0, 24].[79] The legislature would be happiest with expenditures of 5 (point L).[80] However, the legislature prefers every expenditure level

77 Clinton v. City of New York, 524 U.S. 417, 450–51 (1998) (Kennedy, J., concurring).

78 For a related analysis, see Robert Cooter, The Strategic Constitution (2000).

79 In set notation, brackets indicate a closed interval, meaning the end points are included. Thus, the executive is willing to discuss expenditures greater than or equal to 0 and less than or equal to 24. Why would the executive discuss 24 when she is indifferent between 24 and the status quo? We assume the actors will discuss any possibility that leaves them at least as well off as the status quo. This simplifies the presentation without affecting the logic.

80 To simplify, we treat the legislature as a unitary actor. All members agree with each other. The next chapter examines voting among people who disagree with each other.

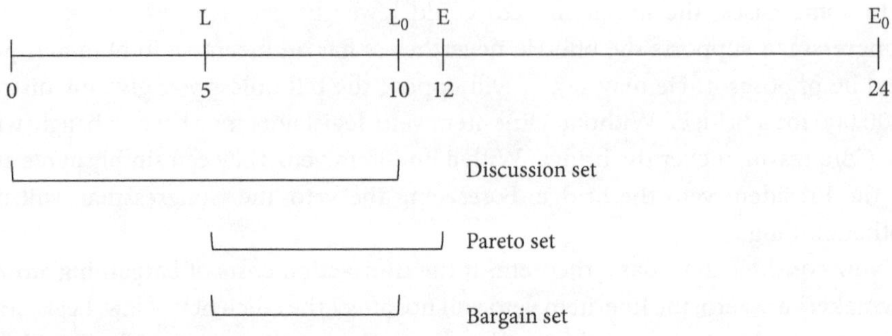

Figure 3.1. Bargaining among Branches

between 0 and 10 (point L_0) to the status quo. Thus, the legislature will discuss every point in the set [0, 10]. The intersection of these two sets, which equals [0, 10], is the set of expenditures that both parties are prepared to discuss. Thus [0,10] is labeled *discussion set* in Figure 3.1.

When the parties begin discussion, they will immediately identify some points preferred by both of them to other points. For example, they both prefer spending 5 to spending 4. Law is *Pareto inefficient* when changing it can make at least one party better off without making anyone worse off. Spending 4 is Pareto inefficient for the legislature and executive—moving from 4 to 5 would make both parties better off. In contrast, spending 5 is *Pareto efficient.* A law is Pareto efficient when changing it makes at least one party worse off. From 5, decreasing expenditures would make both parties worse off, and increasing expenditures would make the legislature worse off.

Now consider the problem from the other side. To do this, ignore the discussion set, and focus only on the concept of Pareto efficiency. Spending 13 is Pareto inefficient, as both parties prefer expenditures of 12 to 13. Spending 12 is Pareto efficient. From 12, increasing expenditures would make both parties worse off, and decreasing expenditures would make the executive worse off.

Expenditures of 5 and 12 are not unique. These expenditures and all points between are Pareto efficient, so Figure 3.1 calls them the *Pareto set.* To see the logic, pick any point in the Pareto set. Moving leftward from that point makes the executive worse off, and moving rightward makes the legislature worse off. For points outside the Pareto set, moving either leftward or rightward can make both parties better off.

Rational parties will not agree to make Pareto-inefficient law. The executive and legislature will not agree to spend 4 when they both prefer 5. Furthermore, they cannot make a law unless they are willing to discuss it. Thus, we can remove points they are unwilling to discuss from the Pareto set. What remains is the *bargain set* [5, 10]. For a point to be in the bargain set, both parties must be prepared to discuss it, and they must disagree about whether any better point exists. Thus, the bargain set equals the intersection of the discussion set and the Pareto set.

The parties will agree on an expenditure level in the bargain set. What point in the bargain set will the parties choose? This question is analogous to one involving Adam and Blair, who bargained over jail cells in the previous chapter. We knew they would settle between \$3,000 and \$4,000, but we could not predict the exact price. Soon we will make sharper predictions.

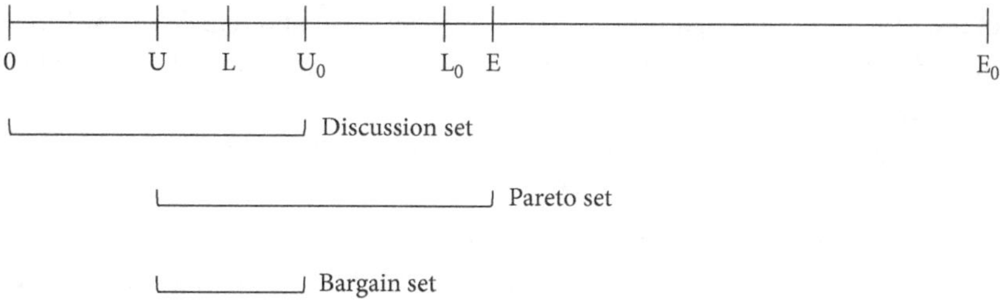

Figure 3.2. Bargaining with More Players

So far, our analysis of bargaining assumes a unicameral legislature. Now consider bargaining under bicameralism. Depicting bargaining between the executive and a two-chamber legislature requires modifications as pictured in Figure 3.2. Instead of thinking of *L* as the legislature, think of it as the lower chamber of the legislature, like the House of Representatives in the U.S. Congress. The new point *U* represents the spending level most preferred by the upper chamber of the legislature, like the Senate in Congress. The point U_0 is the upper chamber's point of indifference with no expenditure. To make the analysis general, we have eliminated numbers.

Compared to the status quo of 0, the upper chamber will discuss expenditures in the set [0, U_0], the lower chamber will discuss [0, L_0], and the executive will discuss [0, E_0]. Thus, the discussion set equals [0, U_0]. All three actors prefer *U* to points leftward, and all three prefer *E* to points rightward. Thus, the Pareto set equals [*U*, *E*]. The bargain set equals the overlap of the two preceding sets, [*U*, U_0].

Compared to Figure 3.1, Figure 3.2 has a narrower discussion set and bargain set. This is not surprising. Adding another actor under unanimity rule tends to make bargaining harder. Compared to Figure 3.1, Figure 3.2 has a wider Pareto set. Again, this is not surprising. The Pareto set captures the points over which the parties disagree about whether any better alternative exists. As the number of parties increases, disagreement tends to increase.

The sets in Figures 3.1 and 3.2 depend on the locations of the points *E*, *L*, and so on. We chose the locations of those points arbitrarily for the sake of example. Now we develop a generalization that does not depend on the exact locations of the points: *additional division of powers weakly decreases the range of bargaining and weakly increases the size of the Pareto set.* Adding another power like a second legislative chamber cannot lengthen, and might narrow, the bargain set. Likewise, it cannot narrow, and might lengthen, the Pareto set.

E. Take It or Leave It

Thomas Hobson had 40 horses in his stable, but customers had just one choice: take the horse near the door or walk. A "Hobson's Choice" offers one option only, which can be accepted or rejected.[81] This is a *take-it-or-leave-it offer*. Take-it-or-leave-it offers help us

[81] Hobson's Choice, Webster's Third New International Dictionary (Philip Babcock Gove ed., 3d ed. 1976).

predict the outcomes of bargaining games. The executive and legislature will reach an agreement in the bargain set, but which point in the set will they choose? Take-it-or-leave-it offers provide an answer.

The previous chapter discussed credible commitments. Commitments are credible when parties are better off following through than reneging. Credible commitments lower the transaction costs of bargaining by facilitating trust. They also affect the distribution of the surplus. The ability to make a take-it-or-leave-it offer gives all the bargaining power to one actor. An actor with this power will make an offer in the bargain set closest to his most preferred point. If they are rational, the other parties will accept this offer because they prefer it to the status quo and no alternatives are possible.

To illustrate, suppose that the executive in Figure 3.2 can make a take-it-or-leave-it offer. He will offer spending at U_0, which is as close to his preferred point as he can get while remaining in the bargain set. Both legislative chambers prefer this to the status quo.[82] Since the offer is final, they cannot hope for a better choice, so they will accept.

What allows the executive to make a take-it-or-leave-it offer? Term limits are a possibility. At the end of a president's term, and with re-election foreclosed by law, he can make a take-it-or-leave-it offer. In general, however, take-it-or-leave-it offers are rare because public actors struggle to make credible commitments. Unlike the buyer and seller of a house, they cannot sign a legally enforceable contract that commits them to their promises. An executive may state that his offer is final, but in reality rejecting the offer may lead to further negotiations. President Trump tried to make a take-it-or-leave-it offer to the House of Representatives, telling its members to vote on a health care bill by March 24, 2017, or lose his support. The House voted on the bill several weeks later—with Trump's support.[83]

Sometimes procedural rules give an official power to make take-it-or-leave-it offers. In the legislature, take-it-or-leave-it offers may take the form of bills drafted in committee and proposed to the whole legislature under a procedural rule requiring legislators to vote for or against the bill without amending it. This is called a *closed rule*. In contrast to an *open rule* that permits amendments on the floor, a closed rule empowers committees to make take-it-or-leave-it offers.[84] To illustrate, making new law requires both houses of Congress to pass the same bill. Sometimes they cannot agree and pass different bills. A "conference committee" with members from both chambers may be appointed to reconcile the different bills. The conference committee reports one bill to both chambers under a closed rule.

[82] Actually, the upper chamber is indifferent between U_0 and the status quo. If the upper chamber "votes for change" when indifferent, the executive offers U_0 as we described. If the upper chamber votes against change when indifferent, the executive makes an offer just left of U_0.

[83] *See* David Lawder & Steve Holland, *Trump Tastes Failure as U.S. House Healthcare Bill Collapses*, REUTERS, Mar. 24, 2017, https://www.reuters.com/article/us-usa-obamacare/trump-tastes-failure-as-u-s-house-healthcare-bill-collapses-idUSKBN16V149; Brian Naylor, *Trump "Confident" About GOP Health Care Bill's Prospects in the Senate*, NPR, May 4, 2017, https://www.npr.org/2017/05/04/526866090/trump-confident-about-gop-health-care-bills-prospects-in-the-senate.

[84] *See* Barry R. Weingast, *Floor Behavior in the United States Congress: Committee Power Under the Open Rule*, 83 AM. POL. SCI. REV. 795 (1989); David P. Baron & John A. Ferejohn, *Bargaining in Legislatures*, 83 AM. POL. SCI. REV. 1181 (1989).

Questions

3.22. In Figure 3.2, suppose the upper house can make a take-it-or-leave-it offer. What level of spending will the upper house propose? If the lower house can make a take-it-or-leave-it offer, what level of spending will it propose?

3.23. A legislative committee sends a bill to the full legislature. Before the legislature votes, the committee circulates a report with details about the bill. The bill passes and becomes a statute that courts must interpret. Courts search the committee report for clues about the statute's meaning. Why is the committee report more reliable if the legislature voted under a closed rule than an open rule?

F. A Cooling Saucer?

Thomas Jefferson and George Washington debated the Constitution over breakfast. Jefferson asked Washington why he had agreed to a bicameral Congress with a Senate rather than a unicameral Congress. Washington replied by asking Jefferson why he poured his coffee in a saucer. "To cool it," Jefferson answered. "Even so," said Washington, "we pour legislation into the senatorial saucer to cool it."[85] This story may be more fiction than fact, but it captures an enduring argument. Bicameralism and the separation of powers moderate and stabilize legislation. They prevent, as the *Federalist Papers* argued, an "excess of law-making" and "improper acts of legislation."[86]

Is this argument correct? Yes and no. Separating powers makes enacting new law difficult. It is hard to get multiple actors to agree. Making new law difficult to enact freezes old law in place, so separating powers promotes stability. Figure 3.3 demonstrates. The government considers changing expenditures on the military. The House of Representatives, Senate, and executive prefer different levels of expenditures, as indicated by *H*, *S*, and *E*. Will they agree to change expenditures? Suppose that the House and Senate can make law without the executive's support (bicameralism). If the existing level of expenditures is outside of the Pareto set under bicameralism, they will agree to change it. But if the existing level of expenditures is inside of the Pareto set under bicameralism, they will not. Expenditures in the Pareto set are stable.

Because law inside it is stable, scholars call the Pareto set the "gridlock zone."[87] The size of the gridlock zone depends on the level of agreement between the House and the Senate. When one political party controls both, *H* and *S* may be close together and the gridlock zone narrows. If different parties control the House and Senate, *H* and *S* may drift apart and the gridlock zone widens. The gridlock zone also depends on the extent

[85] Matthew C. Stephenson, *Does Separation of Powers Promote Stability and Moderation?*, 42 J. LEGAL STUD. 331, 331–32 (2013) (citing 3 MAX FARRAND, THE RECORDS OF THE FEDERAL CONVENTION OF 1787, at 359 (1966)).

[86] THE FEDERALIST NO. 62, 314–15 (James Madison) (Ian Shapiro ed., 2009).

[87] Jason S. Oh, *The Pivotal Politics of Temporary Legislation*, 100 IOWA L. REV. 1055, 1064 (2015); Keith Krehbiel, PIVOTAL POLITICS: A THEORY OF U.S. LAWMAKING (2010); David W. Brady & Craig Volden, REVOLVING GRIDLOCK: POLITICS AND POLICY FROM JIMMY CARTER TO GEORGE W. BUSH (2005).

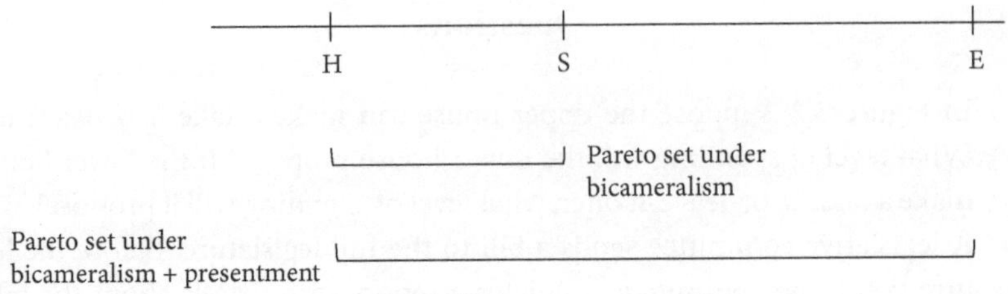

Figure 3.3. Separation of Powers and Stability

to which powers are separated. If making new law requires the President's support (bicameralism and presentment), the zone widens, as Figure 3.3 shows. Increasing powers weakly increases the size of the gridlock zone.

We have shown how separating powers can promote stability. What about moderation? The story is complicated. Getting multiple actors to agree usually requires compromise, so separating powers usually promotes moderation—but not always. Because new law is difficult to enact, old law endures, even when that old law is unpopular or extreme. The promise of endurance incentivizes political actors to pass extreme laws when the opportunity strikes.[88]

To see this clearly, imagine a competitive democracy in which a unicameral legislature has exclusive control over lawmaking. If political liberals control the legislature, they can make liberal laws. However, when the political conservatives gain control, they will repeal those liberal laws. The liberals can prevent this unstable back-and-forth by enacting moderate rather than liberal laws. Repealing laws is costly. Conservatives will pay those costs to repeal liberal laws but not moderate laws. Thus, moderation insulates law from change.[89] To prevent their program from being undermined after the next election, liberals may enact moderate laws. They get some of what they want for a long time rather than all of what they want for a short time.

Now replay this scenario with some changes. The legislature is bicameral, and it must cooperate with the executive to make law. Thus, powers are separated. Political liberals control all branches of government. To repeal the liberals' program, conservatives will have to gain control of all branches of government. It is much harder to gain control over all branches than to gain control over a unicameral legislature. Thus, liberals have confidence that their program will endure. They do not need to enact moderate laws to avoid repeal. They can enact liberal laws and let the separation of powers insulate them from repeal.

This logic amends Washington's metaphor. A second legislative chamber may "cool" legislation. Or, by weakening the threat of repeal, it may encourage extreme legislation.

[88] *See* Matthew C. Stephenson, *Does Separation of Powers Promote Stability and Moderation?*, 42 J. Legal Stud. 331, 331–32 (2013).

[89] Yehonatan Givati & Matthew C. Stephenson, *Judicial Deference to Inconsistent Agency Statutory Interpretations*, 40 J. Legal Stud. 85 (2011); Terry M. Moe & Michael Caldwell, *The Institutional Foundations of Democratic Government: A Comparison of Presidential and Parliamentary Systems*, 150 J. Inst. & Theoretical Econ. 171 (1994).

Questions

3.24. Assume *H* and *S* appear at the points indicated in Figure 3.3. Assume *E* does not appear on the figure. Your job is to add *E* to the figure. This question will help you understand this statement: "Increasing powers weakly increases the size of the gridlock zone."
  (a) Can you find a location for *E* that does not change the size of the gridlock zone?
  (b) Can you identify all of the locations for *E* that would widen the gridlock zone?
  (c) Can you find a location for *E* that narrows the gridlock zone?

Conclusion

The previous chapter develops the theory of bargaining, and this chapter applies it to problems in public law. We first apply the theory to regulations. Bargaining theory clarifies why markets fail, when regulations can correct market failure, and whether regulations should command (Hobbesian solutions) or facilitate bargaining (Coasean solutions). Second, we apply the theory to federalism. Scholars have long debated when national as opposed to state governments should exercise power. Bargaining theory provides an answer. Finally, we apply bargaining theory to the separation of powers. Our analysis shows the consequences of different laws and legal arrangements. Since the meaning of law often depends on consequences, our analysis also aids in legal interpretation.

4

Theory of Voting

In a democracy, citizens vote for legislators, legislators vote on bills, judges vote in panels when interpreting laws, and juries vote when deciding cases. Sometimes citizens vote in a plebiscite (a direct vote of the people), as when Coloradans voted to legalize marijuana. Some people hope that voting in the United Nations will replace war, as when the Security Council sanctions countries for violating international law. Voting is fundamental to democracy, so fundamental that people have fought and died for the right to vote.

What is the connection between voting and bargaining, the subject of the preceding chapters? Recall the example of city council members who bargained over funding for schools and police. Caleb and Dee agreed to the terms of the bargain in Dee's office, and they implemented the bargain by casting votes at the city council meeting. Like signing a contract, voting formalizes a deal that has already been struck. In a democracy, implementing a political bargain often requires voting.

Besides implementing, voting sometimes substitutes for bargaining. California makes laws by legislation and plebiscite. With a plebiscite, the voters make law themselves. The California legislature is small enough for its members to bargain together and enact legislation. However, California has too many citizens (about 40 million) for them to bargain with each other over the terms of a plebiscite. In 2008, California held a plebiscite to prohibit same-sex marriage. The direct vote of the citizens substituted for bargaining among legislators.[1]

We have contrasted voting as implementing political bargaining with voting as substituting for political bargaining. This difference is so fundamental that we will refer to two forms of government: bargain democracy (voting implements bargains) and median democracy (voting substitutes for bargains). To contrast them, this chapter develops the theory of voting, which provides insight into questions like these:

Example 1: Some voters want government to be rich as a symbol of a great society, and other voters want it starved so it cannot cause harm. Most voters favor a position between these extremes. What political platform on government expenditures will command a majority of votes by citizens?

Example 2: Majorities sometimes exclude minorities from power, as when the white majority in the American South excluded the African American minority from politics. When is majority rule desirable and when is it undesirable?

[1] The plebiscite passed, thus prohibiting same sex marriage, but it was then overturned in court.

Public Law and Economics. Robert D. Cooter and Michael D. Gilbert, Oxford University Press. © Oxford University Press 2022.
DOI: 10.1093/oso/9780197655870.003.0004

Example 3: According to a popular slogan, "If voting made any difference, they wouldn't let you do it."[2] Are political outcomes decided by people who cast votes? Or are they decided by agenda setters who structure votes, like the Speaker of the House in the U.S. Congress?

Example 4: In 2014, the U.S. Congress passed a bill to "unlock" cell phones. The same year, Congress passed a 1,600-page bill addressing immigration, tropical diseases, military spending, abortion, gun sales, and other matters.[3] When should legislators cast separate votes on separate issues, and when should they cast a single vote on multiple issues?

To address these questions and others, this chapter draws on positive, normative, and interpretive analysis.

I. Positive Theory of Voting

We build the theory of voting from the ground up. First, we examine how individuals vote, and then we examine how to aggregate votes. Sometimes voting produces a winner, in which case the voters decide the direction of government. Other times, however, voting spins its wheels like a car stuck in mud. Adding structure to the voting process prevents wheel-spinning, but then officials decide where government goes.

A. Why Vote?

In the 1960s, southern states blocked African Americans from voting, leading to violent confrontations.[4] Meanwhile, millions of enfranchised citizens did not bother to vote. Today, roughly half of eligible citizens in the United States vote in major elections. Voter participation rates are similar in other countries. Many commentators ask why citizens choose *not* to vote. Economists turn the question around: Why do citizens choose *to* vote?[5]

Imagine a self-interested person, Larry, who decides whether to vote by comparing the cost and benefit of voting. His benefit from voting lies in electing his preferred candidate. Of course, he may get that benefit whether or not he votes. Larry's vote only affects the election if he is the *decisive voter*. To illustrate, suppose one candidate wins by ten votes. Larry was not decisive because the same candidate would have won whether Larry voted or not. If Larry cast the tie-breaking vote, however, then he was decisive.[6]

For Larry, the benefit of voting must be discounted by the probability that he is decisive. In a large election, the probability of being the decisive voter is negligible. Thus, his

[2] This quote is often misattributed to Mark Twain. The actual source of the quote is unknown.

[3] Unlocking Consumer Choice and Wireless Competition Act, 17 U.S.C. § 1201 (2014); Consolidated Appropriations Act of 2014, Public L. No. 113-76, 128 Stat. 5 (2014).

[4] Disfranchisement was especially salient in the United States in the 1960s, but the practice is much older than that.

[5] This question has been explored in a sizeable literature. For a review, see Timothy J. Feddersen, *Rational Choice Theory and the Paradox of Not Voting*, 18 J. ECON. PERSP. 99 (2004).

[6] The "decisive voter" is also called the "pivotal voter."

expected benefit from voting is very small. Meanwhile, voting imposes costs—learning about candidates, finding the polling station, taking time from work, waiting in line, and so forth. The effort required to vote probably exceeds the expected benefit in large elections.

Some notation and specialized language will clarify this point. Voting imposes costs on Larry, including an *opportunity cost*. He foregoes doing something else in order to vote. To demonstrate, a parent who votes instead of watching her child's championship game has a higher opportunity cost than a college student who votes instead of watching a boring movie. The total cost of voting to Larry, which includes the opportunity cost, can be denoted C. Let p denote the probability that Larry's vote decides the election's outcome (p is sometimes called the "power" of a vote). Let B denote Larry's benefit from his preferred candidate winning the election. His *expected benefit* from voting equals pB. Larry votes when the expected benefit exceeds the opportunity cost, or $pB > C$. In these circumstances, voting is "rational" for Larry. Conversely, he does not vote when the expected benefit is less than the opportunity cost, or $pB < C$.[7] In these circumstances, voting is not rational.

To illustrate concretely, assume that having his preferred candidate win the election is worth \$10,000 to Larry, and assume that voting requires one hour of his time, which he values at \$10. Rationality prompts him to vote if $p(\$10{,}000) > \$10$, which implies $p > 1/1{,}000$. In large elections, the probability of any single citizen's vote being decisive is much smaller than 1/1,000. In 2008, the probability of a voter being decisive in the U.S. presidential election was one in 60 million.[8]

This reasoning leads to the *paradox of voting*.[9] Rationality should prompt citizens to vote at much lower rates than we observe. What explains the paradox? Political theory dating from Aristotle holds that political participation appeals to people's social nature. People express themselves by performing civic duties like voting, and self-expression is intrinsically satisfying. In addition, voting can have social advantages. We often praise voters and criticize nonvoters. Some villages in Italy post public lists of the names of citizens who did not vote. Social pressure may cause people to vote even when they get little self-satisfaction from it. (Are you wearing your "I Voted" sticker?) A combination of self-satisfaction and social pressure, which we call the *civic duty theory of voting*, may explain why people vote.[10]

To represent the civic duty theory of voting, let V denote the intrinsic and instrumental value to Larry of fulfilling his civic duty. In contrast, let B represent his narrowly self-interested benefit from his preferred candidate winning the election. We have separated reasons for voting into narrow self-interest B and civic duty V. Larry votes if $V + pB > C$. In these circumstances, we might say that voting is rational and benevolent. Conversely, he does not vote if $V + pB < C$.

These ideas may help explain high voter participation rates in general elections where the probability of casting a decisive vote is low. The outcome of a presidential election

[7] What happens when costs and benefits are equal? Larry may follow a rule, like "always vote when indifferent," or he may flip a coin or use some other procedure. This does not affect our analysis.

[8] Andrew Gelman, Nate Silver, & Aaron Edlin, *What Is the Probability Your Vote Will Make a Difference?*, 50 ECON. INQ'Y 321 (2012).

[9] *See* ANTHONY DOWNS, AN ECONOMIC THEORY OF DEMOCRACY (1957).

[10] *See* William H. Riker & Peter C. Ordeshook, *A Theory of the Calculus of Voting*, 62 AM. POL. SCI. REV. 25 (1968).

affects many more people than the outcome of a local election for the city council. For people who care about the public interest, the increase in the number of people affected by a national election increases the civic duty V in general elections relative to V in local elections. The increase in civic duty V may offset the decrease in the probability p of casting a decisive vote.[11] This may explain why voter turnout is higher in national elections than local elections.

Questions

4.1. Use the probability p of casting the decisive vote to explain why the rate of voter participation will never fall to zero.

4.2. Until 2014, voters in South Carolina elected the Adjutant General, an official who oversees the state's national guard. Use the aforementioned ideas to explain why participation in South Carolina's statewide election for adjutant general may be lower than participation in New York City's citywide election for mayor.

B. Why Abstain?

The analysis so far implies that people will vote when the intrinsic and instrumental payoff $V + pB$ is high. Yet this is not always the case. Sometimes voters choose to abstain, even when they might tip the election. Such abstention can be rational, as an example demonstrates.

Suppose you are a member of the U.S. Senate, which has 100 members and often uses majority rule (to simplify, we ignore the filibuster). Suppose the Senate votes on a national security bill, specifically a bill on collecting citizens' phone records. Should you vote or abstain? If your vote will be indecisive, meaning the outcome does not depend on it, then your choice does not matter. But suppose your vote will be decisive. Forty-nine Senators have voted in favor of the bill, 49 Senators have voted against it, and one Senator is absent. The bill will pass if you vote for it, and it will fail if you vote against it. If you abstain, the vote ties. In the event of a tie, the Vice President will cast the tie-breaking vote, according to the Senate's voting rules.

Two considerations should guide your choice of whether to vote or abstain: information and values.[12] If you know more than the Vice President about the bill, then you should vote. If the Vice President knows more than you, and if you and the Vice President share the same values concerning national security and privacy, then you should abstain. The hard choice comes when the Vice President knows more about

[11] To express the argument succinctly, if n is the number of voters, the probability of being decisive roughly equals $1/n$. The gain from being decisive, as perceived by the voter, equals the number of people benefited n multiplied by the benefit per person b. Thus the expected benefit from voting roughly equals $(1/n)(n^*b)$. Since the n cancels, the expected benefit from voting is independent of the number of voters. *See* Aaron Edlin, Andrew Gelman, & Noah Kaplan, *Voting as a Rational Choice: Why and How People Vote to Improve the Well-Being of Others*, 19 RATIONALITY & SOC'Y 293 (2007); Aaron Edlin, Andrew Gelman, & Nate Silver, *Vote for Charity's Sake*, 5 ECONOMISTS' VOICE 1 (2008).

[12] In reality, a third value might guide a Senator's choice: popularity. If voting leads to political rewards, a Senator might vote, regardless of information and values.

national security than you, but the Vice President has a different set of values about national security than you do. Now you must balance information and values when deciding whether to vote or abstain.

This analysis shows why ignorance about candidates or issues may cause rational voters to abstain. If a citizen's vote will be indecisive, then voting or abstaining does not affect the outcome. If the vote will be decisive, then the citizen can determine the outcome herself by voting. Or the citizen can abstain, which allows a different citizen to determine the outcome. Call this different citizen the *next-decisive voter*. A rational citizen will decide whether to vote or abstain by asking whether she prefers to decide the outcome herself or to let the next-decisive voter decide. The case for letting the next decisive voter decide grows stronger as the next-decisive voter's information improves and her values align more closely with the decisive voter's values.

The next-decisive-voter theory generates some interesting predictions. It implies that voter participation rates will fall as values become more homogenous (voters agree on the ends, though not necessarily the means). It implies that voter participation rates will fall as information becomes more heterogeneous (some voters have more information than others). Finally, it implies that people who abstain on average have less political information than people who vote.

Questions

4.3. Many state court judges in the United States are elected. As many as 25 percent of voters leave the section of the ballot pertaining to judicial elections blank, presumably because they know little about the candidates.[13] Commentators lament the failure of voters to participate in judicial elections. Are low participation rates in judicial elections indicative of a failure in democracy?

4.4. Why might a rational citizen prefer to cast a *blank* ballot in an election instead of not participating?

C. Representing a Voter's Preferences

In some countries including the United States, elections often come down to two-party competitions (the next chapter explains why). To analyze two-party competitions, imagine a simplified election with two candidates, say, the nominees of the Democratic and Republican parties. In the election campaign, each candidate will announce his or her positions on major issues. Collectively these announcements are called a "platform." A platform encompasses the candidate's general ideology and specific policies on such matters as taxes, national security, and education. In response, each citizen will vote in the simplified election for the candidate whose platform conforms closest to that citizen's political preferences.

[13] Herbert M. Kritzer, *Roll-Off in State Court Elections: The Impact of the Straight-Ticket Voting Option*, 4 J.L. & Cts. 409 (2016); Charles Gardner Geyh, *Judicial Selection and the Search for Middle Ground*, 67 DePaul L. Rev. 333, 337–38, n.14 (2016).

Some notation represents voter preferences in two-party competition. Let x represent political platforms, where x_d denotes the platform announced by the Democrat and x_r denotes the platform announced by the Republican. Each citizen ranks the possible platforms of the candidates from best to worst. The ranking of platforms by, say, the ith citizen is indicated by the *utility function* $u_i = u(x)$. This is just a mathematical expression of a person's preferences. The ith citizen's utility u_i is a function of the platform x. The utility value of platform x_d to citizen i is $u_i(x_d)$, and the utility value of platform x_r to citizen i is $u_i(x_r)$. If citizen i prefers x_d to x_r, then the utility value of the former exceeds the utility value of the latter: $u_i\,(x_d) > u_i(x_r)$.

Here is the ith citizen's voting rule:

If $u_i(x_r) > u_i(x_d)$, then citizen i votes for the Republican.
If $u_i(x_r) < u_i(x_d)$, then citizen i votes for the Democrat.
If $u_i(x_r) = u_i(x_d)$, then citizen i votes by flipping a coin.

In deciding how to vote, all others follow the same procedure as citizen i, except the utility functions are different for different people.

In this brief discussion, political platforms alone determine citizens' votes. In reality, many other considerations affect voting. Beside substance, the framing of issues affects the preferences of voters. "Pro-life" and "pro-choice" sound good. Consequently, people who want to limit access to abortions describe themselves as "pro-life" rather than "anti-choice," whereas people who want to ease access to abortions call themselves "pro-choice" not "anti-life." Like framing, a candidate's appearance and personality sway voters, as does advertising and support from interest groups. The simple model of a two-party election omits these and other complications.

D. Aggregating Votes: Majority Rule

So far, we have focused on how voters behave. In the simple model of two-party competition, where two candidates choose platforms, citizens vote for the party with the preferred platform. Now focus on the candidates. If citizens vote based on platforms, candidates will select the platform that delivers the most votes. Which platform will deliver the most votes? The winning platform will tend toward the political center, not the left or right, and this section explains why.

Imagine three voters: Larry whom we met earlier, and two other rational voters, Mary and Ned. Figure 4.1 depicts their utility on the vertical axis. Their utility is a function of the location on the horizontal axis of political platforms. Thus, the curve $u_l(x)$ depicts Larry's utility function. Consider the change in his utility when starting from the origin on the extreme left and moving to the right. Larry's utility increases until we reach the point x_l^* on the horizontal axis. There Larry's utility is maximized. After passing x_l^*, Larry's utility decreases when moving further to the right. Thus, x_l^* is Larry's *ideal point*, meaning the platform that maximizes his utility on the left-right political dimension. The same analysis reveals that Mary's ideal point is x_m^* and Ned's ideal point is x_n^*. To clarify, Figure 4.1 labels Larry's ideal point and utility curve using both words and notation. For Mary and Ned, the figure shows notation only.

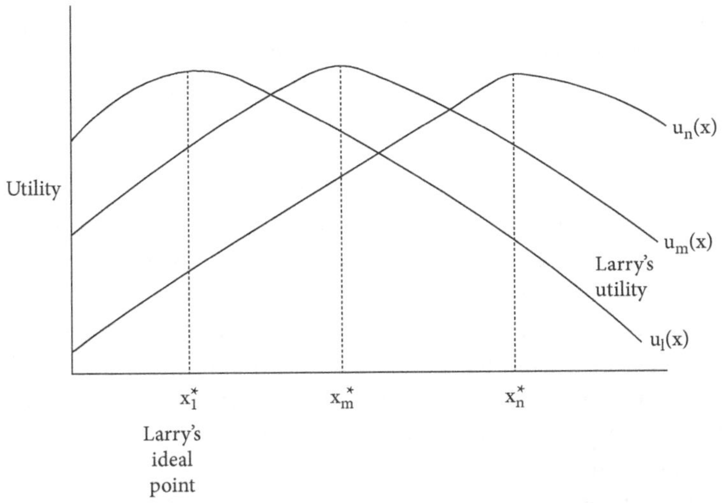

Figure 4.1. The Winning Platform

Now we show how to find the winner in Figure 4.1 by majority rule. Assume that two candidates, a Democrat and a Republican, compete for the votes of Larry, Mary, and Ned. Each candidate chooses a political platform. In this circumstance, the platform x_m^* will beat any other platform.[14] To see why, assume the Democrat chooses x_m^* and the Republican chooses a platform a little to the right of x_m^*. Larry and Mary will get more utility from the Democrat's platform than from the Republican's, whereas Ned will get more utility from the Republican's, so the Democrat will win by a 2 to 1 majority. Reversing the example, assume that the Republican chooses the platform x_m^* and the Democrat chooses a platform a little further to the left. Mary and Ned will get more utility from the Republican's platform, whereas Larry will get more utility from the Democrat's platform, so the Republican will win by a 2 to 1 majority. The party that discovers and announces platform x_m^* is unbeatable in the election.

Note some features of this example. First, the winning platform is the one most preferred by Mary. Mary is in the middle of the distribution of preferences in the sense that one voter's most preferred point lies to the right and one voter's most preferred point lies to the left. In other words, Mary is the *median voter*.

Second, all voters have *single-peaked preferences*. This means that each voter has a single ideal point, and the further the platform moves from that point, whether to the left or right, the more the voter's utility declines. This characteristic causes the graph of the utility function to have a single peak.[15]

[14] To keep the analysis simple, we assume that all three voters have complete information, and each of them votes for the candidate whose platform yields higher utility.

[15] Technically, utility need not always decline—it can remain flat. Single-peakness only requires that, as one moves from a voter's ideal point, utility never increases. As long as a voter choosing between two options always chooses the one closer to his or her ideal point, even if both options yield the same utility, then the presence of "flat spots" in utility curves does not disturb the analysis.

Third, the voters cast votes on a single policy dimension. In the example, all possible platforms are situated on a left-right line. Many other plausible examples involve a single dimension. To illustrate, imagine voting on tax rates, where points near the left end of the line correspond to low rates and points near the right end correspond to high rates.

Fourth, the voters make a *pairwise choice*. This means they choose between two and only two options, the Democrat's platform and the Republican's platform.

Now we can state the voting equilibrium. When voters have single-peaked preferences, and when they cast votes on a single policy issue, the median voter's ideal point defeats all other potential platforms in pairwise voting under majority rule. This is the *median voter theorem*.[16] It implies that, from any starting position, platforms will gravitate toward the center. The voters can make pairwise choices until they reach the median voter's ideal point, and then change will cease. The median is the equilibrium.

This theorem is powerful because of its generality. It does not matter if there are a few voters or millions. It does not matter if voters are motivated by self-interest or civic duty. It does not matter if voters are distributed uniformly (equal numbers of far-left, centrist, and far-right voters) or in another manner (e.g., few voters take extreme positions and many take centrist positions). It does not matter if voters have intense preferences, meaning the peaks of their utility functions are like Mount Everest, or weak preferences, meaning the peaks are like speed bumps. Nor does it matter if intensity varies across voters, meaning some voters' peaks are tall while others are short. In all circumstances, if the requirements of the median voter theorem are satisfied, the median voter's ideal platform wins.

The theorem's requirements are not always satisfied, a point to which we will return. However, they are satisfied often enough to help explain the centrist tendencies in many political systems. For example, many Americans can locate themselves along a left-right continuum, with "liberal Democrat" at one end and "conservative Republican" at the other. A common pattern in U.S. presidential campaigns is for the Republican candidate to take a position on the right wing in the primary elections when seeking his party's nomination, and, once nominated, to move nearer to the middle of the political spectrum. The initial right-wing position appeals to the median voter in the Republican Party, as required to secure the party's nomination, and the moderate position appeals to the median voter among all the citizens, as required to win the general election. Similarly, Democratic Party candidates often start from the left in the primaries and move toward the middle after nomination.

The median voter theorem leaves out important features of real elections, such as party loyalty, voter ignorance, campaign spending, and the personal appeal of candidates. Despite these omissions, the theorem provides a useful starting point for analyses of voting.

[16] The theorem traces to Douglas Black, *On the Rationale of Group Decision-making*, 56 J. Pol. Econ. 23 (1948), and Anthony Downs, An Economic Theory of Democracy (1957). *See also* Harold Hotelling, *Stability in Competition*, 39 Econ. J. 41–57 (1929).

Questions

4.5. Suppose that left-wing voters become so filled with righteous anger at their political choices that they boycott a general election and do not vote. In which direction will their behavior shift the winning platform?

4.6. Majority rule allegedly increases a government's legitimacy and intimidates rebellious opposition by demonstrating publicly that more citizens support the government's policies than oppose them. Defend or criticize this proposition by assuming that majority rule means the median rule.

E. The Median in Governing Bodies

The preceding analysis focused on a general election in which citizens vote for candidates based on their platforms. The analysis applies equally well to voting by legislatures, committees, or other governing bodies. In any such group, there will be some set of policies representing the status quo. From time to time a member will make a new proposal. After debate, the group will vote on the new proposal. If the new proposal fails to gain a majority, the status quo will persist. If the new proposal gains a majority, the group abandons the old status quo, and the winning proposal becomes the new status quo. Each proposal is pitted against the status quo. If the preferences of the voters satisfy the conditions described earlier, the proposal most preferred by the median voter will prevail.

The Median Justice

Decisions by the U.S. Supreme Court can have a profound effect on American society. To demonstrate, in 1954 the Court prohibited racial segregation in the landmark decision *Brown v. Board of Education*.[17] In 2000, the Supreme Court resolved the presidential election by determining that George W. Bush beat Al Gore.[18] The Court consists of nine members appointed by the President. It resolves cases using majority rule. In recent years, the vote has often been 5–4. Many observers focus on the "swing" Justice who casts the decisive vote in a 5–4 decision.

Between 1994 and 2004, the Court consisted of the same nine Justices. By many accounts, those Justices could be arranged from most politically liberal to most politically conservative as follows (we use last names only): Stevens, Ginsburg, Souter, Breyer, O'Connor, Kennedy, Rehnquist, Scalia, Thomas. Justice O'Connor was widely thought to be the swing Justice, and the median voter theorem explains why. As the median member of the Court, her preferred outcome would command a majority of votes when paired against any alternative.

In 2005, John Roberts replaced Chief Justice Rehnquist. Those Justices differ in some respects, but one can situate Roberts in the same place as Rehnquist in the

[17] 347 U.S. 483 (1954).
[18] Bush v. Gore, 531 U.S. 98 (2000).

liberal-to-conservative order described earlier. A more fundamental shift came in 2006 when Samuel Alito replaced Justice O'Connor. Alito occupies the conservative end of the court with Scalia and Thomas. The median voter theorem illuminates this shift. It implies that Kennedy became the new median, and in fact observers considered him the swing Justice for 10 years, with some calling the Court the "Kennedy Court."

In 2018, the Justices could be arranged from liberal to conservative as follows: Ginsburg, Sotomayor, Kagan, Breyer, Kennedy, Roberts, Gorsuch, Alito, Thomas. This changed when Brett Kavanaugh, who lies on the conservative end, replaced Kennedy. Why might a liberal oppose Kavanaugh's appointment more intensely than Roberts' appointment? What happened to the median when the conservative Amy Coney Barrett replaced Justice Ginsburg in 2020?

This short discussion assumes that Justices' political views influence their decisions. A later chapter will examine this assumption.

F. Intransitivity

When the conditions of the median voter theorem hold, majority rule has a unique, stable equilibrium. A situation can arise, however, in which no political equilibrium exists. To appreciate this possibility, recall the childhood game called "rock, paper, scissors." In this game, two players simultaneously thrust forward one hand in the shape of a rock (fist), a piece of paper (flat hand), or scissors (two fingers extended). The rules of the game are "rock breaks scissors," "scissors cut paper," and "paper covers rock." Each choice defeats one alternative and loses to the other. The game has no unique equilibrium.

A unique equilibrium, if it had one, would destroy the game. To illustrate, if rock breaks scissors and paper, then each of the children would learn to show the fist in every round of the game. Given that no pure strategy beats each alternative, the best strategy for each player is to choose randomly among the three alternatives.[19] Chance decides the outcome.

Like "rock, paper, scissors," voting can have no equilibrium. When voting has no equilibrium, it resembles the child's game. To illustrate, suppose Larry, Mary, and Ned consider three political platforms x_l, x_m, and x_n. Ned's preferences have been modified from earlier. Now the preferences of the three voters can be summarized as follows, where ">" means "preferred":

$$\text{Larry: } x_l > x_m > x_n$$
$$\text{Mary: } x_m > x_n > x_l$$
$$\text{Ned: } x_n > x_l > x_m$$

[19] This assumes opponents are fully rational. If an opponent is not fully rational—for example, he plays paper every time—then the best strategy is not to randomize but to play scissors every time.

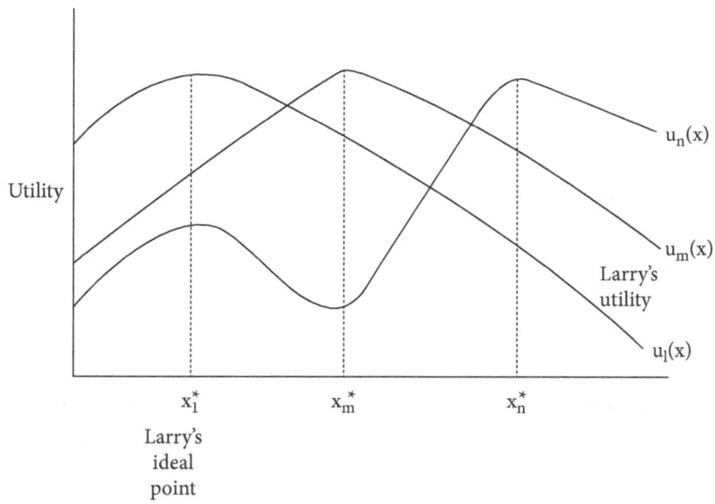

Figure 4.2. Intransitivity

Suppose two candidates competing for the same seat must pick a platform that will appeal to these voters. The two candidates are, in effect, playing "rock, paper, scissors." To see why, apply majority rule to voting among these three alternatives. Larry and Ned prefer x_l to x_m, so x_l defeats x_m by two votes to one. By the same logic, x_m defeats x_n, and x_n defeats x_l. As a group, the voters' preferences can be summarized like this: $x_l > x_m > x_n > x_l$. Instead of converging on the median voter's ideal point, majority voting runs in circles. The mathematical name for circular voting is *intransitivity*.[20]

With intransitivity, each alternative loses to another alternative, as in "rock, paper, scissors." This fact has implications for setting the agenda for voting. If the first candidate chooses a platform, the second candidate can choose an alternative that will win. Consequently, each candidate wants to choose second.

Figure 4.2 clarifies intransitivity by graphing the preferences of Larry, Mary, and Ned. Larry's utility curve is labeled $u_l(x)$, and Mary's utility curve is labeled $u_m(x)$. Both utility curves are single-peaked. However, Ned's utility curve, $u_n(x)$, is double-peaked. Intransitivity can occur when a voter's utility is double-peaked, whereas the median voter theorem applies when every voter's utility is single-peaked.[21]

Constructing examples of intransitive preferences is easy. Consider three alternative expenditures on public schools: low, moderate, and high. There are three groups of voters of equal size. The conservative group prefers less expenditure on public schools rather than more. The centrist group prefers a moderate level of expenditure. Finally,

[20] In mathematics, the relationship ">" is transitive if, for all *a*, *b*, and *c*, $a > b$ and $b > c$ implies $a > c$. When voting runs in a circle, the transitive property is violated, so the relationship is intransitive. Intransitive voting is sometimes called the Condorcet Paradox after the French mathematician who discovered it. *See* Nicolas de Condorcet, *Essai sur l'Application de l'Analyse à la Probabilité des Décisions Rendue à la Pluralité des Voix* [*Essay on the Application of Analysis to the Probability of Majority Decisions*] (1785).

[21] Strictly speaking, a sufficient condition for the most preferred point of the median voter to be a unique equilibrium in majority voting over paired alternatives is that everyone's preferences have a single peak, whereas a necessary condition for intransitivity is the presence of preferences with multiple peaks.

a third group of voters—call them "yuppies"[22]—have more complicated preferences. They most prefer a high level of expenditure, in which case they will send their children to public school. If the level is not high, however, they would prefer it to be low, so they will have enough disposable income to send their children to private school. The worst alternative for them is a moderate level of expenditure on public schools. The preference rankings of the three groups are:

conservative:	low > moderate > high
centrist:	moderate > high > low
yuppie:	high > low > moderate

In a majority vote, low defeats moderate, moderate defeats high, and high defeats low, so voting is intransitive.

Questions

4.7 An election pits two candidates against one another. Assume that the preferences of voters form an intransitive cycle under majority rule. Neither candidate is committed to a political platform at the commencement of the campaign. Would you advise your candidate to profess platitudes or take a firm stand on the issues?

4.8. A beach fills up with sunbathers on a warm afternoon. The sunbathers space themselves evenly such that the density of people is about the same everywhere on the beach. The hot sun makes people want ice cream, and it also makes them reluctant to walk far to get it.

(a) Suppose that two vendors with ice cream carts appear at the beach. If the vendors are competitive and do not cooperate, where will they locate?

(b) Suppose a third ice cream vendor arrives at the beach and competes with the others. Where will the three vendors locate?

G. The Chaos Theorem

The previous section showed how double-peaked preferences can lead to intransitivity. Now consider another cause: multiple dimensions of choice. The preceding figures depicted a single dimension of choice, which can be named "left-right" or "Democrat-Republican." In politics, however, the left-right dimension is often an aggregation of many smaller dimensions. For example, a government budget involves spending on the military, police, roads, schools, air quality, social entitlements, and so on. As the number of alternatives increases, intransitivity rapidly becomes more likely, as we will show.[23]

[22] "Yuppie" is a dated, amusing term for young urban professionals who often prioritize education. At least one author of this book is (or as a younger person was) a yuppie.

[23] *See* WILLIAM H. RIKER, LIBERALISM AGAINST POPULISM: A CONFRONTATIONAL CHOICE BETWEEN THE THEORY OF DEMOCRACY AND THE THEORY OF SOCIAL CHOICE (1982).

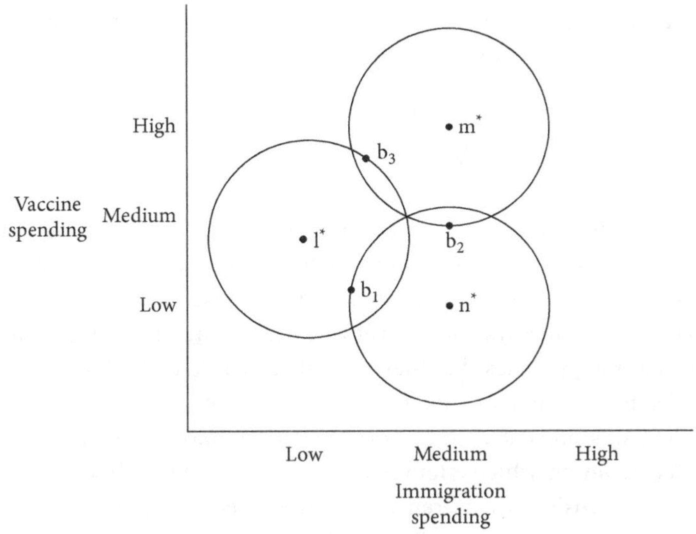

Figure 4.3. Chaos

Instead of voting for legislators, suppose Larry, Mary, and Ned *are* legislators. They vote on spending for two programs: immigration enforcement and vaccines. Larry would most prefer to spend little on immigration and moderately on vaccines. In Figure 4.3, Larry's ideal point is labeled l^*.[24] Larry's ideal point is surrounded by a circle called an *indifference contour*.[25] Every point on the contour represents a different combination of spending on immigration and vaccines. Larry is indifferent between every one of those combinations, meaning he gets the same utility from each. So an indifference contour connects points of constant utility.[26] Points inside a contour are closer to his ideal than points outside of it. Consequently, Larry prefers any point inside the contour to any point outside of it. Mary and Ned have ideal points labeled m^* and n^*, and each has an indifference contour like Larry's.

What combination of spending on immigration and vaccines will voting produce? Consider three possible budgets labeled b_1, b_2, and b_3. Each represents a different combination of spending. Mary and Ned prefer b_2 to b_1, Larry and Mary prefer b_3 to b_2, and Larry and Ned prefer b_1 to b_3. The group's preferences form an intransitive cycle under majority rule: $b_1 > b_3 > b_2 > b_1$. Choosing different budgets cannot solve the problem. For any point on the figure, some other point will defeat it in a pairwise vote.

The source of intransitivity is not multi-peaked preferences. Each voter can have single-peaked preferences on each issue, immigration and vaccines. The source of intransitivity is multiple issues. Combining issues produces intransitivity. As the number of issues increases, the likelihood of intransitivity quickly rises. In a remarkable paper, Richard McKelvey showed that all of the potential outcomes in a multidimensional

24 We simplify notation for this discussion.

25 We use circles for simplicity. Indifference contours can take many shapes, with different shapes implying different configurations of a voter's preferences over the two spending programs.

26 Indifference contours function like points on an indifference curve in microeconomics.

choice lie in a single intransitive cycle.[27] This is the *Chaos Theorem*. It implies that voting simultaneously on multiple issues can lead to any outcome.

H. Why So Much Stability?

Legislators routinely vote on multidimensional choices. The beginning of the chapter referred to a 1,600-page statute on immigration, tropical diseases, military spending, abortion, gun sales, and other issues. Scholars have shown that voting on multidimensional choices can lead to intransitivity, yet we do not routinely see legislatures running in circles by adopting policies that they recently discarded. Cycling is unavoidable in theory but rare in fact. This led scholars to ask, "Why so much stability?"[28]

Two mechanisms prevent cycling from occurring: bargaining and agenda-setting. We start with bargaining, which is familiar from earlier chapters. In general, voting does not account for intensity of preference. Suppose three legislators have the following preferences for expenditures on public schools:

conservative: low > moderate > high
centrist: moderate > high > low
yuppie: high > low > moderate

Voting over these three choices leads to intransitivity,[29] regardless of the strength of the voters' preferences. For example, whether the conservative feels strongly or weakly about low expenditures, she always votes for low over moderate and moderate over high. The other voters behave similarly, producing the cycle: low > moderate > high > low.

Bargaining provides an opportunity to express intensity of preferences. By responding to intensity of preferences, bargaining can prevent intransitivity. Specifically, bargaining delivers each legislator's favorite policy on the issue he or she cares most about, and all the voters may prefer this result to any other feasible outcome. All voters are better off because their most intense desire is satisfied. The result is efficient and stable.

To illustrate, let ">>" denote "very strongly prefers." Rewrite the preceding preferences:

conservative: low >> moderate > high
centrist: moderate > high > low
yuppie: high > low > moderate

Applying majority rule to these preferences yields intransitivity. However, bargaining may avoid this result. The conservative may offer the yuppie a deal: "vote for low spending on schools like I want, and I will vote for high spending on recycling programs

[27] Richard D. McKelvey, *Intransitivity in Multidimensional Voting Models and Some Implications for Agenda Control*, 12 J. ECON. THEORY 472 (1976). *See also* Charles R. Plott, *A Notion of Equilibrium and its Possibility Under Majority Rule*, 57 AM. ECON. REV. 787 (1967) (showing that voting in multidimensional space can be transitive only under a very demanding condition called radial symmetry).

[28] Gordon Tullock & Geoffrey Brennan, *Why So Much Stability*, 37 PUB. CHOICE 189 (1981).

[29] We assume the voters do not vote strategically.

like you want." If the yuppie intensely favors recycling programs, he may accept the offer. If the transaction costs are low, the centrist may bargain too. After bargaining, the legislators vote on multiple issues, but no intransitivity results. As part of the bargain, the yuppie votes for low expenditures on schools instead of high expenditures on schools, breaking the intransitive cycle. Voting implements a stable bargain. This kind of voting among lawmakers is called "logrolling."

Now consider the second mechanism for preventing intransitivity: agenda-setting. Voting is usually structured by rules of procedure, such as Robert's Rules of Order. The procedures usually prohibit reintroducing a defeated proposal. If defeated proposals cannot be reintroduced, an endless cycle of voting cannot occur. Voting ends when the agenda ends.

Given a fixed agenda, the proposal that wins the last vote prevails. The proposal that wins on the last vote is usually predictable from the proposal that wins on the next-to-last vote. The same relationship holds between the next-to-last vote and the vote preceding it. Thus, the final winner in the intransitive set can be determined by whoever sets the agenda. Control of the agenda avoids cycling by giving the agenda setter the power to choose among intransitive alternatives.[30]

To illustrate, suppose three legislators, the conservative, the centrist, and the yuppie, make a decision about school funding: low, moderate, or high. They do not bargain with one another. Instead of bargaining, they vote over pairwise choices. The person controlling the agenda must fill in the "tree" in Figure 4.4 that depicts the order of voting.

Assume that the three alternatives form an intransitive cycle: low > moderate > high > low. Furthermore, assume that the conservative sets the agenda. The conservative wants "low" to prevail. She can set the agenda so that the first vote pits "moderate" against "high." "Moderate" prevails, setting up a final vote between "moderate" and "low." "Low" prevails in the final vote. Thus, the conservative gets her most preferred outcome, as depicted in Figure 4.5.

What if the agenda setter is the yuppie who wants "high" to prevail? He can accomplish this by setting the agenda so that the first vote pits "low" against "moderate" and the final vote pits the winner of the first vote against "high." "High" funding will prevail, as depicted in Figure 4.6.

For the agenda setter to determine the outcome of voting over an intransitive cycle, she must think recursively. Specifically, she must figure out which alternative can be beaten by the one she most favors, pit them against each other in the last round of voting, then repeat the same process of reasoning for the next-to-last round, and so forth back to the beginning. This assumes that the agenda setter is obliged to hold a vote on every alternative. If this is not the case, then her task is simpler. She can hold just one vote, which pits her preferred alternative against the one it can beat.

This discussion focuses on a one-dimensional choice, school funding. Earlier we mentioned the Chaos Theorem, which shows that, except in rare circumstances, all of the potential outcomes in a multidimensional choice lie in an intransitive cycle. For *any* status quo policy, a majority will, given the right sequence of votes, move the policy to *any* final policy. This theorem implies that whoever controls the sequence of votes

[30] *See, e.g.*, ROBIN FARQUHARSON, THEORY OF VOTING (1969); Birgitte Sloth, *The Theory of Voting and Equilibria in Noncooperative Games*, 5 GAMES & ECON. BEHAV. 152 (1993).

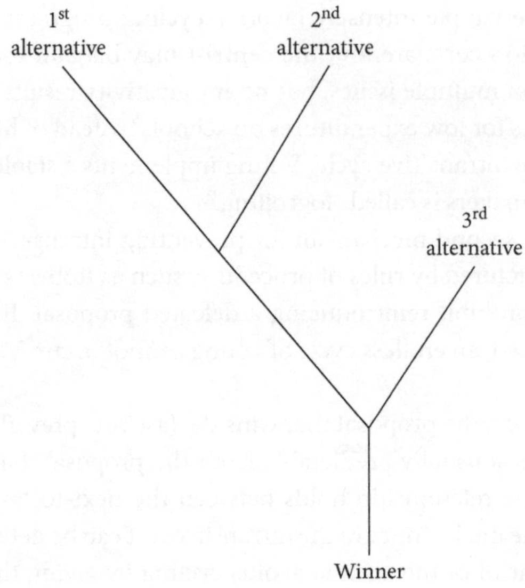

Figure 4.4. Setting the Agenda

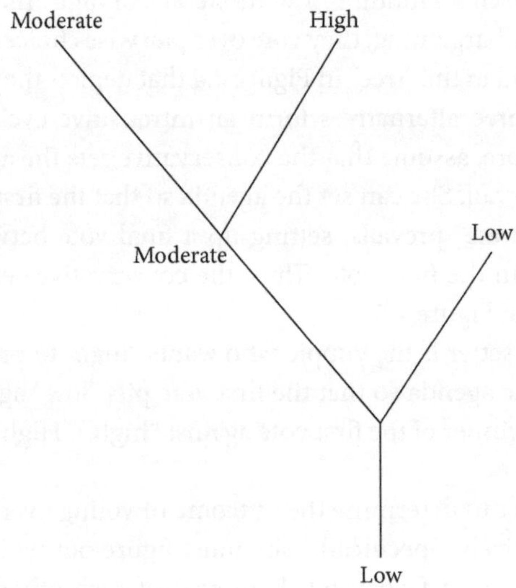

Figure 4.5. Low Wins

dictates policy, even in multiple dimensions.[31] Legislatures and other bodies that vote typically adopt rules giving control over the agenda to particular individuals, such as committee chairs. By choosing the agenda, the chair in effect determines which majority will prevail.

Generalizing, groups can avoid intransitive cycles by empowering someone to determine which majority will prevail. Put more provocatively, groups face a choice between

[31] Richard D. McKelvey, *Intransitivity in Multidimensional Voting Models and Some Implications for Agenda Control*, 12 J. Econ. Theory 472 (1976).

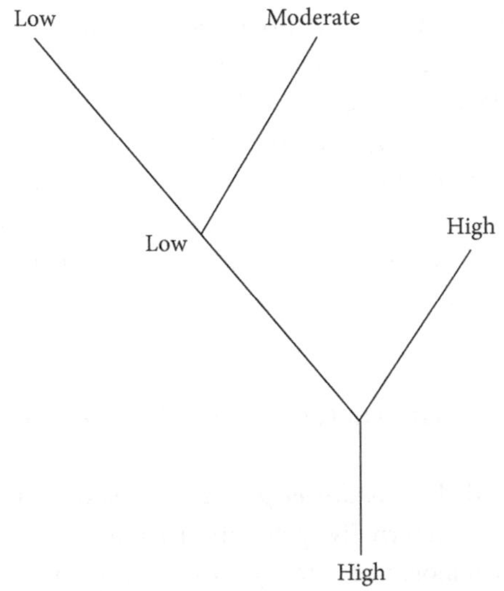

Figure 4.6. High Wins

incoherence and dictatorship. They can suffer from intransitivity, or they can enjoy stability by concentrating power in an agenda setter.[32]

Questions

4.9. Political commentators in the United States sometimes say that the President can use the media to "set the agenda."[33] Assume the government must choose low, medium, or high funding for the military. Voting by majority rule will produce an intransitive cycle: low > medium > high > low. The President wants medium to win. To induce support for medium, how should the President frame the choice? How should the opposition frame the choice?

4.10. A legislature with three members (*A*, *B*, *C*) chooses among three alternatives (*x*, *y*, *z*). Here are the legislators' preference rankings:

$$A: x > y > z$$
$$B: y > z > x$$
$$C: z > x > y$$

The alternatives are to be pitted against each other in majority voting, and a defeated alternative cannot be reintroduced. Assume that *C* is the agenda setter.

[32] Kenneth A. Shepsle, Analyzing Politics: Rationality, Behavior, and Institutions 72 (2d ed. 2010) ("There is, in social life, a trade-off between social rationality and the concentration of power. Social organizations that concentrate power provide for the prospect of social coherence: the dictator knows her own mind and can act rationally in pursuit of whatever it is she prefers. Social organizations in which power is dispersed, on the other hand, have less promising prospects for making coherent choices.").

[33] *See, e.g.*, Dan B. Wood, *Presidents and the Political Agenda*, *in* The Oxford Handbook of the American Presidency 108 (George C. Edwards III & William G. Howell eds., 2009).

(a) If each legislator votes for her preferred alternative in paired voting, describe the agenda that enables *C* to get her most preferred outcome.

(b) Assume that legislators act strategically on the first vote. For example, if the first vote pits *x* against *y*, *A* foresees that voting for *x* in the first vote will cause *z* to win in the second vote. Since *z* is the worst outcome for *A*, she decides to vote for *y* instead of *x* on the first vote. Can *C* still set the agenda such that her most preferred alternative is the winner? (Hint: consider what happens if *C* includes *z* on the first vote.)

I. Alternative Voting Procedures

So far, we have analyzed the *Condorcet procedure*: majority rule in pairwise voting. Under this procedure, each alternative gets paired against every other alternative. If one alternative commands a majority of votes against every other, then that alternative wins. If no alternative defeats every other (intransitivity), then the Condorcet procedure does not produce a winner.

Citizens and lawmakers use many alternative voting procedures, not just majority rule in paired voting. We will briefly discuss a few leading alternatives. Under *simple plurality rule*, every voter casts one vote for a single alternative, and the alternative with the most votes wins, even if that alternative has less than half the votes. To illustrate, if candidates *A*, *B*, and *C* get 40 percent, 35 percent, and 25 percent of the vote, respectively, then *A* wins. Simple plurality rule is used in American presidential elections and in many other settings. People often say "majority rule" when they mean simple plurality rule.

Variations on simple plurality rule abound. Under a *plurality runoff*, every voter casts one vote for a single alternative, and the two alternatives with the most votes proceed to a second round of voting. Every voter votes in the second round, and the alternative with the most votes wins. The state of Georgia, for example, uses a version of a plurality runoff to elect legislators.[34]

Under a *sequential runoff*, every voter casts one vote for a single candidate, the votes get tallied, and one candidate gets eliminated. The voters vote on the remaining candidates, another candidate gets eliminated, and the process repeats until one only candidate remains. Sequential runoffs can be organized in different ways. One way, which is sometimes called "instant-runoff" or "ranked-choice" voting, works like this. Every voter ranks all candidates (first choice, second choice, etc.) simultaneously. The candidate with the fewest first-place votes get eliminated. Each voter who ranked that candidate first has her vote reallocated to the candidate she ranked second, and the process repeats. A version of ranked-choice voting has been used in San Francisco and other places.[35]

[34] Many elections in Georgia follow this rule: if no candidate gets a majority in the first vote, the two candidates with the most votes appear on the ballot for a second vote.

[35] *See* Dean E. Murphy, *New Runoff System in San Francisco Has the Rival Candidates Cooperating*, N.Y. Times, Sept. 30, 2004; Lee Drutman, *Laboratories of Democracy: San Francisco Voters Rank Their Candidates. It's Made Politics a Little Less Nasty*, Vox, July 31, 2019, https://www.vox.com/the-highlight/2019/7/24/20700007/maine-san-francisco-ranked-choice-voting.

The *Borda count* is a voting method that works by a scoring system. Every voter assigns points to each alternative. For example, if there are three alternatives, a voter will assign two points to her favorite alternative, one point to her second favorite, and zero points to her least favorite alternative. All points get added up, and the alternative with the most wins. Versions of the Borda count have been used in Iceland and Slovenia, and this method is used in the United States to select the most valuable player in professional baseball.[36]

Do voting procedures affect outcomes? The answer is yes, as the box illustrates. However, we focus on a different question here: Do voting procedures affect intransitivity? As discussed, majority rule over paired alternatives can result in intransitivity, and this is especially likely when voting on multiple issues. Is there a voting procedure that can always avoid intransitivity? In a monumental generalization, Kenneth Arrow proved that *no* democratic voting rule prevents intransitivity.[37] The appendix to this chapter describes *Arrow's Impossibility Theorem*. People who suppose that tinkering with voting processes can solve the problem of intransitivity are mistaken.

Five Voting Rules, Five Winners

Do voting procedures affect election outcomes? Consider an example.[38] Five candidates are running for office: Olivia, Penny, Quinn, Rhonda, and Steve. Voters rank the candidates from best to worst. The voters can be divided into six groups according to their rankings. Everyone within a group agrees about the ranking. Table 4.1 shows the rankings of candidates by each group. Note that the groups have different numbers of voters in them, as Table 4.1 indicates. To illustrate, Group I has 18 voters, and all of them rank the candidates as follows: Olivia > Penny > Quinn > Rhonda > Steve.

Table 4.1. Voters and Candidates

	Group I 18 voters	**Group II** 12 voters	**Group III** 10 voters	**Group IV** 9 voters	**Group V** 4 voters	**Group VI** 2 voters
Rank 1	Olivia	Steve	Rhonda	Penny	Quinn	Quinn
Rank 2	Penny	Quinn	Steve	Rhonda	Steve	Rhonda
Rank 3	Quinn	Penny	Quinn	Quinn	Penny	Penny
Rank 4	Rhonda	Rhonda	Penny	Steve	Rhonda	Steve
Rank 5	Steve	Olivia	Olivia	Olivia	Olivia	Olivia

36 *See* Thorkell Helgason, Appointment of Seats to the *Althingi*, the Icelandic Parliament, National Electoral Commission of Iceland 18 (2013); Voting FAQ, How Is the Voting Counted?, Baseball Writers' Association of America, https://bbwaa.com/voting-faq/.

37 *See* Kenneth Arrow, Social Choice and Individual Values (1951); *see also* Amartya Sen, Collective Choice and Social Welfare (1970). Details are in the appendix to this chapter.

38 This discussion draws from Joseph Malkevitch, *Mathematical Theory of Elections*, 607 Annals of the N.Y. Acad. of Sci. 89 (1990), and Kenneth A. Shepsle, Analyzing Politics: Rationality, Behavior, and Institutions 192–97 (2d ed. 2010).

The electorate consists of everyone in all six groups. Now consider the different outcomes when the electorate votes under five different methods described earlier. Start with *simple plurality rule*. Everyone votes for his or her favorite candidate, and the one with the most votes wins. Thus, Olivia gets 18 votes, Steve gets 12 votes, Rhonda gets 10 votes, and so forth. Since Olivia get more votes than any other, she wins under simple plurality rule.

What about a *plurality runoff*? In the first round of voting, Olivia gets 18 votes, and Steve gets 12. Everyone else gets fewer votes, so they drop out. The second round of voting pits Olivia against Steve. Voters in Group I vote for Olivia, but everyone else votes for Steve. Steve wins under a plurality runoff by a vote of 37 to 18.

Consider a *sequential runoff* according to which the candidate with the fewest first-place votes in each round gets eliminated. Quinn only gets 6 votes in round one, fewer than anyone else, so he drops out. In round two, everyone votes on the remaining candidates. Penny gets 9 votes in round two, fewer than anyone else, so she drops out. The process repeats until two candidates remain, Olivia and Rhonda. Rhonda wins in the last round by a vote of 37 to 18. Rhonda prevails in the sequential runoff.

The *Borda Count* requires voters to assign points to candidates according to their rank order. In Group I, each of the 18 voters gives 4 points to Olivia, 3 to Penny, 2 to Quinn, 1 to Rhonda, and 0 to Steve. Thus, Olivia gets 72 points from Group I, Penny gets 54, and so on. Adding up all points across all groups produces a final score for each candidate. Penny wins with a high score of 136.

Finally, consider the *Condorcet Procedure*. Quinn is the only candidate who can beat everyone else in pairwise contests. He defeats Olivia by a vote of 37 to 18, Steve by a vote of 33 to 22, and so on. Quinn prevails under the Condorcet Procedure.

We started with 55 voters who rank five candidates. The voters, candidates, and rankings never change, but the voting rule does. Five different voting rules produce five different winners. Is one voting rule better than the others? Arrow proved that all of these voting procedures (and any others you can think of) are subject to intransitivity. It is hard to find a general reason to prefer one procedure over another. Instead of being general, coherent arguments for preferring a particular procedure are often historical, partisan, or pragmatic (e.g., "this procedure is easiest to understand").

II. Normative Theory of Voting

Now we turn to the normative evaluation of voting. Voting is a way for a group of people to make collective decisions. Does it give good results? For economists, a "good result" is one that best satisfies people's preferences. In a democracy, citizens vote on public goods like police and schools. Under certain conditions explained earlier, majority rule produces the outcome preferred by the median voter. Does satisfying the median voter's preferences best satisfy everyone's preferences?

Answering this question requires combining different wants of different people into an overall judgment. In economics, this is the problem of deriving social values from individual values. Different political and moral philosophies derive social value from individual values in different ways. Economic analysis relies on different types of aggregation. As we will show, these concepts of social value provide different normative justifications for voting.

A. Pareto Efficiency

We start with the simplest conception of social value. Under the simplest conception, the outcome of voting is best if no alternative exists that some voters prefer and none oppose. Thus, no change can make someone better off without making someone else worse off. This is the standard of Pareto efficiency applied to voting.[39] In notation, the outcome x_1 is Pareto efficient if there is no alternative x_2 such that at least one voter prefers x_2 to x_1, and no voter prefers x_1 to x_2.[40]

Majority rule ordinarily achieves Pareto efficiency. To see why, assume that citizens vote over platforms, and a party proposes a platform that is Pareto inefficient. For any Pareto-inefficient platform, some voters favor a change and no voters oppose the change. Consequently, a proposal to make the change will normally command a majority of votes. Indeed, the change might receive unanimous support. Thus, a Pareto-inefficient platform usually is not a voting equilibrium.[41] This implies that any voting equilibrium (if one exists) is likely to be Pareto efficient.

These conclusions apply to Figure 4.1, which depicts the utility curves and ideal points of Larry, Mary, and Ned. To find the Pareto-efficient points, begin at the origin of the graph, which corresponds to an extreme left-wing platform, and start moving to the right along the horizontal axis. At first, all three voters prefer the move to the right. However, once the point x_l^* is reached, which is Larry's ideal point, any further move to the right makes Larry worse off. Similarly, start from the extreme right side of the horizontal axis and move to the left. At first, all three voters prefer the move to the left. However, after reaching the point x_n^*, any further move to the left makes Ned worse off. Pareto-efficient points are all the platforms in the interval between x_l^* and x_n^*. The median platform necessarily lies in this interval. Consequently, the median voter theorem yields Pareto-efficient results.

Replacing Pareto-inefficient outcomes with Pareto-efficient outcomes is uncontroversial. Who would oppose a change that makes someone better off and no one worse off? However, choosing among Pareto-efficient outcomes is controversial. Every platform between x_l^* and x_n^* is Pareto efficient. Which should prevail?

B. Social Welfare

Many laws benefit some people and harm others. Pareto efficiency provides no basis for choosing among such laws. Guiding political choices requires a more definite and

[39] This theory traces to VILFREDO PARETO, MANUAL OF POLITICAL ECONOMY (1906).

[40] Here is a complementary explanation. A *Pareto improvement* is a change to the status quo that makes at least one voter better off and no voter worse off. If no Pareto improvement can be made, then the status quo is Pareto efficient.

[41] In complex models with strategic behavior, Pareto-inefficient voting equilibria can exist.

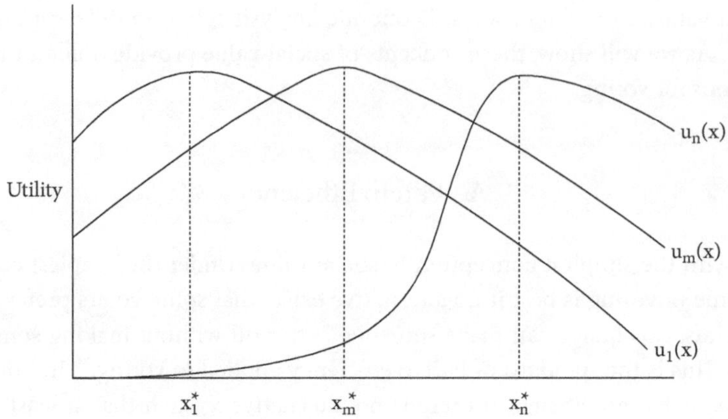

Figure 4.7. Intensity and the Median Rule

controversial standard than Pareto efficiency. Social welfare, or utility aggregated across individuals, provides such a standard. Unlike Pareto efficiency, the standard of social welfare commands changes whose benefits to the winners exceed the losses to the losers. For example, a move from x_l* to x_m* in Figure 4.1 harms Larry and benefits Mary and Ned. The change is no improvement by the standard of Pareto efficiency. If, however, the harm to Larry is less than the sum of the benefits to Mary and Ned, then the change is an improvement by the social welfare standard.[42]

The median rule does not necessarily maximize welfare. To see why, assume that a three-person committee must decide a difficult issue by majority vote. The committee agrees that each person will write his or her vote on a slip of paper. When the slips of paper are collected, the chairperson reports, "I have two slips marked 'Yes' and one marked 'No, no, please, no!'" Apparently, two people favor the proposal and one adamantly opposes it. Majority rule will lead to adopting the proposal, but this might reduce welfare, because the opponent loses more than the two supporters gain.

The underlying problem is that voting does not reflect the intensity voters feel toward issues. To illustrate graphically, assume that Ned develops an intense dislike of left and moderate platforms. Consequently, Ned's utility curve shifts down in the vicinity of x_l* and x_m*, as depicted in Figure 4.7. Larry's and Mary's preferences have not changed. The social welfare standard responds to shifts in sentiment, so it requires the voter equilibrium to shift to the right. However, shifting down Ned's utility curve does not change the median platform, which remains at x_m*. Changes in the intensity of voters' sentiment affects social welfare but not the median outcome.

The median voter theorem does not usually maximize social welfare, but it does under an assumption called *strong symmetry*. Under strong symmetry, the intensity of right-wing feeling exactly offsets the intensity of left-wing feeling. For every voter's utility curve on one side of the median, another voter has an identical curve on the other side of the median. In Figure 4.1, a move from x_l* toward x_n* benefits Ned and harms Larry. Strong symmetry implies that the benefit to Ned exactly offsets the harm to Larry.

42 Here we assume social welfare is simply the sum of the three voters' utility. Conceptualized this way, social welfare is equivalent to cost-benefit efficiency, where costs and benefits are measured in individual utility.

Given strong symmetry in voters' preferences, the median rule maximizes social welfare. To see why, start at the median x_m^* and consider a move to the right. Ned gains, and Larry loses an equivalent amount. The benefits of the move to the right-wing voter exactly offset the costs of the move to the left-wing voter. Meanwhile, the move to the right costs the median voter, and nothing cancels this cost. Consequently, remaining at the median is better than shifting to the right. The same logic applies to shifts from the median to the left.

Strong symmetry must be rare in fact. Even so, it is worth understanding in order to understand approximate symmetry. Given approximate symmetry in voters' preferences, the median rule approximately maximizes welfare. Approximate symmetry might be common.

This discussion of welfare measures costs and benefits of voters. What happens to the result when some people do not vote? If voters are a representative sample of all citizens, then the electoral outcome remains the same, and so do the social welfare implications. Conversely, if voters are a biased sample of all citizens, then the median voter's ideal outcome differs from the median citizen's ideal outcome. To illustrate concretely, if legislators vote on bills in a representative democracy, and if the median legislator is to the right of the median citizen, then the bills that pass will be to the right of the ones preferred by the median citizen.

The preceding analysis omits a perplexing problem in economics: How to measure social welfare? In reality, we do not have graphs with which to measure and compare individuals' utility. Economists often measure the utility that a good conveys to someone by her willingness to pay for it. Thus, if Larry is willing to pay $100 to get his preferred platform chosen, then its value to Larry is $100. This measure does not account for Larry's ability to pay. If Larry is poor, then paying $100 may reduce his utility a lot. He must place a high value on his preferred platform to part with $100. Conversely, if Larry is rich, then paying $100 may reduce his utility only a little. Thus, he might place only a low value on his preferred platform.

When evaluating investment projects, the World Bank sometimes gives extra weight to the net benefits of very poor people.[43] In an earlier chapter, we encountered the underlying rationale for this: an extra dollar spent by the rich on opera tickets increases welfare by a smaller amount than an extra dollar spent by the poor on bread. Citizens in democratic countries vigorously debate how much income the state should redistribute from the rich to the poor. Libertarians oppose most redistribution, and socialists favor much redistribution.

Does majority rule maximize the welfare of voters? We can answer that question when voting satisfies the median rule. The median rule is Pareto efficient, and it is welfare-maximizing if voter preferences are symmetrical.

Questions

4.11. Compare attitudes of citizens toward military expenditures and abortion. In which case are preferences more likely to be strongly symmetrical?

[43] *See, e.g.*, Paul J. Gertler et al., *Impact Evaluation in Practice*, THE WORLD BANK (2011).

4.12. A right-wing minority of American voters wants to outlaw abortion, and a left-wing minority wants to outlaw the death penalty. Assume that each minority has very intense feelings. Would it be better for the intense minority to get its way on each issue or for the majority to get its way on both issues?

4.13. Return to the example of sunbathers on a hot beach. If two ice cream vendors compete with one another, they will both locate in the middle of the beach. Is this location inefficient by the social welfare standard? (Hint: how far must the sunbathers walk to get ice cream?)

4.14. There are three voters (*A*, *B*, *C*) and three alternatives (x_1, x_2, x_3). The voters rank the alternatives based on their utility. To illustrate, voter *A* gets 3 utility from x_1, 2 from x_2, and 1 from x_3. Here are the payoffs of each alternative for the three voters:

$$A: 3 = u_a(x_1), 2 = u_a(x_2), 1 = u_a(x_3)$$
$$B: 3 = u_b(x_2), 2 = u_b(x_1), 1 = u_b(x_3)$$
$$C: 3 = u_c(x_3), 2 = u_c(x_1), 1 = u_c(x_2)$$

(a) Which alternative is the voter equilibrium in paired voting?
(b) Which alternatives are Pareto efficient?
(c) Which alternative maximizes the sum of utilities?

C. No Equilibrium

We have examined the normative implications of majority rule when it yields a unique, stable equilibrium. Recall that a situation can arise in which no equilibrium exists, like the game of "rock, paper, scissors." Is intransitivity in voting good or bad? Intransitivity is irrational for individuals and society, as we will explain.[44]

Suppose that a student takes his desk lamp—call it lamp *A*—to the flea market to trade for another. The student sees lamp *B*, which he prefers to lamp *A*, and he offers to trade lamp *A* and $5 for lamp *B*. The vendor accepts the offer. The student is carrying lamp *B* when he sees lamp *C*, which he prefers to lamp *B*, so he offers to trade lamp *B* and $5 for lamp *C*. The vendor accepts. Now the student turns to leave the flea market, and he sees lamp *A* offered for resale. Since he has intransitive preferences, he likes lamp *A* better than lamp *C*, so he offers to swap lamp *C* and $5 for lamp *A*. The vendor accepts and the student goes home with lamp *A*. He leaves with the same lamp he brought to the flea market, only he wasted time and $15.

Intransitivity is irrational, not just when shopping. A long philosophical tradition holds that a rational person can rank states of the world from bad to good.[45] Without such a ranking, a person has no concept of a better world to strive for. Intransitive

[44] This is the "money pump" argument. For earlier formulations, see Donald Davidson, J.C.C. McKinsey, & Patrick Suppes, *Outlines of a Formal Theory of Value*, I, 22 Phil. Sci. 140 (1955); Frank P. Ramsey, *Truth and Probability*, *in* The Foundations of Mathematics and other Logical Essays (R.B. Braithwaite ed., 1950).

[45] This requirement of rational ethics, which is implicit in the utilitarian tradition, was formulated in a forceful, sustained argument in Henry Sidgwick, The Method of Ethics (1966).

preferences do not yield a ranking from bad to good because they run in a circle. The intransitive student did not have a vision of a better lamp. The objection to intransitive preferences is that they reveal no vision of a better world on the part of the actor.

This characterization of individuals also applies to groups such as a legislature. With intransitive voting, the legislature may prefer statute *A* over *B*, *B* over *C*, and *C* over *A*. Thus, the legislature cannot rank statutes from bad to good. Given intransitive voting, the state lacks coherent goals. Instead of rejecting worse states of the world in favor of better states, intransitive voting goes in a circle. Circular politics does not reveal the goal of a better world to achieve by collective choice.

Political philosophers often justify laws enacted in a democracy on the grounds that they represent the "will of the majority" or the "intent of the people's representatives." Given intransitive voting, however, these phrases make no sense. Voters have no collective "will" because they contradict themselves. The justification of democracy—or anything else—cannot rest on contradictions. Consequently, intransitive voting poses a problem for justifying democracy.[46]

III. Interpretive Theory of Voting

Academics like to discuss the justifications for democracy. Most lawyers, however, do not spend their time on such abstractions. They work to interpret the laws that democracies produce. To illustrate, when Congress passed the Civil Rights Act of 1964, lawyers asked if the act permitted affirmative action programs for on-the-job training,[47] not if Congress had intransitive preferences. Does the theory of voting help interpretation? The following sections argue that the answer is yes. We begin by contrasting two forms of collective choice: median democracy and bargain democracy. Then we use these categories to address intent, a key element in interpretation.

A. Median and Bargain Democracy

The theory of voting exposes a fault line in government: median versus bargain democracy.[48] *Median democracy* refers to a system that empowers the political center to make collective choices. To implement median democracy, separate different political issues from each other and vote on them independently. The median wins in voting.[49] Median democracy is promoted by ballot initiatives, direct election of an executive like the U.S. President, special districts for individual public goods, and a single subject rule (see the next chapter).

In contrast, *bargain democracy* refers to a system for making collective choices by negotiated agreement. To implement bargain democracy, bundle different issues

[46] William H. Riker, Liberalism Against Populism: A Confrontational Choice Between the Theory of Democracy and the Theory of Social Choice (1982).

[47] United Steelworkers of Am. v. Weber, 443 U.S. 193 (1979).

[48] The distinction between median and bargain democracy was developed in Robert D. Cooter, The Strategic Constitution (2000).

[49] Recall that the median voter theorem assumes single-peaked preferences. When one or more voters have multi-peaked preferences, intransitivity may result, in which case the agenda setter decides the vote.

Table 4.2. Preferences on Schools and Police

	School Expenditures		Police Expenditures	
	low	**high**	**low**	**high**
liberals	0	11	1	0
conservatives	1	0	0	11
moderates	2	0	3	0
total	3	11	4	11

together and vote on them simultaneously. Compared to separating issues, deciding multiple issues at the same time facilitates bargaining. The vote implements the bargain. Omnibus bills bundle different subjects into the same legislation, as when the U.S. Congress passed a bill addressing immigration, tropical diseases, military spending, and abortion. Besides omnibus bills, government forms that promote bargaining include representative democracy, bicameralism, presentment, and legislative committees.

What are the consequences of bargain and median democracy? We use a numerical example to explain the difference.[50] Expenditures on schools and police are the two major political issues in a town. Expenditures can be high or low for schools and police. The town has equal numbers of liberal, conservative, and moderate voters. Table 4.2 indicates their preferences for schools and police. The liberals intensely prefer high expenditures on schools and mildly prefer low expenditures on police. The opposite is true of conservatives, who intensely prefer high expenditures on police and mildly prefer low expenditures on schools. The moderates mildly prefer low expenditures on both. The row labeled "total" indicates the sum of net benefits to the three groups.

There are four possible outcomes for expenditures:

(schools, police) = (high, high), (high, low), (low, high), or (low, low).

For each outcome, the net benefits to voters are shown in Table 4.3. For example, (high, high) indicates high expenditures on schools and high expenditures on police, which results in a payoff of 11 for liberals, 11 for conservatives, and 0 for moderates.

Now we contrast the consequences of bargain and median democracy. The town council provides a forum for bargaining and cooperating. To implement bargain democracy, the town council should decide both issues. If bargaining succeeds, council members who care intensely about police may trade votes with council members who care intensely about schools, so that each group gets what it wants most. A platform calling for high expenditures on schools and police allows the liberals and conservatives to get what they want on the issues they prioritize, maximizing the total payoff at 22. The outcome is (high, high), with liberals getting 11, conservatives getting 11, and moderates getting 0.

50 The example draws on ROBERT D. COOTER, THE STRATEGIC CONSTITUTION 120–23 (2000).

Table 4.3. Combinations of School and Police Spending

	Expenditures on Schools and Police, Respectively			
	(high, high)	**(low, low)**	**(high, low)**	**(low, high)**
liberals	11	1	12	0
conservatives	11	1	0	12
moderates	0	5	3	2
total	22	7	15	14

However, political bargaining often fails. If the voters do not bargain and simply vote, majority rule produces an intransitive cycle. Specifically,

(high, high) > (low, low) > (high, low) > (low, high) > (high, high).[51]

To avoid a pointless cycle, the council may empower someone to set an agenda. The order of voting will determine the outcome. Thus, we see bargain democracy's advantage (if bargaining succeeds, voters get what they care about most) and disadvantage (if bargaining fails, the agenda setter chooses an outcome from among intransitive alternatives).

Instead of deciding both issues, the town council could choose police expenditures, and a separately elected school board could choose school expenditures. Without a forum for bargaining over the two issues, the town council and the school board will have difficulty agreeing. Instead of bargaining, they will have separate votes on separate issues. Separate voting by issue implements median democracy. With single-peaked preferences and pairwise voting, the median voter prevails on each dimension of choice. Under median democracy, two out of three groups (conservatives and moderates) vote for low expenditures on schools. Furthermore, two out of three groups (liberals and moderates) vote for low expenditures on police. Thus, median democracy results in low expenditures on schools and police. Moderates represent the median voter in our example, and they get their way on both issues. However, the potential gains from trade are lost. Liberals and conservatives would benefit from a bargain, but separating issues precludes a deal.

In sum, bargain democracy allows each political faction to get its way on the issue it cares about most. However, political factions often cannot agree. Without an underlying agreement, voting in multiple dimensions of choice is usually intransitive. To prevent voting in circles, an agenda setter can impose the order of voting, which determines the outcome. Instead of the agenda setter selecting the outcome, institutions can restrict each vote to a single dimension of choice. The median voter selects the outcome. Bargain democracy is like a risky stock with a high upside and a low downside, whereas median democracy is like a safe stock with a modest, predictable yield.

[51] Two of three groups (liberals and conservatives) prefer (high, high) rather than (low, low). Two of three groups (conservatives and moderates) prefer (low, low) rather than (high, low). Two of three groups (liberals and moderates) prefer (high, low) rather than (low, high). And, finally, two of three groups (conservatives and moderates) prefer (low, high) rather than (high, high).

Questions

4.15. In the previous example, suppose the town council decides both issues. The factions cannot agree, and the agenda setter decides the outcome. In this example, is the agenda setter's decision worse than the outcome under median democracy? In general, is an agenda setter's decision worse than the outcome under median democracy?

4.16. If the transaction costs of bargaining between units of government, like a town council and school board, are low, does separating the issues promote median democracy?

4.17. Maryland's constitution requires state legislators to get approval from a majority of voters before incurring some debts for the state.[52] Explain the relationship between voter-approval requirements like this and bargain democracy.

4.18. The original U.S. Constitution vested state legislatures with the power to select U.S. Senators. The Seventeenth Amendment to the U.S. Constitution replaced this system by providing for the election of U.S. Senators by the people.[53] Explain the relationship between the Seventeenth Amendment and median democracy.

The Unbundled Executive

The Framers of the U.S. Constitution faced an important choice: Should they create a council of executives, or a unitary executive? Many states have "unbundled" executives. In addition to voting for governor, citizens vote for offices like lieutenant governor, secretary of state, attorney general, insurance commissioner, and mine inspector. These are statewide offices that exercise a slice of a state's executive power. In contrast, the U.S. Constitution established a single President who exercises the federal government's executive power.[54] The President exercises some power directly, as with executive orders. The President exercises many other functions indirectly, as with the appointment of cabinet officers like the Secretary of Defense and the Administrator of the Environmental Protection Agency.

Which is better, a unitary executive as in the federal government or an unbundled executive as in many states?[55] Alexander Hamilton argued that "it is far more safe there should be a single object for the jealousy and watchfulness of the people . . . all multiplication of the Executive is rather dangerous than friendly to liberty."[56] This is a claim about accountability. Citizens can monitor a unitary executive better than a plural executive. When a problem arises, everyone knows who should address it. When the executive branch fails, voters know who to blame. As Harry Truman felt

52 Md. Const. art. III, § 34.

53 U.S. Const. amend. XVII.

54 U.S. Const. art. II.

55 This discussion draws on Christopher R. Berry & Jacob E. Gersen, *The Unbundled Executive*, 75 U. Chi. L. Rev. 1385 (2008).

56 The Federalist No. 69, at 430 (Alexander Hamilton) (Clinton Rossiter ed., 1961).

about the presidency, "the buck stops here."[57] Furthermore, a unitary executive can better coordinate the activities of the federal government.

Median and bargain democracy can clarify the choice. A unitary executive is analogous to bargain democracy. One official makes decisions across a range of issues, allowing trade-offs among them. He or she may make a politically popular choice on one issue in order to conserve resources for the unpopular choice on another issue. The upside of this arrangement is gains from trade. The most intense constituencies may get their preferred outcome on each issue. The downside of this arrangement is opacity. Although there is only one executive to monitor, voters often cannot tell if that executive's decisions reflect publicly minded trade-offs or handouts to special interests.

An unbundled executive is analogous to median democracy. An official like Arizona's mine inspector has one responsibility. The inspector cannot make tradeoffs across issues unless he or she bargains with other officials, which may be difficult. Unbundling foregoes gains from trade, but it pushes policy toward the political center. To get re-elected, the inspector needs to satisfy the median voter's preferences on mine safety. To demonstrate the logic, states with elected utility regulators (unbundled executives) have lower electricity prices than states with appointed utility regulators (unitary executives).[58] The median voter is an electricity consumer, not a producer, and elected regulators respond to the median voter.

To repeat an analogy, a unitary executive is like a risky stock with a high upside and a low downside, while an unbundled executive is like a safe stock with a modest, predictable yield. The former can make publicly minded trade-offs across issues—or give handouts to special interests. The latter can do less of both. An unbundled executive responds more to the median voter on each issue.

B. Intentionalism and Intransitivity

As an earlier chapter explained, judges interpreting statutes often seek legislative intent. When a church hired an Englishman to work as a pastor in the United States, it appeared to violate a federal statute on foreign workers. To determine if the church actually violated the statute, the Supreme Court looked beyond the words of the statute and inquired into legislative intent. Did Congress intend for its law to apply to churches and pastors? The Court concluded that the answer was no. Congress only intended the prohibition on foreign workers to apply to low-skill, low-wage workers, and pastors do not fit in that category.[59]

Cases like *Church of the Holy Trinity v. United States* are controversial. Critics argue that legislative intent is hard to discover or even nonexistent. Economics deepens this critique. We explain why using a modified version of the case. Suppose Congress

[57] *See, e.g.*, Buck Stops Here Sign, Harry S. Truman Library, National Archives, https://www.trumanlibrary.gov/photograph-records/77-3799.

[58] Timothy Besley & Stephen Coate, *Elected Versus Appointed Regulators: Theory and Evidence*, 1 J. EUR. ECON. ASSOC. 1176 (2003).

[59] Church of the Holy Trinity v. United States, 143 U.S. 457 (1892).

enacted the statute on foreign workers, and then the church contracted with the pastor as described earlier. To decide if the church broke the law, the Court searches for legislative intent. The legislative history, which provides clues about intent, is not uniform. Instead, the history supports three competing interpretations. Under interpretation *A*, the church violated the law. Under interpretation *B*, the church did not violate the law. Under interpretation *C*, whether the church violated the law depends on whether the pastor is from the "lowest social stratum" (the Court used this language in the real case).[60]

What should the Court do in the face of conflicting legislative history? Judges might reason as follows: the legisla*ture*'s intended interpretation is the one that a majority of legisla*tors* supported. What did the legislators support? Suppose that one-third of Congress (group I) preferred interpretation *A* to *B* and *B* to *C*. One-third of Congress (group II) preferred interpretation *C* to *A* and *A* to *B*. Finally, one-third of Congress (group III) preferred interpretation *B* to *C* and *C* to *A*. Here are the legislators' rankings of interpretations:

I: $A > B > C$.
II: $C > A > B$.
III: $B > C > A$.

A majority of legislators think that *A* is better than *B*, *B* is better than *C*, and *C* is better than *A*. There is no interpretation that a majority of legislators think is better than the alternatives. Like the voters in our school-funding example, the legislators here have intransitive preferences. Therefore, the "legislature's intended interpretation" cannot mean "the majority's intended interpretation." The majority has no coherent intent.

Could the court use a principle other than majority rule to translate individual legislators' intentions into a group intention? No. Congress is a "they," not an "it."[61] Legislatures are collections of individuals, not monoliths. Any effort to take those individuals' interpretations and aggregate them into a collective interpretation will run into the teeth of Arrow's Impossibility Theorem. No democratic voting rule prevents intransitivity. Using these ideas, Kenneth Shepsle concluded that "[l]egislative intent is an internally inconsistent, self-contradictory expression" and "provides a very insecure foundation for statutory interpretation."[62]

The root problem is that statutes usually involve compromising across issues, or deciding in multiple dimensions of choice. Given multiple dimensions of choice, aggregating individuals' intentions will lead to intransitivity. To break an intransitive cycle requires bargaining or agenda-setting. The bargain theory of interpretation introduced in an earlier chapter directs courts to look to bargaining and agenda-setting. What did the parties agree upon? What did the agenda setters insist upon in exchange for permitting a vote? To understand the terms of the deal, courts must ask these questions.

[60] *Id.* at 465.

[61] Kenneth A. Shepsle, *Congress Is a "They" Not an "It": Legislative Intent as Oxymoron*, 12 INT'L REV. L. ECON. 239 (1992).

[62] *Id.* at 239.

Questions

4.19. This chapter began by contrasting two statutes, a narrow one about cellphones and a broad one about immigration, diseases, the military, abortion, guns, and other matters. For which statute is legislative intent more likely to be intransitive?

4.20. Originalism is a theory of constitutional interpretation. It holds that the meaning of the Constitution was fixed at the time of enactment. But what exactly does the Constitution mean? According to "original intentions" originalism, the Constitution means what the Framers intended it to mean when they drafted it. According to "original public meaning" originalism, the Constitution means what the public thought it meant when it was adopted. Is original intentions originalism subject to the problem of intransitivity? Does original public meaning originalism avoid the problem of intransitivity?[63]

C. The Median Theory of Interpretation

The bargain theory of interpretation applies naturally to legislatures, where much political bargaining occurs. However, legislatures are just one forum for making laws. Often citizens can make laws themselves through direct democracy, as when voters in Missouri voted to raise the minimum wage. Like ordinary laws, the products of direct democracy require interpretation.

To illustrate, consider Issue 3, which voters in Ohio approved in 2011. The purpose of Issue 3 was to nullify a federal law that required Americans to purchase health insurance (the "individual mandate" in the Affordable Care Act).[64] Issue 3 failed to achieve that purpose because of the U.S. Constitution's Supremacy Clause, according to which federal laws trump state laws.[65] Even though Issue 3 could not achieve its main purpose, it still affected Ohio. For example, the initiative prohibited laws that prevent "the purchase or sale of health care." Did the initiative invalidate Ohio's restrictions on abortion? Arguably those restrictions prevent "the purchase or sale of health care." This is a matter of interpretation for courts.

Judges interpreting ordinary statutes often seek legislative intent. In direct democracy, judges seek "popular intent."[66] In other words, they seek the intention of voters who enacted the initiative. Some judges believe that voter intent is harder to ascertain

[63] *See* Gary Lawson, *Delegation and Original Meaning*, 88 VA. L. REV. 327, 398 (2002) ("Originalist analysis, at least as practiced by most contemporary originalists, is not a search for concrete historical understandings held by specific persons. Rather, it is a hypothetical inquiry that asks how a fully informed public audience, knowing all that there is to know about the Constitution and the surrounding world, would understand a particular provision.").

[64] *See* Andy Kroll, *The Ohio Tea Party's Big "Obamacare" Fail*, MOTHER JONES, Nov. 3, 2011 ("An early pamphlet created by the Ohio Project, the grassroots group created to promote the amendment, focuses entirely on defusing 'the new federal health care measure passed by Congress.' ").

[65] Here is the text of the Supremacy Clause: "This Constitution, and the laws of the United States which shall be made in pursuance thereof; and all treaties made, or which shall be made, under the authority of the United States, shall be the supreme law of the land; and the judges in every state shall be bound thereby, anything in the Constitution or laws of any State to the contrary notwithstanding." U.S. CONST. art. VI.

[66] *See* Jane S. Schacter, *The Pursuit of "Popular Intent": Interpretive Dilemmas in Direct Democracy*, 105 YALE L.J. 107 (1995).

than legislative intent. In a Supreme Court case involving an Arkansas initiative, Justice Thomas wrote: "inquiries into legislative intent are even more difficult than usual when the legislative body whose unified intent must be determined consists of 825,162 Arkansas voters."[67]

Is Justice Thomas right? Assume for now that direct democracy does not involve bargaining. Instead of casting one vote on a law addressing many issues, citizens cast separate votes on separate issues. Now recall the median voter theorem. When voters make decisions on one issue at a time, law tends to move to the political center. Between two alternatives, a majority prefers the one closer to the median. When law reaches the median, it sticks. Aggregating preferences on one issue leads to a unique equilibrium at the median voter's ideal point.

These ideas lead to a surprising conclusion. Unlike legislative intent, voter intent is a coherent concept. Aggregating the intentions of individual voters on an initiative does not lead to chaos. It leads to the median. Among two plausible interpretations of an initiative, which one did voters intend? A good rule of thumb is that voters intended the interpretation closest to the political center at the time of the vote. This is the *median theory of interpretation*.[68]

Apply this theory to Ohio. The question is whether Issue 3 invalidated the state's law on abortion. Many judges would answer this question based on voter intent. Did voters intend to invalidate the law on abortion when they passed Issue 3? According to the median theory of interpretation, the question is, "Did the median voter intend to invalidate the law on abortion by passing Issue 3?"

Justice Thomas has it backward. Inquiries into voter intent are not harder than inquiries into legislative intent. They are easier, even when voters number in the hundreds of thousands. This assumes that median democracy prevails. Voters cast separate votes on separate issues. Specialized governments force voters to cast separate votes on separate issues, as when the school board makes policy on schools and the water board makes policy on water. In direct democracy, a law called the "single subject rule" forces voters to cast separate votes on separate issues. We address that law in the next chapter.

Questions

4.21. In 2016, British citizens voted on this question: "Should the United Kingdom remain a member of the European Union or leave the European Union?" A majority voted to leave. Leaving the European Union is complicated, as it involves decisions on trade, travel, energy, and other issues. Does the median theory of interpretation help determine what voters wanted on each issue?

4.22. According to the bargain theory of interpretation, courts should not consider the views of legislators who voted against a bill. They were outside the bargain. According to the median theory of interpretation, courts should consider the views of voters who voted against an initiative. Why?[69]

67 U.S. Term Limits, Inc. v. Thornton, 514 U.S. 779, 921 (1995) (Thomas, J., dissenting).
68 *See* Michael D. Gilbert, *Interpreting Initiatives*, 97 MINN. L. REV. 1621 (2013).
69 *See id.* at 1646–49.

4.23. We call the median theory of interpretation a rule of thumb. The theory is often but not always right. To illustrate, consider an example. A policy dimension stretches from zero to one. The median voter prefers policy at 0.5. The old law set policy at 0.2. An initiative replaced that old law, but where it set policy is unclear because the initiative is ambiguous. A court needs to interpret it.

(a) The initiative is subject to two interpretations. The first interpretation would set policy at 0.1, and the second would set policy at 0.3. Which interpretation does the median theory support? Explain why this must be the proper interpretation.

(b) The initiative is subject to two interpretations. The first interpretation would set policy at 0.3. The text of the initiative, statements from its sponsors, and commercials run before the election strongly suggest this is the proper interpretation. The second interpretation would set policy at 0.5. There is little evidence to support this interpretation, but the court cannot rule it out. Which interpretation does the median theory support? Explain why this is not necessarily the proper interpretation.

The Highest Vote Rule

Sometimes voters cast different votes on the *same* issue. In one election, Arizonans considered two initiatives on smoking, and Nevadans considered three initiatives on medical malpractice. Some initiatives not only address the same issue, they conflict. To take an example, consider two California initiatives on alcohol taxes. One would impose a "penny-a-drink" tax, and the other would impose a "nickel-a-drink" tax.[70] These conflicting initiatives appeared on the same ballot.

On occasion, voters approve conflicting initiatives in the same election. This is not necessarily irrational; voters might prefer both alternatives to the status quo. However, it creates an interpretation problem for courts: which initiative controls? The tax cannot be a "penny-a-drink" *and* a "nickel-a-drink." Should the court enforce one initiative and disregard the other, even though a majority of voters supported both? Should the court "harmonize" the initiatives by setting the alcohol tax at, say, "three-cents-a-drink?"

Courts usually resolve this impasse by applying the *highest vote rule*.[71] According to this rule, the initiative that received more affirmative votes controls. Thus, if the "penny-a-drink" initiative had passed by a vote of 100,000 to 50,000, and if the "nickel-a-drink" initiative had passed by a vote of 80,000 to 50,000, the alcohol tax would be a "penny-a-drink." According to courts, the initiative receiving the most votes offers the "clearest expression" of the people's will.[72]

[70] *See* Ted Nace, GANGS OF AMERICA: THE RISE OF CORPORATE POWER AND THE DISABLING OF DEMOCRACY 152–53 (2003) (explaining the alcohol industry introduced the "penny-a-drink" counterinitiative to confuse voters, who rejected both initiatives on election day).

[71] The following discussion is based on Michael D. Gilbert & Joshua M. Levine, *Less Can Be More: Conflicting Ballot Proposals and the Highest Vote Rule*, 38 J. LEGAL STUD. 383 (2009).

[72] In re Interrogatories Propounded by the Senate Concerning House Bill 1078, 536 P.2d 308, 315 (Colo. 1975).

Is this right? Suppose Kim, Larry, Mary, Ned, and Olivia vote on alcohol taxes. The existing tax is zero cents, which matches Kim's ideal. The first initiative would raise the tax to one cent, which matches Larry's ideal. The second initiative would raise the tax to a nickel, which matches Mary's ideal. Ned and Olivia would prefer even higher taxes. The "penny-a-drink" initiative will receive four votes (Larry, Mary, Ned, and Olivia prefer one cent to zero).[73] The "nickel-a-drink" initiative will receive three votes (Mary, Ned, and Olivia prefer five cents to zero). Both initiatives receive a majority of votes, but the "penny-a-drink" initiative prevails under the highest vote rule. However, this is not the "clearest expression" of the voters' will. Given a choice between the two initiatives, a majority of voters would prefer a "nickel-a-drink." This follows from the median voter theorem.

Consider two alternatives to the highest vote rule. In Maine, voters can vote "no" on both initiatives, or they can vote "yes" on one and "no" on the other, but they cannot vote "yes" on both.[74] This prevents conflicting initiatives from passing simultaneously. In Switzerland, voters cast three votes: one between the status quo law and the first initiative; one between the status quo and the second initiative; and one between the conflicting initiatives.[75] If both initiatives pass, the initiative winning the third vote controls. Does the Maine or Swiss approach improve upon the highest vote rule?

Conclusion

This chapter analyzed voting as a method for satisfying the preferences of citizens. With single-peaked preferences and one issue, majority voting over paired alternatives reaches an equilibrium most preferred by the median voter. Instead of reaching equilibrium, however, this voting procedure will cause voting to cycle given multidimensional choices. When voting cycles, outcomes become irrational or arbitrary, and the "will of the majority" has no clear meaning.

"Why didn't the dog bark in the night? The dog must have known the criminal."[76] Sometimes Sherlock Holmes solves a mystery by asking why something that should have occurred did not. Scholars have shown why intransitive cycles should occur, but, like a good detective, you should ask why cycles do not occur in particular political systems. We described two methods to prevent cycling. Bargaining responds to the intensity of voters' preferences, which stops cycling. Voters can trade votes across issues to secure the outcomes they like most. In addition, agenda-setting stops cycling by giving the agenda setter power to choose a final outcome within an intransitive set.

The analyses of voting and bargaining distinguish between median and bargain democracy. Median democracy promotes stable, centrist government. Laws, especially

[73] We assume that the voters vote in favor of every initiative that they prefer to the status quo.

[74] Me. Rev. Stat. Ann. tit. 21-A, § 906(6)(D) (West 2019).

[75] Philip L. Dubois & Floyd Feeney, Lawmaking by Initiative: Issues, Options and Comparisons 50 (1998).

[76] Our language paraphrases Sir Arthur Conan Doyle, *The Adventure of Silver Blaze*, *in* The Memoirs of Sherlock Holmes (1892).

a constitution, that implement median democracy advance political moderation. Unfortunately, median democracy also forgoes gains from political trade. In contrast, bargain democracy satisfies the preferences of citizens through political trade. Laws, especially a constitution, that implement bargain democracy can advance social welfare. However, they can also cause intransitivity.

Appendix: Arrow's Impossibility Theorem

This appendix describes a famous result by Kenneth Arrow, a Nobel Prize–winning economist who founded a field called social choice theory.[77]

Imagine three or more individuals considering three or more alternatives. The alternatives could be, for example, high, medium, or low expenditures on schools. The individuals must choose a method of aggregating their individual preferences into a set of group preferences over the alternatives. How should they do this? Rather than considering particular methods of collective choice like majority rule, Arrow approached the problem differently. He specified five conditions that, at a minimum, any reasonable aggregation must satisfy. Here are the conditions:

Rationality: Every member of the group must be rational, meaning everyone has complete and transitive preferences over all of the alternatives. An individual's preferences are complete when, for all possible pairs of alternatives, he can say which one he prefers or whether he is indifferent between them. An individual's preferences are transitive when they do not turn circles (if $l > m$ and $m > h$, then $l > h$). Likewise, the group's preferences must be complete and transitive.

Universal Domain: Every member of the group can adopt any preference ordering over the alternatives as long as those preferences are complete and transitive. To illustrate, no one is required to prefer *l* to *m*.

Unanimity: If every member of the group prefers one alternative to another (say, *l* to *m*), then the method of collective choice must select the preferred alternative (*l*, not *m*).

Independence of Irrelevant Alternatives: The relative positions of any two alternatives in the group's preference ordering depend only on their relative positions in the individual members' preference orderings. This one is easiest to explain by example. Suppose some individuals prefer *l* to *h*, while others prefer *h* to *l*. Among these two alternatives, the method of aggregation (whatever it may be) yields a group preference of *l* to *h*. Now the individuals discuss *m*. The discussion causes some members to move *m* up in their individual preference orderings, while it causes some others to move *m* down. For this condition to be satisfied, the changes in members' assessments of *m* (the irrelevant alternative) must not affect the group's choice between *l* and *h*. The method of aggregation must continue to yield a group preference of *l* to *h*. Here is a simple story to convey the intuition. Three patrons sit at a restaurant. The waiter gives them a choice of two appetizers, chips or cheese. The patrons choose chips. Then the waiter returns and says there is a third choice, bread. If the patrons say, "in that case we will have cheese," they have violated this condition.

Nondictatorship: There is no individual member of the group whose own preferences dictate the group's preferences. In other words, there is no group member whose own preferences, regardless of what the other members think, determine the group's choice.

Arrow proved mathematically that *no* method of aggregating individuals' preferences into a set of group preferences can satisfy all five conditions simultaneously. Put differently, if the three conditions in the middle of the list are satisfied, then either the first or last condition is not. The method of collective choice will either generate intransitive group preferences, or a dictator will dominate the group.

[77] Kenneth J. Arrow, *A Difficulty in the Concept of Social Welfare*, 58 J. POL. ECON. 328 (1950); KENNETH J. ARROW, SOCIAL CHOICE AND INDIVIDUAL VALUE (1951). Our discussion also draws on KENNETH A. SHEPSLE, ANALYZING POLITICS: RATIONALITY, BEHAVIOR, AND INSTITUTIONS 67–74 (2d ed. 2010).

To be clear, the Impossibility Theorem does not imply that every collective choice violates at least one of these conditions. Instead, it implies that every method of collective choice sometimes violates at least one of these conditions. No method—plurality rule, a sequential runoff, the Condorcet procedure, or any other one you can think of—satisfies all of the conditions all of the time. Arrow uncovered a profound and unavoidable limitation of group choice.

5
Voting Applications

"The ballot," Abraham Lincoln said, "is stronger than the bullet."[1] We need a theory of voting to understand democracy's strength—its capacity for peace, order, and prosperity. Voting theory illuminates issues central to public law. Electing officials implicates the right to vote, voter fraud, gerrymandering, and other matters. Making laws implicates executive, legislative, administrative, and legal processes. This chapter applies voting theory to public law. We address questions like these:

Example 1: Americans living in Pakistan can vote in U.S. elections, even if their connection to the United States is weak. Pakistanis living in the United States cannot vote in U.S. elections, even if their connection to the United States is strong. Who should have a right to vote?

Example 2: Some politicians want to spread faithful voters across districts in order to secure as many seats as possible for their party. Other politicians want to concentrate faithful voters in their districts in order to secure their re-election. How are district boundaries drawn? How should they be drawn?

Example 3: Law requires politicians to publicize the names of people who contribute money to their campaigns. Such disclosure should ameliorate political corruption. But can it worsen corruption? In answering, consider James Huffman, who challenged an incumbent in a Senate race. Huffman claimed that people supported his candidacy but refused to contribute to his campaign. They feared that disclosure would reveal their identities to the incumbent, who would punish them.[2]

To answer such questions, this chapter examines voting by citizens: who gets to vote, and under what conditions. Then it turns to structures of representation, including political districts and legislative committees. Finally, the chapter studies some questions of interpretation.

I. The Right to Vote

Democracy belongs to philosophers in theory and to lawyers in practice. Law structures every aspect of the democratic process. This section focuses on laws governing voting by citizens. Citizens register to vote, gather information on candidates, travel to polling

[1] Abraham Lincoln, *"Lincoln's Lost Speech," in* EARLY SPEECHES, SPRINGFIELD SPEECH, COOPER UNION SPEECH, INAUGURAL ADDRESSES, GETTYSBURG ADDRESS, SELECTED LETTERS, LINCOLN'S LOST SPEECH 127, 159 (Bliss Perry ed., 1902).

[2] James Huffman, *How Disclosure Hurts Democracy*, WALL ST. J., Apr. 11, 2011.

Public Law and Economics. Robert D. Cooter and Michael D. Gilbert, Oxford University Press. © Oxford University Press 2022.
DOI: 10.1093/oso/9780197655870.003.0005

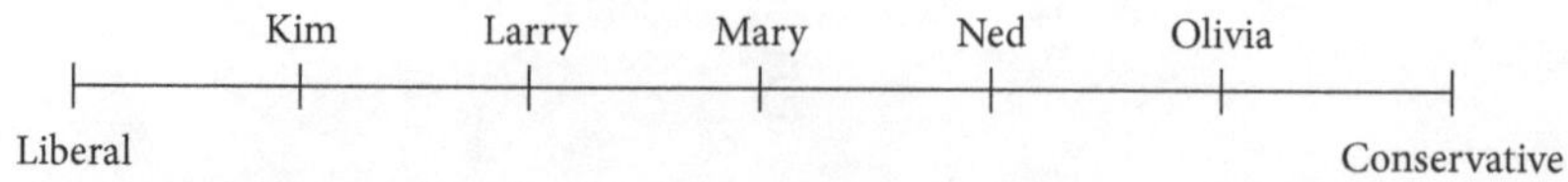

Figure 5.1. Suffrage and the Median Rule

stations at the appointed times, and cast their ballots. The state prints ballots, deters fraudulent voting, and counts votes. We examine some fundamental questions: Who gets to vote, how do they gather information, and what prevents fraud?

A. Inclusive Voting

The original U.S. Constitution granted states discretion to decide who could vote.[3] Originally states gave the vote exclusively to white male property owners. Compared to other countries in the eighteenth century, the right to vote was vastly expanded in the United States. Of course, compared to contemporary standards of morality, the right to vote was wrongly restricted. With time, suffrage extended to women, racial and religious minorities, and poor people. Wider franchise developed by wrenching violence (the Civil War of 1861–1865), grinding struggle (the women's suffrage movement leading to the Nineteenth Amendment in 1920), and debates over political ideals.

Inclusive voting seems to follow from aspirations in the Constitution itself. In a single sentence of 62 words, the Constitution's Preamble lists its aspirations: unity, justice, domestic tranquility, defense, liberty, and the general welfare.[4] To achieve them, the Constitution institutionalized majority rule with checks and balances. With time, Americans increasingly believed that majority rule works better with wider suffrage; that is, wider voting increases unity, justice, domestic tranquility, defense, liberty, and the general welfare. This belief generated political and legal pressure for more inclusive suffrage.

Does majority rule work better with wider suffrage? An abstract answer comes from the median rule. The previous chapter explained that pairwise voting on a single dimension of choice draws law to the political center. To illustrate, assume that five voters can be arrayed from liberal to conservative as indicated in Figure 5.1.

Mary is the median voter. As the prior chapter explained, in an election between two candidates, the platform of the winner should match Mary's preferred platform. Furthermore, the median rule maximizes the voters' welfare under conditions of strong symmetry. Strong symmetry among voters means that people on the left and the right have matching preferences. Specifically, it implies that for every voter left of the median, a voter exists on the right with equal preferences. Strong symmetry must be rare, but

[3] U.S. Const. art. I, § 4, cl. 1 ("The Times, Places and Manner of holding Elections for Senators and Representatives, shall be prescribed in each State by the Legislature thereof; but Congress may at any time make or alter such Regulations, except as to the Place of chusing Senators.").

[4] The Preamble to the U.S. Constitution reads in its entirety: "We the people of the United States, in order to form a more perfect union, establish justice, insure domestic tranquility, provide for the common defense, promote the general welfare, and secure the blessings of liberty to ourselves and our posterity, do ordain and establish this Constitution for the United States of America."

approximate symmetry might be common. Given approximate symmetry, Mary's preferred platform approximately maximizes the voters' welfare.

According to the Preamble, the Constitution's purposes include the "general welfare," which we can interpret as the social welfare of all Americans. Under this definition and the assumption of symmetrical preferences, the median rule predicts that majority rule maximizes the social welfare of Americans, provided that all of them vote.

What happens when some people cannot vote? Then the median rule might not maximize social welfare. To illustrate, assume that the state restricts the voters in Figure 5.1. Say, Kim and Larry cannot vote. Now Ned is the median voter, not Mary, so Ned's platform gets adopted. The change in platforms reduces the total welfare. The problem is that Mary's preferences represent the general welfare, whereas Ned's preferences misrepresent the general welfare. In this example, excluding some voters causes a *representation error*.

Instead of excluding Kim and Larry, assume that Kim and Olivia are the two people prohibited from voting. Mary is still the median among the remaining voters. The election's outcome is the same whether Kim and Olivia are included or excluded from voting. Excluding them does not cause a representation error.[5] The winning platform is constant, and so is social welfare.

Generalizing, *symmetric voting restrictions* disfranchise equal numbers of people on both sides of the median, which does not cause representation errors. In contrast, *asymmetric voting restrictions* disfranchise more people on one side of the median than the other, which causes representation errors. The degree of asymmetry determines the size of the representation error. Imagine 99 people organized from most liberal to most conservative. The fiftieth person is the group's median. If law prevents the first 10 people from voting, then the fifty-fifth person becomes the median voter. If law prevents the first 50 people from voting, then the seventy-fifth person becomes the median voter. The representation error is much larger in the second case.

This analysis helps justify laws like the Fifteenth and Nineteenth Amendments to the U.S. Constitution, which together gave racial minorities and women the right to vote.[6] Insofar as these groups share characteristics and experiences that affect their political views, they cluster on one side of the median. Disfranchising them changes political outcomes and reduces the general welfare.

The Fifteenth Amendment formally gave African Americans the right to vote, but many states denied them the right in practice. States used a variety of nefarious tricks. For example, some states required voters to pay a poll tax before casting a ballot. At that time, few African Americans had money to pay a poll tax. In *Harper v. Virginia State Board of Elections*, the U.S. Supreme Court held that poll taxes violate the Constitution.[7] According to the Court, states cannot make "the affluence of the voter" a condition for voting, because this "invidiously" discriminates in violation of the Equal Protection

[5] Of course, we might object to their exclusion on grounds of autonomy, dignity, and so on.

[6] U.S. CONST. amend XV ("The right of citizens of the United States to vote shall not be denied or abridged by the United States or by any State on account of race, color, or previous condition of servitude."); U.S. CONST. amend XIX ("The right of citizens of the United States to vote shall not be denied or abridged by the United States or by any State on account of sex."). The Fifteenth Amendment was enacted in 1870, and the Nineteenth Amendment followed in 1920.

[7] 383 U.S. 663 (1966). The Court held that requiring payment of poll taxes to vote in state elections violates the Constitution. The Twenty-Fourth Amendment prohibits poll taxes in federal elections.

Clause in the Fourteenth Amendment.[8] In our terms, poorer people tend to cluster on one side of the median, so disfranchising them leads to underrepresenting their preferences. To justify underrepresentation, the Constitution requires states to give a compelling reason. Virginia could not provide a compelling reason for its poll tax.

Questions

5.1. Return to the example of Kim, Larry, Mary, Ned, and Olivia. Suppose Ned and Olivia are excluded from voting.
   (a) Who is the median voter?
   (b) What happens to the representation error if Ned and Olivia feel more intensely than the others?

5.2. Many American states disfranchise people convicted of a felony, sometimes for life. In 2018, voters in Florida approved an initiative to restore felons' voting rights, but the Florida legislature has tried to block it.[9]
   (a) Under what circumstances would enfranchising felons reduce representation errors?
   (b) Many political strategists believe that felons tend to vote for Democrats over Republicans. Why do some states make it easier for felons to vote while others make it harder?

5.3. Some women are liberal and others are conservative, meaning women occupy both sides of the political distribution. Nevertheless, enfranchising women decreases representation errors. Why?

Election Administration

The 2000 presidential election between George W. Bush and Al Gore turned on one state, Florida. After the initial tally, Bush led in Florida by fewer than 2,000 votes, a tiny fraction of the millions cast in the state. As Gore sought recounts, problems mounted. Many ballots had not been counted properly. Some people intended to support Gore, a liberal, but accidentally voted for Pat Buchanan, a third-party conservative. Florida's elections chief was a Bush supporter. In *Bush v. Gore*, the Supreme Court put a controversial end to a controversial election, declaring Bush the winner in Florida and, therefore, the next President of the United States.[10] The case electrified a moribund field: election administration.

Elections require many steps: registering voters, operating polling stations, procuring ballots, counting votes, and so on. Every step has the potential for disfranchisement. To illustrate, suppose a voter arrives at a polling station and discovers a line to vote stretching down the block. One of the voting machines

[8] *Id.* at 666.
[9] Associated Press, *Florida Can't Bar Felons from Vote Over Fines and Fees, Court Rules*, NBCNEWS.COM, Feb. 19, 2020, https://www.nbcnews.com/politics/elections/florida-can-t-bar-felons-vote-over-fines-fees-court-n1138736.
[10] 531 U.S. 98 (2000).

is broken, and errors in the voter registration rolls are causing further delays. He waits for two hours before giving up. He has children to pick up from school and other responsibilities. This voter has not been denied the right to vote—he could vote eventually—but his right has been *burdened*. In addition to long lines (the so-called "time tax"), registration hurdles, transportation challenges, and poll worker mistakes burden voting.

Burdens on voting can be challenged in court. Judges usually review those burdens using the so-called *Anderson-Burdick* test.[11] They balance the burden on voters against the state's interest in its election procedure. To illustrate, Ohio used to permit voters to vote on Election Day or during 35 days beforehand. The state changed its law, reducing the early voting period to 29 days. In theory, this could burden some voters. A federal court upheld the new law, concluding that the burden is minimal and the state's interests—reducing costs and strain on electoral boards—were sufficient.[12] While reducing early voting from 35 days to 29 days was upheld, a reduction to zero days might not have been upheld.[13]

Our discussion of representation errors can illuminate election administration. Take another example from Ohio. The Ohio Secretary of State gave some voters an extra opportunity to vote early. Specifically, voters in the military could vote during the three days before Election Day, whereas nonmilitary voters could not. A federal court applied the *Anderson-Burdick* test and prohibited Ohio from applying its law in this manner.[14] The court concluded that officials cannot "pick and choose among . . . voters to dole out special voting privileges. Partisan state legislatures could give extra early voting time to groups that traditionally support the party in power and impose corresponding burdens on the other party's core constituents."[15] In other words, the mismatch in early voting could cause a representation error. The concept of representation errors complements the *Anderson-Burdick* test, though judges do not speak in these terms.

B. Exclusive Voting and Externalities

We have explained the advantage of majority rule with an inclusive franchise. Taken to its logical extreme, perfect inclusion means that everyone affected by an election's outcome can vote in it.[16] Conversely, perfect exclusion means that no one affected by an

[11] Burdick v. Takushi, 504 U.S. 428 (1992); Anderson v. Celebrezze, 460 U.S. 780 (1983). The *Anderson-Burdick* test "prescribe[s] sliding-scale or multiple-tier scrutiny, with the degree of scrutiny a function of the 'character and magnitude' of the burden on voting or associational rights. Laws that effect a 'severe' burden receive strict scrutiny; laws whose burden is minimal receive lax, rational-basis-like review; and laws whose burden is significant but not severe arguably receive something in between." Christopher S. Elmendorf, *Structuring Judicial Review of Electoral Mechanics: Explanations and Opportunities*, 156 U. Pa. L. Rev. 313, 318 (2007) (internal citations omitted).

[12] Ohio Democratic Party v. Husted, 834 F.3d 620 (6th Cir. 2016).

[13] North Carolina attempted to reduce its early voting days from 17 to 10. A federal court prevented this, concluding that the legislature intended to make voting harder for African Americans. *See* N. Carolina State Conf. of NAACP v. McCrory, 831 F.3d 204, 216 (4th Cir. 2016).

[14] Obama for Am. v. Husted, 697 F.3d 423 (6th Cir. 2012).

[15] *Id.* at 435.

[16] Indeed, taking this logic all the way, everyone in an interdependent world should vote in every election.

election can vote in it. Instead of perfect inclusion or exclusion, the U.S. Constitution creates a federal system with elements of each. The states and localities can set voting rules within limits. Specifically, state and local governments have the power to limit voting to members of the "political community."[17] States and localities usually exclude noncitizens, nonresidents, and felons from voting.

We have seen the advantages of inclusive voting. What are the advantages, if any, of exclusive voting, and how should the state choose between the two? Economics provides an answer based on two factors: externalities and administration. We will consider them in turn.

An earlier chapter discussed legal externalities, where one government's laws affect another place. State and local restrictions on voting create legal externalities. To illustrate, school boards make decisions that affect nearly everyone in a community, including noncitizens who cannot vote. To be concrete, imagine two neighbors. The first neighbor is a U.S. citizen without children. The second is a Chinese citizen with two children in public school. Both of them reside in Berkeley, California, where they also work and pay taxes. Berkeley schools are governed by an elected school board. Who can vote in Berkeley school board elections? The answer is U.S. citizens who reside in Berkeley. Thus, the American neighbor can vote for the Berkeley school board, but the Chinese neighbor cannot, even though she has children and arguably a larger stake in the public schools.

To generalize, an American city can exclude a foreigner from voting for a school board, even though the foreigner resides lawfully in the district, has children in school, and pays school taxes. Conversely, an American city cannot exclude a childless citizen who resides in the district from voting for a school board.[18] This structure can create a representation error. The error causes a legal externality. The school board's decisions affect foreigners, but since foreigners cannot vote, the board might not account for their interests when making decisions.

In a federal system, elections inevitably affect people who cannot vote in them. A person who lives in Kansas City, Kansas, and works across the bridge in Kansas City, Missouri, has a stake in both states, but she can vote in only one of them. When Delaware changes its corporate law, the change affects Mainers owning stock in Delaware-based companies. Utah, which is upstream on the Colorado River, makes laws affecting Arizona, which is downstream, but Arizonans cannot vote in Utah's elections. In these examples and others, exclusive voting leads to externalities.

In a previous chapter, we identified two methods for correcting legal externalities. The first is to create a single polity, such as merging a county and a city, or forming a special district on air quality encompassing two states. A single polity internalizes the externality. The second method is bargaining between separate jurisdictions such as states (Iowa negotiates with Nebraska) or localities (Los Angeles County negotiates with Ventura County).

To illustrate the two methods for correcting legal externalities, recall our example of the mother who cannot vote for the school board. The mother could bargain with the school board, possibly offering a gift to the school in exchange for a policy that benefits

[17] *See* Skafte v. Rorex, 553 P.2d 830 (Colo. 1976).
[18] *See* Kramer v. Union Free School District No. 15, 395 U.S. 621 (1969).

her child. In the United States, such bargaining might be illegal and will likely fail. Alternatively, the community could extend the franchise, permitting foreigners with schoolchildren to vote. Giving the mother a vote makes the school board more likely to internalize rather than externalize her interests.

If bargaining will fail, then the only option is to extend the franchise. Yet most state and local governments do not extend the franchise. In general, law in the United States prohibits noncitizens from voting. Politics helps to explain the exclusion. Usually the people who exercise political power do not want to share it with others, even if sharing power would improve representation and welfare. However, politics is not entirely to blame. Economics can explain and even justify exclusion in some circumstances, as we will show.

Questions

5.4. The chapters on bargaining introduced two concepts, production and distribution. Can you use these concepts to explain why politicians restrict the franchise even when expanding it would reduce representation errors?

5.5. Private citizens cannot order elite universities to admit their children. However, by making large donations to elite universities, private citizens can "buy" admission for their children. Does "buying" admission corrupt education? Does it create or cure any externalities?

C. Offsetting Errors

We have explained how extending the franchise can reduce errors. Now we explain how it can exacerbate errors. Many people lived outside of Tuscaloosa, Alabama, but inside the city's "police jurisdiction," a three-mile-wide ring around the city. Residents of the police jurisdiction were subject to some city laws, including criminal laws. However, they were exempt from other city laws. Residents of the police jurisdiction could not vote in city elections. In *Holt Civic Club v. City of Tuscaloosa*, the Supreme Court upheld the prohibition on voting, stating:

> A city's decisions inescapably affect individuals living immediately outside its borders. The granting of building permits for high rise apartments, industrial plants, and the like on the city's fringe unavoidably contributes to problems of traffic congestion, school districting, and law enforcement immediately outside the city. . . . The condemnation of real property on the city's edge for construction of a municipal garbage dump or waste treatment plant would have obvious implications for neighboring nonresidents. . . . Yet no one would suggest that nonresidents likely to be affected by this sort of municipal action have a constitutional right to participate in the political processes bringing it about.[19]

[19] 439 U.S. 60, 69 (1978).

Does the Court's decision reflect bad economics? You might think the answer is yes. The solution to the externalities the Court describes, one might argue, is to expand the franchise, not restrict it. But this is not quite right. Some decisions by the city, like building a garbage dump on the edge of town, will impose externalities on the police jurisdiction. With respect to those decisions, excluding the police jurisdiction from voting leads to a representation error. This is an error of *underrepresentation*—the police jurisdiction gets too little weight. However, other decisions by the city, like building a small park downtown, will not impose externalities on the police jurisdiction. With respect to those decisions, including the police jurisdiction in voting leads to an error of *overrepresentation*—the police jurisdiction gets too much weight.

The problem is that one city council makes two kinds of decisions: those that only affect the city, and those that affect the city and the police jurisdiction. Enfranchising the police jurisdiction will worsen the first kind of decision but improve the second kind of decision, and vice versa. We can characterize the problem in terms of externalities. If the police jurisdiction cannot vote, the city will externalize costs on the jurisdiction. If the police jurisdiction can vote, its residents will externalize costs on the city.

We can generalize from this discussion. When elections affect people differently, extending the franchise has cross-cutting effects. It improves underrepresentation at the cost of overrepresentation.

An earlier chapter introduced the internalization principle. According to this principle, we should assign power to the smallest unit of government that internalizes the effects of its exercise. Applied to *Holt*, the internalization principle implies that one government should make laws for the city only, and everyone in the city should vote in its elections, and another government should make laws for the city and the police jurisdiction, and everyone in both places should vote in its elections. Having two governments instead of one would mitigate externalities. However, it would create costs. Running two governments costs more than running one. Furthermore, and as discussed in a prior chapter, assigning issues to different government units tends to make bargaining across the issues harder.

Questions

5.6. In *Holt*, the Supreme Court held that the Constitution gives states discretion to exclude nonresidents from voting. Is this a good rule of thumb for balancing the costs of under- and overrepresentation?

5.7. Use a spatial model to explain these statements: "I am underrepresented when the median citizen is closer than the median voter to me. I am overrepresented when the median voter is closer than the median citizen to me."

5.8. Concurring in *Holt*, Justice Stevens wrote: "[T]here is nothing in the Federal Constitution to prevent a suburb from contracting with a nearby city to provide municipal services for its residents, even though those residents have no voice in the election of the city's officials or in the formulation of the city's rules."[20] If

[20] Holt Civic Club v. City of Tuscaloosa, 439 U.S. 60, 76 (1978) (Stevens, J., concurring).

transaction costs are low and representation is good, should courts worry about excluding the police jurisdiction from voting? What if transaction costs are high and representation is poor?

D. The Optimal Political Community

Deciding who should vote requires balancing the advantages and disadvantages of inclusion and exclusion. Exclusion of voters causes legal externalities—some people cannot vote on decisions that affect them. To overcome externalities from underrepresentation, extend the franchise. At the logical extreme, everyone can vote on all decisions that affect them. However, if elections affect some people more than others, extending the franchise too far creates the opposite problem. Some people can vote on decisions that do not affect them, or do not affect them much. To overcome externalities from overrepresentation, restrict the franchise.

Separate from externalities, more voting increases administrative costs to government—printing ballots, opening voting booths, counting votes, and so on.

The *optimal political community* balances these considerations. To find the optimum, extend the political community until the marginal benefit from improved representation just equals the marginal cost of administration.[21] The optimal political community is useful because courts balance such considerations when interpreting election laws. However, the optimal political community is an ideal that resonates with the purpose of constitutional democracy, not a rule of law.

Questions

5.9. The United States had soldiers in Afghanistan for 20 years. The President is Commander-in-Chief of the military. During that time, should Afghans have voted in U.S. presidential elections?

5.10. Australia makes voting compulsory. If you can vote, you must. Use the concept of an optimal political community to analyze compulsory voting.

5.11. In 1957, Alabama passed a law that redrew the boundary of the City of Tuskegee. The old boundary, a square, was replaced by a "strangely irregular twenty-eight-sided figure."[22] The new boundary placed nearly every African American resident outside the city's limit. Every white resident remained inside the city's limit. Only city residents could vote in the city's elections. In *Gomillion v. Lightfoot*, the Supreme Court invalidated the new boundary.[23] Use the concept of an optimal political community to defend the Court's decision.

[21] Buchanan and Tullock developed a similar principle: "the group should be extended so long as the expected costs of the spillover effects from excluded jurisdictions exceed the expected incremental costs of decision-making resulting from adding the excluded jurisdictions." JAMES M. BUCHANAN & GORDON TULLOCK, THE CALCULUS OF CONSENT: LOGICAL FOUNDATIONS OF CONSTITUTIONAL DEMOCRACY 113 (1965).

[22] 364 U.S. 339, 341 (1960).

[23] *Id.*

5.12. New York law limited voting in some school board elections to two groups: parents with children in public schools, and owners of real property like houses (their property taxes paid for the schools). In *Kramer v. Union Free School District No. 15*, the Supreme Court struck down this law.[24] Thus, people who could vote in ordinary elections could also vote in school board elections, even if they had no children or property. Can you use the concept of an optimal political community to critique the Court's decision?

The Twenty-Sixth Amendment

Statisticians distinguish two kinds of errors. When you conclude something is true that is false, your conclusion is a "false positive." When you conclude something is false that is true, your conclusion is a "false negative." To illustrate, consider a blood test designed to reveal the risk of disease. If the test shows the risk is high when it is low, the test result is a false positive, and vice versa. If the blood test makes too many errors, doctors seek better tests.

Like doctors, lawyers are familiar with false positives and false negatives. However, lawyers use different words to describe them. Rules are *overinclusive* if they forbid what they were designed to permit, and rules are *underinclusive* if they permit what they were designed to forbid. To illustrate, consider the Twenty-Sixth Amendment to the U.S. Constitution, which enfranchises Americans aged 18 years or older.[25] We can reformulate (and simplify) the amendment as follows: "people 18 or older, and no one else, can vote." Assume that the purpose of this amendment is to extend suffrage to those with the maturity and knowledge necessary to vote responsibly. The rule is overinclusive because it forbids what it should permit: some 17-year-olds are mature, knowledgeable, and responsible, yet they cannot vote. The rule is underinclusive because it permits what it should forbid: some 18-year-olds are not mature, knowledgeable, or responsible, yet they can vote.

Good rules minimize over- and underinclusiveness like good blood tests minimize false positives and false negatives. The optimal political community directs courts to minimize the costs of over- and underinclusiveness in representation. Can you use the concept of optimal political community to assess the Twenty-Sixth Amendment? The following information might influence your thinking. Support for the Twenty-Sixth Amendment was tied to the Vietnam War and the draft. The slogan was "old enough to fight, old enough to vote."[26] The Twenty-Sixth Amendment enfranchises Americans aged 18 years or older in all elections, not just federal elections.

[24] 395 U.S. 621 (1969).

[25] U.S. Const. amend XXVI ("The right of citizens of the United States, who are eighteen years of age or older, to vote shall not be denied or abridged by the United States or by any State on account of age.").

[26] Joseph P. Williams, *"Old Enough to Fight, Old Enough to Vote": The 26th Amendment's Mixed Legacy*, US News, July 1, 2016.

E. Voter Information

To vote intelligently, voters need information about politics. However, polling confirms that many voters lack basic information about political life. They cannot name their representative or describe the Constitution or federal agencies. They cannot explain laws constraining officials (can the Secretary of State store government secrets on a private email server?). Nor can they identify the positions of candidates (what is the Republicans' plan for health care?). "The best argument against Democracy is a five-minute conversation with the average voter."[27]

Some states required voters to prove that they could read and write before casting a ballot. In *Lassiter v. Northampton County Board of Elections*, the Supreme Court held that literacy tests do not violate the Constitution.[28] "The ability to read and write," the Court wrote, "has some relation to standards designed to promote intelligent use of the ballot."[29] In principle, perhaps a nondiscriminatory test could promote an informed electorate as the Court said.[30] In practice, literacy tests were applied in a discriminatory manner. They did not promote voter information; they intentionally disfranchised African Americans. The Voting Rights Act of 1965 prohibits literacy tests.

Literacy tests are thankfully gone, but the lack of information persists. Many people bemoan the shallowness of voters' information. What good is the right to vote if voters don't understand their choices?

Many economists have a different view. Voters are *rationally ignorant*.[31] Ignorance is rational when the cost of acquiring information exceeds the benefits to the decision maker. Rational ignorance characterizes voters in large elections where the probability of being decisive is minuscule. Voters cannot justify the cost of gathering information when their vote, whether informed or not, is unlikely to matter.

Rational ignorance does not imply total ignorance. Rational voters acquire some information in low-cost ways. Rather than reading detailed news reports, they use information shortcuts, or *heuristics*.[32] For example, suppose a politician proposes to restructure retirement savings plans. A retired voter could read the politician's bill, which is long and complicated. Or the voter could find out if the AARP, a powerful interest group that supports retirees, endorses or opposes the bill. The AARP's position is a heuristic. *Heuristics are helpful when they lead voters to make the same decision they would have made if they had acquired detailed information.*

[27] The underlying sentiment might be true, although the usual attribution to Winston Churchill is probably false.

[28] 360 U.S. 45 (1959).

[29] *Id.* at 51.

[30] As explained previously, if illiterate voters cluster on the same side of issues, then a literacy test worsens representation. This analysis, however, assumes that voters have the "correct" political preferences. Ignorant voters may have no preferences, or they may mistakenly prefer the wrong candidate, meaning the candidate who would do a worse job of representing them.

[31] Anthony Downs, *An Economic Theory of Political Action in a Democracy*, 65 J. Pol. Econ. 2 (1957).

[32] *See, e.g.*, Samuel L. Popkin, The Reasoning Voter: Communication and Persuasion in Presidential Campaigns (1991).

Political parties provide a common heuristic in voting. In the United States, most ballots list a candidate's political party. For many voters, knowing whether a candidate is a Democrat or a Republican is a reasonable heuristic.[33]

Questions

5.13. Nike's swoosh symbol and McDonald's golden arches are trademarks. Nike and McDonald's sue people who use their trademarks without permission. These suits are not only good for Nike and McDonald's, they are good for consumers of shoes and French fries. Why?

5.14. Many state court judges in the United States are elected. Some of these elections are partisan, meaning the judicial candidates are associated with political parties (Democrats, Republicans). Some of these elections feature attack ads ("Candidate X is a crook!"). Do partisan elections and attack ads harm the integrity of the judiciary, or do they inform voters?[34] What information do voters need to decide if a candidate will be a good judge?

Heuristics on the Ballot

The state of Washington implemented a "blanket" primary. All candidates for office—Democrats, Republicans, third-party candidates, and independents—appeared on the same primary ballot, and the candidates receiving the most votes advanced to the general election. Washington allowed candidates on the primary ballot to list a "party preference" next to their names, even if they had no affiliation with the party. Thus, a candidate could place an "R" for Republican next to his name, even if he had never associated with Republicans.

The Republican Party claimed that the law violated the First Amendment. The First Amendment protects the right to associate, and Republicans claimed that the law forced them to associate with people who did not share their values.[35] The Supreme Court rejected the party's claim.[36] According to the Court, the question was whether "voters will be confused as to the meaning of the party-preference designation."[37] If the party had evidence of voter confusion, then the law might be

[33] Scholars have examined when heuristics succeed and when they appear to fail. *See, e.g.*, Richard R. Lau & David P. Redlawsk, *Advantages and Disadvantages of Cognitive Heuristics in Political Decision Making*, 45 Am. J. Pol. Sci. 951 (2001).

[34] *See* Shanto Iyengar, *The Effects of Media-Based Campaigns on Candidate and Voter Behavior: Implications for Judicial Elections*, 35 Ind. L. Rev. 691 (2002) ("The spread of negative campaigning in judicial races is likely to have adverse consequences for the court system."). *But see* James L. Gibson, *Campaigning for the Bench: The Corrosive Effects of Campaign Speech?*, 42 Law & Soc'y Rev. 899 (2008) ("[M]ost Kentuckians are not off-put by general statements of policy positions, and most do not object to even fairly vigorous attack ads. At least some elements of traditional political campaign activity are acceptable to most people, even within the context of judicial elections.").

[35] For an example of this kind of problem, consider Arthur Jones, a self-proclaimed Nazi who ran for office in Illinois. Jones claimed to be a Republican, to the consternation of the Republican Party. *See* Natasha Korecki, *"I Snookered Them": Illinois Nazi Candidate Creates GOP Dumpster Fire*, Politico, June 29, 2018.

[36] Washington State Grange v. Washington State Republican Party, 552 U.S. 442 (2008).

[37] *Id.* at 454.

unconstitutional. But the party did not have evidence. Without evidence, the Court held that Washington's "interest in providing voters with relevant information about the candidates on the ballot" was sufficient to uphold the law.[38]

The Court wrote as though the interests of the party and the state conflict. In fact, they appear to align. The theory of heuristics shows why. For the "R" next to a name to provide "relevant information" to voters, it must send an accurate signal. Voters must interpret the "R" to mean Republican values when the candidate in fact holds Republican values. If the signal is accurate, the state is happy (voters get a helpful heuristic) and the party should be happy (no forced association takes place because the "Rs" are actually Republicans). Consider the opposite case where "R" sends an inaccurate signal. Voters assume the "R" means Republican values, but the candidate does not hold Republican values. The state is unhappy (voters get a misleading heuristic), and the party is forced to associate (the "Rs" are not Republicans).

If the interests align, why did the party sue the state? Here is one possibility. The party prioritizes control over candidates. You cannot put an "R" next to your name unless the party approves. To get party approval, you must compromise with party leaders. The law permitted candidates to signal their values without compromising, whereas the party wanted to make candidates compromise to signal their values.

F. Disclosure

In the United States, disclosure laws require candidates for office and their supporters to publicize information about themselves and their political spending.[39] For example, suppose the National Rifle Association (NRA), a well-known advocate of gun owners' rights, runs a television ad supporting the President's re-election campaign. Federal law requires the ad to state that the NRA paid for it.

Disclosure laws have provoked a legal controversy. The First Amendment protects political speech, including the NRA's ads. Disclosure laws burden political speech. In California, supporters of a ballot measure on same-sex marriage received death threats.[40] Priests, therapists, salesmen, teachers, lawyers—people like these can suffer professional harm when their political spending is publicized. Organizations may face boycotts. To avoid sanctions, people may choose not to speak. Thus, disclosure "chills" political speech in violation of the First Amendment, or so goes the argument.

Despite the chilling effect, courts have consistently upheld disclosure laws on the basis of the "information interest." "[T]he public," the Supreme Court wrote, "has an interest in knowing who is speaking about a candidate shortly before an election."[41] Translating into our language, disclosure laws generate heuristics. Viewers who know little about politics but strongly favor or disfavor gun owners' rights benefit from knowing that the NRA supports the President.

38 *Id.* at 458.
39 A later chapter describes campaign finance in detail.
40 Brad Stone, *Prop 8 Donor Web Site Shows Disclosure Law Is 2-Edged Sword*, N.Y. Times, Feb. 7, 2009.
41 Citizens United v. Fed. Election Comm'n, 558 U.S. 310, 369 (2010).

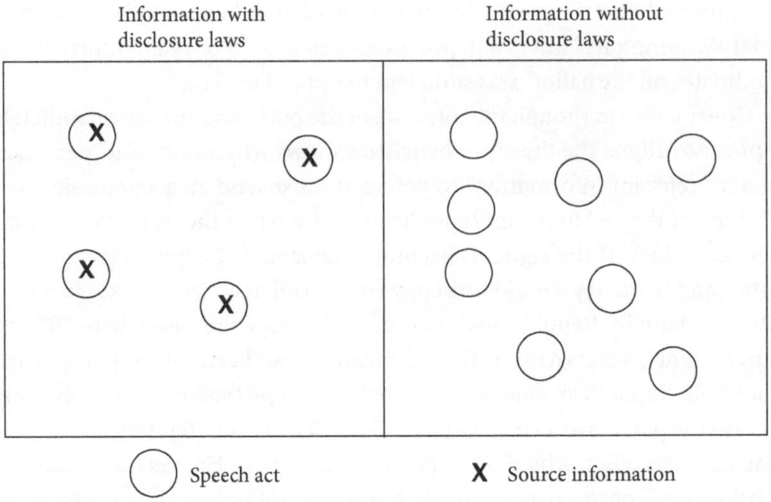

Figure 5.2. Voter Information with and without Disclosure

The connection between information and disclosure is more complicated than it appears.[42] Voters gain information through two mechanisms. The first is political speech. Thus, the content of an advertisement about the President provides voters with some information. Call this "content information." The second is the source of political speech—who wrote it, who paid for it? Call this "source information." Disclosure laws require speakers to disclose source information.

Disclosure laws increase voters' source information. However, disclosure laws can *decrease* voters' content information. This follows from the chilling effect. Without disclosure laws, many speech acts take place, and with disclosure laws relatively few speech acts take place. Thus, disclosure creates an information trade-off. Figure 5.2 illustrates. Each circle represents a speech act, which conveys content information, and each "X" represents a disclosure, which conveys source information. With disclosure laws, voters get fewer speech acts but more source information, and without disclosure voters get more speech acts but less source information.

On balance, do disclosure laws actually make voters better informed? Once you understand the two opposite effects, you see that the question is harder than it appears. These two effects imply a prescription: *to maximize voter information, expand disclosure laws until the information gained through source revelation just equals the information lost from chilled speech*. This prescription is an ideal, not a reality. Judges seem unaware of this balancing problem. To apply the prescription with precision requires empirical evidence that we lack.

As explained, disclosure chills speech by enabling sanctions from the speaker's opponents. If you know who speaks, you can exact revenge. However, disclosure laws also "thaw" speech by increasing the credibility of speakers.[43] Consider the following

[42] The following discussion draws on Michael D. Gilbert, *Campaign Finance Disclosure and the Information Tradeoff*, 98 Iowa L. Rev. 1847 (2013).
[43] *Id.*

scenario. Penny wishes to contribute to a politician who will enact policies to combat climate change. Two politicians have promised to do so. But talk is cheap, and Penny is not sure if she can trust them. Law requires the politicians to disclose the sources of contributions. Penny sees that the first politician has received support from the coal industry every year, and the second politician only receives support from environmentalists groups. Because of disclosure, Penny is confident that the second politician will pursue her preferred policies. Disclosure made the second politician's speech credible, causing Penny to spend money supporting him. In this case, disclosure facilitates political speech.

Consistent with this example, some remarks by politicians suggest that disclosure works to their advantage. During the 2016 presidential election, the candidates Hillary Clinton and Donald Trump encouraged their supporters to give generously and "see your name on a major FEC report."[44] (The Federal Election Commission, or "FEC" for short, is the federal agency that publicizes disclosures.) Implicit in this claim is the fact that Clinton, Trump, and everyone else would see the names. Thus, the state would certify that a political donation was made. That certification could be valuable for people seeking influence, jobs, or solidarity with a political group. Clinton and Trump took advantage of this fact and used disclosure to entice contributions.

Questions

5.15. Suppose disclosure thaws more speech than it chills. In this case, expanding disclosure laws must improve voter information. Use the distinction between content and source information to explain why.

5.16. Disclosure laws have loopholes that result in "dark money ads," meaning political ads whose source cannot be traced. Expanding disclosure laws could eliminate those loopholes. Would that improve voter information?

5.17. An Ohio law prohibited anonymous campaign literature. Margaret McIntyre, a private citizen, violated the law by distributing handmade leaflets that encouraged people to vote against a new tax. Many of the leaflets were unsigned. In *McIntyre v. Ohio Elections Commission*, the Supreme Court struck down Ohio's law on the ground that it violated the First Amendment's right to free speech.[45] Is this decision consistent with the economic analysis of disclosure and voter information?

Disclosure and Corruption

Some people make political speech for ideological or expressive reasons. Others have sinister motives: they want something in return. Corruption occurs when a person supports a politician in exchange for a favor. Disclosure laws are supposed to prevent quid pro quos of this kind. The logic works like this. By publicizing the money

[44] Abby K. Wood & Michael D. Gilbert, *Disclosure Can Encourage Political Speech*, THE HILL, Oct. 21, 2016.
[45] 514 U.S. 334 (1995).

flowing to politicians—who gave what to whom—disclosure reveals the "quid" in corrupt transactions. Fearful of exposure, corrupt actors do not give, and corruption is deterred. "Sunlight is said to be the best disinfectant."[46]

Courts have upheld disclosure laws on this basis. They reason that although disclosure chills speech (a questionable conclusion, as we explained in the text), it deters corruption. The benefits outweigh the costs.

Does disclosure actually deter corruption?[47] Quinn's company manufactures tanks. He wants to buy a senator's vote on a defense bill. Whom should he approach? An offer to the wrong senator could lead to an attempted bribery charge. Assuming Quinn identifies a corruptible senator, what should he offer? A campaign contribution? How large should it be? Assuming Quinn and the senator agree on a price, can they commit to seeing the deal through? They cannot sign an enforceable contract under which Quinn agrees to make a contribution to the senator's campaign, and the senator agrees to give him the vote. Contracts for illegal exchanges are unenforceable. Without a contract, Quinn and the senator have to rely on trust. If Quinn's promise to support the senator is credible, and if the senator's promise to deliver the vote is credible, they will exchange a vote for a contribution. Otherwise the deal will fail.

To buy a vote, Quinn must overcome all of these obstacles to bargaining. Disclosure laws make that easier. Which senator should Quinn approach with his corrupt offer? Disclosure records identify good candidates by telling Quinn who other tank manufacturers support. How much money should Quinn offer? Disclosure records show how much others give to the senator. Can Quinn trust the senator, and can the senator trust him? Disclosure records allow them to assess one another's credibility. The records tell Quinn who has supported the senator in the past. By comparing them to the senator's voting record, Quinn can determine if the senator rewards his benefactors. Likewise, disclosure records tell the senator whom Quinn has supported. By comparing them to voting records, the senator can determine if Quinn rewards compliant legislators. In sum, disclosure records lower the transaction costs of corrupt bargaining.

Consider an example. Tom "the Hammer" Delay was once a powerful and feared member of Congress. Delay kept a book with detailed information on "Friendly" contributions to members of his party and "Unfriendly" contributions to his opponents.[48] He would show lobbyists requesting favors where they stood. Delay's book was like a crude menu of prices. The book became legendary in Washington. When asked by an aide whether the legend should be tamped down, Delay responded, "No, let it get bigger."[49] How could Delay have kept track of lobbyists' contributions, including to members of the other political party? Disclosure records, of course.

[46] Louis D. Brandeis, *What Publicity Can Do*, Harper's Weekly, Dec. 20, 1913.

[47] This discussion is based on Michael D. Gilbert & Benjamin F. Aiken, *Disclosure and Corruption*, 14 Election L.J. 148 (2015). *See also* Michael D. Gilbert, *Transparency and Corruption: A General Analysis*, 2018 U. Chi. L. Forum 117 (2018).

[48] Michael Weisskopf & David Maraniss, Tell Newt to Shut Up: Prize-Winning Washington Post Journalists Reveal How Reality Gagged the Gingrich Revolution 111 (1996).

[49] *Id.*

To summarize, transparency of political donations (everyone knows who gave how much) dampens corruption through exposure to the public. Anonymity in political donations (no one knows who gave how much) dampens corruption by inhibiting dealmaking.[50] Thus, disclosure law creates a trade-off. More disclosure deters corruption by exposing it, and less disclosure deters corruption by raising the transaction costs of bargaining.

G. Voter Fraud

We discussed how poor information can affect representation in elections. Another cause of misrepresentation is election fraud, which occurs in many ways. A fraudster can vote multiple times, tinker with voting machines, or steal, buy, or forge mail-in ballots. Dictatorships can have democratic forms without substance. "The people who count the votes," Joseph Stalin said, "decide everything."[51] Even strong democracies are vulnerable to fraud. George Washington bought votes with liquor.[52] In 2019, North Carolina held a new congressional election after a scandal over ballot "harvesting."[53]

Allegations of voter fraud cause a firestorm in American politics. One side argues that fraud is rampant. Many states have responded by enacting "voter ID" laws that require people to present government-issued photo identification, like a driver's license, before casting a ballot. Critics argue that these laws are unjustified. Some poor, disabled, and elderly people do not have a driver's licenses and cannot assemble the documents, complete the forms, or pay the fees to get them. Also, an ID requirement only targets voters who misrepresent their identity in person (e.g., Renee says she is Samantha). They do not deter fraud by other means like mail-in ballots, which is probably more common. According to critics, the real objective of voter ID laws is to suppress votes. Republican legislators, the argument goes, are intentionally disfranchising Democratic voters.

Courts have waded into this debate. Consider the case *Crawford v. Marion County Election Board*.[54] Voters challenged Indiana's voter ID law, claiming that it burdened their right to vote. Their challenge suffered from weak evidence. They could identify only a handful of voters who struggled to produce identification. The state defended its ID law on antifraud grounds, which also suffered from weak evidence. Indiana could not identify a single instance of in-person voter fraud in its history. The Supreme Court applied the *Anderson-Burdick* test described earlier in this chapter. It weighed the burden on voters, which seemed minimal to the Court, against the state's interest in protecting its elections, which in principle seemed strong. The Court upheld the law.

50 Ian Ayres & Jeremy Bulow, *The Donation Booth: Mandating Donor Anonymity to Disrupt the Market for Political Influence*, 50 Stan. L. Rev. 837 (1998).

51 This quote is often attributed to Stalin, but there is little evidence he said it.

52 Tracy Campbell, Deliver the Vote: A History of Election Fraud, an American Political Tradition—1742–2004, at 5, 62–64, 86 (2005).

53 John Bowden, *House Clerk to Take Over Constituent Services for Contested North Carolina District*, The Hill, Mar. 14, 2019. "Harvesting" is a derogatory term for gathering and submitting other people's ballots. A wrong occurs if one *fills out* or otherwise unduly influences other people's ballots.

54 553 U.S. 181 (2008).

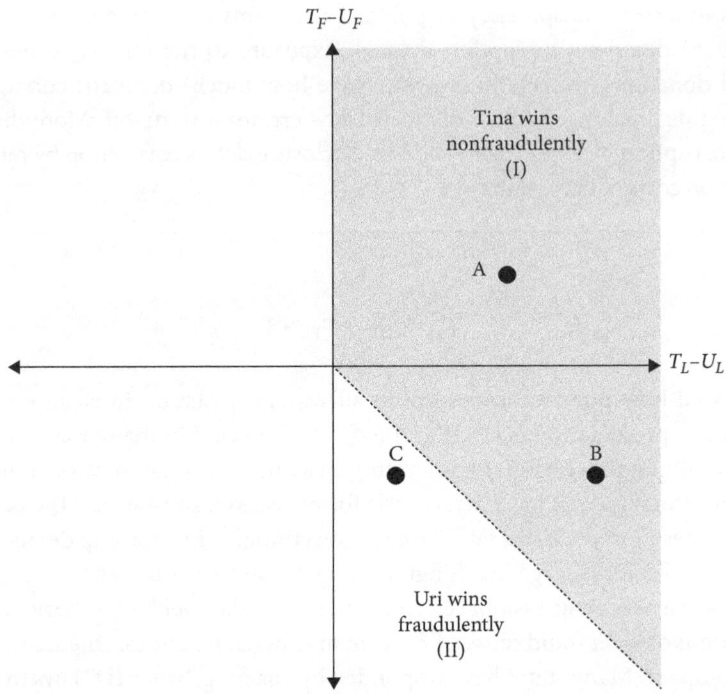

Figure 5.3. Election without Voter ID

Consequences matter a lot under the *Anderson-Burdick* test. Thus, courts should tend to invalidate voter ID laws that mostly suppress votes, and they should tend to sustain voter ID laws that mostly stop fraud.

We can clarify these considerations.[55] For the sake of example, we will assume in this discussion that elections feature more than a trivial number of fraudulent votes. Whether this is a reasonable assumption to make about modern elections in the United States seems rather doubtful.[56] However, this is a reasonable assumption about some older elections in the United States and elections elsewhere in the world.

Imagine an election between two candidates, Tina and Uri. Tina gets lawful votes totaling T_L, and Uri gets lawful votes totaling U_L. Likewise, Tina gets fraudulent votes totaling T_F, and Uri gets fraudulent votes totaling U_F. Let's assume that Tina gets more *lawful* votes than Uri ($T_L > U_L$), so Tina should win the election. Will she? The answer depends on whether she gets more *total* votes than Uri ($T_L + T_F > U_L + U_F$).

Figure 5.3 captures the possibilities. The horizontal axis represents the margin of lawful votes separating the candidates. At the origin, the candidates get the same number of lawful votes ($T_L = U_L$). As we move rightward from the origin, Tina's lead in lawful votes grows. The vertical axis represents the margin of fraudulent votes separating the candidates. At the origin, Tina and Uri have the same number of fraudulent votes ($T_F = U_F$). Above the origin, Tina leads in fraud, and below the origin Uri leads in fraud.

55 The following analysis draws on Michael D. Gilbert, *The Problem of Voter Fraud*, 115 Colum. L. Rev. 739 (2015).

56 Following the 2020 presidential election, Donald Trump and his supporters claimed widespread voter fraud. Many audits, investigations, and court cases took place. None revealed significant fraud.

To clarify Figure 5.3, consider some examples. The point A represents an election in which Tina leads in both lawful and fraudulent votes. To be specific, let's assume that at point A $T_L = 10$, $T_F = 3$, $U_L = 7$, and $U_F = 1$. Tina wins 13 to 8. The point B represents an election in which Uri leads in fraudulent votes, but not by enough to overcome Tina's lead in lawful votes. Specifically, at point B $T_L = 10$, $T_F = 1$, $U_L = 6$, and $U_F = 3$. Tina wins 11 to 9. For all points in the shaded region I, Tina wins (as she should) and the election is nonfraudulent (fraud does not affect the outcome). The point C represents an election in which Uri leads in fraudulent votes by enough to overcome Tina's lead in lawful votes. Specifically, at point C $T_L = 10$, $T_F = 1$, $U_L = 9$, and $U_F = 3$. Uri wins 12 to 11. For all points in the triangle region II, Uri wins (he should not) and the election is fraudulent.

What happens if we introduce a voter ID law to the election between Tina and Uri? As discussed, the law can have two effects. First, it can suppress lawful votes. If more of Uri's voters are suppressed, then Tina gains an advantage in lawful votes. If more of Tina's voters are suppressed, then Uri gains an advantage in lawful votes. Second, the voter ID law can deter fraud. Suppose Tina leads in fraud to start. The voter ID law could increase her lead (if more of Uri's fraud gets deterred), shrink her lead (if more of her fraud gets deterred), or even cause Uri to lead in fraud.

Figure 5.4 shows the possibilities. Suppose that *without* a voter ID law Uri would win fraudulently. Specifically, the election would lie at point C in region II, where $T_L = 10$, $T_F = 1$, $U_L = 9$, and $U_F = 3$. Suppose that running the election *with* a voter ID law would eliminate fraud. Thus, $T_L = 10$, $T_F = 0$, $U_L = 9$, and $U_F = 0$. Uri would lose to Tina, the rightful winner, by a vote of 10 to 9. The voter ID law moves the election from C in

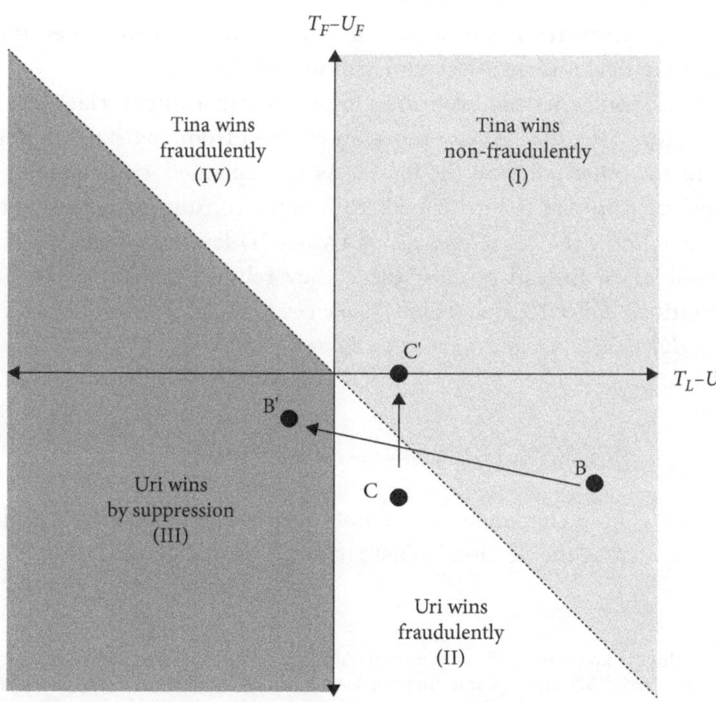

Figure 5.4. Election with Voter ID

region II to C' in region I. It "cleans up" the election, just like many supporters of ID laws claim.

Consider another possibility. Without a voter ID law, Tina would win nonfraudulently (region I). Specifically, the election would lie at point B in Figure 5.4, where $T_L = 10$, $T_F = 1$, $U_L = 6$, and $U_F = 3$. With a voter ID law, Tina's voters are suppressed, so Uri takes a decisive lead. Following the suppression, the vote totals are $T_L = 5$, $T_F = 0$, $U_L = 6$, and $U_F = 1$.[57] Uri wins through suppression by a vote of 7 to 5. Voter ID moves the election from B in region I to B' in region III. This scenario captures what many opponents of voter ID laws fear.

We have shown what supporters and opponents of voter ID imagine. However, these scenarios are not exhaustive. Voter ID laws can have effects that commentators do not appreciate. Take another numerical example. Without a voter ID law, Tina would receive 13 lawful votes and 4 fraudulent votes, and Uri would receive 10 lawful votes and 6 fraudulent votes. Tina wins nonfraudulently, 17 to 16. Now rerun the election with a voter ID law. To simplify, suppose no votes are suppressed, so Tina and Uri still get 13 and 10 lawful votes, respectively. However, some fraud is deterred. Tina gets only 1 fraudulent vote and Uri gets only 5. Uri wins the election fraudulently, 15 to 14. In Figure 5.4, voter ID causes a fraudulent election by moving it from region I to II.

To understand this example better, focus on vote margins. The law decreases the total number of fraudulent votes from 10 to 6. However, it increases the margin of fraudulent votes from 2 (Uri gets 6 to Tina's 4) to 4 (he gets 5 to her 1). The law increases the margin by deterring fraud asymmetrically. As the margin of fraudulent votes increases, the risk of fraud deciding the election grows. This is true even if the total number of fraudulent votes shrinks.

The same analysis applies to suppression. If a voter ID law suppresses the votes of Tina and Uri symmetrically, it cannot affect who wins in lawful votes. If the law suppresses asymmetrically, it can affect who wins in lawful votes.

Once you understand vote margins, you see that voter ID laws can have many effects. In Figure 5.4, voter ID can move an election from any starting point in regions I or II to any other point on the figure. As we explained, consequences matter under the *Anderson-Burdick* test, which determines the constitutionality of voter ID laws. Judges cannot know the consequences of a voter ID law with certainty; there are too many possibilities. Instead of clear facts, they rely on intuitions. This analysis sharpens intuitions. *Voter ID laws cannot make elections safer unless they narrow the margin of fraudulent votes separating the candidates.*

Questions

5.18. "Both candidates in the last race received 1,000 fraudulent votes. Fraud decided the election." What's wrong with this statement?

[57] This example assumes that the voter ID law deters some fraud and suppresses a large percentage of lawful votes. In reality, ID laws appear to suppress a small percentage of lawful votes, if any. For a review of empirical studies on this topic, see Emily Rong Zhang, *Questioning Questions in the Law of Democracy: What the Debate over Voter ID Laws' Effects Teaches about Asking the Right Questions*, UCLA L. Rev. (Forthcoming 2022).

5.19. Without a voter ID law, *A* and *B* would each get 50 fraudulent votes. With a voter ID law, *A* would get 5 fraudulent votes and *B* would get 0 fraudulent votes. Thus, the voter ID law would reduce fraudulent votes by 95 percent. Should the state adopt the voter ID law?

5.20. In Figure 5.4, a voter ID law can move an election from region II to III, or from region I to IV. Demonstrate these possibilities with numerical examples involving Tina and Uri.

5.21. Some states want voters to prove their citizenship before casting ballots. Some states want to "purge" their voter registration rolls, removing voters who have moved or died. Some states want to cut back on early voting. Some people want to eliminate voting by mail. Many of these proposals are supposed to reduce fraudulent votes, and all of them could suppress lawful votes. What does the preceding analysis suggest about differences and similarities in the effects of these laws?

II. Structures of Representation

A republic, James Madison wrote, will "refine and enlarge the public views, by passing them through the medium of a chosen body of citizens, whose wisdom may best discern the true interest of their country."[58] The "chosen body" are the people's representatives who hold office. Here, we focus on how the chosen body is organized. Legislatures can be big or small, and legislators can represent many citizens or few. Legislative districting can produce competitive elections or anticompetitive gerrymanders. Economics clarifies these possibilities. After discussing the "chosen body's" organization, we discuss its motivation. Does the chosen body care about the public interest?

A. The Size of Legislatures

In Bleckley County, Georgia, a single commissioner exercised all of the county's executive and legislative functions. African Americans claimed that this arrangement violated the Constitution and the Voting Rights Act. Their argument ran like this. If the commission*er* were replaced by a five-member commiss*ion*, and if the five commissioners were elected from five districts, African Americans could constitute a majority in one district. Thus, they would exercise more political power. In *Holder v. Hall*,[59] the Supreme Court rejected this claim. No one could say how large the commission *should be*, the Justices reasoned, and thus there was no benchmark against which to compare the county's government. "There is no principled reason why one size should be picked over another[.]"[60]

[58] THE FEDERALIST NO. 10, at 51 (James Madison) (Ian Shapiro ed., 2009).
[59] 512 U.S. 874 (1994).
[60] *Id.* at 881.

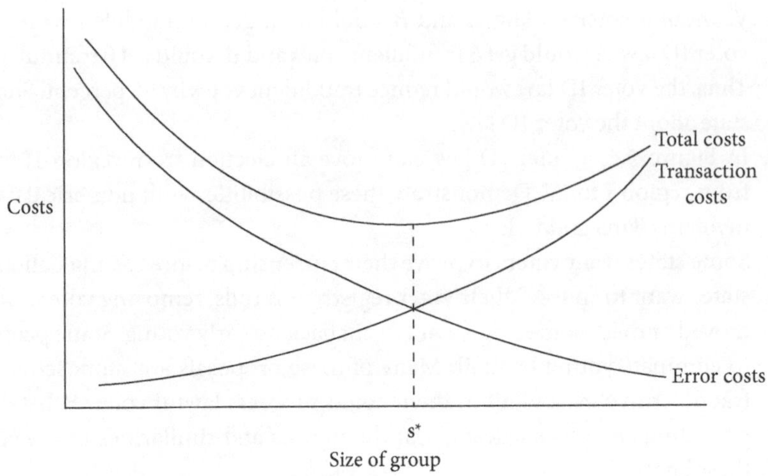

Figure 5.5. Optimal Size of Legislature

Unlike the Supreme Court, we can offer a prescription for choosing a governing body's size using concepts from economics. Suppose that a constitutional convention must decide the size of the legislature. The legislature could consist of a single person, every person, or any number in between. What is the best size? Two considerations seem especially relevant.[61]

First, legislation requires costly negotiation. As an earlier chapter discussed, the cost of negotiating tends to fall as the number of negotiators decreases. Thus, a legislature consisting of a single representative minimizes the transaction costs of political bargaining, and a legislature consisting of every person maximizes the transaction costs of political bargaining.

Second, a larger legislature has a higher ratio of representatives to citizens. As the ratio increases, citizens are more likely to know their representatives, and representatives are more likely to know their constituents. With fewer constituents a legislator can more easily identify his or her constituents' preferences. For example, to win a majority of votes in a district, a candidate for representative may need to identify the median voter. This becomes easier as the ratio of citizens to representatives decreases. With fewer constituents, a legislator makes fewer mistakes in representing them. Taken to its extreme, a legislature consisting of every citizen makes no representation errors.

The optimal size of the legislature balances errors in representation and the costs of political negotiations. As a legislature grows, representation errors decrease and the transaction costs of legislative bargaining increase. Taking both factors into account, the legislature's size is optimal when one more member improves representation by an amount equal to the increase in transaction costs of legislative bargaining. To illustrate the optimum, the horizontal axis in Figure 5.5 indicates the size of the group making the decision, and the vertical axis indicates costs. According to the graph, transaction costs increase with the group's size, whereas representation costs diminish, at least up to a point. The total costs, which equal the sum of transaction costs and error costs, decrease

[61] *See* Robert Cooter, The Strategic Constitution 175 (2000).

at first and then increase with the group's size. The minimum point on the total cost curve, denoted s*, indicates the optimal size of the group.

This trade-off is inevitable in representative government, so we call it the *republican compromise*. In a republic, where officials represent citizens, improving representation usually comes at the expense of higher transaction costs.

The republican compromise seems to explain a fact about some troubled democracies. If the legislature is large and political parties are fragmented, majority rule stalls—the legislature can argue but not act. Consequently, from time to time a "strongman"—maybe a party boss, general, or secret policeman—seizes the state and preempts the legislature. The strongman can get things done, but he lacks legitimacy. He does not represent anyone, so he does not do what people want. Thus, democracy pauses, but it does not end. Eventually, power shifts back from the strongman to the legislature. This democracy is troubled because it cannot find the balance between error costs in representation and transaction costs.

Questions

5.22. Recall *Holder v. Hall.* Would a five-member commission be preferable to a one-member commission? Does the answer depend on the population of Bleckley County?

5.23. The state of Nebraska has about two million people, and the state legislature has one chamber consisting of 49 members. The state of New Hampshire has about 1.4 million people, and the state legislature has two chambers, an upper chamber with 24 members and a lower chamber with 400 members. Use our analysis to predict some differences in the performance of the legislatures in these two states.

5.24. Suppose that immigration diversifies the population of a country. Predict the resulting shift, if any, in the curves in Figure 5.5.

B. Bicameralism

Constitutions often create two chambers of the legislature with different principles of representation. In the U.S. Congress, the House of Representatives (lower house) consists of 435 members, each representing approximately equal numbers of voters. The Senate (upper house) consists of two representatives elected from each of the 50 states.[62] Similarly, the European Parliament consists of 705 members, with more members coming from more populous countries.[63] To make law, the European Parliament must cooperate with Europe's Council of Ministers, which consists of one representative from each nation in the European Union.

62 Representation by states implies disproportionate representation of people. To illustrate, Wyoming and California each have two senators, even though Wyoming's population is less than 2 percent of California's population.

63 Following the United Kingdom's withdrawal from the European Union, the number fell from 751 to 705.

An earlier chapter related bicameralism to bargaining. Here we connect bicameralism to representation. With bicameralism, new legislation is harder to pass, which prevents the minority from exploiting the majority, and also prevents the majority from exploiting the minority. To explain this fact, we will contrast unicameral and bicameral representation.

Assume that a nation has a unicameral legislature, and districts of equal size elect one representative by majority rule. In principle, the party representing one-fourth of the population could control the legislature. To do so, the party would need to win 51 percent of the votes in 51 percent of the districts. Thus, the party that wins slightly more than one-fourth of the votes in the nation holds a majority of the seats in the legislature. The party representing one-fourth of the population could enact laws opposed by most citizens. (To achieve this outcome, districts must be "gerrymandered," a topic we consider later.)

Figure 5.6 depicts these facts. Assume that a nation consists of three states, labeled *A*, *B*, and *C*. Assume there are two parties, named Left and Right. The shaded area represents the number of Right voters, and the blank area represents the number of Left voters. The upper half of the figure shows the party allegiances of voters in states *A*, *B*, and *C*. The lower half of the figure divides the states into five districts and shows the party allegiances of voters by district.

With unicameralism, the lower chamber is the only chamber. So focus on the bottom half of the figure. In districts 1, 3, and 5, 51 percent of the voters are Right, whereas in districts 2 and 4, zero percent of the voters are Right. Each district elects one representative to the legislature. Consequently, in the unicameral legislature, Right controls three seats, and Left controls two seats. Thus, the Right can rule over the Left. However, the Right's percentage of the popular vote in the nation as a whole is much less than 50 percent, and the Left's percentage of the popular vote in the nation as a whole is much more than 50 percent.

Bicameralism changes this result. Assume the second chamber represents states, where districts 1 and 2 constitute State *A*, districts 3 and 4 constitute State *B*, and district 5 constitutes State *C*. The top half of Figure 5.6 represents these facts. Each state elects one representative to the second chamber, so Right controls one seat and Left

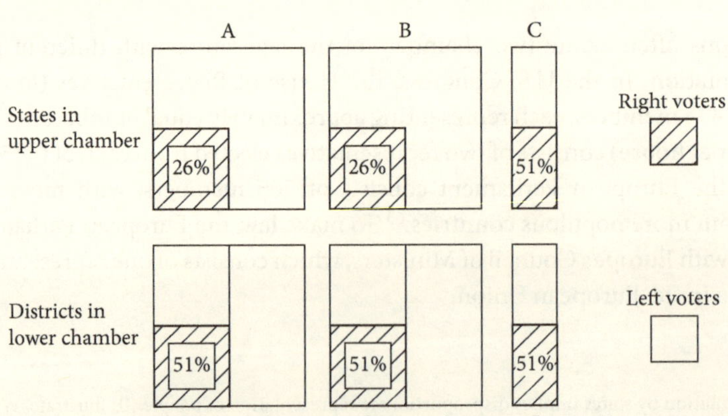

Figure 5.6. Unicameralism and Bicameralism

controls two seats. The minority in the whole polity controls the first chamber, and the majority in the whole polity controls the second chamber. So the Right controls the lower chamber and the Left controls the upper chamber.

In this example, bicameralism blocks the minority from dominating the majority. Note, however, that the same facts can be viewed in another way: adding a second chamber blocks the majority from dominating the minority. To see why, begin with a unicameral legislature consisting of the chamber depicted in the top half of Figure 5.6. The Left holds two of the three seats, and the Left receives almost 70 percent of the popular vote. A unicameral legislature consisting of this chamber permits the Left majority to rule. Now add another chamber as depicted in the bottom half of Figure 5.6. The lower chamber has 5 seats and the Right holds 3 of them. So under bicameralism, the Right minority with roughly 30 percent of the popular vote can block the Left majority with roughly 70 percent of the vote.

In general, bicameralism can protect the majority from the minority, and bicameralism can protect the minority from the majority. This can reduce representation errors. However, improved representation comes with a price. Successful legislation requires bargaining between the two houses of the legislature. Thus, in the preceding figure, successful legislation requires the Right in the lower chamber to agree with the Left in the upper chamber. Getting many legislators across two chambers to agree is harder than getting few legislators in one chamber to agree. Bicameralism increases the transaction costs of legislating.

In sum, bicameralism tends to improve representation but increase the transaction costs of political bargaining. This is the republican compromise.

Questions

5.25. We explained that bicameralism can protect minorities from majorities. A more conventional approach protects minorities by entrenching rights in the constitution. If you have bicameralism, why might you still want rights? (We discuss rights in a later chapter.)

5.26. Recall the Line-Item Veto Act, which (prior to its invalidation by the Supreme Court in *Clinton v. New York*) gave the President power to veto individual provisions in spending bills. The act empowered the President to sidestep bicameralism by changing the terms of deals that the House and Senate struck. Analyze the implications of the act for the nation's political majority and minority.

C. Plurality Rule and Proportional Representation

In the United States, the Democratic and Republican parties dominate politics. This system leaves many voters frustrated. Ralph Nader, a consumer advocate, called it "a political prison."[64] In 2000, he ran for president as the candidate of a third party called the Green Party, receiving support from progressives and about 3 percent of the nationwide vote. In addition to progressives, other groups like libertarians and communists feel

[64] Michelle Goldberg, *The Folly of Ralph Nader*, SLATE, Sept. 15, 2016.

unrepresented in the American system. While some citizens demand more choice, two parties continue to dominate U.S. politics. Why? Economics provides an answer.

Recall plurality rule: the candidate who receives the most votes in a single election wins the office. To illustrate, if votes were divided among three candidates in the proportions 40 percent, 31 percent, and 29 percent, then the candidate receiving 40 percent would win. Countries like the United States with plurality rule tend to have two dominant parties. This proposition is called *Duverger's Law* after the scholar who developed it.[65]

To see the logic, return to our five voters: Kim, Larry, Mary, Ned, and Olivia. Suppose Kim and Larry are represented by the Democratic Party, and Ned and Olivia are represented by the Republican Party. Mary is the median voter, and she votes Democratic or Republican depending on which one appeals to her more in the election. So both parties compete for the vote of Mary. Now suppose the Tea Party forms. This conservative third party attracts the support of Olivia. Olivia's support will not cause the Tea Party to win, but it may cause her second choice (the Republican Party) to lose and her last choice (the Democratic Party) to win. This is a bad result for everyone on the right end of the political spectrum. To avoid it, the Republican Party has an incentive to bargain with the Tea Party and induce it to join the Republicans. Merging the Republicans and the Tea Party will reduce the number of parties from three to two. This is Duverger's Law at work. Plurality rule tends to eliminate third parties.

Following this logic, what keeps the two competing parties—Republican and Democratic—from merging into one grand coalition? If the parties remain separate, the winning party enjoys the spoils of power (offices, contracts, grants, etc.). If the parties merge, they must share the spoils of power with each other. Thus, the desire to concentrate the spoils of power usually prevents mergers between the two dominant parties.

We have explained that plurality rule stifles third parties. What electoral rule animates them? Proportional representation. In a proportional representation system, each political party receives seats in the legislature in proportion to the votes it receives in the election. To demonstrate, citizens in Israel do not vote for individual candidates. Instead, they vote for political parties.[66] If the Likud Party wins 20 percent of the vote, then the party gets 20 percent of the seats in the national legislature. In a proportional representation system, a citizen does not "waste" a vote by voting for a small party. Likewise, a small party does not have to join a large one to exercise political power. To generalize, proportional representation fragments parties by empowering them all, whereas plurality rule consolidates parties by stripping power from small ones.

Proportional representation tends to improve representation. To formalize this idea, define the *error in representing a party* as the difference between the party's fraction of the popular vote and the fraction of its seats in the legislature. To illustrate, assume that the fraction of the popular vote for Israel's legislature equals 0.6 (60 percent) for the

[65] Maurice Duverger, Political Parties 209–10 (Barbara North & Robert North trans., 1969). This law is not absolute but rather a generalization with exceptions.

[66] This is a closed-list system. An open-list system gives voters some influence over the parties' candidates. Proportional representation systems come in many varieties.

Likud Party, 0.3 for the Labor Party, and 0.1 for the Kulanu Party. Now, compare plurality rule and proportional representation. In a system of plurality rule, the Likud Party wins all of the seats, so the error in overrepresenting the Likud Party equals $|1 - 0.6|$. (The mathematical notation | . . . | means "absolute value," so the difference is always expressed as a positive number.) Similarly, the error in underrepresenting the Labor Party and the Kulanu Party equals $|0 - 0.3|$ and $|0 - 0.1|$, respectively. The total error under plurality rule equals $|1 - 0.6| + |0 - 0.3| + |0 - 0.1| = 0.8$. In contrast, a system of proportional representation assigns 60 percent of the seats to the Likud Party, 30 percent to the Labor Party, and 10 percent to the Kulanu Party. The error in representation equals $|0.6 - 0.6| + |0.3 - 0.3| + |0.1 - 0.1| = 0$.

Proportional representation reduces representation errors. However, by fragmenting parties, it raises the transaction costs of political bargaining. In proportional representation systems, individual parties often do not get a majority of seats. In Germany's 2017 election, the largest and most popular party, the Christian Democratic Union (CDU), won only 33 percent of the vote.[67] To govern, the CDU must form a coalition with other parties. Together, the coalition must command over half the votes in the legislature to be effective. In general, legislators from different parties do not share the same political platform, so they have a harder time agreeing with each other.

We can relate the choice between plurality rule and proportional representation to the republican compromise. Plurality rule consolidates parties, which raises the cost of representation errors and lowers the transaction costs of political bargaining. Proportional rule fragments parties, which lowers the cost of representation errors and raises the transaction costs of political bargaining.

Questions

5.27. During the 2000 election, the conservative George W. Bush defeated the liberal Al Gore by about 500 votes in Florida. Bush's victory in Florida made him President. During that same election, the very liberal Ralph Nader won about 97,000 votes in Florida. Why did John Kerry, the liberal in the 2004 presidential election, discourage Nader from running again? Why did Nader run anyway?

5.28. Pure proportional representation matches a party's seats in the legislature to its votes in the election. In a 100-person legislature, a party receiving just 1 percent of the vote will get a seat. Many countries adopt *minimum* proportional representation. To illustrate, political parties in Israel must win at least 3.25 percent of the vote to get any seats in the legislature. Suppose Israel increased its threshold from 3.25 percent to 32.5 percent. What would happen to the number of political parties, representation errors, and the transaction costs of bargaining in the legislature?

[67] Sean Clarke, *German Elections 2017: Full Results*, THE GUARDIAN, Sept. 25, 2017, https://www.theguardian.com/world/ng-interactive/2017/sep/24/german-elections-2017-latest-results-live-merkel-bundestag-afd.

Minor Parties and Stability

Democrats and Republicans dominate American politics like Duverger's Law predicts, but minor parties do exist. In U.S. presidential elections, minor parties fielding candidates usually include Libertarian, Green, Constitution, and Reform. Often these parties struggle for ballot access. Consider the case of *Munro v. Socialist Workers Party*.[68] Dean Peoples ran for a U.S. Senate seat in Washington State as the candidate of the small Socialist Workers Party. Under state law, Peoples could not compete in the general election unless he won at least 1 percent of the vote in the primary. (Washington used a "blanket primary," meaning all candidates appeared on the same ballot, and only those winning a certain number of votes advanced to the general election.) Peoples failed to win 1 percent. He challenged the ballot access law, claiming that it violated the First and Fourteenth Amendments.[69] The Supreme Court rejected his challenge.

Courts resolve cases like this using a balancing test.[70] Judges weigh the rights of parties and voters against the interests of the state in limiting ballot access. Some state interests are self-explanatory, like avoiding cluttering ballots with many candidates' names. But one state interest deserves attention: stability. In upholding a ballot access restriction, the Supreme Court concluded that states can "enact reasonable election regulations that may, in practice, favor the traditional two-party system, and that temper the destabilizing effects of party-splintering and excessive factionalism."[71]

What is "excessive factionalism," and why do states have an interest in preventing it? This sounds like an excuse to squelch political competition. Legislators from major parties make ballot access laws, and they conspire to keep minor parties—their rivals—off the ballot. No doubt self-preservation helps explain these laws. But something more objective is also at work. Notwithstanding the name, Duverger's Law is not a law. Plurality rule does not guarantee a stable two-party system, and minor parties can destabilize the state.

Imagine voters distributed uniformly[72] on a one-unit political spectrum. The furthest left voter is at 0, and the furthest right voter is at 1. The median voter is at 0.5. If two parties compete for votes under plurality rule, they have an incentive to set their platforms at 0.5. Once there, they will not change their platforms. This is the logic of the median voter theorem. What happens if a third party joins the competition? That party might set its platform at, say, 0.7. The first two parties split the votes of all voters between 0 and 0.6, winning 30 percent apiece, but the third party wins the votes of all voters above 0.6, winning 40 percent. The third party wins. Foreseeing this, the first party does not remain at 0.5 when the third party enters the race. It may move

[68] 479 U.S. 189 (1986).

[69] Specifically, Peoples argued that denying him ballot access burdened the First Amendment right of association (Peoples could not associate with his supporters, and they could not associate with him) and the Fourteenth Amendment's equal protection clause (Peoples' supporters could not cast effective votes, while voters whose candidates made it on the general election ballot could).

[70] *See* Timmons v. Twin Cities Area New Party, 520 U.S. 351 (1997); *see also* Munro v. Socialist Workers Party, 479 U.S. 189 (1986).

[71] *Timmons*, 520 U.S. at 367.

[72] A "uniform distribution" means all possible outcomes are equally likely. Our example imagines voters lined up between zero and one. In this context, "uniform distribution" means the voters are spread evenly, not clustered in one or more places.

its platform to, say, 0.3. Now the first and third parties each get 40 percent of the vote. Foreseeing this, the second party may relocate to, say, 0.71. The other parties will react, and the game continues.

The parties do not reach a stable equilibrium. Instead, they cycle over platforms. This is analogous to voters in the previous chapter whose group preferences were intransitive. States can reduce this instability by limiting the number of parties on the ballot.

D. One Person, One Vote

"Legislators represent people, not trees or acres."[73] This quote from the Supreme Court foreshadowed its historic holding in *Reynolds v. Sims*. Some background clarifies the case. Officials divide each state into districts whose residents elect representatives to the state legislature. To illustrate, if a state has a 50-person senate, then officials ordinarily divide the state into 50 districts. Voters in each district elect one person to the state senate.

In the 1960s, many districts were "malapportioned," meaning their populations varied widely. In New Hampshire, one state legislative district had over 3,000 people in it while another had just three. In California, one state senate district had six million people in it while another had just 14,000. *Reynolds* involved a challenge to districts in Alabama. Voters claimed that malapportionment denied them "equal suffrage" in violation of the Fourteenth Amendment. The Supreme Court agreed and announced the one-person, one-vote principle, which requires districts to be equal in size.[74]

Reynolds involves inequalities in the *power of the vote*, which refers to the statistical probability that a person's vote affects the election's outcome. For voters in low-population districts, the power of each vote was relatively high. With few voters, a change in one of them is likely to change the outcome. For voters in high-population districts, the power of each vote was relatively low. With many voters, a change in one of them is unlikely to change the outcome. Thus, many voters "dilute" the power of each individual voter. Equalizing the number of voters in each district approximately equalizes the power of each person's vote.

Did *Reynolds* improve representation? Presumably the answer is yes, though not for every voter. In response to *Reynolds*, the boundaries of malapportioned districts were redrawn. Moving voters out of a district concentrated the vote among those who remained, so the power of their votes increased. Conversely, moving voters into a district diluted the voting power of existing residents.

To illustrate mathematically, imagine a state with only two districts. The first district has one voter and one representative. The second district has nine voters and one representative. Thus, the first district's fraction of total voters is 0.1, and the second district's

[73] Reynolds v. Sims, 377 U.S. 533, 562 (1964).

[74] To be precise, state-level districts must be "substantially equal" in size. *See* Reynolds v. Sims, 377 U.S. 533, 568 (1964). Courts have elaborated on what exactly this means. *See, e.g.*, Larios v. Cox, 300 F. Supp. 2d 1320 (N.D. Ga.) (*aff'd*, 542 U.S. 947 (2004)).

fraction of total voters is 0.9. Define the error in representing a constituency as the difference between the constituency's seats in the legislature and its fraction of the popular vote. The overrepresentation error in the first district is $|0.5 - 0.1|$, which equals 0.4. The underrepresentation error in the second district is $|0.5 - 0.9|$, which also equals 0.4. Thus, the total representation error for the two districts equals 0.8. The districts are malapportioned.

Now, suppose the two districts are equalized under the one-person, one-vote principle, so each district has five voters. The representation error in each is $|0.5 - 0.5|$, for a total representation error of zero. The districts are equally apportioned. Note that equalization decreases the power of the vote in the first district and increases it in the second district.

This example supports the Court's decision in *Reynolds*. Nevertheless, *Reynolds* was controversial. The Supreme Court required dozens of states to redistrict. In addition, consider Supreme Court Justice Stewart's dissent to the one-person, one-vote cases:

> [P]opulation factors must often to some degree be subordinated in devising a legislative apportionment plan which is to achieve the important goal of ensuring a fair, effective, and balanced representation of the regional, social, and economic interests within a State. . . . [T]hroughout our history the apportionments of State Legislatures have reflected the strongly felt American tradition that the public interest is composed of many diverse interests, and that in the long run it can better be expressed by a medley of component voices than by the majority's monolithic command.[75]

To clarify Stewart's argument, return to the example of two districts, one with one voter and the other with nine. The voter in the first district is a farmer who lives in the country. The other nine voters are bankers who live in the city. The farmer and the bankers have different concerns and opinions. With malapportioned districts, each group gets a seat in the legislature. To legislate, they need to cooperate with each other. Conversely, with equalized districts, the bankers control both seats. The bankers do not need to cooperate with the farmer to legislate. Consequently, according to Justice Stewart's argument, malapportioning seats expresses the diverse interests of farmer and bankers better than equal apportioning. Equalizing district size can reduce the majority's need to cooperate with the minority.

Questions

5.29. Suppose the two districts in our example are equalized, so two bankers get elected. Suppose the transaction costs of bargaining between private citizens and legislators are zero. Does the one-person, one-vote principle constrain the surplus from political bargaining?

[75] Lucas v. Forty-Fourth Gen. Assembly of State of Colo., 377 U.S. 713, 751 (1964).

5.30. The republican compromise implies that, in the right circumstance, malapportioned districts could strike the best balance between representation and transaction costs. Can you explain why? Do you think legislators who create malapportioned districts seek the best balance between representation and transaction costs?

5.31. "One person, one vote" is the headline from *Reynolds* but not the full story. The Supreme Court declared that state legislative districts must be "substantially equal" in size. In practice, population deviations across districts can reach 10 percent or more without violating the Constitution. Why might giving states some discretion, rather than demanding perfect equality across districts, be a good idea?

5.32. *Reynolds* requires districts to be approximately equal, but it does not mandate any particular size. Districts can be small (North Dakota's state senate districts have about 16,000 people apiece) or large (Texas's state senate districts have about one million people apiece). What is the optimal district size?

One Person or One Voter?

Reynolds required states to equalize the power of the vote. Or did it? Ordinarily states equalize *populations* across districts, not voters. To see the difference, suppose District *A* has nine voters and one noncitizen (noncitizens cannot vote), whereas District *B* has one voter and nine noncitizens. The populations of the districts match, so *Reynolds* is satisfied, but the power of the vote is unequal. In District *A*, nine voters share power, and in District *B* one voter monopolizes power.

A voter in Texas sued over this kind of discrepancy. She claimed that the Constitution required the state to equalize voters, not populations. In *Evenwel v. Abbott*, the Supreme Court rejected her claim.[76] According to the Court, the Constitution does not require states to equalize voters.

Should the Constitution *permit* states to equalize voters? Commentators assume that equalizing voters would harm the representation of nonvoters. They imagine a circumstance like this: District *A* has five voters, and District *B* has five voters and 10 noncitizens. This is not inevitable. District *A* and District *B* could each have five voters and five noncitizens. In general, states can draw districts that equalize both total populations and voter populations.[77] However, achieving this might violate other norms, like making districts compact.

If equalizing voters means harming nonvoters, then states face the trade-off that commentators imagine. What would happen if nonvoters were "packed" as in the previous example? This is a complicated question on which we offer one perspective. The representation error in a district worsens as the gap between the median voter and the median resident grows. In the abstract, we cannot predict if equalizing voters across districts would shrink or grow the gap between medians.

[76] 136 S. Ct. 1120 (2016).

[77] *See* Paul Edelman, Evenwell, *Voting Power and Dual Districting*, 45 J. Legal Stud. 203 (2016).

E. Gerrymandering

Between 2000 and 2010, about 250,000 people moved out of Detroit. In contrast, about 100,000 people moved into Las Vegas. To keep track of migrations, the federal government conducts a census every 10 years. By ascertaining the population of each state, the census determines the allocation of seats in the U.S. House of Representatives. The census also determines compliance with *Reynolds*. Districts that were equal in size when drawn are often unequal in size 10 years later. Thus, each census marks the beginning of an important political event: the redrawing of districts to comply with the one-person, one-vote principle.

Who draws the districts? In general, state legislators. Legislators in the United States are subject to legal constraints when drawing districts. In addition to the one-person, one-vote principle, districts should be compact (they should look more like squares than octopuses) and contiguous (you can draw the district's boundary on a map without lifting your pen), and they should protect communities of interests (a town should not be splintered across districts). The Voting Rights Act prevents some districting that would disadvantage racial minorities.

In practice, however, these constraints leave discretion. Like a soccer team choosing its own rules, legislators can manipulate their districts to advantage themselves and disadvantage their opponents. This practice is called *partisan gerrymandering*, and it has deep roots. Governor Elbridge Gerry of Massachusetts, the namesake for strategic districting, initiated the practice in 1812. In the 1980s, President Ronald Reagan accused the Democratic Party of gerrymandering to produce a Democratic majority in Congress. After 2010, the Republican Party was accused of gerrymandering to produce a Republican majority in Congress.

To understand gerrymandering, consider an example. A state consists of 50 people who must be divided into five districts of equal size. Thirty of the people are Republicans, and 20 are Democrats. Figure 5.7.a shows this setup.[78] Each gray square represents a Republican, and each white square represents a Democrat. The legislature could create three districts with 10 Republicans apiece and two districts with 10 Democrats apiece. This is the "Proportional Plan" in Figure 5.7.b. Under this approach, Republicans and Democrats control three and two districts, respectively, which is proportional to their shares of the population. Alternatively, the legislature could create five districts, each containing six Republicans and four Democrats. Figure 5.7.c depicts this approach, which we label "Republican Plan." Under this approach, Republicans control all of the districts. Republicans gain this advantage by "cracking" Democrats across districts. Finally, the legislature could divide the voters as pictured in Figure 5.7.d. This "Democratic Plan" gives Democrats control of 60 percent of the districts, even though they are the minority. Democrats gain this advantage by "packing" Republicans in two districts.

What's wrong with gerrymandering? Critics offer two main arguments. First, gerrymandering leads to disproportional representation. Under the Republican Plan in Figure 5.7.c, Republicans control all of the districts despite constituting just 60 percent

[78] This figure resembles one in Christopher Ingraham, *This Is the Best Explanation of Gerrymandering You Will Ever See*, WASH. POST, Mar. 1, 2015.

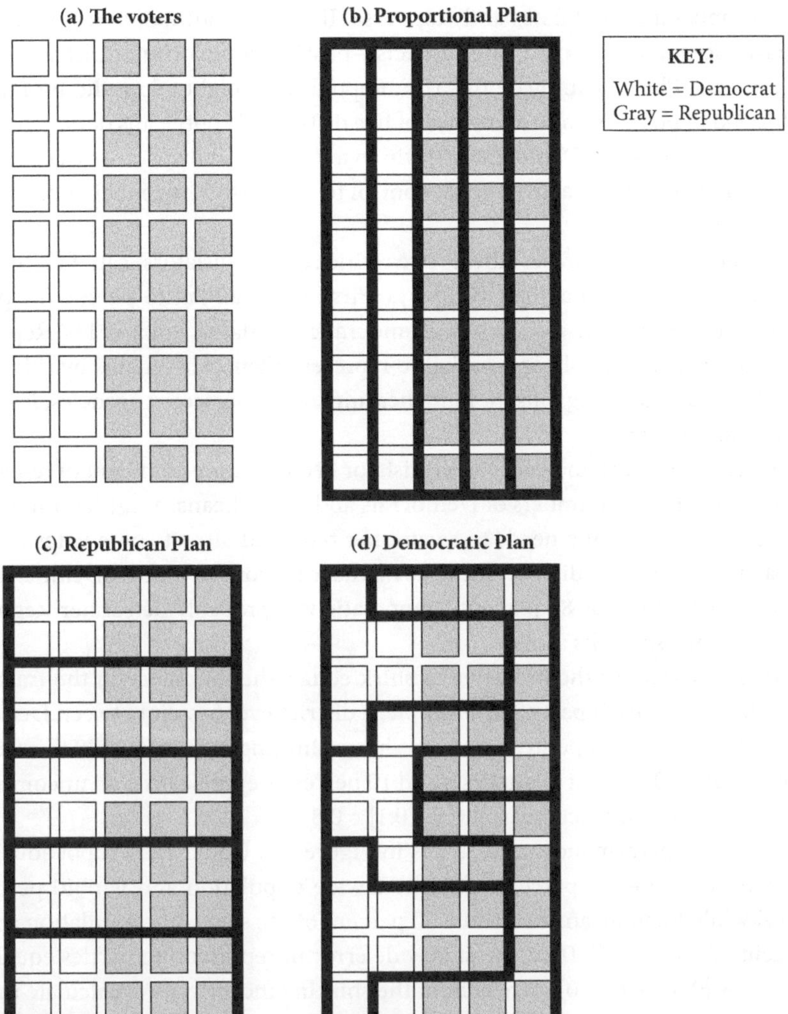

Figure 5.7. Gerrymandering

of the population. Under the Democratic Plan in Figure 5.7.d, Democrats control 60 percent of the districts despite constituting just 40 percent of the population. The Democratic Plan seems especially bad. In a democracy, the majority is supposed to govern. Under the Democratic Plan, the minority governs. As Justice Breyer wrote, "gerrymandering that so entrenches a minority party in power violates basic democratic norms."[79]

The second criticism is that gerrymandering suppresses political competition.[80] Suppose Republicans control the legislature. If they adopt the Republican Plan, and if all voters vote as predicted, Republicans will control all five districts, maximizing their power. However, voters are not always predictable. Sometimes Republicans

[79] Vieth v. Jubelirer, 541 U.S. 267, 361 (2004) (Breyer, J., dissenting).

[80] Samuel Issacharoff, *Gerrymandering and Political Cartels*, 116 Harv. L. Rev. 593 (2002).

vote for Democratic candidates and vice versa. If just a handful of voters vote against their party, Republicans could lose districts—possibly a majority of districts—under the Republican Plan. To mitigate this risk, Republicans might adopt the Proportional Plan. Instead of possibly controlling five of five districts, Republicans definitely control three of five districts. No Democrat will win in a Republican district, or vice versa. The Proportional Plan gives stable political control to the parties by reducing competition between them.

Economic analysis clarifies these two criticisms. Legislators can fail to represent their constituents in at least two ways. First, they can fail to pursue the policies their constituents prefer, as when a Democratic legislator ignores his Republican constituents. Second, legislators can fail to represent their constituents by shirking on the job. Instead of drafting bills, holding hearings, and overseeing agencies, legislators play golf and drink wine.

The incentive to shirk increases as a legislator become more confident of re-election. In a district with equal numbers of Democrats and Republicans, a legislator must work hard to get re-elected. She needs to secure her base and attract some votes from the other party. In a lopsided district, she does not have to work so hard. A Democratic legislator in a district that is 80 percent Democratic will probably defeat her Republican opponent, even if she golfs a lot.

A simple measure of the incentive to shirk equals the difference in the fraction of voters belonging to each party. For example, a district evenly split between Democrats and Republicans—a competitive district—has a shirking incentive of $|0.5 - 0.5| = 0$. A district that is 90 percent Democrats and 10 percent Republicans—an uncompetitive district—has a shirking incentive of $|0.9 - 0.1| = 0.8$.

Return to the gerrymandered districts in Figure 5.7. Under the Proportional Plan, Democrats constitute 40 percent of the statewide population and win 40 percent of the seats, while Republicans constitute 60 percent of the statewide population and win 60 percent of the seats.[81] Thus, the statewide error in representing parties equals zero ($|0.4 - 0.4| + |0.6 - 0.6| = 0$). What about the shirking incentive? We calculate these by district. In every district, one party constitutes 100 percent of the population and the other constitutes 0 percent of the population. Thus, the shirking incentive in each district is $|1 - 0| = 1$, and the average shirking incentive across districts is 1.

Consider the Democratic Plan. Statewide, Democrats constitute 40 percent of the population and win 60 percent of the seats, and Republicans constitute 60 percent of the population and win 40 percent of the seats. Thus, the statewide error in representing parties is $|0.4 - 0.6| + |0.6 - 0.4| = 0.4$. As for the shirking incentive, in three districts Democrats constitute 60 percent of the population and Republicans constitute 40 percent of the population. In those districts the shirking incentive is $|0.6 - 0.4| = 0.2$. In two districts Republicans constitute 90 percent of the population while Democrats constitute 10 percent of the population. The shirking incentive in those districts is $|0.9 - 0.1| = 0.8$. The average shirking error across districts is 2.2/5, or about 0.4.

Finally, consider the Republican Plan. Statewide, Republicans constitute 60 percent of the population and win 100 percent of the seats, while Democrats constitute 40 percent

[81] We assume throughout the example that all voters vote for their party.

Table 5.1. Errors under Three Districting Plans

	Error in Representing Parties	Error from Shirking
Proportional Plan	0	1
Democratic Plan	0.4	0.4
Republican Plan	0.8	0.2

of the population and win zero seats. Thus, the statewide error in representing parties is $|0.6 - 1| + |0.4 - 0| = 0.8$. As for the shirking incentive, in every district Republicans constitute 60 percent of the population and Democrats constitute 40 percent of the population. The shirking incentive in each district is $|0.6 - 0.4| = 0.2$, and the average shirking incentive across districts is 0.2.

Table 5.1 summarizes the costs of misrepresentation and shirking under three plans for districting.

As we move down the first column, from the Proportional to the Democratic and then Republican Plan, representation errors increase while shirking errors decrease.

Recall the two criticisms of gerrymandering: it leads to disproportionate representation (what we call errors in representing parties), and it stifles competition (less competition means larger incentives to shirk). If gerrymandered districts have both problems, non-gerrymandered districts must have neither, right? This logic is wrong, as Table 5.1 shows. The Proportional Plan avoids disproportionality—party representation is perfect—but leads to uncompetitive districts and shirking. The Republican Plan creates disproportionality. However, Republicans under that plan have small margins in each district and so must work hard, reducing shirking.[82]

We can generalize from this discussion. The party empowered to draw districts has two basic strategies: pack or crack.[83] It can pack its opponents' voters in relatively few districts (a low-risk, low-return strategy). With packing, senior legislators get safe seats. Packing reduces errors in party representation and also reduces competition. Alternatively, it can crack its opponents' voters across many districts (a higher risk, higher return strategy). With cracking, the party drawing the lines gets more seats, but they are less safe. Cracking increases errors in party representation and also increases competition.

How does law treat partisan gerrymandering? In 2019, the U.S. Supreme Court decided *Rucho v. Common Cause*.[84] The case involved a challenge to districts in Maryland, which had been gerrymandered to favor Democrats, and districts in North Carolina, which had been gerrymandered to favor Republicans. The Court wrote, "Excessive partisanship in districting leads to results that reasonably seem unjust."[85] But then the

[82] On this trade-off, see Nathaniel Persily, *In Defense of Foxes Guarding Henhouses: The Case for Judicial Acquiescence to Incumbent-Protecting Gerrymanders*, 116 HARV. L. REV. 649, 663 (2002); BRUCE E. CAIN, THE REAPPORTIONMENT PUZZLE 154–55 (1984).

[83] John N. Friedman & Richard T. Holden, *Optimal Gerrymandering: Sometimes Pack, But Never Crack*, 98 AM. ECON. REV. 1, 113–44 (2008).

[84] 139 S. Ct. 2484 (2019).

[85] *Id.* at 2506–07.

Court held that partisan gerrymandering is a "political question."[86] Courts do not have jurisdiction to resolve political questions. Consequently, after *Rucho*, complaints about partisan gerrymandering in the United States cannot be brought in federal court.

Did the Court make the right decision in *Rucho*? People disagree. The Constitution does not specify how to balance the errors in representing parties against the errors from shirking. Without such guidance, it is difficult for judges to know what to do.

Questions

5.33. Proportional districting plans decrease errors in representing parties, but they increase errors from shirking. If primary elections were competitive, errors from shirking would decrease. Could we combine proportional districting and competitive primaries to decrease both kinds of errors? Why are primary elections usually uncompetitive?

5.34. Suppose that voters develop stronger commitments to political parties. Republicans will never vote for Democrats, and Democrats will never vote for Republicans. With strong partisanship, a series of districts that are 51 percent Republicans and 49 percent Democrats will produce errors in representing parties (Democrats get no seats) and shirking (the Republicans will win, even if they are lazy). Assuming strong partisanship, did the Court err in *Rucho*?

Term Limits

Officials shirk more when their re-election is secure. Gerrymandering can make re-election secure, as when 70 percent of the voters in a district belong to the same party. Incumbency can also make re-election secure. In 2016, 97 percent of the members of the U.S. House of Representatives won re-election. In 2018, the "blue wave" election in which Democrats gained control of the House, 91 percent of members won re-election. Incumbents have many advantages over challengers, including name recognition, experience, and usually money.

To mitigate the incumbency advantage, voters in many states enacted term limits. In Arkansas, for example, voters approved a state constitutional amendment limiting members of the House of Representatives to three terms. The same voters who approved term limits re-elected their incumbents, baffling observers. Why would voters disfavor incumbency but support incumbents? Scholars have different explanations. One relates to seniority.[87] Compared to junior legislators, senior legislators can direct more resources to their constituents, like money for schools and subsidies for farmers. By favoring incumbents, voters keep senior legislators in

[86] *Id.* at 2506.

[87] Dick Andrew & John Lott, *Reconciling Voters' Behavior and Legislative Term Limits*, 50 J. PUB. ECON. 1, 1–14 (1993); James M. Buchanan & Roger D. Congleton, *The Incumbency Dilemma and Rent Extraction by Legislators*, 79 PUB. CHOICE 47 (1994).

office and, over time, make their junior legislators senior. Thus, voters trade shirking for resources.

On this view, voters face a collective action problem akin to the prisoner's dilemma. The best *outcome* for voters is not to advantage incumbents. Without an advantage, incumbents will work harder and shirk less. But the best *strategy* for voters is to favor incumbents. If other voters do not favor incumbents, the ones who do benefit because their legislators are more senior.

Term limits are a Hobbesian solution to failed cooperation. Voters cannot overcome the incentive to favor incumbents by bargaining, so they impose a solution on themselves.[88] In *U.S. Term Limits, Inc. v. Thornton*, the Supreme Court rejected that solution.[89] The Constitution specifies some qualifications for federal office (for example, "No Person shall be a Representative who shall not have attained to the Age of twenty five Years"[90]). According to the Court, states lack the authority to add term limits to those qualifications.

People disagree on whether the Court got the law right.[91] Did the Court get the policy right? By discouraging shirking, term limits reduce representation errors. However, term limits have a second effect. By replacing incumbents with newcomers, term limits presumably increase the transaction costs of political bargaining. Inexperienced strangers must have more trouble cooperating than experienced colleagues. The republican compromise strikes again.

F. The Electoral College

In the United States, presidential elections unfold in three steps. First, voters vote for candidates. Second, states appoint "electors" to the Electoral College based on the vote. In general, states with more people get more electors. Third, the Electoral College officially selects the President. This structure is controversial. George W. Bush and Donald Trump won in the Electoral College, and therefore became President, while losing the popular vote. Given this experience, many commentators have argued that the Electoral College is antidemocratic. However, the Electoral College is mandated by the Constitution, so reforming it is difficult.[92]

Why does the Electoral College sometimes produce antidemocratic results? The answer lies in the method for appointing electors. Nearly every state appoints electors on a winner-take-all basis. To illustrate, Florida's size entitled it to 25 seats in the Electoral

[88] This logic might explain why voters in Arkansas adopted term limits for state officials. It probably cannot explain why voters in Arkansas adopted term limits for federal officials. Can you see why? *See* Edward L. Glaeser, *Self-Imposed Term Limits*, 93 Pub. Choice 389 (1997).

[89] 514 U.S. 779 (1995).

[90] U.S. Const. art. I, § 2 ("No Person shall be a Representative who shall not have attained to the Age of twenty five Years, and been seven Years a Citizen of the United States, and who shall not, when elected, be an Inhabitant of that State in which he shall be chosen.").

[91] *See, e.g.*, U.S. Term Limits, Inc. v. Thornton, 514 U.S. 779 (1995) (Thomas, J., dissenting) ("Nothing in the Constitution deprives the people of each State of the power to prescribe eligibility requirements for the candidates who seek to represent them in Congress. The Constitution is simply silent on this question. And where the Constitution is silent, it raises no bar to action by the States or the people.").

[92] U.S. Const. art. II, § 1.

College during the 2000 election. George W. Bush won Florida by about 500 votes, or about 0.01 percent of the total number of votes cast. Rather than giving 13 electors to Bush and 12 electors to his opponent Al Gore, Florida awarded all 25 electors to Bush. This gave Bush a decisive lead in the Electoral College. Meanwhile, Al Gore won California by over one million votes, giving him a decisive lead in the popular vote.

The Constitution mandates the Electoral College, but it does not mandate appointing electors on a winner-take-all basis. States could appoint electors in proportion to the vote. If states appointed electors in proportion to the vote, the outcome in the Electoral College would match the outcome of the popular vote, or nearly so.[93]

Why don't states connect electors to the popular vote?[94] Consider a thought experiment. Suppose one state appointed electors winner-take-all, while every other state appointed electors proportionally. For presidential candidates, the stakes in the winner-take-all state would be especially high. If a candidate won the state, even by a single vote, he or she would get all of the state's electors. With such high stakes, the candidates would have a strong incentive to invest in the state—to spend time there, to meet local officials, and possibly to promise the state rewards (for example, subsidies or tax breaks for local industries). Other states would like that kind of attention from presidential candidates, so other states would have an incentive to adopt winner-take-all. Soon every state might adopt winner-take-all, benefiting themselves individually but leaving the nation with a peculiar and occasionally antidemocratic system for choosing a president.

Thomas Jefferson understood this collective action problem. Some states used winner-take-all, while others, including Jefferson's home state of Virginia, awarded electors by congressional district. Whichever candidate won the vote in a given district won an elector. Compared to winner-take-all, appointment by district better approximates the popular vote.[95] In the presidential election of 1796, Jefferson lost to John Adams by three votes in the Electoral College. Afterward he pressured Virginia to adopt winner-take-all. In a letter to James Monroe, he explained the problem: "[A]n election by districts would be best, if it could be general; but while 10 states chuse either by their legislatures or by a general ticket, it is worse than folly for the other 6 not to do it."[96]

Questions

5.35. The National Popular Vote Compact is an agreement among states to change the allocation of electors. States that ratify the Compact agree to award all of their electors to whichever candidate wins the national popular vote. If enough states ratify the Compact, the winner in the Electoral College will always match

[93] Each state gets a number of electors equal to the sum of its representatives and senators in Congress. Each state has two senators, no matter its population, so states with small populations have disproportionate influence in the Electoral College. This could cause the outcome in the Electoral College to differ from the outcome of the popular vote, even if all states appointed their electors in proportion to the vote.

[94] The following is based on Michael Weisbuch, *Winner-Take-All as a Collective Action Problem*, 35 J.L. & Pol. 67 (2019).

[95] Note that the "popular vote" wasn't so meaningful in 1796 because the franchise was severely restricted.

[96] *Letter from Thomas Jefferson to James Monroe* (Jan. 12, 1800) *in* 31 The Papers of Thomas Jefferson 300–01 (Barbara Oberg ed., 2005).

the winner of the popular vote.[97] According to a proviso, the Compact does not take effect until it becomes decisive—that is, until states that collectively control a majority of electors in the Electoral College have signed on.

(a) The proviso is essential to solve the collective action problem. Explain why.
(b) Which states do you predict will ratify the Compact: States that tend to support the Democratic candidate in presidential elections, or states that tend to support the Republican?
(c) An earlier chapter argued that the Constitution's General Welfare Clause authorizes Congress to act when states suffer from collective action problems that they cannot overcome through bargaining. Following this logic, should Congress require states to appoint electors in a proportional manner? Would this be constitutional?[98] Under what circumstances would a sitting President support a bill requiring proportional appointment?

III. Government Competition

We have analyzed competition among candidates. This section analyzes competition among governments. Governments compete with one another in different ways. New Mexico and Indiana offer financial incentives to Hollywood to make movies in their states. San Francisco and Oakland offer different public goods and services in an effort to attract residents and businesses in the Bay Area. Uruguay lures wealthy people from Argentina with the promise of lower taxes. We focus on two forms of government competition: direct democracy and mobility. With direct democracy, people can make laws with their votes. With mobility, people can choose laws with their feet.

A. Direct Democracy

The previous chapter introduced direct democracy, and here we provide more detail. Direct democracy comes in two basic forms: initiatives and referenda.[99] *Initiatives* are statutes or constitutional amendments that originate among citizens. Individuals propose them, collect enough signatures to qualify them for the ballot, and then, along with other voters in the relevant jurisdiction, vote on them. The initiative process sidesteps representative bodies such as legislatures and city councils. *Referenda* are statutes or constitutional amendments that a representative body refers to the citizens for approval or rejection. Legislators may refer a bill to the people voluntarily, because the state

[97] This assumes the compact is constitutional. It might not be. *See* Norman R. Williams, *Why the National Popular Vote Compact Is Unconstitutional*, 2012 BYU L. Rev. 1523 (2012).

[98] *See* U.S. Const. art. 2 § 1 ("Each State shall appoint, in such Manner as the Legislature thereof may direct, a Number of Electors, equal to the whole Number of Senators and Representatives to which the State may be entitled in the Congress: but no Senator or Representative, or Person holding an Office of Trust or Profit under the United States, shall be appointed an Elector.").

[99] These distinctions, and the following discussion, are based on Robert D. Cooter & Michael D. Gilbert, *A Theory of Direct Democracy and the Single Subject Rule*, 110 Colum. L. Rev. 687, 687–730 (2010). Our terminology is common but not universal. The Initiative and Referendum Institute has a helpful website with more definitions and distinctions.

constitution requires it, or because a sufficient number of citizens demand that they do so. Importantly, referenda originate with legislative processes.

Twenty-four U.S. states have the initiative power, and almost all states have a version of the referendum. About 70 percent of the national population lives in a city with a citywide initiative process, and nearly all American cities have a version of the referendum. Sometimes voters use direct democracy to make important laws. When voters in Colorado approved an initiative that discriminated against gay people, the Supreme Court struck it down in *Romer v. Evans*.[100] The case paved the way for the eventual legalization of same-sex marriage. Other times voters use direct democracy on smaller matters, like whether hunters can use doughnuts as bait.[101]

Direct democracy competes with ordinary government—legislatures, city councils, and so on—by providing an alternative lawmaking mechanism. If voters do not get their preferred laws through legislation, they can make their preferred laws through initiatives. If legislators produce laws voters oppose, voters can negate them with referenda. Like diners choosing between two restaurants, voters choose between two lawmaking institutions for satisfying their tastes.

Why don't voters use direct democracy to make all laws? Recall the republican compromise: improvements in representation often come at the expense of higher transaction costs. Direct democracy may improve representation. Voters make decisions for themselves rather than entrusting representatives, each with many constituents, to do it for them. However, direct democracy raises transaction costs to prohibitive levels. Thousands or millions of voters cannot negotiate with one another over hunting and doughnuts, let alone more complicated policy questions (remember Brexit).

The previous chapter presented the Chaos Theorem. When voters make decisions across multiple issues at once, their collective preferences are almost certainly intransitive. They will turn in circles, replacing old proposals with new ones again and again, until they bargain or permit an agenda setter to impose stability. Sometimes voters in direct democracy make decisions over multiple issues. Consider the California Bill of Rights, an initiative proposed in that state in 1948. The initiative had about 21,000 words (about the length of this chapter) and addressed taxes, pensions, voting by Native Americans, health, gambling, oleomargarine, districting, and mining.[102]

How can voters in direct democracy avoid cycling over issues? Not by bargaining, because high transaction costs preclude it. Not by an agenda setter, because any citizen can propose just about any initiative. The two methods of avoiding intransitivity in a representative assembly—bargaining and agenda-setting—are unavailable for direct democracy.

Law supplies a different solution to this problem. Nearly every U.S. state and many countries have a "single subject" rule.[103] The rule limits initiatives to one "subject."

[100] 517 U.S. 620 (1996).

[101] Christine Dell'Amore & Virginia Morell, *After Vote, Baiting Bears with Doughnuts Poised to Stay Legal in Maine*, NAT'L GEOGRAPHIC, Nov. 6, 2014.

[102] *See* Daniel H. Lowenstein, *California Initiatives and the Single-Subject Rule*, 30 UCLA L. REV. 936, 950 (1983). The initiative was never presented to voters because the California Supreme Court struck it down. The court held that the initiative constituted a "revision," not an "amendment," to the California Constitution. McFadden v. Jordan, 196 P.2d 787 (Cal. 1948). In California, the initiative power is limited to "amendments."

[103] *See, e.g.*, NEB. CONST. art. III, § 14 ("No bill shall contain more than one subject, and the subject shall be clearly expressed in the title.").

With a single subject rule, voters must cast separate votes on separate issues, rather than casting one vote on multiple issues like taxes, pensions, environmental protection, and highways. By dividing initiatives into individual issues, law tends toward the political center. When law reaches the center, it stabilizes, just as the median voter theorem predicts. Thus, the single subject rule makes direct democracy into median democracy.

Questions

5.36. Thousands of citizens cannot bargain with each other, but a handful of initiative drafters can. Suppose drafters bargain and agree to combine two issues, *A* and *B*, in one initiative. Suppose a majority of voters vote to enact the initiative. Does *AB* reflect the "will of the majority?" Is *AB* stable law?

5.37. Many states impose limits on defeated initiatives. In Wyoming, an initiative is forbidden if it is "substantially the same" as another initiative voted down in the prior five years.[104] Can you relate Wyoming's rule to stability and the Chaos Theorem?

5.38. The single subject rule sits in the constitution of nearly every U.S. state. In many states, the rule applies to laws made by the legislature as well as laws made through initiatives. When should a single subject rule apply to laws made by the legislature?[105]

5.39. "[T]he United States shall guarantee to every state in this Union a republican form of government."[106] This is the Guarantee Clause in the U.S. Constitution. The Supreme Court has not interpreted this clause,[107] but we can speculate about its meaning. Why might applying the single subject rule to lawmaking by state legislators violate the clause?

B. What's a Subject?

Suppose an initiative addresses the death penalty and spotted owls. The single subject rule is easy to apply: the initiative violates the rule because the death penalty and spotted owls are clearly different subjects. Now consider a harder case that many judges faced in the early 2000s. One initiative bans same-sex marriage and also same-sex civil unions. (Civil unions were contractual arrangements that granted couples some, but not all, of the rights and responsibilities of marriage.) On one view, the initiative contains two subjects, marriage and civil unions. On another view, the initiative contains just one

104 Wyo. Const. art. 3 § 52(d) ("An initiative petition may be filed at any time except that one may not be filed for a measure substantially the same as that defeated by an initiative election within the preceding (5) years.").

105 *See* Michael D. Gilbert, *Single Subject Rules and the Legislative Process*, 67 U. Pitt. L. Rev. 803 (2006).

106 U.S. Const. art. 4, § 4. Here is the complete text of the clause: "The United States shall guarantee to every State in this Union a Republican Form of Government, and shall protect each of them against Invasion; and on Application of the Legislature, or of the Executive (when the Legislature cannot be convened), against domestic Violence."

107 Pacific States Telephone & Telegraph Co. v. State of Oregon, 223 U.S. 118 (1912). *See also* Luther v. Borden, 48 U.S. 1 (1849).

subject, relationships. Whether the initiative violates the rule—whether it stands or falls—depends on how abstractly one categorizes its contents.

Consider another example. An initiative in California changed the penalties for gang-related crimes ranging from vandalism to murder, reformed sentencing of repeat offenders, and revised the juvenile justice system. Challengers argued that the initiative had three subjects: gangs, repeat offenders, and juvenile crime. The court held that the initiative had just one subject, "the problem of violent crime committed by juveniles and gangs."[108] To generalize, any initiative can be categorized as one subject through a general category or multiple subjects through specific categories. When drafting an initiative under the single subject rule, abstraction is constitutional and granularity is unconstitutional.

Judges have little faith in their ability to achieve a convincing interpretation of a "single subject." Consider this statement from Justice Kogan of the Florida Supreme Court:

> [The single subject rule] requires an initiative to contain a logical and natural "oneness of purpose." . . . However, the erratic nature of our own case law . . . shows just how vague and malleable this "oneness" standard is. What may be "oneness" to one person might seem a crazy quilt of disparate topics to another. "Oneness," like beauty, is in the eye of the beholder; and our conception of "oneness" thus has changed every time new members have come onto this Court.[109]

The problem of single subject interpretation looms large. Initiatives work best when voters consider one issue at a time and the median rule applies. The single subject rule is the principal mechanism for achieving this, but judges do not know how to interpret it.

Economics offers a method for interpreting the single subject rule.[110] We begin as courts often do by identifying the law's purpose. Courts agree that the single subject rule has one central purpose: to prevent "logrolling."[111] Logrolling is a technique for political bargaining. It means combining issues to achieve majority support overall, even though a majority would oppose some issues if considered separately. Courts call logrolling a "vexatious worm" and a "perversion of majority will."[112]

If preventing logrolling is the purpose of the single subject rule, what interpretation fulfills this purpose? The traditional approach to the rule—what Justice Kogan calls the search for a natural oneness of purpose—disincentivizes logrolling across wholly disparate topics, like the death penalty and spotted owls, same-sex marriage and drunk driving, or sushi and drones. However, the traditional approach allows logrolling on related topics like vandalism and gangs (the subject is "juvenile crime") or taxes and government spending (the subject is "taxes and expenditures").[113]

[108] Manduley v. Superior Court, 41 P.3d 3, 29 (Cal. 2002).

[109] Advisory Opinion to Attorney Gen.—Ltd. Political Terms in Certain Elective Offices, 592 So. 2d 225, 231 (Fla. 1991) (Kogan, J., concurring in part and dissenting in part).

[110] This discussion is based on Robert D. Cooter & Michael D. Gilbert, *A Theory of Direct Democracy and the Single Subject Rule*, 110 COLUM. L. REV. 687, 687–730 (2010).

[111] Many judges believe that the rule has a secondary purpose, which is to prevent "riding." On the distinction, see Michael D. Gilbert, *Single Subject Rules and the Legislative Process*, 67 U. PITT. L. REV. 803 (2006).

[112] *See id.* at 814–15.

[113] Buchanan v. Kirkpatrick, 615 S.W.2d 6, 14 (Mo. 1981).

What interpretation of the single subject rule would disincentivize all logrolling, including logrolling on related topics? Answering this question involves some additional concepts. A voter has *separable* preferences for two policy proposals when she can decide how to vote on each without knowing whether the other will become law.[114] To illustrate, imagine two policy proposals, one on vaccines and another on satellites. For most voters, their vote on the first proposal is unaffected by whether the second becomes law and vice versa. Thus, most voters have separable preferences for these proposals.[115]

A voter has *inseparable* preferences for two policy proposals when she cannot decide how to vote on one without knowing whether the other will become law. This occurs when a voter only votes for one proposal if she is certain to get the other proposal (in economic terms, the proposals are *complements*). This also occurs when a voter only votes for one if she is certain *not* to get the other (the proposals are *substitutes*). To illustrate, imagine a proposal to reduce property tax rates by half, and a proposal to reduce property valuations for tax purposes by half.[116] If a voter favors reducing property taxes but believes that passing both measures would have disastrous consequences for the budget, the voter has inseparable preferences. She cannot decide how to vote on the first proposal without knowing whether the other will pass.

Now turn to logrolling. A logroll occurs under four conditions: (1) two or more proposals, have (2) *minority* support individually but (3) *majority* support when combined, and (4) members of the majority accept a proposal they dislike in order to enact a proposal they like more. Return to our old friends Caleb and Dee, who traded votes to pass two proposals, one on schools and one on police. The two proposals had minority support individually and majority support when combined. Caleb and Dee each accepted something they did not like to get something they liked. Caleb and Dee logrolled.

Logrolling has a precise connection to separability: voters cannot logroll when they have inseparable preferences. To illustrate, suppose Caleb and Dee have inseparable preferences over the proposals on police and schools. They will support one of the proposals only if the other proposal does not pass (substitutes). Or, they will support one of the proposals only if both proposals pass (complements). With substitutes, a bill combining the proposals will fail. With complements, a bill combining the proposals

[114] We do not use the term "separable preferences" in the way economists usually do. A more precise label for our concept is "*sufficiently* separable preferences." Translating preferences into votes requires an assumption about voters' behavior. We assume voters vote simultaneously on proposals, and they discount future elections because they cannot forecast the agenda. Consequently, voters vote sincerely, by which we mean that they vote for every proposal that yields at least as much utility as the status quo. Now we can express our concept of separability using game theory. A voter has a *weakly dominant strategy* for voting on a proposal when always voting the same way—for or against—yields a payoff at least as great as the payoff from voting any other way, regardless of whether other proposals pass or fail. The voter does not have a weakly dominant strategy if her optimal vote on one proposal hinges on whether other proposals pass or fail. If a voter votes sincerely and has a weakly dominant strategy for voting on each of two policy proposals, then she has what we call separable preferences for them.

[115] This example involves independent proposals. A voter also has separable preferences for two policy proposals when those proposals are weakly conjoined. Proposals are weakly conjoined when they weakly complement or weakly substitute for one another. Two proposals weakly complement each other when passage of the first increases a voter's support for the second, but not by so much that her vote on the second depends on whether the first passes. Likewise, two proposals weakly substitute for each other when passage of the first diminishes a voter's support for the second, but not by so much that her vote on the second depends on whether the first passes.

[116] We base this example on Measures 9 and 11, voted on simultaneously by Oregonians in November 1986.

will pass, but no one accepts a proposal they dislike to get another proposal they like more. On police and schools, there is no log to roll.

As explained, voters cannot logroll when they have inseparable preferences. Conversely, voters can logroll when they have separable preferences. Go back to our original assumptions about Caleb and Dee. Caleb wants more funding for schools. He would support a proposal to increase school funding whether or not police funding increases. Dee wants more funding for police. She would support a proposal to increase police funding whether or not school funding increases. They have separable preferences over these issues. They can trade votes to pass a combination of proposals that would fail on their own. Caleb and Dee each give something up to get something in return.

Generalizing, our analysis yields the following interpretation of the single subject rule: *First, separate policy proposals over which most voters have separable preferences.* When voters have separable preferences for two proposals, they can vote on those proposals in isolation, as required by the single subject rule. Combining the proposals facilitates logrolling, which violates the single subject rule's purpose. *Second, unite policy proposals over which most voters have inseparable preferences.* When voters have inseparable preferences for two proposals, they cannot vote on those proposals in isolation. Instead of voting in isolation, combining the proposals helps voters decide how to vote. With inseparable preferences, combining the proposals does not cause logrolling, so it does not violate the single subject rule's purpose.

Questions

5.40. An initiative implemented public financing for elections and funded that program with a tax on oil.[117] A court held that the initiative presented a "substantial and plain violation of the single-subject rule."[118] Suppose the court decided the case using the method of interpretation that we just proposed. Would the court have reached a different conclusion?

5.41. Policy proposal *y* and policy proposal *z* are popular. Both would pass if presented to voters individually. Instead, the proposals are combined into an omnibus initiative, *yz*, that would also pass. Most voters have separable preferences for *y* and *z*.

(a) Does the omnibus initiative *yz* constitute a logroll?

(b) Does the method of interpretation that we proposed require a judge to invalidate initiative *yz* for violating the single subject rule?

(c) The central purpose of the single subject rule is to prevent logrolling. However, many courts say the rule has a second purpose: to improve transparency and voter information. Voters have an easier time, the argument goes, when making a decision about one subject than many subjects. Should courts use the single subject rule to invalidate the initiative *yz*, even though it does not constitute a logroll?

[117] *See* Croft v. Parnell, No. 3AN-07-9339 CI, at *10 (Alaska Super. Ct. June 26, 2008).
[118] *Id.*

Prescription or Description?

Policymakers considering a new proposal care about what law *ought* to be. Judges, on the other hand, usually care about what existing law *is*. Judges benefit from descriptions of what the law is, as when professors write articles or litigators write briefs that clarify the meaning of a statute. For judges, prescriptions for what the law ought to be are often a waste of time. Consequently, prescriptions for what the law ought to be are often a waste of time for people who want to influence judges.

Is our interpretation of the single subject rule prescriptive or descriptive? We think the latter. As courts often do, we began by identifying the purpose of the single subject rule. Once we identified the purpose—preventing logrolling—we developed an interpretation to achieve it. Our interpretation mirrors judges' intuitions. To satisfy the single subject rule, judges say the parts of an initiative must be "reasonably germane" to one another,[119] they must have a "rational unity,"[120] they must not be "disconnected and incongruous,"[121] and so on. If voters have inseparable preferences over two proposals, and therefore cannot decide whether to support one without knowing whether the other will become law, then the proposals are "reasonably germane" to one another. They have a rational unity, connection, and congruity. Judges permit such proposals to be combined, and so would we. Conversely, if voters have separable preferences, they can make independent decisions about two proposals, so the proposals do not have a rational unity, connection, or congruity. Judges separate such proposals, and so would we.

Our theory clarifies the law by providing a framework for understanding it. Our theory describes, rather than prescribes, the meaning of the single subject rule. Courts use intuitions to apply the rule, and our theory makes those intuitions precise. To prove this, a study collected data on single subject cases. It recorded details about initiatives and whether courts held that they satisfied or violated the single subject rule. Students read the initiatives and indicated whether they could make independent judgments about the elements in each initiative. Higher numbers meant that students found it relatively easy to make independent judgments. In other words, higher numbers indicated separable preferences. According to our theory, separable preferences should be associated with courts striking initiatives down for violating the single subject rule. The research finds exactly this relationship.[122]

C. Mobility

Having discussed direct democracy, we now consider another form of government competition: mobility. To understand mobility, consider the development in the United

[119] Cal. Ass'n of Retail Tobacconists v. State, 135 Cal. Rptr. 2d 224, 237 (Ct. App. 2003) (internal citations, quotations, and emphasis omitted).

[120] Amalgamated Transit Union Local 587 v. State, 11 P.3d 762, 782 (Wash. 2000) (en banc).

[121] Jones v. Polhill, 46 P.3d 438, 440 (Colo. 2002) (en banc) (internal citations and quotations omitted).

[122] Michael D. Gilbert, *Does Law Matter? Theory and Evidence from Single Subject Adjudication*, 40 J. Legal Stud. 333 (2011).

States of the right to travel. In the 1800s, Nevada imposed a tax of one dollar on every person leaving the state by "railroad or stagecoach."[123] In the 1900s, the Secretary of State refused to grant passports to U.S. citizens who joined the Communist Party. In both cases, the Supreme Court intervened, rejecting the tax and the Secretary's authority. "[T]he right of exit," the Court wrote, "is a personal right included within the word 'liberty[.]' "[124] These cases helped establish the right to travel. In general, U.S. citizens can travel inside and outside the country without undue government interference.

Economics can illuminate the right to travel. People with similar tastes voluntarily cluster together in order to enjoy amenities, including local laws and public goods. Thus, people who prioritize culture, nightlife, and a walkable lifestyle move to city centers. Laws on commercial zoning, noise, and public transportation help sustain the features of city centers. Likewise, people who want to raise children in convenience move to suburbs. Laws on residential zoning, traffic, and public parks help sustain the features of suburbs. The right to travel contributes to voluntary clustering.

To refine thinking about clustering, we extend the concepts of equilibrium and efficiency. A *location equilibrium* exists when no one prefers to move from one jurisdiction to another. If relocating people cannot increase anyone's satisfaction without decreasing someone else's satisfaction, then the location equilibrium is Pareto efficient.

What conditions make a location equilibrium Pareto efficient? Scholars have studied the question extensively.[125] We reduce their answers to two unrealistic conditions. First, people must enjoy "free mobility," which means no obstacles to moving. Legal obstacles to moving include residence permits or exclusionary zoning, economic obstacles include the cost of moving, and so on. Second, jurisdictions must be sufficiently numerous to accommodate differences in taste among different types of people. If 10 kinds of people exist, the highest order of efficiency requires 10 jurisdictions. Given free mobility and many jurisdictions, people with similar tastes will voluntarily cluster to obtain the highest order of efficiency in the supply of laws and public goods. This is called the *Tiebout Model* after the economist Charles Tiebout, who first addressed it.[126]

The Tiebout Model implies competition among governments. To attract residents, jurisdictions offer different baskets of laws and amenities. People who favor a jurisdiction's offerings will move there, just like consumers who favor a store will shop there. Rather than creating good laws with their votes, people move to good laws with their feet. Thus, voluntary sorting is called "voting with your feet." [127] By voting with your feet, mobility diversifies culture. Many people in the United States are mobile, yet Salt Lake City and New Orleans have different city cultures, and Texas and Wisconsin have different state cultures.

In reality, moving comes with professional, financial, and personal costs. Jurisdictions are limited in number. Mobility costs obstruct movements toward efficiency, and too few jurisdictions cause too much similarity in jurisdictions relative to differences in people. With costly mobility and few jurisdictions, people with similar tastes still cluster

[123] Crandall v. State of Nevada, 73 U.S. 35, 39 (1867).

[124] Kent v. Dulles, 357 U.S. 116, 129 (1958).

[125] *See, e.g.*, Daniel L. Rubinfeld & Robert Inman, Democratic Federalism: The Economics, Politics, and Law of Federal Governance 37–75 (2020).

[126] Charles M. Tiebout, *A Pure Theory of Local Expenditures*, 64 J. Pol. Econ. 5 (1956).

[127] *See generally* Ilya Somin, Free to Move: Foot Voting, Migration, and Political Freedom (2020).

together to obtain more of their preferred amenities, but the result falls short of the highest order of efficiency.

Questions

5.42. The European Union guarantees the right of workers to compete for jobs throughout Europe. To implement this right, the European Union has tried to dismantle obstacles to mobility, notably the incompatibility of housing, health, and pension benefits in different nations. Are the European Union's efforts better characterized as a Coasean or a Hobbesian solution to locational inefficiencies?

5.43. "Exclusionary zoning" is the term for laws that aim to exclude poor people. To illustrate, one town's law mandated a minimum lot size of four acres in residential areas.[128] Do exclusionary zoning laws encourage or discourage locational efficiency? In answering, consider the effects of exclusionary zoning on the diversity of jurisdictions and mobility costs.

D. Local Governments and Home Rule

California enacted a statewide law forbidding people from accepting "public moneys for the purpose of seeking elective office."[129] Two years later, Los Angeles enacted a citywide law providing public moneys for people seeking elective office. Can a person seeking elective office in Los Angeles accept public money?[130] The answer depends on whether the state or the city has authority over the city's elections. Under California's constitution, cities have authority to make laws "in respect to municipal affairs."[131] Are city elections "municipal affairs"? This is a question for courts.

Questions like this arise frequently in federal systems. Like conflicts between national and state power, conflicts arise between state and local governments. Beyond campaign finance, these conflicts involve the minimum wage, benefits for government employees, training for police officers, collective bargaining, confinement of livestock, and so on.[132]

How do courts determine the boundary between state and local power? The answer varies, but they often apply a flexible balancing test. According to the Supreme Court of California, its "inescapable duty" is to "allocate the governmental powers . . . in the most sensible and appropriate fashion as between local and state legislative bodies."[133] To that end, courts often focus on whether the local law has "extramunicipal"[134] or

[128] Nat'l Land & Inv. Co. v. Kohn, 215 A.2d 597 (Pa. 1965).

[129] Cal. Gov. Code § 85300 (West 2017).

[130] This question was addressed in Johnson v. Bradley, 841 P.2d 990 (Cal. 1992) (en banc).

[131] *Id.* at 994.

[132] *See, e.g.*, Richard Briffault & Laurie Reynolds, Cases and Materials on State and Local Government Law 348–414 (7th ed. 2008).

[133] Johnson v. Bradley, 841 P.2d 990, 996 (Cal. 1992) (internal citation omitted). *See also* Farris v. Blanton, 528 S.W. 2d 549, 551 (Tenn. 1975) ("The whole purpose of the Home Rule Amendment was to vest control of local affairs in local governments, or in the people, to the maximum permissible extent. The sole constitutional test must be whether the legislative enactment, irrespective of its form, is local in effect and application.").

[134] *Johnson*, 841 P.2d at 996.

"extraterritorial"[135] effects. Laws without such effects are usually upheld (in the language of California's constitution, they address "municipal affairs"). Laws with "extramunicipal" effects are usually struck down.

Economics provides a prescription for allocating governmental powers in the "most sensible and appropriate fashion." The prescription involves externalities, bargaining, and mobility.

Begin with externalities. Like Nebraska's feedlots, a city's laws can affect its neighbors. Legal externalities cause inefficiency. To correct an externality, internalize it. Thus, if Los Angeles' law affects San Diego, replace the city law with state law because the state encompasses both cities. This is the internalization principle discussed in an earlier chapter. Courts embrace the internalization principle when they ask if a law has "extramunicipal" effects.

Internalization offers one solution to the problem of externalities. Bargaining offers another. If the nightclub's noise harms the neighbor, and if they can bargain costlessly, they will achieve efficiency. Likewise, if Los Angeles harms San Diego, and if the cities can bargain costlessly, they will achieve efficiency. This is the Public Coase Theorem. Given zero transaction costs, parties bargain to abate negative externalities and to promote positive externalities.

Finally, consider the Tiebout Model. Given zero mobility costs and many jurisdictions, people cluster in the locations that offer the laws and amenities they like best. More jurisdictions imply greater locational efficiency, just as more choices at the store imply greater satisfaction among shoppers. If municipalities cannot make local laws, they cannot distinguish themselves. State control makes jurisdictions homogenous, reducing choice.

We can combine these considerations into a prescription. *Given zero transaction costs between local governments, make control local.* Local control leads to diversity in jurisdictions, which empowers people to vote with their feet. Bargaining will correct externalities associated with local control. *Given high transaction costs between local governments, make control local if the benefits of clustering exceed the costs of externalities, and vice versa.* If governments cannot bargain, then local control will lead to inefficient externalities. However, local control will also promote diversity in jurisdictions, which promotes locational efficiency. The optimal balance between local and state control depends on which effect dominates. In practice, judges cannot know which effect dominates. They must rely on intuitions. Here are some intuitions: local control becomes more desirable as transaction costs, mobility costs, and externalities decrease.

Questions

5.44. The Supreme Court of California upheld Los Angeles' law on public financing of campaigns. Does the economic approach to local power support the court's decision?

5.45. Municipalities cooperate over public transportation, schools, and other matters. Under the "mutuality of powers" approach, municipalities can act on

[135] Fraternal Order of Police, Colorado Lodge No. 27 v. City & Cty. of Denver, 926 P.2d 582, 589 (Colo. 1996).

a matter jointly if *all* have authority to act on it individually. Under the "power of one unit" approach, municipalities can act on a matter jointly if *one* has authority to act on it individually.[136] Which approach facilitates bargaining?

5.46. "Dillon's Rule" directs courts to interpret narrowly grants of power to local governments. According to this rule, local governments only have those powers expressly delegated to them. Is Dillon's Rule good policy? Relate your answer to transaction costs, mobility costs, and externality costs.

5.47. Some scholars argue that local governments are especially corrupt. To reduce corruption by local governments, should states adopt Dillon's Rule, or should states improve mobility?[137]

5.48. An earlier chapter explained collective action federalism. Applied to the U.S. Constitution, this theory empowers Congress to act on interstate externalities when the transaction costs of bargaining among states are high. Is our prescription for delineating state and local power the same as collective action federalism? Why might mobility matter more for questions of local-state power than questions of state-national power?

Conclusion

The previous chapter develops the theory of the median rule, and this chapter applies it to electoral law. We first apply the theory to voting rights of citizens, specifically to inclusive and exclusive voting, legal externalities, and information costs. These applications provide critiques of hotly contested cases on voter identification and disclosure. Second, we apply the theory to structural problems of representation, specifically, legislative size, the number of houses, legislative decision rules, and one person, one vote. Finally, we apply the theory to direct democracy, the single subject rule, and localism. In each section, we aim to help you analyze the cases, not to provide a solution for you. A better analysis leads lawyers and judges to a deeper understanding of what law requires.

[136] *See* Richard Briffault & Laurie Reynolds, Cases and Materials on State and Local Government Law 543 (7th ed. 2008).

[137] *See* Clayton P. Gillette, *Local Redistribution, Living Wage Ordinances, and Judicial Intervention*, 101 Nw. U.L. Rev. 1057 (2007). *But see* Richard C. Schragger, *Mobile Capital, Local Economic Regulation, and the Democratic City*, 123 Harv. L. Rev. 482 (2009).

6
Theory of Entrenchment

Law is hierarchical, like the military. Constitutions trump statutes, statutes trump regulations, and regulations trump the common law. To stabilize the hierarchy, higher laws are usually harder to change. In the United States, enacting a federal statute requires majority support in both houses of Congress, but amending the Constitution requires supermajority support in both houses of Congress and ratification by three-fourths of the states.[1] When a law is hard to amend, it is *entrenched*, like the British army in World War I. Entrenchment is fundamental to law. Constitutions, treaties, and countless other laws are entrenched.

Why do we entrench law? Scholars offer many answers—to secure minority rights, to stabilize law, and to protect us from ourselves. During the Peloponnesian War, Athenians crushed a revolt and in the furious aftermath executed all conquered men. "The morrow," Thucydides wrote, brought "reflection on the horrid cruelty of a decree which condemned a whole city to the fate merited only by the guilty."[2] Entrenchment keeps our passions in check.

These justifications appear sound but disjointed. What connects minority rights to stability? Furthermore, they provide little guidance. Rights, stability, and passions all seem important. But what laws should we entrench, and to what degree?

This chapter uses economics to analyze entrenchment. We unite the justifications for entrenchment with a single theory: credible commitments. We study the optimal level of entrenchment using voting models. We use the theory of entrenchment to study legal design and constitutional collapse. The chapter helps answer questions like these:

Example 1: "It is impossible," James Madison wrote, "for the man of pious reflection not to perceive in [the Constitution] a finger of that Almighty Hand."[3] Many believe that constitutions should declare a society's sacred ideals. Yet most constitutions do not prohibit murder, and others address narrow topics like fishing nets.[4] What should go in a constitution?

Example 2: The nation of Japan and the state of Alabama have comparable procedures for amending their constitutions. Japan's constitution has not changed since 1947, while Alabama's changes about eight times per year.[5] What explains constitutional amendments?

[1] U.S. Const. art. V ("The Congress, whenever two thirds of both Houses shall deem it necessary, shall propose Amendments to this Constitution," which shall become "Part of this Constitution, when ratified by the Legislatures of three fourths of the several States[.]").

[2] Jon Elster, Ulysses Unbound 122 (2000). In fact, the Athenians rescinded the initial decision and spared the Mytilenians.

[3] The Federalist No. 37, at 184 (James Madison) (Ian Shapiro ed., 2009).

[4] Fl. Const. art. X, § 16.

[5] *See* Satoshi Yokodaido, *Constitutional Stability in Japan Not Due to Popular Approval*, 20 German L.J. 263 (2019); Albert P. Brewer, *Constitutional Revision in Alabama: History and Methodology*, 48 Ala. L. Rev. 583 (1997).

Public Law and Economics. Robert D. Cooter and Michael D. Gilbert, Oxford University Press. © Oxford University Press 2022.
DOI: 10.1093/oso/9780197655870.003.0006

Example 3: In the United States, the majority prefers more regulation of guns, and the minority intensely prefers less regulation of guns. Should intense minorities get what they want?

Example 4: New technology lets police see through walls and monitor suspects with drones. Courts update the U.S. Constitution, which forbids unreasonable searches, to this changing reality. Should courts update constitutions slowly and gradually, or should courts make radical change?

We begin with the positive theory of entrenchment before examining its normative properties. We conclude by connecting entrenchment to legal interpretation.

I. Positive Theory of Entrenchment

To resist the sirens, Ulysses tied himself to the mast of his ship. Similarly, to resist everyday politics, lawmakers bind themselves to laws by entrenching them. Entrenchment binds lawmakers by permitting a few actors to prevent collective action by many. To illustrate, since amending the U.S. Constitution requires ratification by three-fourths of the 50 states, any 13 states can prevent an amendment. The 13 smallest states have a combined population of about 16 million, and the national population is about 320 million. Entrenchment empowers the few to prevent legal change by giving them veto power. Enacting a new law requires agreement from everyone holding a veto.

As with the U.S. Constitution, lawmakers can entrench law with a demanding voting rule. Securing support from three-fourths of the states is harder than securing support from a bare majority. However, entrenchment can be achieved in other ways. Compared to unicameralism, bicameralism entrenches law by creating a second veto player. Either chamber of the legislature can prevent a new law from passing. Changing law often requires approval from executives or even citizens. As with bicameralism, these requirements entrench law by giving more actors a veto. In the United States, congressional committee chairs, the Speaker of the House, the Senate Majority Leader, and the President all have a veto over ordinary legislation. This helps explain why Congress enacts so few laws.

We will analyze all forms of entrenchment, but first we consider a threshold question: Why do lawmakers bind themselves to the mast?

A. Credible Commitments

Today people everywhere recognize the horrors of slavery. However, when the Framers of the U.S. Constitution met in 1787, their moral commitments were not so strong. Northern states tended to oppose slavery, but southern states supported it. The Framers were willing to compromise on this cruel practice to unify the states. The North could have made a promise to the South: join the United States by ratifying the Constitution, and in exchange we promise to allow slavery in your territory. The South would have scoffed at the North's cheap talk. If the northern states gained control of the new Congress, they would renege on the promise. To solve this problem, the Framers added

Article I, Section 9, to the Constitution, which forbade Congress from stopping the slave trade for 20 years.[6] To renege now would require the northern states to do more than break a promise. It would require a violation of the nation's fundamental law. Confident that the North would respect the bargain, the slave states ratified the Constitution.[7]

This is a tragic story with an important point: entrenchment is powerful. Entrenchment replaces cheap talk with credible commitments. Credible commitments lower transaction costs. Bargaining gets easier when people believe each other's promises. An earlier chapter explained that making credible commitments in public law often requires institutions. Entrenchment—in this example, a demanding rule for amending the Constitution—is such an institution.

Entrenchment lowers transaction costs in more than one way. Entrenching Article I, Section 9, lowered the costs of *constitutional* bargaining among states. Without the article, the North and South could not cut a deal. Likewise, entrenching the Constitution lowered the costs of *legislative* bargaining among politicians. Bargaining gets easier when its consequences are more certain. By stabilizing background conditions, the Constitution increases certainty over the consequences of statutes. Likewise, the Constitution channels political disagreements into predictable forums like legislatures and courts. When lawmakers seek change to lower laws, they follow procedures established by the Constitution. Crafting rules for each soccer match would cripple the sport, and restructuring government for each law would cripple the state.

We have explained that politicians entrench laws to lower their transaction costs of bargaining. According to the Public Coase Theorem, low transaction costs benefit lawmakers and, when they represent their constituents, society as a whole. This is the economic theory of entrenchment.

The economic theory does not compete with legal theories of entrenchment; it subsumes them. Legal scholars justify entrenchment on three grounds: to secure minority rights, to stabilize law, and to protect us from our passions. To secure minority rights is to make a credible commitment not to violate them. To stabilize law is to make a credible commitment not to change it. To protect us from our passions is to make a credible commitment not to pursue short-term interests. The legal justifications for entrenchment are instantiations of the economic theory.

If entrenchment lowers transaction costs, should lawmakers entrench all laws to the fullest extent? The answer is no because lawmakers face a trade-off. If changing law is too easy, commitments are not credible. But if changing law is too hard, commitments become untenable because they cannot be undone. Had the Constitution protected the slave trade forever, free states would not have signed.

Figure 6.1 depicts these ideas. The horizontal axis represents the entrenchment of the constitution. The vertical axis represents transaction costs. "Constitutional" lawmaking involves enacting a constitution, while "statutory" lawmaking involves enacting statutes. As we move rightward on the horizontal axis, constitutional entrenchment deepens. At first, this decreases the transaction costs of constitutional lawmaking by

[6] U.S. CONST. art. I, § 9.

[7] On the history of Article I, Section 9, see, for example, Paul Finkelman, *Slavery and the Constitutional Convention: Making a Covenant with Death*, *in* BEYOND CONFEDERATION: ORIGINS OF THE CONSTITUTION AND AMERICAN NATIONAL IDENTITY 188–225 (Richard Beeman, Stephen Botein, & Edward C. Carter II eds., 1987).

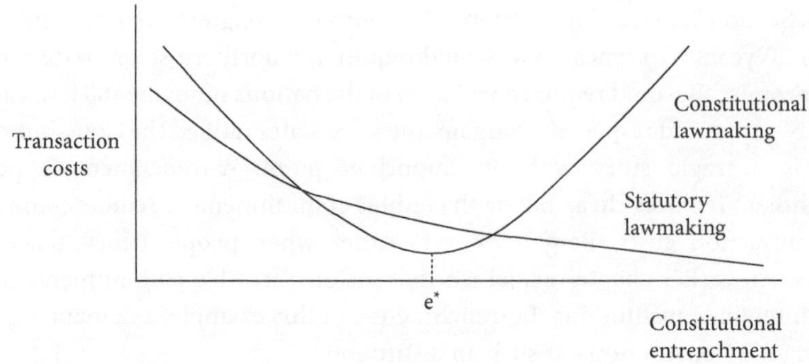

Figure 6.1. Entrenchment and Bargaining

making commitments more credible. Eventually, however, entrenchment becomes so deep that transaction costs increase. They increase because bargainers become reluctant to enact a constitution that will be very difficult to amend or replace. Entrenching beyond the tipping point e* increases the transaction costs of constitutional lawmaking. Deepening entrenchment always decreases the transaction costs of statutory lawmaking by making the state's processes and actions fixed and predictable.

We have connected entrenchment and political bargaining. Some political bargaining features lawmakers on both sides of the transaction, as with free and slave states. Other political bargaining includes private actors. To illustrate, suppose a nation wants a company to build factories within its borders. The factories would bring jobs and growth. Politicians promise not to expropriate the factories after completion, but the company has doubts. Thus, the nation adds a Takings Clause to its constitution that prevents the government from seizing property without compensation.[8] Entrenching the clause gives the company confidence to build the factories.

"Stability in government," Madison wrote, "is essential . . . to that repose and confidence in the minds of the people."[9] If Madison is right, then lawmakers who represent the people well should entrench fundamental laws. In fact, even lawmakers who represent the people *poorly* entrench fundamental laws. Economics explains why. All lawmakers benefit from credible commitments because all lawmakers benefit from successful bargaining. Stability in government for citizens is a consequence, but not necessarily a cause, of entrenchment.

Questions

6.1. The Contract Clause in the U.S. Constitution forbids any individual state from enacting a law "impairing the Obligation of Contracts."[10] How does the Contract Clause lower the transaction costs of public and private bargaining?

[8] *See, e.g.*, U.S. CONST. amend. V.

[9] THE FEDERALIST No. 37, at 181 (James Madison) (Ian Shapiro ed., 2009).

[10] U.S. CONST. art. I, § X ("No State shall enter into any Treaty, Alliance, or Confederation; grant Letters of Marque and Reprisal; coin Money; emit Bills of Credit; make any Thing but gold and silver Coin a Tender in Payments of Debts; pass any Bill of Attainder, ex post facto Law, or Law impairing the Obligation of Contracts, or grant any Title of Nobility.").

6.2. The philosopher John Locke helped draft a constitution for the colony of Carolina in 1669. It said this "shall be and remain the sacred and unalterable form and rule of government . . . forever."[11] Under what circumstances would lawmakers favor unalterable laws?

6.3. An earlier chapter distinguished Coasean and Hobbesian solutions to inefficiency. Hobbesian solutions are imposed on feuding parties, while Coasean solutions lower feuding parties' transaction costs of bargaining. The creation of a legislature is a Coasean solution. It provides a forum in which representatives of feuding parties can bargain. Why are legislatures usually entrenched in constitutions?

Parchment Barriers

The Framers of the U.S. Constitution divided the federal government into three branches—legislative, executive, and judicial—that would vie for power. They reasoned that separating powers should restrain the state and protect rights. The argument worked in theory, but what about in practice? Would the branches stay in their assigned roles, or would one aggrandize itself at the expense of the others? James Madison feared the latter. He worried that simply "mark[ing], with precision, the boundaries of these departments, in the constitution" would fail. Mere "parchment barriers" could not protect the state from "the encroaching spirit of power."[12]

Constitutions are not self-enforcing. Simply writing something, even in a fundamental legal document, does not ensure success. The constitutions of Equatorial Guinea and North Korea grant freedoms like speech, press, assembly, and dignity, but both regimes brutally oppress their citizens. Many constitutions worldwide are "shams."[13]

If leaders can ignore constitutions, then entrenchment cannot lower transaction costs. People cannot credibly promise to follow a rule that they are free to ignore. Recall the factories example. No company will invest in new factories if the Takings Clause in the constitution is a sham and the government can expropriate the factories at will.

To lower transaction costs, entrenchment must create a strong, not merely a parchment, barrier. To create a strong barrier, violating entrenched law must be costly. To illustrate, suppose a nation entrenches a Takings Clause in its constitution. To cancel the Takings Clause through legal means would require the executive to propose an amendment and persuade two-thirds of the legislature to support it. This would cost the executive a lot of time and effort. To make it concrete, suppose this would cost the executive 10. Alternatively, the executive could cancel the Takings Clause through extralegal means by ignoring it and ordering soldiers to expropriate factories. This would cost the executive political capital and future investments, and it could even

[11] David Armitage, *John Locke, Carolina, and the Two Treatises of Government*, 32 Pol. Theory 602, 603–07 (2004).

[12] The Federalist No. 48, at 252 (James Madison) (Ian Shapiro ed., 2009).

[13] David Law & Mila Versteeg, *Sham Constitutions*, 101 Cal. L. Rev. 863 (2013).

lead to criminal charges against him. If this cost is greater than 10, then the executive will not use extralegal means. Thus, the executive can commit to obeying the constitution. However, if this cost is less than 10, then the executive cannot commit to obeying the constitution. If the executive cannot commit to the constitution, then entrenching law in the constitution does not make the executive's promises credible.

Consider two implications of this logic. First, the credibility gains from entrenchment are bounded by the costs of violating law. Suppose the executive can violate the Takings Clause at a cost to himself of 10, the same cost as amending the clause through legal means. Deepening entrenchment—say, switching from a two-thirds to a three-quarters voting rule in the legislature—would increase the executive's cost of amending the clause, but it would not make the executive's commitment to the clause any more credible. Second, if lawmakers value credibility, they have an incentive to increase the costs of acting extralegally. To make companies trust the Takings Clause, the executive must find a way to punish *himself* for violating it.

When is acting extralegally costly for lawmakers? We will address this and related questions in the chapters on enforcement. For now, consider what scholars call *audience costs*.[14] Acting extralegally can reduce lawmakers' support among the public. Who is more likely to comply with the constitution, an elected president or a dictator?

B. Entrenchment and Equilibria

Commitments become more credible as reneging gets harder. Entrenchment makes reneging harder by multiplying the number of actors who must agree to renege. In public law, reneging on a legal commitment usually requires a vote, as when legislators vote to amend the constitution or administrators vote to scrap a regulation. This section integrates voting and entrenchment by drawing on spatial models from an earlier chapter. As before, the models are abstract, and they omit many features of the real world. Nevertheless, they provide an instructive foundation for understanding entrenchment.

Suppose that seven voters make law. To simplify, their names are *j*, *k*, *l*, *m*, *n*, *o*, and *p*. These voters use pairwise voting, and they consider each issue individually. The voters all have single-peaked preferences, meaning they prefer laws closer to their ideal points. Figure 6.2 shows the voters' ideal points. To simplify, we omit utility curves.

The point labeled *SQ* represents the status quo law. *SQ* is far from the political center at *m*. Suppose the voters choose between *SQ* and the proposal labeled *P1*, which is closer to the center. Will *P1* defeat *SQ*? The answer depends on the voting rule. To begin, suppose the voters use bare majority rule, meaning it takes just four votes to win (i.e., 4/7ths voting rule). *P1* lies closer to the ideal points of four voters, *m*, *n*, *o*, and *p*, so *P1* defeats *SQ*.[15] By the same logic, the proposal *P2* defeats *P1* (*j*, *k*, *l*, and *m* prefer *P2*). According

[14] *See* James D. Fearon, *Domestic Political Audiences and the Escalation of International Dispute*, 88 Am. Pol. Sci. Rev. 577 (1994). In international relations, the term "audience costs" means the political costs imposed on leaders by a domestic audience for foreign policy decisions. *See id.* We use the term more broadly.

[15] We assume, as does the median voter theorem, that voters do not behave strategically.

to the median voter theorem, law will change until it reaches *m* and stabilizes. The median is the sole equilibrium, so majority rule produces an *equilibrium point.*

If the median voter's ideal point never changes, law remains stable at *m*. In reality, ideal points change. Voter *m* could become more conservative over time, as some Americans have on issues like gun rights and immigration. The median swings to the right. If the median voter's ideal point changes, law moves to match her new ideal point.

To stabilize law, the state can replace majority rule with supermajority rule. Returning to Figure 6.2, suppose that changing law requires five voters to agree (5/7ths voting rule). If the law equals *m*'s ideal point, it cannot change. No more than three voters would support a change in either direction, and under the new voting rule it takes five votes to win. Suppose the law equals *P2* instead. Again, the law cannot change. No more than three voters would support moving leftward from *P2*, and no more than four voters would support moving rightward from *P2*. By this logic, every point between *l* and *n* is stable under a 5/7ths voting rule. Supermajority rule produces an *equilibrium set.*

Under majority rule, law destabilizes every time it deviates from the median voter's ideal point. In contrast, under supermajority rule law only destabilizes if it exits the equilibrium set. The voters' preferences may evolve—*m* moves leftward, *n* drifts rightward, and so forth—but law remains stable so long as it sits between *l* and *n*. This demonstrates the stabilizing power of entrenchment.

Stability grows with the depth of entrenchment. Replacing majority rule with a 5/7ths rule replaces an equilibrium point with an equilibrium set. Replacing a 5/7ths rule with a 6/7ths rule widens the set, as Figure 6.2 shows. To see the logic, consider a law at *P1*. Under a 5/7ths rule, the law is unstable. Five voters—*j*, *k*, *l*, *m*, and *n*—would prefer some points to the left. However, under a 6/7ths rule *P1* is stable. No more than five voters would support moving leftward, and no more than two voters would support moving rightward. It takes six voters to make a change.

We have shown that stability grows with the depth of entrenchment. Stability also grows as voters diverge. In Figure 6.2, the equilibrium set under a 5/7ths voting rule stretches from *l* to *n*. Suppose voters *l* and *n* become more extreme, meaning their ideal points move toward the left and right ends of the figure, respectively. The equilibrium set widens, even though the voting rule has not changed. A supermajority rule in a heterogeneous society entrenches more than the same rule in a homogeneous society.

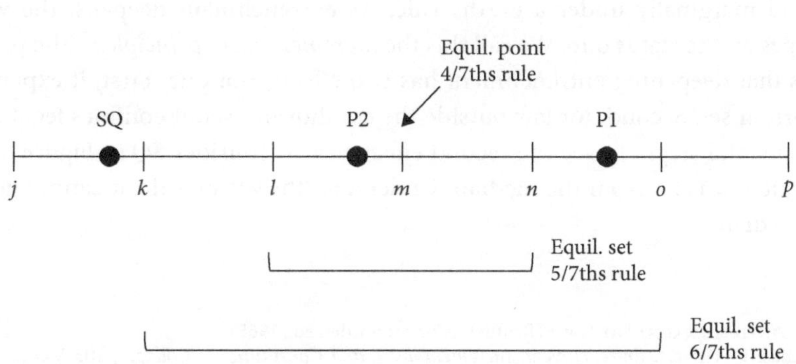

Figure 6.2. Equilibrium with Entrenchment

Questions

6.4. Suppose lawmakers want stable law, but entrenching is costly in terms of time and effort. Should lawmakers entrench laws over which the median voter's preferences tend not to change, like prohibitions on theft?

6.5. Explain why a politically fragmented country like Iraq might change its constitution less often than a politically unified country, even if both have the same amendment procedure.

6.6. Under what circumstance will switching from a 5/7ths voting rule to a 6/7ths voting rule *not* widen the equilibrium set?

6.7. The Anti-Federalists opposed adoption of the Constitution, arguing that it would only benefit members of the "Aristocratick combination" like bankers and lawyers.[16] Suppose drafters write the constitution to benefit themselves rather than the public. Would they prefer majority rule or supermajority rule for amendments?

C. Entrenchment and Incrementalism

We have explained that entrenchment creates an equilibrium set. Law inside the set stays fixed. What happens to law outside the set? Consider Figure 6.3. The status quo law is labeled *SQ*, and it began at the median. However, the voters' preferences lurched to the right, so relative to them the law now lies on the far left. *SQ* is out of equilibrium whether the voting rule is 4/7ths, 5/7ths, or 6/7ths. (If the voters use a unanimity rule, meaning a 7/7ths rule, then *SQ* is in the equilibrium set. Can you explain why?)

Law out of equilibrium is unstable, but what proposals can defeat it? Figure 6.3 has the answer. If the voters use bare majority rule, then any proposal in the first, wide win set would defeat *SQ* in a pairwise vote. At least four voters prefer every point in the win set to *SQ*. The law could move, for example, from *SQ* to a point near *p* and then back again, oscillating until it converges on *m*. What if the voters use a 5/7ths voting rule instead? Then only those proposals in the second, narrower win set would defeat *SQ*. At least five voters prefer every point in that set to the status quo. Under a 6/7ths rule, only those proposals in the third, narrowest win set would defeat *SQ*.

From *SQ*, law can change drastically under majority rule, moderately under a 5/7ths rule, and marginally under a 6/7ths rule. As entrenchment deepens, the win set converges on the status quo. We call this the *incrementalism principle*.[17] The principle teaches that deepening entrenchment has two effects, not one. First, it expands the equilibrium set. Second, for law outside the equilibrium set, it confines legal change to incremental steps. To see the second effect clearly, consider *SQ* in Figure 6.3. The status quo law is far from the median. Under a 6/7ths voting rule, it cannot get back to the median.

[16] THE ANTIFEDERALIST NO. I, at 1 (Brutus) (Morton Borden ed., 1965).

[17] Michael D. Gilbert, *Entrenchment, Incrementalism, and Constitutional Collapse*, 103 VA. L. REV. 631 (2017). *See also* John O. McGinnis & Michael B. Rappaport, *Our Supermajoritarian Constitution*, 80 TEX. L. REV. 703 (2002).

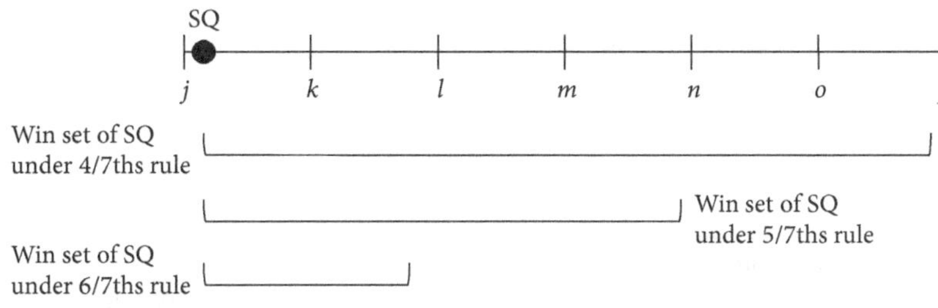

Figure 6.3. Incrementalism Principle

We have explained the incrementalism principle with a graph. To sharpen the intuition, consider an example. The tax rate equals 1 percent, and three legislators, Van, Wanda, and Xavier, have authority to change it. They prefer rates of 2, 10, and 20 percent, respectively. If the legislators make decisions using majority law—the law is not entrenched—they might change the rate to 10 percent. Wanda and Xavier prefer 10 percent to 1 percent, and they constitute a majority. If the legislators make decisions under unanimity rule—the law is entrenched—they cannot make such a drastic change because Van opposes it. Van would support an incremental change, like from 1 percent to 2 percent, but not a large change.

The incrementalism principle exacerbates a downside of entrenchment. Entrenchment stabilizes law regardless of its content. Thus, special interests like to entrench self-serving laws whenever possible. Next to religious liberties and property rights, state constitutions limit mechanics' working hours[18] and forbid caging pregnant pigs.[19] The incrementalism principle shows that entrenchment is even more appealing to special interests than you might think. In addition to freezing special interest laws in place, at least for a time, entrenchment limits future changes to those laws. Mechanics and pregnant pigs may lose some of their protections, but probably not much and probably not quickly.

D. Generalizing from Supermajority Rule

Our analysis of entrenchment has focused on voting rules in a single decision-making body. In reality, entrenchment usually takes more complicated forms. One can entrench law by requiring not one but two legislative chambers to approve amendments (bicameralism), executive approval (presentment), or both. States like Nevada require voter approval to change their constitutions,[20] while others like Delaware require multiple approvals by the same body.[21] These requirements often combine with supermajority rules. Amending Germany's Basic Law requires supermajority support in both chambers of the national legislature.[22] Our simple model generalizes to these complicated settings.

[18] *See* Cal. Const. art. XIV, § 2.
[19] *See* Fla. Const. art. X, § 21.
[20] *See* Nev. Const. art. XVI, § 1.
[21] *See, e.g.*, Del. Const. art. XVI, § 1 (amending Delaware's constitution requires supermajority support in the General Assembly and "in the General Assembly next after").
[22] German Const. of 1949 art. 79, § 1.

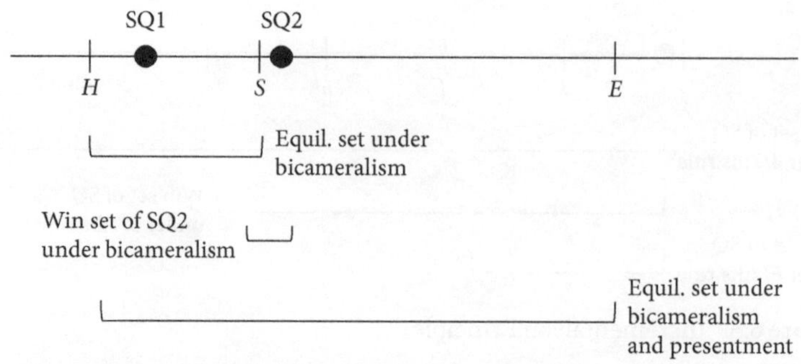

Figure 6.4. Entrenchment and the Separation of Powers

To illustrate, suppose law gets entrenched through bicameralism. Two chambers, a House of Representatives and a Senate, must agree for law to change. In Figure 6.4, *H* represents the ideal point of the House and *S* represents the Senate.[23] A law at *SQ1* is stable. The House will oppose any proposal to move it rightward. Likewise, the Senate will oppose any proposal to move law leftward. *SQ1* is not the only stable law. Bicameralism creates an equilibrium set between *H* and *S*. If the chambers diverge—for example, if *S* moves rightward—the equilibrium set grows.

What happens when law exits the equilibrium set? Suppose *S* moved leftward over time. A law that used to lie in the equilibrium set now lies just outside of it, as illustrated by *SQ2*. Both chambers support replacing *SQ2* with a new law, but the scope of potential change is narrow as the win set shows. *SQ2* lies close to *S*, and the Senate will only approve an incremental change that moves law even closer.

Suppose entrenchment deepens. In addition to bicameralism, changing law requires support from the executive, who has ideal point *E*. Now the equilibrium set runs from *H* to *E*. Deepening entrenchment made unstable laws like *SQ2* stable. If the executive's ideal point moved rightward, the equilibrium set would grow and vice versa.

These examples demonstrate a broad point. Amending entrenched law requires a certain number of actors to agree. One can represent these actors and the rules that govern them (supermajority requirements, for example) on the line. Thereafter, precise details of amendment techniques disappear, and a general model remains.[24] The general model has the same features as the seven-voter model. The ideas developed in the simple case extend to complicated cases.

Questions

6.8. In 2016, the Electoral College made Donald Trump the President of the United States, even though he lost the nationwide popular vote. Some Americans would like to eliminate the Electoral College, which requires amending the U.S. Constitution. Amending the U.S. Constitution is notoriously difficult. Use a spatial model to sketch an equilibrium set for the Electoral College.

[23] Attributing one ideal point to each chamber simplifies the analysis. In reality, the House and Senate each comprise many individual legislators with different ideal points.
[24] *See* GEORGE TSEBELIS, VETO PLAYERS (2000).

6.9. Adding an executive to Figure 6.4 expanded the equilibrium set. Will adding an executive to a bicameral system always expand the equilibrium set? Will it ever shrink the equilibrium set?

6.10. Suppose a constitutional designer chooses between two methods of entrenchment: a bicameral legislature, each chamber of which operates under majority rule, or a unicameral legislature operating under supermajority rule. Which method seems more democratic?[25]

6.11. Under bicameralism, we call the space between *H* and *S* the equilibrium set. An earlier chapter called the same space the Pareto set. Are these concepts the same? Does the answer depend on whether *H* and *S* represent the institutions or the median members of the institutions?

Unpopular Constitutionalism

Constitutions are supposed to reflect the will of the people, yet many constitutions are unpopular among the people they govern.[26] Public views on topics like homosexuality and abortion do not track constitutional protections for gay rights and reproductive choice. Consider another puzzle. Scholars report that constitutions are "sticky": new ones closely resemble their predecessors.[27] In a comprehensive study of the world's constitutions, researchers found that the "average amended constitution covers 97 percent of the same topics as the previous document, prior to amendment."[28]

Many constitutions are unpopular, and apparently amendments do not solve the problem. Why? Scholars have offered answers rooted in psychology, judicial behavior, and so on. We offer a simpler explanation: constitutions are entrenched, and entrenchment forces incrementalism. As citizens' preferences change, the median voter's ideal moves away from the existing law, contributing to its unpopularity. When the law falls out of the equilibrium set, an amendment becomes possible. However, the incrementalism principle shows that the amendment will likely be minor. Amendment can move an unpopular constitutional law closer to the political center, but often it cannot return the law to the center. Suddenly the puzzles seem less puzzling. Of course constitutions are sticky and unpopular. Preferences change, and entrenchment stops amendments from keeping up.

E. Entrenchment and Instability

On some issues, preferences change quickly. In 20 years, Americans' views on same-sex marriage and marijuana changed dramatically. On other issues preferences evolve

[25] *See* Saul Levmore, *Bicameralism*, 12 Int'l Rev. L. Econ. 145 (1992).

[26] Mila Versteeg, *Unpopular Constitutionalism*, 89 Ind. L.J. 1133, 1137 (2014).

[27] *See* Ozan O. Varol, *Constitutional Stickiness*, 49 U.C. Davis L. Rev. 899, 902, 904 (2016) (observing that "amendment processes around the globe . . . produce relatively little change in constitutional substance").

[28] Zachary Elkins, Tom Ginsburg, & James Melton, The Endurance of National Constitutions 59 (2012).

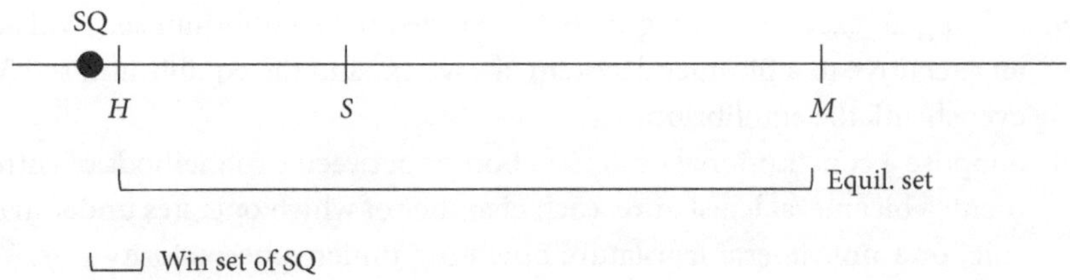

Figure 6.5. Constitutional Instability

gradually. Support for the rights of racial minorities in the United States has changed slowly over time. The pace of social change affects the path of legal change, sometimes in surprising ways.

Consider these events in the state of Texas. In 2007, a constitutional amendment empowered the state to exempt "totally" disabled veterans from some property taxes. In 2011, an amendment extended the exemption to the surviving spouse of a "totally" disabled veteran. In 2013, another amendment extended the exemption to "partially" disabled veterans and their surviving spouses. In 2015, yet another amendment allowed the legislature to extend the tax break to the surviving spouse of a "totally" disabled veteran who died before the 2011 amendment took effect. Texas changed the same section of its constitution four times in eight years, repeatedly expanding the tax break.[29]

This sequence seems surprising. Amending the Texas constitution requires supermajority support in both chambers of the legislature and majority support among citizens. That level of entrenchment suggests that constitutional change should be rare, not common. What explains the instability? Rapid changes in preferences could be the cause. However, rapid changes are not necessary.

To see why, consider Figure 6.5. Suppose the dimension represents support for veterans. *H* is the ideal point of the Texas House of Representatives. *S* is the ideal point of the Texas Senate.[30] The median voter among Texans has ideal point *M*. Thus, the equilibrium set for constitutional support of veterans stretches from *H* to *M*. Suppose the status quo law supporting veterans lies just to the right of *H*. It lies in the equilibrium set, but just barely. Now suppose the House gradually becomes more supportive of veterans. The point *H* slides rightward. Eventually it moves past the status quo law, meaning the law slips out of the equilibrium set, as the point *SQ* illustrates. When the status quo falls out of the equilibrium set, an amendment becomes possible, but note the narrowness of the win set. *SQ* lies just left of *H*, and the largest-possible amendment will create a new law just right of *H*.

Suppose a new law just right of *H* gets enacted. The law is in the equilibrium set. If *H* stops moving rightward on the line, or if it oscillates leftward, then the new law will stick. But suppose *H* keeps drifting rightward. That evolution pushed *SQ* out of the

[29] *See* Tex. Legislative Council, Amendments to the Texas Constitution Since 1876, 92–93 (Feb. 2016).

[30] To simplify, we assume that every member of the Texas House has ideal point *H* and every member of the Texas Senate has ideal point *S*.

equilibrium set to begin with, and it might continue. When *H* slips out of equilibrium, a narrow win set opens, a new but similar law replaces the old, and the process repeats.[31]

To make this concrete, reconsider Van, Wanda, and Xavier. The status quo tax rate equals 1 percent, and they prefer rates of 2, 10, and 20 percent, respectively. Because they operate under unanimity rule, they cannot increase the rate drastically. Van will agree to move from 1 percent to, say, 2 percent, but not much more. Suppose they change the rate to 2 percent. Now their views evolve, and they prefer rates of 3, 11, and 21 percent. All prefer to increase the tax rate again, but the change will have to be small. They might switch the rate from 2 to, say, 3 percent, and the process continues.

In this scenario, entrenched law is unstable. Like a wagon, it trails behind as voters march, never lurching ahead but never resting. Entrenched law changes just as often as law under majority rule. However, the law is less popular because it never reaches the political center.

This analysis might illuminate events in Texas. More importantly, it leads to predictions about when entrenchment will and will not stabilize law. If the views of voters evolve consistently in one direction, even entrenched law may change frequently, as in the example of Van, Wanda, and Xavier. Conversely, if voters vacillate, shifting right and then left and back again, entrenched law may never change. Perhaps this explains why democratic constitutions address election procedures (the "rules of the game") and the allocation of power among branches of government. When a political party gains control of Congress but loses the presidency, it wants more power concentrated in legislators and less in the executive, and vice versa. The views of lawmakers on fundamental institutions oscillate as one party or the other wins elections. Entrenchment prevents the rotation of lawmakers from destabilizing the state.

Questions

6.12. In Figure 6.5, suppose *S* and *M* drift leftward while *H* drifts rightward. When will the law stabilize?

6.13. The U.S. Constitution has operated for two centuries, while the constitution of France's Fourth Republic lasted just 12 years. Some constitutions endure while others collapse. What poses a greater risk to constitutional endurance: occasional, dramatic changes in preferences or persistent, small changes in preferences?

Amend or Convene?

How should constitutions change? The U.S. Constitution and many others authorize two methods for changing constitutional text: amendments and conventions. In general, amendments focus on discrete issues, like the Nineteenth Amendment addressing women's right to vote.[32] Conventions can encompass bundles of issues. In

[31] This phenomenon is explored in Michael D. Gilbert, *Entrenchment, Incrementalism, and Constitutional Collapse*, 103 VA. L. REV. 631 (2017).

[32] The single subject rule constrains many state constitutional amendments. The rule does not apply to federal constitutional amendments, though the Framers anticipated that federal amendments would have

the 1960s, a convention to rewrite the state of Michigan's constitution met for nearly a year, and voters cast one vote to approve the whole package, which included 12 articles and dozens of sections.[33]

Amendments are more likely to fit our analysis, which assumes decisions happen on one issue at a time. Thus, changing law through amendment will more likely produce the incrementalism described earlier. Conventions, on the other hand, might involve bargaining across multiple issues, and bargaining can generate greater change. Reconsider Figure 6.5. Absent bargaining, the House will not approve replacing *SQ* with a law at *S*. With bargaining, the House might agree to this change if it gets, say, more school funding as part of the deal. Bargaining can produce significant change even when law is entrenched.

Amendments and conventions differ in another way: the former can only move law *closer* to the political center. In every previous example, a new law closer to the median replaces the status quo. Conventions are not so constrained. A political actor might approve moving the law on religious minorities further from the political center if in exchange she gets a right to health. In short, conventions work better when the objective is unpopular or drastic change, including change that seeks to replace an unstable status quo with a law deep in the equilibrium set. Amendments work better when the objective is popular, incremental change.[34]

Many lawyers fear constitutional conventions, and there has never been one for the U.S. Constitution. We can use a concept from an earlier chapter to explain why. Amendments resemble median democracy and conventions resemble bargain democracy. Bargain democracy is better than median democracy when transaction costs are low and representation is good. Bargain democracy is worse when transaction costs are high or representation is poor. Transaction costs increase with the number of issues. A convention to remake the entire Constitution could bog down or become unpredictable (a "runaway convention"). Limiting the scope of a convention could lower transaction costs, but Article V does not provide for any such limitation.[35]

Nor does California. The California Supreme Court once described the state's convention process like this: "[T]he entire sovereignty of the people is represented in the convention. The character and extent of a constitution that may be framed by that body is freed from any limitations."[36] Economics provides perspective on the court's reasoning. An unconstrained convention raises transaction costs, which may harm citizens rather than help them.

limited scope. *See* THE FEDERALIST NO. 85, at 443 (Alexander Hamilton) (Ian Shapiro ed., 2009) ("[E]very amendment to the Constitution, if once established, would be a single proposition, and might be brought forward singly. There would then be no necessity for management or compromise, in relation to any other point–no giving nor taking.").

33 JAMES K. POLLOCK, MAKING MICHIGAN'S NEW CONSTITUTION, 1961–1962 (1962).

34 Michael D. Gilbert, *Entrenchment, Incrementalism, and Constitutional Collapse*, 103 VA. L. REV. 631, 666–68 (2017).

35 *See* U.S. CONST. art. V. Perhaps Congress or the states could impose a limit on a constitutional convention.

36 Livermore v. Waite, 36 P. 424, 426 (Cal. 1894).

II. Normative Theory of Entrenchment

Drafted in 1901, Alabama's constitution mandates "separate schools . . . for white and colored children."[37] Efforts to remove that racist language have failed.[38] Entrenchment may check passions and deliver other benefits, but it comes with a cost: law can diverge from popular values. When it diverges too far, society suffers and the state may fail. "We might as well require a man to wear still the coat which fitted him when a boy," Thomas Jefferson wrote, "as civilized society to remain ever under the regimen of their barbarous ancestors."[39]

The last section showed how different degrees of entrenchment affect law's development. Here we ask what degree of entrenchment is best for society. In answering, we consider the three justifications for entrenchment: minority rights, stability, and passions.

A. Welfare and Democracy

An earlier chapter explained that if voters have equally intense preferences, then majority rule can maximize social welfare. To reiterate the logic, return to voters *j* through *p*. If law shifts a little leftward from *m*'s ideal point, three voters (*j*, *k*, and *l*) gain while the other four suffer. Because of the equality of intensity, the gains to *j*, *k*, and *l* exactly offset the losses to *n*, *o*, and *p*. However, nothing offsets *m*'s loss, so the net effect of the leftward shift is a decline in total utility. The same would hold if law shifted right of the median.

Setting law at the median maximizes social welfare, so moving law closer to the median must increase it.[40] However, moves of equal distance do not increase social welfare by equal amounts. The curve in Figure 6.6 demonstrates. Assume that each voter gains one when law moves one ideal point closer to his or her own and vice versa. Thus, preferences are equally intense. From a status quo of *j*, moving law to *k* will help six voters and hurt one, leading to a net gain of five. Moving from *k* to *l* helps five voters and hurts two, leading to a net increase in three. These changes are additive. Moving from *j* to *m* increases total utility by nine,[41] while moving from *k* to *n* increases it by three.[42]

We can relate the positive analysis of entrenchment to democracy. Under majority rule law converges on the median voter, maximizing welfare. In Figure 6.6, the curve peaks at *m*. Under supermajority rule, law does not necessarily move to the median, leading to a welfare loss. To illustrate, suppose the status quo law in Figure 6.6 equals *l*. Under a 5/7ths voting rule, that law lies in the equilibrium set, so it cannot change. The

[37] Ala. Const. § 256.

[38] The language has no effect because of the Supreme Court's decision in *Brown v. Board of Education*, 347 U.S. 483 (1954). Efforts to revise Alabama's constitution are finally underway. *See* Tariro Mzezewa, *Alabama Begins Removing Racist Language from Its Constitution*, N.Y. Times, Sept. 19, 2021.

[39] Thomas Jefferson, *Letter to Samuel Kercheval, July 12, 1816*, *in* The Works of Thomas Jefferson (Paul Leicester Ford ed., 1904–5).

[40] We set social welfare equal to the sum of individuals' utility.

[41] This move decreases *j*'s utility by three and *k*'s by one. It increases *l*'s utility by one and *m*'s, *n*'s, *o*'s, and *p*'s by three. The net gain equals nine.

[42] This move decreases *j*'s and *k*'s utility by three and *l*'s by one. It increases *m*'s utility by one and *n*'s, *o*'s, and *p*'s by three. The net gain equals three.

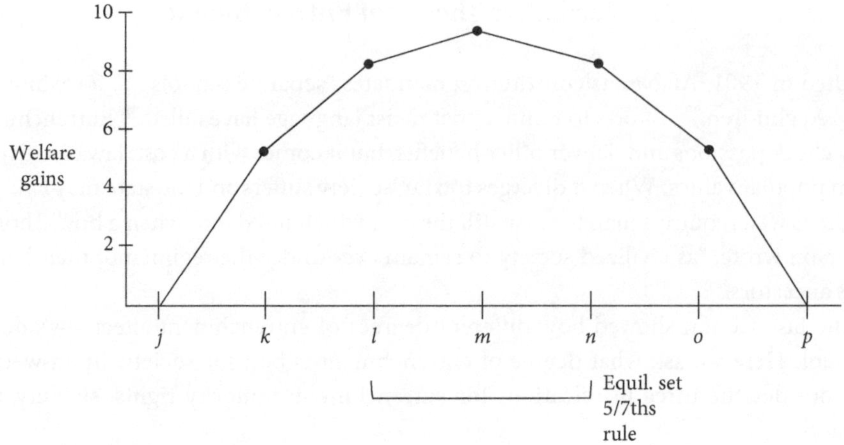

Figure 6.6. Social Welfare and the Median

lack of democratic responsiveness costs society. Switching to majority rule would make law responsive to the majority. Law would move from *l* to *m*, increasing social welfare.

We have shown that entrenchment can harm society when voters have equally intense preferences by preventing law from reaching the median. In fact, entrenchment can harm society when voters have *un*equally intense preferences. Consider abortion rights. Some people oppose abortion in all cases, even if the pregnancy resulted from rape, is not viable, or threatens the life of the mother. Others support abortion rights in all or nearly all cases. These passionate minorities take extreme positions. Most people have less-intense preferences and take moderate positions. How do these preferences affect the analysis of entrenchment?

Return to Figure 6.6. Assume that voters *j* and *p* have opposing but equally intense preferences. Voter *j* strongly opposes abortion rights, and *p* strongly supports them. To make this concrete, let's assign some numbers. When law moves one ideal point away from *j*'s, voter *j* suffers a loss of three, and vice versa. The same goes for voter *p*. The other voters gain or lose only one as law moves one ideal point closer or further from theirs. From a status quo law of *j*, moving one ideal point to the right would cost *j* three, benefit *k*, *l*, *m*, *n*, and *o* one apiece, and benefit *p* three. The net gain would equal five—just like the curve in Figure 6.6 shows. From *j*, moving law two ideal points to the right would cost *j* six, voter *k* would be indifferent, voters *l*, *m*, *n*, and *o* would gain two apiece, and voter *p* would gain six. The net gain would equal eight—again, just like the curve shows. The gains to *p* exactly offset the losses to *j*, so their intensity does not affect the analysis.

To generalize, setting law at the median maximizes social welfare when preferences are equally intense *and* when preferences are symmetrically intense. Preferences are symmetrically intense when the utility curve of every person whose ideal is left of the median matches the curve of a person whose ideal is right of the median. Symmetrical intensity means that folding the political dimension in half makes all points on both sides align, like a snowflake.[43]

[43] Symmetry requires alignment of the voters' ideal points and utility curves, which are not pictured in the figures.

Equally intense preferences are just a special case of symmetrically intense preferences. Symmetrically intense preferences must be rare in fact, but approximately symmetrical preferences might be common. On many issues voters with passionate liberal views might more-or-less offset voters with passionate conservative views. When preferences are approximately symmetrical, the median rule approximately maximizes social welfare.

If preferences tend to be symmetrical, then majority rule tends to be optimal because it pushes law toward the median. In reality, majority rule is rare. In the United States, most statutes get enacted through bicameralism and presentment. Thus, we entrench laws even when preferences are approximately symmetrical. The following sections explain why.

Questions

6.14. In Figure 6.6, suppose the status quo law matches *p* and the voting rule is 6/7ths. What is the win set of the status quo? If law moves as close to *m* as the 6/7ths rule allows, by what amount will social welfare increase?

6.15. Imagine two laws, one far from the political center and the other near the political center. Legislators move the first law closer to the center and make the second law match the center. Which change reflects majority will? Which change does more for society?

B. Welfare and Minorities

The Reconstruction Amendments banned slavery, promised at least some equality before the law, and forbade racial discrimination in voting.[44] Those laws hurt some southern whites a little and helped African Americans and others a lot. Constitutional law often addresses this situation: a majority supports an issue (in that case, the power to own and brutalize slaves), while a minority intensely opposes it. By protecting intense minorities, entrenchment can increase social welfare.

To illustrate this idea, imagine three people voting on the use of peyote, a mood-altering substance. Native Americans have used peyote in rituals for centuries. The first voter prefers a complete ban on peyote, the second prefers to permit limited use during religious practices, and the third strongly prefers unlimited use during religious practices.[45] Majority rule causes law to gravitate to the second voter's position, but this

[44] U.S. Const. amend. XIII ("Neither slavery nor involuntary servitude, except as a punishment for crime whereof the party shall have been duly convicted, shall exist within the United States, or any place subject to their jurisdiction."); U.S. Const. amend. XIV ("All persons born or naturalized in the United States and subject to the jurisdiction thereof, are citizens of the United States and of the State wherein they reside. No State shall make or enforce any law which shall abridge the privileges or immunities of citizens of the United States; nor shall any State deprive any person of life, liberty, or property, without due process of law; nor deny to any person within its jurisdiction the equal protection of the laws."); U.S. Const. amend. XV ("The right of citizens of the United States to vote shall not be denied or abridged by the United States or by any State on account of race, color, or previous condition of servitude.").

[45] For an important case on peyote and religion, see Employment Div., Dept. of Human Resources of Oregon v. Smith, 494 U.S. 872 (1990).

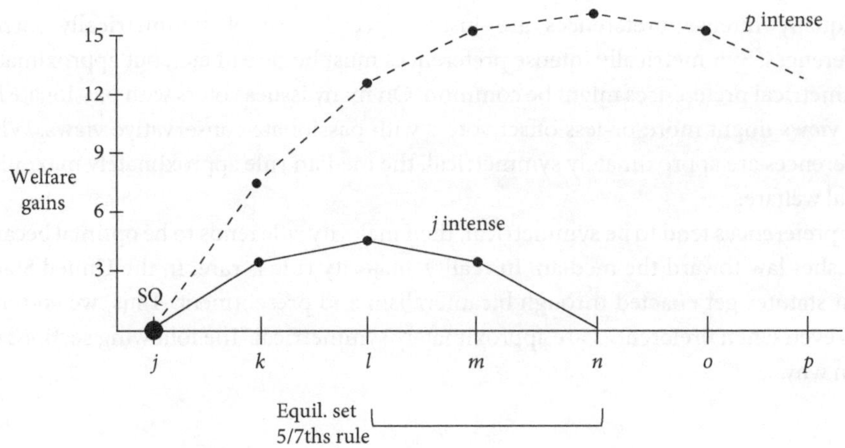

Figure 6.7. Asymmetrical Preferences

is suboptimal.[46] Permitting unlimited use for religion would help the third voter more than it would hurt the other two. Legalizing unlimited use, and entrenching that law with unanimity rule, would maximize welfare.

To clarify, Figure 6.7 shows the ideal points of our seven voters, *j* through *p*. Unlike before, voter *j* has intense preferences compared to the others. When law moves one ideal point closer to hers (for example, from *k* to *j*), her utility grows by three. When law moves one ideal point further from hers, she loses three. The other voters gain only one when law moves one ideal point closer and lose only one when law moves one ideal point further.

The status quo law aligns with *j*'s ideal point, so the law satisfies her intense preferences. However, the law does not maximize social welfare.[47] The solid curve shows the total utility gains from moving law from the status quo toward the center. Replacing the status quo with a law one ideal point to the right would cost *j* three but benefit *k*, *l*, *m*, *n*, *o*, and *p* one apiece. The net gain would equal three, as the solid curve shows. From *j*, moving law two ideal points to the right would cost *j* six. Voter *k* would be indifferent, and voters *l*, *m*, *n*, *o*, and *p* would gain two apiece, so the net gain would equal four. The solid curve peaks at *l*, which means that moving law from *j* to *l* would maximize social welfare.

To generalize, given asymmetrically intense preferences, setting law at the median fails to maximize social welfare. Instead, the social welfare–maximizing law skews toward the intense minority. In Figure 6.7, the optimal law equals *l*, not *m*. If voter *j* had more intense preferences, the optimal law would lie between *j* and *l*, and if she had less intense preferences, it would lie to the right of *l*.

Suppose the optimal law lies at *l* as the solid curve shows. Lawmakers could make the law *l*, but majority rule will cause the law to gravitate toward *m*. Entrenching the law with a 5/7ths voting rule will stabilize it at *l* by creating an equilibrium set. In general, entrenchment benefits society when it stabilizes a law favoring intense minorities.

[46] We discussed majority rule and the intensity of preferences in an earlier chapter on voting.
[47] Again, we assume that social welfare is simply the sum of individuals' utility.

This proposition has an inverse. Entrenchment harms society when it stabilizes a law disfavoring intense minorities. Return to Figure 6.7, and suppose voter *p* has intense preferences instead of voter *j*. He gains and loses three as law moves one ideal point closer or further from his. The others gain or lose only one. If the status quo law equals *j*, great gains can be had from moving law toward *p*, as the dashed curve shows. Ideally, law would move from *j* to *n*. Whether this is possible depends on the level of entrenchment. Under a 5/7ths voting rule, law could move to *n*, but under a 6/7ths rule it could not. The incrementalism principle strikes again.

Questions

6.16. In *United States v. Carolene Products Co.*, the Supreme Court addressed laws that harm "discrete and insular minorities."[48] The Court reserved the power to conduct a "searching judicial inquiry" of such laws when "political processes ordinarily to be relied upon to protect minorities" might fail.[49] In Figure 6.7, where voter *j* has intense preferences, should a court conduct a searching inquiry if the political process moves the law from *SQ* to *p*? What if it moves the law from *SQ* to *m*?

6.17. In Figure 6.7, suppose the status quo law equals *j*. Voter *o* gains three when law moves one ideal point closer to his and loses three when law moves one ideal point further from his. The other six voters gain or lose one. Given a 5/7ths voting rule, can law move from the status quo to the social welfare–maximizing point?

Voting Externalities

Three voters using majority rule consider a proposal for road repairs.[50] According to the proposal, each voter would pay a tax of $30 to cover the cost of the repair. The repaired road would provide a benefit of $40 to the first voter and $40 to the second, both of whom live nearby. The repaired road would provide no benefit to the third voter. As to these three voters, building the road is inefficient. The cost of $90 exceeds the benefit of $80. Nevertheless, the road might get built. For two of the three voters, the proposal yields a net benefit of $10 apiece.

This example involves expropriation: a majority of voters take money from a minority for their own use. Expropriation of money may seem different from the religious oppression in the peyote example. To an economist, however, the scenarios are identical. In both cases, the majority cares a little (two feel weakly about peyote, two stand to gain just $10), and the minority cares a lot (one feels strongly about peyote, one stands to lose $30). Asymmetry like this causes inefficiency under majority rule.

[48] 304 U.S. 144, 152 n.4 (1938).

[49] *Id.*

[50] This example resembles one in JAMES M. BUCHANAN & GORDON TULLOCK, THE COLLECTED WORKS OF JAMES M. BUCHANAN, VOL. 3. THE CALCULUS OF CONSENT: LOGICAL FOUNDATIONS OF CONSTITUTIONAL DEMOCRACY 291–92 (1999).

The problem with majority rule is familiar from earlier chapters: externalization. Voting usually changes the law for everyone, including people who oppose the new law. Those opponents pay a cost, but supporters do not internalize that cost. Rational voters consider their own costs and benefits, not everyone's costs and benefits.

"Peculiarly Narrow" Governments

The United States has one federal government, 50 state governments, and tens of thousands of local governments. Many of these governments, including counties and cities, perform multiple functions: police, firefighters, roads, parks, hospitals, and so on. These are "general" units of government. Thousands of other governments perform only one function. School districts manage schools. Gas districts manage natural gas. The Bay Area Rapid Transit District manages commuter trains around San Francisco. These are "special-purpose" districts.

Citizens who live within a general government's borders have a right to vote in its elections. What about citizens who live in a special-purpose government's borders? The answer comes from a case called *Salyer Land Co. v. Tulare Water District*.[51] In California, a water district had just one function: managing water for the district's farms. Landowners in the district could vote in the district's elections under a "one acre–one vote" system. The more acres a person (or company) owned, the more votes he or she (or it) got. Non-landowners—renters who lived in the district, leaseholders who farmed but did not own their land—could not vote. The Supreme Court upheld this arrangement. According to the Court, constitutional protections for voting do not apply to special-purpose governments "whose duties are so far removed from normal governmental activities" and that "disproportionately affect different groups."[52] In *Ball v. James*, the Supreme Court upheld another water district's one-acre, one-vote arrangement, emphasizing the district's "peculiarly narrow function."[53]

These cases are controversial. How can a modern democracy condition the franchise on property ownership? The normative theory of entrenchment has an answer. General units of government make decisions across multiple issues, whereas special units of government make decisions on one issue. Thus, we can situate voters in a special unit of government on a single dimension, as in the previous figures. If a special unit of government disproportionately affects different groups, that might mean that voters on one side of the median care more than voters on the other side of the median. This asymmetry makes majority rule suboptimal. The best policy is "off median." To sustain an off-median policy, the government can entrench it. Alternatively, the government can keep majority rule but adjust the electorate. By

51 410 U.S. 719 (1973).
52 *Id.* at 727–28.
53 451 U.S. 355 (1981).

limiting the franchise to the actors who care the most, the government can align the median with the optimal policy.

To clarify the logic, return to the example involving the use of peyote in religion. The first person would prohibit all peyote use, the second person would permit some, and the third person would permit unlimited use. Because the third person cares much more intensely than the others, the welfare-maximizing law would permit unlimited use. To sustain that law, the state can enact and entrench it with unanimity rule. Alternatively, the state can permit only the third person to vote. If no one else can vote, then the third person is the median voter by definition. Law gravitates to the (new) median's ideal, which is the socially optimal outcome. In special districts, limiting the franchise to disproportionately affected groups is akin to limiting the franchise to the intense supporter of peyote.

This analysis shows how limiting the franchise in special units of government can promote social welfare in theory. Does it promote social welfare in fact? In *Salyer*, the answer depends on whether the landowners who could vote cared more than the non-landowners who could not. Who do you think had more intense preferences: agricultural companies whose profits depended on the district's decisions? Or renters whose homes flooded because of the district's decisions?[54]

C. Stability and Transition Costs

We have shown that entrenchment benefits society when it protects an intense minority from the majority. This helps explain why minority rights are often entrenched, either through constitutions (constitutional rights) or bicameralism and entrenchment (statutory rights). We address rights in the next chapter. Here we consider a puzzle. Many laws that do not appear to involve intense minorities, including laws on mundane topics like speed limits and horsemeat, are entrenched. Why entrench law when preferences seem more-or-less symmetrical? The following sections have an answer.

The Framers of the U.S. Constitution faced a dilemma. They wanted a nimble national government. "Energy in government," Madison wrote, is necessary for "security" and "prompt and salutary execution of the laws."[55] But they also wanted a stable national government. People had suffered under the "vicissitudes and uncertainties" of the states. "Stability in government," Madison declared, "is essential."[56]

[54] Salyer Land Co. v. Tulare Lake Basin Water Storage Dist., 410 U.S. 719, 737–39 (1973) (Douglas, J., concurring in part, dissenting in part) ("[T]his district has had repeated flood control problems. . . . South of Tulare Lake Basin is Buena Vista Lake. In the past, Buena Vista has been used to protect Tulare Lake Basin by storing Kern River water in the former. That is how Tulare Lake Basin was protected from menacing floods in 1952. But that was not done in the great 1969 flood, the result being that 88,000 of the 193,000 acres in respondent district were flooded. The board of the respondent district—dominated by the big landowner J. G. Boswell Co.—voted . . . to table the motion that would put into operation the machinery to divert the flood waters to the Buena Vista Lake. The reason is that J. G. Boswell Co. had a long-term agricultural lease in the Buena Vista Lake Basin and flooding it would have interfered with the planting, growing, and harvesting of crops the next season.").

[55] The Federalist No. 37, at 181 (James Madison) (Ian Shapiro ed., 2009).

[56] *Id.*

Why is stability essential? What value does it produce? Consider some examples. An entrepreneur builds a whiskey distillery. Then the Eighteenth Amendment to the U.S. Constitution passes, prohibiting the manufacture and sale of alcohol. The distillery is worthless. A farmer invests in new cages for chickens. Then voters approve a ballot initiative on animal cruelty. The cages are too small to use. An administrative agency spends years designing a regulation to prevent workplace injuries. Then the legislature passes a statute stripping the agency's authority. In each case changing law squanders an investment. Stable law would preserve the investment.

For lawyers, these examples implicate *reliance interests*. The entrepreneur, the farmer, and the agency relied on existing law when they invested their time and resources. Changing law undermined their reliance interests.

As described, reliance interests are backward-looking. Changing law threatens an investment already undertaken. But reliance interests can also be forward-looking. People have interests in predictability and planning. The entrepreneur and the farmer make predictions before they build distilleries and buy cages. If they predict stable law, they will invest. If they predict unstable law—the law could change anytime, possibly in unfavorable ways—they hesitate. Unpredictability in law creates costs. In 2017, British citizens surprised the world by voting to exit the European Union. Employers, investors, and many others in the United Kingdom and throughout Europe suddenly had to spend time and money planning for uncertainty. Predictability is so important that scholars consider it fundamental to the rule of law.[57]

If stable law benefits society, changing law must cost society. We have focused on one, foundational cost of legal change: the loss of reliance. Now consider another cost: the mechanics of changing law. New laws must be researched, drafted, reviewed, amended, and approved. They must be implemented, which requires training, adaptation, enforcement, and adjudication. To demonstrate, the Affordable Care Act remade the market for health insurance in the United States, causing states, insurers, and millions of consumers to change their behavior. It triggered rule-making by regulators, disputes in court, and at least one statewide ballot initiative.[58]

An earlier chapter labeled all impediments to bargaining "transaction costs." Here we label all harm associated with legal change "transition costs." Transition costs capture the losses to society from changing law.

The Paradox of Compensation

When law changes, people incur transition costs, like the entrepreneur who lost his distillery. The state could pay the entrepreneur for his loss. More generally, the state could compensate people or otherwise ease their legal transitions. For example, if the state enacts stricter pollution laws for power plants, it could pay plants for their losses, subsidize the purchase of new abatement technology, or exempt the plants from the new laws (this is called "grandfathering"). Should

[57] *See, e.g.*, LON L. FULLER, THE MORALITY OF LAW 39 (1964).

[58] *See* Michael D. Gilbert, *Interpreting Initiatives*, 97 MINN. L. REV. 1621, 1621–22 (2013) (describing Issue 3, a ballot initiative that tried unsuccessfully to undercut the individual mandate in the Affordable Care Act and that had other, surprising implications).

the state compensate for transition costs? Many people think the answer is yes. Economists are not sure.[59]

Compensation can distort decisions. To illustrate, suppose a constitutional amendment barring the manufacture of alcohol is pending. There is a 60 percent chance the amendment will pass and a 40 percent chance it will fail. An entrepreneur considers building a whiskey distillery. The expected cost of building and operating the distillery equals 75. If the amendment fails, the distillery will operate and generate revenue of 100. If the amendment passes the distillery will not operate and generate nothing.

The entrepreneur should not build the distillery. The expected cost of 75 exceeds the expected benefit of 40 (0.6*0 + 0.4*100). If the entrepreneur will not receive compensation for the legal transition, then he reasons as previously and does not build the distillery. What if the entrepreneur will receive compensation? Then the entrepreneur reasons like this. There is a 40 percent chance the amendment fails and the distillery operates, earning 100. There is a 60 percent chance the amendment passes and the state pays him 100. Regardless of whether the amendment passes, the entrepreneur will receive 100. Thus, he builds the distillery because his expected benefit of 100 exceeds his expected cost of 75. Building is individually rational but inefficient.[60]

The root problem is externalization. Like an insurance policy, compensation lets the entrepreneur externalize the costs of a legal transition. When people externalize the costs of an activity, they usually do too much of it—here they build too many distilleries. This suggests the state should not compensate for legal transitions.

But there is another side to the story. Suppose the state enacts new regulations on pollution by power plants. Complying requires plants to install scrubbers on their smokestacks. New plants can be designed to accommodate the scrubbers. For new plants, the cost of complying with the regulation equals 5, and the social benefit of cleaner air equals 10. Old plants must be retrofitted to accommodate the scrubbers. For old plants, the cost of complying with the regulation equals 12, and the social benefit of cleaner air equals 10. If the state does not compensate plants for the legal transition, it does not internalize the costs of its regulation. It might require old plants to comply with the regulation even though this produces more costs than benefits. If the state must compensate the plants, then it internalizes the costs of its regulation. The state probably will not pay an old plant 12 to secure cleaner air worth 10. The state will apply the regulation to new plants but not old plants.

To generalize, compensation creates a paradox. Paying for legal transitions creates bad incentives for regulated parties, like distillers. Conversely, not paying for legal

[59] The phrase "paradox of compensation" comes from Robert Cooter, *Unity in Tort, Contract, and Property: The Model of Precaution*, 73 CAL. L. REV. 1 (1985). This discussion draws on Louis Kaplow, *An Economic Analysis of Legal Transitions*, 99 HARV. L. REV. 509 (1986), and Steven Shavell, *On Optimal Legal Change, Past Behavior, and Grandfathering*, 37 J. LEGAL STUD. 37 (2008), which study the paradox in regulatory settings. *See also* DANIEL SHAVIRO, WHEN RULES CHANGE (2000).

[60] Building is inefficient because its expected cost to society of 75 exceeds its expected benefit to society of 40 (remember there is only a 40 percent chance that the distillery can operate). This is true regardless of whether the prohibition on alcohol is a good policy.

transitions creates bad incentives for the state.[61] One party or the other externalizes costs, so one party or the other has bad incentives.

Good public law mitigates the paradox. The state can compare incentives. If compensating power plants leads to worse incentives than not compensating power plants, then the state should not compensate power plants. Alternatively, the state can try a creative solution. To promote efficient behavior, regulated parties and the state should internalize the costs of their decisions. If the state pays compensation, but regulated parties do not receive it, then both parties internalize costs. To illustrate, suppose the state prohibits the manufacture of alcohol, making the distillery worthless. Instead of paying the distiller 100, the state can *burn* 100. Can you explain why burning the money would improve both parties' incentives?[62]

D. Stability and Rationality

We have explained that changing law creates transition costs. If those transition costs are sufficiently high, then law—even unpopular law—should not change. However, many people believe it will change in a democracy. They argue that fickle majorities will change law on a whim, satisfying themselves but destabilizing society. To prevent instability, people argue, entrench the law.

Is this argument right? Start with a simple question: who incurs transition costs? The answer is the people who compose society. If people incur transition costs, they should hesitate to change laws when their transition costs are high. The political scientist Adam Przeworski captured the point: "If people value legal stability, then simple majorities should be hesitant to change laws. . . . [S]imple majority rule is sufficient to prevent capricious legal changes."[63]

One might respond as follows. Given high transition costs, rational people will not change law, but *passionate* people will. In lawmaking, people succumb to passions. In the heat of the moment, they make bad decisions like the Athenians in the Peloponnesian War. Entrenchment protects against shortsighted behavior.

The danger of passion in lawmaking is well known. One can imagine lawmakers impassioned over matters like security, immigration, religion, and abortion. But passion only partly solves the puzzle. Governments entrench laws that do not engender passions. Next to the freedoms of speech and religion, the U.S. Constitution addresses postal roads.[64] In Alabama, the state constitution addresses traffic, bingo, and shrimp sales.[65] Statutes entrenched through bicameralism and presentment address mundane

[61] In theory, making the state pay compensation will force it to internalize the cost of its regulations. In reality, the money for compensation comes from the state's budget, not from regulators' pockets. Consequently, regulators do not fully internalize the costs of their regulations. This might cause them to regulate too much. On the other hand, regulators do not fully internalize the benefits of regulation, and this might cause them to regulate too little. *See generally* Daryl J. Levinson, *Making Government Pay: Markets, Politics, and the Allocation of Constitutional Costs*, 67 U. CHI. L. REV. 345 (2000).

[62] *See* Robert D. Cooter & Ariel Porat, *Anti-Insurance*, 31 J. LEGAL STUD. 203 (2002).

[63] ADAM PRZEWORSKI, DEMOCRACY AND THE LIMITS OF SELF-GOVERNMENT 139 (2010).

[64] *See* U.S. CONST. art. I, § 8(7).

[65] ALA. CONST. amends. 756, 743, 744, 766.

topics like government leases.[66] Passions cannot justify the widespread entrenchment we observe in practice.

We develop an economic justification for entrenchment.[67] Rather than passions, our theory involves transition costs and externalities. We can demonstrate the theory with an example. Suppose the majority approves higher taxes. The majority benefits from the policy change, and the minority suffers. Separate from those gains and losses, which result from the policy change itself, changing taxes creates transition costs. When the sales tax rises, people adjust their behavior, and this creates transition costs. For example, they might spend time and effort searching for cheaper stores. Suppose the majority can force the minority to bear all transition costs. Thus, the minority faces a double loss: they suffer from the policy change, and they suffer from the transition costs. That double loss might outweigh the benefit to the majority. Nevertheless, members of the majority will support the change because they only see benefits, not costs. The majority externalizes the minority's losses.

In that example, the majority forced the minority to pay all transition costs. In reality, transition costs may be hard to externalize (can someone pay your cost of adjusting to a new sales tax?). Consider an example without that kind of externalization. Four of seven voters, a majority, support a change in law. For them the change would provide a benefit of one apiece. The other three voters oppose the change in law, as it would come with a cost of one apiece. Separate from those gains and losses, which follow from the substance of the new law, the change would come with a transition cost. The transition cost is 0.25 apiece. For the majority, the change in law delivers a net benefit of 0.75 apiece, so they support it. For members of the minority, the change in law delivers a net loss of 1.25 apiece, so they oppose it. If law is not entrenched, the majority will enact the change, harming society. The gains to the majority total 3 (0.75 * 4), but the losses to the minority total 3.75 (1.25 * 3).

To generalize, transition costs create an asymmetry between the winners and losers from a change in law. The majority supporting the new law gain the *difference* between their benefit from the new law and the transition cost they pay. The minority opposing the change suffer the *sum* of their loss from the new law and the transition cost they pay. Each loser loses more than each winner wins. Given this asymmetry, majority rule can harm society.

We have already seen how asymmetry in payoffs can make majority rule inefficient (remember the peyote example). The difference here is the mechanism: transition costs. Transition costs do not involve minorities with intense preferences over policy. In the seven-voter example we just presented, each voter gained or lost one from the change in the substance of law, meaning no one felt more intensely than anyone else. Transition costs do not involve extractions, as when the majority taxes the minority to build its road. The seven-voter example did not involve redistribution.

Transition costs are ubiquitous. Some changes to law redistribute to the majority, and some changes to law involve intense minorities. Nearly *all* changes to law involve

[66] *See* 38 U.S.C. § 8103(d)(3)(A) ("The Secretary [of Veterans' Affairs] may enter into a lease for the use of any facility described in paragraph (2)(B) of this subsection for not more than 35 years[.]").

[67] This discussion is based on Michael D. Gilbert, *The Law and Economics of Entrenchment*, 54 Ga. L. Rev. 61 (2019).

transition costs. This implies that many changes to law have asymmetric benefits and costs.

In sum, voters may approve welfare-reducing changes to law—even when they rationally account for their own transition costs, and even when no intense minority is present. This helps justify the widespread use of entrenchment, whether through supermajority rules or other means. The stability justification holds even when passions run cold.

Questions

6.18. Colorado enacts many laws through ballot initiatives. In 2016, Colorado raised the voting threshold for enacting ballot initiatives from a bare majority to 55 percent. Defend this change.

6.19. Apply the Public Coase Theorem to the seven-voter example where transition costs equal 0.25 apiece. How can bargaining prevent the majority from enacting the welfare-reducing law?

6.20. Entrenchment protects intense minorities and stabilizes law. Are these justifications for entrenchment distinct, or are they the same?

E. On Optimal Entrenchment

We have explained how transition costs can make majority rule inefficient. Entrenchment can prevent inefficiency by making law harder to change. But what level of entrenchment is optimal? Should lawmakers operate under, say, a two-thirds or three-quarters voting rule? Here we sketch an answer.[68]

Transition costs divide into two categories, fixed and variable. Fixed costs accrue in the same amount every time law changes, whether the change is small or large. For example, suppose a state changes its sales tax. Every cash register in the state must be reprogrammed, but reprogramming costs the same amount of time and money whether the rate changes by one percentage point or 10. Likewise, elections officials must change their forms and procedures if the voting age jumps from 18 to 19 or to 29. Any change to a program like Social Security (government payments to older people) interjects a baseline of insecurity for recipients.

Variable costs accrue with the magnitude of legal change. As the sales tax rises, consumers make increasingly drastic changes to their consumption patterns. As the voting age rises, politicians make greater changes to their platforms, and citizens make greater adjustments to their lives in anticipation of new representation and policies. Slashing Social Security causes more disruption than trimming it.

Figure 6.8 adds transition costs to our analysis of seven voters.[69] The status quo law matches *j*. The curve shows the benefits of moving law toward the political center. Voters have symmetrically intense preferences, so the curve peaks at *m*. The four lines reflect

[68] *Id.* at 61.
[69] This figure resembles one in *id.* at 94.

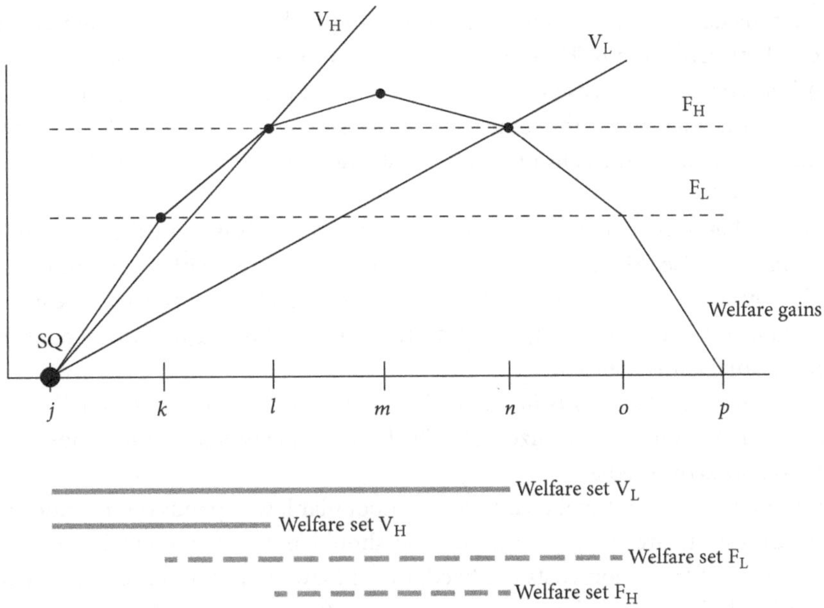

Figure 6.8. Transition Costs and Social Welfare

transition costs. The upward-sloping lines V_L and V_H show variable transition costs.[70] Starting at *j*, transition costs grow as law moves further to the right. The flat lines F_L and F_H show fixed transition costs. With fixed costs, the magnitude of legal change does not matter. Moving from *j* to any other point always creates the same cost.

To begin, focus on the line V_L (the subscript stands for "low"). Moving law from the status quo at *j* to the right creates benefits indicated by the curve and transition costs indicated by V_L. The benefit curve lies above V_L between *j* and *n*. Thus, moving law from *j* to any point between *j* and *n* creates a net benefit. The points between *j* and *n* are the *welfare set*. Every point in the welfare set represents an improvement over the status quo. However, only one point represents the best improvement: *l*. Starting at *j*, moving law to *l* creates the largest net benefit. The largest net benefit is achieved when the gap between the benefit curve and the cost line is maximized.

Suppose that stability in law becomes more valuable. This is equivalent to saying that transition costs increase. In Figure 6.8, V_H (the subscript means "high") replaces V_L. Starting at *j*, any move rightward comes with a higher cost than before. The increase in transition costs shrinks the welfare set. Given V_L, the welfare set stretched from *j* to *n*, but given V_H, it stretches from *j* to *l*. Every point in the new welfare set represents an improvement over the status quo at *j*. The point representing the best improvement over the status quo is *k*.

To generalize, *when variable transition costs increase, the welfare set recedes toward the status quo*. Given variable transition costs, law should modernize incrementally. As variable costs increase, the optimal changes to law get smaller.

[70] To simplify, we assume that variable transition costs are linear. Nonlinearity would not affect the basic analysis as long as the function is monotonic.

Now consider fixed transition costs, beginning with line F_L. The benefit curve lies above F_L between *k* and *o*. Thus, moving law from the status quo at *j* to any point between *k* and *o* would increase welfare. The point with the greatest net payoff is *m*. This is intuitive: the fixed cost is the same whether the law moves a little or a lot. Meanwhile, the benefit is greatest when law moves all the way to the median. So move the law all the way to the median.

Suppose that stability in law becomes more valuable. This is equivalent to saying that transition costs rise. Figure 6.8 captures this by replacing F_L with F_H. From the status quo of *j*, any change in law comes with a higher cost than before. The increase in transition costs shrinks the welfare set; now it stretches from *l* to *n*. The welfare set has shrunk, but the optimal law remains *m*.

In general, *when fixed costs increase, the welfare set collapses on the median*. Given fixed costs, law should modernize fully. The best change to law requires moving from the status quo to the median.

To summarize, the optimal change to an unpopular law depends on transition costs. If transition costs are variable, the old law should move incrementally toward the modern ideal. If transition costs are fixed, the old law should move all the way to the modern ideal. Of course, if transition costs are sufficiently high, then law should not change at all.

We have analyzed what changes *should* be made to law. What changes *can* be made to law? The answer depends on the amendment rule. Figure 6.9 combines Figures 6.3 and 6.8.[71] The law starts at *j*. The win sets on top indicate the possible changes to that status quo law under different voting rules.[72] The wins sets reflect the incrementalism principle. As entrenchment deepens, the set of possible changes to law collapses on the status quo. Moving law rightward from *j* would create benefits and costs. The welfare sets on bottom indicate the net beneficial changes to law. As before, welfare sets with the label "*V*" assume variable transition costs, and welfare sets with the label "*F*" assume fixed transition costs.

Comparing welfare sets and win sets reveals some important features of entrenchment. Let's start with variable transitions costs. As variable costs increase, the solid welfare sets on bottom collapse on the status quo law at *j*. As entrenchment deepens, the win sets on top collapse on the status quo at *j*. Thus, the changes to law we *should* make correspond to the changes we *can* make.

Given variable transition costs, entrenchment has two benefits, not one. It prevents law from changing when, because of transition costs, law should not change. And it encourages optimal reform when law should change. The win sets and welfare sets align.

Now consider fixed transition costs. As fixed costs increase, the dashed welfare sets on bottom collapse on the median at *m*. As entrenchment deepens, the win sets on top collapse on the status quo at *j*. A wedge opens between the changes to law we *should*

[71] Figure 6.9 resembles one in Michael D. Gilbert, *The Law and Economics of Entrenchment*, 54 GA. L. REV. 61, 98 (2019).

[72] In Figure 6.9, all three win sets imply that the group would vote to move law from *j* to points just right of *j*. In fact, voters might not support such a change. The transition cost each voter pays might outweigh his or her benefit from such a minor policy improvement. We ignore this possibility. We draw the wins sets as if the voters ignore their transition costs when voting. This simplifies the figure without affecting our basic conclusions. *See id.* at 107–09 (2019).

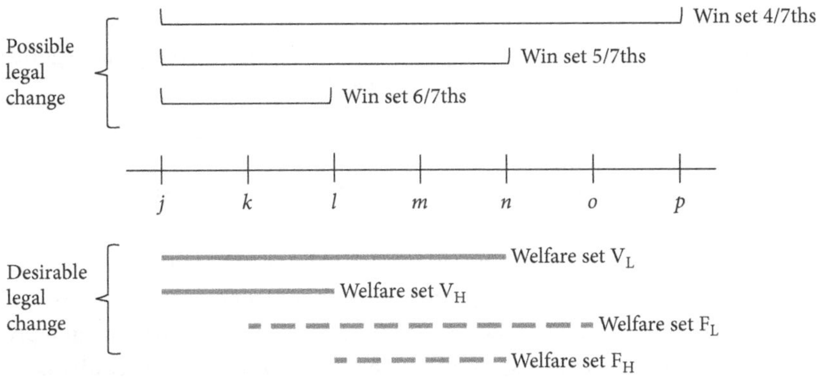

Figure 6.9. Optimal Legal Change

make and the changes to law we *can* make. To see this starkly, suppose fixed transition costs are high (F_H) and the voters use a 6/7s voting rule. The "welfare set F_H" shows beneficial changes to law, and the "win set 6/7ths" shows possible changes to law. They do not overlap. Every possible change to law would create more costs than benefits.

This uncovers a flaw in entrenchment. Given fixed transition costs, entrenchment can encourage welfare-*reducing* changes to law. To appreciate the depth of this problem, consider a thought experiment. A law is outdated. A legal designer with power to choose an amendment rule for that law is told that legal stability is very valuable. In other words, transition costs are high. The legal designer's intuition is to deepen entrenchment to keep the law steady. But if transition costs are fixed, this intuition might lead to the wrong decision. To overcome the fixed transition costs, law must move a lot, not a little. To ensure that law moves a lot, the best decision is to entrench *less*, not more.

In sum, optimal entrenchment depends on transition costs. Variable transition costs support smaller legal change and deeper entrenchment, while fixed transition costs support larger legal change and shallower entrenchment.

Questions

6.21. "As the value of stable law increases, entrenchment should always deepen." What is wrong with this statement?

6.22. In *Furman v. Georgia*, the Supreme Court held that states were administering the death penalty in an unconstitutional way.[73] Afterward, many states enacted new laws on the death penalty. Did the Court's decision generate fixed transition costs, variable transition costs, or both?

6.23. The Real ID Act established new federal standards for state identification cards, like drivers' licenses. To board a commercial airplane or enter a federal building, people's state IDs must meet the federal standard. Does changing the federal standard create fixed or variable transition costs?

[73] 408 U.S. 238 (1972).

6.24. The human rights in Ghana's constitution are harder to amend than other provisions in Ghana's constitution. Are "tiered" amendment rules a good idea? Which parts of the constitution should be hardest to amend?[74]

III. Interpretive Theory of Entrenchment

We have analyzed when and why law should be entrenched. Most lawyers, however, do not consider such questions. They consider what entrenched law means. To illustrate, lawyers ask if the Second Amendment to the U.S. Constitution, which protects the right to keep and bear arms, prevents the government from requiring trigger locks on rifles.[75] Lawyers do not ask if the voting threshold for amending the Second Amendment should be higher or lower. Does the theory of entrenchment help interpretation? We think the answer is yes. Our discussion of entrenchment illuminates a question of interpretation that lawyers and judges face every day: Should we follow precedent?

A. On Precedent

To interpret a law, lawyers consider its text, structure, and history. They also consider precedents, meaning prior decisions about the law's meaning. The principle of *stare decisis* directs judges to follow precedents. If an earlier court concluded that a law forbids the use of peyote, today's court should reach the same conclusion.

Stare decisis promotes stability in law.[76] This gives it independent force in legal arguments. Even if the earlier court erred (or arguably erred) when analyzing the law's text, structure, or history, stability supplies a reason to follow the court's precedent. As Justice Louis Brandeis wrote, "*Stare decisis* is usually the wise policy, because in most matters it is more important that the applicable rule of law be settled than that it be settled right."[77]

Stare decisis works better in theory than practice. Identifying precedents is hard. Does a case about boat accidents set a precedent for cases about car, bicycle, or skiing accidents? Does a case in New York set a precedent for cases in Connecticut? We defer questions like these and focus on a different point. Stare decisis is a rule of thumb, not a command. Judges should follow a precedent unless the precedent is wrong and correcting it would not cause too much trouble.

Consider some examples of the U.S. Supreme Court's treatment of precedents. In 1922, the Court considered whether federal antitrust law applied to professional baseball leagues. Congress can regulate commerce between states but not commerce within states. Thus, the question was whether professional baseball constituted in*ter*state or

[74] *See* David Landau & Rosalind Dixon, *Tiered Constitutional Design*, 86 Geo. Wash. L. Rev. 438 (2018).

[75] District of Columbia v. Heller, 554 U.S. 570 (2008).

[76] According to the U.S. Supreme Court, stare decisis "promotes the evenhanded, predictable, and consistent development of legal principles" and "fosters reliance on judicial decisions." Payne v. Tennessee, 501 U.S. 808, 827 (1991).

[77] Burnet v. Coronado Oil & Gas Co., 285 U.S. 393, 406 (1932) (Brandeis, J., dissenting).

in*tra*state commerce. The Court concluded the latter. Although players and coaches crossed state lines, the "essential thing" was the exhibition, a "purely state" affair.[78] Thus, federal antitrust law did not apply to baseball. In 1953, the Court considered the same issue and gave the same answer.[79]

Then the Court changed course. It held that professional boxing, football, and basketball involve in*ter*state commerce, so federal antitrust law applied. Meanwhile, technology evolved. Radio and television made sporting events in one state accessible to audiences in many states. In 1972, in a case called *Flood v. Kuhn*, the Court considered yet again whether professional baseball constituted interstate commerce and was therefore subject to federal antitrust law.[80] Developments in other sports and technology indicated the answer was yes, but the Court's precedents indicated the answer was no. The Court followed the precedents and held that baseball remained exempt from the antitrust laws. Baseball's exemption, the Court wrote, is an "aberration that has been with us now for half a century" and is "fully entitled to the benefit of stare decisis."[81]

In *Flood*, the Court placed a lot of weight on stare decisis. Now consider a case where the Court did the opposite. For decades, laws regulated how corporations spent money on political activities. In general, corporations could not use their treasuries to make so-called independent expenditures (for example, television ads promoting a candidate). In *Austin v. Michigan Chamber of Commerce*, a litigant argued that these laws violate the First Amendment.[82] The Court disagreed, concluding that corporate spending has a "corrosive and distorting" effect on politics that outweighs the First Amendment concerns.[83] Consequently, states could limit corporate political spending.

Twenty years later, the Court reconsidered. In *Citizens United v. Federal Election Commission*, the Court concluded that the First Amendment grants corporations a right to engage in political speech.[84] Thus, the state cannot prevent corporations from funding things like television ads supporting candidates. In overruling *Austin*, Chief Justice Roberts wrote:

> Fidelity to precedent—the policy of *stare decisis*—is vital to the proper exercise of the judicial function. . . . At the same time, *stare decisis* is neither an inexorable command . . . nor a mechanical formula of adherence to the latest decision. . . . *Stare decisis* is instead a principle of policy. When considering whether to reexamine a prior erroneous holding, we must balance the importance of having constitutional questions *decided* against the importance of having them *decided right*.[85]

The formula seems right, but what about the application? Was the Court right to reject precedent in *Citizens United* and follow precedent in *Flood*? Or did the Court get it backward?

[78] Fed. Baseball Club v. Nat'l League, 259 U.S. 200 (1922).
[79] Toolson v. New York Yankees, Inc., 346 U.S. 356 (1953).
[80] 407 U.S. 258 (1972).
[81] *Id.* at 282.
[82] 494 U.S. 652 (1990).
[83] *Id.* at 660.
[84] 558 U.S. 310 (2010).
[85] *Id.* at 377–78 (2010) (Roberts, J., concurring) (internal quotation marks and citations omitted).

B. The Transitions Theory of Interpretation

A main purpose of stare decisis is to promote stability in law. Thus, stare decisis substitutes for entrenchment. Law does not require the Supreme Court to use a supermajority voting rule, an intriguing possibility we discuss later. Instead, law requires the Court to consider the dangers of instability when contemplating a break with precedent. As Chief Justice Roberts wrote, judges "must balance the importance of having constitutional questions *decided* against the importance of having them decided *right*." We can translate this idea into economic language. *Courts should follow precedent when the transition costs of rejecting the precedent exceed the benefits of error correction, and vice versa.* This is how stare decisis directs judges to make decisions. In other words, this is what law requires judges to do. Thus, the statement is interpretive, not normative.

We have sharpened the language but not the inquiry. To make progress we deploy the aforementioned analysis. In Figure 6.10, *P* reflects the precedent, meaning the status quo interpretation. For example, *P* could reflect the holding in *Austin* that the First Amendment allows the state to regulate corporate political speech. Suppose that interpretation is incorrect. The Court should have held that the state cannot regulate corporate political speech.[86] The correct outcome is indicated with *A*. Rejecting *P* and replacing it with *A* would create a *correction benefit* indicated by the solid curve. "Correction benefit" is the value to society from properly interpreting law. The correction benefit peaks when the actual interpretation matches the correct interpretation.

Replacing the precedent with a new interpretation would create a transition cost indicated by the upward-sloping line. Switching from *P* to *A* would create more costs than benefits, as the figure indicates. Between *P* and *A*, stare decisis directs courts to follow the precedent *P*, even though the precedent is incorrect.

Suppose *A* is not the only plausible interpretation. The interpretation at *B* also finds support in legal materials like text, structure, and history. If *B* is the correct interpretation, then moving law to *B* would create a correction benefit indicated by the dashed curve. If *B* is the correct interpretation, then the precedent *P* makes a small rather than a large error. The benefit of correcting a small error is limited, so the dashed curve has a lower peak than the solid curve. The correction benefit from moving law to *B* exceeds the transition cost, so stare decisis directs judges to reject *P* and select *B*.

In reality, judges do not know the benefits of error correction or the costs of legal transitions. Graphs like Figure 6.10 do not appear in lawyers' briefs. Instead, judges rely on intuitions. Our analysis sharpens intuitions.

Should we maintain an erroneous precedent or correct it? When confronting this question, judges should ask themselves not only whether correcting the law would create transition costs (the answer is almost certainly yes). They should ask themselves about the nature of those transition costs. Do they seem mostly fixed or mostly variable? If they seem mostly fixed, then judges should retain the precedent or make a large correction. Conversely, if transition costs seem mostly variable, then judges should retain the precedent or make a small correction. These are not normative statements about

[86] We assume this only for the purpose of analysis. The legal soundness of the decisions in *Austin* and *Citizens United* is controversial, and we take no positions on those cases.

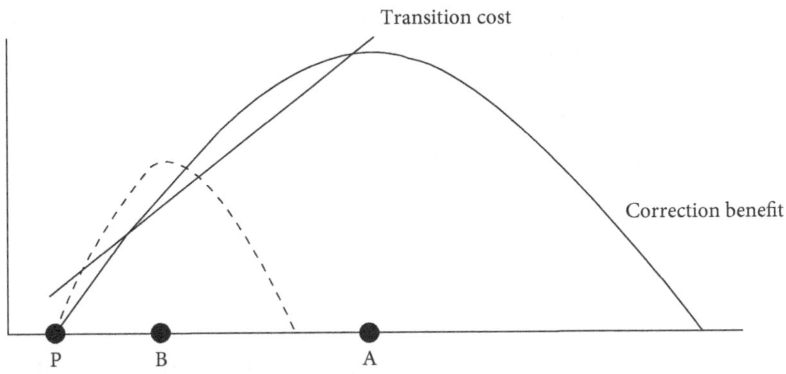

Figure 6.10. Stare Decisis

how we prefer judges to behave. These are interpretative statements about how stare decisis requires judges to behave. This is a *transitions theory of interpretation*.

The transitions theory does not identify correct outcomes for every case. Because transition costs are unobservable, judges will make mistakes. However, the transitions theory should reduce mistakes by sweeping away bad options.

Apply the transitions theory of interpretation to *Flood*. According to the precedent, existing federal antitrust law did not apply to baseball. Suppose the Supreme Court had multiple options: follow the precedent, hold that the law imposed minor constraints on baseball, or hold that the law applied to baseball in full. We believe that the second and third options would have created a large fixed cost. Changing course by holding that existing law applied to baseball could upend the industry. For decades, baseball developed free from that existing law, just like the Court in *Flood* said. Given a large fixed cost, the transitions theory directs judges to avoid small corrections. In fact, the Court did not consider a small correction. It chose between following the precedent and making a large correction (holding that existing antitrust law applied to baseball in full). Because we cannot observe transition costs, we cannot say if the Court in *Flood* made the right choice by following precedent. But the transitions theory suggests the Court chose among the best options.

Now consider *Citizens United*. The precedent permitted major regulation of corporate political speech (the government could prohibit it). The Court chose between following the precedent and an interpretation permitting almost no regulation of corporate political speech.[87] This constituted a large correction. We believe a large correction in this area of law created variable transition costs. The freer corporations can spend, the greater the adjustments by corporations and other actors in the political system, including candidates, political parties, interest groups, and lobbyists. Given variable costs, the transitions theory directs judges to avoid large corrections. The Court rejected the precedent and made a large correction.

[87] This is a simplification. Citizens United permits a particular kind of regulation of corporate political speech, which is mandated disclosure. *See* Daniel R. Ortiz, *The Informational Interest*, 27 J.L. & Pol. 663 (2012).

Because we cannot observe transition costs, we cannot say if the Court in *Citizens United* made the wrong choice. But the transitions theory suggests the Court did not choose among the best options. Perhaps the Court should have made the smaller correction suggested by four dissenting Justices. They argued that the First Amendment does not forbid regulation of any corporate political speech. It forbids regulation of political speech by nonprofit corporations that receive little or no funding from business.[88]

Questions

6.25. The common law developed incrementally over time, with judges making small adjustments to the rules of contracts, property, and torts. Some scholars say that constitutional law develops the same way.[89] Observers applaud courts for being cautious, minimalist, and incremental. Given the transitions theory of interpretation, should courts always be cautious, minimalist, and incremental?

6.26. In *Roe v. Wade*, the Supreme Court held that the Constitution protects a woman's right to have an abortion.[90] Thus, the Court severely limited the government's authority to regulate abortion. Twenty years later, the Court reconsidered in a case called *Planned Parenthood v. Casey*.[91] The Court in *Casey* could have followed *Roe*, or it could have rejected it entirely by holding that the Constitution does not protect a woman's right to have an abortion. Instead, the Justices chose a middle path. They permitted regulations that do not pose an "undue burden" on a woman's ability to have an abortion. Use the transitions theory of interpretation to analyze *Casey*.

Statutory Stare Decisis

Citizens United involved a constitutional precedent. An earlier case established a precedent about the meaning of the Constitution, and the Court in *Citizens United* decided not to follow it. *Flood* involved a statutory precedent. An earlier case established that a statute, the Sherman Act, does not apply to professional baseball. The question in *Flood* was whether to sustain that interpretation of the statute or adopt a new one.

In the United States, stare decisis operates with extra force in statutory cases. In other words, statutory precedents have more influence in subsequent cases than constitutional precedents. Why? One justification involves acquiescence. Unlike constitutional precedents, legislators can override statutory precedents. When the Court held that the Sherman Act does not apply to baseball, Congress could have responded by amending the Sherman Act so that it does apply to baseball.[92] When

[88] Citizens United v. Fed. Election Comm'n, 558 U.S. 310 (2010) (Stevens, J., concurring in part, dissenting in part).

[89] *See* David A. Strauss, *Common Law Constitutional Interpretation*, 63 U. Chi. L. Rev. 877 (1996).

[90] 410 U.S. 113 (1973).

[91] 505 U.S. 833 (1992).

[92] To be clear, Congress could not have done this in 1922, which is when the Supreme Court first considered this question. At that time the Court considered baseball *intra*state commerce, and Congress cannot regulate

legislators do not respond in this way—when they let interpretations of statutes stand—judges say they "acquiesce." Acquiescence suggests that a precedent is correct and should be followed, or so goes the argument.

Consider a different reason for statutory stare decisis: information. Changes to law come with benefits and costs. This is so regardless of the source of legal change. Thus, courts create benefits and costs when they replace old interpretations with new ones, and legislators create benefits and costs when they replace old statutes with new ones. The Affordable Care Act, for example, altered the health plans of millions of consumers. No one can measure these benefits and costs with precision, so everyone relies on intuitions. Who has better intuitions, a handful of cloistered judges, or hundreds of elected legislators who talk to lobbyists and voters? Probably the latter.

In addition to information, legislators have another advantage over judges: they can legislate prospectively. The Affordable Care Act changed health insurance going forward. The old law applied before, and the new law applied after. Statutes are usually prospective, not retroactive. In contrast, interpretation by judges is usually both. In *Citizens United*, the Court held that corporations have a right to political speech. This not only meant corporations have the right going forward. It meant corporations *always* had the right in the past.

Retroactive changes to law usually create more transition costs than purely prospective changes. To illustrate, suppose the Court in *Flood* had reached the opposite conclusion. Then past and future baseball transactions would be subject to antitrust laws. If Congress changed the law by statute, then only future baseball transactions would be subject to antitrust laws. This helps explain why the Court in *Flood* wrote that "the remedy" to baseball's exemption "is for congressional, and not judicial, action."[93]

Legislators usually have better information and act prospectively. This suggests that legislators are better than judges at minimizing the transition costs of legal change. Does this mean courts should always follow statutory precedents? Or should they update statutes like they update the Constitution? These questions connect to acquiescence. We address them later.

Conclusion

Law should align with the political center when voters have symmetrical preferences. Conversely, law should deviate from the political center when voters have asymmetrical preferences. Entrenchment stabilizes law that deviates from the political center by creating an equilibrium set. The size of the equilibrium set grows with the depth of entrenchment and the heterogeneity of voters. Equilibrium sets promote social welfare by protecting intense minorities from the majority and preventing legal changes for which transition costs exceed the benefits.

intrastate commerce. Later it became clear that baseball was *inter*state commerce. At that point, Congress could have amended the federal antitrust law to apply to baseball.

[93] 407 U.S. 258, 285 (1972).

Equilibrium sets come at a price. Law in equilibrium cannot change, even if voters' preferences evolve and change becomes optimal. When law falls out of equilibrium, entrenchment forces it to change incrementally, even if dramatic change is best. Optimal entrenchment balances these considerations and others, notably the variable or fixed character of transition costs.

These ideas illuminate the design of new laws. They also illuminate the interpretation of existing laws. When interpreting constitutions, statutes, regulations, and the common law, judges weigh the benefit from correcting a legal error against the cost of a legal transition. The theory of entrenchment clarifies this choice.

The next chapter applies these principles to concrete legal problems involving rights, special governments, and other matters.

7
Entrenchment Applications

In the previous chapter we studied entrenchment dispassionately, like scientists in a lab. In reality, lawmakers often practice entrenchment like battlefield surgeons. Hamilton awaited adoption of the U.S. Constitution with "trembling anxiety."[1] Decades later, Lincoln pushed the Thirteenth Amendment through Congress during the Civil War. Sometimes judges interpreting entrenched laws face similar pressures. During World War II, the U.S. Supreme Court had to decide if the Constitution permitted the government to force Japanese Americans into camps.[2]

This chapter applies the theory of entrenchment to pressing problems in and out of court. We concentrate on problems involving rights, the archetype of entrenched law. We address questions like these:

Example 1: Same-sex couples have a right to marry in the United States. Thus, the state cannot refuse them wedding certificates. Can a baker refuse them wedding cakes?[3] Should the answer depend on whether the baker has a monopoly on wedding cakes?

Example 2: Many states have enacted laws prohibiting obscene material, like pornographic books. These laws might violate rights like speech and expression. In *Roth v. United States*, Justice Harlan suggested that whether one state could ban obscenity depends on whether obscenity is permitted in other states.[4] Should rights be contingent like Justice Harlan suggested, or should rights be universal?

Example 3: In *New York Times v. Sullivan*, the Supreme Court made it hard to sue journalists for defamation.[5] The Court's decision was meant to make debate on public issues "uninhibited, robust, and wide-open."[6] Does the Court's decision increase or decrease the supply of fake news?

Example 4: The Equal Rights Amendment to the U.S. Constitution sought to give women equal treatment in matters like employment and property. The amendment failed to pass.[7] Around the same time, the Supreme Court began subjecting laws that discriminated on the basis of sex heightened review, meaning more were struck down. Some people connect these events. They say that the Supreme

[1] The Federalist No. 85, at 445 (Alexander Hamilton) (Ian Shapiro ed., 2009).

[2] Korematsu v. United States, 323 U.S. 214 (1944).

[3] *See* Masterpiece Cakeshop, Ltd. v. Colorado Civil Rights Comm'n, 138 S. Ct. 1719 (2018).

[4] 354 U.S. 476, 506 (1957) (Harlan, J., concurring in part and dissenting in part) ("The fact that the people of one State cannot read some of the works of D. H. Lawrence seems to me, if not wise or desirable, at least acceptable. But that no person in the United States should be allowed to do so seems to me to be intolerable, and violative of both the letter and spirit of the First Amendment.").

[5] 376 U.S. 254 (1964).

[6] *Id.* at 270.

[7] To be precise, it failed to pass in the allotted time. It eventually passed with Virginia's ratification. *See generally* Saikrishna Bangalore Prakash, *Of Synchronicity and Supreme Law*, 132 Harv. L. Rev. 1220 (2019).

Public Law and Economics. Robert D. Cooter and Michael D. Gilbert, Oxford University Press. © Oxford University Press 2022.
DOI: 10.1093/oso/9780197655870.003.0007

Court's decisions reduced demand for the amendment. Should the Court be celebrated or condemned for protecting women's rights?

To answer these questions, this chapter combines positive, normative, and interpretive analysis. It begins by defining and justifying an important type of entrenched law: rights. Then it addresses the geographic reach of rights: should they be local, national, or universal? Afterward we analyze two rights in detail, equality and speech. Finally, we analyze whether courts should "update" rights and other entrenched laws through interpretation.

I. Rights

Some trace rights to the Magna Carta, which King John of England signed in 1215. Others trace rights to Cyrus the Great, who ruled Mesopotamia in the sixth century BC. Whatever their origin, rights have long been central to the rule of law. Why? To answer this question, we define rights, and then we relate them to familiar concepts: entrenchment, bargaining, and representation.

A. Definitions of Rights

Rights are a multipurpose tool in the box of legal concepts.[8] Some rights are entitlements created by a duty. To illustrate, the promisor's duty to perform on a contract creates the promisee's right to performance. In this case, someone is entitled to a benefit because someone else has a duty to provide it. Instead of a contract, a statute can impose the duty creating the right. To illustrate, a law that forbids employers from interfering with unionization gives workers the right to organize into unions.

These rights have a clear practical effect when the person with the right can obtain a legal remedy for violation of the duty. To illustrate, the victim of breach of contract can sue for damages, and workers can seek an injunction against their employer's interfering with their efforts to organize a union. In general, law strengthens a right whenever it supplies a remedy for breach of the associated duty.

These "work-a-day" rights are ubiquitous and important. However, when people speak of "rights" they often mean something grander. They mean special rights enshrined in constitutions like the freedom of speech, press, assembly, and religion. These rights protect individual autonomy. They give the individual a zone of discretion to make life's fundamental choices without interference from the state. Individual rights provide the legal foundation for a society of autonomous people.

We refer to rights that provide autonomy as *liberties*. Two aspects of law help to secure liberty. First, the individual who possesses a liberty is neither obligated nor forbidden to do the act in question. Second, other people are generally forbidden to interfere with the liberty's exercise. To illustrate, a person who enjoys freedom of speech is not legally obligated to keep silent or to speak, and, if he chooses to speak, he is not legally

[8] This discussion draws on ROBERT COOTER, THE STRATEGIC CONSTITUTION 244–46 (2000).

obligated to say anything in particular. He has *permission* to speak. Furthermore, other people are prohibited from interfering with his speech, for example, by silencing him with threats. His autonomy to speak is *protected*. Given this logic, a liberty can be defined as a protected permission.

Are liberties absolute? Some defenders of liberty say yes. Many libertarians, for example, believe that liberties trump other values. An economist might disagree. For many economists, liberties trade off against other values. To illustrate, the Fourth Amendment to the U.S. Constitution prohibits "unreasonable searches and seizures." A libertarian might argue that the Fourth Amendment always forbids police from using a radar that "sees" through the walls of a home. To an economist, whether the Fourth Amendment forbids the radar might depend on things like the dangerousness of the person inside. Economists might view liberties as *presumptively* protected permissions, not absolutely protected permissions.

We have sketched some simple concepts of rights. Philosophers have offered many refinements and distinctions, including natural rights, group rights, human rights, and civil rights.[9] Though important and interesting, we do not focus on these matters. Instead, we focus on connections between rights and economics.

B. Rights and Entrenchment

The prior chapter discussed three justifications for entrenchment: to stabilize law, cool passions, and protect minorities. We united these justifications with the concept of credible commitments. In some areas of law, credible commitments by the state not to do certain things are especially important, perhaps because the temptation to do those things is especially strong. We can understand many constitutional rights in these terms. Rights represent important commitments by the state, and entrenching them in constitutions makes them credible.

To illustrate, many constitutions protect the right to private property. Ireland's constitution forbids the government from "abolish[ing] the right of private ownership or the general right to transfer, bequeath, and inherit property."[10] The U.S. Constitution forbids the government from taking private property without paying compensation.[11] Property rights protect minorities, as when the state seeks to seize land from a poor community to build a road. Furthermore, property rights stabilize law. Whether cold and calculating or consumed by passions, the party in power might like to change the law and expropriate the property of its rivals. Entrenchment makes this difficult.

Entrenchment protects rights, but usually the protection has limits. A sufficiently large group can take away a right by amending the constitution. Why not make rights unamendable? An earlier chapter explained that making law too hard to amend raises transaction costs. Like other people, constitutional drafters resist making agreements that

[9] *See, e.g.*, Wesley Newcomb Hohfeld, Fundamental Legal Conceptions as Applied in Judicial Reasoning (1919); Max Radin, *A Restatement of Hohfeld*, 51 Harv. L. Rev. 1141 (1938); Georg Henrik von Wright, Norm and Action (1963); Carl Wellman, A Theory of Rights: Persons under Laws, Institutions and Morals (1985); William A. Edmundson, An Introduction to Rights (2d ed. 2012).

[10] Const. of Ireland art. 43.

[11] *See* U.S. Const. amend. V.

they cannot undo. A later chapter explains that unamendable laws give judges power—perhaps too much. Here we focus on a different reason for avoiding unamendable rights.

Like many laws, rights are generalizations. Consider the freedom of religion. The right protects all religions, but in practice it often matters most for religious minorities. Protecting religious minorities is usually a good idea, but not always. Consider the "I Am" religious movement started by Guy Ballard in the 1930s. I Am followers should be permitted to worship Ballard as a divine messenger, but they should not be permitted to sell Ballard's "supernatural" healing powers to naïve consumers.[12] I Am should enjoy some but not total religious freedom. A broad right to religion could empower the I Am movement to defraud consumers, and if the right were unamendable, lawmakers could not solve the problem. Given amendable rights, they can.

What should it take to overcome a generalization? Consider an example. A legislature consists of 29 people. Fifteen members, a majority, would like to enact a new law limiting the minority's religious liberty. The other 14 members, who are part of the religious minority, oppose the law. Minorities often gain more from exercising their religion than majorities gain from restricting it. Consequently, permitting 15 members to change the law might reduce social welfare. If the 15 supporters gain one apiece from the law and the 14 opponents lose just 1.1 apiece from the law, then the law creates gains of 15 and losses of 15.4. Support from 15 legislators should not overcome the generalization that restricting a religious minority does more harm than good. To ensure that 15 legislators cannot restrict the minority, law might entrench the freedom of religion in the constitution. Instead of majority support, restricting religion might require, say, three-fourths support. Given a three-fourths rule, limiting religion would require support from 22 of the 29 legislators. If 22 legislators want to restrict a religious minority, then perhaps the generalization should be overcome. The gains to a majority that large might outweigh the losses to a minority that small.

This example draws on the theory from the prior chapter. Sometimes even entrenched law should change. For an economist, the natural question is whether changing the law creates a net gain in utility. As the proportion of people favoring the change grows, the probability of a net gain in utility increases.

To summarize, citizens worldwide demand commitments from their governments. They especially demand commitments about property, religion, equality, speech, and so on. Governments formulate their commitments as rights, and they make them credible by entrenching them in constitutions. Entrenchment often provides substantial but not absolute protection. With enough political support, governments can weaken or eliminate constitutional rights. This is not necessarily problematic. Like many laws, rights are generalizations, and generalizations can lead to bad outcomes.

Questions

7.1. People should have a right to defend themselves from intruders in their home. In the United States, people do have this right, but it does not appear in the U.S.

[12] *See* United States v. Ballard, 322 U.S. 78 (1944) (holding that while the truth or falsity of one's religious beliefs is protected by the First Amendment, fraudulent conduct because of those beliefs is not protected).

Constitution. In most states the right grows from statutes or the common law. Why? When a right is universally respected, do we need to constitutionalize it?

7.2. In the United States, the Americans with Disabilities Act (ADA) protects disabled people from discrimination. The ADA creates a statutory rather than constitutional right. Is the ADA entrenched?

7.3. If the right to religion allows the I Am movement to defraud consumers, lawmakers can respond by amending the right. Or judges can respond by reinterpreting the right not to protect this activity. If judges can reinterpret the right, is the right entrenched?

C. Transaction Costs and Rights

We related rights to the theory of entrenchment. Next, we relate rights to the theory of bargaining.

"[A] bill of rights," Jefferson argued, "is what the people are entitled to against every government on earth."[13] The Bill of Rights in the U.S. Constitution protects liberties like speech, assembly, and religion. Few people question the value of the Bill of Rights today. However, the Bill of Rights was controversial at the time of the Founding. James Wilson, a member of the Constitutional Convention, thought it was "superfluous and absurd."[14] According to Wilson, the Constitution's enumerated powers so limited the authority of the federal government that additional protections were unnecessary. What is wrong with Wilson's argument? Why are rights important even when the government is circumscribed?

We provide an economic justification for rights rooted in bargaining theory. Recall this statement of the Public Coase Theorem: as the transaction costs of political bargaining among representative lawmakers approach zero, laws will become socially efficient. This proposition holds regardless of rights. If everyone has representation in the legislature, and if legislators can bargain costlessly, then law achieves efficiency even without rights. The government will not infringe on speech unless the sum of benefits exceeds the sum of costs. Likewise, the government will protect religious minorities when the benefits exceed the costs, which we usually assume they do. With good representation and costless bargaining, we do not need rights to speech and religion—at least not when the objective is to maximize social welfare.

Now suppose lawmakers are *not* representative. A religious minority lacks representation in the legislature. Alternatively suppose the minority has representation but transaction costs are high. Legislators who represent the minority struggle to bargain with other legislators. In this case, law will not achieve social efficiency through bargaining. A majority might enact a law that benefits them but harms a religious minority more.

An earlier chapter distinguished two methods for resolving a bargaining failure: lower transaction costs or impose a solution. Recall the example of consumer loans, which

[13] *Letter from Thomas Jefferson to James Madison* (Dec. 20, 1787), *in* 2 THOMAS JEFFERSON, at 330 (H.A. Washington ed., 2012).

[14] JAMES WILSON, THE COLLECTED WORKS OF JAMES WILSON 172 (Kermit L. Hall & Mark D. Hall eds., 2007).

are sometimes inefficient because of information asymmetry between lenders and borrowers. To address the inefficiency, the state can permit the loans and require banks to disclose their terms (lower transaction costs), or the state can ban high-interest loans (impose a solution). Just as regulations can address bargaining failures in loans, rights can address bargaining failures in politics.

The right to vote and the right to petition the government improve representation. The freedoms of speech and press produce information that tends to improve the legislative process. These rights facilitate socially efficient bargaining, so we call them *Coasean rights.*[15] Coasean rights relate to what jurists call "process rights" or "political process theory."[16] Meanwhile, rights like equality and the freedom of religion bind the state. They constrain the outcomes of bargaining. Lenders cannot charge interest above a certain rate, and politicians cannot legislate beyond certain bounds. These rights impose limits when legislative bargaining threatens social welfare. We call them *Hobbesian rights* to match the language from earlier chapters. (Recall that an order imposed upon people who cannot bargain successfully among themselves is a "Hobbesian solution.") Hobbesian rights relate to what jurists call "substantive" rights.

In sum, Coasean rights help realize the Public Coase Theorem, and Hobbesian rights provide insurance when the theorem fails.

Questions

7.4. We characterize the freedom of speech as a Coasean right. Is it also a Hobbesian right?

7.5. Can you relate the freedom of religion to efficiency? In answering, use the Tiebout Model.

7.6. Sometimes people discount the future too much, like students partying before an exam. We can conceptualize this in terms of representativeness. Prudent lawmakers consider today's and tomorrow's interests, but impassioned lawmakers consider today's interests only. No one representing tomorrow's interests has a seat at the table. Explain how this representation error precludes law from achieving social efficiency, and explain how rights can help.

Democracy and Distrust

People disagree about the meaning and proper interpretation of constitutions. An approach called *originalism* emphasizes language and original understanding. The constitution means what its drafters intended or what readers would have understood it to mean at the time of enactment. According to some originalists, the Equal Protection Clause in the U.S. Constitution forbids racial discrimination in property ownership and jury composition. However, it does not grant same-sex couples a right

[15] Of course, these rights also give people a zone of autonomy to enjoy. Reciting poetry in a public park may not affect lawmaking, but it creates pleasure for the speaker and her audience.

[16] *See* John Hart Ely, Democracy and Distrust: Theory of Judicial Review (1981).

to marry. The clause does not mention same-sex marriage, and no one supported (or contemplated) this issue when the clause was drafted in the 1860s.

Consider an alternative: *pragmatism*.[17] Constitutional meaning evolves over time. Proponents of pragmatism argue that constitutional drafters intended meaning to evolve, readers at the time of enactment expected it to evolve, evolution is necessary, or some combination of the above. According to pragmatists, the prohibition on cruel and unusual punishment in the U.S. Constitution forbids whipping and immolation, punishments the Framers knew and opposed. However, it also forbids punishment that offends today's mores, like life imprisonment for people who committed crimes as minors.

Both methods of interpretation have shortcomings. Originalism can generate bad or nonsensical outcomes. The First Amendment forbids "Congress" from abridging the freedom of speech.[18] Can the President abridge speech? The drafters of the Equal Protection Clause opposed slavery but perhaps not school segregation. Does that mean the Supreme Court erred in *Brown v. Board of Education*? Pragmatism can turn law into politics. Today a majority supports reproductive and sexual choice. Does that mean the Constitution protects abortion and same-sex marriage? As fickle voters change their minds, what else will the Constitution protect?

In *Democracy and Distrust*, John Hart Ely sought a middle ground.[19] He championed *representation-reinforcement*. According to this theory, courts should avoid questions about substantive values like whether the Constitution contains an unwritten right to privacy. Instead, courts should concentrate on improving democratic processes. They should "clear the channels of political change" by defending the right to vote, prohibiting malapportioned districts, and protecting the press and political speech.[20] Furthermore, courts should protect minorities when the political system "malfunctions" and oppresses them.[21] Under Ely's account, women deserve no special constitutional protection because they can vote and constitute half the population. However, noncitizens deserve protection because they cannot vote and constitute a small fraction of the population.

We can frame Ely's theory in economic terms. According to the Public Coase Theorem, bargaining among representative lawmakers produces social efficiency when transaction costs are zero. Under that ideal, lawmakers resolve questions about values—abortion, privacy, radars that see through walls—in the welfare-maximizing way. By encouraging courts to make lawmakers representative, Ely pushed the political system toward that ideal. Recognizing that the ideal could never be fully achieved, Ely encouraged courts to protect minorities when the system fails.

Ely missed something crucial. The most representative legislature consists of every member of society. Though perfectly representative, this legislature will fail to

[17] In the United States, pragmatism sometimes goes by other names, including "living constitutionalism."
[18] *See* U.S. CONST. amend. I ("Congress shall make no law . . . abridging the freedom of speech, or of the press[.]").
[19] JOHN HART ELY, DEMOCRACY AND DISTRUST: THEORY OF JUDICIAL REVIEW (1981).
[20] *Id.* at 105.
[21] *Id.* at 136

get anything done. Transaction costs will be too high. To achieve efficiency, representatives need to be able to bargain. Does improving representation tend to help or hinder bargaining (recall the republican compromise)?

D. Coase versus Hobbes Revisited

"Give us the ballot, and we will no longer have to worry the federal government about our basic rights."[22] Martin Luther King, Jr. made this statement while pursuing equality for African Americans during the Civil Rights Movement. Economics illuminates his logic.

Two goods are substitutes when having one reduces demand for the other, as with a watch and a clock. In public law, representation and rights are often substitutes.[23] To protect a minority, law can improve the minority's representation in the legislature, or law can grant the minority rights that the legislature cannot infringe. King pushed the state to improve representation. Enfranchising African Americans would help them influence the lawmaking process. Influence ex ante reduces the need for rights ex post.

This idea applies in many settings. For example, in *Strauder v. West Virginia*, the U.S. Supreme Court held that a law prohibiting African Americans from serving on juries violates the Constitution.[24] Since then the Court has held that juries must reflect a "fair cross-section" of the community.[25] Decisions like these make juries more representative. More representative juries mean fewer (but not zero) discriminatory convictions and less (but not no) need for criminal defendants' rights.

Are representation and rights good substitutes? We can reframe the question in familiar terms. Should society try to satisfy the Public Coase Theorem by designing a constitution that achieves perfect representation and zero transaction costs? Or should society design a constitution that protects against bargaining failures with rights? In other words, should we seek a Coasean or Hobbesian solution? In answering this question, we will analyze efficiency and distribution separately.

Start with efficiency. According to the Public Coase Theorem, costless bargaining by representative lawmakers leads to socially efficient laws. If improving representation—by, for example, enfranchising a minority—actuates the Public Coase Theorem, then improving representation achieves social efficiency. The political process will produce efficient laws, so rights that prevent inefficient laws are unnecessary, at least when the objective is efficiency.

If the Public Coase Theorem holds, Hobbesian rights are not harmful in an efficiency sense. They do not cause inefficiency. They are irrelevant to efficiency. Recall Coase's example involving the farmer and the rancher. The farmer can fence the cows out for $10, or the rancher can fence the cows in for $20. If the transaction costs of bargaining are

[22] The Papers of Martin Luther King, Jr. Volume IV: Symbol of the Movement, January 1957–December 1958 (Clayborne Carson, Susan Carson, Adrienne Clay, Virginia Shadron, & Kieran Taylor eds., 2000).

[23] *See* Daryl J. Levinson, *Rights and Votes*, 121 Yale L.J. 1286 (2012).

[24] 100 U.S. 303 (1880).

[25] Taylor v. Louisiana, 419 U.S. 522 (1975).

zero, the farmer will fence the cows out for $10. This efficient outcome results whether the law is "open range" or "closed range." The law is irrelevant to efficiency.

The same logic applies to rights. Suppose a proposed law would ban animal sacrifices in religion. For the sake of example, assume the law would create a benefit for the majority and a smaller cost for a religious minority. Thus, enacting the law would increase social welfare. If the transaction costs of bargaining among representative lawmakers are zero, the law will pass. If the minority does not have a right, lawmakers will simply pass the law. If the minority has a right, lawmakers will pay the minority to waive it, just like the rancher will pay the farmer to build the fence. If the Public Coase Theorem holds, rights are irrelevant to efficiency.

We have explained that actuating the Public Coase Theorem promotes social efficiency. Can Hobbesian rights promote efficiency? Yes. Returning to Coase's example, efficiency requires the farmer to build the fence. Law can achieve that with "open range." The property law mandates the efficient solution. Likewise, rights can mandate the efficient solution by precluding the state from adopting an inefficient solution. For example, suppose that welfare requires permitting animal experiments in medicine and banning animal sacrifices in religion. A perfect combination of rights—animal rights, religious rights, a human right to health—could achieve this ideal.

Finding the perfect combination of rights is difficult. Lawmakers need to specify and prioritize the rights carefully. Furthermore, the perfect combination of rights may change over time. Today welfare requires permitting animal experiments. If scientists invent an alternative method for testing medicine, welfare might require banning animal experiments. If the Public Coase Theorem is satisfied, then rights do not need to evolve over time to achieve efficiency (bargaining will yield efficiency regardless of rights). However, if the Public Coase Theorem is not satisfied, then rights need to adjust to achieve efficiency. Because rights are entrenched, they might not adjust.

In sum, society can achieve efficiency by actuating the Public Coase Theorem or optimizing Hobbesian rights. In practice, both approaches have limits. Representation is rarely perfect, transaction costs are never zero, and rights are rarely optimal. Whether we should facilitate bargaining or impose solutions depends on costs and benefits. Economists take all costs into account. If the net benefit of facilitating bargaining exceeds the net benefit of imposing with rights, then we should facilitate bargaining, and vice versa.

We have analyzed the choice between Coasean and Hobbesian solutions with efficiency in mind. Now consider distribution. Suppose the majority wants to enact a law that would harm a minority. To make this concrete, suppose the gain to the majority from the law would equal 10, and the loss to the minority from the law would equal 20. Thus, the law is inefficient. If representation is good and transaction costs are low, the law will not pass. The minority will bargain with the majority and offer a proposal like this: we will pay you 15 if you will not enact the law. The minority prefers −15 to −20, so the deal makes the minority better off. The majority prefers 15 to 10, so the deal makes the majority better off. Bargaining achieves efficiency, and the payoffs to the majority and the minority, respectively, are 15 and −15.

Now consider this example with a right that protects the minority. Because of the right, the majority cannot enact the law. Thus, the right achieves efficiency, and the payoffs to the majority and the minority respectively are 0 and 0.

To generalize, rights give the people they protect a stronger position in bargaining. This increases their payoffs, as the example shows. This leads to a restatement of the Public Coase Theorem: *If transaction costs are zero, the cooperative surplus is maximized, and rights give their beneficiaries a greater share.*

"Proportionate Interest Representation"

Following passage of the Voting Rights Act, African American citizens began voting in large numbers, and African American candidates began winning elections. However, African American representatives had little political power. White representatives outnumbered them in legislatures, and white representatives voted as a bloc. Thus, African American representatives and their constituents were largely ignored. Legislatures enacted some of the same laws they would have enacted if no African American representatives had been elected.

To improve politics, Lani Guinier advocated for "proportionate interest representation."[26] According to her theory, if white representatives refused to bargain with black representatives, then simple majority rule would be replaced with some form of supermajority rule. Her objective was to give African American representatives power to block legislation that would negatively affect African American citizens. She called this a "minority veto."[27]

Economics can illuminate Guinier's proposal. A minority veto would affect distribution. By giving black representatives leverage, it would ensure that they get more of the surplus from political bargains. To illustrate, suppose a law would create a benefit of 10 for the majority and a cost of 4 for the minority. Without the veto, the law would pass, and the payoffs to the majority and minority would be 10 and −4, respectively. With the veto, the law could pass, but only if the majority secured the minority's support. The majority might pay the minority, say, 7, to enact the law, meaning the final payoff for each group would be 3. The minority's payoff is higher with the veto than without it.

A minority veto could also affect efficiency. It could increase efficiency by blocking negative-sum laws. To illustrate, suppose a law would create a benefit of 10 for the majority and a cost of 40 for the minority. If the transaction costs of bargaining are high, then without the veto this harmful law would pass. With the veto it would not. Of course, a minority veto could also decrease efficiency by blocking positive-sum laws.[28] If a law would create a benefit of 10 for the majority and a cost of 4 for the minority, then efficiency requires the law to pass. However, disagreement over dividing the surplus could prevent this. If the majority offered a payment of 6 to the minority, and the minority held out for a payment of 8, the law might not pass.

[26] Lani Guinier, *The Triumph of Tokenism: The Voting Rights Act and the Theory of Black Electoral Success*, 89 Mich. L. Rev. 1077 (1991).

[27] These ideas are described in *id. See also* Lani Guinier, The Tyranny of the Majority: Fundamental Fairness in Representative Democracy (1994).

[28] *See, e.g.*, Richard Briffault, *Lani Guinier and the Dilemmas of American Democracy*, 95 Colum. L. Rev. 418, 465 (1995) ("a supermajority rule is likely to result less in 'taking turns' and more in deadlock").

Now we can summarize much of Guinier's argument: the benefits of distributing surplus to minorities and blocking negative-sum laws exceed the costs of holdouts. Whether Guinier got the balance of benefits and costs right is debatable, of course.

Perhaps a minority veto could improve efficiency through another channel. Recall that any impediment to bargaining counts as a transaction cost. Thus, racism counts as a transaction cost when it precludes people—say, white and black representatives—from bargaining. If they were forced to bargain, representatives might discover that hatred is irrational and cooperation is fruitful. Could a minority veto lower the transaction costs of bargaining?

E. Rights for Sale

A rancher can sell beef, a publisher can sell e-books, and a lawyer can sell legal advice. Most goods and services can be sold. However, some goods and services cannot be sold. Law prohibits people from selling sex, babies, or kidneys. Things like heroin and bombs cannot be given away. These things are "inalienable," meaning they cannot be sold or transferred.

Are rights inalienable? For work-a-day rights the answer is usually no. If a buyer owes money to a seller, the seller has a right to get paid. The seller can waive the right by forgiving the debt, or the seller can sell the right to a third-party debt collector. For grand rights associated with constitutions, the answer is more complicated.[29] According to the Declaration of Independence, the rights to life, liberty and the pursuit of happiness are inalienable.

Inalienability impedes bargaining. To see why, recall the example of a law that would ban animal sacrifices in religion. The law would create a benefit for the majority and a smaller cost for a religious minority, so enacting the law would be efficient. Suppose the freedom of religion protects animal sacrifices. If the freedom of religion is alienable, then the majority can pay the minority to waive it and enact the law. If the freedom of religion is inalienable, then the majority cannot enact the law. The minority's freedom is protected whether or not they prefer it to the majority's offer. Inalienable rights raise the transaction costs of political bargaining, and this can lead to inefficiency.

This example suggests that rights should be alienable. In fact, many rights are alienable, despite the Declaration of Independence. In the United States, a person can waive his right to sue the police in exchange for a reduction in criminal charges.[30] Likewise, defendants can waive their right to a jury trial in exchange for a shorter prison sentence (we will discuss plea bargaining in a later chapter).[31] However, some rights are not alienable, like the right to vote. In an election for public office, one person cannot sell her vote to another.

[29] Many scholars have addressed the alienability of liberties. *See, e.g.*, Margaret Jane Radin, *Market-Inalienability*, 100 Harv. L. Rev. 1849 (1987); Kathleen M. Sullivan, *Unconstitutional Conditions*, 102 Harv. L. Rev. 1413 (1989); Richard A. Epstein, *Why Restrain Alienation?*, 85 Colum. L. Rev. 970 (1985).

[30] *See* Town of Newton v. Rumery, 480 U.S. 386 (1987).

[31] *See* Brady v. United States, 397 U.S. 742, 748 (1970).

Why can't you sell your vote? According to the Supreme Court, "No body politic worthy of being called a democracy entrusts the selection of leaders to a process of auction or barter."[32] This sounds like moral condemnation. People often use moral arguments to justify prohibitions on alienability. With respect to voting, however, economics can justify inalienability.

As the previous chapter explained, voting creates externalities.[33] The pivotal vote determines the outcome for everyone, not just the pivotal voter. Thus, one person's vote to build a road raises another person's taxes. Externalities lead to inefficiency. Recall our five voters arranged from left to right: Kim, Larry, Mary, Ned, and Olivia. The voters have equally intense preferences, and law begins at Larry's ideal. Moving the law from Larry's ideal to Mary's would cost Kim and Larry one apiece and benefit Mary, Ned, and Olivia one apiece. To maximize social welfare, we should set the law at Mary's ideal, and voting under majority rule will ordinarily produce that result. However, suppose Kim and Larry conspire to buy Mary's vote. Each will pay her 0.6 if she will vote for Larry's ideal rather than her own. Instead of losing one apiece, Kim and Larry lose 0.6 apiece. Instead of gaining 1, Mary gains 1.2. Kim, Larry, and Mary prefer this deal to no deal, so Larry's ideal triumphs by a vote of 3 to 2. This outcome is suboptimal. Moving the law from Larry's ideal to Mary's would create a net benefit for the group of 1. The source of inefficiency is an externality: the deal for Mary's vote imposes a cost on Ned and Olivia.

To correct externalities, law can lower transaction costs or impose a solution. Making votes alienable lowers transaction costs. If vote buying is easy and legal, everyone can bargain. In the example, all four voters can bargain with Mary. Given costless bargaining, the Public Coase Theorem predicts that bargaining will achieve efficiency, meaning in this example that the law will move to Mary's ideal. However, bargaining is never costless, especially in large elections. High transaction costs imply that bargaining cannot solve the externalities of voting.

In voting, the Coasean solution fails, so the law adopts the Hobbesian solution. The Hobbesian solution makes votes inalienable.

Should people be able to sell their rights? Usually, the answer is no because of morality. When it comes to the right to vote, the answer is (also) no because of economics.

Questions

7.7. Children can't sign enforceable contracts. Should children be able to sell their rights? Why not?

7.8. Selling your right to vote creates an externality, which can lead to inefficiency. What about other rights? Would selling yourself into servitude create an externality?[34] What about taking a payment in exchange for not exercising your religion?

[32] Brown v. Hartlage, 456 U.S. 45, 54 (1982).

[33] On voting externalities and inalienability, see Pamela S. Karlan, *Politics by Other Means*, 85 Va. L. Rev. 1697 (1999); Richard Epstein, *Why Restrain Alienation?*, 85 Colum. L. Rev. 970 (1985).

[34] *See* Guido Calabresi & A. Douglas Melamed, *Property Rules, Liability Rules, and Inalienability: One View of the Cathedral*, 85 Harv. L. Rev. 1089, 1112 (1972) ("If Taney is allowed to sell himself into slavery, or to take undue risks of becoming penniless, or to sell a kidney, Marshall may be harmed, simply because Marshall is a sensitive man who is made unhappy by seeing slaves, paupers, or persons who die because they have sold a kidney. Again

7.9. Yala wants the legislature to enact a bill. The legislature has three members and uses majority rule. Enacting Yala's bill would cost each legislator $100. Yala makes the following offer: if you vote for my bill and your vote is pivotal (i.e., necessary to enact it), I will pay you $150; if you vote for my bill but your vote is not pivotal, I will pay you $1; and if you vote against my bill I will pay you nothing. If the legislators cannot bargain with one another, they will unanimously approve the bill, accepting a total of $3 for a bill that costs them $300. Why?[35]

F. Unconstitutional Conditions

Some rights are alienable, but only under certain conditions. To illustrate, in the United States, the First Amendment protects the freedom of association. When members of labor unions go on strike—no work until wages improve—they engage in protected acts of association. In 1981, Congress enacted a law denying food stamps to workers on strike. Congress offered workers a trade: we will fund your food stamps if you do not strike. Can workers trade their First Amendment rights for food? In *Lyng v. International Union, UAW*, the Supreme Court said yes.[36] Congress has the power to deny food stamps to workers who strike.

Consider a different case. An untenured professor at a state college criticized his superiors. When his teaching contract expired, his superiors refused to renew it. The professor claimed that the state fired him in retaliation for engaging in speech protected by the First Amendment. The state had offered him a trade: you can work if you keep quiet. Can the state demand that public employees trade their free speech for a job? In *Perry v. Sindermann*, the Supreme Court said no.[37]

Cases like these implicate the *doctrine of unconstitutional conditions*.[38] The doctrine determines when the exercise of a right is conditioned in an unconstitutional way.

To analyze the doctrine, consider the related problem of duress.[39] A criminal points a gun and offers his victim a deal: "pay me or I'll shoot." The gun gives the criminal a strong position in bargaining (would you haggle?). The victim will give the criminal her money. Thus, duress affects distribution; value travels from one person to another. Duress also affects efficiency. To facilitate the crime, the criminal buys a gun. To prevent the crime, the victim installs an alarm on her home. These acts are individually rational but inefficient. The criminal and victim burn resources, but not to create new value. They burn resources squabbling over the distribution of existing value: the money in the victim's pocket.

Marshall could pay Taney not to sell his freedom to Chase the slaveowner; but again, because Marshall is not one but many individuals, freeloader and information costs make such transactions practically impossible.").

[35] *See* Ernesto Dal Bo, *Bribing Voters*, 51 Am. J. Pol. Sci. 789 (2007).

[36] 485 U.S. 360 (1988).

[37] 408 U.S. 593 (1972).

[38] For a comprehensive if somewhat dated overview of the doctrine, see Kathleen M. Sullivan, *Unconstitutional Conditions*, 102 Harv. L. Rev. 1413 (1989).

[39] On the economic analysis of duress, see Robert Cooter & Thomas Ulen, Law and Economics 343–47 (6th ed. 2016); Mark Seidenfeld & Murat C. Mungan, *Duress as Rent Seeking*, 99 Minn. L. Rev. 1423 (2015); Steven Shavell, *Contractual Holdup and Legal Intervention*, 36 J. Legal Stud. 325 (2007); Oren Bar-Gill & Omri Ben-Shahar, *The Law of Duress and the Economics of Credible Threats*, 33 J. Legal Stud. 391 (2004).

We can apply these ideas to the doctrine of unconstitutional conditions.[40] To begin, consider distribution. A member of a labor union values her right to strike. To make it concrete, suppose she values striking at 10. If she loses food stamps, without which she cannot eat, she loses 11. If the state cannot condition the right to strike, then the worker can choose to strike or not (10 versus 0) and she can choose between accepting food stamps or not (0 versus −11). She will choose to strike and accept food stamps for a payoff of 10. If the state *can* condition the right to strike, then the worker must choose between striking without food stamps for a payoff of −1, or not striking with food stamps for a payoff of 0. She will choose not striking with food stamps for a payoff of 0. Conditioning the right to strike harms the worker and helps her employer (she will work instead of strike). This is analogous to pointing the gun, which harms the victim and helps the criminal. Value grows for one person and declines for another.

We have shown how conditioning rights can affect distribution. Now consider how it can affect efficiency. In the earlier example, the criminal buys a gun so he can threaten his victim, and the victim installs an alarm so she can avoid being threatened. Those investments are individually rational but inefficient. Does a comparable inefficiency arise with unconstitutional conditions? The state might make people reliant on food stamps today in order to pressure them tomorrow, perhaps by threatening to take the stamps away. People might refuse food stamps today so the state cannot pressure them later. These possibilities seem unlikely. The decision to offer and accept food stamps probably depends on other factors. However, once food stamps exist, then the state and recipients might burn resources—legislating, lobbying—in an effort to gain leverage over the other. Those efforts are costly.

When the state, like a criminal, wastes resources on threats to redistribute value, courts should intervene. Courts should forbid the state from attaching conditions to rights. Often, however, the state does not resemble a criminal. Often the state conditions rights to create value, not to redistribute it. To illustrate, consider the Central Intelligence Agency. To work at the CIA, an employee must agree not to share the government's secrets. Thus, the state conditions employment on sacrificing the right to free speech. This condition costs employees, but value does not get redistributed like money from a victim to a thief. Employees lose speech rights, but U.S. citizens gain safety and security. The benefit to hundreds of millions of Americans surely outweighs the cost to CIA workers.[41]

These ideas lead to a prescription. *The state should not be permitted to condition rights to redistribute value. The state should be permitted to condition rights to create value.*

Questions

7.10. As with the professor and the CIA, many cases involving the doctrine of unconstitutional conditions involve speech. The state offers someone a benefit in exchange for keeping quiet.

[40] *See generally* Richard A. Epstein, *Foreword: Unconstitutional Conditions, State Power, and the Limits of Consent*, 102 Harv. L. Rev. 4 (1988).

[41] This example comes from *Snepp v. United States*, 444 U.S. 507 (1980) (holding that a former CIA employee was bound to his employment contract under which he sacrificed some speech rights).

(a) Does selling your right to free speech create a negative externality? Does the answer depend on what kind of speech (political, commercial, chitchat about sports) you give up?
(b) Assume selling your speech creates a negative externality. Does this mean the government should not be allowed to buy your silence? Or does this mean the government should pay extra for your silence?
(c) An earlier chapter explained how a Pigouvian tax can prevent the inefficiency of negative externalities. Can a Pigouvian tax help courts analyze unconstitutional conditions?

"A Gun to the Head"

Sometimes the government pressures people to give up their rights. Other times the government pressures states. Consider Medicaid, a program started in 1965 under which the federal government gives states subsidies to provide health care to the poor. In 2010, the Affordable Care Act (ACA) required states to meet a new Medicaid standard. Specifically, it required states to extend Medicaid coverage for people up to a certain income level as a condition for continuing to receive Medicaid subsidies for *anyone* at *any* income level. In *National Federation of Independent Business v. Sebelius* (*NFIB*), the Supreme Court found that this condition unconstitutionally coerced the states.[42] According to the Court, the ACA was akin to "a gun to the head."[43]

Some notation represents the court's holding. Let *X* denote no Medicaid program; let *O* denote the old program before the ACA; and let *N* denote the new program after the ACA. The Court held that Congress can give states the choice of *O* or *N*. States can keep the old program or adopt the new program, which requires more coverage for more people but comes with an additional subsidy. However, Congress cannot give states the choice of *X* or *N*. This is unconstitutional coercion.

As before, we can analyze coercion in terms of distribution and efficiency. Coercion allows the federal government to harm states in the same way that it can harm strikers by threatening their food stamps. Likewise, coercion can cause the federal government and the states to spend resources in a distributional squabble. Once Medicaid exists, and given that changes to Medicaid have distributional implications, both sides might burn resources—legislating, lobbying—not to improve the program but to strengthen their position.

In addition to distribution and efficiency, coercion between governments affects credibility. Suppose the Court held that the federal government *can* offer states the choice of *X* or *N*. Now imagine the federal government bargaining with the states over a new program to provide internet access to rural areas. The federal government offers to pay subsidies to the states if the states will provide the service. States might reason as follows: "After we start this program, the federal government will coerce us by making us choose between expanding the program more than we want or canceling it. To avoid coercion later, we reject the offer today." To overcome this

42 567 U.S. 519 (2012).
43 *Id.* at 581.

resistance, the federal government would like to make a credible commitment not to coerce. Without the decision in *NFIB*, making that commitment is hard. With *NFIB*, making that commitment is easy.

These ideas illuminate a controversy in *NFIB*. Congress could repeal Medicaid and then offer states the choice of no Medicaid or new, expanded Medicaid. In notation, Congress could change the law from *O* to *X* and then pass a new law giving states the choice of *X* or *N*. So why can't Congress skip the repeal and offer the choice of *X* or *N* immediately? Justice Ginsburg wrote, "A ritualistic requirement that Congress repeal and reenact spending legislation . . . would advance no constitutional principle and would scarcely serve the interests of federalism."[44]

This is an argument about costs. Congress can expand Medicaid at low cost (do not repeal *O*, offer *X* or *N* immediately) or high cost (repeal *O*, then offer *X* or *N*). Why make Congress incur the higher cost? The theory of credible commitments provides perspective. Burning the boats raised the cost of retreat, committing the army to advance. Likewise, requiring repeal raised the cost of making a coercive offer, committing the federal government not to coerce.

In sum, the doctrine of unconstitutional conditions as deployed in *NFIB* frustrated the federal government today but lowered its transaction costs of bargaining tomorrow. That is a descriptive analysis of the case, not a normative or interpretive analysis. Did the Court make the right decision?

G. Local or Universal Rights

In *Obergefell v. Hodges*, the U.S. Supreme Court held that the Constitution grants same-sex couples the right to marry.[45] Prior to the case, the legal right to same-sex marriage was local: some states had it, others did not. After the case, the right became universal. Should rights be local or universal? Some people reject the distinction. They think rights are universal by definition and all governments should recognize them. For others the question is not so simple. Sometimes local rights have advantages over universal rights.[46]

Start with a mundane example: architectural regulations. Some people like architectural purity. To achieve this, many municipalities restrict neighborhood architecture to certain styles. Thus, some neighborhoods in London feature Georgian houses only. Private mechanisms like covenants usually fail to produce uniform architecture. To keep buildings in one style, the state prohibits building in another style.

These ideas generalize beyond architecture. People who cluster in a neighborhood to perpetuate a culture may want to exclude other practices and people. If given the choice, some religious communities will forbid commerce on the Sabbath and consumption of pork, and some family neighborhoods will prohibit sales of alcohol and pornography. Private mechanisms usually fail to produce uniformity. An agnostic will open his store

44 Nat'l Fed'n of Indep. Bus. v. Sebelius, 567 U.S. 519, 624 (2012) (Ginsburg, J., dissenting).
45 135 S. Ct. 2584 (2015).
46 This discussion draws on Robert Cooter, The Strategic Constitution 129–43 (2000).

on the Sabbath, and a magazine store will sell pornography near a school. Achieving uniformity requires local restrictions.

Local restrictions create conflicts. The agnostic who works on the Sabbath may allege that the local restrictions violate his individual rights. The municipality that enacted the restriction may claim that enforcing community values protects religious rights and the distinctiveness of neighborhoods.

How should the state respond to such conflicts? The answer depends on the state's objectives. If the social goal is diversity *within* each community, the state should forbid local governments from enforcing local values. This will induce "mixed" communities like Paris, where some people choose to work on Saturdays and others choose not to work on Saturdays. If the social goal is diversity *across* communities, the state should permit local governments to enforce local values. This will induce "pure" communities that differ from one another. In some towns in Israel, no one works on Saturdays, and in other towns they do.[47]

The costs of mobility determine the severity of the trade-off between individual rights and community values. Local restrictions are not oppressive when nonconformists can easily move to unrestricted communities. To demonstrate, "dry counties" prohibit the sale of alcohol. If a distiller can easily move his business, or at least his whiskey, to a "wet county," then the dry county's law does not harm him. Conversely, local restrictions are oppressive when costs preclude nonconformists from moving. If the distiller cannot move, the dry county's law will ruin his business.

An earlier chapter introduced the Tiebout Model, according to which people vote with their feet. This model has implications for rights. Low relocation costs give a reason to allow local communities to develop different interpretations of individual rights. High relocation costs give a reason for imposing the same respect for individual rights on different local governments. The strength of the right to resist community norms should depend in part on the cost of leaving. *In general, local rights fit mobile societies and universal rights fit immobile societies.*

Questions

7.11. In general, national constitutions contain more rights than city charters. Why?

7.12. *Roe v. Wade* established a nationwide right to abortion under some circumstances.[48] If the Supreme Court overturns *Roe*, some jurisdictions will permit abortions and others will not. Whether overturning *Roe* would affect the number and availability of abortions depends on mobility. Why? Use your answer to analyze this statement from Justice Ginsburg: "There will never be a woman of means without [reproductive] choice anymore."[49]

7.13. In the 1950s, laws in the United States prohibited distribution of "obscene" material like pornography. Do such laws violate individual rights? According to Justice Harlan, *federal* prohibitions on obscenity are impermissible because

[47] Israeli law prohibits working on Shabbat, but the law is often unenforced.
[48] 410 U.S. 113 (1973).
[49] Emily Bazelon, *The Place of Women on the Court*, N.Y. TIMES, July 7, 2009.

they create a "deadening uniformity."[50] In contrast, *state* prohibitions on obscenity are generally permissible. Justice Harlan saw "no overwhelming danger . . . from the suppression of a borderline book in one of the States so long as there is no uniform nationwide suppression of the book."[51] Justice Harlan was criticized for suggesting that individual rights are contingent, not universal. Do you agree with Harlan or his critics?

H. Balancing Rights

A gay couple wanted a baker to supply a custom-made cake for their wedding. The baker refused because of his religious opposition to same-sex marriage. Their dispute led to a case called *Masterpiece Cakeshop*.[52] The Supreme Court ruled in favor of the baker, but on narrow grounds. The Court did not resolve the fundamental question: When equality and religion collide, who wins?

How should judges balance competing rights? In *Masterpiece Cakeshop*, the Court could have held that equality always trumps religion or religion always trumps equality. Neither approach seems sound. Legally, the Constitution does not seem to prioritize one right over the other. Normatively, categorical approaches will generate errors, meaning cases where one right should control but the other right does control.

To illustrate the potential for error, let's attach some numbers to the case. For the sake of example, we assume equality and religion can be quantified and compared. The couple suffers a loss of 8 when denied equal treatment, and the baker suffers a loss of 4 when denied his religion. In this case, a rule that prioritizes equality produces the best result. The couple wins, and the baker bears the loss of 4, which is better than the alternative loss of 8. But the numbers may look different in a future case. The next baker might suffer a loss of 9 instead of 4, in which case the rule prioritizing equality yields an inferior result. The loss is 9 instead of 8.

To reduce errors, judges can reject categorical approaches and balance rights case by case. Case-by-case decision-making has many costs and benefits, as a later chapter explains. Here we focus only on its capacity to prevent errors. In the first example, judges can prioritize equality to minimize costs at 4, and in the second example they can prioritize religion to minimize costs at 8. Case-by-case decision-making yields the best outcome in each case.

For judges to decide case by case, they need good information, which they often lack. Judges can count money but not utility or dignity. They cannot observe the couple's or the baker's losses. However, judges can observe their choices.

To explain this idea, let's set rights aside for a moment and concentrate on something else, accidents. A train and truck collide at a crossing. Who must pay for the damage, the train company or the truck's owner? To answer, we might ask a different question: How could the parties have avoided the accident? The train could have stopped to let the truck pass, or the truck could have stopped to let the train pass. Either approach would

[50] In *Roth v. United States*, 354 U.S. 476 (1957), the Supreme Court said no. Writing separately, Justice Harlan said "maybe." *Id.* at 506 (Harlan, J., dissenting).
[51] *Id.*
[52] Masterpiece Cakeshop, Ltd. v. Colorado Civil Rights Comm'n, 138 S. Ct. 1719 (2018).

have worked. However, stopping trains is hard, or "costly" in the language of economics. Trains require a lot of time and track to stop, and passengers and cargo get delayed. In contrast, trucks stop quickly and easily. Restarting a train is difficult, whereas restarting a truck is not. All things considered, stopping the truck to avoid the accident would have been cheaper than stopping the train. Consequently, we should make the truck's owner liable. This prevents future accidents at low cost by encouraging trucks to stop.

This is *least cost avoidance*, an influential theory in law and economics.[53] The theory compares the choices available to the parties at the time they came into conflict. How could each side have avoided the accident? How costly would an alternative course of action have been? The party that could have avoided the conflict at lowest cost loses.

Scholars have applied least cost avoidance to accidents. Here we adapt the theory to rights.[54] Consider the conflict between the gay couple and the religious baker. Suppose the couple could have gotten a cake of equal quality from another shop nearby. Meanwhile, the religious baker is a sole proprietor, so he could not have asked a non-objecting coworker to bake the cake. Loosely speaking, the baker resembles the train and the couple resembles the truck. The couple could have avoided the conflict at relatively low cost by shopping elsewhere. In this rights conflict, the couple should lose.

Turn the facts around. Suppose that no other store would have served the couple. Meanwhile, the religious baker had a coworker without objections to same-sex marriage. The religious baker could have avoided the conflict by simply referring the couple to his coworker. Under these facts, the baker should lose.

These examples generate a principle for resolving hard conflicts among rights: decide against the party who could have more easily avoided the conflict in the first place. This is the *conflict avoidance principle*.[55] This logic is familiar from earlier. Local restrictions do not oppress when people can easily relocate. Likewise, one rightsholder does not oppress another when the latter can easily avoid the conflict.

The conflict avoidance principle makes cases manageable by replacing nebulous questions about equality, religion, and dignity with simpler, concrete inquiries, like whether other bakers serve gay couples. But simpler isn't always better. A critic might argue that ignoring equality, religion, and dignity cuts the heart from the case. Here are two responses. First, if courts can balance fundamental values carefully and objectively, then they should. The conflict avoidance principle is a tiebreaker for the many cases where they cannot. Second, courts often concentrate on particular interests, like getting a cake, rather than fundamental values. In our accident, the train company might have a fundamental interest in property rights, especially if it owns the track, and the truck owner might have a fundamental interest in the right of travel. Both sides have interests in freedom and safety. These interests are fundamental, but courts usually ignore them, probably because they lack the capacity to balance them. Instead, courts resolve accidents by asking specific, concrete questions, like "How hard would it have been to stop the truck?" Emphasizing particular interests instead of fundamental values is common in law.

[53] *See* GUIDO CALABRESI, THE COSTS OF ACCIDENTS: A LEGAL AND ECONOMIC ANALYSIS 135 (1970). Least cost avoidance induces precautions by one party or the other, but efficiency usually requires precautions by both parties. Thus, least cost avoidance promotes but does not usually maximize efficiency.

[54] The following ideas are developed in Charles L. Barzun & Michael D. Gilbert, *Conflict Avoidance in Constitutional Law*, 107 VA. L. REV. 1 (2021).

[55] *See id.* at 3.

Questions

7.14. How costly would it be for the gay couple to get a cake from another store? The answer depends in part on the psychological harm to them of shopping elsewhere to avoid discrimination. How costly would it be for the religious baker to have a coworker bake the cake? The answer depends in part on the psychological harm to him of condoning a gay wedding in this limited way. Psychological harms are relevant to the parties' costs of avoiding the conflict. Can courts measure and compare psychological harms? If not, what avoidance costs can courts measure and compare?

7.15. *Fulton v. City of Philadelphia* involved another conflict between equality and religion.[56] Same-sex couples wanted to foster children. One religious organization refused to connect children in need with same-sex couples. Over two dozen other organizations would connect children in need with same-sex couples. According to the conflict avoidance principle, which party should win?[57]

7.16. A photographer refused to photograph a same-sex wedding, citing religious objections.[58] According to Andrew Koppelman, the photographer should prevail in the ensuing rights conflict, but only if she publicly identifies herself as discriminatory.[59] How could the photographer publicly identify as discriminatory? Would this prevent or provoke rights conflicts?

II. Equality

We have analyzed rights in general. Now we focus on two specific rights, beginning with equality.[60] In *Brown v. Board of Education*, the U.S. Supreme Court rejected the doctrine of "separate but equal" and required racial integration in public schools.[61] *Brown* took a first, tentative step toward racial equality, and today few people question its moral force. Yet discrimination persists. Some discrimination leads to grave injustice, as when police officers target racial minorities. Other discrimination generates almost no attention, as when young men pay higher premiums for automobile insurance than young women. Sometimes people *demand* discrimination. Young men are more likely to bomb an airplane than elderly women. Shouldn't airport security search more young men than elderly women?

Race, sex, age, ethnicity, religion, and other characteristics form part of each person's identity. Discrimination based on these traits involves an indignity that provokes

[56] 141 S. Ct. 1868 (2021).

[57] *See* Michael Gilbert, *Conflicts Among Rights: An Economic Approach*, 9 REVISTA FACULTAD DE JURISPRUDENCIA 66 (2021).

[58] Elane Photography, LLC v. Willock, 309 P.3d 53 (N.M. 2013).

[59] Andrew Koppelman, *Gay Rights, Religious Accommodations, and the Purposes of Antidiscrimination Law*, 88 S. CAL. L. REV. 619, 620 (2015).

[60] In the United States, many cases about the right to equality involve the U.S. Constitution's Fourteenth Amendment. Here is the relevant text: "No State shall make or enforce any law which shall abridge the privileges or immunities of citizens of the United States; nor shall any State deprive any person of life, liberty, or property, without due process of law; nor deny to any person within its jurisdiction the equal protection of the laws." U.S. CONST. amend. XIV, § 1.

[61] 347 U.S. 483, 495 (1954).

powerful emotions and motivates strong moral judgments. However, the moral judgments of different people conflict. These conflicts make analysis urgent and controversial. Economics cannot solve the problem of discrimination, but it can inform the debate.

A. Discrimination by the State

The city of San Francisco refused to let Chinese immigrants operate laundries.[62] The state of Virginia forbade marriage between white and "colored" people.[63] The U.S. government forced Japanese Americans into internment camps.[64] Everyone agrees that these examples involve discrimination. The government treats one group of people differently from the rest. Now consider other examples. Only speeding drivers get tickets, and only strong people get hired as firefighters. Again, the government treats one group—speeders, strong people—differently from the rest, but most people would not call this discrimination.

What's the difference? In general, "discrimination" in law does not mean treating people differently. It means treating people differently because of a characteristic that is or should be irrelevant. Thus, the government does not discriminate when it imprisons people based on their crimes. The government *does* discriminate when it imprisons people based on their skin color.

A *protected class* is a group of people who share a characteristic that should be irrelevant to decision-making. In the United States, racial minorities have been a protected class for decades. Today people divide over whether and when sexual minorities are a protected class.[65]

Often the characteristic uniting a protected class is *immutable*. You cannot change your race, age, ethnicity, or national origin. Many people believe that religion is immutable. Immutability implies the absence of choice. A driver can choose to comply with a law that forbids speeding, but can a Christian choose to comply with a law that forbids Christianity? Some people think the answer is no. In the Soviet Union, the ban on religion caused much more oppression than speed limits.

Our opening examples—Chinese laundries, interracial marriage, Japanese internment—involve discrimination by governments. Government discrimination is especially harmful because governments operate as monopolies. Only the state issues licenses for marriage, and only the city issues licenses for laundries. If the government discriminates against you, you have only two choices: exit or obey. If the characteristic driving discrimination is immutable, then you cannot exit from the class of targeted people—an old person cannot make herself young. Likewise, if mobility costs are high or other jurisdictions also discriminate, then you cannot exit from the jurisdiction, trading a bad government for a good one. This leaves you only one choice: obey.

62 *See* Yick Wo v. Hopkins, 118 U.S. 356 (1886).

63 Loving v. Virginia, 388 U.S. 1 (1967).

64 Korematsu v. United States, 323 U.S. 214 (1944).

65 *See* Bostock v. Clayton County, Georgia, 140 S. Ct. 1731 (2020). In *Bostock*, the Supreme Court held that the Civil Rights Act prohibits employment discrimination based on sexual orientation or identity. Three Justices dissented, and many people have criticized the decision.

This discussion connects equality to choice, and it generates a prediction. The clearest cases of impermissible discrimination arise when the national government treats people differently based on immutable characteristics.

Questions

7.17. Usually discrimination involves the majority discriminating against the minority. How does entrenching a right to equality prevent this? Why isn't the U.S. Constitution's Equal Protection Clause unamendable?

7.18. The state can require prison guards to be men, at least when the prison contains many violent male prisoners. According to the Supreme Court, being male is a "bona fide occupational qualification" for the job of prison guard.[66] Does refusing to hire women prison guards constitute discrimination?

B. Tiers of Scrutiny

Can the government forbid 16-year-olds from buying alcohol? In general, the answer is yes, even though this involves discrimination based on age, an immutable characteristic. Not all discrimination violates law or offends morality. To sort permissible from impermissible discrimination, courts apply different tests. In many European countries they apply "proportionality analysis." In the United States, courts apply the "tiers of scrutiny." We focus on the latter, though the tests have similarities.[67]

In brief, courts begin by asking if the government's law discriminates among people. If the answer is yes, courts then force the government to justify its action. The government must identify its "interest" (what end does it seek?), and the government must defend its means (how well does it achieve the end?). The rigor of review depends on the tier that applies. For discrimination based on race or religion, courts apply "strict scrutiny." The government needs a "compelling" interest, and it must show "narrow tailoring" (to restate, the government's action must be "narrowly tailored" to achieve its "compelling" interest). For discrimination based on characteristics like income, the demands on the government are less onerous. This is because rich people are not a protected class, nor are poor people.

To demonstrate, consider *Grutter v. Bollinger*.[68] The University of Michigan Law School, a state institution, gave a "plus" to applicants who were racial minorities. Thus, the state discriminated based on race. The Supreme Court applied strict scrutiny to the university's admissions policy. The Court concluded that the university had a compelling interest in achieving a diverse student body. Furthermore, the Court concluded that the admissions policy was narrowly tailored. It did not grant admission to all racial minorities or create a racial quota. That would advantage some applicants regardless of

[66] Dothard v. Rawlinson, 433 U.S. 321, 336–37 (1977).

[67] *See* Judkins Mathews & Alec Stone Sweet, *All Things in Proportion? American Rights Doctrine and the Problem of Balancing*, 60 Emory L.J. 799 (2010).

[68] 539 U.S. 306 (2003).

whether they would diversify the school. (To illustrate, if the class already includes five African Americans from New York, admitting a sixth might not diversify the school as much as admitting a white student from Alaska.) Instead, the admissions policy gave each applicant "individualized, holistic review."[69] The Court upheld the admissions policy.

To an economist, the tiers of scrutiny framework resembles cost-benefit analysis.[70] Can the state discriminate? The answer depends on whether the costs of discrimination outweigh its benefits. Courts assess the costs in part by identifying the existence of and basis for discrimination. Courts assess the benefits by analyzing the state's interest (is the end compelling?) and its means (will the discrimination further the interest, will it have costly side effects, etc.?).

If judges were omniscient, perhaps they could adjudicate discrimination cases perfectly, permitting only cost-justified discrimination (affirmative action might be an example, though of course some people will disagree). In reality, judges make mistakes. The tiers can be conceptualized as guidance to minimize mistakes, like rules of thumb. Discrimination based on immutable characteristics tends to be costliest, so it triggers strict scrutiny, making it hard for the state to sustain its law. Discrimination based on characteristics like income is not considered so costly, so it triggers more deferential review. If the discrimination will not further the state's interest, then it serves no benefit, so it is not cost-justified.

Even with the tiers, judges have a lot of discretion when weighing costs and benefits. The U.S. Constitution does not specify which government interests are "compelling." We will return to judicial discretion in a later chapter.

Questions

7.19. The state can require firefighters to be strong. However, the state cannot require firefighters to be men, even though men tend to be stronger than women. Why?

7.20. To become a police officer, applicants had to take a test. African Americans tended to do worse on the test.[71] They claimed that the test violated their right to equality. In *Washington v. Davis*, the Supreme Court held that government policies like the test can violate the Constitution only if they have a discriminatory effect *and* are motivated by discriminatory intent.[72] Apparently, the government did not intend to discriminate, so the test was permissible. Is the Court's holding consistent with cost-benefit analysis? Why or why not?

[69] *Id.* at 337.

[70] However, it is not identical to cost-benefit analysis. *See* Louis Kaplow, *On the Design of Legal Rules: Balancing Versus Structured Decision Procedures*, 132 Harv. L. Rev. 992 (2019).

[71] A rich literature examines the relationships between race and standardized tests. *See, e.g.*, Roland G. Fryer & Steven D. Levitt, *Understanding the Black-White Test Score Gap in the First Two Years of School*, 86 Rev. Econ. Stat. 447, 447–64 (2004).

[72] 426 U.S. 229, 240 (1976).

C. Discrimination in a Perfect Market

In 1960, four African American students in North Carolina sat at a Woolworth's lunch counter and demanded service. The staff refused to serve them. Instead of leaving, the "Greensboro Four" sat in protest until the store closed. Their sit-in galvanized the Civil Rights Movement and facilitated integration. Instead of protesting discrimination by the state, the students protested discrimination by private actors, our next topic.

To begin, we consider the economics of the labor market.[73] Imagine employers competing with one another in the market for employees. If the market is perfectly competitive, employers who discriminate will suffer the costs of their discrimination. To illustrate, suppose a professional chess team only hires male players. It will lose to teams that hire the best players regardless of sex. Competition punishes employers who discriminate, discouraging discrimination.

Having discussed how competition affects discriminatory employers, now consider how competition affects discriminatory employees. Imagine a painting company whose employees are white or black, and suppose some of the white painters refuse to work with black painters. All of the painters are equally good at painting. The paint company must pay the extra cost of segregating its discriminating white painters. Segregating might involve time-consuming scheduling, separate break rooms, and so on. To the company, the value of a discriminatory painter equals the value of a nondiscriminatory painter minus the cost of segregation. Because discriminatory painters are worth less to the employer, they will get paid less. Perfect competition in the market for painters imposes the cost of segregation on the workers who demand it.

We have discussed the labor market. Now consider the market for goods and services. The lunch counter involved buyers (the students) and a seller (the restaurant). The buyers did not discriminate, but the seller did. In a perfectly competitive market, discriminatory sellers bear the cost of their discrimination. A restaurant that serves only white customers will earn less than a restaurant that serves everyone. Likewise, a restaurant that has to erect a wall to segregate its customers by race will have higher costs than a restaurant that integrates. If buyers do not discriminate, then discriminatory sellers pay the costs of their discrimination.

Turn the example around. Suppose sellers do not discriminate but buyers do, as when white people refuse to dine next to African Americans. Segregation is costly. Restaurants have to turn away customers or devise means to segregate them. Nondiscriminatory sellers will not incur those costs unless discriminatory buyers are willing to pay for them.

In sum, when markets are perfectly competitive, discriminators pay the costs of discrimination. In reality, the targets of discrimination often pay the costs. Thus, markets must not be perfectly competitive. Next we consider why.

[73] This discussion draws on GARY BECKER, THE ECONOMICS OF DISCRIMINATION (1957). *See also* John J. Donohue, *Antidiscrimination Law*, *in* HANDBOOK OF LAW AND ECONOMICS 1387–1472 (A. Mitchell Polinsky

Questions

7.21. In 2016, North Carolina enacted a law requiring transgender people to use bathrooms matching their biological sex. In response, major sporting events and concerts were canceled, and businesses threatened to move jobs out of the state.[74] The legislature retracted its law. Use the analysis of discrimination in competitive markets to analyze these facts.

7.22. Hospitals seek female nurses to deliver babies. Does this sex-based discrimination benefit expectant mothers and the female nurses who get these jobs? Does it harm men who cannot get these jobs?[75]

D. Discrimination in an Imperfect Market

In promoting the Civil Rights Act, Senator Hubert Humphrey summarized the plight of many African Americans: "How can a Negro child be motivated to take full advantage of integrated educational facilities if he has no hope of getting a job where he can use that education?"[76] In the United States, the targets of discrimination historically received lower wages than others with equivalent skills. The model of perfect competition cannot explain this fact. Market failures allow people to shift the burden of discrimination to victims. We focus on one kind of market failure: racial cartels.[77]

Consider a model of discrimination based on power, not competition. Just as producers sometimes collude to fix prices, social groups sometimes collude to obtain monopoly control over markets. To enjoy the advantages of monopoly, a social group must reduce competition from others by excluding them from markets. In this way, the more powerful social group can shift the cost of segregation to its victims, so that the victims of discrimination are worse off and the discriminators are better off.

To illustrate, imagine a trucking company with white truckers and minority truckers.[78] Suppose that the discriminatory white truckers organize themselves and acquire enough power to disrupt the workplace. They threaten employers—"we will skip work or drive slowly"—who fail to discriminate against minorities. Faced with the power of the white truckers, employers might be better off discriminating against minorities and avoiding disruption. The white truckers benefit themselves by reducing competition for jobs. Less competition means higher wages. The white truckers harm minorities by foreclosing a job opportunity, pushing them to other, often lower-skill work. As more minorities compete for the other work, competition drives down wages. The victims of discrimination bear its cost.

& Steven Shavell eds., 2007).

[74] *See* Dan Levin, *North Carolina Reaches Settlement on "Bathroom Bill"*, N.Y. Times, July 23, 2019.

[75] *See* Kimberly A. Yuracko, *Private Nurses and Playboy Bunnies: Explaining Permissible Sex Discrimination*, 92 Cal. L. Rev. 147 (2004).

[76] United Steelworkers of Am., AFL-CIO-CLC v. Weber, 443 U.S. 193, 203 (1979). "Negro" is an outdated term that is now considered offensive.

[77] For more, see John J. Donohue, *Antidiscrimination Law*, *in* Handbook of Law and Economics 1387–1472 (A. Mitchell Polinsky & Steven Shavell eds., 2007). *See also* Daria Roithmayr, Reproducing Racism: How Everyday Choices Lock In White Advantage (2014).

[78] For a real case involving a similar set of facts, see *Int'l Brotherhood of Teamsters v. United States*, 431 U.S. 324 (1977).

In this example, the discriminatory white truckers resemble a cartel, and their discriminatory norm resembles a price-fixing agreement. In practice, cartels are unstable because each member can benefit by defecting from the group.[79] For example, the Organization of Petroleum Exporting Nations (OPEC) tried to fix oil prices in the early 1970s, but members like Algeria secretly discounted oil to sell more of it. As a cartel grows, detecting and preventing "cheating" by members becomes harder. Large cartels usually collapse.

Like Algeria, members of a racial cartel can profit from violating the agreement. To prevent their employer from hiring minorities, white truckers must bear the inconvenience and danger of threatening the employers and disrupting work. As long as the employers discriminate, white truckers benefit, regardless of whether they participate in these activities. Thus, white truckers have an incentive to free ride on the efforts of other white truckers.

In general, sustaining discriminatory norms across markets requires the collusion of many people. Why doesn't free riding cause large racial cartels to collapse? Informal sanctions such as gossip, ostracism, boycotts, and violence can discourage free riding. In the past, many people in the United States used informal sanctions like these to punish people who failed to discriminate. However, informal sanctions were insufficient to sustain some forms of discrimination. To sustain racial cartels required law and other formal mechanisms. Southern states enacted laws preventing planters from competing for black labor.[80] Municipalities enacted laws preventing black families from moving to white neighborhoods.[81] The threat of legal sanctions discouraged free riding and supported racial cartels.

The Civil Rights Act of 1964 and new interpretations of the Constitution by judges swept away some discriminatory laws and local practices. By undermining sanctions for nondiscriminators, federal law weakened the discriminatory norms. As with business cartels, a good policy against a racial cartel aggravates its natural instability.

Our analysis of racial cartels imagines discriminatory employees pressuring their nondiscriminatory employers for personal advantage. In reality, some people discriminate without pressure and without the promise of any advantage. Racists simply "prefer" discrimination.[82] If enough members of the majority are racist in this way, they will force minorities to compete with each other for a small number of jobs. Rather than collusive strategy, preferences for segregation might best explain why the victims of discrimination pay its costs.

Questions

7.23. In the trucking example, we imagined white workers pressuring their employer not to hire racial minorities. The pressure increases white workers' wages and

[79] Instability of cartels is a standard topic in the economic theory of monopoly. *See, e.g.*, LESTER G. TELSER, ECONOMIC THEORY AND THE CORE (1978).

[80] William Cohen, *Negro Involuntary Servitude in the South, 1865–1940: A Preliminary Analysis*, 42 J. SO. HIST. 31 (1976). *See also* Jennifer Roback, *Racism as Rent Seeking*, 27 ECON. INQ'Y 661 (1989).

[81] Werner Troesken & Randall Walsh, *Collective Action, White Flight, and the Origins of Racial Zoning Laws*, 35 J.L. ECON. & ORG. 289 (2019).

[82] For influential work on "taste-based" discrimination, see GARY BECKER, THE ECONOMICS OF DISCRIMINATION (1957).

decreases minorities' wages. Why doesn't the employer fire the white workers and hire only minorities?

7.24. Coercive law aims to change behavior through threats: behave a certain way or suffer a penalty. Expressive law aims to change behavior through persuasion: behave a certain way because it's superior.[83] The Civil Rights Act of 1964 forbade companies from hiring only white workers. Is this coercive or expressive law?

7.25. Economists usually take all costs and benefits into account when assessing social welfare. Some people have discriminatory preferences, as when white people in the 1950s refused to share drinking fountains with black people. Should satisfying the preferences of racists count as a "benefit" when assessing social welfare?[84] (This is an easy question for most people but a surprisingly hard question for social welfarists. We will return to it later in the book.)

E. Discriminatory Signals

We have connected discrimination to monopoly power. Next we connect discrimination to another kind of market failure, asymmetric information. To begin with a familiar example, consider automobile insurance. Insurers cannot charge every driver a low premium; the accidents of unsafe drivers will bankrupt the company. Likewise, insurers cannot charge every driver a high premium because safe drivers will not pay a lot for insurance they are unlikely to need. To maximize profits, insurers must distinguish safe and unsafe drivers and charge them different rates. To do this, insurers need to overcome an information asymmetry: drivers know something about their own safety, but insurers do not.

How do insurers overcome this asymmetry? With statistics. Young drivers cause more accidents on average than middle-aged drivers, and young males cause more accidents on average than young females. The sex and age of policyholders predict the risk of accidents. The predictions are not perfect; some young men are safe drivers, and some middle-aged women are unsafe drivers. But the predictions are sufficiently accurate to be useful when setting insurance rates. Thus, insurance companies charge higher premiums for being young and male.

Just as insurance companies know little about individual policyholders, employers know little about job applicants. In choosing among applicants, employers rely on *signals*. For example, suppose an employer seeks to hire an accountant. The employer cannot read the minds of applicants and assess their fitness for the job. Instead, the employer looks for signals, like whether an applicant has a college degree in accounting. Having a degree signals interest in and talent for accounting, just what the employer seeks.[85]

83 Scholars use the term "expressive law" in many ways, including some that differ from our usage.

84 *See, e.g.*, Joseph William Singer, *Normative Methods for Lawyers*, 56 UCLA L. REV. 899 (2009); Daphna Lewinsohn-Zamir, *The Objectivity of Well-Being and the Objectives of Property Law*, 78 NYU L. REV. 1669 (2003).

85 Moreover, smart people inclined to reason like accountants find getting accounting degrees easier. *See* A. MICHAEL SPENCE, MARKET SIGNALING: INFORMATIONAL TRANSFER IN HIRING AND RELATED SCREENING PROCESSES (1974).

A good signal is cheap to observe, hard to manipulate, and it predicts accurately on average. Observing a college transcript is easy. Faking a college transcript is hard, and getting a degree in accounting is excruciating if you hate the topic. The average holder of an accounting degree is better at accounting than the average among everyone else. Thus, an accounting degree is a good signal for employers seeking accountants. Other examples of good signals include the smell of a melon, the height of a basketball player, the rating of a bond, the political party of a candidate, and the brand name of a smartphone.[86] People search for good signals to surmount information asymmetry.

Some signals cause controversy. To illustrate, one can often—though of course not always—make a good guess about another person's sex based on physical appearance. In contrast, observing a person's strength can be relatively difficult. Men are physically stronger than women on average, so some employers use sex as a signal and reject female applicants for jobs requiring strength. Sex is a *discriminatory signal*.[87]

As with regular signals, discriminatory signals trade off accuracy and cost. Signals cause mistakes, as when employers reject strong women and hire weak men. This error is equivalent to insurers overcharging safe drivers and undercharging dangerous drivers. However, using sex as a signal is cheap for employers, much cheaper than testing the strength of every job applicant. These ideas generate guidance for assessing discriminatory signals. *If mistakes of generalization cost the user less than gathering more individualized information, then use of the discriminatory signal is rational for the user.* It reflects rational discrimination. *If the cost of generalization to the user exceeds the cost of gathering more individualized information, then use of the discriminatory signal is irrational for the user.* It reflects irrational prejudice, or at least a persistent mistake.[88]

In a competitive market without prejudice, competition will eliminate inefficient signals. If employers compete for strong workers, and if a different signal—say, weight—does a better job of sorting strong and weak applicants, employers will stop sorting by sex and start sorting by weight. Banning signals that persist in a competitive market causes inefficiency. If sex is an efficient signal of strength, banning its use will force employers to adopt a different, costlier signal, like results of a strength test. Administering strength tests will drive up costs for the employer and its customers.

We have explained how competition can promote the use of efficient signals. However, efficiency is not the only objective of many public laws. Other objectives include distribution and equality. Preventing the use of discriminatory signals like sex might worsen efficiency but improve distribution and equality.

Suppose the state wants to prevent the use of discriminatory signals. It could simply ban them. However, banning signals can backfire, as the following box shows. In general, *a superior strategy for preventing the use of discriminatory signals is to increase the*

[86] Our list includes different kinds of signals. The smell of a melon tells you something about its flavor, but the melon didn't choose its smell, and the melon doesn't have private information. In contrast, candidates for office choose their political parties, and they possess information about themselves that voters lack. A candidate's party is a true signal, whereas smell might best be described as a proxy—in this case, a proxy for the melon's taste.

[87] Discriminatory signals relate to statistical discrimination. For pioneering work on this concept, see Kenneth J. Arrow, *Models of Job Discrimination*, *in* Racial Discrimination in Economic Life 83–102 (A.H. Pascal ed., 1972); Kenneth J. Arrow, *Some Mathematical Models of Race Discrimination in the Labor Market*, *in* Racial Discrimination in Economic Life 187–204 (A.H. Pascal ed., 1972).

[88] Similar propositions appear in Robert Cooter, The Strategic Constitution 349 (2000).

flow of information to the market so that relying on them is unnecessary. To demonstrate, suppose the state wants employers to stop using sex as a signal for strength. The state could pay for job applicants to get strength tests and share the results. Strength tests are better predictors of strength than sex. If employers do not have to pay for the tests, they will use them rather than sex as a signal.

We have analyzed the connection between signals and competitive markets. Now consider uncompetitive markets. The absence of competition can cause signals to persist even when they are inaccurate and inefficient. A telling example comes from criminal courts.[89] When the state charges a person with a crime, the person is jailed and the judge sets bail. If the accused posts bail (i.e., if he pays a certain amount of money), then he can go free pending trial. The state returns the bail to the accused if he appears for trial, whereas the state keeps the bail if the accused fails to appear for trial.

High bail strongly encourages people to appear for trial, but it causes hardship for poor defendants. To balance this trade-off, the law instructs judges to set bail at the smallest amount that will "reasonably assure the appearance of the arrested person in court."[90] One study found that bail amounts averaged 35 percent higher for black people charged with a particular crime than for white people charged with the same crime.[91] This suggests that judges used a discriminatory signal, race, to assess a defendant's propensity to flee.

Is race a good signal for propensity to flee? Many people post bail by borrowing money from a lender called a bail bond agent. In exchange for a fee, the agent pays the bail and assumes the risk that the defendant will not appear for trial. Like insurers, bail bond agents need to distinguish among customers to maximize their profits. They charge more from defendants more likely to flee, and vice versa. Bail bond agents in the study charged black defendants *less* than white defendants. They thought black people were less likely than white people to flee when facing the same bail.

Apparently bail bond agents and judges attach opposite signs to the racial signal. Who is right? The authors of the study believe that competition among the agents causes them to estimate probabilities accurately, whereas the absence of competition among judges permits their prejudices to go uncorrected.[92] To restate the idea, if a bond agent makes a mistake, she loses money. This encourages her to make fewer mistakes. If a judge makes a mistake, she loses nothing, so she faces no pressure to make corrections.

To generalize, stifling competition allows bad signals to persist. Competition is especially stifled in the nonprofit and government sectors. In addition to bail rates, this might explain why police stop and search more black motorists, even if black people are no more likely than white people to commit crimes. It might also explain events at Chicago's O'Hare Airport. U.S. Customs officers thought that female African American passengers were especially likely to be drug couriers, so they targeted them for invasive searches. In fact, being female and black was a poor predictor. When officers stopped relying on these bad signals, they detected more drug smugglers than before.[93]

[89] Ian Ayres & Joel Waldfogel, *A Market Test for Race Discrimination in Bail Setting*, 46 Stan. L. Rev. 987 (1994).

[90] *Id.* at 989. This was the law in the relevant state at the time of the study.

[91] *See id.* at 992.

[92] *Id. See also* David Arnold, Will Dobbie, & Crystal S. Yang, *Racial Bias in Bail Decisions*, 133 Q.J. Econ. 1885 (2018).

[93] *See* Fred Schauer, Profiles, Probabilities, and Stereotypes 176–78 (2003).

Questions

7.26. A male employer says, "If you want me to use your strength instead of your sex as a signal, you must pay for your strength test." A female job applicant responds, "I should not have to pay for your discrimination." Who has the better argument?

7.27. "Profiling" occurs when enforcers rely on a trait to signal criminality, as when police officers pull over African American drivers and airport security searches Arab passengers.

(a) Men commit more crimes than women. Does this justify profiling men for searches and arrests?

(b) In the United States, police statistics show that racial minorities commit more crimes than white people. Does this justify profiling racial minorities? In answering, consider whether the government polices white and minority communities in the same way. Might different approaches to policing affect the statistics?

(c) Suppose that white and black people commit crimes at the same rate, but (for whatever reason) searches of white people are half as likely as searches of black people to lead to a conviction. To equalize conviction rates across groups, should police search twice as many white people as black people?[94]

Ban the Box

Employers want to know if people applying for jobs have been convicted of any crimes. To gather this information, employers ask job applicants to tick a box on their applications if they have criminal records. Predictably, employers reject otherwise-qualified applicants who tick the box. Thus, the box makes it harder for people who have committed crimes and served their sentences to secure jobs and reintegrate themselves in society. In particular, the box makes it harder for black men to secure jobs, as they are more likely than other groups in the United States to have criminal records.

To correct this problem, some U.S. states and other jurisdictions have passed laws "banning the box." Employers cannot ask job applicants about their criminal records, at least not during the initial screening. Employers can ask about criminal records after the initial screening, but, according to proponents of these laws, those records will matter less after employers meet applicants in person.

Does banning the box achieve its goal? Apparently, the answer is no.[95] A study found that before the box was banned, black applicants were 7 percent less likely

[94] *See* John Knowles, Nicola Persico, & Petra Todd, *Racial Bias in Motor Vehicle Searches: Theory and Evidence*, 109 J. Pol. Econ. 203, 227 (2001) ("searching some groups more often than others may be *necessary* to sustain equality in the proportions guilty across groups.").

[95] The following discussion is based on Amanda Agan & Sonja Starr, *Ban the Box, Criminal Records, and Racial Discrimination: A Field Experiment*, 133 Q.J. Econ. 191 (2018). *See also* Jennifer L. Doleac & Benjamin Hansen, *The Unintended Consequences of "Ban the Box": Statistical Discrimination and Employment Outcomes When Criminal Histories Are Hidden*, 38 J. Labor Econ. 321 (2020).

than white applicants to get called for a job interview. After the box was banned, black applicants were *43 percent* less likely than white applicants to get called for a job interview. Banning the box worsened racial disparities in hiring.

Signals can explain this perverse result. Employers want to identify and reject job applicants with bad qualities. Bad qualities are hard to observe, so employers use criminal records as a signal. When the law forbade employers from using criminal records as a signal, they used another signal instead: race. Employers in the study apparently assumed that black applicants were more likely than white applicants to have bad qualities. Without the box, white applicants with criminal records got interviews, and black applicants without criminal records did not get interviews.

Earlier we argued that a good strategy for preventing the use of discriminatory signals is to increase the flow of information to the market. Rather than banning the box, law could expand the box.[96] Details about criminal records could help employers sort applicants with good and bad qualities. To illustrate, imagine a store hiring someone to take payments from customers. The store wants someone who can be trusted with money. The store owner would benefit if she could distinguish an applicant convicted of, say, vandalism from an applicant convicted of theft.

If details about criminal records would benefit employers, why don't employers ask for details? Here's a hypothesis. Good signals are not only accurate, they are cheap to observe. Details about criminal records are not cheap to observe. Have you ever reviewed a rap sheet? Could you make sense of it?

III. Speech

People praise God, find love, do business, debate politics, litigate cases, and perform plays. Speech is the medium of social life. Without speech, people and their leaders cannot communicate. For these reasons we call speech a Coasean right. Speech and its complements, press and assembly, facilitate bargaining and good representation. But speech is also a Hobbesian right. Speech promotes self-expression, which is part of human flourishing, not a means for good government. Speech is so important that it comes first among rights in the U.S. Constitution.[97] Here we use economics to illuminate the freedom of speech.

A. Speech and Monopoly

Speakers and listeners often resemble sellers and buyers. Speakers create a product, which is information, and they try to sell it in the marketplace of ideas. Speeches by candidates for office and commercials by companies touting their products fit this

[96] *Cf.* Lior Strahilevitz, *Privacy versus Antidiscrimination*, 75 U. Chi. L. Rev. 363 (2008).

[97] Here is the text of the First Amendment: "Congress shall make no law respecting an establishment of religion, or prohibiting the free exercise thereof; or abridging the freedom of speech, or of the press; or the right of the people peaceably to assemble, and to petition the Government for a redress of grievances." U.S. Const. amend. I.

characterization. If listeners consider the information valuable, they will trade time, attention, and occasionally money to consume it. Described this way, the market for information seems indistinguishable from the market for other goods and services.

An earlier chapter explained that absent transaction costs, markets achieve efficiency on their own. Does the market for speech achieve efficiency on its own? The answer is no. Speech suffers from persistent sources of inefficiency, including monopoly.

Consider *Red Lion Broadcasting Co. v. FCC.*[98] A radio station hosted Reverend Billy Hargis, who besmirched the character of Fred Cook on the air. When Cook learned of the slight, he demanded an opportunity to respond pursuant to the "fairness doctrine." In brief, that doctrine required broadcasters to cover both sides of public issues.[99] The station refused, arguing that the doctrine violated the freedom of speech. The Supreme Court disagreed. "[N]o constitutional right," the Court wrote, authorizes a broadcaster "to monopolize a radio frequency to the exclusion of his fellow citizens."[100]

According to the Court, broadcasters like Red Lion resembled monopolists. By controlling the airwaves, they controlled information. An earlier chapter explained monopolies with an example involving a bridge. By controlling passage over the river, the bridge owner could charge high tolls, enriching himself but harming commuters and reducing efficiency. By the same logic, a broadcaster could charge a high price for airtime or refuse to air opposing views. Instead of a free market for ideas, one broadcaster could dominate.

The Court's reasoning is flawed. Red Lion did not have a monopoly. Radio stations on other frequencies competed with it, as did television stations and newspapers. The threat of a private monopoly on speech seems especially unlikely today, as radio, TV, and newspapers compete with communications made possible by the internet.

Suppose Red Lion *did* have a monopoly. Would government regulation help? In assessing regulations, economists compare their costs with the costs of the market failure they aim to correct. Sometimes the costs of regulation are so high that the market failure is preferable. The costs of regulation depend in part on the character of the officials who make them. Competent officials who pursue the public good make better regulations than venal politicians who seek personal gain.

Many politicians seek personal gain. In particular, they resist giving up the power and prestige that comes with holding office. To prevent dictatorship and sustain democracy requires political competition, which in turn requires free debate and wide dissemination of information. Now we can state the economic logic for the freedom of speech. Allowing the state to regulate speech would empower politicians to create a public monopoly. Rather than supporting the marketplace of ideas, politicians might squelch debate and choke off information to support themselves. The freedom of speech prevents this. It tolerates the risk of private manipulation of speech to block a public monopoly on power.

To illustrate these ideas, consider *Near v. State of Minnesota.*[101] A newspaper reported that officials, including the chief of police, had conspired with gangsters. Officials sought

98 395 U.S. 367 (1969).

99 *See* Dominic E. Markwordt, *More Folly Than Fairness: the Fairness Doctrine, the First Amendment, and the Internet Age*, 22 REGENT U.L. REV. 405 (2010).

100 395 U.S. 367, 389 (1969).

101 283 U.S. 697 (1931).

to prevent publication of the newspaper's articles under a law prohibiting "malicious, scandalous and defamatory" reporting. The Supreme Court described the law as follows:

> Under this statute, a publisher of a newspaper . . . undertaking to conduct a campaign to expose and to censure official derelictions, and devoting his publication principally to that purpose, must face not simply the possibility of a verdict against him . . . but a determination that his newspaper or periodical is a public nuisance to be abated[.][102]

The Court invalidated the law, calling it "the essence of censorship."[103]

Monopoly theory illuminates the dangers of censorship. It also explains the Supreme Court's special skepticism toward "prior restraints." A prior restraint is a law requiring a speaker to get approval from the state before speaking. To illustrate, a local law in Georgia prohibited the distribution of "literature of any kind . . . without first obtaining written permission from the City Manager."[104] The Supreme Court struck down the law.[105] According to the Court, "Any prior restraint on expression comes . . . with a heavy presumption against its constitutional validity."[106] The danger of prior restraints is obvious. If you were trying to control information, what would you prefer: the power to punish people after they speak, or the power to stop people from speaking in the first place?

Questions

7.28. Newspapers reported on top-secret documents connected to the Vietnam War. President Nixon tried to stop them. In the "Pentagon Papers" case, the Supreme Court sided with the newspapers, but the Justices disagreed among themselves about why.[107] Justice Black concluded that the President could never stop newspapers from reporting, even on classified material. Justice Brennan suggested the President could make newspapers stop, but only if the reporting would create a grave risk, like "set[ting] in motion a nuclear holocaust."[108] Do you agree with Justice Black or Brennan? What risks accompany each of their positions?

7.29. Law often entrenches rights to protect the minority from the majority. Do you suppose a majority of Americans wanted President Nixon to silence the press? When we entrench free speech, who gets protected from whom?

7.30. Private companies provide high-speed internet access. In many communities there is only one provider.

(a) Should the government require "net neutrality" so that these companies cannot block or favor certain internet traffic?[109]

[102] *Id.* at 711.
[103] *Id.* at 713.
[104] Lovell v. City of Griffin, Ga., 303 U.S. 444, 447 (1938).
[105] *Id.*
[106] Org. for a Better Austin v. Keefe, 402 U.S. 415, 419 (1971) (internal quotation marks omitted).
[107] New York Times Co. v. United States, 403 U.S. 719 (1971).
[108] *Id.* at 726 (Brennan, J., concurring in the judgment).
[109] *See, e.g.*, 33 FCC Rcd 311 (2018). The FCC committed to net neutrality in 2015 but then changed its position, creating controversy. *See, e.g.*, Nelson Granados, *No Surprise: FCC to Abandon Net Neutrality Rules*, FORBES, Nov. 21, 2017.

(b) 5G networks provide high-speed internet access through cellphone towers. Will 5G networks increase or decrease demand for net neutrality?

B. Speech and Positive Externalities

Separate from monopoly, the market for speech suffers from another inefficiency: positive externalities.[110] Speech usually conveys ideas, and ideas are public goods. Recall that public goods have two characteristics, non-rivalry and non-excludability. Ideas are non-rivalrous; your use of the Pythagorean Theorem does not preclude me from using it. Likewise, ideas are non-excludable, especially in the information age. Preventing people from using your idea is much harder than preventing people from using your car. These characteristics give rise to externalities. When an inventor explains his new product to investors, everyone benefits, including eavesdroppers who copy the idea.

As an earlier chapter explained, the free market undersupplies activities that create positive externalities. Without regulation, inventors and artists will create too few ideas, stifling innovation and creativity. (Would you write a novel if your editor could steal it?) Law responds to this problem with intellectual property. By conveying ownership over ideas, patents and copyrights empower creative people to exclude others from exploiting their work. Intellectual property promotes speech by letting speakers internalize the value that their speech creates.

We have explained that speech with commercial value comes with positive externalities. What about speech with political value, like reporting on the Pentagon Papers? Many political speakers seek influence, not wealth. When speakers seek influence, they want to maximize their audience. Every listener is welcome; no one is an unintended beneficiary. Such speech has value, but it does not have positive externalities. Now consider other scenarios. An orator practices in the park, inspiring students who overhear her. A leader's speech gets broadcasted across the border, improving politics in another state. Some political speech does have positive externalities.

How can society correct an undersupply of political speech? Intellectual property law must help. Some political speech appears in books and articles that cannot lawfully be copied. Without copyright, that speech might never have been produced. However, solving the undersupply of speech probably requires more than copyrights. It would require state subsidies and regulations that, for reasons described, might do more harm than good. Remember those venal politicians.

Although law cannot solve the undersupply of political speech, it can minimize the problem. Law minimizes the problem by lowering the cost of political speech, boosting its production. In the United States, the First Amendment lowers the cost of speech by making public forums available for debate and assembly.[111] More fundamentally,

[110] *See, e.g.*, Daniel A. Farber, *Free Speech without Romance: Public Choice and the First Amendment*, 105 Harv. L. Rev. 554 (1991).

[111] The First Amendment especially protects speech made in public fora. *See id.* at 574.

the First Amendment lowers the cost of speech by stopping the government from punishing speakers.

Questions

7.31. Consider these statements that presidential candidates in the United States made to private groups: Barack Obama said that small-town voters "cling to guns or religion"; Mitt Romney said "47 percent" of voters are "dependent on government"; and Hillary Clinton called "half" of Donald Trump's supporters "a basket of deplorables."[112] All three statements leaked and became public.
   (a) Did these acts of political speech have positive externalities?
   (b) The people who leaked these statements were protected from recriminations by the First Amendment. Does that protection promote voter information? Does it discourage political speech?

7.32. Rather than making their own building code, some municipalities bought a model building code from a private company and enacted it into law. When the building code was posted online, the company sued for copyright infringement.[113] Should law be copyrightable? In answering, consider two issues. First, good law requires good ideas, and good ideas are public goods. Second, according to a long tradition in philosophy, the rule of law requires all laws to be publicly accessible.

C. Speech and Congestion

The Lord of the Flies is a famous novel about boys stranded on an island who struggle to govern themselves. They quickly develop a rule: you cannot speak to the group unless you are holding the conch. The boys in the novel experienced something fundamental about free speech: it leads to congestion. When two people speak simultaneously, no one communicates.

An earlier chapter introduced congestion with common resources, as when one rancher's grazing affects another rancher's livelihood. Congestion implies a negative externality that leads to inefficiency—too much grazing. Negative externalities in speech follow the same logic. Instead of congested pastures, we have congested wavelengths, and instead of too little grass, we have too much noise.

To see this problem in law, recall our discussion of the electromagnetic spectrum. If multiple people use the same frequency at the same time, everyone's signal gets jammed. In 1910, "irresponsible operators" jammed the U.S. Navy's signals, imperiling

[112] Ed Pilkington, *Obama Angers Midwest Voters with Guns and Religion Remark*, The Guardian, Apr. 14, 2008; Mark Memmott, *Romney's Wrong and Right about the "47 Percent"*, NPR, Sept. 18, 2012; Domenico Montanaro, *Hillary Clinton's "Basket of Deplorables," in Full Context of This Ugly Campaign*, NPR, Sept. 10, 2016.

[113] *See* James M. Sweeney, Note, *Copyrighted Laws: Enabling and Preserving Access to Incorporated Private Standards*, 101 Minn. L. Rev. 1331 (2017); Veeck v. Southern Building Code Congress International, Inc., 293 F.3d 791 (5th Cir. 2002) (en banc) (holding that municipal law was not copyrightable).

communication at sea.[114] The Communications Act of 1934 authorized the Federal Communications Commission (FCC) to regulate allocation and use of the spectrum. The law created free speech concerns—"the FCC won't let me broadcast my speech." However, the Supreme Court upheld the law, stating that the FCC did not violate the First Amendment by acting as a "traffic officer, policing the wave lengths to prevent stations from interfering with each other."[115] The First Amendment permits the government to manage congestion.

Consider another case. A state-owned television broadcaster hosted a debate among candidates for a seat in Congress. Three people ran for the seat, but only two were invited to the debate. The third candidate, who ran as an independent and had almost no public support, was excluded. That candidate was named Ralph Forbes, and he sued the broadcaster for violating his speech rights. In *Arkansas Educational Television Commission v. Forbes*, the Supreme Court rejected Mr. Forbes' claim.[116] Including all candidates in a debate, the Court reasoned, could "actually undermine the educational value and quality of debates."[117] We can understand this as an argument about congestion. Increasing speakers can decrease communication.

Some readers might bristle at the Court's conclusion. Including 10 or 15 candidates might make a debate pointless, but including three would not. To promote free speech, the broadcaster should have let Mr. Forbes participate. However, the free speech calculation is more complicated than that. Good lawyers look beyond the facts of the individual case to the general principle. Should broadcasters have wide discretion to choose the number of debaters, or should they have to include more or less everyone? If broadcasters must include more or less everyone, then broadcasters might not hold debates. The Supreme Court made this argument when rejecting Mr. Forbes' claim: "[F]aced with the prospect of cacophony, on the one hand, and First Amendment liability, on the other, a public television broadcaster might choose not to air candidates' views at all . . . and by so doing diminish the free flow of information and ideas."[118]

Questions

7.33. Use the Coase Theorem to explain why boys on an island can solve congestion but radio operators cannot.

7.34. Many organizations march, protest, and picket on the National Mall in Washington, DC. Those activities require a permit. Permits are prior restraints, yet U.S. courts do not interpret the freedom of speech to forbid requiring permits. Why?

[114] Ronald H. Coase, *The Federal Communications Commission*, 2 J.L. Econ. 1, 2 (1959).

[115] Nat'l Broad. Co. v. United States, 319 U.S. 190, 215 (1943). The Court held that the FCC had broader authority that went beyond simply coordinating spectrum.

[116] 523 U.S. 666 (1998).

[117] *Id.* at 681 (internal quotations marks and citation omitted).

[118] *Id.* (internal quotations marks and citation omitted).

D. Harmful Speech

We have explained how one person's speech can interfere with another's. This is an important but narrow type of negative externality. Here we generalize. Speech causes a negative externality whenever it causes harm to another that the speaker does not take into account. Consider some examples: hate speech, as when Nazis march by Jewish synagogues; incitement, as when a protester burns the national flag; and obscenity, as when a club exposes passersby to sexual images. All of these cases involve a negative externality: the listener (or viewer) suffers a cost that the speaker doesn't properly take into account. The speaker either ignores the cost to the listener or treats the cost as a benefit.

Does free speech always prevail? In the United States, you might think the answer is yes. The First Amendment says, "Congress shall make *no* law . . . abridging the freedom of speech."[119] In fact, the answer is no. The government routinely regulates negative externalities in speech. This is consistent with economic reasoning.

To economists, nothing is free. Every act comes with costs, including speaking. Whether an act should be permitted depends on whether its costs outweigh its benefits. Judge Learned Hand developed a framework for weighing the costs and benefits of free speech in a case called *United States v. Dennis*.[120] Members of the Communist Party USA were convicted of advocating the violent overthrow of the U.S. government. The case pitted the value of free speech against the danger of incitement. To resolve the case, Judge Hand asked "whether the gravity of the 'evil,' discounted by its improbability, justifies such invasion of free speech as is necessary to avoid the danger."[121] Judge Hand's reasoning can be expressed algebraically. Let B equal the burden on speech from government regulation, let p equal the probability that unregulated speech leads to harm, and let H equal that harm. The government should regulate when $B < p * H$.[122]

This formula is simple and illuminating. If the probability of harm is small, then the case for regulation weakens, even if the actual harm, should it materialize, is large. If the probability is large, then regulation may be justified even if the actual harm is small.

To illustrate, let's apply the formula to the facts in *Brandenburg v. Ohio*.[123] A leader of the Ku Klux Klan advocated violence against racial minorities and threatened government institutions for "suppress[ing] the white, Caucasian race."[124] He was convicted of violating a statute prohibiting incitement. The Supreme Court overturned his conviction. According to the Court, the state cannot forbid speech unless it will likely cause "imminent lawless action."[125] We can interpret *Brandenburg* as follows: p was too

[119] U.S. CONST. amend. I (emphasis added).

[120] 183 F.2d 201 (2d Cir. 1950). *Dennis* is central to an influential analysis of the First Amendment from which we draw. *See* Richard A. Posner, *Free Speech in an Economic Perspective*, 20 SUFFOLK U.L. REV. 1 (1986). Though never overruled, *Dennis* is not prominent in contemporary First Amendment doctrine.

[121] United States v. Dennis, 183 F.2d 201, 212 (2d Cir. 1950), *aff'd*, 341 U.S. 494 (1951).

[122] This matches the Hand Formula applied in tort law. Judge Hand expressed that formula three years before *Dennis* in *United States v. Carroll Towing Co.*, 159 F.2d 169 (2d. Cir. 1947). To find the optimal regulation in an economic sense, we must understand the formula's inputs in marginal terms.

[123] 395 U.S. 444 (1969). We apply the *Dennis* test to the facts of *Brandenburg* for the sake of example. The Court in *Brandenburg* cited *Dennis* but did not endorse or follow its test. *Dennis* is a curiosity in First Amendment doctrine, not the controlling precedent.

[124] *Id.* at 446.

[125] *Id.* at 447.

small. Abstract advocacy in the Ohio countryside was unlikely to provoke imminent lawlessness.

Instead of abstract advocacy, suppose Brandenburg had directed his supporters to target a particular, vulnerable person nearby. H would have been smaller because violence against one causes less harm than violence against many. However, p would have been much larger. On balance, Judge Hand's equation may have supported a restriction on speech.

We have focused on the costs of speech (in the equation, p and H). Now consider the costs of regulating it (B). When the government restricts speech, the speaker suffers, as do listeners who desired the speech. More speakers, listeners, and positive externalities mean higher costs. In addition, regulations have a "chilling effect" when they discourage more speech than lawmakers intend. Chilling valuable speech drives up costs. Finally, making and enforcing regulations takes time and resources.

Our chapters on enforcement will examine some of these costs in detail. Here we focus on two legal doctrines that affect the costs of speech regulations. The first is the preference for content-neutral, as opposed to content-based, laws. A content-neutral law applies to speech regardless of its message, whereas a content-based law applies to speech because of its message. To illustrate, a city ordinance prohibited picketing near a public school, unless the picketing happened near a school involved in a labor dispute. The law was content-based. It treated expression about one issue, labor, differently from the rest. The Supreme Court invalidated the law, stating that "government has no power to restrict expression because of its message, its ideas, its subject matter, or its content."[126]

Content-based laws create special costs. First, they encourage monopoly. A politician intent on staying in power will not ban all political speech, just speech that criticizes him. By insisting on content neutrality, courts prevent officials from targeting the speech of their opponents.[127]

Second, content-neutrality reduces disruptions in the marketplace of ideas. To see why, consider a topic that might seem quite different: taxes. Suppose that growing a pumpkin costs \$1 and growing a melon costs \$2. If each has a market value of \$5, then farmers should grow pumpkins (net value of \$4 apiece), not melons (\$3 apiece). If the government imposes a tax of \$1.50 on pumpkins, farmers will switch to melons. They prefer profit of \$3 per melon to a profit of \$2.50 per pumpkin. This is inefficient. Even with the tax, pumpkins produce more value than melons. The problem is that farmers don't internalize that value. Some of the value gets transferred to the state. To avoid this kind of inefficiency, the state should tax melons *and* pumpkins. A \$1.50 tax on all produce would cause farmers to grow pumpkins (profit of \$2.50 apiece, net value of \$4 apiece) rather than melons (profit of \$1.50 apiece, net value of \$3 apiece).

To generalize from this example, broader taxes cause fewer distortions in decision-making, reducing inefficiency. Content-neutral restrictions on speech resemble broad taxes, whereas content-based restrictions resemble narrow taxes.[128] To illustrate, a

[126] Police Dep't of City of Chicago v. Mosley, 408 U.S. 92, 95 (1972).

[127] Content-based restrictions limit all speech on a topic ("Don't discuss the war"), whereas viewpoint-based restrictions limit *particular* speech on a topic ("Don't criticize the war"). This is an interesting and important distinction, but we mostly ignore it.

[128] *See* Daniel A. Farber, *Free Speech without Romance: Public Choice and the First Amendment*, 105 Harv. L. Rev. 554, 577–78 (1991). Viewpoint-based restrictions resemble even narrower taxes.

content-neutral law might prohibit proselytizing with a loudspeaker after dark. The law does not change what proselytizers say, it just changes when they say it. A content-based law might prohibit proselytizing on a particular topic. The content-based law forces the speaker to talk about something less valuable or meaningful to him.

This discussion leads to time, place, and manner restrictions. The state cannot ban picketing near public schools, but it can require picketing to happen after students go home. Likewise, the state can move parades to quiet streets, and it can move protesters away from funerals and abortion clinics. Time, place, and manner restrictions reorganize speech, which imposes fewer costs than banning it.

In sum, legal doctrines in the United States push officials to make content-neutral restrictions on the time, place, and manner of speech. Restrictions with these characteristics create smaller costs than the alternatives.

We have analyzed speech and its spillovers abstractly. In practice, courts scrutinize restrictions on speech using tests that resemble the tiers of scrutiny discussed previously. To illustrate, content-based restrictions draw strict scrutiny, meaning the state must show that its regulation is "necessary" to serve a "compelling" interest.[129] For time, place, and manner restrictions, the government only must show "narrow" tailoring to achieve a "significant" interest.[130] Instead of exploring these details, we will generalize across them. Rights, including free speech, are confident generalizations about the best course of action. The government should not be able to overcome them easily. Courts reserve the strictest tests for speech restrictions that seem likely to cause the most harm. Many First Amendment doctrines seem to produce results consistent with Judge Hand's test in *Dennis*.

Questions

7.35. One restriction on incitement applies to many speakers, and another applies to just one speaker. Does Judge Hand's formula imply that the state has more authority to enact the latter (smaller cost to speakers)? Why might his formula suggest the opposite?

7.36. In the United States, some speech and expression—obscenity, libel, speech integral to committing crime—receive no constitutional protection. Is this consistent with Judge Hand's formula?

7.37. Time, place, and manner restrictions must "leave open ample alternative channels for communication of the information."[131] Thus, the state can move a parade across town but not 100 miles away. Officials can limit a demonstration to two hours but not two minutes. Use Judge Hand's formula to justify this requirement.

7.38. An artist calls the sculpture in his yard art. The state calls it pornography that offends passersby. Should the state ban the sculpture? Or should the state tax the artist for displaying it?[132]

[129] Simon & Schuster, Inc. v. Members of New York State Crime Victims Bd., 502 U.S. 105, 118 (1991).
[130] Ward v. Rock Against Racism, 491 U.S. 781, 796 (1989).
[131] *Id.* at 791 (internal quotation marks omitted).
[132] *See* Peter N. Salib, *The Pigouvian Constitution*, 88 U. Chi. L. Rev. 1081 (2021).

The Captive Audience Doctrine

To drum up business, advertisers mailed material to people's homes. Some of the material included explicit images, like ads for pornographic magazines. Congress enacted a law allowing homeowners to opt out of receiving such offensive mail. If a homeowner opted out, the sender had to stop sending the material and delete the homeowner from its mailing list. Advertisers challenged the law, claiming that it violated their freedom of speech and expression. In *Rowan v. United States Post Office Department*, the Supreme Court upheld the law, stating, "the right of every person 'to be let alone' must be placed in the scales with the right of others to communicate."[133]

Rowan involved the "captive audience doctrine." In brief, that doctrine protects people from unwanted speech that they cannot avoid. Homeowners cannot avoid their own mailboxes. Thus, they can prevent unwanted ads from filling them, even if doing so stifles the senders' speech. Likewise, homeowners cannot avoid their front doors, so they can bar unwanted salesmen from knocking on them.[134] The doctrine permits the state to ban picketing in front of a home[135] and political ads on public transportation.[136]

The doctrine has limits. A man walked through a courthouse wearing a jacket that said, "Fuck the Draft." In *Cohen v. California*, the Supreme Court held that the state could not prohibit this.[137] The Court conceded that there were probably "unwitting listeners or viewers" of the message.[138] However, they could "avoid . . . bombardment of their sensibilities simply by averting their eyes."[139] In the Court's view, no one in the courthouse was forced to bear the offensive expression.

The captive audience doctrine might seem puzzling. Hate speech, "fighting words," and other kinds of expression harm some listeners, yet courts usually protect it. What about a captive audience changes the legal calculation?

Earlier we analyzed cases where two rights conflict. In *Masterpiece Cakeshop*, for example, the gay couple's right to equality conflicted with the baker's right to religion. We provided guidance for resolving such cases: courts should favor the party with fewer options because fewer options imply larger losses. Can you use this to defend the captive audience doctrine? Does it support the Court's decision in *Cohen*?

E. Commercial Speech

So far we have concentrated on political speech, meaning speech about politics, policy, and ideas. When the magazine sellers in *Rowan* mailed advertisements, they engaged in a different kind of speech called commercial speech. Commercial speech supplies information to generate profits, as when a company encourages you to buy soda or movie

133 397 U.S. 728, 736, (1970).

134 *Id.* at 737 ("The Court has traditionally respected the right of a householder to bar, by order or notice, solicitors, hawkers, and peddlers from his property.").

135 Frisby v. Schultz, 487 U.S. 474 (1988).

136 Lehman v. City of Shaker Heights, 418 U.S. 298 (1974).

137 403 U.S. 15 (1971).

138 *Id.* at 21.

139 *Id.*

tickets. People are constantly exposed to commercial speech on television, radio, signs, and the internet.

Beginning in the 1970s, the U.S. Supreme Court held that the First Amendment provides some protection for some commercial speech. However, the protection is limited. We will not explore the doctrine in detail, but here are some highlights.[140] The government can regulate commercial speech that promotes illegality ("buy heroin here") or misleads people ("cigarettes are good for your health"). Even if the commercial speech involves lawful activity and does not mislead, the government can still regulate it in some circumstances. To illustrate, the state can limit advertising on billboards to beautify cities and reduce distractions while driving.[141]

As a policy matter, one might wonder if commercial speech deserves special protection from the government. The preceding analysis supplies a reason. Just as regulating political speech can stifle competition in politics, regulating commercial speech can stifle competition in business. To demonstrate, rules in some states forbade lawyers from advertising their services and specialties.[142] Virginia enacted a law that prohibited pharmacists from advertising drug prices.[143] Courts invalidated many of these restrictions on the ground that they block the flow of information to consumers.[144] Protecting commercial speech stops the government from restricting competition in business.

Competition in markets is important. It helps consumers and some producers, like junior lawyers who need advertising to establish their practice. However, competition in markets is not as important as competition in government. This might help explain why political speech gets more protection than commercial speech.

Questions

7.39. Does commercial speech have positive externalities? Can you give an example?

7.40. In the United States, federal law permits alcohol makers to advertise their products to children. However, you will not see a beer commercial during a cartoon. Alcohol makers self-regulate, meaning they voluntarily refrain from marketing to minors.[145] Why? Would they self-regulate if commercial speech were protected like political speech?

7.41. A company wanted to post online instructions for making guns with a 3D printer. A federal court stopped it.[146] Should the First Amendment protect the company's right to promote the Second Amendment?

140 For the key precedent, see *Central Hudson Gas & Elec. Corp. v. Public Service Commission of New York*, 447 U.S. 557 (1980).

141 *See* Metromedia, Inc. v. San Diego, 453 U.S. 490 (1981). Courts review restrictions on commercial speech that involves lawful activity and that does not mislead using "intermediate" scrutiny.

142 For a concise overview of restrictions and litigation, see Ronald D. Rotunda & John E. Nowak, Principles of Constitutional Law 747–53 (5th ed. 2016).

143 *See* Virginia State Bd. of Pharmacy v. Virginia Citizens Consumer Council, Inc., 425 U.S. 748 (1976).

144 *Id.* at 765 ("Advertising, however tasteless and excessive it sometimes may seem, is nonetheless dissemination of information as to who is producing and selling what product, for what reason, and at what price. . . . [T]he allocation of our resources in large measure will be made through numerous private economic decisions. It is a matter of public interest that those decisions . . . be intelligent and well informed. To this end, the free flow of commercial information is indispensable.").

145 *See Alcohol Industry Self-Regulation: Who Is It Really Protecting?*, 112 Addiction 57 (2017).

146 Deanna Paul, *Federal Judge Blocks Publication of 3-D Printed Gun Blueprints*, Wash. Post, Aug. 21, 2018.

F. Defamation

Like commercial speech, political speech can mislead. Politicians routinely make false statements.[147] A prominent reporter fabricated stories about crime and war.[148] If political speech can mislead like commercial speech, why not regulate it like commercial speech?

In fact, some misleading political speech is regulated. Consider the law of defamation. Defamation occurs when one person makes a false statement about another that harms her reputation. For example, suppose a person falsely accuses another person of committing crimes, cheating on a spouse, or voting against a bill. Courts permit victims of defamation to sue for damages. In general, a victim must show that the statement asserted a fact ("he's a drug addict") instead of an opinion ("he's a jerk"), a third-party heard the fact, the fact is false, the victim suffered harm, and the person making the false statement acted negligently.

Consider that last requirement. What is negligence? A speaker acts negligently when she makes insufficient efforts to find the truth. What counts as insufficient can vary. It might be insufficient if a speaker fails to make "reasonable efforts" to find the truth. Or it might be insufficient only if the speaker acts with "reckless disregard," meaning she fails to make *any* real effort to find the truth.

This difference matters, as *New York Times v. Sullivan* shows.[149] The newspaper ran an ad accusing police in Alabama of acting against civil rights protesters. Parts of the ad were inaccurate, and an official sued. The Supreme Court announced a new rule: the Constitution "prohibits a public official from recovering damages for a defamatory falsehood relating to his official conduct unless he proves that the statement was made with 'actual malice'—that is, with knowledge that it was false or with reckless disregard of whether it was false or not."[150] The official could not satisfy the Court's demanding test.

Sullivan is celebrated for protecting speech and the free press. By making it hard for officials to sue, *Sullivan* prevents them from pressuring journalists to keep quiet. However, the case does limit some political speech. If speakers lie about politicians, or if they do not attempt to corroborate their claims, they might be liable.

Sullivan balanced free speech against officials' right to defend their reputations. By requiring actual malice, the Court tilted the balance in favor of speech. Economics might justify this. Journalists internalize all of the costs of political speech that turns out to be misleading—they have to pay damages in defamation suits. However, journalists probably do not internalize all of the benefits of political speech that turns out to be truthful. Some benefits accrue to listeners and society. Externalizing benefits encourages journalists to speak less. By limiting defamation suits, *Sullivan* let journalists externalize costs, encouraging them to speak more.

[147] The *Washington Post* reports that Donald Trump made 10,000 misleading claims as President. Glenn Kessler, Salvador Rizzo, & Meg Kelly, *President Trump Has Made More Than 10,000 False or Misleading Claims*, WASH. POST, Apr. 29, 2019. No doubt other Presidents have made many false or misleading claims as well.

[148] Dan Barry, David Barstow, Jonathan D. Glater, Adam Liptak, & Jacques Steinberg, *Correcting the Record; Times Reporter Who Resigned Leaves Long Trail of Deception*, N.Y. TIMES, May 11, 2003.

[149] 376 U.S. 254 (1964).

[150] *Id.* at 279–80.

Sullivan encourages more speech, but does it encourage truthful speech? By shielding speakers from liability, *Sullivan* empowers them to tell the truth, even in the face of powerful opposition. However, the same protection permits speakers to shade the truth with impunity. Thus, we predict that *Sullivan* increases both truthful and misleading speech.

If listeners can costlessly sort truth from lies, then more speech is always better. In this case, *Sullivan* promotes good government. What if listeners cannot easily distinguish truth from lies? Here the law, at least in the United States, falls back on the theory of monopoly. We are better with free speech and political competition, even if some voters are confused, than restricted speech and the risk of political monopoly. Of course, this is contestable.

Questions

7.42. An editor knows that her reporter's story is 60 percent likely to be true. Publishing the story will increase the paper's profits by $100,000. If true, the story will produce a net social benefit of $1 million. If false, the story will cause $500,000 in damages to a public official, who will sue for defamation. Should the editor publish the story? Does *Sullivan* encourage the editor to make the efficient choice?[151]

7.43. Yuri has a good reputation, meaning he has a lot to lose if someone defames him. Zephyr has a bad reputation. Who does *Sullivan* encourage to run for office, Yuri or Zephyr?[152]

7.44. Suppose a speaker cares about two things: whether she will be liable for her speech, and whether her listeners will believe her. If defamation is easy to prove, she might be liable. That "chills" her speech. However, if defamation is easy to prove, her listeners are more likely to believe her. Explain why the threat of liability can encourage people to speak.[153]

Fake News and the First Amendment

Speakers accused politicians of running a child sex ring in a pizza parlor. The accusations were false, yet they spread online, causing a man to storm the restaurant with a gun (he was arrested) and possibly affecting a presidential election.[154] "Pizzagate" is a prominent example of "fake news." Fake news is a new term for an old problem: misleading political speech.

151 This question is based on Daniel A. Farber, *Free Speech without Romance: Public Choice and the First Amendment*, 105 Harv. L. Rev. 554, 569 (1991).

152 Richard A. Epstein, *Was* New York Times v. Sullivan *Wrong?*, 53 U. Chi. L. Rev. 782, 799 (1986) ("[H]onest people are vulnerable to serious loss if defamed. The greater their reputations, the greater their potential losses. If the remedies for actual defamation are removed, or even watered down, one response is for these people to stay out of the public arena [.]").

153 *See* Daniel Hemel & Ariel Porat, *Free Speech and Cheap Talk*, 11 J. Legal Analysis 46 (2019); Yonathan A. Arbel & Murat Mungan, The Case against Expanding Defamation Law, 71 Ala. L. Rev. 453 (2019).

154 Gregor Aisch, Jon Huang, & Cecilia Kang, *Dissecting the #PizzaGate Conspiracy*, N.Y. Times, Dec. 10, 2016.

Can law solve fake news? The challenge is difficult. To see why, consider an analogous problem: misleading commercial speech. When lying is profitable, people have an incentive to lie. To make this concrete, imagine a used car salesman who has good cars and bad cars on his lot. Good cars sell for more, so the salesman has an incentive to lie and say that every car is good. The salesman's lies distort the market. Buyers pay for cars they don't want. Or, recognizing that the salesman can't be trusted, buyers don't buy anything, even though some cars are good.[155]

Here are three strategies for addressing commercial lies. First, the state can prohibit them.[156] If the salesman can't lie, no one gets duped. Second, the state can prohibit the product the speaker lies about. If the salesman can't sell a bad car, then buyers can trust that all cars on the lot are good. Third, the state can help people distinguish products. If buyers can tell the difference between good and bad cars, then the salesman's lies can't mislead them. The state helps people distinguish products by, for example, requiring disclosure. To demonstrate, packaging for homeopathic remedies must say things like, "the health benefits of this product have not been tested."

Apply these strategies to fake news. Can the state prohibit lying about politics? Can it forbid selling a newspaper with misleading political stories? No. The state can forbid defamation, but in general it cannot prohibit political speech because the Constitution protects it. Can the state help people distinguish true and fake news? Probably not. The state cannot make people say, "my speech is fake" or "I'm not a real journalist." This would require the government to sort political truths (or truth-tellers) from all the rest. The First Amendment denies it that power.

Our analysis shows why public solutions to fake news fail. What about private solutions? Companies like Facebook try to discourage fake news with fact checkers and artificial intelligence. Economics suggest another solution. The makers of good products offer a warranty ("our product is good"). The threat of state enforcement (if the product is bad, you can sue) makes the warranty credible. Credible warranties help consumers sort good and bad products.

Speakers could offer a warranty ("my speech is true"). The First Amendment might prevent state enforcement, but it doesn't prevent private enforcement. Why don't speakers warranty the truthfulness of their speech?[157] Why don't they commit to private arbitration if someone claims a breach of the warranty?

IV. Constitutional Updating

This chapter has analyzed the creation and interpretation of rights, especially the rights to equality and speech. Here we extend the analysis to a pressing topic: the evolution of rights. As with any law, drafting a "perfect" right presents a challenge. Over time, facts

[155] George A. Akerlof, *The Market for "Lemons": Quality Uncertainty and the Market Mechanism*, 84 Q.J. Econ. 488 (1970).

[156] Recall that in the United States the government can regulate misleading commercial speech.

[157] *Cf.* Yonathan Arbel, *Slicing Defamation by Contract*, U. Chi. L. Rev. Online (Mar. 2020).

change and opinions transform. Consequently, a situation can arise in which a right—or, for that matter, any entrenched law—falls out of step with society. Consider an example. Should same-sex couples have a right to wed? Twenty years ago most Americans said no, but today most say yes.

How should we modernize outdated law? Two solutions are available: enact a new law, or reinterpret the old law. To illustrate, legislators can protect the right of same-sex couples to wed by adding new language to the U.S. Constitution. Or judges can protect the right by interpreting the existing Equal Protection Clause to encompass it. Scholars call reinterpretation of existing law "judicial updating." In *Obergefell v. Hodges*, the Supreme Court held that the Equal Protection Clause grants same-sex couples the right to marry.[158] The Court engaged in judicial updating.

The choice between amendment and judicial updating has descriptive, normative, and interpretive dimensions. The descriptive dimension involves facts: which institution *can or does* modernize law? In the United States, many people would say the Supreme Court. The Court appears to update the Constitution frequently, while legislators have amended it just 27 times. The normative question involves predictions and values: Which institution *should* modernize law? Finally, the legal question involves interpretation: Which institution is *authorized* to modernize law? Legislators are always authorized, assuming they follow the required procedures. Whether courts have authority to update depends on the law in question and approaches to interpretation like originalism and pragmatism.

In the United States, people disagree bitterly over the choice between amendment and judicial updating. Economics cannot resolve their disagreement, but it can sharpen the debate.

A. Updates Constrain Amendments

A thermal imaging device reveals heat. Police pointed the device at Danny Kyllo's home and saw heat in his garage. They investigated and found dozens of marijuana plants growing under indoor lights. Growing marijuana was against the law. Kyllo argued that use of the thermal device was illegal. Specifically, he argued that pointing the device at his home constituted a "search" under the Constitution's Fourth Amendment.[159] In general, police cannot conduct a search, or use any evidence they retrieve, without a warrant, which they did not have.

Was pointing the device at Kyllo's home a "search?" The Supreme Court said yes.[160] Scholars disagree over how to characterize that decision. For the sake of example, let's stipulate that the decision constituted judicial updating. Prior to the case, the Fourth Amendment permitted use of the device, but the Court updated the Constitution and forbade it.

[158] 576 U.S. 644 (2015).

[159] U.S. Const. amend. IV ("The right of the people to be secure in their persons, houses, papers, and effects, against unreasonable searches and seizures, shall not be violated, and no Warrants shall issue, but upon probable cause, supported by Oath or affirmation, and particularly describing the place to be searched, and the persons or things to be seized.").

[160] Kyllo v. United States, 533 U.S. 27 (2001).

Is this act of (hypothesized) judicial updating problematic? The answer depends in part on whether the action informs or preempts the legislature's amendment process.

One action informs another when it supplies information but no constraint. Encouraging your spouse to carry an umbrella does not constrain him; he can choose to leave the umbrella at home. The encouragement can, however, supply information (perhaps you checked the weather forecast) that might lead to a better decision. Encouraging an umbrella *informs* another's choice. In contrast, preemption blocks an action. When you order your child to carry an umbrella, you prevent her from leaving without an umbrella, regardless of whether carrying one is a good idea. Your action *preempts* another's choice.

Let's characterize the decision in *Kyllo* as informing the legislature. The Court had to make a decision at the intersection of law enforcement, privacy, and technology. The Court concluded that the best decision precluded thermal imaging without a warrant. That decision informs legislators by conveying the considered views of judges about the issue. However, the Court's decision does not bind the legislature. The Court decided just one case about one criminal. Legislators can resolve all future cases in their preferred way by amending the constitutional law on thermal imaging. They have the same freedom to do so before and after the case.

Characterized this way, judicial updating might not seem controversial. However, this characterization is inaccurate. Judicial updating does not simply inform the amendment process, it can preempt it. Figure 7.1 shows why. The figure gives us an opportunity to review tools from the prior chapter.

Seven legislators, *j* through *p*, have authority to amend the constitution, and they appear in the figure at their ideal points. The status quo constitutional law matches *j*. The law is outdated in the sense that it lies far from the political center. The legislators operate under a 5/7ths voting rule.

If the legislators amend the law, they can move it from *j* to any point in the win set that stretches from *j* to *n*. They have many choices. Suppose the legislature's preferred choice is *m*. If the legislature moves the law to *m* it will stabilize. The legislators cannot amend the law once it moves inside the equilibrium set.

Instead of legislators amending the law, suppose a court updates the law instead. If the court updates the law into the equilibrium set, it fully preempts the legislature. To illustrate, suppose the court moves the law to *n*. No more than four legislators support moving law leftward from *n*, and no more than two support moving law rightward from *n*. It takes five votes to amend the law. Thus, the law remains at *n*, even though the legislature preferred *m*. Judicial updating preempts the legislature's choice.

Judicial updating does not always preempt the legislature. Instead of *n*, suppose the court moves the law to the point labeled *I* (where *I* stands for "interpretation"). This act of updating is less dramatic. The point *I* lies outside the equilibrium set, meaning the legislature can amend the law. However, the legislature is constrained. From *I*, the legislators can only move law to points in the narrow win set. They cannot move law to their preferred point *m*.

To generalize, updating by judges constrains amendment by legislators. When judges move law closer to the political center, they reduce legislative choice. When judges move law sufficiently close to the center, they preempt legislative choice.

The Supreme Court decided *Kyllo* in 2001, when thermal imaging devices were rare. Back then people had a reasonable expectation that others could not see heat emanating from their homes. Today anyone can buy a thermal device for a low price. Privacy has changed, yet police use of a thermal device still constitutes a search. Congress has not amended the constitutional law on thermal imaging. If the Court's decision in *Kyllo* merely informed Congress, then you might conclude that Congress's failure to amend the law means the Court got it right. Once you understand entrenchment you can see the flaw in that conclusion.

Questions

7.45. In Figure 7.1, suppose the court updates the law by moving it to a point left of *j*. What effect does this have on the legislature's power to amend?

7.46. Updating by the U.S. Supreme Court preempts Congress more than updating by Alabama's supreme court preempts the Alabama legislature. Why?

B. Institutional Advantage and Constitutional Change

We have shown that judicial updating constrains the amendment process. Is this harmful? It depends. If legislatures tend to make better decisions than courts, meaning decisions that better promote welfare, then updating should be discouraged. Courts interfere with a superior institution. However, if courts tend to make better decisions than legislatures, then judicial updating should be encouraged.

Scholars have made many arguments about whether and when courts make better decisions than legislatures. We reduce the debate to two factors: information and transition costs.

Start with information. The best decision in business maximizes profit, which equals revenues minus expenses. To make the best decision, CEOs need information about the revenues and expenses associated with different business strategies. Like profit in business, the best decision in law promotes one or more values. The value could be social welfare, or it could be something like equality, freedom, or whatever else. For the sake

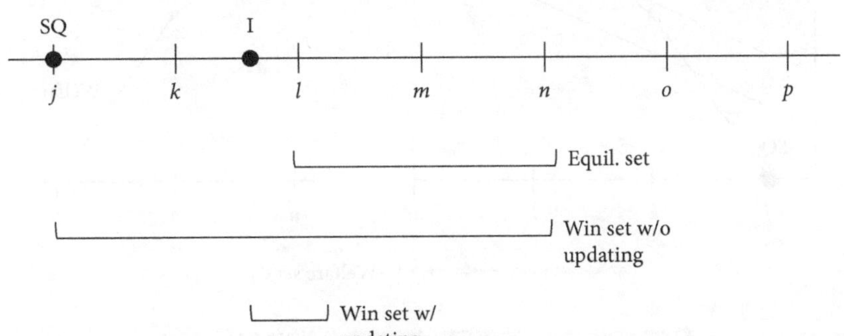

Figure 7.1. The Effect of Judicial Updating on Amendments

of this example, we will focus on social welfare. To maximize welfare, lawmakers need information about the benefits and costs of legal change.

To sharpen our discussion of benefits and costs, consider Figure 7.2. Voters *j* through *p* appear at their ideal points, and the status quo constitution matches *j*. The curve captures the benefit associated with moving the constitution from *j* toward the political center. The line labeled C_L shows transition costs. Given this setup, moving the constitution from *j* to any point in the "welfare set C_L" would increase welfare. Moving the constitution from *j* to *l* would maximize welfare.

If lawmakers were omniscient, they might move the constitution from *j* to *l* in order to maximize social welfare. In reality, lawmakers lack information. They do not know the shape of the benefit curve. If voter *k* has intense preferences, the curve will skew leftward, but if voter *o* has intense preferences it will skew rightward. Likewise, they do not know the details of transition costs. The line might originate higher or lower, and it might be steeper or flatter. Instead of a line, transition costs might follow a curve. Without good information, lawmakers make suboptimal choices. They might fail to maximize welfare, as when they maintain the status quo at *j* in Figure 7.2. They might reduce welfare, as when they move the constitution to *k* in Figure 7.2.

To generalize, good information promotes beneficial legal change, whereas bad information permits harmful legal change.

In contrast to legislators, most judges are insulated from politics. Instead of talking to voters and lobbyists about many issues, judges adjudicate cases about few issues. Instead of specializing in policy areas (legislatures divide into committees, like the Finance Committee in the U.S. Senate), judges are generalists. Court cases are not always representative of society's disputes, as a later chapter will explain. For these reasons, legislators probably have better information than judges.

Having discussed information, we now consider transition costs. Some transition costs do not depend on the institution causing the transition. When the Eighteenth

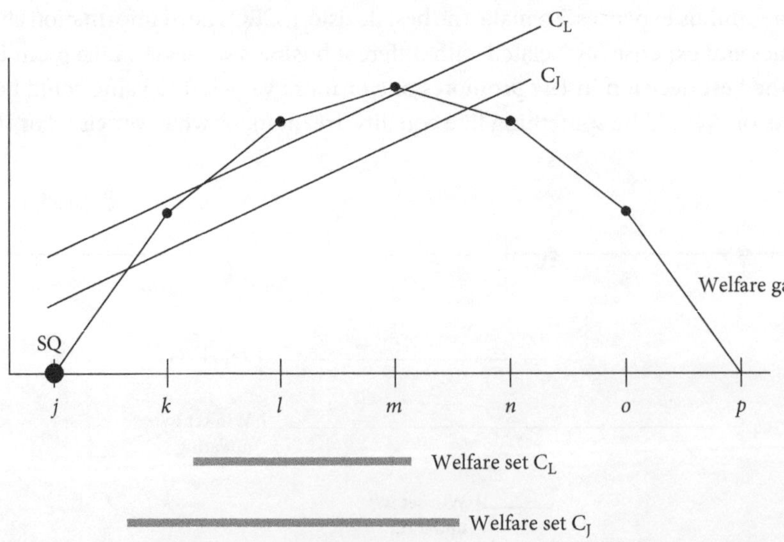

Figure 7.2. Updating by Legislators and Judges

Amendment to the U.S. Constitution prohibited alcohol, distillers, bar owners, and others incurred costs. The same people would have incurred the same costs if prohibition had originated with judges instead of Congress. Other transition costs do depend on the institution. To see why, recall that transition costs encompass all costs associated with legal change. Thus, transition costs include the mechanics of changing law: gathering information, deliberating, and voting. Transition costs also include opportunity costs. Time spent on one issue, like prohibiting life imprisonment for minors, is time that cannot be spent on other issues like terrorism, immigration, and budgeting.

In the United States, amending the Constitution requires support from two-thirds of the members of both houses of Congress. In addition, amendments require support from at least 38 states. The costs of gathering information, deliberating, and voting (not to mention haggling, threatening, grandstanding, and holding out) are much higher for thousands of far-flung legislators than for nine Supreme Court Justices. Likewise, the opportunity costs to thousands of legislators considering constitutional change must exceed the opportunity costs of a few judges.

Figure 7.2 captures these ideas. The line C_L shows transition costs when legislators amend the constitution, and the line C_J shows transition costs when judges update the constitution. Because transition costs are lower for judges, the welfare set C_J is relatively wide. Judges have more room for error.

Now we can characterize the choice between constitutional amendments and judicial updating. Amendments place the burden of constitutional change on legislators, who have better information than judges. Updating places the burden on judges, who create fewer transition costs than legislators. Legislators should tend to make more-informed decisions at high cost, while judges should tend to make less-informed decisions at relatively low cost. Amendments outperform updating when legislators' advantage in information exceeds the transitions advantage of courts.

Framed this way, the choice between amendment and updating resembles a delegation problem. The next chapter will analyze the theory of delegation in detail. For now, consider a thought experiment to make the point. An experienced doctor is performing surgery on one patient when another patient arrives with a sore throat. Should the doctor delay the surgery to see the second patient? Or should the doctor let an inexperienced nurse see the second patient? The doctor knows more but has higher opportunity costs. Sometimes the nurse should see the patient instead. In this example, the doctor resembles a legislature and the nurse resembles a court.

Questions

7.47. In Figure 7.2, would society be better off if legislators moved the constitution from j to l or judges moved the constitution from j to m?

7.48. "Amicus briefs" are submitted to court by third parties. They provide information that judges and the parties to the case might not otherwise have. In the 1800s, amicus briefs were rare, but today they are common. Do amicus briefs strengthen or weaken the argument for updating?

7.49. In general, transition costs are lower when people can anticipate legal change. Is it easier to anticipate legal change when legislators vote or judges adjudicate?

7.50. Is the argument for updating stronger in states that elect their judges than in states that appoint their judges?[161]

7.51. Some legislators are captured by special interests, and some judges are aloof or incompetent. Should these facts affect the choice between amendments and judicial updating?

C. Entrenchment and Updating

We have tied the case for judicial updating to information and transition costs. Our reasoning especially discourages updating on technical issues where the legislature knows much better. Conversely, our reasoning especially encourages updating when, for example, the country faces war or other national emergencies. In such cases, judges' opportunity costs, which are a component of transition costs, are much lower than legislators' opportunity costs.

In fact, low transition costs are not the only advantage that courts possess over legislators. Unlike amendment processes in legislatures, judges usually are not bound by supermajority rules. Consequently, judges can make changes to law that legislators cannot.

Recall the distinction between variable transition costs, which grow with the magnitude of legal change, and fixed transition costs, which always accrue in the same amount. Incremental legal change is best given variable costs, while substantial change is best given fixed costs. Figure 7.3 illustrates. From a status quo law of *j*, and given variable costs indicated by the line *V*, law should move incrementally into the "welfare set *V*." Given fixed costs indicated by the line *F*, law should move substantially into the "welfare set *F*."

In Figure 7.3, the change to law that *should* be made depends on transition costs. However, the change that *can* be made depends on the voting rule. Suppose voters *j* through *p* use a 6/7ths voting rule. They will replace the law at *j* with a law in the win set. This is optimal given variable costs; the "welfare set *V*" and the win set align. All possible changes to law increase welfare. However, this is harmful given fixed costs. The win set does not align with the "welfare set *F*." If transition costs are fixed, all possible changes to law reduce welfare.

In Figure 7.3, a constitutional amendment cannot solve the problem of fixed costs. Judicial updating can. A court can update the constitution by moving law from *j* to a point in welfare set *F*. Courts can achieve what legislators cannot.

This observation follows from the transitions theory of interpretation described in the prior chapter. If judges are going to update constitutional law, they should attend to transition costs. Fixed transition costs imply that legislators cannot promote welfare, courts can, and substantial rather than incremental updating is best.

We have shown that judges can improve social welfare when legislators cannot. This does not imply that judges should update. Legislators are constrained by voting rules and high transition costs, but they tend to have better information. Judges with poor information might make harmful decisions. Our objective is not to argue that updating outperforms amendment, just to show when and why it might.

161 *Cf.* David E. Pozen, *Judicial Elections as Popular Constitutionalism*, 110 COLUM. L. REV. 2047 (2010).

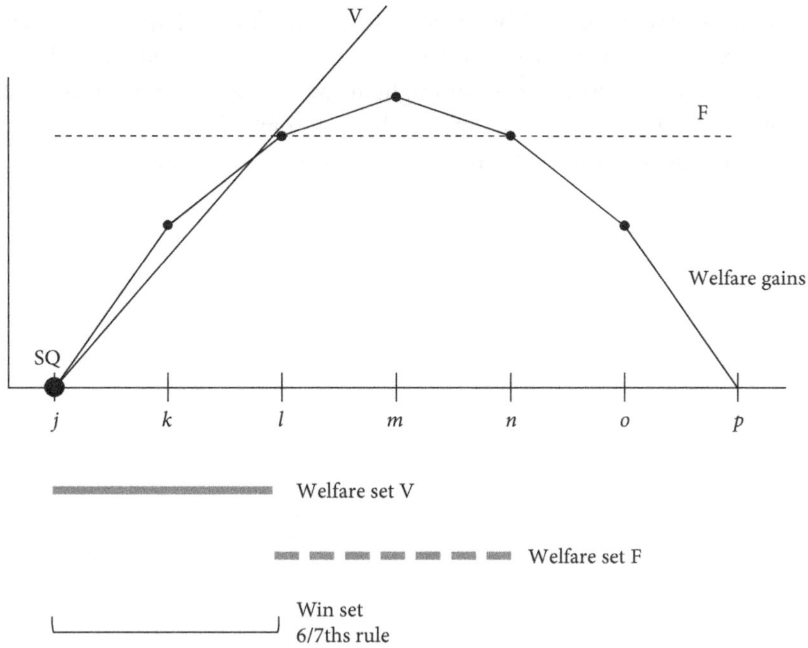

Figure 7.3. Legal Change and Transition Costs

Questions

7.52. According to the preceding analysis, a well-informed court can promote welfare by making larger changes to law than legislators can make. Can a well-informed court promote welfare by making a smaller change to law than legislators seek to make?

7.53. In the nineteenth and twentieth centuries, judges in the United States gradually updated the common law. Today scholars argue that the U.S. Supreme Court updates the Constitution in the same gradual way.[162] Use the transitions theory of interpretation to critique the Supreme Court's practice.

Conclusion

This chapter applies the theory of entrenchment to problems in public law. Specifically, the chapter focuses on rights, a common and important form of entrenched law. We distinguished Coasean and Hobbesian rights, analyzed the alienability of rights, and considered conflicts among rights. Then we considered two fundamental rights in detail, equality and speech. We showed that both rights give way in certain circumstances. This is consistent with our interpretation of rights as confident generalizations about the best course of action. In some circumstances, the state can overcome those confident

[162] *See, e.g.*, David Strauss, The Living Constitution (2010).

generalizations. We concluded by examining constitutional change. Entrenched law changes through amendment by legislators and updating by courts. Each approach has advantages and disadvantages. Throughout the chapter we have aimed to sharpen thinking about public law. Economics cuts through some of the fog surrounding rights and constitutional law, though it cannot always find the best solution.

8
Theory of Delegation

The Attorney General relies on her employees to enforce civil rights statutes, rather than doing it herself. The Administrator of the Environmental Protection Agency relies on scientists to test polluted water, rather than doing it himself. The police chief relies on officers to issue speeding tickets to motorists, instead of doing it herself. In a hierarchy, higher officials delegate authority to lower officials. Political theorists often describe representative government as the delegation of authority. Instead of making laws themselves, citizens in a democracy elect representatives to make laws on their behalf.

Delegation saves the delegator's effort, time, energy, concentration, and material resources. However, delegation also gives discretion to the delegate. A perfectly loyal delegate uses discretion to advance the delegator's purposes. An imperfectly loyal delegate uses discretion to advance her own purposes. Thus, delegation saves effort and risks diversion of purpose. To illustrate, appeals courts in the United States make decisions on law themselves (*de novo* review), but they defer to lower courts' findings of fact. Appeals courts effectively delegate fact-finding to trial courts.[1] Most of the time lower courts perform their role conscientiously. Sometimes, however, lower courts might manipulate fact-finding to advance their preferred outcome. By manipulating facts, the lower court dictates the higher court's decision on law.

The effort-diversion trade-off is fundamental when someone decides whether to exercise authority directly or delegate to another. Part I of this chapter models this trade-off as the "delegation game." Besides deciding when to delegate, a leader must decide whether to impose rules on the delegate or permit the delegate to exercise discretion. By constraining the delegate's choices, rules make diversion of purpose harder. However, rules also reduce flexibility. Part II models this trade-off as the "rule game." Part III provides a normative analysis of the delegation and rule games, and part IV applies the analysis to problems of interpretation. The chapter helps answer questions like these:

Example 1: In a 1935 case called *Schechter Poultry*, the Supreme Court struck down a law that empowered the President to make and enforce codes of "fair competition."[2] The Court reasoned that the legislative branch (Congress) could not delegate such authority to the executive branch (President). Today Congress routinely

[1] Some readers might say that appellate courts do *not* delegate fact-finding to trial courts because they do not have a choice. The Federal Rules of Civil Procedure require appellate courts to defer on facts unless the fact-finding is "clearly erroneous." We will say more about what delegation means in public law below. For now, we note that although law requires deference on fact-finding, appellate courts have some discretion in deciding what counts as "clearly erroneous."

[2] A.L.A. Schechter Poultry Corp. v. United States, 295 U.S. 495 (1935).

Public Law and Economics. Robert D. Cooter and Michael D. Gilbert, Oxford University Press. © Oxford University Press 2022.
DOI: 10.1093/oso/9780197655870.003.0008

delegates authority to the executive branch. Has the meaning of the Constitution changed since 1935?

Example 2: Citizens can enact many state and local laws through ballot initiatives, but they cannot enact federal laws. The U.S. Constitution vests all federal legislative power in Congress. Why should citizens delegate the making of all federal laws but not all state and local laws?

Example 3: U.S. Attorneys are prosecutors appointed by the President to enforce federal laws. Their assistants are accomplished attorneys hired through less political means. In 2006, President George W. Bush dismissed several U.S. Attorneys in the middle of his term in office, but he did not (and could not) dismiss their assistants.[3] When deciding who will enforce federal laws, where should politics end?

Example 4: In *Brown v Board of Education*, the Supreme Court ordered states to end racial segregation with "all deliberate speed."[4] That vague language allowed some states to remain segregated for many years. The Court could have used precise language, ordering integration by, say, "January 1, 1957." When should orders be vague, and when should orders be precise?

In its many forms, delegation pervades public law. This chapter develops its positive, normative, and interpretative theory.

I. The Delegation Game

In 2016, Congress enacted 216 statutes, and federal agencies enacted 3,853 regulations. As the numbers show, most federal rules come from administrative agencies like the Environmental Protection Agency (EPA), Securities and Exchange Commission, and Department of Education. Every agency and regulation implies an act of delegation. Agencies and delegation go together like butter and bread. Thus, we use an agency example to study the positive theory of delegation. We begin by studying binary choices, as when a person chooses between delegating or not. Then we consider continuous choices, as when a person can delegate more or less. Finally, we analyze a situation common in law: multiple actors, like Congress and the President, cooperate in delegating authority to a single agency like the EPA.

A. Principals and Agents

The Department of Health and Human Services aims to protect the health and well-being of U.S. citizens. Suppose the Secretary of Health and Human Services, who leads the Department, proposes to improve prenatal care by tying payments to performance. Doctors whose patients experience better outcomes will make more money. The Secretary could implement the plan directly by overseeing its details, but that would

[3] Ari Shapiro, *Timeline: Behind the Firing of Eight U.S. Attorneys*, NPR, Apr. 15, 2007.
[4] Brown v. Board of Educ. of Topeka, Kan., 349 U.S. 294, 301 (1955).

distract her from other important business. Alternatively, she could delegate power to an administrator, which would save her valuable time. After delegating power, the Secretary will be too remote from daily operations to observe the administrator's work in detail. Instead of improving prenatal care, the administrator would prefer to focus on emergency care, which is his specialty. Should the Secretary delegate authority to the administrator to execute her plan?

Economists ask a related question. The owner of a valuable resource—say, a dump truck, a house, a corporation, money, stocks, or an antique vase—gives control over it to someone else. The owner is called the *principal* and the controller is called the *agent*. Lawyers encounter these terms in the fiduciary relationship, as found in corporate, banking, and commercial law. In contracting with the agent, the principal's problem is to incentivize the agent to advance the principal's purpose, rather than diverting resources to the agent's purposes. Should the principal give the agent control over the asset? This is similar to the question of whether the Secretary should delegate authority to the administrator to implement her plan. To make use of agency theory in economics, this chapter treats delegation problems in government as principal-agent problems.

Outside of government, principals and agents control the details of their relationship. The principal decides whether to employ an agent, what she can do, how to compensate her, when to fire her, and so on. Inside government, principals sometimes have less flexibility. In the United States, the President appoints the Attorney General, but the President does not set the Attorney General's salary. Law gives the Attorney General responsibilities that the President cannot take away, even if he wants to. In situations like this, agency theory does not apply perfectly to government. However, it often applies well. Agency theory provides a helpful starting point for analysis.

When a principal delegates power, she hopes the agent will loyally implement her purpose. In reality, many agents fall short of this ideal. Many factors influence an agent's fidelity, including private interests, affection, prudence, boldness, and information. For simplicity, we begin by modeling interests.

A self-interested agent will divert resources to his advantage when the probability of detection by the principal is low. The probability of detection depends on what the principal can observe. After delegating authority, the principal cannot observe many of the agent's actions, but the principal usually can observe the project's overall success or failure. Unusually good results imply that the agent was loyal. Unusually bad results imply that the agent was disloyal. With intermediate results, the principal cannot determine the agent's loyalty.

In addition to loyalty, luck affects a project's success or failure. In the agency example, the Secretary's plan may fail because her administrator is disloyal, or because of uncontrollable events like a shortage of nurses or a health insurer's bankruptcy. When the Secretary observes intermediate results, she cannot tell if the administrator was loyal but unlucky, or disloyal and lucky.

Questions

8.1. Who is the principal and who is the agent: governor and constituent in a state; partner and associate in a law firm; professor and teaching assistant in a university; clerk and judge in a court; police chief and officer in a city; CEO and the company's general counsel; President and central banker?

8.2. *Agency cost* refers to the cost to the principal from the agent's disloyalty. Which of the following are agency costs: citizens suffer when politicians steal tax revenues; the President suffers when the Attorney General of New York investigates the President's businesses; the Administrator of the EPA suffers when his staff makes policy he opposes; cities suffer when states preempt local decision-making?

B. The Strategic Game

To understand the Secretary's problem better, Figure 8.1 embodies it in a game tree.[5] In the first branching of the tree, the principal decides whether to delegate authority or exercise it directly. Assuming nondelegation, the agent has nothing to decide. Assuming delegation, the agent, acting in the second branch of the tree, decides whether to implement (act loyally) or divert (act disloyally). In the final branch of the tree, good or bad luck affects the project's success. Economists call luck "nature," good luck a "good state of nature," and bad luck a "bad state of nature."

Having described what the principal and agent can do, now we describe what they get. Consider the right side of Figure 8.1, where the game tree ends in payoffs. At each terminal point, the principal's payoff is the first number and the agent's payoff is the second number. We explain the numbers from top to bottom. If the principal delegates and the agent implements, in a good state of nature the principal receives 1 and the agent receives 1, and in a bad state of nature the principal receives 0.5 and the agent receives 0.5. Moving down, if the principal delegates and the agent diverts, in a good

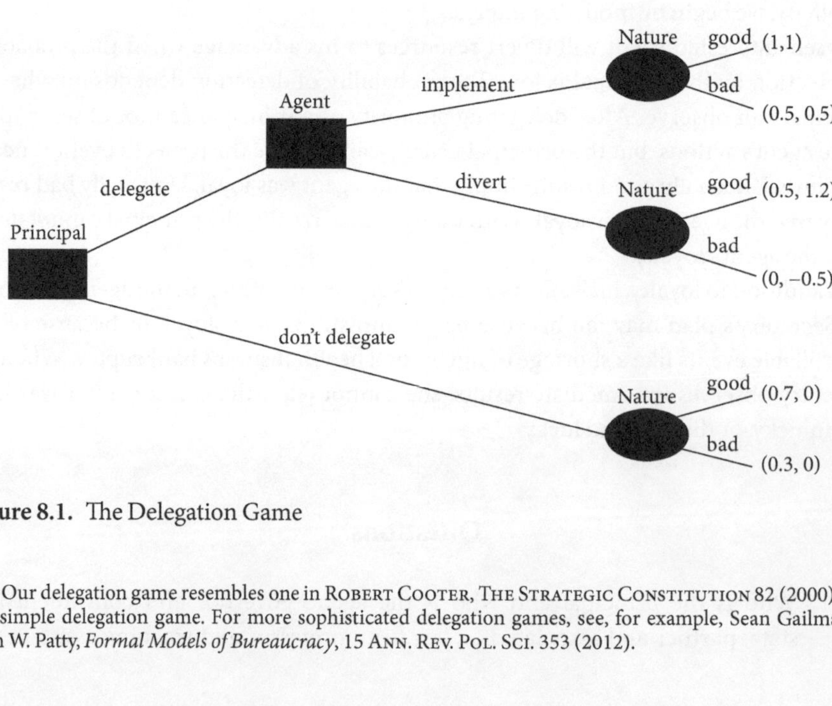

Figure 8.1. The Delegation Game

[5] Our delegation game resembles one in Robert Cooter, The Strategic Constitution 82 (2000). This is a simple delegation game. For more sophisticated delegation games, see, for example, Sean Gailmard & John W. Patty, *Formal Models of Bureaucracy*, 15 Ann. Rev. Pol. Sci. 353 (2012).

state the principal receives 0.5. and the agent receives 1.2, and in a bad state the principal receives 0 and the agent receives −0.5. The agent's negative payoff comes from the principal punishing him after detecting his disloyalty. Moving further down, if the principal exercises power directly ("don't delegate"), the agent has no choice to make. In a good state the principal receives 0.7 and the agent receives 0, and in a bad state the principal receives 0.3 and the agent receives 0.

Questions

8.3. If the principal in Figure 8.1 gets a payoff of 0, should she punish the agent? Why or why not?

8.4. If the principal in Figure 8.1 gets a payoff of 0.5, should she punish the agent? Why or why not?

C. When to Delegate

Now we can find the game's equilibrium, meaning the choices that a self-interested principal and agent will make. To solve the game, work from the last decision on the right to the first decision on the left (this is called *backward induction*). Assuming the principal delegates, the last decision on the right is the agent's choice between implementing and diverting. In a good state, the agent's payoff from diverting exceeds his payoff from implementing ($1.2 > 1$), so the agent's best strategy is to divert. Conversely, in a bad state the agent's payoff from implementing exceeds his payoff from diverting ($0.5 > -0.5$), so the agent's best strategy is to implement. Thus, the agent's best strategy depends on whether luck is good or bad.

Assume the parties know that luck will be good with probability p and bad with probability $1 - p$. If probability p is high, the agent expects to gain from diverting; conversely, if probability p is low, the agent expects to gain from implementing.[6]

Having considered the agent's strategy, now consider the principal's strategy. The principal must choose between delegating and not delegating. When p is high, the principal understands that delegating will cause the agent to divert, so the principal gains by not delegating. The principal prefers 0.7 (don't delegate/good luck) to 0.5 (delegate/divert/good luck). Alternatively, when p is low, the principal understands that delegating will cause the agent to implement, so the principal gains by delegating. The principal prefers 0.5 (delegate/implement/bad luck) to 0.3 (don't delegate/bad luck).

In sum, the principal exercises power directly or delegates depending on whether the agent will implement or divert, and the agent implements or diverts depending on the probability of a good state. To be precise, the tipping point in Figure 8.1 is $p = 5/6$.[7] The game's solution is:

[6] The probability p of good luck does not depend on the choices of the principal and agent. Luck is *exogenous*, meaning it gets determined outside of the game.

[7] The tipping point is found by setting the agent's expected payoff from implementing equal to the agent's expected payoff from diverting and solving for p. Thus, 5/6 is the solution to $1p + 0.5(1 - p) = 1.2p - 0.5(1 - p)$.

if $p \geq 5/6$, principal exercises power directly
if $p < 5/6$, principal delegates, agent implements.

We can apply this logic to our example. The Secretary is better off delegating given a loyal administrator, and she is better off administering the plan herself given a disloyal administrator. The administrator is better off acting disloyally if he won't be detected, and he is better off acting loyally if he will be detected. Good luck means disloyalty will not be detected, and bad luck means it will. So the Secretary should delegate if bad luck is likely and not delegate if good luck is likely.

Questions

8.5. Efficiency is achieved when the sum of the parties' payoffs is maximized. In Figure 8.1, is diverting ever efficient?

8.6. Optimal contracts mitigate agency costs. Given the payoffs in Figure 8.1, suppose the principal offers the agent the following deal: "If I receive a payoff of 1, you will receive your usual payment of 1 plus a bonus payment from me of 0.3." Explain why this offer will cause the agent to implement rather than divert.

8.7. Consider three principal-agent relationships: a CEO and her managers, the President and the Secretary of Defense, the Supreme Court and lower courts. In which of these relationships, if any, can the principal offer the optimal contract described in the prior question?

8.8. In Figure 8.1, suppose the agent's payoff from diverting in a good state increases from 1.2 to 2. What is the game's new solution?

D. How Much to Delegate

Figure 8.1 represents delegation as a binary choice: the principal does or does not delegate. In reality, delegation is often a continuous choice. Appellate courts can always defer to lower courts on facts (complete delegation), never defer on facts (no delegation), or defer unless the lower court committed "clear error" on facts (partial delegation). The Secretary in our example can delegate all, some, or none of her plan to the administrator.

Figure 8.2 represents delegation as a continuous choice. The horizontal axis measures the proportion of power directly exercised by the principal. Moving from left to right, the principal's direct exercise of power increases from 0 percent to 100 percent, and the principal's delegation of power decreases from 100 percent to 0 percent. The vertical axis measures two kinds of costs: administrative and diversion. As the principal devotes more time to exercising power directly (moving rightward in the figure), her administrative costs increase.[8] Conversely, as the principal devotes more time to exercising power directly, her diversion costs decrease.[9]

[8] We assume that as the principal exercises more direct power, she focuses first on matters that can be administered at lowest cost, and later on matters that are more costly to administer. She does the easiest things first. Consequently, the total cost of administration rises at an increasing rate with more direct exercise.

[9] We assume that as the principal exercises more direct power, she focuses first on matters that save the most diversion costs, and later on matters that save less diversion costs. She fixes the worst problems first. Consequently, the total cost of diversion falls at a decreasing rate with more direct exercise.

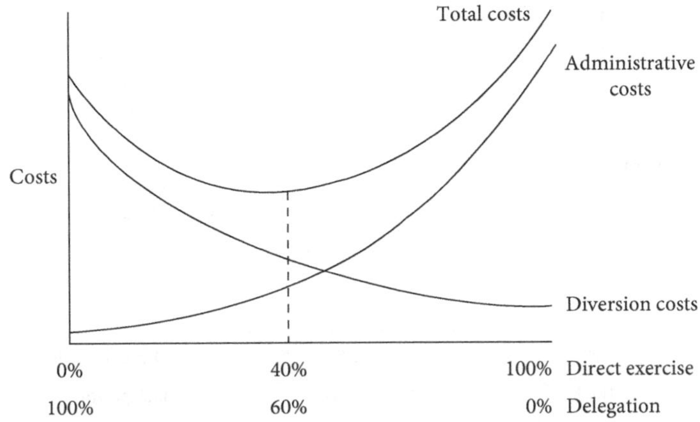

Figure 8.2. Administrative and Diversion Costs

Adding the two cost curves yields the u-shaped curve labeled "total costs." To minimize total costs, the principal selects the level of delegation corresponding to the lowest point on the total costs curve—60 percent, or a little more than half her power. That is the principal's optimal level of delegation in Figure 8.2.

Focus on the total cost curve in the figure. Starting at the origin, a marginal move to the right—say, from 0 percent direct exercise to 1 percent—creates low administrative costs but saves high diversion costs. The total cost curve slopes down. Likewise, another marginal move from 1 percent direct exercise to 2 percent is associated with a decrease in total costs. This pattern continues until we reach 40 percent direct exercise. A marginal move rightward from 40 percent creates more administrative costs than it saves in diversion costs. The total cost curve slopes up. Figure 8.3 captures this reasoning by graphing marginal costs (the solid curves). Optimal delegation is achieved when marginal administrative costs equal marginal diversion costs.[10]

Figure 8.3 helps us visualize how various factors affect delegation. In the preceding binary model, an increase in the probability of good luck cloaks disloyalty. Figure 8.3 captures this idea. As the probability of good luck increases, the agent becomes more likely to divert, shifting upward the marginal diversion cost in Figure 8.3 (dotted curve). Optimal delegation decreases. Specifically, the principal's optimal direct exercise increases from 40 to 50 percent. Equivalently, the principal's optimal delegation decreases from 60 to 50 percent.

This reasoning is general. If *anything* makes it harder for the principal to monitor the agent, the diversion cost curve shifts up, and optimal delegation decreases. Conversely, if anything makes it easier to monitor the agent, the diversion cost curve shifts down. If the principal hires auditors or adopts a better accounting system, optimal delegation increases.

Another factor affecting delegation is the divergence of interests between principal and agent. In our running example, the Secretary prioritizes pre-natal care and the administrator prioritizes emergency care. This divergence causes the administrator to act disloyally sometimes, frustrating the Secretary. As their interests converge, the

[10] For the principal, decreases in marginal diversion costs are effectively marginal benefits.

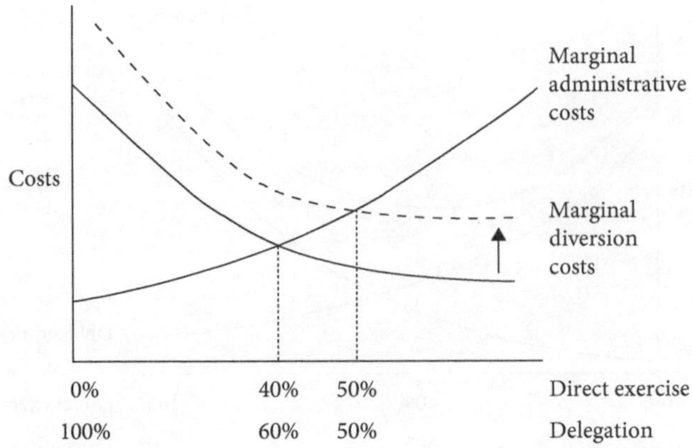

Figure 8.3. Optimal Delegation

administrator has less incentive to divert. The diversion cost curve shifts down, and the Secretary delegates more. To generalize, the *ally principle* predicts that principals delegate more when agents share their objectives.[11]

Questions

8.9. Trash collectors are easier to monitor than spies. Should officials delegate more authority to trash collectors than spies?

8.10. Explain why the optimal delegation of authority from the President to agencies like the Department of Agriculture might increase during times of war.

8.11. The Secretary asks her administrator how much her plan will cost. If the plan will cost more than $50 million, she will not pursue it. The administrator reports that the plan will cost $51 million. Should the Secretary trust the administrator? Does the answer depend on whether the Secretary and her administrator have the same objectives?[12]

The President's Removal Power

In 1920, President Woodrow Wilson fired Frank Myers, a postmaster in Oregon. Myers sued, arguing that the President had violated a federal statute stating "Postmasters . . . shall be appointed and may be removed by the President by and with the advice and consent of the Senate."[13] Wilson had not consulted the Senate before firing Myers. The Supreme Court rejected Myers' claim, holding that the

[11] John D. Huber & Nolan McCarty, *Bureaucratic Capacity, Delegation, and Political Reform*, 98 Am. Pol. Sci. Rev. 481, 489 (2004). *See also* Jonathan Bendor & Adam Meirowitz, *Spatial Models of Delegation*, 98 Am. Pol. Sci. Rev. 293 (2004).

[12] Jonathan Bendor, Amihai Glazer, & Thomas H. Hammond, *Theories of Delegation*, 4 Ann. Rev. Pol. Sci. 235, 249–51 (2001).

[13] Myers v. United States, 272 U.S. 52, 107 (1926).

Constitution gives the President power to remove executive-branch officials like Myers at will.[14] Because the Constitution trumps statutes, the President was not required to consult the Senate.

The delegation game can help justify the Court's decision. The President appoints many agents, including postmasters. According to the ally principle, diversion costs decrease as the values of the principal and agent converge. In giving the executive broad removal powers, the Constitution empowers the President to dismiss agents whose values diverge from his or her own.

The President's removal power does have limits. In 1933, President Franklin D. Roosevelt fired William Humphrey, a member of the Federal Trade Commission (FTC), for political reasons. This violated a federal statute, which permitted the President to dismiss an FTC member only for "inefficiency, neglect of duty, or malfeasance in office."[15] In *Humphrey's Executor v. United States*, the Supreme Court upheld the statute.[16] Whereas Myers performed purely executive functions (delivering mail), Humphrey performed quasi-legislative functions (investigating trade practices, reporting to Congress) and quasi-judicial functions (adjudicating cases about unfair competition). In *Morrison v. Olson*, the Court elaborated, holding that statutes requiring the President to show "cause" before firing an executive official are permissible if they do not unduly interfere with the President's constitutional duty to enforce the law.[17]

Rather than focusing on the law in these cases, we focus on their consequences. By limiting the President's removal power, *Humphrey's Executor* and *Morrison* undercut the ally principle. The President might have to tolerate an agent with different values, increasing the President's diversion costs. However, there are countervailing benefits.

Consider the problem of credible commitments. Congress and the President bargain over the creation of a new agency. Both would prefer a powerful agency to a weak agency. However, Congress is reluctant to support a powerful agency if the President has complete control over its administrator. By threatening removal, the President can pressure the administrator to pursue the President's priorities and ignore Congress's priorities. Thus, Congress will only support a weak agency, making both Congress and the President worse off. To overcome this impasse and create a powerful agency, the President needs to make a credible commitment not to control the administrator. Limiting the President's removal power makes the President's commitment credible.[18] *Humphrey's Executor* and *Morrison* increase the President's diversion costs but decrease transaction costs between the President and Congress.

In addition to Congress, limiting the removal power lets the President make credible commitments to citizens. Voters prefer low inflation. However, the President is tempted to print money, boosting the economy in the short term (before the next election) but causing high inflation later. By limiting the President's power to fire

[14] *See id.*

[15] Humphrey's Ex'r v. United States, 295 U.S. 602, 619 (1935).

[16] *See id.*

[17] 487 U.S. 654 (1988).

[18] These themes are addressed in Nolan McCarty, *The Appointments Dilemma*, 48 Am. J. Pol. Sci. 413 (2004).

central bankers, *Humphrey's Executor* and *Morrison* help the President commit to low inflation.

Finally, consider information. Principals delegate to take advantage of agents' expertise. Most Presidents know little about airplanes. Rather than drafting airplane regulations themselves, they delegate to an agent, the Federal Aviation Administration (FAA). Does the FAA have the best information on airplanes? Researching airplanes is costly, especially when technology changes. To induce the FAA to gather information, the President needs to give the FAA discretion to use that information to pursue its vision of good policy. (Would you do costly research if you couldn't then use the information?) Limiting the President's power to fire civil servants gives the FAA discretion and thus an incentive to gain expertise.[19]

E. Accountability versus Expertise

We have analyzed the optimal degree of delegation given two kinds of costs, administrative and diversion. This language may seem strange to lawyers. When discussing agencies like the FTC and FAA, lawyers usually describe a different trade-off: accountability versus expertise.[20] Delegating power from Congress and the President to agencies sacrifices accountability. Instead of elected officials, insulated bureaucrats make decisions. However, those bureaucrats possess expertise. Designing sensible regulations on aviation, uranium mining, bridges, the internet, medical procedures, and workplace safety requires technical knowledge that most politicians lack. For lawyers, agencies balance losses in accountability against gains from expertise.

Our analysis captures this trade-off. To begin, consider accountability. Democracy features chains of delegation. Citizens are the principal; the President is the citizens' agent and the administrators' principal; and administrators are the President's agents. Sometimes the President pursues his own interests—getting rich, getting re-elected—rather than citizens' interests. This imposes diversion costs on citizens.

Just as presidents can impose diversion costs on citizens, administrators can impose diversion costs on the President. Pilots like to fly, engineers like to build, and surgeons like to operate. Rather than pursuing the President's agenda, administrators like to pursue their own interests. Without the threat of elections, and given the technical, opaque nature of their work, they have room to pursue those interests. This imposes diversion costs on the President, as well as on citizens.

In Figure 8.3, "marginal diversion costs" capture the lawyers' concern over accountability. As accountability decreases, diversion costs increase, implying that less delegation is optimal.

Now consider expertise. When the principal delegates less, she exercises more power directly. This increases her administrative costs. The exact increase in administrative costs

[19] Sean Gailmard & John W. Patty, Learning While Governing: Expertise and Accountability in the Executive Branch 25–54 (2013). On information acquisition generally, see Matthew C. Stephenson, *Information Acquisition and Institutional Design*, 124 Harv. L. Rev. 1422 (2011).

[20] *See, e.g.*, Francesca Bignami, *From Expert Administration to Accountability Network: A New Paradigm for Comparative Administrative Law*, 59 Am. J. Comp. L. 859 (2011).

depends on the activity the principal undertakes. For technical activities that require expertise, the principal's administrative costs are high—she must learn about aviation, uranium mining, and so on. To generalize, as a policy problem becomes more complex, the administrative costs curve shifts up, implying that more delegation is optimal. "Marginal administrative costs" in Figure 8.3 capture the value to the principal of the agent's expertise.

Sometimes economic analysis generates new ideas, and other times it clarifies existing ideas. The delegation game clarifies the debate over accountability and expertise by reducing many arguments to one graph.

Beyond clarifying the debate, the delegation game uncovers a solution. Diversion costs decrease when the principal can monitor and punish the agent. The principal usually cannot monitor the agent's day-to-day activities. However, in the case of technical problems, the citizens and their representatives often can monitor outcomes—did the plane crash, the mine leak, the bridge fall, the internet connect, the patient survive? So the key to controlling the experts is to make the outcomes clearly observable.[21] When outcomes are clearly observable, the laymen can make value judgments and the experts can make technical judgments.

Questions

8.12. A judge gets a difficult case. To find the right solution requires expertise, which the judge can acquire by researching statutes, the Constitution, precedents, and other legal materials. Who bears the cost of that research, the judge or society? Who enjoys the benefit if the judge finds the right solution? Will the judge spend enough time acquiring expertise?[22]

8.13. In the United States, the Office of Information and Regulatory Affairs (OIRA) reviews rules promulgated by administrative agencies before they take effect. The OIRA Administrator is appointed by the President. OIRA used to review all rules, between 2,000 and 3,000 per year. In 1993, President Bill Clinton issued Executive Order 12866, which directed OIRA to concentrate on "economically significant" rules—about 500 to 700 annually.[23] Did Executive Order 12866 increase or decrease the President's administrative costs? What about the President's diversion costs?

Delegation and Courts

The delegation game applies to the President, administrative agencies, governors, mayors, admirals, police chiefs, and many other government actors. What about courts? Judges do not have administrators to whom they can delegate decisions (though they do have clerks). Even so, scholars have long conceptualized the judiciary in principal-agent terms.

[21] *See* Bengt Holmstrom & Paul Milgrom, *Aggregation and Linearity in the Provision of Intertemporal Incentives*, 55 Econometrica 303 (1987).

[22] *See* Gordon Tullock, *Public Decisions as Public Goods*, 79 J. Pol. Econ. 913, 914–15 (1971).

[23] Regulatory Planning and Review, 58 Fed. Reg. 51735 (Sept. 30, 1993).

Like courts elsewhere, U.S. federal courts are organized in a hierarchy, with trial (district) courts on bottom, appellate (circuit) courts in the middle, and the Supreme Court on top. Trial courts make factual determinations, and appellate courts review those facts for clear error, meaning they accept the trial court's conclusions of fact unless they see an obvious mistake. This is tantamount to delegating authority to trial courts. The upside for appellate courts is that delegation saves them the time and effort of revisiting the facts. The downside is that trial courts may make (small) mistakes of fact or even misconstrue facts to achieve their desired outcomes. Appellate courts review trial courts' conclusions of law *de novo*, meaning they do not defer. This is tantamount to exercising power directly.

In general, appellate courts must accept all appeals from trial courts, but the Supreme Court controls its own docket, and it accepts only a small fraction (like 1 or 2 percent) of the cases appealed to it. In the appeals it accepts, the Supreme Court exercises power directly, and in the rest, it delegates final decision-making authority to the appellate courts.

A key feature of the delegation game is the principal's ability to sanction the agent. The threat of a sanction helps keep the agent in line. In business, principals can usually hire and fire agents, but higher court judges usually cannot hire or fire lower court judges. However, higher court judges can punish lower court judges in other ways: by overturning their decisions, which can harm their reputations; by remanding cases, which forces lower court judges to do more work; and by humiliating them. Appellate courts occasionally humiliate trial courts by overturning their decisions, remanding for further proceedings, and ordering that *a different* trial judge handle those proceedings.[24]

F. Unilateral Oversight

We have explained that the agent's ability to divert depends on the principal's ability to monitor and punish. Here we express this idea using spatial models familiar from other chapters. Figure 8.4 depicts a single dimension of choice for public policy. The dimension could reflect money spent on farm subsidies, the number of migrants permitted to enter, or the ideological location (liberal or conservative) of the government's policy on fetal tissue research. The principal has ideal point *P*, and the agent has ideal point *A*. The difference between them captures the divergence in their preferences, as when the Secretary in our example prioritizes prenatal care and her administrator prioritizes emergency care.

The agent chooses the policy. If unconstrained, he would set policy at *A*. However, the principal has the power to oversee the agent and, if he makes an unsatisfactory choice, punish him. So where will the agent set policy? The answer depends on the principal's ability to monitor and punish. If the principal can monitor and punish perfectly at zero cost, then the agent will set policy at *P*. Any other choice would trigger punishment that

[24] *See* Toby J. Heytens, *Reassignment*, 66 STAN. L. REV. 1 (2014).

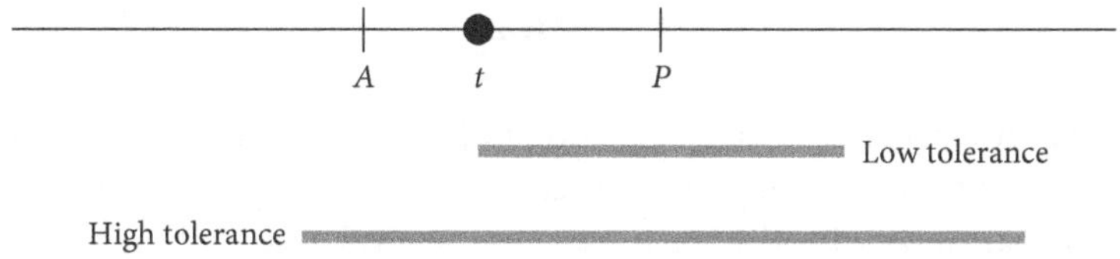

Figure 8.4. Unilateral Oversight with Tolerance Intervals

the agent does not want. In reality, exercising oversight imposes costs on principals, and those costs give the agent some discretion.

Figure 8.4 visualizes this trade-off. Suppose the policy moves leftward from *P*. As the policy gets further from *P*, the principal's diversion costs increase. At some point the costs become so large that the principal is better off overseeing and disciplining the agent. The dot *t* marks the principal's tipping point. For policies between *t* and *P*, the principal's oversight costs exceed her diversion costs, so she will not intervene. For policies left of *t*, the principal's diversion costs exceed her oversight costs, so she will intervene.

Just as the agent cannot set policy too far left of *P*, he cannot set policy too far right of *P*. Figure 8.4 captures these limitations on the agent with the shaded bars called *tolerance intervals*.[25] If the agent makes a decision inside the principal's tolerance interval, the principal will not intervene, and the policy will stand. For the principal, the costs of oversight exceed her diversion costs. If the agent makes a decision outside the principal's tolerance interval, the principal will intervene and punish the agent.

Focus on the interval labeled "Low tolerance." This interval implies that the principal has relatively low oversight costs. The agent can deviate from the principal's ideal, but not by much. In Figure 8.4, a rational agent will set policy at *t*, the end of the tolerance interval. This is the policy closest to the agent's ideal that does not trigger oversight. Now focus on the interval labeled "High tolerance." This interval implies that the principal has relatively high oversight costs. A rational agent will set policy at *A*. Given the high costs of oversight, the agent can choose his ideal policy without triggering oversight.

Tolerance intervals have a natural interpretation: they represent the agent's *discretionary power*. As the principal's oversight costs increase, the agent's discretion grows.

To make this discussion concrete, we apply it to our example involving the Secretary of Health and Human Services. The Secretary delegates her plan for prenatal care to the administrator. The Secretary does not monitor the administrator's day-to-day work. However, she monitors outcomes, like the budget showing outlays to obstetricians. She expects her plan to cost $50 million. If the budget shows costs of, say, $46 million, she will not investigate. However, if the budget shows costs below $46 million, she will investigate. Below $46 million, the difference between her expectation and reality is large enough to justify the cost of oversight. Foreseeing oversight, the administrator will devote $46 million to the Secretary's plan, but no more. Once he reaches $46 million, he will direct resources to his priority, emergency care, rather than prenatal care. In Figure 8.4, *t* equates to $46 million.

[25] *See, e.g.*, Lee Epstein, Jack Knight, & Olga Shvetsova, *The Role of Constitutional Courts in the Establishment and Maintenance of Democratic Systems of Government*, 35 Law & Soc'y Rev. 117 (2001).

Questions

8.14. In Figure 8.4, the principal starts with the low tolerance interval, but monitoring costs go up, so the interval expands. Will the agent's behavior change? If the principal starts with the high tolerance interval and monitoring costs go up, will the agent's behavior change?

8.15. The Freedom of Information Act lets people, including journalists, gather and publish information on the workings of administrative agencies. Whistleblower statutes protect civil servants who publicize malfeasance within their departments. Businesses complain to their representatives when agencies burden them. Predict the effects of these laws and practices on the President's tolerance interval and agencies' behavior.

G. Multiple Principals

Figure 8.4 depicts a single principal with power to oversee the agent. Sometimes, however, multiple principals have powers of oversight. To illustrate, both the President and Congress oversee federal agencies. The President can punish administrators by firing them (but see the preceding box on removal), and Congress can punish administrators by cutting their budgets or launching investigations.

Multiple principals can oversee an agent unilaterally or cooperatively. With *unilateral oversight*, any principal can exercise oversight on its own. For example, the President and Congress each have unilateral power to investigate an agency's behavior. With *cooperative oversight*, no principal can exercise oversight without agreement by the other(s). Suppose an agency issues a new rule on fuel standards for automobiles. If Congress dislikes the rule, it can override it by passing new legislation. However, enacting new legislation requires the President's agreement.[26]

Figure 8.5 represents unilateral and cooperative oversight. As before, *A* is the agent's ideal point. *P* depicts the President's ideal point, and *C* depicts Congress's ideal point. Each principal has a tolerance interval, as shown.

Under unilateral oversight, either principal can discipline the agent. To avoid discipline, the agent must make a choice that satisfies both principals. Points inside both tolerance intervals represent choices that will satisfy both principals. This set of points is labeled "unilateral discretion." Given unilateral oversight, the agent has discretion to choose any point in that set without provoking discipline. The agent will choose the leftmost point in the set, which is closest to his ideal point *A*.

Compared to unilateral oversight with one principal, unilateral oversight with two principals decreases the agent's discretionary power. To see why, suppose the agent answers only to the President. In Figure 8.5, the agent could choose any point in the President's tolerance interval. If the agent answers only to Congress, he could choose any point in Congress's tolerance interval. When the agent answers to both, he must choose from the union of the tolerance intervals, which is narrower. To generalize,

[26] We ignore congressional overrides.

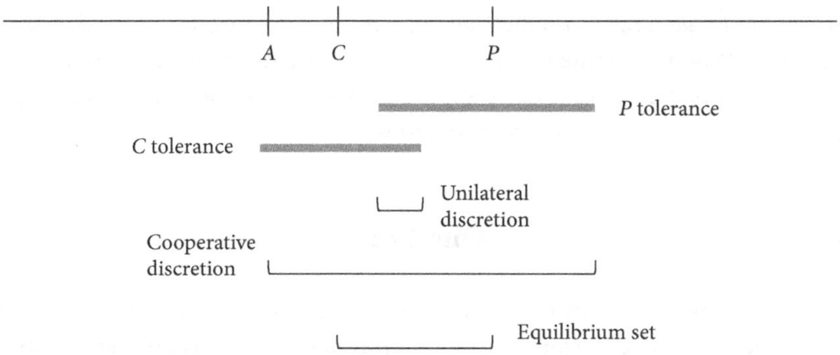

Figure 8.5. Unilateral and Cooperative Oversight

adding principals with unilateral oversight usually decreases, and cannot increase, the agent's discretionary power.[27]

Having analyzed unilateral oversight, now we consider cooperative oversight. Under cooperative oversight, disciplining the agent requires the President and Congress to agree. The President will not agree to discipline the agent unless he makes a decision outside the President's tolerance interval. Likewise, Congress will not agree to discipline the agent unless he makes a decision outside Congress's tolerance interval. Points inside either tolerance interval represent choices that will satisfy at least one principal. In Figure 8.5, this set is labeled "cooperative discretion." Given cooperative oversight, the agent has discretion to choose any point in that set, and he will choose *A*.

Compared to oversight with one principal, cooperative oversight with two principals increases the agent's discretionary power. Instead of choosing within one tolerance interval or the other, the agent can choose within either. To generalize, *adding principals with cooperative oversight usually increases, and cannot decrease, the agent's discretionary power.*[28]

With cooperative oversight, the agent's discretion depends in part on the principals' costs of monitoring and enforcement. However, it also depends on the principals' level of disagreement. To understand why, assume that monitoring and disciplining the agent is costless for the principals. In Figure 8.5, this assumption eliminates the tolerance internals. If the agent answers only to Congress, he will have to choose *C*, and if he answers only to the President, he will have to choose *P*. Under cooperative oversight, he has more choices. Suppose the agent chooses the point halfway between *C* and *P*. Congress would like to move the agent leftward, but the President will not agree, and the President would like to move the agent rightward, but Congress will not agree. The agent's choice is stable. To generalize, the agent can choose any point between *C* and *P*. This is the equilibrium set, as shown in the figure. The agent's discretion results from divergence in the principals' ideal points, not from the costs of monitoring. As the principals disagree more, the agent's discretion grows.

27 *See* Robert Cooter, The Strategic Constitution 158–59 (2000).

28 *See id.* at 159–61. *See also* Craig Volden, *A Formal Model of the Politics of Delegation in a Separation of Powers System*, 46 Am. J. Pol. Sci. 111 (2002).

This analysis generates predictions about agency discretion under different governments. When the same party controls the legislative and executive branches of government, agency discretion narrows. When different parties control the legislative and executive branches, agency discretion grows.

Questions

8.16. A federal statute set targets for government spending. If the government's budget exceeded the targets, the Comptroller General recommended spending cuts to the President, who was (with some exceptions) required to order them. The Comptroller General was appointed by the President. However, the statute gave Congress power to remove the Comptroller General. In *Bowsher v. Synar*, the Supreme Court held that this arrangement violated the separation of powers.[29] The Court wrote: "Congress could simply remove, or threaten to remove, an officer for executing the laws in any fashion found to be unsatisfactory to Congress. This kind of congressional control over the execution of laws . . . is constitutionally impermissible."[30] We will analyze *Bowsher* using Figure 8.5, where *C* is Congress's ideal point, *P* is the President's ideal point, and both actors have tolerance intervals as indicated in the figure.

(a) The President nominates the Comptroller General from a list of three candidates recommended by Congress. In Figure 8.5, would Congress ever recommend a candidate with an ideal point known to be left of *C* or right of *P*?

(b) If Congress and the President had to cooperate to remove the Comptroller General, what would be the Comptroller General's range of discretion? Given your answer to question (a), in what subset of that range of discretion would you expect the Comptroller General to set policy?

(c) If Congress alone had power to remove the Comptroller General, what would be the Comptroller General's range of discretion? Given your answer to question (a), in what subset of that range of discretion would you expect the Comptroller General to set policy?

(d) If the Comptroller General can only be removed by impeachment ("treason, bribery, or other high crimes and misdemeanors"[31]), what happens to the tolerance intervals in Figure 8.5? Can voters benefit from having such an independent agent?

The Legislative Veto

Jagdish Chadha, a noncitizen, remained in the United States illegally. Rather than deport him, the Attorney General decided to let Chadha remain because deporting

[29] 478 U.S. 714 (1986).
[30] *Id.* at 726–27.
[31] *Id.* at 729.

him would result in extreme hardship. The House of Representatives exercised a "legislative veto" and reversed the Attorney General's decision. A legislative veto allows either chamber of Congress to reverse a decision by an executive official, like the Attorney General or an agency head. The immigration statute included a legislative veto, so the House could act against Chadha alone, without support from the Senate or the President.

In *INS v. Chadha*, the Supreme Court invalidated the legislative veto.[32] According to the Court, overturning an agency decision is a legislative act, and the Constitution only permits legislative acts that follow a "single, finely wrought and exhaustively considered, procedure": bicameralism and presentment.[33] The legislative veto sidesteps that procedure.

Our model of delegation illuminates the Court's decision. Bicameralism and presentment imply cooperative oversight. To reverse an agency, the House, Senate, and President must agree. Cooperative oversight tends to increase agency discretion, especially when different political parties control the different branches. The legislative veto sought to replace cooperative oversight with unilateral oversight, reducing agency discretion. The Court held that Congress could not replace cooperative with unilateral oversight. The Court's decision eliminated legislative vetoes from about 200 federal statutes.

Dissenting in *INS v. Chadha*, Justice White emphasized the consequence of the Court's decision:

> Without the legislative veto, Congress is faced with a Hobson's choice: either to refrain from delegating the necessary authority, leaving itself with a hopeless task of writing laws with the requisite specificity to cover endless special circumstances across the entire policy landscape, or . . . to abdicate its law-making function to the executive branch. . . . To choose the former leaves major national problems unresolved; to opt for the latter risks unaccountable policymaking by those not elected to fill that role.[34]

Justice White expressed a functional view of the separation of powers. *Functionalism* permits flexibility, experimentation, and some blending of powers to achieve government's ends, so long as each branch retains its core function and authority. In contrast, *formalism* emphasizes rigid adherence to the structure described in the Constitution, even if it frustrates government's ends.[35]

Readers might assume that economists favor functionalism. Once you understand the difference between unilateral and cooperative oversight, you can see why the legislative veto might reduce agency costs.[36] However, things are not so simple. Just as administrators can abuse the discretion granted by politicians, politicians can

[32] 462 U.S. 919 (1983).

[33] *Id.* at 951.

[34] *Id.* at 968 (White, J., dissenting).

[35] *See, e.g.*, Peter L. Strauss, *Formal and Functional Approaches to Separation-of-Powers Questions—A Foolish Inconsistency?*, 72 Cornell L. Rev. 488 (1987).

[36] *See* Willian N. Eskridge, Jr. & John Ferejohn, *The Article I, Section 7 Game*, 80 Geo. L.J. 523, 540–43 (1992).

abuse the discretion granted by citizens. Formalism gives politicians less discretion, like a rule. Functionalism gives politicians more discretion, like a standard. Rules and standards are our next topic.

II. Rule Game

Laws can be precise, like a speed limit of 65 miles per hour. Or laws can be imprecise, like the state of Montana's directive to drive at "reasonable and prudent" speeds.[37] Legal scholars call precise laws "rules" and imprecise laws "standards." The distinction between rules and standards is apparent throughout law. The U.S. Constitution, for example, features both rules (the President must be 35 years old, each state gets two Senators) and standards (people have a right to "equal protection," Congress can provide for the "general Welfare").

In the following pages, we explain the connection between rules, standards, and delegation. After making the connection, we study a binary choice: give the agent a rule, or give the agent a standard. Then we study a continuous choice, as when a principal can make her instructions more or less precise.

A. Rules, Standards, and Delegation

Many factors affect the choice between rules and standards. We concentrate on one important factor: the allocation of decision-making authority. When lawmakers adopt a rule, they reserve decision-making authority for themselves. When lawmakers adopt a standard, they allocate decision-making authority to someone else. To illustrate, contrast the speed limits "65 miles per hour" (rule) and "reasonable and prudent speeds" (standard). In adopting the rule, the legislature decides when people drive too fast. Patrol officers merely enforce the legislature's decision. In adopting the standard, the legislature lets patrol officers decide when people drive too fast. Officers observe drivers' speed, consider factors like traffic, weather, and the condition of the road, and then decide for themselves when someone has broken the law.

As this example shows, rules and standards relate to delegation. A principal can choose between constraining her agent with a rule or liberating her agent with a standard.

We can apply these ideas to our running example. The Secretary of Health and Human Services has a plan to improve prenatal care. Rather than implementing the plan herself, she has decided to delegate implementation to her administrator. Now she has a choice. She can constrain the administrator with a rule, like "spend $50 million on the plan," "hire ten more specialists to study the problem," or "distribute 1,000 copies of

[37] *See* State v. Stanko, 974 P.2d 1132 (Mont. 1998). *See also* Cass R. Sunstein, *Problems with Rules*, 83 Cal. L. Rev. 953 (1995).

best practices to obstetricians." Alternatively, she can give the administrator discretion with a standard, like "spend resources as necessary to improve prenatal care."

The Secretary prioritizes prenatal care, but the administrator prioritizes emergency care. Given the opportunity, the administrator will divert resources to his priority, creating diversion costs for the principal. By limiting the administrator's discretion, rules reduce the administrator's opportunity to divert resources. However, rules also limit the administrator's flexibility. Recall our discussion of luck. Many factors affect the success of the Secretary's plan, like a shortage of nurses, the behavior of doctors, and the policies of insurance companies. Compared to rules, standards give the administrator flexibility to respond to these unpredictable circumstances.

In sum, rules decrease diversion costs but increase inflexibility costs, whereas standards increase diversion costs but decrease inflexibility costs. For principals, the choice between a rule and a standard depends on this trade-off.

Questions

8.17. The Religious Freedom Restoration Act (RFRA) states, "Government shall not substantially burden a person's exercise of religion."[38] RFRA limits the power of agencies to regulate in a way that interferes with people's religious beliefs. Is RFRA a rule or a standard? Would agencies have more or less discretion without RFRA?

8.18. In the United States, many federal laws establish regulatory "floors." To demonstrate, a federal environmental statute might forbid pollution levels above *X* (that's the floor) but allow states that want a cleaner environment to set even stricter limits. Do laws establishing regulatory floors give discretion to states? Are such laws rules or standards?

B. Strategic Game

We have described the principal's choice between standards and rules in general terms. Here we make the choice precise with a game tree.[39] In Figure 8.6, the principal first decides whether to give the agent a standard or a rule. Second, luck is good or bad. The agent observes the state of nature, but the principal does not. Third, the agent responds to luck, as far as the discretion given to him allows. We can clarify this last step using our example. If luck is good, the administrator can implement the Secretary's prenatal plan, which would be best for the Secretary, or the agent can divert, meaning redirect resources to emergency care. The administrator prefers to divert, and good luck masks his disloyalty. If luck is bad, the agent can implement the principal's plan, but this will harm

[38] 42 U.S.C. § 2000bb-1.

[39] Our rule game resembles one in Robert Cooter, The Strategic Constitution 82 (2000). Our rule game is simple. For more sophisticated analyses, see, for example, Louis Kaplow, *Rules Versus Standards: An Economic Analysis*, 42 Duke L.J. 557 (1992); Jeffrey K. Staton & Georg Vanberg, *The Value of Vagueness: Delegation, Defiance, and Judicial Opinions*, 52 Am. J. Pol. Sci. 504 (2008); Gillian K. Hadfield, *Weighing the Value of Vagueness: An Economic Perspective on Precision in the Law*, 82 Cal. L. Rev. 541 (1994).

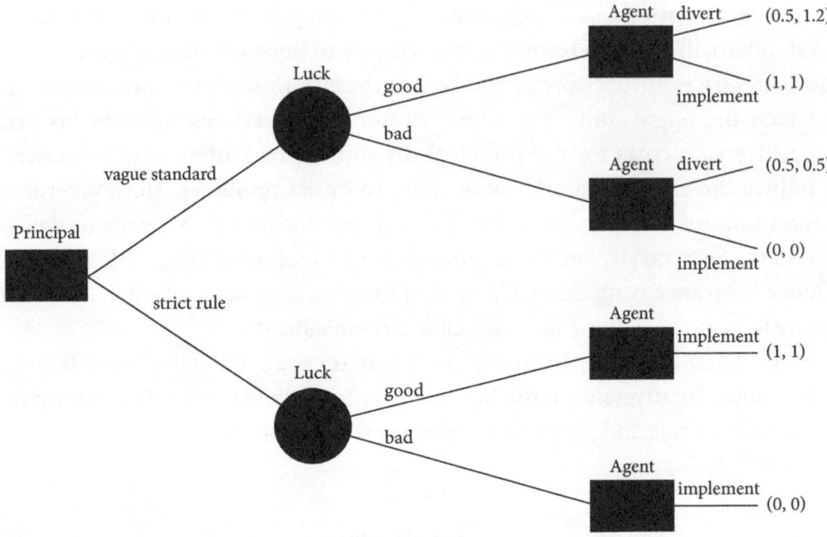

Figure 8.6. The Rule Game

everyone given the state of nature. The doctors do not cooperate, so the plan is doomed to fail. Alternatively, the agent can divert some resources to improving emergency care, which both he and, given the circumstances, the Secretary would prefer.

Note that Figures 8.1 and 8.6 differ in a small but important way. Figure 8.1 depicts the agent making a choice between diverting and implementing *before* luck occurs. The agent must decide under uncertainty. To illustrate with the example of the Secretary, the administrator must make some decisions before knowing whether or not doctors will cooperate. In contrast, Figure 8.6 depicts the agent deciding what to do *after* luck occurs. The agent can respond differently to different circumstances. Thus, the administrator can make some decisions after he knows whether or not the doctors will cooperate. A standard allows the agent to respond flexibly to new information, whereas a rule precludes the agent from responding flexibly.

Now we explain the payoffs in Figure 8.6, proceeding from top to bottom. If the principal imposes a standard, luck is good, and the agent diverts, the principal receives 0.5 and the agent receives 1.2. If the principal imposes a standard, luck is good, and the agent implements, the principal receives 1 and the agent receives 1. If the principal imposes a standard, luck is bad, and the agent diverts, the principal receives 0.5 and the agent receives 0.5. If the principal imposes a standard, luck is bad, and the agent implements, the principal receives 0 and the agent receives 0.

Continuing down, we see the payoffs when the principal imposes a rule that the agent must implement. If the principal imposes a rule and luck is good, the principal receives 1 and the agent receives 1. The rule fits the circumstances, as when the Secretary orders the administrator to spend $50 million on prenatal care, and doctors put the money to good use. If the principal imposes a rule and luck is bad, the principal receives 0 and the agent receives 0. The rule does not fit the circumstances, as when the Secretary orders the administrator to spend $50 million, but doctors do not cooperate and the money is wasted.

Questions

8.19. If the principal in Figure 8.6 gives the agent a rule and gets a payoff of 0, should she punish the agent? Why or why not?
8.20. If the principal in Figure 8.6 gives the agent a standard and gets a payoff of 0, should she punish the agent? Why or why not?
8.21. If the principal in Figure 8.6 gives the agent a standard and gets a payoff of 0.5, should she punish the agent? Why or why not?

C. When to Use Rules and Standards

Having described the rule game, we can now find its solution using recursive reasoning. If the principal imposes a standard and luck is good, the agent diverts (he prefers the payoff of 1.2 from diverting to the payoff of 1 from implementing). The agent diverts resources to his own interests, leaving the principal with a payoff of 0.5. If the principal imposes a standard and luck is bad, the agent diverts (he prefers the payoff of 0.5 from diverting to the payoff of 0 from implementing). The principal gets 0.5. So imposing a standard pays the principal 0.5 regardless of whether luck is good or bad.

Alternatively, if the principal imposes a rule and luck is good, the principal gets 1. If the principal imposes a rule and luck is bad, the principal gets 0. By imposing a strict rule, the principal's payoff depends on the probability of good luck. If the probability of good luck is p and the probability of bad luck is $1 - p$, the principal's expected payoff from a rule is $1^*p + 0^*(1 - p)$, which equals p. In sum, the game's solution is

if $p \geq 0.5$, principal imposes a rule
if $p < 0.5$, principal imposes a standard.

Thus, the principal imposes a rule when good luck is likely, meaning the agent will pursue his own interests. The principal imposes a standard when bad luck is likely, meaning the agent will respond flexibly and pursue everyone's interests.

We can apply the game's solution to our medical example. If the probability of good luck is greater than 0.5, the Secretary imposes a rule to prevent the administrator from diverting resources away from prenatal care and toward emergency care. If the probability of good luck is less than 0.5, the principal will impose a standard to allow the administrator flexibility if, say, the doctors do not cooperate. The agent will respond to bad luck by reallocating resources.

As explained, standards give more flexibility to the agent than rules. When uncertainty increases, flexibility becomes more important. Consequently, we expect more standards and fewer rules when circumstances change unpredictably.

Questions

8.22. In Figure 8.6, suppose the principal gives a standard and luck is good, so the agent diverts. Is diverting by the agent efficient? If the transaction costs of bargaining between the principal and agent are zero, will the agent divert? What could the principal offer the agent to incentivize him to implement?

8.23. In Figure 8.6, suppose that the principal's payoff when the plan gets implemented in a good state increases from 1 to 1.5. What is the game's solution?

Does Vagueness Cause Litigation?

In 1938, Congress enacted the Food, Drug, and Cosmetic Act, which gave the Food and Drug Administration (FDA) authority to regulate "drugs." The statute defines "drugs" as "articles (other than food) intended to affect the structure or any function of the body." Is nicotine a drug? Can the FDA regulate cigarettes? In 1996, the FDA concluded that the answer is yes. However, the Supreme Court later concluded that the answer is no.[40] The Court held that Congress did not intend the word "drug" to include tobacco, so the FDA did not have authority to regulate cigarettes.

FDA v. Brown & Williamson Tobacco Corp. is a famous case in statutory interpretation. We use it to make a point about rules and standards. In the Food, Drug, and Cosmetic Act, Congress (the principal) delegated authority to the FDA (the agent). The principal could have imposed a rule by listing exactly those articles that the agent can regulate (e.g., "acetaminophen," "ascorbic acid," "erythrosine"). With a rule, the FDA's authority would be easy to determine: Does "nicotine" appear on the list? Instead, the principal imposed a standard (the FDA can regulate "drugs"). With a standard, the FDA's authority was hard to determine, and the Supreme Court had to intervene.

Generalizing from cases like this, some scholars conclude that vague laws encourage litigation.[41] How? The first topic in the book, bargaining theory, supplies an answer. Litigating is costly for the parties (time, money, energy, emotion). Thus, parties are usually better off settling their dispute out of court and avoiding those costs. Different factors impede settlement, including optimism. If the plaintiff expects to win in court, she will sue and demand a lot to settle. If the defendant expects to win in court, he will fight back and offer only a little to settle. Parties struggle to settle out of court when each expects to win in court. At least one of the parties is falsely optimistic, and false optimism causes litigation.

Vague laws can encourage optimism. Regulators assume the word "drug" must include nicotine, and the tobacco company assumes the word "drug" must exclude nicotine. Each side expects to win, so the tobacco company sues, and the agency refuses to back down. Consider another example. When the speed limit is "reasonable and prudent speeds," the officer assumes the law prohibits driving 75 miles per hour, and the motorist assumes the law permits driving 75 miles per hour. Each side expects to win, so the officer issues the ticket, and the motorist challenges it in court.

[40] Food & Drug Admin. v. Brown & Williamson Tobacco Corp., 529 U.S. 120 (2000).

[41] *See, e.g.*, Frederick Schauer, *Easy Cases*, 58 S. CAL. L. REV. 399, 404 (1985). For the opposite view, see Richard Craswell & John E. Calfee, *Deterrence and Uncertain Legal Standards*, 2 J.L. ECON. & ORG. 279 (1986).

This analysis implies that litigation is a cost of the principal imposing standards rather than rules. Do principals like Congress bear those costs? Who internalizes the costs of litigation?

D. Continuous Precision

Figure 8.6 represents a binary choice: the principal can impose a standard or a rule. In reality, the choice is often continuous. The principal can impose an especially vague standard, an especially precise rule, or directives in between. To illustrate, a legislature could direct a transportation agency to "promote safety," "promote safety by requiring vehicles to have seat belts," or "promote safety by requiring vehicles to have three-point seat belts with locking retractors, pretensioners, and web clamps."

Figure 8.7 represents rule-making as a continuous choice about precision. The horizontal axis measures precision from 0 percent (vague standard) to 100 percent (precise rule). Moving from left to right implies a more precise rule and greater constraint of the agent, while moving from right to left implies a vaguer standard and less constraint of the agent. The vertical axis measures two kinds of marginal costs: inflexibility and diversion. With more precision, inflexibility increases and diversion decreases.[42] In Figure 8.7, the optimum is 55 percent—the point where marginal inflexibility costs equal marginal diversion costs.

Figure 8.7 predicts how various factors affect the principal's optimal level of precision. Shifting inflexibility costs down, or shifting diversion costs up, causes the optimum level of precision to increase. Thus, the dotted lines depict the shifting curves and the increase in the optimum from 55 to 75. We will discuss a few of the many causes of these shifts in inflexibility and diversion costs.

Suppose the probability *p* of good luck increases, so diversion is harder for the principal to detect. Figure 8.7 represents this fact by shifting up the diversion cost curve. Thus, an increase in the probability of good luck causes an increase in the principal's optimal precision of rules. To generalize, when the agent's opportunity for diversion improves, the principal's incentive to constrain the agent with stricter rules strengthens. When the agent's opportunity for diversion worsens—perhaps monitoring or punishing the agent becomes easier—the principal's incentive to constrain the agent with stricter rules weakens.

Recall the ally principle. In general, convergence between the interests of the principal and agent support more delegation. Figure 8.7 represents this fact. As the interests of the principal and agent converge, the diversion cost curve shifts down, implying that less precision is optimal. Conversely, as the interests of the parties diverge, the diversion cost curve shifts up, so more precision is optimal.

[42] We assume that as a principal increases the precision of rules, she focuses first on those matters where diversion costs are highest. This explains why the diversion costs curve gets flatter as we move to the right. Furthermore, as the principal increases the precision of rules, she constrains the agent, which prevents him from reallocating resources as circumstances demand. This explains why inflexibility costs rise. We assume that as a principal imposes more rules, she focuses first on those matters where flexibility is less valuable. This explains why the inflexibility costs curve gets steeper as we move to the right.

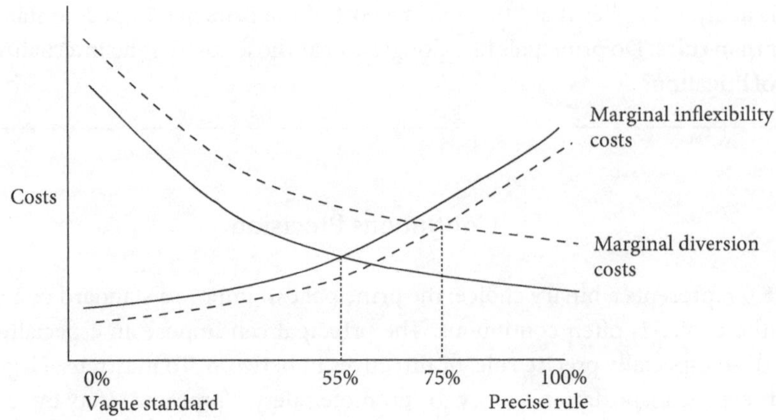

Figure 8.7. Optimal Precision

Finally, suppose that technical and social conditions change faster. Agents need more flexibility to respond to changed circumstances. Figure 8.7 represents this fact by shifting up the inflexibility cost curve, which implies a decrease in the optimal precision of rules.

Questions

8.24. Compared to standards, rules lower diversion costs. Why? Is it because agents must obey rules—patrol officers, for example, must ticket everyone who drives faster than the 65-mile-per-hour limit? Or is it because principals can detect violations of rules more easily than they can detect violations of standards?

8.25. Do you expect Google to apply rules or standards to its employees? Explain how rapid technological change in an industry affects the strictness of rules within a company.

8.26. Explain why military rules allow more discretion after a battle begins than before it starts.

8.27. Some federal agencies, although part of the executive branch, are largely beyond the President's control. For example, the President cannot easily remove the head of the Federal Reserve Board, the nation's central bank. Should Congress and the President give the Federal Reserve Board rules or standards?

E. Drafting and Applying—Invest Now or Later?

We have discussed the costs of inflexibility and diversion. Here we address the cost of drafting. A standard describes the end that the principal wants to achieve. To draft a standard, the principal has to know her objectives. Drafting a description of objectives is relatively easy. In contrast, a rule describes the means to the end. To draft a rule, the principal has to know about causes and effects. Drafting a description of the means that will achieve her end is relatively hard. So according to conventional wisdom, rules are costlier to draft than standards.[43]

To illustrate by the medical example, before drafting a standard the Secretary needs to know that she wants to improve prenatal care. Before drafting a rule, however, she needs to know the effects of alternative medical procedures on prenatal care. Specifying the goal is easier than specifying the means. Similarly, little information is required to draft a standard stating that drivers should go a "reasonable and prudent speed." Conversely, drafting a precise speed limit requires a lot of information. Identifying the best speed limit requires understanding driving practices and their connection to accidents.

As this discussion shows, standards are cheaper to draft than rules. However, standards are costlier to apply than rules. Suppose the Secretary directs her administrator to "improve prenatal care." Her drafting costs are low, but the administrator's application costs are high. The heavy information requirement comes after drafting, when the administrator has to determine what steps will best improve prenatal care. Similarly, if the legislature adopts a speed limit of "reasonable and prudent speeds," the patrol officer has to decide whether each driver's speed is reasonable. The heavy information requirement comes when the law is applied, not when it is drafted.

We have explained that increasing the precision of rules shifts costs to the principal who drafts them, whereas decreasing the precision of rules shifts costs to the agent who applies them. Who can bear the burden best? If drafting costs are lower for the principal than application costs for the agent, then total costs fall when the principal drafts precise rules. Conversely, if drafting costs are higher for the principal than application costs for the agent, then total costs fall when the principal drafts standards. The costs to the principal and agent depend on their access to information. If the principal has good information today, she can draft the rule at relatively low cost. If the agent will have better information later, after the standard is enacted, the agent can apply the law later at relatively low cost.

This discussion addresses the optimal precision of law based on drafting and application costs. These considerations are distinct from inflexibility and diversion costs. The best law takes all costs into account, including the costs to regulated parties like doctors and drivers.

Questions

8.28. In the United States, police apply speed limits to millions of drivers. Meanwhile, regulators apply nuclear energy laws to about 60 power plants. Why might legislators make speed limits more precise than nuclear energy laws?

8.29. Does the principal internalize application costs? Do you expect principals to make their directives too precise, or not precise enough?

8.30. When airplanes crash, citizens might blame Congress or the Federal Aviation Administration (FAA). Is the FAA more likely to get blamed if Congress drafts a rule or the FAA applies a standard? Why might Congress impose a standard even if its drafting costs are low?

[43] This discussion draws on Louis Kaplow, *Rules Versus Standards: An Economic Analysis*, 42 DUKE L.J. 557 (1992). *See also* Isaac Ehrlich & Richard A. Posner, *An Economic Analysis of Legal Rulemaking*, 3 J. LEGAL STUD. 257 (1974).

Vagueness or Ambiguity?

Like the delegation game, the rule game applies to courts. In *Brown v. Board of Education*, the Supreme Court declared the fundamental principle that "separate is not equal."[44] The decision required public schools to integrate, but how quickly? The Supreme Court could have required integration by a particular date—say, January 1, 1957. Given that rule, lower courts would have to conclude that any school remaining segregated after January 1, 1957, violated the Constitution. Instead, the Supreme Court gave a standard, holding that schools must integrate "with all deliberate speed."[45] Given that standard, lower courts had flexibility to decide when a school violated the Constitution. Flexibility allowed courts to consider local circumstances, like school capacity and the availability of buses. However, compared to a precise date of January 1, 1957, flexibility prolonged segregation.

Sometimes Justices decide how much discretion to give courts, as in *Brown*. Other times legislators decide. If the legislature enacts a speed limit of "65 miles per hour," judges have little discretion. Conversely, if the legislature enacts a speed limit of "reasonable and prudent speeds," judges have much discretion. The patrol officer decides whom to ticket, but the judge (or jury) makes the final decision on whom to convict.

Instructions from legislatures to courts can create a special problem of interpretation. The problem involves vagueness and ambiguity.[46] An expression is vague if it refers to a range with uncertain borders. "Drive at a reasonable speed" is a vague expression. Many speeds are reasonable (the range), and the border at which speed becomes unreasonable—75 mph? 82 mph?—is uncertain. An expression is ambiguous if it has a particular meaning, but readers might not discern it. Here is an amusing example. Suppose law prohibits "possession of arms in a public library." The word "arms" could mean weapons, or it could mean the limbs attached to your shoulders. (Common sense, but not the words of the statute, tell you it means weapons.)

In general, vague expressions represent delegations. The legislature intends for the court to exercise discretion. In contrast, ambiguous expressions represent errors in drafting. Legislators intend a particular meaning. They want courts to find and apply that meaning, not exercise discretion.

To find the correct meaning of an ambiguous expression requires effort. How hard should courts work to find the correct meaning? To an economist, the answer depends in part on the difference between the correct and the incorrect meaning. If the difference is trivial, courts should not work so hard. After making some effort, they should guess. If the difference is significant—does "arms" mean guns or limbs?—they should work harder.

44 347 U.S. 495 (1954) ("Separate educational facilities are inherently unequal.").
45 349 U.S. 294, 301 (1955).
46 For a brief and helpful discussion, see Caleb Nelson, Statutory Interpretation 77–80 (2011).

III. Normative Analysis of Delegation

We have analyzed the positive properties of delegation, including when we expect principals to delegate and to what degree. Now we turn to normative analysis. Does delegation give good results? As explained in an earlier chapter, a "good result" in economics is one that best satisfies people's preferences. In the simplest case, delegation involves two people, the principal and the agent. We begin by considering when delegation satisfies the preferences of the principal, the agent, or both. Then we consider the hard case where delegation involves many people: millions of citizens, dozens of executives, hundreds of administrators. In government, delegation usually resembles the hard case, not the easy case.

A. Delegation as Offer or Command

Imagine a single principal and a single agent, like the Secretary and administrator in our medical example. The principal will delegate when she expects a greater return from delegating than from exercising power directly. Thus, delegation makes the principal better off. Does delegation make the agent better off? If the agent can refuse the delegation of authority, then the answer must be yes. The agent will only accept delegation when accepting makes him better off than not accepting. In this situation, delegating looks like bargaining. Instead of exchanging money for a car, the principal and agent exchange authority for effort. Assuming the principal and agent are rational, they will only agree to arrangements that make them both better off. Thus, delegation is Pareto efficient.

Like the choice to delegate, the extent of delegation is Pareto efficient. If the principal would benefit from more (or less) delegation, she will offer more (or less) to the agent. The agent will accept more (or less) delegation when doing so makes him better off. To generalize, the principal and agent will agree to a Pareto efficient allocation of authority between them.

We have explained that the principal and agent will achieve Pareto efficiency. Will they achieve cost-benefit efficiency? To see the difference, imagine three levels of delegation from the principal to the agent: none, low, and high. "None" would give the principal and agent payoffs of 0 and 0; "low" would give them payoffs of 2 and 2; and "high" would give them payoffs of 1 and 4. The principal will offer "low," which has the highest payoff for her at 2. The agent prefers "low" with a payoff of 2 to none with a payoff of 0, so the agent will accept. "Low" is Pareto efficient.[47] However, "high" is cost-benefit efficient. The total payoff of "high" is 5, whereas the total payoff from "low" is 4. To achieve cost-benefit efficiency, the agent could offer the principal a side payment of, say, 1.5 in exchange for "high" delegation. Then both parties would prefer "high" (payoffs of 2.5 and 2.5) to "low" (payoffs of 2 and 2).

[47] Recall that Pareto efficiency is achieved when there is no change that would make someone better off without also making someone worse off. From "low," moving to "none" would make both parties worse off, and moving to "high" would make the principal worse off.

To generalize, if the agent can refuse the principal's offer, then delegation will achieve Pareto efficiency. If the transaction costs of bargaining between the principal and agent are zero, delegation will achieve cost-benefit efficiency. This is an application of the Public Coase Theorem.

We have assumed that the agent can refuse a delegation of authority. In private law, this assumption is often reasonable. Before a sports agent represents a star player, they must agree to terms in a contract, and either can walk away from negotiations.[48] However, in public law, this assumption is often unreasonable. Many public agents must accept delegations of authority, even if they dislike them. If the Supreme Court imposes a standard, lower court judges must apply it, even if they would prefer a rule. When agents cannot refuse, delegation becomes a command rather than an offer. Commands are not necessarily Pareto efficient. The principal benefits, but the agent might not.

We have explained that forced delegation can be Pareto inefficient. Similarly, forced delegation can be cost-benefit inefficient. To benefit a little, the principal might impose or take away authority and harm the agent a lot.

As always, bargaining can prevent inefficiency. If the transaction costs of bargaining between the principal and agent are zero, they will achieve efficiency.[49] However, in public law the transaction costs of bargaining between the principal and agent are often high. Suppose the administrator in the medical example would like more authority to promote emergency care. He can talk to the Secretary, but what can he offer her? Money? Loyalty? Even if they had something to exchange, can they sign an enforceable contract?

In sum, delegation in public law often resembles an order rather than a bargain. Delegation by order may or may not be Pareto efficient, and it may or may not be cost-benefit efficient.

Questions

8.31. Sometimes law forces an agent to accept authority from a principal. Does law ever force a principal to give authority to an agent? Analyze these possible examples from the U.S. Constitution: Article III requires the judiciary, not the President, to interpret law; Article I grants some legislative power to Congress, with the rest reserved for the states; the Sixth Amendment requires a trial by jury rather than by a judge.

8.32. Does law really *force* agents to accept authority they do not want? If the Supreme Court gives lower courts too many standards, or if Congress gives agencies too many responsibilities, why don't lower court judges and civil servants resign? Can an agent's threat to resign discipline a principal's urge to overdelegate?

[48] Even when the agent can refuse a delegation, the parties may still fail to achieve cost-benefit efficiency. Agency costs present a very difficult problem to solve, as a large literature in economics shows.

[49] If the agent cannot refuse delegation, then he has a weak position in bargaining. His weak position will affect distribution—he will get a smaller payoff—but it will not affect efficiency. To see why, recall Coase's example involving the farmer, the rancher, and the fence. Efficiency requires the farmer to build the fence. If the law is "farmer's rights," then the rancher has a weak position in bargaining. The farmer will build the fence, but the rancher's payoff will be low. If the law were "rancher's rights," the farmer would build the fence, but the rancher's payoff would be higher. When the agent cannot refuse delegation, he resembles the rancher where law is "farmer's rights," and when the agent can refuse delegation, he resembles the rancher where law is "rancher's rights."

B. Externalization and Allies

We have explained that delegation in public law might not achieve efficiency as to the principal and agent. We can sharpen the point with the concept of externalization. When the principal decides on delegation, she considers her own costs and benefits but not the agent's. The principal externalizes the agent's interests. As an earlier chapter explained, people usually do too much of an activity with negative externalities and too little of an activity with positive externalities. Thus, we expect principals to delegate too much when delegation harms the agent and too little when delegation benefits the agent.

We can make the same predictions for the agent. When the agent exercises delegated authority, she considers only her own costs and benefits. The agent externalizes the principal's interests. Thus, we expect agents to divert resources too much when diversion harms the principal, we expect agents to be too rigid when flexibility would help the principal, and so on. Externalization by the agent imposes agency costs on the principal.

As we have explained throughout the book, bargaining can solve inefficiencies from externalization. To achieve this in public law, the transaction costs of political bargaining must be low. Often the transaction costs of political bargaining are high. This does not mean principals and agents can never bargain to efficiency, only that bargaining cannot systematically prevent inefficiency when delegating in public law.

If bargaining fails, principals and agents can achieve efficiency by internalizing one another's interests. One way to approximate internalization is through the appointment of like-minded people. In our example, the Secretary favors prenatal care and the administrator favors emergency care. This difference leads to inefficiency, as when the administrator diverts too much. To solve the inefficiency, the Secretary could choose an administrator who shares her opinion on prenatal care. The new administrator does not internalize the Secretary's values; he shares them.[50] In exercising authority to suit himself, the agent acts in the best way for the principal. Likewise, in delegating to suit herself, the principal delegates in the best way for the agent.

In general, *delegation maximizes efficiency as to the principal and agent as their values converge*. In economics, to say that two people's values converge means their utility functions align. When utility functions align, the act that best promotes one person's utility best promotes the other person's utility. Thus, we can restate the generalization more abstractly. *Delegation maximizes welfare as to the principal and agent as their values converge*. No two people are identical, so no combination of principal and agent automatically maximizes their joint welfare. But greater similarity between principal and agent can promote welfare.

Earlier we presented the ally principle as a positive prediction: principals will delegate more to agents whose values resemble their own. The ally principle also has a normative implication. It justifies giving principals broad power to select their agents.

[50] Instead of sharing the principal's values, the agent's value may be to serve the principal loyally. In that case the agent *behaves* as though he shares the principal's values, even though he doesn't. From the principal's point of view, this difference is immaterial.

Questions

8.33. In what ways does choosing an ally lower the transaction costs of bargaining between a principal and her agent?

8.34. The President nominates ambassadors, and the Senate confirms them. The President and the Senate would each like to choose an ambassador who internalizes their interests. Is this possible?

8.35. Suppose the Secretary in our medical example chooses an administrator who, like her, prioritizes prenatal care. She rejects the administrator who prioritizes emergency care. The Secretary's choice increases her welfare and her chosen administrator's welfare, but it probably decreases the welfare of the administrator whom she rejects. In public law, whose welfare should we prioritize?

Is Your Lawyer Your Ally?

A politician sues you for defamation, a neighbor crashes into your car, or the tax agency investigates your business. How should you respond? You could try to learn the law and represent yourself. But law is complicated and time is short. Most people hire lawyers instead, creating an agency relationship. The client is the principal, and the lawyer is her agent.

Like all principals, clients prefer to delegate to allies.[51] Sometimes this is possible, as when a civil rights advocate hires a public interest lawyer who wants to advance civil rights. However, few clients can find perfect allies. The person whose business gets investigated wants to avoid fines and jail time. The lawyer just wants to get paid.

As in business, the success or failure of agency relationships in law often depends on contracting.[52] The client signs a contract with her lawyer in which she agrees to exchange money for legal services. Clients can pay lawyers by the hour (actually, by the minute). This creates an incentive problem. The lawyer gets paid whether the client wins or loses, meaning she externalizes the costs of working on the case. The lawyer might encourage the client to litigate even if the case is weak, or the lawyer might spend more time on the case than is warranted. Instead of paying by the hour, clients can pay by the service. To illustrate, a lawyer could charge $500 for every employment contract that she writes, or she could charge $5,000 for every divorce case that she argues. This creates a different incentive problem. The lawyer gets paid the same whether her work is good or mediocre. She externalizes the benefits of doing careful work, so she might do careless work instead. Finally, the client can pay the lawyer a contingency fee, like 40 percent. If a plaintiff wins $100,000 in damages, the lawyer gets $40,000, but if the plaintiff loses the lawyer gets nothing. Contingency fees create yet another incentive problem. The lawyer does not internalize all of the benefit from

[51] Sometimes principals can benefit from delegating to "enemies," but only in narrow circumstances. *See* Jacob E. Gersen & Adrian Vermeule, *Delegating to Enemies*, 112 Colum. L. Rev. 2193 (2012).

[52] The ideas in the following paragraphs draw from Robert Cooter & Thomas Ulen, Law and Economics 427–28 (6th ed. 2016). For other discussions and proposed solutions to agency problems in lawyering, see, for example, Robert D. Cooter & Ariel Porat, *Anti-Insurance*, 31 J. Legal Stud. 203 (2002); A. Mitchell Polinsky & Daniel L. Rubinfeld, *Aligning the Interests of Lawyers and Clients*, 5 Am. L. Econ. Rev. 165 (2003).

working on the case (she gets 40 percent, not 100 percent). Consequently, she will not work as hard as she should.

According to the Coase Theorem, parties will bargain to efficiency provided transaction costs are zero. Clients and their lawyers face a persistent transaction cost that prevents efficient bargaining: information asymmetry. Usually the lawyer knows much more than the client about the strength of the case and the best litigation strategy. The lawyer's expertise attracts the client in the first place. But the lawyer's expertise also makes it hard for the client to monitor her. Did the case fail because the lawyer erred or because the judge got it wrong? Usually the client cannot tell.

Society has developed solutions to agency problems in the market for lawyers. Law schools and bar associations impose ethical obligations on lawyers, pushing them to prioritize their clients' interests over their own. And reputation matters a lot. Lawyers with good reputations prosper, while lawyers with bad reputations usually founder. To build and sustain good reputations, lawyers must produce good outcomes for their clients—so good that clients will promote them to others. New lawyers can generate good reputations by going to work for large firms with recognizable names. The importance of reputation may help explain why dozens of big firms, rather than hundreds of small ones, dominate the largest legal markets.

C. Delegation and Representation

We have analyzed delegation from one principal to one agent. We have shown that the principal and agent can maximize their joint welfare by bargaining or, alternatively, by aligning interests, as when the principal delegates to a close ally. In business, one principal often delegates to one agent. In public law, however, delegation is rarely so simple. Sometimes the principal is a natural person like the President, a governor, or the Secretary of Health and Human Services. However, the principal is often a group like Congress, the Supreme Court, or the United Nations General Assembly. Similarly, some agents are natural persons, but many others are groups like a congressional committee, the Department of Treasury, or the Office of Information and Regulatory Affairs.

Delegation in public law has other important features. The chains of delegation are long. Congress and the President delegate to the Secretary of Homeland Security, who delegates to the Director of U.S. Citizenship and Immigration Services, who delegates to the Chief of the Office of Policy and Strategy, who delegates to a subordinate. The last "link" in the chain is an agent who only has principals. In a democracy, the first "link" in the chain is the people. The people only have agents, including Congress and the President.

In theory, the same tools for promoting welfare between one principal and one agent apply in the public law setting. If all principals and agents can bargain costlessly, then delegation will achieve efficiency as to all principals and agents. This is an application of the Public Coase Theorem. Of course, no democracy can realize this ideal, though some public law promotes it. Debates, hearings, reviews, committee sessions, party caucuses, political campaigns, budget processes—these activities and others offer forums for principals and agents to negotiate.

Separate from bargaining, principals in public law can promote welfare through the ally principal. The people benefit when the President shares their values, the President benefits when the Secretary of Defense shares her values, and so on. In practice, no democracy enjoys rule by a chain of perfect allies. The people disagree among themselves about values, so no agent can perfectly mirror them. Similarly, the agents disagree among themselves about values (see Congress), so no subagents—administrators, subcommittees, civil servants—can perfectly mirror them. Each link in the chain of delegation involves slippage. Public law tries to minimize the slippage through activities like elections, congressional hearings, and the President's removal power. However, public law can never eliminate the slippage.

We have discussed two mechanisms for promoting welfare in delegation, bargaining and the ally principle. Now we consider a third mechanism: punishment. Principals can encourage agents to behave loyally by punishing them for acting disloyally. This strategy does not require agents to share the principals' preferences. Instead, agents are incentivized to behave *as if* they share the principals' preferences. In the delegation and rule games analyzed previously, the threat of punishment discourages the agent from shirking.

Punishment might not maximize welfare between the principal and the agent, especially when the agent cannot refuse the delegation. When President Trump ordered immigrants seeking asylum to wait in Mexico, U.S. asylum officers objected, but they obeyed under the threat of dismissal.[53] As this example shows, the threat of punishment can benefit the principal while harming the agent.

To maximize welfare, public law should account for the preferences of all actors, including agents. To approximately maximize welfare, public law should account for the preferences of the *people*, the first principal in the chain. The people vastly outnumber their agents, so satisfying the people tends to promote welfare even if some agents are dissatisfied. Public law tries to satisfy the people by punishing their wayward agents through elections, anti-bribery laws, and lawsuits against abusive police officers. Before punishing a disloyal agent, people must observe their bad acts. The freedoms of speech and press, the Freedom of Information Act, whistleblower-protection statutes, and other laws help the people observe disloyalty by their agents.

In sum, delegation in public law promotes welfare as the transaction costs of bargaining decrease, the preferences of principals and agents converge, and the capacity of the people to monitor and punish their agents grows. In a republic, agents are the people's representatives. When delegation promotes welfare, we can say that representation is good.

Questions

8.36. In *Gregory v. Ashcroft*, the Supreme Court upheld a law requiring state judges to retire at age 70.[54] Are judges representatives of the people? Why might a

[53] Maria Sacchetti, *U.S. Asylum Officers Say Trump's "Remain in Mexico" Policy Is Threatening Migrants' Lives, Ask Federal Court to End It*, WASH. POST, June 27, 2019.

[54] 501 U.S. 452 (1991).

mandatory retirement age for judges, but not for legislators or executives, improve representation?

8.37. When electing leaders, voters could exhaustively research candidates' positions on many issues. Instead, some voters just search for candidates with whom they share characteristics like sex, age, race, and background. How might this strategy promote good representation?

8.38. In 2008, a financial crisis in the United States triggered a global recession. Many people blamed officials like the Secretary of the Treasury, the Chairman of the Federal Reserve Board, and the Chairman of the Securities and Exchange Commission. When officials like those mismanage policy, does the President internalize all of the costs? Can the people count on the President to monitor those officials?

IV. Interpretive Theory of Delegation

When will principals delegate authority to agents? When will delegation benefit society? We have addressed these questions with positive and normative theory. Now we turn to interpretive theory. Interpretive theory addresses the questions of lawyers. With respect to delegation, lawyers ask questions like: Did Congress delegate more authority than the Constitution allows? Is a statute requiring "humane" disposal of fetal remains unconstitutionally vague?[55] These questions involve the Constitution. Other questions involve statutes: Can the EPA interpret the phrase "stationary source" in the Clean Air Act to mean an industrial plant?[56]

In the United States, constitutional questions about delegation are rare, whereas statutory questions about delegation are common. Every day courts decide if agencies act within the scope of authority delegated to them by statute. Because statutory questions are common, we focus on them first. Economics cannot answer all statutory questions in delegation, but it can help.

A. The Canons of Construction

In government, principals often delegate authority to agents by statute. Thus, the Clean Water Act delegates authority over "navigable waters" to the EPA, and the Food, Drug, and Cosmetics Act (FDCA) delegates authority over "drugs" to the FDA. Agencies use their authority to make and enforce regulations. Often agencies act in ways that the statute clearly authorizes, but sometimes they push the limit. To demonstrate, the FDCA clearly gave the FDA authority over prescription drugs, but it did not clearly give the FDA authority over cigarettes. To decide if the FDA had authority over cigarettes, courts had to interpret the FDCA.

55 City of Akron v. Akron Ctr. for Reprod. Health, Inc., 462 U.S. 416 (1983).

56 Chevron, U.S.A., Inc. v. Natural Resources Defense Council, Inc., 467 U.S. 837 (1984).

Courts begin interpreting a statute by reading its text. Sometimes the text is clear. To illustrate, the Endangered Species Act makes it unlawful to "take" an endangered animal, where "take" is defined to mean, among other things, "shoot." The Endangered Species Act clearly prohibits shooting an endangered animal with a gun.[57]

Many cases are not so easy. Recall the law prohibiting "possession of arms in a public library." The language might seem clear, but it isn't. "Arms" might mean guns, swords, bombs, clubs, the limbs attached to your shoulders, or all of the above. To interpret statutes like this, judges rely on *canons of construction*. Canons are background principles that guide interpretation. For example, the "whole act rule" is a canon that directs courts to read words in the context of the complete statute.[58] Applying the whole act rule, a judge might read the statute about arms in libraries and discover that the preamble addresses "the danger of firearms in public places." This is a good clue about the meaning of "arms." The whole act rule suggests that the statute prohibits guns but not knives or limbs.

Judges rely on dozens of canons of construction.[59] Some apply in narrow situations, like the canon directing courts to interpret statutes about veterans in favor of veterans. Other canons apply broadly, like the presumption of consistent usage. According to that canon, courts should interpret the same word to mean the same thing throughout a statute.

Scholars divide canons into two categories, descriptive and normative.[60] *Descriptive* canons provide guidance on what the legislature enacting the statute probably meant. They help "describe" the bargain the legislators struck. The whole act rule is a descriptive canon. To determine what legislators meant by "arms," read the whole statute. *Normative* canons direct courts to resolve questions of interpretation in favor of certain goals. For example, when a criminal statute is subject to two interpretations, one lenient on defendants and one harsh on defendants, the rule of lenity directs courts to adopt the lenient interpretation. The rule of lenity reflects a policy judgment. When judges cannot determine the meaning of the statute, they should "break the tie" in favor of lenience.

Canons of construction are not foolproof. Sometimes different canons support different interpretations. To illustrate, let's revisit our statute prohibiting "possession of arms in a public library." Does this statute forbid pocketknives in public libraries? Suppose the preamble addresses "dangerous objects in public places." Pocketknives can be "dangerous objects," so maybe pocketknives are "arms." But most people would not call pocketknives "arms," and punishing people for carrying pocketknives seems harsh. The whole act rule suggests pocketknives are "arms," and the rule of lenity suggests they are not.

As this example shows, the canons do not always provide clear answers. Rather than guiding judges to correct interpretations, canons can give judges discretion. A harsh judge will hold that pocketknives are prohibited and cite the whole act rule, while a lenient judge will hold that pocketknives are not prohibited and cite the rule of lenity.

[57] *See* Babbitt v. Sweet Home Chapter of Communities for a Great Oregon, 515 U.S. 687 (1995).

[58] *See* William N. Eskridge, Jr., *Gadamer/Statutory Interpretation*, 90 COLUM. L. REV. 609 (1990).

[59] For a comprehensive list, see WILLIAM N. ESKRIDGE, JR., PHILIP P. FRICKEY, & ELIZABETH GARRETT, CASES AND MATERIALS ON STATUTORY INTERPRETATION 851–870 (2012).

[60] This categorization comes from Stephen F. Ross, *Where Have You Gone, Karl Llewellyn—Should Congress Turn Its Lonely Eyes to You?*, 45 VAND. L. REV. 561 (1992). Many canons fit under both headings. Other scholars offer different categorizations. *See, e.g.*, CALEB NELSON, STATUTORY INTERPRETATION 81–83 (2011); Cass R. Sunstein, *Interpreting Statutes in the Regulatory State*, 103 HARV. L. REV. 405 (1989).

Judges do exercise discretion, as a later chapter will show. However, not all judges seek discretion at all times. Judges often appear to seek the best interpretation of the statute before them. In some cases, canons can help them find the best interpretation.

B. The Delegation Canon

Does the Food, Drug, and Cosmetics Act give the FDA authority over cigarettes?[61] Does the Clean Water Act give the EPA authority to regulate isolated wetlands?[62] Judges confront questions like these in important cases about delegation. Sometimes the statutes provide clear answers to the questions, but in hard cases they do not. Judges would benefit from a principle of interpretation, like a canon of construction, that guides them to correct answers in hard cases. The economic analysis of delegation supplies such a principle.

As discussed, delegation involves a fundamental trade-off between effort and diversion. By delegating, a principal saves the administrative costs of doing the work herself, but she risks diversion of purpose. According to the preceding analysis, rational principals will delegate until their expected savings in administrative costs just equal their expected losses from diversion.

We can apply this prediction to law. In cases about delegation, judges ask if an agency had authority to take a certain action. This is equivalent to asking if the principal delegated the power to take the action. If delegating the power would have saved the principal more administrative costs than it created in diversion costs, the principal probably delegated the power. Conversely, if delegating the power would have saved the principal less in administrative costs than it created in diversion costs, the principal probably did not delegate the power.

As an earlier chapter explained, judges interpreting law often ask what the legislature "intended." As reformulated by economists, the question is "What bargain did the legislators strike?" In general, legislators would not agree to a bargain that imposed more costs on them than necessary. If they could reduce their total costs by delegating more or less, presumably they would.

Now we can state the principle of interpretation. To determine if a legislature delegated a certain power to an agency, and assuming legal materials like the text of the statute do not answer the question, judges should ask: Would the legislature's administrative savings from this delegation exceed the legislature's diversion costs? If the answer is yes, then the legislature intended to delegate the power, and vice versa. This is the delegation theory of interpretation, or the *delegation canon*.

The delegation canon is descriptive, not normative. It provides a guide for determining what legislators agreed to in the actual statute. The canon does not address what legislators *should* have agreed to in an *ideal* statute. Determining what legislators should have agreed to is a normative inquiry involving the complications above—whether the agent could refuse delegation, the transaction costs of bargaining between principals and agents, whether the legislators are good or bad representatives of the people, and so

[61] Food & Drug Admin. v. Brown & Williamson Tobacco Corp., 529 U.S. 120 (2000).
[62] Rapanos v. United States, 547 U.S. 715 (2006).

on. The delegation canon sweeps aside those complications to address the interpretive question: Did the legislators delegate the power?

Courts cannot measure administrative and diversion costs with precision. Even if they could, the delegation canon might sometimes lead them astray. Legislators do not always make choices to minimize their administrative and diversion costs. For example, they might delegate even when diversion costs are high. In such cases, the canon might lead courts to the wrong answer rather than the right one. Like all canons, the delegation canon is a rule of thumb, not a law of nature. It sharpens intuitions and guides reasoning.

Questions

8.39. Legislators expect a policy decision to be politically unpopular. Rather than making the decision themselves, the legislators agree to delegate authority to an agency to make the decision. However, the legislators do not draft the statute clearly. A court applies the delegation canon and concludes that the legislators did not delegate authority to make the decision to the agency. In this case, does the delegation canon lead to a good answer as a matter of law? Does it lead to a good answer as a matter of policy?

8.40. "Independent" agencies are run by administrators whom the President cannot easily replace. Some commentators argue that courts should grant less discretion to independent agencies than to other agencies.[63] Does the delegation canon support this argument?

C. Applying the Delegation Canon

You will not find the phrase "delegation canon" in legal opinions, nor will you find talk of "administrative" and "diversion" costs. Judges do not write in these terms. However, judges sometimes reason in these terms. Consequently, the delegation canon is not a proposal for a new method of statutory interpretation. Rather, the canon labels and synthesizes a form of reasoning that courts already deploy. The following examples illustrate.

The Clean Air Act required permits for certain "stationary sources" of air pollution. The EPA interpreted the phrase "stationary source" to mean industrial grouping. To clarify, suppose one factory emits pollution from two smokestacks. Under the EPA's interpretation, there is only one "stationary source" (the factory), not two (each smokestack). This interpretation made it easier for polluters to acquire permits. Did the Clean Air Act authorize the EPA's interpretation? In *Chevron v. Natural Resources Defense Council*, the Supreme Court said yes.[64]

[63] *See, e.g.*, Randolph J. May, *Defining Deference Down: Independent Agencies and Chevron Deference*, 58 Admin. L. Rev. 429 (2006).

[64] 467 U.S. 837 (1984).

The Court's decision established the *Chevron* doctrine, which we will address later. For now, consider some of the Court's reasoning. After noting that the Clean Air Act is "technical and complex" and requires balancing environmental and economic interests, the Court wrote:

> Congress intended to accommodate both interests, but did not do so itself on the level of specificity presented by these cases. Perhaps that body consciously desired the [EPA] Administrator to strike the balance . . . , thinking that those with great expertise . . . would be in a better position to do so; perhaps it simply did not consider the question at this level; and perhaps Congress was unable to forge a coalition on either side of the question[.][65]

We can restate these arguments in our language: the administrative costs to Congress of defining "stationary source" were high. Meanwhile, the EPA's interpretation seemed reasonable, meaning the diversion costs seemed low. According to the delegation canon, these facts suggest that Congress intended to let the agency decide, and that's what the Court held.

Here is another example. The Supreme Court had to decide if the Department of Labor had authority under the Black Lung Benefits Act to issue certain regulations on government benefits. The Court held that it did. In justifying its decision, the Court wrote:

> The Benefits Act has produced a complex and highly technical regulatory program. The identification and classification of medical eligibility criteria necessarily require significant expertise and entail the exercise of judgment grounded in policy concerns. In those circumstances, courts appropriately defer to the agency entrusted by Congress to make such policy determinations.[66]

Because the decisions required technical expertise, the administrative costs to Congress of making them would be high. Meanwhile, the regulations seemed reasonable, suggesting that diversion costs were low. These facts suggest that Congress intended to delegate, and that's what the Court held.

Consider a different kind of delegation problem: subdelegation. The Clean Water Act requires a permit to discharge certain pollutants. According to the act, "the Secretary of the Army, acting through the Chief of Engineers" issues the permits.[67] A company building a gas pipeline got a permit, but not from the Chief of Engineers. Instead, the permit came from a District Engineer, a subordinate of the Chief of Engineers. The question in *United States v. Mango* was whether the Clean Water Act allows the Chief of Engineers to delegate permitting authority to District Engineers.[68] The court held that it does. The Chief of Engineers processed up to 11,000 permits per year. "[T]he magnitude of the task," the court wrote, "is such that it is reasonable to assume Congress did not contemplate it would be performed by one person."[69]

65 *Id.* at 865.
66 Pauley v. BethEnergy Mines, Inc., 501 U.S. 680, 697 (1991).
67 33 U.S.C. § 1344(d).
68 199 F.3d 85 (2d Cir. 1999).
69 *Id.* at 91.

The court in *Mango* reasoned consistently with the delegation canon. The administrative costs of not delegating were exceptionally high. The Chief of Engineers would bear the costs directly—he would process thousands of permits per year—but Congress would bear the costs indirectly. Burdened by permitting, the Chief of Engineers could not achieve the other goals Congress set for him. Meanwhile, the subdelegation did not appear to create meaningful diversion costs. These facts suggest that Congress intended to let the Chief of Engineers delegate. That's what the court held.

We have examined some cases where courts reasoned according to the delegation canon and permitted the agency action. Now consider some cases where courts used the same kind of reasoning but forbade the agency action.

The state of Oregon permitted doctors to prescribe lethal drugs to terminally ill patients who wished to end their lives. The drugs were regulated by the federal Controlled Substances Act (CSA). The U.S. Attorney General determined that the drugs had no legitimate medical purpose. Without a legitimate purpose, the CSA forbade doctors from prescribing the drugs. Thus, the Attorney General's determination blocked physician-assisted suicide in Oregon. Did the CSA delegate power to the Attorney General to decide what constituted a legitimate medical purpose? In *Gonzalez v. Oregon*, the Supreme Court said no.[70] Among other arguments, the Court stated that the CSA would not "cede medical judgments to an executive official who lacks medical expertise."[71]

The delegation canon supports this reasoning. All else equal, higher diversion costs suggest that Congress did not mean to delegate. Diversion costs are higher when agents lack expertise. An agent who knows little is less likely to achieve Congress's objectives, especially in a technical area, than an agent who knows a lot.[72] Having concluded that the Attorney General had no expertise on assisted suicide, the Court held that Congress did not delegate.

Consider a case on subdelegation. The Telecommunications Act of 1996 sought to make the market for telecommunications more competitive. It required "incumbent local exchange carriers"—the companies owning the wires running from house to house—to permit competitors to use their wires in exchange for a reasonable fee.[73] The act gave the Federal Communications Commission (FCC) authority to work out the details. The FCC subdelegated authority over the details to state-level communications agencies. A court held that the FCC could not subdelegate this authority:

> [T]he cases recognize an important distinction between subdelegation to a *subordinate* and subdelegation to an *outside party*. . . . [T]he case law strongly suggests that subdelegations to outside parties are assumed to be improper absent an affirmative showing of congressional authorization. . . .

[70] 546 U.S. 243 (2006).
[71] *Id.* at 266.
[72] Here is an illustration of the point. Suppose your sick relative needs an operation, and your objective is to make her well. You could perform the operation yourself, but you have no medical expertise. Alternatively, you could delegate the operation to a surgeon or to a lawyer who, like you, has no medical expertise. The surgeon is more likely to achieve your objective than the lawyer. If the lawyer claims you delegated the operation to him, a judge should be skeptical.
[73] 47 U.S.C. § 251(c)(3) (1996).

> This distinction is entirely sensible. When an agency delegates authority to its subordinate, responsibility—and thus accountability—clearly remain with the federal agency. But when an agency delegates power to outside parties, lines of accountability may blur. . . . [D]elegation to outside entities increases the risk that these parties will not share the agency's "national vision and perspective," . . . and thus may pursue goals inconsistent with those of the agency and the underlying statutory scheme. In short, subdelegation to outside entities aggravates the risk of policy drift inherent in any principal-agent relationship.[74]

The court's reasoning matches the delegation canon. Subdelegation by the FCC to state agencies would increase the diversion costs to Congress. All else equal, higher diversion costs imply Congress did not authorize the delegation.

As these examples show, judges often reason like economists about delegation. The delegation canon captures reasoning that courts already deploy.

Questions

8.41. The presumption against extraterritoriality is a canon of construction. It directs courts not to apply statutes outside of the United States absent clear authorization from Congress. The presumption against extraterritoriality limits agency authority.[75] For example, U.S. agencies cannot apply Title VII of the Civil Rights Act in Saudi Arabia, only in the United States, because Title VII does not clearly state that it applies abroad.[76] Is the presumption against extraterritoriality consistent with the delegation canon? Why might diversion costs be higher when agencies act outside of the United States?

8.42. The Food, Drug, and Cosmetic Act of 1938 gave the FDA authority to regulate "drugs." Is tobacco a "drug?" You know from our description of *FDA v. Brown & Williamson Tobacco Corp.* that the Supreme Court said no. To reach that conclusion, the Court identified six statutes enacted by Congress after 1938 that regulated tobacco. According to the Court, the existence of those statutes implied that Congress intended to regulate tobacco itself, not delegate authority to the FDA.[77] Is this consistent with the delegation canon? What, if anything, do those six statutes tell you about Congress's administrative costs?

[74] U.S. Telecom Ass'n v. F.C.C., 359 F.3d 554, 565–66 (D.C. Cir. 2004).

[75] *See* Cass R. Sunstein, *Nondelegation Canons*, 67 U. Chi. L. Rev. 315, 316 (2000).

[76] *See* E.E.O.C. v. Arabian Am. Oil Co., 499 U.S. 244 (1991). This has changed since the case. *See* Renee S. Orleans, *Extraterritorial Employment Protection Amendments of 1991: Congress Protects U.S. Citizens Who Work for U.S. Companies Abroad*, 16 Md. J. Int'l L. & Trade 147 (1992).

[77] Food & Drug Admin. v. Brown & Williamson Tobacco Corp., 529 U.S. 120, 122–23 (2000) ("Under these circumstances, it is evident that Congress has ratified the FDA's previous, long-held position that it lacks jurisdiction to regulate tobacco products as customarily marketed. Congress has created a distinct scheme for addressing the subject, and that scheme excludes any role for FDA regulation.").

Conclusion

Political parties offer programs to voters, voters choose among programs in elections, and agency heads or ministers direct administrators to implement the programs. Each link in the chain of authority consists of a principal and an agent. Delegating authority to agents saves administrative costs for principals and gives agents the opportunity to divert resources. Principals prefer to delegate power when their opportunity costs are high and when they can monitor and punish diversion by agents. These ideas illuminate the choice to delegate by citizens, presidents, legislators, and judges. Similarly, they illuminate the choice between rules and standards. The next chapter applies these generalizations to a variety of legal problems and cases.

9

Delegation Applications

In *The Federalist Papers*, Madison reviewed the "power delegated by the proposed Constitution to the federal government."[1] He reached an "undeniable" conclusion: "no part of the power is unnecessary or improper for accomplishing the necessary objects of the Union."[2] The Framers fixated on delegation when drafting the U.S. Constitution. Today, lawmakers fixate on delegation when drafting other public laws—treaties, statutes, city ordinances, and judicial opinions. Delegation is fundamental to public law. The prior chapter provided a general analysis of the positive, normative, and interpretive aspects of delegation. Here we apply those ideas to particular legal problems. We address questions like these:

Example 1: Agencies produce thousands of regulations every year. Like statutes, regulations require interpretation. Agencies often interpret their own regulations. In *Auer v. Robbins*, the Supreme Court held that judges must defer to agency interpretations of their own regulations unless the interpretation is "plainly erroneous or inconsistent with the regulation."[3] *Auer* gives agencies much discretion to determine the meaning of their regulations. Does this benefit the agencies? Does it benefit their principals (Congress, the President, citizens)?

Example 2: The mayor of Fort Lee, New Jersey, did not support Governor Chris Christie's re-election bid. To punish him, officials concocted a fake traffic study and changed the lanes on a bridge, causing gridlock in Fort Lee. The officials were convicted under a federal statute criminalizing "any scheme or artifice to defraud, or for obtaining money or property by means of false or fraudulent pretenses, representations, or promises."[4] In *Kelly v. United States*, the Supreme Court ordered the officials released.[5] According to the Court, the officials' realignment of lanes was an exercise in regulatory power, not a taking of money or property, so they did not violate the law. Do you agree?

Example 3: In *Citizens United*, the Supreme Court held that the First Amendment grants U.S. corporations the right to spend unlimited amounts on ads to influence U.S. elections.[6] Justice Kennedy wrote, "Factions should be checked by permitting them all to speak . . . and by entrusting the people to judge what is true

[1] THE FEDERALIST NO. 44, at 233 (James Madison) (Ian Shapiro ed., 2009).

[2] *Id.*

[3] 519 U.S. 452, 461 (1997). *But see* Kisor v. Wilkie, 139 S. Ct. 2400, 2416 (2019) ("[N]ot every reasonable agency reading of a genuinely ambiguous rule should receive *Auer* deference.").

[4] 18 U.S.C. § 1343.

[5] 140 S. Ct. 1565 (2020).

[6] Citizens United v. F.E.C., 558 U.S. 310 (2010). Specifically, corporations have the right to spend unlimited amounts on "independent political expenditures." *See id.*

Public Law and Economics. Robert D. Cooter and Michael D. Gilbert, Oxford University Press. © Oxford University Press 2022.
DOI: 10.1093/oso/9780197655870.003.0009

and what is false."[7] Justice Scalia wrote, "We should celebrate rather than condemn the addition of this speech to the public debate."[8] If more speech is better, why does U.S. law prohibit foreign corporations from running ads to influence U.S. elections?

As the questions show, some delegation problems in public law involve the daily operations of government, as when agencies issue regulations. Other delegation involves the structure of government, or "the rules of the game." We will discuss both, beginning with agencies and regulations and then turning to topics like corruption, campaign finance, and lobbying. To analyze these topics, we combine positive, normative, and interpretive reasoning.

I. Agencies and Administrative Law

In the United States, Congress and the President enact few statutes, whereas administrative agencies enact many regulations. Regulations address topics like food safety, energy conservation, immigration procedures, student loans, communicable diseases, and migratory birds. To enact those regulations, agencies follow certain procedures, some optional and some mandatory. A vast body of law called "administrative law" governs those procedures. Much of administrative law concerns one question: How should courts review agency actions? Should they defer, meaning agencies have more discretion, or should they not defer, meaning agencies have less discretion? We will analyze this choice.

A. The *Chevron* Doctrine

The previous chapter introduced *Chevron v. Natural Resources Defense Council*, a famous case in U.S. administrative law.[9] Here we describe the details. The Clean Air Act of 1963 aimed to control air pollution on a national level. Pursuant to the act, the Environmental Protection Agency set air quality standards. Not every state met the standards. In 1977, a new statute required noncomplying states to regulate "new or modified major stationary sources" of air pollution. Under the new law, one could not build or change certain "stationary sources" of pollution without a permit. Getting a permit was hard. Consequently, the definition of "stationary source" was important. If every smokestack constituted a "stationary source," then factories would need many expensive permits.

The statute did not include a definition of "stationary source." So the EPA supplied one, choosing a "plantwide" definition. The definition treated industrial plants, rather than their individual parts, as "stationary sources." To see the difference, imagine a factory with two buildings. The boss wants to close production in the first building,

[7] *Id.* at 355.
[8] *Id.* at 393 (Scalia, J., concurring).
[9] 467 U.S. 837 (1984).

eliminating a smokestack, and start production in the second building, adding a new smokestack. Under a narrow definition of "stationary source," the boss would need a permit to add the new smokestack. Under the EPA's definition, the boss would not need a permit as long as the total pollution from the factory did not increase.

Environmental groups challenged the EPA's definition. The question was interpretive: What does "stationary source" mean? The Supreme Court could not find an answer. The statute did not provide a definition, and the legislative history was inconsistent. To make the law work, someone had to pick a definition, and the question was who. Should the EPA select a definition, or should judges?

The Supreme Court announced a two-step test for cases like this. First, judges should ask if "Congress has directly spoken to the precise question at issue."[10] In other words, did Congress supply an answer to the interpretive question? If so, Congress's choice governs. If not, then judges should turn to the second step and ask if the agency chose "a permissible construction of the statute."[11] In other words, did the agency supply a reasonable answer to the interpretive question? If so, the agency's choice governs.

To clarify the *Chevron* two-step, consider an example. Congress enacts a confusing statute that could mean *A*, *B*, or *C*. An agency interprets the statute to mean *C*. Under *Chevron*, the first question for courts is whether Congress made a choice among *A*, *B*, or *C*. Judges read the statute, apply the canons of construction, and consult other legal sources. If they conclude that the answer is yes (say, Congress chose *B*), then Congress's choice governs (the agency erred in choosing *C*, it must choose *B*). If the answer is no, then the question for courts is whether the agency's interpretation is reasonable. If the legal sources support *A* and *B* but preclude *C*, then the agency erred; it must choose between *A* and *B*. If the legal sources support *B* and *C* but preclude *A*, then the agency's choice of *C* is permissible.

Judges have applied the *Chevron* doctrine in thousands of cases. Meanwhile, scholars have analyzed it in hundreds of papers. They disagree sharply on whether the case was decided correctly as a matter of law and whether it promotes good or bad behavior by agencies. Economics can illuminate this controversy.

Questions

9.1. According to Justice Gorsuch, *Chevron* empowers "bureaucracies to swallow huge amounts of core judicial and legislative power . . . in a way that seems more than a little difficult to square with the Constitution of the framers' design."[12] Is he right? Consider the following:

(a) *Chevron* grants agencies discretion when the statute is vague *and* when the statute is ambiguous. Vagueness usually signals a delegation of authority, whereas ambiguity usually signals a mistake in drafting. Who is better at resolving drafting mistakes, agencies or courts?[13]

[10] *Id.* at 842.

[11] *Id.* at 843.

[12] Gutierrez-Brizuela v. Lynch, 834 F.3d 1142, 1149 (10th Cir. 2016) (Gorsuch, J., concurring). Justice Gorsuch wrote this as a circuit judge, prior to his appointment to the Supreme Court.

[13] *See* Cass R. Sunstein & Adrian Vermeule, *The Unbearable Rightness of* Auer, 84 U. Chi. L. Rev. 297, 307 (2017).

(b) The statute is subject to three interpretations, *A*, *B*, and *C*. The agency chooses *C*. After careful review, a judge determines that *C* is a reasonable interpretation. However, the judge thinks *B* is the best interpretation. Does the *Chevron* doctrine require the agency to switch from interpretation *C* to *B*?

(c) "It is emphatically the province and duty of the judicial department to say what the law is."[14] Chief Justice Marshall's statement means judges have the final say when interpreting law. Suppose a statute is vague. The lower court interprets the statute and concludes that the best interpretation is *A*. Afterward the agency in charge of the statute concludes that the best interpretation is *B*. Under *Chevron*, the lower court's interpretation controls if it concluded that the statute *unambiguously* means *A*. However, if the lower court admitted that the statute is unclear, then the agency's interpretation controls over the court's.[15] Does this contradict Chief Justice Marshall?

B. What Do Agencies Maximize?

Chevron directs courts to defer to agencies in certain cases. Does this promote good policy? The answer depends on agency competence. An agency's competence depends in part on the objectives of the people who staff it. CEOs maximize profits, monks maximize enlightenment, and doctors maximize health. What do bureaucrats maximize?

Like good representatives, agencies might try to maximize the public interest. A beneficent agent regulates and enforces until the marginal benefits to society of her efforts just equal the marginal costs. Figure 9.1 depicts this possibility.[16] The horizontal axis represents the agency's size, which might be measured in terms of its budget, staff, or power. The vertical axis indicates the benefits to society (net social benefits, or benefits minus costs) created by the agency. Starting from the left and moving to the right, the agency expands and net social benefits increase. Net social benefits reach their maximum when the agency's size equals x^*, the social optimum.

Agencies often impose costs on the parties they regulate, as when the EPA forces power plants to reduce emissions. But not every regulated party suffers from regulation. Some parties seek regulation to restrict competition. Airlines might want regulators to set fares and routes to choke their competitors, or farmers might want extensive subsidies (we will say more about subsidies later). New, lenient regulations can replace old, strict regulations, lowering the costs to regulated parties. Under President Trump, the EPA issued new regulations that relaxed gas mileage requirements on cars. In extreme cases, industry *captures* the agency that regulates it. The regulated use the regulator to extract value for themselves, like monopoly profits.[17] Capture implies that the agency does not regulate enough in the public interest. In Figure 9.1, the agency has a size like x_c, which is suboptimal.

[14] Marbury v. Madison, 5 U.S. 137, 177 (1803).

[15] *See* Nat'l Cable & Telecomm. Ass'n v. Brand X Internet Servs., 545 U.S. 967 (2005).

[16] This figure and analysis draw on Robert D. Cooter, The Strategic Constitution 151–52 (2000).

[17] *See* Einer Elhauge, *Does Interest Group Theory Justify More Intrusive Judicial Review?*, 101 Yale L.J. 31 (1991); George Stigler, The Citizen and the State (1975).

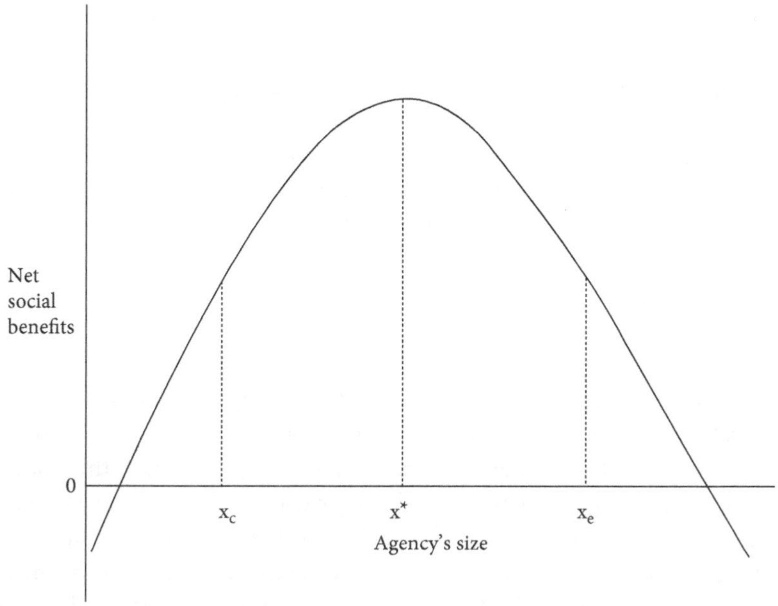

Figure 9.1. Agencies and Social Benefits

Now we consider a final possibility: the regulators serve themselves. Regulators have their own interests. Being human, they confuse what is best for themselves with what is best for society. As an agency expands, its administrators often gain responsibilities, prestige, power, and pay. Consequently, administrators might favor expansion beyond the socially optimal size. According to the *engorgement principle*, administrators strive to maximize their agency's size as measured by budget or staff.[18] In Figure 9.1, an engorging agent wants to go as far to the right on the horizontal axis as possible, say, to point x_e.

Figure 9.1 depicts the interests of regulators, regulated, and the general public. Regulators might prefer a bloated organization at x_e, the regulated prefer a small organization at x_c, and the general public prefers the social optimum x^*. In politics, who usually wins? Sometimes results follow the median rule, which can yield the social optimum as the chapters on voting explained. However, the general public is often unorganized, uninformed, and uninfluential. In contrast, regulated parties and administrators often have an intense interest in a particular agency, so they organize for better information and more influence. Sometimes the administrators win the political competition and the agency becomes too large, and sometimes the regulated win the political competition and the agency becomes too small.

Questions

9.2. Critics argue that judicial review of agency action imposes high costs on agencies by requiring demanding procedures. Supporters argue that judicial review improves the quality and "legitimacy" of agency action.

[18] *See* William A. Niskanen, Bureaucracy and Representative Government (1971).

(a) Does the argument for judicial review depend on what the agency maximizes?

(b) Imagine a spectrum of judicial review ranging from complete deference (no review) to zero deference (demanding review). As a matter of theory, what is the optimal degree of deference to agency action? What information would you need to determine if the existing degree of deference is optimal? Does anyone have this information?

Police Patrols versus Fire Alarms

Lawyers worry about diversion by agencies, as when a captured administrator serves industry rather than the public. Does Congress worry about diversion by agencies? For many years, scholars thought the answer was "no." They based this conclusion on the absence of congressional oversight. After delegating power to agencies, one might expect Congress to monitor their behavior. For example, one might expect Senators to hold hearings on agency activities, demand monthly reports from agency experts, or even tour agency buildings. In fact, Congress did little of those things. Rather than oversee agencies, Congress appeared to ignore them. One scholar wrote, "[O]versight is a vital yet neglected congressional function."[19]

Mathew McCubbins and Thomas Schwartz thought otherwise.[20] They distinguished two forms of oversight. First, Congress might monitor agencies in a systematic, ongoing manner. This could involve routine hearings, reports, and inspections. This is called *police patrol* oversight because it resembles cops walking the beat. Most review turns up nothing, but occasionally it deters or uncovers problems. Second, Congress might empower private citizens and interest groups to monitor agencies. For example, statutes might require agencies to hold public hearings, solicit comments from regulated parties, and publicize their decisions. Furthermore, statutes might permit challenges in court, where judges can correct agency actions. This is called *fire alarm* oversight. Congress installs fire alarms, and private actors pull them when agencies misbehave.

McCubbins and Schwartz argue that Congress prefers fire alarms. Much police patrol oversight wastes time and effort. In contrast, fire alarm oversight is focused. Congress only pays attention when a constituent sounds the alarm. Relatedly, members of Congress seek re-election. Fire alarms help Congress respond to constituents in need, generating political support, whereas routine, police patrol oversight does not. Finally, fire alarms transfer costs. Instead of burning its own resources on ongoing monitoring, much of which turns up nothing, Congress empowers private actors to monitor. Those actors burn their own resources keeping agencies in line.

[19] James Pearson, *Oversight: A Vital Yet Neglected Function*, 23 Kan. L. Rev. 277, 288 (1975). For a prominent argument that Congress abdicates its responsibility and lets agencies run amuck, see Theodore J. Lowi, The End of Liberalism (1969).

[20] *See* Mathew D. McCubbins & Thomas Schwartz, *Congressional Oversight Overlooked: Police Patrols versus Fire Alarms*, 28 Am. J. Pol. Sci. 165 (1984).

According to McCubbins and Schwartz, Congress does not neglect oversight of the administrative state. Rather, Congress uses fire alarms, which are decentralized and harder for ordinary citizens to observe than police patrol oversight. This arrangement is probably best for Congress. Is it best for courts? For society?

C. Institutional Competence

Scholars have studied agency design, capture, and engorgement extensively. However, most lawyers are not involved in agency design. In the courthouse, judges do not ask questions like, "What did the agency maximize?" or "How would you restructure the EPA?" They ask questions like, "Is the EPA's definition of 'stationary source' reasonable?" Questions of interpretation seem independent from questions of agency design. Consequently, design might seem irrelevant to interpretation.

But this is not quite right. Some interpretive questions have no ascertainable solution. Many smart judges analyzed the legal materials in *Chevron*, and they could not agree on a definition of "stationary source." Some statutes permit multiple interpretations from which interpreters must choose. In such cases, the answer to interpretive questions depends on the deference that courts give to agencies. If courts defer, then agencies resolve interpretive questions, as in *Chevron*. If courts do not defer, then judges resolve interpretive questions.

Decisions about deference are usually made by judges and influenced by lawyers. Courts often *choose* whether to defer. That choice does and should depend on an agency's competence.[21] Agency competence depends on design.

To elaborate, recall that delegation raises a fundamental trade-off: the principal saves administrative costs but incurs diversion costs. In administrative law, the President and Congress are the principals, and agencies like the EPA are agents. Courts are a third player in the game. They are not exactly agents of the President or Congress. As Chief Justice Marshall wrote, judges serve "the will of the law."[22] What law requires may differ from what the President and Congress, or at least *today's* President and Congress, want.[23] Likewise, courts are not principals of agencies. Agencies get most of their directions and rewards from lawmakers enacting statutes, not from judges deciding cases. Thus, courts complicate the game.

Suppose that Congress and the agencies are "enemies" (agencies will divert when they can), whereas Congress and the courts are allies (what is good for Congress is good for the courts). Courts will impose fewer diversion costs than agencies. Holding all else constant, courts should resolve interpretive questions themselves rather than deferring

[21] *See* Cass R. Sunstein & Adrian Vermeule, *Interpretation and Institutions*, 101 MICH. L. REV. 885 (2003).

[22] Osborn v. Bank of United States, 22 U.S. 738, 866 (1824).

[23] Here is Chief Justice Marshall's complete quote: "Judicial power is never exercised for the purpose of giving effect to the will of the Judge; always for the purpose of giving effect to the will of the Legislature; or, in other words, to the will of the law." Marshall equates the "will of the legislature," or what we might call legislative intent, with the "will of the law." This is controversial among some modern jurists, but set that aside. Legislators might intentionally enact a statute that violates the Constitution, but the Constitution trumps. Thus, judges cannot be perfect agents of Congress.

to agencies. This will reduce Congress's diversion costs. If Congress represents the citizens, this will also reduce society's diversion costs.

Are courts allies of Congress as we have assumed? Perhaps. The Senate confirms federal judges, and presumably Senators will not confirm "enemies." But judges often remain on the bench long after the Senators who confirmed them leave office. Furthermore, judges are independent. Independence might make them disinterested interpreters. But independence means power, and power can corrupt. The Anti-Federalists who opposed the U.S. Constitution worried about making judges "independent of the people, of the legislature, and of every power under heaven."[24] We will say more about judicial independence later. For now, the point is that agencies are accountable to Congress and the President, whereas judges are not. Consequently, judges might impose *higher* diversion costs than agencies.[25] If they do, and holding all else constant, judges should defer to agencies.

Having discussed diversion costs, we now consider administrative costs. Delegation saves Congress time and resources. Those savings increase when the matter requires expertise. To illustrate, few members of Congress know medicine. Consequently, it would be difficult for Congress to write good rules for preventing a pandemic, like the coronavirus that began spreading in 2019. Delegating to a competent agent saves Congress a lot of effort. If an agency like the Department of Health and Human Services is more competent than courts, then courts should defer to its interpretations, holding all else constant. Of course, agencies are not always competent. The Food and Drug Administration spent 12 years defining the term "peanut butter."[26] If courts are more competent than agencies, judges should not defer.

In sum, courts should defer when agencies have lower diversion and administrative costs, and courts should decide themselves when agencies have higher diversion and administrative costs. In reality, judges might have lower diversion costs (because they tend to respect legislative bargains), and agencies might have lower administrative costs (because they tend to possess more expertise). Courts should defer when the agency's advantage in expertise exceeds the court's advantage in diversion costs. Note that these are statements about good policy, not about law. Law might require courts to defer even when doing so causes bad policy, and vice versa.

We have analyzed courts and agencies separately, as though decisions by one do not affect the other. In reality, their decisions interact. A court's decision about deference ex post, meaning after the agency acts, affects the agency's behavior ex ante. In reviewing an agency's decision, courts usually do more than read the statute. They subject many agency actions to "hard look" review.[27] Did the agency gather facts, hold hearings, use

[24] *Essays of Brutus* XV, *in* THE ANTI-FEDERALIST: WRITINGS BY THE OPPONENTS OF THE CONSTITUTION 182, 183 (Herbert J. Storing ed., 1985).

[25] Cass R. Sunstein & Adrian Vermeule, *Interpretation and Institutions*, 101 MICH. L. REV. 885, 935 (2003) ("If judges are corrupt, biased, poorly informed, or otherwise unreliable, it would hardly make sense to entrust them with [the power to review agencies].").

[26] President Jimmy Carter said, "[I]t should not have taken 12 years and a hearing record of over 100,000 pages for the FDA to decide what percentage of peanuts there ought to be in peanut butter." Angie M. Boyce, *"When Does It Stop Being Peanut Butter?": FDA Food Standards of Identity, Ruth Desmond, and the Shifting Politics of Consumer Activism, 1960s–1970s*, 57 TECH. & CULTURE 54 (2016). The arduous process was not entirely the FDA's fault. *See* Richard A. Merrill & Earl M. Collier, Jr., *"Like Mother Used to Make": An Analysis of FDA Food Standards of Identity*, 74 COLUM. L. REV. 561 (1974).

[27] *See, e.g.*, Cass R. Sunstein, *In Defense of the Hard Look: Judicial Activism and Administrative Law*, 7 HARV. J.L. & PUB. POL'Y 51 (1984).

science, consult industry, consider costs and benefits, and explain its decision? If courts scrutinize carefully, then agencies must use exhaustive procedures, otherwise courts will reject their decisions.

Economics clarifies this relationship. Demanding review by courts drives up the costs of agency action. When the cost of producing cars increases, people produce fewer cars. Likewise, when the cost of regulating increases, agencies issue fewer regulations. Instead of using minimal procedures to make two regulations quickly, both of which courts will reject, agencies might use exhaustive procedures to make one regulation that courts will accept. In sum, demanding review by courts should tend to reduce agency action. Legal scholars who noticed this phenomenon called it "ossification."[28]

Is ossification good or bad? The answer depends on many factors. If regulations tend to be harmful because agencies are incompetent, then ossification is good. If exhaustive procedures just waste time, they should be abandoned. If exhaustive procedures improve regulations, then demanding review by courts creates a trade-off: agencies produce few, high-quality regulations rather than many, low-quality regulations. To illustrate this trade-off, imagine two social problems, poverty and disease. The Department of Health and Human Services can address poverty with one high-quality regulation, leaving disease unaddressed, or it can address poverty and disease with two lower-quality regulations. Sometimes the first option is better, sometimes the second option is better.

Consider another complication: the cost of review. Careful scrutiny by judges increases the costs of agencies, and it also increases the costs of courts. Instead of quickly reading a statute, judges must consult records, read transcripts, and review procedures. This takes time and attention away from other cases. To decide if demanding review is worthwhile, one must take all costs into account, including the costs to the court system.

Finally, consider a topic from an earlier chapter: transition costs. They include the costs to people of adapting to new laws. Transition costs increase when law changes more frequently. Judicial review of agency action can cause law to change more frequently. To illustrate, consider air pollution in the United States. In 2005, the EPA promulgated the Clean Air Interstate Rule. In 2008, a federal court vacated the rule, stating that the "EPA must redo its analysis from the ground up" regardless of any "disruptive consequences."[29] In 2011, the EPA promulgated a replacement called the Cross-State Air Pollution Rule (CSAPI). In 2012, a federal court vacated the CSAPI.[30] In 2014, the Supreme Court reversed the lower court and reinstated the CSAPI.[31] Without judicial review, the regulation of air pollution might have remained stable. Instead, it changed four times in ten years. Whatever its benefits, judicial review of the EPA introduced many transition costs.

[28] *See* Thomas O. McGarity, *Some Thoughts on "Deossifying" the Rulemaking Process*, 41 DUKE L.J. 1385 (1992).

[29] *See* North Carolina v. E.P.A., 531 F.3d 896, 930 (D.C. Cir. 2008). On rehearing, the court decided to remand without vacating. 550 F.3d 1176 (D.C. Cir. 2008).

[30] EME Homer City Generation, L.P. v. E.P.A., 696 F.3d 7 (D.C. Cir. 2012).

[31] E.P.A. v. EME Homer City Generation, L.P., 572 U.S. 489 (2014).

Questions

9.3. Without court oversight, a technical agency might hire many scientists who focus on regulating. With court oversight, the agency must replace some scientists with lawyers who focus on litigating. Oversight by judges changes the personnel and priorities of agencies.[32] Is this good or bad?

9.4. Suppose an agency wants to enact three rules. It can enact them individually, yielding three minor regulations, or it can "bundle" them into one major regulation. Would you advise the agency to bundle? In answering, consider these facts. Agencies need approval from the Office of Information and Regulatory Affairs to enact "economically significant" rules, but not for other rules. Courts defer more when regulations are technical and complicated, but they defer less when they perceive bad faith by agencies.[33]

D. *Chevron* Revisited

According to the *Chevron* doctrine, courts should defer to an agency's reasonable interpretations of unclear statutes. Is this good policy? We have shown that the optimal degree of deference to agencies depends on many factors—the relative competence of agencies and courts, their responsiveness to Congress, the cost of judicial review, and so on. With so many factors, deciding if a court should defer in a given case seems challenging. Deciding if *all* courts should defer in *most* cases seems impossible, yet this is what *Chevron* requires.[34] Once you understand the depth of the problem, you can see why assessing *Chevron* is difficult.

Economics cannot resolve the controversy over *Chevron*. That would require data on costs and benefits that we do not possess. However, economics can illuminate the debate. Beyond the institutional considerations described earlier, which are relevant to all judicial review of agencies, economics offers perspective on two features of *Chevron* in particular.

Chevron deference does not apply to all agency actions. According to *United States v. Mead*, it only applies in certain circumstances.[35] That case began when the U.S. Customs Service classified the Mead Corporation's "day planners" as "diaries, notebooks, and address books." That classification meant a tariff applied to Mead's product. Mead challenged the classification in court. The Supreme Court noted that the Customs Service issues thousands of tariff classifications every year, and none has precedential value. Thus, the decision about Mead's day planners applied only to Mead's day planners. It did not provide a general principle governing other companies' products. The Court did not apply *Chevron* deference. According to the Court, *Chevron* only applies when "Congress delegated authority to the agency generally to make rules

[32] *See* Frank B. Cross, *Pragmatic Pathologies of Judicial Review of Administrative Rulemaking*, 78 N.C. L. Rev. 1013 (2000).

[33] On this question, see Jennifer Nou & Edward Stiglitz, *Regulatory Bundling*, 128 Yale L.J. 1174 (2019).

[34] For reasons like this, Justice Breyer resists applying one doctrine to different kinds of cases. *See* Stephen Breyer, *Judicial Review of Questions of Law and Policy*, 38 Admin. L. Rev. 363 (1986).

[35] 533 U.S. 218 (2001).

carrying the force of law," and the agency interpretation at issue "was promulgated in the exercise of that authority."[36]

We can simplify the Court's language. *Chevron* applies when (1) Congress gave the agency power to make rules, and (2) the agency acts pursuant to that power.[37] The classification of Mead's day planners was not an exercise of rule-making power. No general rule was created; the classification did not bind any party other than Mead. Consequently, *Chevron* did not apply.

Economics provides support for the Court's decision in *Mead*. The previous chapter introduced the delegation canon, a rule of thumb for determining if Congress authorized a particular agency action. The delegation canon invites a thought experiment: Would the legislature's administrative savings from this delegation exceed its diversion costs? If the answer is yes, then the legislature probably intended to delegate. In general, Congress would not grant an agency power to make rules unless it expected its administrative savings to exceed its diversion costs. When the agency exercises that power, it furthers Congress's plan. Consequently, when (1) Congress gave the agency power to make rules, and (2) the agency acts pursuant to that power, the delegation canon supports the agency action. *Mead* applies *Chevron* in these circumstances. By directing courts to defer, *Chevron* supports the agency action.

Economics supports *Mead* in another way. The Supreme Court decides fewer than 100 cases per year. Thus, most challenges to agency action get resolved in federal district courts, of which there are 94, or courts of appeal ("circuit courts"), of which there are 13. Judges sometimes disagree with one another about interpretation. Together these facts mean that judicial review of agency action can generate inconsistencies. A district court might vacate the agency action only to have the circuit court reinstate it. One circuit court might uphold an agency action, while another circuit court rejects it.

A later chapter discusses inconsistent adjudication in detail. Here we make just one point. For onetime decisions like the tariff classification in *Mead*, the costs to agencies of inconsistent adjudication are low. For rules like the definition of "stationary source," the costs to agencies of inconsistent adjudication are much higher. Instead of a unified, national program, the agency rule becomes a patchwork. "Stationary source" could mean one thing in Arizona, where the Ninth Circuit Court of Appeals has jurisdiction, and something else in the neighboring state of New Mexico, where the Tenth Circuit has jurisdiction.[38]

The decision in *Mead* can mitigate this problem. It directs courts to apply *Chevron*—that is, usually to defer to agencies—when those agencies make rules. Instead of many courts reaching different conclusions, most courts reach the same conclusion: the agency action is permissible. This preserves national regulatory programs. This benefits agencies, and it probably benefits Congress too.[39]

[36] *Id.* at 226–27. The language we quoted might suggest that *Chevron* never applies to adjudication, meaning an agency decision about a particular case, but that's incorrect. If Congress authorizes an agency to engage in "formal adjudication," the outcomes of such adjudication might get *Chevron* deference.

[37] This statement aims to summarize the holding in *Mead*, but it does not capture the full range of circumstances under which courts defer to agencies under *Chevron* and related cases.

[38] In fact, Congress anticipated this problem. The Clean Air Act channels review of EPA rules to a single circuit court. *See* 42 U.S.C.A. § 7607 (West).

[39] These themes are discussed in Peter L. Strauss, *One Hundred Fifty Cases per Year: Some Implications of the Supreme Court's Limited Resources for Judicial Review of Agency Action*, 87 COLUM. L. REV. 1093 (1987).

We will address one final issue: the "major questions" exception. In *Mead*, the Supreme Court held that *Chevron* deference applies when (1) Congress gave the agency power to make rules, and (2) the agency acts pursuant to that power. However, subsequent cases seem to have modified this formula. The Supreme Court has suggested that *Chevron* does not apply when agencies interpret "major" statutory provisions, even if the two requirements from *Mead* are met.

To illustrate, consider *FDA v. Brown & Williamson*, which we mentioned in an earlier chapter.[40] A federal statute gave the Food and Drug Administration (FDA) authority to regulate "drugs." The FDA concluded that nicotine is a "drug" and, consequently, that it had authority to regulate cigarettes. The FDA had power to make rules, and it regulated cigarettes pursuant to that power. Nevertheless, the Court rejected the agency's interpretation, stating:

> Deference under *Chevron* to an agency's construction of a statute that it administers is premised on the theory that a statute's ambiguity constitutes an implicit delegation from Congress to the agency to fill in the statutory gaps. . . . In extraordinary cases, however, there may be reason to hesitate before concluding that Congress has intended such an implicit delegation. . . .
>
> This is hardly an ordinary case. Contrary to its representations to Congress since 1914, the FDA has now asserted jurisdiction to regulate an industry constituting a significant portion of the American economy.[41]

The problem was not that the agency's interpretation was unreasonable under *Chevron*'s second step. Rather, the Court doubted that Congress intended to delegate authority on a "major" question like tobacco. Consequently, *Chevron* did not apply, and the Court did not defer.

The major questions exception has mystified scholars. The Court has not explained what counts as a "major" statutory provision. Nor has the Court applied the exception consistently.[42] The delegation canon can help. The canon assumes that legislators aim to minimize the sum of their administrative and diversion costs. Thus, if the administrative savings from delegating a decision to an agency exceed the diversion costs, the legislators intended to delegate the decision.

Compared to "minor" decisions, delegating "major" decisions probably creates more diversion costs. The FDA can impose more harm on Congress when it regulates tobacco, a multibillion dollar industry, than when it regulates small-market products like minced clams.[43] However, delegating "major" decisions probably saves Congress more administrative costs. It must be harder for legislators to regulate a large industry than to regulate one product.[44] Given these cross-cutting effects, Congress might intend *more* delegation of major issues, not less.

[40] 529 U.S. 120 (2000). *See also* Util. Air Reg. Grp. v. E.P.A., 573 U.S. 302 (2014); Massachusetts v. E.P.A., 549 U.S. 497 (2007).

[41] F.D.A. v. Brown & Williamson Tobacco Corp., 529 U.S. 120, 159 (2000).

[42] After reviewing several cases involving the exception, one commentator writes, "The major question exception defies doctrinal justification, and it is tempting to dismiss it as an inexplicable, but fortunately rare, judicial wild card." *Major Question Objections*, 129 Harv. L. Rev. 2191, 2203 (2016).

[43] 21 C.F.R. § 102.49 addresses the labeling of a "nonstandardized" food, "fried clams made from minced clams."

[44] To restate the point, agency expertise might be especially valuable on major questions. *See* Cass R. Sunstein, Chevron *Step Zero*, 92 Va. L. Rev. 187, 236–44 (2006).

The advantages and disadvantages of delegating do not depend on whether the issue is "minor" or "major." Rather, they depend on administrative and diversion costs. This suggests a refinement of the Supreme Court's test. The question should not be whether the agency's interpretation involves a "major" provision of the statute. The question should be whether it involves a "major" provision of the statute *about which the agency lacks expertise*. This follows from the delegation canon. Diversion costs especially increase when agencies tackle major issues outside of their specialty. As diversion costs increase, legislators probably mean to delegate less, meaning courts should scrutinize agencies more carefully.

To see this logic in a case, consider *King v. Burwell*.[45] The Affordable Care Act provides tax credits to people who purchase health insurance from an exchange "established by the State." Is an exchange created by the federal government—as opposed to, say, the state of California—an exchange "established by the State"? The Internal Revenue Service (IRS) said yes. The Supreme Court had to decide if it should defer to the IRS's determination. The Court applied the major question exception and concluded that it did not have to defer to the IRS:

> The tax credits are among the Act's key reforms, involving billions of dollars in spending each year and affecting the price of health insurance for millions of people. Whether those credits are available on Federal Exchanges is thus a question of deep "economic and political significance" that is central to this statutory scheme. . . . It is especially unlikely that Congress would have delegated this decision to the *IRS*, which has no expertise in crafting health insurance policy of this sort. . . . This is not a case for the IRS.[46]

Without expertise, the IRS was not particularly likely to achieve Congress's objectives. The importance of the issue compounded the problem. Thus, diversion costs were likely to be high. All else equal, higher diversion costs imply that Congress did not mean for the agency to make the decision.[47]

King v. Burwell suggests that the major question exception requires a major question and a lack of expertise. This is consistent with the economic theory of delegation.

Questions

9.5. Agencies make general rules and issue onetime decisions. General rules, like the EPA's Cross-State Air Pollution Rule, affect many people. Onetime decisions, like the classification of Mead's day planners, affect few people. Judicial review of general rules must create more transition costs than judicial review of onetime decisions. Should courts defer more to agency rules than to onetime decisions?

9.6. Inconsistent adjudication by lower courts can fragment national regulations, as when "stationary source" means one thing in the Ninth Circuit Court of Appeals and something else in the Tenth Circuit Court of Appeals.

[45] 135 S. Ct. 2480 (2015).
[46] *Id.* at 2489.
[47] In the end, the Court reached the same decision as the IRS, holding that the federal government's exchange constitutes an exchange "established by the State."

(a) If you ran an agency, would you prefer review by lower courts, each with regional jurisdiction? Or would you prefer review by the Supreme Court, which has national jurisdiction?
(b) Regulation *G* addresses growing soybeans, and Regulation *S* addresses selling soybeans. Why might the Department of Agriculture prefer lower courts to review Regulation *G* and the Supreme Court to review Regulation *S*?

Entrench *Chevron*?

In certain cases, *Chevron* directs courts to defer to an agency's reasonable interpretations of statutes. Do courts actually defer? Empirical studies show that some courts defer more than others, while some agencies prevail in court more than others.[48] Furthermore, politics seems to influence adjudication under *Chevron*. Liberal judges, for example, appear to approve liberal regulations more often than conservative regulations.[49]

Why does *Chevron* yield inconsistent results? The answer probably relates to the flexibility of the doctrine. To apply *Chevron*, courts ask: Did Congress supply a clear answer to the interpretive question? Is the agency's interpretation reasonable? Judges disagree about interpretation, so they disagree about these questions. "It is thus relatively rare," Justice Scalia wrote, "that *Chevron* will require me to accept an interpretation which, though reasonable, I would not personally adopt."[50]

To promote deference to agencies, *Chevron* places a doctrinal constraint on judges. Flexibility in the doctrine weakens the constraint. What if *Chevron* imposed a procedural constraint instead? Courts decide cases using majority rule. To promote deference to agencies, courts could review them using a supermajority rule.[51]

Consider Figure 9.2, which depicts nine Supreme Court Justices at their ideal points. The dimension represents a range of interpretations of a statute. To illustrate, what is a "stationary source"? Justice 1 has a very narrow interpretation (every pollution-emitting device is a "stationary source"), whereas Justice 9 has a very broad interpretation (every industrial zone is a "stationary source"). The agency's interpretation corresponds to point *A*.

Chevron gives the Justices much discretion. Five of them, a majority, prefer points left of *A*, so they might reject the agency's interpretation rather than defer. Instead of majority rule, suppose the Court used a two-thirds voting rule. Only five Justices prefer points left of *A*, and only four Justices prefer points right of *A*. Under a

[48] For recent empirical studies of *Chevron* and reviews of the literature, see, for example, Kent H. Barnett & Christopher J. Walker, Chevron *in the Circuit Courts*, 116 MICH. L. REV. 1 (2017); William N. Eskridge, Jr. & Lauren E. Baer, *The Continuum of Deference: Supreme Court Treatment of Agency Statutory Interpretations from* Chevron *to* Hamdan, 96 GEO. L.J. 1083 (2008).

[49] *See* Kent Barnett, Christina L. Boyd, & Christopher J. Walker, *The Politics of Selecting Chevron Deference*, 15 J. EMPIRICAL LEGAL STUD. 597 (2018). For evidence that politics affects the decisions of all judges applying *Chevron*, not just liberals, see Thomas J. Miles & Cass R. Sunstein, *Do Judges Make Regulatory Policy? An Empirical Investigation of Chevron*, 73 U. CHI. L. REV. 823 (2006).

[50] Antonin Scalia, *Judicial Deference to Administrative Interpretations of Law*, 1989 DUKE L.J. 511, 521 (1989).

[51] *See* Jacob E. Gersen & Adrian Vermeule, Chevron *as a Voting Rule*, 116 YALE L.J. 676 (2007).

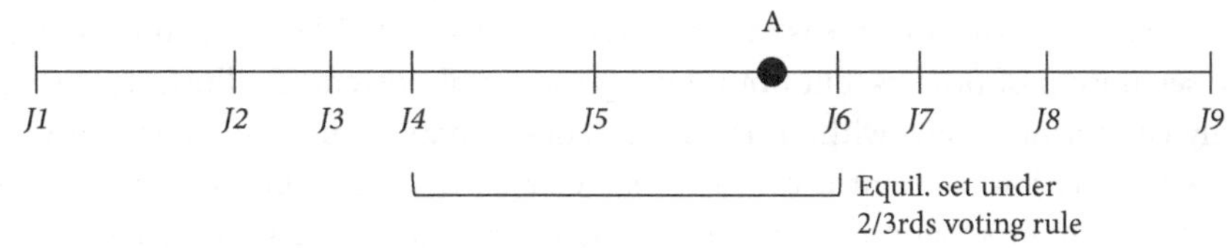

Figure 9.2. Supermajorities on the Supreme Court

two-thirds voting rule, it would take six Justices to reject the agency's interpretation, so the interpretation would stand. By creating an equilibrium set, supermajority rule would convey discretionary power to agencies.

Would the "hard" constraint of a two-thirds voting rule elicit more deference from the Supreme Court than the "soft" constraint of doctrine?[52] The answer depends on obvious factors, like how seriously judges take the doctrine. It also depends on nonobvious factors, like the level of disagreement between Justices 4 and 6.

II. Legal Limits on Delegation

During the Great Depression, millions of people lost their jobs, the stock market plunged, and poverty soared. To stimulate the economy, Congress enacted the National Industrial Recovery Act of 1933 (NIRA). NIRA empowered the President to regulate industry—wages, hours, prices, working conditions, and so on. In *Schechter Poultry v. United States*, the Supreme Court held that NIRA violated the Constitution.[53] According to the Court, the statute gave too much power to the President. He could "regulate the entire economy on the basis of no more precise a standard than stimulating the economy by assuring 'fair competition.' "[54]

Most economists consider NIRA a failure, but set that aside. Was the Court right to invalidate the statute? Why does the Constitution limit the power that Congress can delegate? This section has answers.

A. The Nondelegation Doctrine

NIRA authorized the President to make law. According to the Court in *Schechter Poultry*, this violated Article I of the Constitution, which vests "All legislative Powers" in Congress. *Schechter Poultry* established a principle called the *nondelegation doctrine*. According to that doctrine, one branch of government cannot delegate its constitutional authority to another. Thus, Congress (legislative branch) cannot delegate law-making power to the President (executive branch), the Supreme Court (judicial branch) cannot delegate adjudicatory power to Congress, and so on.

52 *See id.*
53 A.L.A. Schechter Poultry Corp. v. United States, 295 U.S. 495 (1935).
54 This language comes from *Whitman v. Am. Trucking Ass'ns*, 531 U.S. 457 (2001), where the Court explains its holding in *Schechter*.

The nondelegation doctrine is easier to state than to apply. The Constitution requires some separation of powers, but not total separation of powers. To illustrate, Congress usually cannot make law without the President's signature, and the President usually cannot execute law without a budget from Congress. This is probably good policy. A strict view of the separation of powers could prevent government from achieving the ends it was designed to achieve.

The Supreme Court has recognized this. In a case about the nondelegation doctrine, the Court wrote:

> Congress manifestly is not permitted . . . to transfer to others the essential legislative functions. . . . [But] [u]ndoubtedly legislation must often be adapted to complex conditions involving a host of details with which the national Legislature cannot deal directly. The Constitution has never been regarded as denying to the Congress the necessary resources of flexibility and practicality, which will enable it to perform its function in laying down policies . . . while leaving to selected instrumentalities the making of subordinate rules within prescribed limits. . . . Without capacity to give authorizations of that sort we should have the anomaly of a legislative power which in many circumstances . . . would be but a futility.[55]

To balance practicability and the separation of powers, the Court has developed the *intelligible principle* test. If a delegation from Congress contains an "intelligible principle" to guide the delegate's discretion, then the delegation is permissible, otherwise it is impermissible. To demonstrate, NIRA contained no intelligible principle; the President could regulate industry as he saw fit. This violated the nondelegation doctrine. In contrast, consider the Sentencing Reform Act of 1984. The statute transferred some lawmaking power from Congress to a commission in the judicial branch with authority to reform criminal sentencing. The Supreme Court upheld the statute, stating that the "delegation of authority . . . is sufficiently specific and detailed to meet constitutional requirements."[56] The Sentencing Reform Act did not violate the nondelegation doctrine.

The Sentencing Reform Act involved a delegation from Congress to the judiciary. Many other statutes involve delegations from Congress to the executive. Agencies like the Environmental Protection Agency and Department of Transportation exist in the executive branch, and they routinely issue regulations that bind like ordinary legislation. Thus, the nondelegation doctrine does not forbid *all* delegation. It forbids too much delegation.

Questions

9.7. In the 1930s, the Supreme Court used the nondelegation doctrine to invalidate two statutes. The Court has not used the doctrine since. Some scholars say the doctrine is "dead." Does the Court's failure to invoke the doctrine during the last 80 years mean the doctrine no longer exists? Does it mean the doctrine does not affect delegations of power among branches?

[55] Panama Refining Co. v. Ryan, 293 U.S. 388, 421 (1935).
[56] Mistretta v. United States, 488 U.S. 361, 374 (1989).

9.8. The Sex Offender Registration and Notification Act requires people convicted of certain sex crimes to register their names, addresses, and other information with authorities. This information helps track offenders following their release from prison. The act provides detailed instructions for people convicted of sex crimes after the act's passage. For people who committed crimes beforehand, the statute states:

> The Attorney General shall have the authority to specify the applicability of the requirements of this subchapter to sex offenders convicted before the enactment of this chapter . . . and to prescribe rules for the registration of any such sex offender.[57]

Does this language satisfy the "intelligible principle" test? Other language in the statute and its legislative history suggest that the act *must* apply to prior offenders, meaning the Attorney General only has discretion to determine how and when to apply it. Does this help?[58]

Void for Vagueness

On April 20, 1969, Margaret Papachristou and Betty Calloway, two white women, rode in a car with Eugene Eddie Melton and Leonard Johnson, two black men. They stopped near a used car lot that had recently been burglarized, but they engaged in no wrongdoing. A police officer approached the car at 2:20 a.m. and charged the occupants with violating Florida's law on vagrancy. The law stated the following:

> Rogues and vagabonds, or dissolute persons who go about begging; common gamblers, persons who use juggling or unlawful games or plays, common drunkards, common night walkers, thieves, pilferers or pickpockets, traders in stolen property, lewd, wanton and lascivious persons, keepers of gambling places, common railers and brawlers, persons wandering or strolling around from place to place without any lawful purpose or object, habitual loafers, disorderly persons . . . shall be deemed vagrants and, upon conviction in the Municipal Court shall be punished.[59]

This language raises many questions of interpretation. Is an insomniac who walks at night to relax a "common night walker?" Are teenagers hanging out on a corner "habitual loafers"? Did the four occupants of the car engage in any of the listed activities?

In *Papachristou v. City of Jacksonville*, the Supreme Court reviewed Florida's law on vagrancy.[60] The Court held that the law was *void for vagueness*, meaning that it

[57] 34 U.S.C.A. § 20913(d) (West).

[58] This question is based on *Gundy v. United States*, 139 S. Ct. 2116 (2019). The Supreme Court held that the statute satisfied the intelligible principle test. Three Justices dissented.

[59] Papachristou v. City of Jacksonville, 405 U.S. 156, 158 (1972).

[60] 405 U.S. 156 (1972).

violated the Constitution because it failed to provide adequate notice of what conduct it prohibited. According to the Court, the language gave "unfettered discretion" to police that could result in "arbitrary and discriminatory enforcement of the law."[61] Police could exploit that discretion and charge anyone with a crime. The police could even target a particular group, such as black men.[62]

Like the intelligible principle requirement, the void for vagueness doctrine requires some statutes to achieve a certain level of specificity. There is no "void for specificity" doctrine. Why not?

B. The Cost of Prohibiting Delegation

Our analysis from the prior chapter illuminates the nondelegation doctrine. Without legal restrictions, a principal will balance diversion and administrative costs to reach her optimal degree of delegation. With a prohibition against delegation, the principal may not strike this balance. Law might prevent her from delegating as much as she would like.

To illustrate, consider Figure 9.3. Moving from left to right, the principal's direct exercise of power increases from 0 percent to 100 percent, and the principal's delegation of power decreases from 100 percent to 0 percent. The vertical axis measures administrative and diversion costs. As the principal devotes more time to exercising power directly (moving to the right in the figure), her administrative costs increase, and her diversion costs decrease.

To minimize her costs, the principal should delegate 30 percent of her authority, which corresponds to the low point on the total cost curve. That imposes a total cost on her of *A*, as indicated on the vertical axis. Now assume the law prohibits the principal

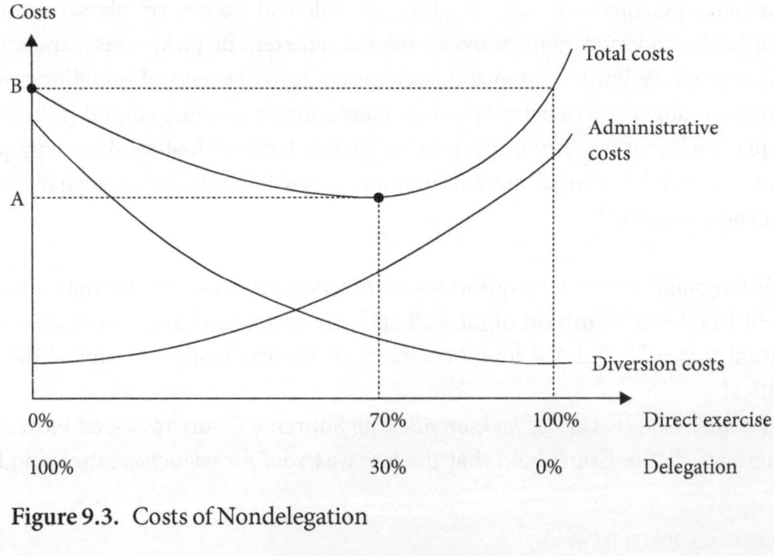

Figure 9.3. Costs of Nondelegation

[61] *Id.* at 170.

[62] Scholars believe that the officer in that case was motivated by racism. *See, e.g.*, Risa Goluboff, Vagrant Nation: Police Power, Constitutional Change, and the 1960s, at 308 (2016).

from delegating authority. Delegation moves from 30 percent to zero, and total costs rise to B. The prohibition on delegation imposes costs on the principal of $B - A$.

The costs of making a power nondelegable depend on the total costs curve, which depends on diversion and administrative costs. If the principal's time becomes more valuable, if monitoring the agent becomes easier, or if the agent becomes more loyal, optimal delegation increases. Consequently, the cost of prohibiting delegation rises. Conversely, if punishing an agent becomes harder, or if a principal has more free time, the optimal degree of delegation decreases. The cost of prohibiting delegation falls. To generalize, the nondelegation doctrine imposes larger costs when diversion by the agent is less likely and the principal's time is more valuable.

Questions

9.9. Suppose the nondelegation doctrine forbids the principal in Figure 9.3 from delegating more than 40 percent of her power. Does this affect the principal's decision to delegate? What if the doctrine forbids delegating more than 20 percent of her power?

9.10. We can adapt Figure 9.3 to the void for vagueness doctrine. Moving rightward from the origin, the legislature makes the law less vague and more precise.
  (a) Why do the legislature's administrative costs increase as we move rightward?
  (b) What do diversion costs mean in this context, and why do they decrease as we move rightward?

C. Nondelegation and Representation

Our analysis shows that prohibitions on delegation can impose costs on principals. So why do the prohibitions exist?[63] The answer relates to representation. Sometimes society may gain from a prohibition on delegation, even as the principal suffers, because the principal does not represent society's interests.

In the previous chapter, we interpreted "diversion" in the delegation game as the agent following his preferences rather than implementing the principal's policy. To illustrate, the administrator in our medical example devoted resources to emergency medicine rather than to prenatal care. Both ends are valuable, but they differ. A more sinister interpretation of diversion concerns corruption. Rather than channeling resources to his preferred policy, an agent may channel resources to his own pocket. Administration often suffers from corruption, even in the modern United States. Recently, employees at the U.S. Internal Revenue Service were accused of using other people's private information to file fraudulent tax returns.[64]

[63] The U.S. Supreme Court has not used the nondelegation doctrine to invalidate a delegation of authority from Congress to an administrative agency since 1935. Some legal scholars say that the doctrine is "dead."

[64] Cleve R. Wootson, Jr., *Her Job Was to Help Victims of Identity Theft. Instead, She Used Them to Steal from the IRS*, Wash. Post, Aug. 11, 2016.

Corrupt officials break laws and distort policies in exchange for bribes. By diffusing and obscuring responsibility, delegation increases opportunities for corruption. Americans have a hard time monitoring their representatives in Congress, let alone employees of the IRS. While corruption may harm principals in government, it may harm the public even more. Consequently, the public might benefit from more direct administration by the principal than the principal would voluntarily choose.

We can state these ideas more precisely. When agents divert resources, they impose costs, some of which their principals internalize and some of which their principals externalize to *their* principals. When IRS employees engage in corruption, the Commissioner of the Internal Revenue Service (their principal) bears some costs, the President (the Commissioner's principal) bears some costs, but the general public (everyone's principal) bears even more. When principals externalize costs of diversion, they delegate too much. Prohibitions on delegation prevent principals from delegating too much. The argument for prohibiting delegation strengthens as principals externalize more of the costs from delegating.

Now consider another rationale for limiting delegation in government. Delegation of power can occur within a branch of government or between branches of government. *Intra*branch delegation may occasionally violate constitutional law. In *INS v. Chadha*, the Supreme Court held that the Constitution forbids Congress from delegating its legislative power to the House or Senate individually.[65] In general, however, intrabranch delegation does not upset the constitutional equilibrium. The balance of power between the executive, legislature, and judiciary stays the same whether the Secretary of Health and Human Services administers the program herself or delegates to a subordinate. *Inter*branch delegation, on the other hand, often upsets the balance of power. To illustrate, the U.S. Constitution separates the judiciary and the legislature, so while the Supreme Court can remand a case to a trial court, it cannot remand a case to Congress.

Interbranch delegation revises the Constitution without following the procedures prescribed for a constitutional amendment. That is a legal problem, of course, but also a potential source of social harm. Interbranch delegation tends to concentrate state powers.[66] Just as concentration in industry can lead to economic monopoly, concentration in government can lead to political monopoly, better known as dictatorship. To illustrate, courts could destroy the rule of law by delegating their power over legal disputes to the executive. Prohibiting interbranch delegation helps maintain competitive government, which defines democracy and restrains dictatorship.

If interbranch delegation risks dictatorship, why would courts or the President or other government officials engage in it? The answer again relates to representation. If the President's party enjoys a majority of seats in the legislature, then the legislature may eagerly vote to give some of its power to the President. By reducing competition, interbranch delegation benefits politicians in the ruling party, even as it harms the public. Connecting this to the previous ideas, officials who engage in interbranch delegation externalize some of the costs of that delegation (they do not suffer the full harm of dictatorship), which causes them to delegate too much. Given this logic, the

[65] 462 U.S. 919 (1983).

[66] Note that interbranch delegation can disperse powers rather than concentrate them. For example, a relatively powerful legislature might delegate powers to a relatively weak executive. The usual case, however, goes in the opposite direction.

fact that legislators and the executive both want to concentrate power without formally revising the Constitution is no reason for a court to allow it. Courts should not require a disagreement between the executive and legislature to justify policing the separation of powers.

We have explained why interbranch delegation can lead to social harm, but we have not explained how to determine when such delegation takes place. Disputes over interbranch delegation often involve vagueness in the definitions of constitutional powers. To illustrate, Article I of the U.S. Constitution vests "All legislative powers" in Congress, and Congress cannot delegate this power to the executive. Does the executive exercise "legislative powers" in violation of Article I by imposing wage and price controls on the economy, or by imposing burdensome regulations on employers?[67] Does the Comptroller General, a legislative office, exercise "executive powers" by imposing limits on government expenditures to reduce the deficit?[68] Similarly, the German Parliament must resolve disputes that are "political," whereas the German constitutional court must decide disputes that are "constitutional." Thus, the question of who must decide whether nuclear missiles may be deployed in Germany turns on whether it is a political or legal question.[69]

Jurists have developed techniques for helping to answer these questions, but some seem more formal than logical. In deciding whether a delegation of power by Congress to an administrative agency violates the Constitution, American courts ask if Congress has provided an "intelligible principle" to which the agency must conform. A better approach may be to ask whether the delegation concentrates power. Behind their rhetoric, courts may be asking exactly that question.

Questions

9.11. *Unified government* means one political party controls the legislature and the executive, whereas *divided government* means different political parties control the branches. Does a delegation under unified government threaten to concentrate power more or less than a delegation under divided government?[70] Can you relate your answer to the transaction costs of bargaining among politicians?

[67] *See, e.g.*, Indus. Union Dep't, AFL-CIO v. Am. Petroleum Inst., 448 U.S. 607 (1980); Mistretta v. United States, 488 U.S. 361 (1989).

[68] Bowsher v. Synar, 478 U.S. 714 (1986).

[69] Pershing II and Cruise Missile . . . Decision II, BVerfGE 68, 1 2 BvE 13/83 (1984) ("Assessments and evaluation of a foreign-policy or defence-policy nature are up to the Federal Government. The Basic Law sets only the bound of obvious arbitrariness to the power of judgment that is accordingly due to the Federal Government. Within this extreme limit, the Federal Constitutional Court does not have to review whether evaluations or assessments of the Federal Government are right or wrong, since legal criteria for this are not present; they have to be taken responsibility for politically.").

[70] Daryl J. Levinson & Richard H. Pildes, *Separation of Parties, not Powers*, 119 HARV. L. REV. 2311, 2358–68 (2006). For evidence that the legislature delegates more under unified government, see DAVID EPSTEIN & SHARYN O'HALLORAN, DELEGATING POWERS: A TRANSACTION COST POLITICS APPROACH TO POLICY MAKING UNDER SEPARATE POWERS 121–62 (1999). *See also* JOHN D. HUBER & CHARLES R. SHIPAN, DELIBERATE DISCRETION? THE INSTITUTIONAL FOUNDATIONS OF BUREAUCRATIC AUTONOMY 139–70 (2002).

9.12. According to the Supreme Court, "the degree of agency discretion that is acceptable varies according to the scope of the power congressionally conferred. . . . While Congress need not provide any direction to the EPA regarding the manner in which it is to define 'country elevators,' which are to be exempt from new-stationary-source regulations governing grain elevators, . . . it must provide substantial guidance on setting air standards that affect the entire national economy."[71] Why?

9.13. Politicians might delegate to take advantage of agencies' expertise. Or, they might delegate to shift blame (if a plane crashes, blame the FAA).[72] Can courts tell the difference? In answering, consider this fact: the Supreme Court has not used the nondelegation doctrine to invalidate a statute since the 1930s.

9.14. When principals externalize the costs of delegation, they delegate too much. Can you think of circumstances in which principals externalize the benefits of delegation?

III. Lobbying, Rent-Seeking, and Agency Capture

We have discussed agency problems in administrative law. Now we consider agency problems in democracy more generally. In a democracy, officials elected to represent the people do most of the political bargaining. So political bargaining is good for the representatives. But is it good for the people? Politicians have blood in their veins and ambition in their hearts. In political competition, self-promotion often outruns idealism. For successful politicians, power is often their first priority. In a democracy, politicians get power by winning elections. Ideally, they win elections by doing what voters want.

In the best scenario, political competition resembles economic competition. In Adam Smith's characterization, an "invisible hand" directs businesses to increase the nation's wealth by increasing their own wealth.[73] Similarly, an "invisible hand" in elections can direct politicians to advance the public interest by advancing their own interests. Elections fill offices by popular vote in the way that markets supply goods by popular demand. The private interest of politicians and the public interest of citizens converge through electoral competition.

Unfortunately, political competition does not always work well. As an earlier chapter explained, most voters know little about politicians' day-to-day activities. Voters often have information about outcomes, such as unemployment rates, food prices, the condition of roads, and the quality of schools, but the information is crude. This leads to errors in accountability. For example, the President gets credit and blame for the business cycle that he cannot control. Voters suffer from free riding; we each wait for someone else to monitor our representatives. Finally, voters have few tools for punishing wayward politicians. Elections happen years apart.

[71] Whitman v. Am. Trucking Ass'ns, 531 U.S. 457, 475 (2001).

[72] On blame shifting, see Peter H. Aranson, Ernest Gellhorn, & Glen O. Robinson, *A Theory of Legislative Delegation*, 68 CORNELL L. REV. 1, 55–63 (1982); Morris P. Fiorina, *Legislative Choice of Regulatory Forms: Legal Process or Administrative Process?*, 39 PUB. CHOICE 33, 46–54 (1982).

[73] ADAM SMITH, AN INQUIRY INTO THE NATURE AND CAUSES OF THE WEALTH OF NATIONS 335 (Charles Jesse Bullock ed., 1909).

For reasons like these, politicians resemble the agent in the delegation game. They can pursue their own interests rather than the principal's. When a politician's ambition diverges from her conception of the public interest, she must make a choice: "Should I do well for myself or do good for society?" Many politicians help themselves first and society second. In some countries, the strain between ambition and morality is so great that politicians have blood on their hands, not just in their veins.

A. Subsidies and Regulations

To understand why and how politicians help themselves first, let's contrast two government activities: subsidies and regulations. A *subsidy* is a transfer of money or other resource from the government to private actors. One country or another subsidizes telephones, banking, electric cars, railroads, steel manufacturing, farmers, airplane flights, windmills, coal mines, internet providers, minority-owned businesses, and so forth. To pay the subsidy to one group, the government must collect it from another. Subsidies go in opposite directions in different countries. To illustrate, farmers subsidized city workers in Peron's Argentina and Stalin's Russia, whereas today city workers subsidize farmers in the United States, the European Union, and Japan.[74]

Subsidies offer one method for enriching the supporters of politicians. Regulations offer another method. They work by restricting competition. In different sectors and countries, all kinds of people enjoy legal protection against competition—pharmacists, defense contractors, bond analysts, teachers, union workers, and so on. Devices for restricting competition include licenses, charters, permits, orders, privileges, and government contracts. By such devices, administrators and politicians determine where a factory can locate, what goods it can produce, to whom it must sell, and whom it employs.

To make this concrete, consider some typical regulations restraining competition: permits to operate taxi cabs ("medallions"), zoning that prevents building apartments, certification requirements to practice law (you must be a member of the bar), or permits required to export coffee. One country or another forbids selling aspirin without a license, advertising prices by optometrists, and locating your dry-cleaning shop within a mile of another. One country or another requires banks to lend to political favorites at below-market rates, farmers to sell coffee beans exclusively to a state agency, and trains to charge passengers less than the cost of their carriage. To enrich yourself, obtain an exclusive license to operate cabs at an international airport, build cars behind tariff walls, or control the regulators who set prices in your industry. Carlos Slim became one of the richest people in the world when the government of Mexico gave him a monopoly on phone service.

Economists have special language for describing profits from regulatory restrictions on competition. A "rent" is income from owning something that is scarce, such as an apartment building in a college town or an oil well in the gulf. Regulations that restrain competition create artificial scarcity that yields rents. Private parties engage in politics

[74] ROBERT D. COOTER & HANS-BERND SCHÄFER, SOLOMON'S KNOT: HOW LAW CAN END THE POVERTY OF NATIONS 41 (2012).

in the hope of obtaining regulations that will restrain competition. Their pursuit is called *rent-seeking*.[75] Regulations enrich the friends of politicians by shielding them from competition, and the friends repay the politicians with electoral support, donations, and bribes. Rent-seeking is political competition to avoid economic competition.

So far we have described subsidies and regulations in negative terms. In fact, some subsidies and regulations transfer wealth to private interests for no defensible reason. However, other subsidies and regulations protect the public for good reason. As an earlier chapter explained, regulations can clean the air, inform consumers, and break monopolies. Subsidies can redistribute wealth from rich to poor.

Regardless of whether subsidies and regulations serve the public or enrich special interests, their beneficiaries describe them in positive terms: fairness, employment, economic growth, national security, equal opportunity, social justice, public health, consumer protection, pollution abatement, and so on. The same lofty claims are made whether the policy has a public purpose or not. Conflicting ideologies about subsidies and regulations grind against each other like ice in the Arctic Sea. Do most regulations benefit or harm the public? Your answer says a lot about your politics.

In sum, subsidies and regulations benefit some people and impose costs on others. Like ice cream, people are willing to pay for favorable laws. Sometimes the promise of payment causes representatives to favor narrow interests at the expense of the public good.

Questions

9.15. To determine the cost to taxpayers of sugar subsidies, read the public budget. How can one determine the cost to consumers of sugar tariffs? Why might sugar companies prefer tariffs to subsidies?[76]

9.16. Subsidies transfer money from one group to another. The act of transferring money uses some of it up (paying tax collectors, for example). So subsidies decrease money. Do subsidies increase welfare?

9.17. Uber flooded the streets with ordinary drivers who transport people in ordinary cars. By increasing competition in the market for rides, Uber drove down prices and bankrupted many taxi drivers. In New York City, the price of a taxi medallion (a medallion is required to operate a taxi lawfully) dropped from $1.3 million to $160,000.[77] To achieve its success, Uber broke many laws. In general, Uber drivers do not have the commercial insurance, commercial registration, special plates, special driver's licenses, or medallions required of taxi drivers. For years Uber drivers did not undergo background checks.[78] Did Uber hurt consumers by flouting public-spirited laws? Or did Uber help consumers by breaking the taxi monopoly?

[75] *See* Anne O. Krueger, *The Political Economy of the Rent-Seeking Society*, 64 AM. ECON. REV. 291 (1974). *See also* Gordon Tullock, *The Welfare Costs of Tariffs, Monopolies and Theft*, 5 WESTERN ECON. J. 224 (1967).

[76] *See* Dan T. Coenen, *Business Subsidies and the Dormant Commerce Clause*, 107 YALE L.J. 965, 985–93 (1998).

[77] Sam Harnett, *Cities Made Millions Selling Taxi Medallions, Now Drivers Are Paying the Price*, NPR, Oct. 15, 2018.

[78] *See id.*; Benjamin Edelman, *Uber Can't Be Fixed—It's Time for Regulators to Shut It Down*, HARV. BUS. REV., June 21, 2017.

Professionalism or Monopoly?

John Bates and Van O'Steen opened a law office to serve low-income clients in Arizona. To keep costs down, they focused on simple matters, like uncontested divorces. Rather than earning large profits from a few clients, they hoped to earn small profits from many clients. To attract many clients, they placed an ad in the newspaper offering "legal services at very reasonable fees." Their ad violated Disciplinary Rule 2-101(b), which stated:

> A lawyer shall not publicize himself, or his partner, or associate, or any other lawyer affiliated with him or his firm, as a lawyer through newspaper or magazine advertisements, radio or television announcements, display advertisements in the city or telephone directories or other means of commercial publicity, nor shall he authorize or permit others to do so on his behalf.[79]

The Supreme Court of Arizona had adopted Disciplinary Rule 2-101(b) pursuant to its regulation of the Arizona bar.

Bates and O'Steen argued that the rule violated their freedom of speech. Do lawyers have a constitutional right to advertise their prices? In *Bates v. State Bar of Arizona*, the Supreme Court said yes.[80] In reaching this conclusion, the Court considered the rationale for Disciplinary Rule 2-101(b). According to the State Bar of Arizona, the rule promoted professionalism:

> [A]dvertising will bring about commercialization, which will undermine the attorney's sense of dignity and self-worth. The hustle of the marketplace will adversely affect the profession's service orientation, and irreparably damage the delicate balance between the lawyer's need to earn and his obligation selflessly to serve. Advertising is also said to erode the client's trust in his attorney: once the client perceives that the lawyer is motivated by profit, his confidence that the attorney is acting out of a commitment to the client's welfare is jeopardized. And advertising is said to tarnish the dignified public image of the profession.[81]

The Court rejected this explanation. Even without advertising, people know that many lawyers work to earn money.[82] Doctors and engineers advertise, yet their professions remain dignified. And failing to advertise might do more harm than good. Rather than preserving professionalism, it could hamper representation. Without ads, some people cannot find lawyers to vindicate their rights.

[79] Bates v. State Bar of Arizona, 433 U.S. 350, 355 (1977).

[80] Within limits. Here's the Court's language: "In holding that advertising by attorneys may not be subjected to blanket suppression, and that the advertisement at issue is protected, we, of course, do not hold that advertising by attorneys may not be regulated in any way." *See id.* at 383.

[81] This is the Supreme Court's summary of the argument. *See id.* at 368.

[82] *See id.* at 368–69 ("[T]he argument presumes that attorneys must conceal from themselves and from their clients the real-life fact that lawyers earn their livelihood at the bar. We suspect that few attorneys engage in such self-deception. And rare is the client . . . who enlists the aid of an attorney with the expectation that his services will be rendered free of charge.").

These arguments involve common sense. The Court made a final argument about economics: "cynicism with regard to the profession may be created by the fact that it long has publicly eschewed advertising, while condoning the actions of the attorney who structures his social or civic associations so as to provide contacts with potential clients."[83] The ban on ads did not stop attorneys from competing. It just shifted the locus of competition from newspapers and radio waves to civic meetings and private events. Any lawyer could advertise in the former by paying, whereas only more senior, experienced lawyers could advertise in the latter by schmoozing. Thus, the bar association's ban on advertising stifled competition. It favored older lawyers who already had reputations and disfavored younger lawyers trying to build reputations.

Do you agree that the First Amendment protects a lawyer's right to advertise? Should it protect a tobacco company's right to advertise to children?

B. Lobbying

How do groups secure favorable laws? The usual answer is through lobbying. In exchange for money, lobbyists inform and influence representatives. In the United States, people and organizations spend billions of dollars on lobbyists every year. Sometimes lobbyists encourage representatives to write bills that favor their clients. Other times lobbyists write the bills themselves and ask representatives to sponsor them.

For many private actors, paying a lobbyist is rational. To illustrate, assume that Abe manufactures computer screens and has money to invest in two activities: making more screens, or lobbying for tariffs against imported screens. Spending the money on more screens would generate profits of $1 million, while spending the money on lobbying would dampen competition, generating profits of $2 million. Abe maximizes profits by investing in lobbying. To generalize, *rational people invest in lobbying until the marginal rate of return equals the marginal rate of return on other activities*, like manufacturing more computer screens.

Manufacturing and lobbying differ in an important way: whereas manufacturing benefits the manufacturer, lobbying benefits the entire industry. A tariff on imported screens benefits all domestic screen makers, not just Abe. With lobbying, everyone in the industry has an incentive to free ride on the efforts of others. For example, all public-school teachers benefit from subsidies to public schools, but many public-school teachers prefer for others to pay the lobbyists who get the laws enacted.

Overcoming free riding is easier when free riders are few and the stakes for each are high. Suppose Abe and Brianna are the only domestic manufacturers of computer screens. A tariff on imported screens would earn them each $2 million. With so much money at stake, both Abe and Brianna find lobbying worthwhile. With only two people, each can monitor the other and confirm that neither free rides. Who pays the costs of the tariff that benefits Abe and Brianna? Buyers of computer screens. As a consequence of the tariff, thousands or even millions of buyers will pay a little more for each screen—say, $400

[83] *Id.* at 370–71.

Table 9.1. Diffusion-Concentration Matrix

	Diffuse Benefits	Concentrated Benefits
Diffuse Costs	Social Security, infrastructure spending	Computer tariffs, sugar subsidies
Concentrated Costs	Free trade, tobacco tax	Occupational health standards, wage bargaining

instead of $350. With so little money at stake, most buyers will not find lobbying worthwhile. With so many people, preventing free riding among buyers seems impossible.

To generalize, concentrated groups can organize and lobby more easily than diffuse groups. This difference is fundamental to the political logic of rent-seeking. Table 9.1 summarizes that logic.[84] Sometimes democracy produces laws in the top-left box, where diffuse costs (taxes that nearly everyone pays) fund policies with millions of beneficiaries. Sometimes, however, democracy produces laws in the top-right box. Concentrated beneficiaries like Abe and Brianna lobby for favorable laws, and the diffuse opposition (millions of screen buyers) fail to organize and resist. Free trade hurts concentrated industries like steel manufacturers, but it lowers prices on products made of steel for millions of consumers, so free trade fits in the bottom-left box. Unions help millions of employees organize, and employers are relatively few in number. Both sides can overcome free riding and lobby, so much labor and employment law fits in the bottom-right box.

These ideas travel under the heading of *interest group theory*. The theory helps explain many features of political life in a democracy. Through unions, public-school teachers become strong, whereas taxpayers' unions do not exist (how could they strike?). To overcome free riding, many organizations finance lobbying by compulsory dues. For example, most doctors need to belong to the American Medical Association, which collects dues and finances lobbying for all doctors. In contrast, clean air and water have diffuse beneficiaries who do not need to belong to a dues-collecting organization. Donations to the Environmental Defense Fund are purely voluntary, unlike dues paid to the American Medical Association. A double failure afflicts the environment: market externality and political free riding. Thus, legislators often focus on doctors and health insurers instead of the environment.

Questions

9.18. Use interest group theory to explain how a small industry could "capture" an administrative agency like the Securities Exchange Commission or the Environmental Protection Agency.

[84] The figure is based on JAMES Q. WILSON, POLITICAL ORGANIZATIONS 332–37 (1973). The foundation for interest group theory is MANCUR OLSON, THE LOGIC OF COLLECTIVE ACTION: PUBLIC GOODS AND THE THEORY OF GROUPS (1971). *See also* George J. Stigler, *The Theory of Economic Regulation*, 2 BELL J. ECON. & MGMT. SCI. 3 (1971); Sam Peltzman, *Toward a More General Theory of Regulation*, 19 J.L. ECON. 211 (1976).

9.19. In our example, the tariff on computer screens earns Brianna $2 million and costs each buyer $50.
(a) How much would Brianna pay lobbyists to secure the tariff?
(b) How much would each buyer pay lobbyists to prevent the tariff?
(c) Is money spent on lobbying productive, like building more screens? Or is it redistributive, like robbing a bank?[85]

9.20. Federal law requires disclosure of some lobbying activities. Many people do not want to disclose their lobbying. Consequently, the law might discourage people from engaging in political speech and petitioning the government, activities protected by the First Amendment. In *United States v. Harriss*, the Supreme Court upheld lobbying disclosure against constitutional challenge.[86] The Court stated that without disclosure, "the voice of the people may all too easily be drowned out by the voice of special interest groups seeking favored treatment while masquerading as proponents of the public weal."[87]
(a) Use interest group theory to support or critique the Court's statement.
(b) The Court in *Harriss* also stated that prohibiting disclosure would "deny Congress . . . the power of self-protection."[88] How might lobbying disclosure "protect" members of Congress?

9.21. In the United States, lawyers cannot practice law without a license. To get a license, most lawyers must attend law school (three years of time, expensive tuition), pass the state bar exam (months of studying, a fee to take the test), and join the bar association (payment of annual dues).
(a) By increasing the cost of becoming a lawyer, these requirements reduce the supply of lawyers. What does reducing the supply of lawyers do to lawyers' salaries?[89]
(b) What's better for society: fewer, expensive lawyers with higher quality on average? Or more, cheaper lawyers with lower quality on average?
(c) Should we require licenses for lawyers arguing in the Supreme Court but not for lawyers arguing in traffic court?

Unions and Free Riding

Thousands of employees cannot bargain with their employer, nor can they lobby legislators. Collective action is too difficult. To overcome this challenge, employees organize themselves into unions. Instead of different, conflicting demands, unions present unified demands to employers. By threatening to call a strike, unions strengthen their position in bargaining (a strike by all costs employers much more than a strike by one). Unions can organize and lobby more effectively than

85 *See, e.g.*, Gordon Tullock, *The Welfare Costs of Tariffs, Monopolies and Theft*, 5 Western Econ. J. 224 (1967).
86 347 U.S. 612 (1954).
87 *Id.* at 625.
88 *Id.*
89 *See* Mario Pagliero, *What Is the Objective of Professional Licensing? Evidence from the US Market for Lawyers*, 29 Int'l J. Indus. Org. 473 (2011).

individuals. In the language of interest group theory, unionization converts diffuse workers into a concentrated group.

Unions need money—to pay officers, organize elections, and hire lobbyists. To raise money, unions collect fees from the workers they represent. The collection of fees invites free riding. In general, all workers benefit from favorable employment terms and laws, even if they do not help to enact them. So workers have an incentive to free ride on the efforts of others. Workers might not join the union, even if they benefit from the union's activities. The same free riding that prevents workers from negotiating and lobbying on their own can bankrupt the unions that negotiate and lobby for them.

To prevent free riding, states required workers to pay fees to the union that represented them, even if they did not join or support the union. Mark Janus challenged one of these laws in court. He worked for the state of Illinois, and the union representing him advocated policies that he opposed, like pay raises for state employees during a budget crisis. Janus argued that the law on fees forced him to subsidize political speech with which he disagreed in violation of the First Amendment.

In *Janus v. AFSCME*, the Supreme Court agreed.[90] According to the Court, "Compelling individuals to mouth support for views they find objectionable violates that cardinal constitutional command" of the First Amendment.[91] Furthermore, the Court held that "free-rider arguments . . . are generally insufficient to overcome First Amendment objections."[92] To defend this conclusion, the Court wrote the following:

> Suppose that a particular group lobbies or speaks out on behalf of what it thinks are the needs of senior citizens or veterans or physicians. . . . Could the government require that all seniors, veterans, or doctors pay for that service even if they object? It has never been thought that this is permissible. . . . [T]he First Amendment does not permit the government to compel a person to pay for another party's speech just because the government thinks that the speech furthers the interests of the person who does not want to pay.[93]

This argument certainly seems compelling. No one wants to subsidize every group that purports to represent them. But consider a limit on this logic. Like unions, governments engage in many different activities, some of which constitute speech. Government speech can include statements on license plates ("Live Free or Die"), slogans ("Only you can prevent forest fires"), and foreign policy positions ("Iran sponsors terrorism," "communism is bad"). Citizens who oppose this speech nevertheless support it by paying taxes. Do taxes compel people to subsidize speech in violation of the First Amendment? The Supreme Court said no.[94] According to the Court, people "have no First Amendment right not to fund government speech."[95]

90 138 S. Ct. 2448 (2018).
91 *Id.* at 2463.
92 *Id.* at 2466.
93 *Id.* at 2466–67.
94 Johanns v. Livestock Mktg. Ass'n, 544 U.S. 550 (2005).
95 *Id.* at 562.

This conclusion might seem hard to justify.[96] To prevent free riding, the state can compel you to pay for the state's speech, but it cannot compel you to pay for the union's speech. Why does the First Amendment work differently in these cases? Economics supplies a justification. The number of people who pay taxes far exceeds the number of workers represented by a union. The threat of free riding grows with the number of people. Without compelled fees, free riding might bankrupt the union. Without compelled taxes, free riding would certainly bankrupt the state (remember the Articles of Confederation).

After the Court decided *Janus*, many people worried that union funding would collapse. Apparently, they were mistaken. According to one report, union membership dropped by only 1 percent in the six months following the case.[97] To retain membership, unions can offer members exclusive benefits. In New York, for example, only dues-paying members get free legal advice and financial counseling from their union. If unions do collapse, states could rescue them with subsidies.[98]

C. Lochnerism

Interest group theory illuminates an important period in U.S. constitutional history called the Lochner era. In 1894, the state of Louisiana enacted a law forbidding its citizens from contracting with out-of-state insurance companies, unless those companies employed an agent within the state. A Louisiana company violated the law by insuring a shipment of cotton through an insurer in New York. Rather than pay the fine, the company challenged Louisiana's law in the Supreme Court.

In *Allgeyer v. Louisiana*, the Court invalidated the law based on the Due Process Clause of the Fourteenth Amendment.[99] That clause forbids states from depriving "any person of life, liberty, or property, without due process of law."[100] According to the Court, the word "liberty" in that clause:

> means not only the right of the citizen to be free from the mere physical restraint of his person, as by incarceration, but the term is deemed to embrace the right of the citizen to be free in the enjoyment of all his faculties, to be free to use them in all lawful ways, to live and work where he will, to earn his livelihood by any lawful calling, to pursue any livelihood or avocation, and for that purpose to enter into all contracts which may

96 The Court hardly bothered to justify its conclusion, only noting that "government speech is subject to democratic accountability." *Id.* at 563. But union speech is too; union leaders are elected by workers. Who is more accountable: a union leader with thousands of members, or a governor or Senator with millions of constituents? For a critique of this case, see Robert Post, *Compelled Subsidization of Speech:* Johanns v. Livestock Marketing Association, 2005 Sup. Ct. Rev. 195 (2005).

97 Rebecca Rainey & Ian Kullgren, *1 Year after Janus, Unions Are Flush*, Politico, May 17, 2019.

98 *See* Aaron Tang, *Life After* Janus, 119 Colum. L. Rev. 677, 709–10 (2019).

99 165 U.S. 578 (1897).

100 *See* U.S. Const. amend. XIV, § 1 ("All persons born or naturalized in the United States, and subject to the jurisdiction thereof, are citizens of the United States and of the state wherein they reside. No state shall make or enforce any law which shall abridge the privileges or immunities of citizens of the United States; nor shall any state deprive any person of life, liberty, or property, without due process of law; nor deny to any person within its jurisdiction the equal protection of the laws.").

> be proper, necessary, and essential to his carrying out to a successful conclusion the purposes above mentioned.[101]

Louisiana's law infringed on liberty by preventing people from voluntarily entering into contracts to earn a living.[102] In short, it violated the "freedom of contract."

Eight years after *Allgeyer*, the Court expanded on the freedom of contract in *Lochner v. New York*.[103] State law prohibited bakers from working more than 10 hours per day and 60 hours per week. A bakery owner named Joseph Lochner argued that the law violated the Due Process Clause. The state of New York defended the law, arguing that it protected the health and safety of bakers, who often worked long hours in hot rooms full of flour dust. The Supreme Court swept aside the state's defense and invalidated the law. The Court wrote:

> The act is not, within any fair meaning of the term, a health law, but is an illegal interference with the rights of individuals, both employers and employees, to make contracts regarding labor upon such terms as they may think best. . . . Statutes of the nature of that under review, limiting the hours in which grown and intelligent men [and women] may labor to earn their living, are mere meddlesome interferences with the rights of the individual[.][104]

Writing in dissent, Justice Harlan challenged the Court's conclusion that New York's law did not constitute a "health law." He argued that although the facts were unclear, the law might promote health, and the Court should respect the legislature's judgment on this question.[105] But Justice Peckham, who wrote the majority opinion, rejected this argument without explanation. He just asserted that the "limitation of the hours of labor . . . has no such direct relation to, and no such substantial effect upon, the health of the employee[.]"[106] According to Justice Peckham, the law was "in reality, passed from other motives."[107]

What motives? Justice Peckham never said, but interest group theory might hold the answer. Rather than pursuing the public good, lawmakers might respond to the wishes of concentrated, organized groups. Take New York's baking industry at the time of *Lochner*. Large bakeries competed with small ones. A limitation on baker hours would not affect the large bakeries, whose unionized workers already worked short shifts. However, a limitation on hours would hamper small bakeries, where non-unionized bakers worked very long shifts. According to one account, New York enacted its limitation on hours in response to pressure from the baker's union. The union did not care about health; it wanted to suppress competition from small bakeries.[108]

101 Allgeyer v. Louisiana, 165 U.S. 578, 589 (1897).
102 Note that this is substantive, not procedural, due process.
103 198 U.S. 45 (1905).
104 *Id.* at 61.
105 *See id.* at 65–74 (1905) (Harlan, J., dissenting).
106 *Id.* at 64.
107 *Id.*
108 This account is developed in DAVID E. BERNSTEIN, REHABILITATING LOCHNER: DEFENDING INDIVIDUAL RIGHTS AGAINST PROGRESSIVE REFORM (2011), and David E. Bernstein, Lochner v. New York: *A Centennial Retrospective*, 83 WASH. U. L.Q. 1469 (2005). *See also* BERNARD H. SIEGAN, ECONOMIC LIBERTIES AND THE CONSTITUTION 113–20 (1980). For a lucid discussion, see MAXWELL STEARNS, TODD J. ZYWICKI, & THOMAS J. MICELI, LAW AND ECONOMICS: PRIVATE AND PUBLIC 456–57 (2018).

Interest group theory provides a similar account of Louisiana's law on insurance agents. The law might have protected citizens from fraud, as when an out-of-state insurer sells bogus coverage.[109] But the law also protected Louisiana's insurance companies. By making it harder for out-of-state companies to operate, the law favored in-state companies, who earned profits insuring shipments to and from the busy port of New Orleans. Like a baker's union, one can imagine a concentrated group of insurers lobbying for favorable laws.

The *Lochner* era endured for 40 years. During that time, the Supreme Court invalidated dozens of statutes. For example, in *Coppage v. Kansas*, the Court struck down a law prohibiting "yellow-dog" contracts.[110] (A yellow-dog contract makes employment conditional on the employee not joining a union.) In *Adkins v. Children's Hospital*, the Court struck down a law mandating a minimum wage for women.[111] In the infamous case of *Hammer v. Dagenhart*, the Court invalidated a federal law meant to limit child labor.[112]

Why did the Court strike down so many laws, especially on employment matters? Many people attribute it to judicial activism. The "freedom of contract" does not appear in the Constitution.[113] Some people say the Justices invented this idea to protect wealthy elites at the expense of poor workers and consumers.[114] This account might have some merit, but it is incomplete. Legal historians have offered a different interpretation according to which the Court pursued the "principle of neutrality."[115] This principle rejected "special" or "class" legislation that redistributed property from one private actor to another, irrespective of the wealth or status of the beneficiary.[116]

In 1937, the Supreme Court decided *West Coast Hotel Co. v. Parrish*.[117] The question in the case was whether a minimum wage law for women violated the Constitution. Earlier the Court had struck down a minimum wage, but in *West Coast Hotel*, it reversed course and upheld the minimum wage. The Court wrote:

> [T]he violation alleged by those attacking minimum wage regulation for women is deprivation of freedom of contract. What is this freedom? The Constitution does not speak of freedom of contract. It speaks of liberty. . . . The guaranty of liberty does not

[109] *See* Herbert Hovenkamp, *The Political Economy of Substantive Due Process*, 40 Stan. L. Rev. 379, 447 (1988) ("An argument can be made, however, that the statute condemned in *Allgeyer* was designed to protect consumers from fraudulent insurance practices.").

[110] 236 U.S. 1 (1915).

[111] 261 U.S. 525 (1923).

[112] 247 U.S. 251 (1918).

[113] In fact, the Supreme Court rarely relied on the freedom of contract when invalidating statutes in this era. *See* Barry Cushman, *Teaching the* Lochner *Era*, 62 St. Louis U. L.J. 537 (2018).

[114] For recitations of the conventional view, see *id.* at 540–41 n.9. *See also* Lochner v. New York, 198 U.S. 45, 75 (1905) (Holmes, J., dissenting) ("This case is decided upon an economic theory which a large part of the country does not entertain.").

[115] Howard Gillman, The Constitution Besieged: The Rise and Demise of Lochner Era Police Powers Jurisprudence 61–100 (1993).

[116] *See* Barry Cushman, *Teaching the* Lochner *Era*, 62 St. Louis U. L.J. 537 (2018). *See also* John Harrison, *Substantive Due Process and the Constitutional Text*, 83 Va. L. Rev. 493, 518 (1997) ("The A-to-B law is the archetypal legislative deprivation and always has been."); Charles W. McCurdy, *Justice Field and the Jurisprudence of Government Business Relations: Some Parameters of Laissez-Faire Constitutionalism, 1863–1897*, 61 J. Am. Hist. 970, 971–73 (1975) (discussing Justice Field's efforts to distinguish permissible regulation from impermissible confiscation).

[117] 300 U.S. 379 (1937).

> withdraw from legislative supervision that wide department of activity which consists of the making of contracts, or deny to government the power to provide restrictive safeguards. Liberty implies the absence of arbitrary restraint, not immunity from reasonable regulations[.][118]

The Court's decision in *West Coast Hotel* ended the *Lochner* era. Judges stopped scrutinizing and invalidating economic legislation.

What caused the Court's change of heart? Politics offers a common answer. President Franklin D. Roosevelt enjoyed immense support,[119] and he favored the kind of economic legislation that the Court had opposed. When Roosevelt threatened to "pack" the Court with new, handpicked Justices, the existing Justices surrendered.[120] But perhaps this account is too simple. According to legal historians, *Lochner* depended on a set of assumptions that crumbled as the economy grew and new cases emerged.[121] *West Coast Hotel* resulted from gradual changes in law and society, not sudden political pressure.

Interest group theory offers perspective on the demise of Lochnerism. Most laws advantage one group or another, so most laws have advocates, including advocates with concentrated interests as stake. Consider the child labor laws in *Hammer v. Dagenhart*.[122] Prohibiting children from working in dangerous conditions, and encouraging them to play and attend school, benefits children and society. But it also benefits some narrow interests. Large manufacturers supported the child labor laws, not because they necessarily opposed child labor but because many small manufacturers relied on it. By prohibiting child labor, big business could dampen competition.[123] Even benign laws enjoy support from interest groups.

Courts cannot invalidate every law that benefits an interest group at the expense of others. This would paralyze democracy. Instead, courts can sort, as the *Lochner* Court did when attacking "class" legislation. Judges can uphold laws that benefit society overall and invalidate laws that only benefit concentrated groups. But making this distinction is hard. What is good for society? Does a minimum wage for women benefit a concentrated group? Few people think judges have the expertise or authority to answer these questions.

If judges cannot invalidate most economic regulations, and if they cannot distinguish among "good" and "bad" regulations, what choice remains? Judges can defer, leaving the choice of law to legislators. Consider the case *Williamson v. Lee Optical of Oklahoma*.[124] A state law forbade opticians from making eyeglasses without a doctor's prescription. Even mundane transactions, like placing existing lenses into a new frame, often required a trip to the doctor. Did the law promote health by encouraging eye exams? Or did it enrich eye doctors at the expense of opticians and consumers? The Supreme Court did not answer:

[118] *Id.* at 391–92.

[119] In the 1936 election, Roosevelt won 60.8 percent of the popular vote and 98.5 percent of the electoral college vote.

[120] The conventional account is presented in caricatured form in BARRY CUSHMAN, RETHINKING THE NEW DEAL COURT: THE STRUCTURE OF A CONSTITUTIONAL REVOLUTION (1998).

[121] *See id.* at 139–225.

[122] 247 U.S. 251 (1918).

[123] *See* Audrey B. Davidson, Elynor D. Davis, & Robert B. Ekelund, Jr., *Political Choice and the Child Labor Statute of 1938: Public Interest or Interest Group Legislation?*, 82 PUB. CHOICE 85 (1995).

[124] 348 U.S. 483 (1955).

> The Oklahoma law may exact a needless, wasteful requirement in many cases. But it is for the legislature, not the courts, to balance the advantages and disadvantages of the new requirement. . . .
>
> The day is gone when this Court uses the Due Process Clause of the Fourteenth Amendment to strike down state laws, regulatory of business and industrial conditions, because they may be unwise, improvident, or out of harmony with a particular school of thought. . . . For protection against abuses by legislatures the people must resort to the polls, not to the courts.[125]

Lee Optical demonstrates the Court's retreat from policing economic legislation. Today courts in the United States subject such legislation to rational basis review, meaning they ask if the law is "reasonably related" to a "legitimate government interest." The answer is almost always yes.

In sum, interest group theory helps explain some puzzles in democracy, like why small groups with few votes often gain at the expense of large groups with many votes. But not every special interest law harms society. Raises for teachers can benefit the public, as can subsidies that push power plants to modernize. Wealth transfers from one group to another can increase welfare, as an earlier chapter discussed. The Constitution does not supply a formula for distinguishing good economic regulations from bad ones, and judges usually lack the capacity to make the distinction on their own. The Court in *Lee Optical* seemed to appreciate that fact.

Questions

9.22. Legislation might begin with a preamble stating a high-minded purpose and end with special interest giveaways. The general purposes stated in the preamble have little connection to the law's substance. One proposal would permit judges to void legislation whose provisions could not advance the purposes stated in the preamble.[126] To illustrate, judges might void a law that purports to enhance education and then reduces spending on school science labs. Do you support this proposal?

9.23. Scholars have argued that interest group theory should affect how courts interpret statutes. According to one account, courts should narrowly interpret statutes that benefit a small, concentrated group at the expense of a large, diffuse group. This would weaken laws giving landowners access to national forests (helps owners at the expense of the public), milk producers the right to set minimum prices (helps farmers at the expense of consumers), and so on.[127] Should courts interpret statutes this way?[128]

[125] *Id.* at 487–88 (internal quotation marks and citations omitted).

[126] Susan Rose-Ackerman, *Judicial Review and the Power of the Purse*, 12 INT'L REV. L. ECON. 191 (1992). Note that some state constitutions have clear title requirements. Barbara J. Van Arsdale, Tracy Bateman Farrell, & Tom Muskus, *Constitutional Provision Requiring Subject of Statute to be Stated in Title*, 73 AMERICAN JURISPRUDENCE 2D STATUTES § 47 (2020).

[127] *See* William N. Eskridge, Jr., *Politics Without Romance: Implications of Public Choice Theory for Statutory Interpretation*, 74 VA. L. REV. 275 (1988). *See also* Leo Sheep Co. v. United States, 440 U.S. 668, 681–82 (1979); Block v. Cmty. Nutrition Inst., 467 U.S. 340, 352 (1984).

[128] *See* Einer R. Elhauge, *Does Interest Group Theory Justify More Intrusive Judicial Review?*, 101 YALE L.J. 31 (1991).

9.24. In the 1800s, state legislatures enacted laws granting a specific person a divorce, paying compensation to a specific state employee, or granting benefits to a specific company. To stop these practices, reformers enacted state constitutional amendments prohibiting "special" legislation. The Supreme Court of Florida explained their rationale: "to prevent state action benefiting local or private interests and to direct the Legislature to focus on issues of statewide importance."[129]

(a) Explain this statement: "Permitting general legislation and forbidding special legislation should weaken interest groups by encouraging free riding among them."

(b) A ballot initiative in Alaska imposed pollution controls on large-scale metallic mineral (LSMM) mines. The initiative only affected two mines, but the court upheld it, concluding that the law was general: "Although the Pebble and Donlin Creek mines may be the only proposed mines currently affected . . . , the language of the initiative is sufficiently broad that it would apply to any new LSMM mines."[130] Meanwhile, a law in Florida affected the governance of two private hospitals owned by the same corporation. The court invalidated it, stating, "It is apparent from the express language . . . that the law was intended to affect only those privately operated hospitals located in St. Lucie County. Therefore, the [law] is unquestionably a special law affecting a private corporation."[131] Without changing its effect, could the Florida legislature have made its law general like the Alaska initiative?

(c) State courts invalidate very few laws for being "special." Why? Can you tell the difference between "general" and "special" laws?

IV. Corruption and Campaign Finance

Sometimes legislatures resemble markets. Like traders at an auction, representatives sell legislation to the highest bidder. The last section analyzed the buyers. We explained that concentrated groups can overcome free riding and hire lobbyists, giving them an advantage in the market for subsidies and regulations. Here we extend the analysis to sellers. In exchange for favorable laws, politicians receive votes, endorsements, campaign contributions, and even bags of cash.

How should we reward lawmakers for good representation? Most people support paying politicians with votes (the essence of democracy) and oppose paying politicians with cash. Money implies corruption. However, this distinction does not track law in the United States. The Constitution protects the right of donors to spend, and politicians to raise, billions of dollars. Meanwhile, trading one vote for one government contract can lead to a bribery charge and imprisonment.

[129] Lanwood Med. Ctr., Inc. v. Seeger, 990 So. 2d 503, 513 (Fla. 2008). *See also* Justin R. Long, *State Constitutional Prohibitions on Special Laws*, 60 CLEV. ST. L. REV. 719 (2012).

[130] Pebble Ltd. P'ship *ex rel.* Pebble Mines Corp. v. Parnell, 215 P.3d 1064, 1080 (Alaska 2009).

[131] Lawnwood Med. Ctr., Inc. v. Seeger, 990 So. 2d 503, 510 (Fla. 2008).

Hard cases in law often require fine distinctions, like the distinction between lawful bargaining and unlawful bribery. Lawyers and judges have tried to make that distinction throughout public law. Economics helps us understand their successes and failures.

A. Bribery Law

Corruption is endemic to government, including in the United States. Officials trade votes and other favors for cars, clothing, and cash, like the $90,000 discovered in a Congressman's freezer.[132] Many laws prohibit corruption. We focus on one law, the U.S. bribery statute, which states:

> Whoever . . . corruptly gives, offers or promises anything of value to any public official or person who has been selected to be a public official . . . with intent . . . to influence any official act . . . shall be fined . . . or imprisoned for not more than fifteen years, or both[.][133]

The statute appears to prohibit exchanges. To illustrate, return to an example from early in the book. A legislator named Caleb plans to vote for increased spending on schools and police. Another legislator named Graham strongly opposes the bill. Caleb tells Graham, "I will vote against the bill on schools and police if you will support my bill on gambling." Caleb appears to have violated the bribery statute. He has "offer[ed]" or "promise[d]" something "of value" (a no vote on schools and police) "with intent . . . to influence any official act" (Graham's vote on gambling).

In fact, Caleb probably did not violate the law. To see why, we must read the statute carefully. Offering or promising a favor is insufficient. To commit bribery, the official must "*corruptly*" offer or promise a favor. Courts have interpreted the word "corruptly" to mean acting with a "bad purpose" or "an intent to induce an official to misuse his position."[134] Has Caleb acted with a bad purpose? Has he induced Graham to misuse his office? Many people would say no. Legislators routinely trade votes. As an earlier chapter showed, vote trading can benefit lawmakers and their constituents.

Mens rea means "guilty mind." If a person takes an action that she knows is wrong, lawyers say she has mens rea. Federal bribery law uses mens rea to distinguish lawful political compromise from unlawful bribery. Whether a political trade violates law depends on the trader's state of mind. But we cannot observe states of mind. Many politicians believe they are selfless and never have mens rea. President Nixon covered up a burglary (he also failed to pay over $400,000 in taxes). While resigning he said with sincerity, "I have always tried to do what was best for the Nation."[135]

132 *See* Frank James, *William "Cold Cash" Jefferson Convicted of Corruption*, NPR, Aug. 5, 2009.
133 18 U.S.C. § 201(b)(1)(A)–(4).
134 Samuel W. Buell, *Culpability and Modern Crime*, 103 Geo. L.J. 547, 567–68 (2015). *See also* Int'l B.V. v. Schreiber, 327 F.3d 173, 182 (2d Cir. 2003); United States v. McElroy, 910 F.2d 1016, 1026 (2d Cir. 1990).
135 Richard M. Nixon, Resignation speech (Aug. 8, 1974) (PBS.org).

Questions

9.25. In addition to *paying* bribes, federal law forbids *requesting* or *accepting* bribes. The law punishes any public official who "corruptly demands, seeks, receives, accepts, or agrees to receive or accept anything of value personally . . . in return for . . . being influenced in the performance of any official act[.]"[136] Congress approved about $400 million in military aid to Ukraine. In a call with the Ukrainian president, President Trump seemed to condition the release of those funds on Ukraine investigating Trump's political rival, Joe Biden. Did President Trump break the law?[137]

9.26. Assemblyman Alan Hochberg made an offer to Charles Rosen. Hochberg would give Rosen a job in the legislature if Rosen did not run against him in the primary election. Hochberg was convicted of corruption.[138] Do you agree that Hochberg's offer was corrupt? What if Hochberg had offered to endorse Rosen if he ran for a different office? What if Hochberg had offered to make a campaign contribution to Rosen if he ran for a different office?

B. Bargaining and Bribes

Economics can help distinguish bribery from lawful political bargaining. We make the distinction with the help of a numerical example. Linda the legislator will cast the tie-breaking vote on a government contract that would benefit her constituent Dani. Paula, another constituent, would suffer if Dani got the contract. To simplify, assume that the contract does not affect anyone besides Dani, Linda, and Paula. If Dani wins the contract, she will get 2 and Paula will get −5. Linda will get −1; she pays a price for making Paula angry. If Dani does not get the contract, she will get zero, Paula will get 2, and Linda will get zero. Table 9.2 shows the payoffs to the parties under the heading "no side payments."

Maximizing the group's payoff requires that Dani not get the contract. Since Linda prefers getting zero to −1, she will not award the contract. Linda's personal interest aligns with the group's interest—unless Dani offers a side payment. Dani might say, "I will give you 1.2 if you award me the contract." Table 9.2 shows the parties' payoffs with the side payment from Dani under the heading "offer from D." Dani prefers 0.8 to zero, so she will make the payment. Linda prefers 0.2 to zero, so she will accept the payment. Linda's personal payoff has changed, so she will vote for the contract, even though she should vote against it. Linda harms the group to help herself and Dani.

Has Dani bribed Linda? The answer might not matter. Paula will suffer if Dani and Linda make the deal. To prevent the deal, Paula might say to Linda, "I will give you 1.5 if you vote against the contract." Table 9.2 shows the payoffs from the dueling offers under the heading "offers from both." Paula prefers 0.5 to −5, so she will make the offer.

136 18 U.S.C. § 201 (b)(2)(A).

137 Rebecca Ballhaus & Natalie Andrews, *Senate Acquits Trump on Both Impeachment Articles*, WALL ST. J., Feb. 5, 2020. Trump was impeached in the House and exonerated in the Senate. Impeachment requirements don't track federal bribery law.

138 People v. Hochberg, 62 A.D. 2d 239 (N.Y. App. Div. 1978).

Table 9.2. Bribery and Bargaining

	No side payments			Offer from D			Offers from both		
	D	L	P	D	L	P	D	L	P
D gets contract	2	−1	−5	0.8	0.2	−5	0.8	0.2	−5
D does not get contract	0	0	2	0	0	2	0	1.5	0.5

Linda prefers 1.5 to 0.2, so she will accept Paula's offer. Linda votes against the contract, maximizing the group's payoff. Dani's offer, whether it constitutes bribery or not, does not affect Linda's choice. If Dani anticipates Paula's offer, she might not bother making her offer in the first place.

Dani's offer shows how bribery can distort policy decisions, decreasing efficiency and social welfare. Paula's offer shows how bargaining can correct this deficiency. Given zero transaction costs, parties will bargain to the social optimum. Successful bargaining can squelch corruption. This is an application of the Public Coase Theorem.

Our example features three people and full information. Dani knows Linda's payoffs, so she makes her offer. Paula knows about Dani's offer, so she makes a counteroffer, and so on. In simple settings, transaction costs might approach zero, and bargaining can mitigate the harms of corruption. However, most settings in public law are complicated, not simple.

Let's make the example more realistic. Instead of Paula, let "*P*" in Table 9.2 represent the public, which consists of thousands or millions of people. If Linda votes for the contract, the public will suffer. The public could prevent the deal with Dani by offering Linda a payment of 1.5, but doing so raises many challenges. The public is large, diffuse, and prone to free riding. By contrast, Dani is one person. Individuals cannot free ride on themselves. Dani can make an offer more easily than the public.

Separate from free riding, the public faces another impediment to bargaining with Linda: credibility. In general, law prohibits giving politicians cash for personal use. The public could try to pay Linda in cash anyway, but who would raise the money and make the illegal payment? How could thousands or millions of people keep the payment secret? In lieu of cash, the public could offer votes. "Vote against the contract, and we will support you in the next election." Linda likes votes, but the promise is not credible. People might change their minds. Linda cannot tell who votes for whom, so she cannot punish voters who break their word. In contrast, Dani can make the payment and keep the secret. Cash today is more credible than a promise to vote tomorrow.

Finally, consider information. Dani has a concentrated interest in the contract, so she has an incentive to monitor and lobby Linda. The public might not know about the contract. Furthermore, Dani and Linda have an incentive to keep Dani's offer secret. Without knowledge of Dani's offer, the public has no reason to make a counteroffer.

In sum, Dani can bargain with Linda more easily than the public can bargain with Linda. Asymmetry in transaction costs permits bribery between Dani and Linda at the public's expense.[139]

[139] *See* Randall G. Holcombe, *The Coase Theorem Applied to Markets and Government*, 23 Indep. Rev. 249 (2018).

So far our analysis of bribery resembles the theory of interest groups described earlier. Instead of Dani, let *D* in Table 9.2 represent defense contractors (companies that sell jets and missiles to the government). Compared to the public, defense contractors have concentrated interests and can overcome free riding. Like Dani offering cash, defense contractors can lobby and make campaign contributions, and the unorganized public cannot respond. Linda might favor the defense contractors, harming the public.

What distinguishes lawful interest group politics from unlawful bribery? Scholars have identified many factors.[140] We focus on three. First, bribery involves few people, whereas interest groups involve many. Larger groups internalize more of the costs and benefits when law changes.[141] So compared to individuals, groups are less likely to promote welfare-reducing laws.[142] Second, officials internalize the full benefit of bribes (as with cash in their pocket), whereas they do not internalize the full benefit of interest group pressures. Lobbying and campaign contributions can create information that benefits others. Third, ideal interest groups promote competition. Instead of hidden cash, ideal interest groups lobby, run ads, and make campaign contributions. Like rival bidders at an open auction, everyone sees the offers and can respond. Bribery dampens competition. Parties to a bribe hide their exchange, preempting bids by rivals. Uncompetitive markets harm consumers, and uncompetitive politics harm voters.

These ideas can improve law. In the United States, the federal bribery statute sorts permissible political bargaining from forbidden bribery. The distinction depends on whether a person acted "corruptly," meaning with bad intentions. Economics sharpens the inquiry into intentions. Did the official's act benefit one or few people? Did the official internalize most or all of the "payment" for the act? Did the bargain happen in an uncompetitive market? If so, the official engaged in bribery.

"Bob's for Jobs"? Or for Bribes?

In 2009, Robert McDonnell was elected governor of Virginia. His campaign slogan was "Bob's for Jobs." Jonnie Williams ran a company in Virginia that made a nutritional supplement from anatabine, a compound found in tobacco. Williams spent lavishly on Governor McDonnell and his wife, giving them rides on a private jet, $20,000 in designer clothing, a Rolex watch, vacations, and loans. The items had a combined value of $175,000. In exchange for his spending, Williams wanted a favor. He wanted public universities in Virginia to test the health benefits of his supplement. The tests could grow Williams' company. McDonnell set up meetings between Williams and health officials and encouraged state universities to study the product.

140 For a discussion, see Toke S. Aidt, *Rent Seeking and the Economics of Corruption*, 27 Const. Pol. Econ. 142 (2016).

141 To see why, imagine all people organized in one group. The group internalizes all costs and benefits of a new law.

142 Johann Graf Lambsdorff, *Corruption and Rent-Seeking*, 113 Pub. Choice 97 (2002). This assumes that transaction costs of bargaining within the group are low.

Prosecutors charged McDonnell with a variety of crimes, including seeking bribes.[143] Did the governor "corruptly" demand, seek, receive, accept, or agree to receive or accept anything of value in return for being "influenced in the performance of any official act"? The jury decided yes, convicting the governor.

In *McDonnell v. United States*, the Supreme Court reversed the jury's decision.[144] To violate the statute, McDonnell had to accept favors in exchange for an "official act." According to the Court, arranging meetings and events are not "official acts." The Court based its decision on the language of the statute and on a policy concern:

> [C]onscientious public officials arrange meetings for constituents, contact other officials on their behalf, and include them in events all the time. The basic compact underlying representative government assumes that public officials will hear from their constituents and act appropriately on their concerns—whether it is the union official worried about a plant closing or the homeowners who wonder why it took five days to restore power to their neighborhood after a storm. The Government's position could cast a pall of potential prosecution over these relationships if the union had given a campaign contribution in the past or the homeowners invited the official to join them on their annual outing to the ballgame. Officials might wonder whether they could respond to even the most commonplace requests for assistance, and citizens with legitimate concerns might shrink from participating in democratic discourse.[145]

The Court's argument seems sensible. People often give or promise to give politicians "things of value," including votes and campaign contributions. Politicians regularly arrange meetings and seek help for their constituents. If every act by a politician constitutes an "official act," then many routine, low-stakes exchanges could become bribes. Whether a politician engaged in bribery would depend only on whether he acted "corruptly," meaning whether he had bad intentions. Determining intentions is difficult and prone to error.

Instead of narrowing the definition of "official act," what if the Court had elaborated on the meaning of "corruptly"? We identified three questions that help distinguish bribery from lawful bargaining: (1) Did the politician's act benefit one or few people? (2) Did the official internalize most or all of the "payment" for the act? (3) Did the bargain happen in an uncompetitive market? In the exchange between Williams and McDonnell, the answer to questions two and three is "yes," and the answer to question one is "probably yes" (this is debatable—perhaps the governor's help would have benefited not just Williams but his employees). What about the hypothetical union official and homeowners discussed by the Supreme Court? Would their imaginary exchanges constitute bribery?

[143] McDonnell v. United States, 136 S. Ct. 2355 (2016). McDonnell was charged with honest services fraud and Hobbs Act extortion, but the parties agreed that they would define the charges with reference to the federal bribery statute. *See id.* at 2375.

[144] *See id.*

[145] *Id.* at 2372.

C. Campaign Contributions

Candidates for political office need money—to hire staff, make signs, mail flyers, and run ads on the internet. In the United States, candidates usually fund their campaigns with donations. *Campaign contribution* refers to a donation to a political campaign, as when a student gives $10 online to the candidate of her choice. Anything of value given to influence a federal election in the United States counts as a contribution. Thus, one can make a contribution by donating office furniture to a campaign, offering discounted advertising, or renting a bus to a candidate at below-market rates. However, most contributions are money, like the student's $10 payment.

The First Amendment protects the freedoms of speech and association. According to the Supreme Court, contributions become political speech when candidates spend the money on ads, like a commercial stating the candidate's view on health care.[146] Furthermore, making a contribution offers a means of associating with a candidate or political party. Because contributions are acts of speech and association, the First Amendment protects the right to make contributions. However, the protection is not absolute. The First Amendment permits contribution regulations that are "closely drawn" to match a "sufficiently important interest."[147]

Law regulates the size of campaign contributions. In 2020, individuals could give presidential candidates like Joe Biden up to $2,800 for the primary election and up to $2,800 more for the general election, for a total contribution of $5,600. Giving a penny more would violate the law. In addition to presidential candidates, candidates for Congress, governor, and many other offices face contribution limits.[148] Courts usually uphold contribution limits.[149] The limits are "closely drawn" to further the government's "important interest" in preventing "quid pro quo" corruption and its appearance.

How do contribution limits prevent corruption? They do not forbid or punish corruption. Bribery laws do that. However, bribery laws are difficult to enforce. Like animal abuse and littering, some bribery takes place even though law forbids it. Contribution limits supplement bribery laws by restraining the size of the "quid." By limiting how much one can give to a campaign, law discourages politicians from doing favors in return. To illustrate, presidential candidates raise hundreds of millions of dollars for their campaigns. They are unlikely to engage in corruption, or significant corruption, for a measly $5,600. By restraining the "quid," contribution limits prevent the "quo."

We have related the size of contributions to corruption. Next we relate their uses to corruption. How do candidates spend the money? Usually they pay for things like ads, flyers, travel, signs, and consultants. This kind of spending benefits some members of the public. People see the candidate, watch her ads, read her signs, and discuss her policy platform. Without the spending, many voters would lack the information necessary to choose among candidates. However, sometimes candidates spend selfishly.

146 *See, e.g.*, Buckley v. Valeo, 424 U.S. 1 (1976).

147 Nixon v. Shrink Missouri Gov't PAC, 528 U.S. 377 (2000). *See also* Randall v. Sorrell, 548 U.S. 230 (2006) (plurality opinion).

148 The Federal Election Campaign Act imposed contribution limits on candidates for federal office. Laws on contributions to candidates for state and local office vary by jurisdiction.

149 For a rare exception, see Randall v. Sorrell, 548 U.S. 230 (2006) (plurality opinion).

Congressman Duncan Hunter used campaign contributions to pay for video games, vacations, and a plane ticket for his rabbit.[150]

Recall a question that helps identify unlawful bribes: Did the official internalize most or all of the "payment" she received? The more value the official internalizes, the greater the potential for corruption. Whether a candidate internalizes the value of a contribution depends on how he spends it. Spending on signs and flyers has positive externalities, whereas spending on video games and rabbits does not. Law tracks this distinction by prohibiting the "personal use" of campaign funds.[151] Video games and rabbit flights constitute "personal use," so Congressman Hunter went to prison.[152]

Notwithstanding the ban on "personal use," law allows candidates for federal office to pay themselves a salary using contributions.[153] This risks corruption. Suppose a candidate for Congress pays herself $4,000 each month from her campaign. The first $4,000 she raises every month amounts to cash, the value of which she fully internalizes. Despite the risk, law permits salaries to promote good representation. Campaigning for office requires months of work. Many people who would make good representatives cannot afford to go months without a paycheck. The law on salaries balances the risk of corruption against the benefit of good representation.

In general, law in the United States requires disclosure of contributions to the public. An internet search reveals who has given what to whom. Many people do not want to disclose their political giving. Rather than donate and disclose, they do not donate. Thus, mandatory disclosure "chills" political speech and association. Nevertheless, the Supreme Court has upheld laws mandating disclosure, in part because they deter corruption.

Economics complicates the relationship between disclosure and corruption. Disclosure reveals information about political giving to everyone. That information helps law enforcement track the "quid," but it also lowers the transaction costs of bargaining among corrupt actors (it simplifies the "pro"). We explained this idea in an earlier chapter. Here we make a different point. Recall a question that helps distinguish lawful political bargaining from unlawful bribery: Did the bargain happen in an uncompetitive market? By publicizing contributions, disclosure makes the market for politics more competitive. Like bidders at an open auction, everyone can observe the "offers" and make counteroffers. The combination of bribery laws, campaign contributions, and disclosure discourages bribery and encourages interest group politics.

We have focused on contributions by private individuals to candidates. Other actors can make and receive contributions, including political action committees, or "PACs."[154] PACs receive contributions from at least 50 individuals, and they use some of the money to make contributions to candidates. To illustrate, suppose Elena wants to contribute $1,000 to candidate Faraz. She could contribute the money to Faraz directly. Or she could contribute the money to a PAC that supports Faraz. Elena might give to the

[150] Brakkton Booker, *Former Rep. Duncan Hunter Gets 11 Months in Prison for Misusing Campaign Funds*, NPR, Mar. 17, 2020.

[151] *See* 11 C.F.R. § 113.2(e) (2016).

[152] Brakkton Booker, *Former Rep. Duncan Hunter Gets 11 Months in Prison for Misusing Campaign Funds*, NPR, Mar. 17, 2020. Facing an indictment alleging 60 counts, Hunter pleaded guilty to a single count of unlawfully using campaign funds.

[153] *See* 11 C.F.R. § 113.1(g)(1)(i)(I) (2016).

[154] There are different types of PACs. We focus on one common type, "nonconnected multi-candidate PACs."

PAC because it has better information. For example, if Faraz will easily win re-election, then he does not need Elena's contribution. The PAC can direct Elena's money to a like-minded candidate in a different race.[155]

Federal law allows PACs to make larger contributions than individuals. In 2020, a citizen like Elena could give a presidential candidate up to $5,600 ($2,800 for the primary election, and another $2,800 for the general election). A PAC could give the same candidate up to $10,000 ($5,000 for each election). Economics provides perspective on the difference. By requiring PACs to receive contributions from at least 50 people, law turns PACs into groups. Compared to individuals, groups internalize more of the costs and benefits of policy change. Consequently, groups are less likely to support socially harmful laws.[156] Furthermore, PACs can replace multiple individuals with a single actor. Fewer actors lower the transaction costs of political bargaining. Finally, PACs can help with free riding and coordination. Suppose a labor union wants to support pro-union candidates. It could ask 100,000 workers to make many contributions to many candidates. Or it could ask the workers to make one contribution to one PAC.

This discussion suggests that PACs help actuate the Public Coase Theorem. But many people think the opposite. Political markets are imperfect. According to critics, PACs raise and spend large amounts of money to corrupt government. Do PACs help or hurt democracy? We cannot settle this debate.

To summarize, campaign contributions risk corruption and promote speech, association, and information. Limits on contributions reduce these costs but also these benefits. In *Randall v. Sorrell*, Justice Breyer wrote:

> [C]ontribution limits that are too low also can harm the electoral process by preventing challengers from mounting effective campaigns against incumbent officeholders, thereby reducing democratic accountability. . . . [A] statute that seeks to regulate campaign contributions could itself prove an obstacle to the very electoral fairness it seeks to promote.[157]

In other words, contribution limits can make it harder for principals (citizens) to choose their agents. This reality must be balanced against the risk of corruption. Good law strives for the right balance.

Questions

9.27. "Bundlers" combine contributions from many individuals and present the candidate with one large contribution, only a fraction of which came from the bundler's pocket. Many bundlers gave $500,000 or more to Barack Obama's presidential campaigns, and many received posts in his administration like ambassadorships. The Federal Election Commission does not require disclosure of bundling unless the bundler is a registered lobbyist. Should all bundlers disclose?

155 This assumes the contribution is not earmarked. *See* 11 C.F.R. § 110.6 (2019).
156 This assumes the transaction costs of bargaining within the group are low.
157 548 U.S. 230, 248–49 (2006) (plurality opinion).

9.28. Politicians cannot spend contributions on ski trips and surf equipment. However, they can hire family members for their campaigns and use contributions to pay their salaries. Duncan Hunter's wife managed his campaign for $3,000 per month.[158] Is paying a family member with contributions more like running ads (positive externality) or taking a ski trip (no positive externality)?

9.29. Corporations cannot make contributions to candidates for federal office. However, the Constitution protects the right of corporations to make contributions to ballot initiative campaigns, like a Massachusetts initiative on taxes.[159] Can contributions to initiative campaigns cause corruption? In answering, consider these facts. Initiative campaigns do not have candidates, just issues. Sometimes politicians endorse and strongly support initiatives.

Aggregate Corruption

Congress has enacted two kinds of contribution limits. The *base* limit caps contributions to individual candidates. The *aggregate* limit caps total contributions to all candidates. In 2014, the base limit equaled $5,200 per election cycle, and the aggregate limit equaled $48,600.[160] A contributor could give, say, $2,000 apiece to 24 candidates and $600 to a twenty-fifth candidate, but then he could not contribute anything to any other candidate. Shaun McCutcheon wanted to contribute generously to many candidates. He argued that the aggregate limit burdened his freedom of speech and association. In *McCutcheon v. Federal Election Commission*, the Supreme Court agreed.[161]

Why did the Court invalidate the aggregate limit? The Justices conceded that the government has an interest in preventing quid pro quo corruption and its appearance. However, they perceived a "substantial mismatch" between this objective and "the means selected to achieve it."[162] We can summarize their reasoning in two steps. First, if one complies with the base limits, channeling no more than $5,200 to any candidate, corruption does not pose a risk. Second, "anticircumvention measures" ensure compliance with the base limits. To illustrate, laws prohibit a contributor from giving $5,200 to a candidate and another $5,200 to a PAC that channels the money to the same candidate.

We can use economics to critique the Court's reasoning.[163] What does it cost to bribe a politician? The answer depends on the favor sought and the risk of prosecution. Buying a vote on a billion dollar contract costs more than buying

[158] Lauryn Schroeder, *Rep. Duncan Hunter Points to His Wife and "Whatever She Did" in Campaign Finance Scandal*, L.A. Times, Aug. 25, 2018.

[159] First Nat'l Bank of Boston v. Bellotti, 435 U.S. 765 (1978).

[160] Of the $5,200, one could give $2,600 for the primary and another $2,600 for the general. The aggregate limit for contributions to candidates equaled $48,600, and the aggregate limit for contributions to other political committees (for example, PACs) equaled $74,600. In total, one could contribute up to $123,200 to candidate and noncandidate committees during a two-year election cycle.

[161] 572 U.S. 185 (2014) (plurality opinion).

[162] *Id.* at 199.

[163] This discussion is based on Michael D. Gilbert & Emily Reeder, *Aggregate Corruption*, 104 Ky. L.J. 651 (2016).

an internship. The contract has greater value, and prosecutors do not monitor internships. So a $5,200 contribution probably cannot buy the contract, but it can buy the internship. To generalize, small contributions can buy small favors. The Court erred in concluding that contributions within base limits cannot cause corruption.[164]

With respect to circumvention, law blocks direct evasion of base limits.[165] However, it cannot block indirect evasion. Suppose a donor gives $5,200 to a party leader and $5,200 to a candidate of the same party in a tight race. Control of the legislature depends on that race. If the candidate wins, the leader's power and prestige soar—thanks in part to the donor. The donor gave the leader $5,200 directly and, by supporting the pivotal candidate, additional value indirectly. In a typical federal election, major political parties field hundreds of candidates.

Before *McCutcheon*, a donor could contribute $5,200 to one party leader and about eight of those candidates. After *McCutcheon*, a donor could contribute $5,200 to the leader and *all* of those candidates.

These ideas lead to generalizations about campaign finance. Base limits affect the magnitude of corruption: the more one can give, the bigger the favor one can buy and the more harm to society. Aggregate limits affect frequency: the more politicians one can support, the more corrupt acts one can buy. The total costs of corruption depend on its magnitude and frequency, which depend on base and aggregate contribution limits. By eliminating the aggregate limit, the Court surely increased corruption.

Did the Court make a mistake? Good campaign finance law balances the harm from corruption against the benefits of speech, association, and voter information. In *McCutcheon*, the Court prohibited Congress from using aggregate limits to strike that balance.

D. Independent Expenditures

The Watergate scandal involved more than a burglary. Investigators discovered that several companies had made illegal payments to President Nixon's re-election campaign. Afterward, Congress amended the Federal Election Campaign Act. The revised statute limited campaign contributions (see earlier) and expenditures. To see the difference, suppose Gloria wants to spend $100 to support Hank, a candidate for office. Gloria could contribute the money to Hank's campaign. Or she could use the money to make and distribute flyers that say "Vote for Hank." If Gloria spends the money on flyers, she makes an expenditure.

164 Technically, the Court did not argue that lawful contributions do not cause corruption. It argued that Congress *does not believe* that lawful contributions cause corruption. *See* McCutcheon v. F.E.C., 572 U.S. 185, 210 (2014) ("But Congress's selection of a $5,200 base limit indicates its belief that contributions of that amount or less do not create a cognizable risk of corruption."). This position is easy to critique. Congress might have held that belief because aggregate limits are in place. That is, Congress might tolerate the corruption that lawful contributions engender if and only if aggregate limits place a cap on it. The Court did not address this possibility.

165 The dissenting opinion in *McCutcheon* challenges the claim that the law effectively blocks circumvention. *See id.* at 244–50 (Breyer, J., dissenting).

Coordinated expenditures involve interaction with the campaign. If Hank gives Gloria advice—where to distribute the flyers, what to write—then Gloria's expenditure is coordinated. If Gloria makes and distributes the flyers on her own, with no advice or assistance from Hank or his staff, then her expenditure is *independent*.

Expenditures can convey value to politicians. Thus, expenditures can supply the "quid" in a quid pro quo. Concern about corruption helps explain why Congress limited expenditures. However, the Supreme Court rejected this concern. In *Buckley v. Valeo*, the Supreme Court struck down limits on independent expenditures by people:

> Unlike contributions [and coordinated expenditures], such independent expenditures may well provide little assistance to the candidate's campaign and indeed may prove counterproductive. The absence of prearrangement and coordination of an expenditure with the candidate or his agent not only undermines the value of the expenditure to the candidate, but also alleviates the danger that expenditures will be given as a quid pro quo for improper commitments from the candidate.[166]

The Court's first argument involves value. Without input from the campaign, independent expenditures cannot convey much benefit. Gloria might make helpful flyers ("Vote for Hank"), or she might make harmful flyers (use your imagination—"Hank's for Banks," "Vote for Hanky-Panky"). The Court's second argument involves bargaining. Corruption requires bargaining, and bargaining requires communication. If Gloria and Hank do not communicate about her flyers (i.e., her spending is independent), then they cannot execute a quid pro quo.

The Supreme Court extended this reasoning in *Citizens United v. Federal Election Commission*.[167] A nonprofit corporation wanted to make an independent expenditure on a video criticizing Hillary Clinton, a prominent politician. The expenditure would violate a federal law. The Court held that the law violated the First Amendment. The Court wrote, "[W]e now conclude that independent expenditures, including those made by corporations, do not give rise to corruption or the appearance of corruption."[168] After *Citizens United*, corporations can make unlimited independent expenditures to influence elections.[169] The largest companies could spend billions of dollars on one campaign, dwarfing the sums spent by individuals.

Citizens United led to the creation of "super PACs." Whereas PACs make contributions and expenditures, super PACs only make independent expenditures. Because independent expenditures "do not give rise to corruption," the government cannot limit their spending. Thus, super PACs can receive unlimited amounts (a wealthy company or individual could give a super PAC, say, $1 billion), and they can make unlimited independent expenditures.

The decision in *Citizens United* follows from the Court's two arguments in *Buckley*: (1) independent expenditures cannot convey much benefit to candidates, and

[166] 424 U.S. 1, 47 (1976).

[167] 558 U.S. 310 (2010).

[168] *Id.* at 357.

[169] However, law bans spending by foreigners, including foreign corporations. What constitutes a "foreign corporation" is subject to dispute. *See* Matt A. Vega, *The First Amendment Lost in Translation: Preventing Foreign Influence in U.S. Elections After* Citizens United v. F.E.C., 44 Loy. L.A. L. Rev. 951 (2011).

(2) independence implies no bargaining and therefore no exchange. Let's consider each argument, starting with the second.[170]

Law cannot forbid politicians and private actors from conversing—at fundraisers, restaurants, baseball games, and on the subway. Law can only forbid them from saying and doing particular things, like making corrupt deals. Usually, we cannot tell if a conversation included a corrupt deal. Consequently, some corruption occurs, even though bribery law forbids it.

The same idea applies in campaign finance. Politicians, CEOs, and super PACs communicate. Did they coordinate on an expenditure in violation of law? Usually, we cannot tell. So some coordination occurs, even though law forbids it. Here is a stark example of the problem. Gabriel Rothblatt ran for Congress, and a super PAC raised over $200,000 to support him. Rothblatt's parent ran the super PAC. Did the super PAC spend the money independently, or did Rothblatt and his parent coordinate in violation of law? The answer depends on what the family discussed over the dinner table.[171]

We have analyzed one of the Supreme Court's argument in *Buckley*. Now we consider the other: independent expenditures cannot convey much benefit to candidates. We can conceptualize the value of political spending to a candidate as the product of two numbers: the amount spent, and the Efficiency Factor, or *EF*. *EF* takes a value between −1 and 1, where higher values indicate greater efficiency of spending.[172] Contributions and coordinated expenditures have maximal effect; the candidate determines how to spend the money, and the candidate knows best. So *EF* equals 1. A contribution of $2,000 conveys $2,000 in value to the candidate. What about independent expenditures? An outsider with little knowledge of a campaign's needs may spend $2,000 on an unflattering ad. That expenditure may have an *EF* of zero, meaning it conveys no value, or even a negative *EF*, meaning it harms the candidate. Conversely, an outsider with a lot of knowledge about the campaign might spend $2,000 on a helpful ad. If the ad has an *EF* of 0.9, it conveys $1,800 in value.

In *Buckley*, the Court assumed that *EF* has an average value of zero. In the digital age, that assumption is surely wrong. Politicians advertise their platforms and agendas on the internet for all to see. One party placed its ad buy schedule online, allowing outside groups to fill the gaps.[173] People use this information to improve the effectiveness of their spending. To give an amusing example, Senator Mitch McConnell posted silent videos of himself on YouTube smiling, shaking hands, and looking like a leader.[174] Super PACs (or anyone else) could download the video and incorporate it into ads. No parties communicated, so no coordination took place. Meanwhile, this information sharing pushed the value of *EF* toward 1.

[170] This discussion is based on Michael D. Gilbert & Brian Barnes, *The Coordination Fallacy*, 43 FLA. ST. L. REV. 399 (2016).

[171] *See* The Editorial Board, *The Custom-Made "Super PAC"*, N.Y. TIMES, Aug. 3, 2014 (editorial). Rothblatt claimed that he had "taken pains" not to communicate with his parent, stating, "You don't want to, in a casual conversation, cross a [coordination] line that can turn around and bite you." Fredreka Schouten & Christopher Schnaars, *Some Candidates' Super PACs Are a Family Affair*, USA TODAY, July 18, 2014.

[172] We assume the maximum value of an expenditure can convey is the face value of the money spent (i.e., *EF* cannot exceed 1) and the most harm an expenditure can cause is the negative face value of the money spent (the smallest value of *EF* is −1). This simplifies the math without affecting the logic.

[173] *See* Jeanne Cummings, *GOP Groups Coordinated Spending*, POLITICO, Nov. 3, 2010.

[174] Ashley Parker, *Viral Video Turns Senator into a Silent Comedy Star*, N.Y. TIMES, Mar. 16, 2014.

Could stricter laws improve matters? Suppose a new regulation prohibited candidates from posting their platforms and plans online, and super PACs could not listen to their speeches or download and use their videos. (This regulation would probably violate the First Amendment, but set that aside.) By putting more distance between candidates and political spenders, the regulation would decrease *EF*. However, wealthy and determined spenders could offset the decrease by spending more money. To illustrate, suppose a candidate demands $100,000 in value to deliver a vote. If the buyer has good information about the candidate's strategy (*EF* equals 1), she can spend $100,000 on an ad and convey that amount in value. With the new regulation, the buyer would have worse information, so *EF* would decrease from 1 to, say, 0.5. The buyer could make her payment by spending $200,000 on the ad.

To summarize, the Supreme Court concluded that independent expenditures, including by for-profit corporations, do not cause corruption. The Court based this conclusion on two arguments: forbidding coordination blocks bargaining, and independent expenditures convey little value to politicians. We have challenged both arguments. Observing coordination is hard, maybe harder than observing bribery. And independent expenditures do convey value.

Most Americans oppose the decision in *Citizens United*.[175] Do corporations support it? Earlier we stated that rational people invest in lobbying until the marginal rate of return equals the marginal rate of return on other activities. In other words, if you can earn more by investing $100 in lobbying than in anything else, invest in lobbying. *Citizens United* extended this logic to political spending. If a business can earn more by investing $100 in independent expenditures than anything else, it will make the expenditures. *Citizens United* created a new income stream for corporations.

Nevertheless, many corporations oppose the Court's decision. To understand why, imagine a venal politician named Izzy. Izzy calls a corporation's CEO and pressures him to support her campaign.[176] Before *Citizens United*, the CEO had a good reason to rebuff Izzy: law forbade corporate political expenditures.[177] After *Citizens United*, the CEO no longer has an excuse. *Citizens United* created a new vehicle for extortion by politicians.

According to the Supreme Court, the First Amendment prohibits limits on independent political expenditures. Without limits, independent expenditures increase corruption and increase speech, association, and (possibly) voter information. On balance, did *Buckley* and *Citizens United* improve democracy?

Questions

9.30. A crooked CEO wants a favor from a politician. To get it, he could offer to spend money supporting the politician. Or he could threaten to spend money opposing the politician.

[175] Leah Field, *10 Years Later, Americans Stand Opposed to Citizens United*, The Hill, Jan. 17, 2020.

[176] This call might be illegal depending on what Izzy says. However, monitoring calls is often difficult.

[177] From the corporation's treasury. Even before *Citizens United*, corporations could spend money on politics through their connected PACs. However, connected PACs often have much less money than corporate treasuries.

(a) Explain the relationship between *Citizens United*, the credibility of the CEO's offer or threat, and the transaction costs of corrupt bargaining.
(b) If you were the CEO, would you make the offer or the threat? Why?
(c) The U.S. government spends and redistributes trillions of dollars every year. One might expect corporations and interest groups to spend trillions of dollars on politics to secure some of that money. In fact, they spend much less. Scholars have remarked that spending on U.S. politics is surprisingly small given the stakes.[178] Does the total amount spent on politics capture the extent of interest group influence?[179]

9.31. Senator Susan Collins held the pivotal vote on Brett Kavanaugh's nomination to the U.S. Supreme Court. Civic groups in her home state opposed the nomination. They raised over $1 million through a crowdfunding website and made a threat: if Senator Collins voted in favor of Kavanaugh, they would spend the money supporting her opponent. Could this independent expenditure by the civic groups cause corruption?[180]

9.32. Super PACs collect data of value to candidates, like voters' names, addresses, and phone numbers. However, super PACs cannot give the data to candidates. That would constitute an "in-kind" contribution, and super PACs cannot make contributions. Instead, super PACs can sell the data to candidates at the "usual and normal rate."[181] Suppose a super PAC sells data to a candidate for the "usual and normal rate" of $100,000, and then the super PAC spends the $100,000 on ads supporting the candidate. Did the campaign get the data for free? Did the super PAC make an illegal contribution?[182]

Public Financing of Elections

In the United States, most candidates fund their campaigns with private money. They solicit contributions and benefit from independent expenditures. This system involves citizens and groups in the political process. However, it also engenders corruption and misrepresentation. Wealthy interests seem to wield more influence than ordinary citizens. Every day we read about candidates golfing with CEOs and charming billionaires in "wine caves." Furthermore, private fundraising creates an arms race. Every candidate expects her opponent to keep raising money, so she keeps raising money, spending more time asking for contributions. Talented people do not enter politics because they cannot bear "dialing for dollars."[183]

[178] *See, e.g.*, Stephen Ansolabehere, John M. de Figueiredo, & James M. Snyder, Jr., *Why Is There So Little Money in U.S. Politics?*, 17 J. ECON. PERSP. 105 (2003).

[179] *See* Marcos Chamon & Ethan Kaplan, *The Iceberg Theory of Campaign Contributions: Political Threats and Interest Group Behavior*, 5 AM. ECON. J: ECON. POL'Y 1 (2013).

[180] Mahita Gajanan, *Activists Raise over $1 Million to Pressure Sen. Susan Collins to Oppose Brett Kavanaugh*, TIME, Sept. 12, 2018.

[181] 11 C.F.R. § 100.52(d)(1) (2014).

[182] *See* Samir Sheth, *Super PACs, Personal Data, and Campaign Finance Loopholes*, 105 VA. L. REV. 655 (2019).

[183] Cyra Master, *"60 Minutes": Fundraising Demands Turning Lawmakers into Telemarketers*, THE HILL, Apr. 24, 2016.

Private financing is not inevitable. In the United States, candidates for many offices can accept public funding. In general, candidates who opt in receive money from the government in exchange for promises to limit the campaign's fundraising and spending. Public funding for U.S. presidential candidates began after the Watergate scandal. Every presidential candidate accepted public funding until 2008, when Barack Obama declined. Instead of accepting $84 million from the government, Obama raised hundreds of millions in private money. No presidential candidate since Obama has accepted public funding for the general election.[184]

Can law encourage candidates to accept public funding by making it more generous? Yes, but within limits. An earlier chapter addressed the doctrine of unconstitutional conditions. According to that doctrine, the government cannot condition benefits on the sacrifice of a right, like the right to free speech. Courts have applied this doctrine to public funding of elections.[185] According to one court, "public financing schemes are permissible if they do not effectively coerce candidates to participate[.]"[186]

How could public financing coerce a candidate? Coercion involves an undesirable offer, as when a criminal "offers" not to harm you if you pay. Public funding involves a desirable offer. Instead of dialing for dollars, candidates can accept public funding, albeit with limitations on their ability to raise and spend. More generous funding makes the offer more desirable. So most public funding programs would seem to satisfy the First Amendment.

But not all. Arizona implemented a public funding program for state elections. The state gave candidates who accepted public funding $21,479 for their campaigns. If a candidate opted for private funding, and if he raised or spent more than $21,479, then his publicly funded opponents would get matching funds from the state, up to a maximum of $64,437.[187] The Supreme Court held that Arizona's program violated the First Amendment, stating that matching imposed "an unprecedented penalty" on a privately funded candidate's speech.[188] "[T]he vigorous exercise of the right to use personal funds to finance campaign speech" leads to "advantages for opponents"[189]

The Court's decision is puzzling. Instead of giving candidates $21,479 with a promise to match up to $64,437, the state could have given candidates a lump sum of $64,437 to start. The lump sum would have helped publicly funded candidates (it could only increase their funding) and harmed their privately funded opponents (it could only increase their competitors' funding). Instead of "penalizing" speech through matching, a lump sum could chill speech entirely—why bother speaking if you can't compete with $64,437?[190] Nevertheless, Arizona apparently should have

[184] *See* James Sample, *The Last Rights of Public Campaign Financing?*, 92 NEB. L. REV. 349 (2013).

[185] Application of the doctrine to public funding traces to the Supreme Court's opinion in *Buckley*, though the Court said very little about this topic. *See* Buckley v. Valeo, 424 U.S. 1, 57 (1976) (holding that the government can "condition acceptance of public funds on an agreement by the candidate" to limit fundraising and spending if the candidate makes the agreement "voluntarily").

[186] N.C. Right to Life Comm. Fund for Indep. Pol. Expenditures v. Leake, 524 F.3d 427, 436 (4th Cir. 2008).

[187] For a fuller description of the complicated program, see Arizona Free Ent. Club's Freedom Club PAC v. Bennett, 564 U.S. 721 (2011).

[188] *Id.* at 736.

[189] *Id.*

[190] For an analysis of matching funds and its implications for speech, see Tilman Klumpp, Hugo M. Mialon, & Michael A. Williams, *Leveling the Playing Field? The Role of Public Campaign Funding in Elections*, 17 AM. L. ECON. REV. 361 (2015).

opted for the lump sum. To preserve public funding, Arizona should have made the public funding too good to refuse.

Conclusion

Delegation is fundamental to modern government. Citizens delegate power to elected officials, who delegate power to high-level administrators, who delegate power to lower-level administrators. The previous chapter used economics to analyze delegation, and this chapter applied the analysis to problems in public law. We began with administrative law, which governs the choices and processes of government agencies. Then we examined limits on delegation to agencies. Turning from agencies, we studied delegation to legislatures. Citizens expect legislators to bargain for society's benefit. However, lobbying, rent-seeking, and bribery can warp the political process. Instead of bargaining for society, legislators benefit themselves and narrow groups. We concluded with campaign finance law. Like a sword with two edges, political spending can help and hurt. It promotes speech, association, and debate. But money in government can corrupt.

Courts patrol delegation throughout public law. Was the agency's interpretation reasonable? Did Congress delegate too much? When do constituent services, like setting up meetings, become bribery? Courts answer these questions. In answering, they do not act as principals. Courts do not delegate power to legislators, and agencies do not "serve" them. Nor do courts act as agents, at least not in the usual sense. Judges do not take orders from politicians, bureaucrats, or citizens. As Chief Justice Marshall wrote, judges serve only "the will of the law."[191] What does this mean? What motivates judges, how do they decide cases, and why? Judges play a critical role in public law and democracy. Can we trust them? We tackle these questions in the next two chapters.

[191] Osborn v. Bank of United States, 22 U.S. 738, 866 (1824).

10
Theory of Adjudication

People disagree—about money, politics, religion, love, and law. Most disagreements resolve privately, as when a landlord and renter compromise over a leaky sink. But some disagreements proceed to litigation. Parties present their disagreement, which lawyers call a case, to a court. The judge (or jury) hears the facts and applies the law to make a decision. Often the decision affects the parties only, as when a homeowner sues a painter over a botched job. However, some decisions affect people outside of the case. This is especially true in public law. Thousands of customers had a stake when the U.S. government sued the bank Wells Fargo for fraud. Millions of votes hung in the balance when President Trump sued over the 2020 election.

Adjudication requires many disciplines. Judges use probabilities to weigh evidence, humanities to interpret law, and social science to predict effects. Good adjudication combines these disciplines to produce just outcomes at low cost. Bad adjudication bungles evidence, misinterprets law, and wastes time and resources. Bad adjudication creates sympathy for Dick the Butcher's famous line: "[L]et's kill all the lawyers."[1]

Whether good or bad, adjudication is central to public law. Courts resolve many of society's fundamental disputes—abortion, equality, environment, health, religion, and so on. Judicial opinions create precedents with the force of law. Those precedents convert vague laws into more precise directives. In the United States, lawyers spend little time reading the Constitution and much time reading judicial opinions about its meaning.

This chapter applies economics to adjudication. Our analysis illuminates questions like these:

Example 1: Chief Justice John Marshall wrote, "Judicial power is never exercised for the purpose of giving effect to the will of the Judge; always for the purpose of giving effect to the will of the Legislature; or, in other words, to the will of the law."[2] President Donald Trump blamed a ruling against him on the judge's "Mexican heritage."[3] He blamed another ruling on an "Obama judge," meaning a judge nominated by President Obama, one of Trump's opponents.[4] Are judges neutral oracles of law, or are they biased and political?

Example 2: Workers used the Fair Labor Standards Act to sue their employer for unpaid wages. The employer agreed to pay the workers, and the workers agreed

[1] William Shakespeare, Henry VI, Part 2, Scene 2.

[2] Osborn v. Bank of United States, 22 U.S. 738, 866 (1824).

[3] *See* Brent Kendall, *Trump Says Judge's Mexican Heritage Presents "Absolute Conflict"*, Wall St. J., June 3, 2016.

[4] *See* Katie Reilly, *President Trump Escalates Attacks on "Obama Judges" After Rare Rebuke from Chief Justice*, Time, Nov. 21, 2018.

Public Law and Economics. Robert D. Cooter and Michael D. Gilbert, Oxford University Press. © Oxford University Press 2022.
DOI: 10.1093/oso/9780197655870.003.0010

to drop all claims against the employer, including future claims they had not yet raised. A court intervened, refusing to let the workers "forfeit claims designed to advance public values through private litigation."[5] According to the court, settlement "deprives courts of their duty to explicate and give force to the values embodied in authoritative texts such as the Constitution and statutes."[6] Should judges let parties settle voluntarily, or should judges force them to litigate?

Example 3: An antitrust case involved 30,000 factual allegations. After 14 weeks of trial, the transcript exceeded 12,000 pages. Yet only two witnesses had testified, with dozens to go. The judge concluded that he had "an obligation to the proper administration of justice . . . to take appropriate action to curtail the length of this trial."[7] He ordered the plaintiff to make his case within seven and a half weeks. Do time limits promote justice?[8]

To address these questions, we begin with a positive analysis of adjudication, covering topics like settlement, evidence, precedent, and judicial behavior. Then we present a normative theory of adjudication. We explore when adjudication benefits litigants and society. Finally, we present an interpretive theory of adjudication. According to the incentive principle, the correct interpretation of law creates the best incentives for achieving its purpose.

I. Positive Theory of the Legal Process

A company named Dominion makes voting machines used throughout the United States. Rudy Giuliani, a prominent politician, claimed that fraud distorted the 2020 election, and he blamed "phony Dominion voting machines."[9] The CEO of Dominion responded: "[T]hese lies damaged the good name of my company" and "undermined trust in American democratic institutions."[10] Dominion sued Giuliani for defamation, demanding over $1 billion. So began the complex ritual of adjudication.

Adjudication involves many steps: filing a complaint, discovering facts, examining witnesses, instructing juries, submitting briefs, and writing opinions. In this section, we apply economics to some of these steps.[11] Our analysis is positive, meaning we aim to explain how adjudication works. We begin by analyzing the value of a legal claim. Then

[5] Trout v. Meggitt-USA Services, Inc., 2018 WL 1870388, at *4 (C.D. Cal. Apr. 17, 2018).

[6] *Id.* (quoting Owen M. Fiss, *Against Settlement*, 93 YALE L.J. 1073, 1085 (1984)).

[7] SCM Corp. v. Xerox Corp., 77 F.R.D. 10, 13 (D. Conn. 1977).

[8] *See* Nora Freeman Engstrom, *The Trouble with Trial Time Limits*, 106 GEO. L.J. 933 (2018).

[9] Nick Corasaniti, *Rudy Giuliani Sued by Dominion Voting Systems Over False Election Claims*, N.Y. TIMES, Jan. 25, 2021.

[10] *Id.*

[11] A large literature in economics addresses these topics. *See, e.g.*, William M. Landes, *An Economic Analysis of the Courts*, 14 J.L. ECON. 61 (1971); Richard A. Posner, *An Economic Approach to Legal Procedure and Judicial Administration*, 2 J. LEGAL STUD. 399 (1973); John P. Gould, *The Economics of Legal Conflicts*, 2 J. LEGAL STUD. 279 (1973); Robert D. Cooter & Daniel L. Rubinfeld, *Economic Analysis of Legal Disputes and Their Resolution*, 27 J. ECON. LIT. 1067 (1989); ROBERT G. BONE, THE ECONOMICS OF CIVIL PROCEDURE (1st ed. 2003); Bruce H. Kobayashi, *Economics of Litigation*, *in* 3 THE OXFORD HANDBOOK OF LAW AND ECONOMICS (Francesco Parisi ed., 2017).

we consider why some disputes settle and others proceed to litigation. We conclude by analyzing trials, evidence, and appeals.

A. The Value of a Legal Claim

The Fourth Amendment to the U.S. Constitution protects people from "unreasonable searches and seizures," including by police.[12] If an officer injures someone without cause, the officer commits an "unreasonable . . . seizure."[13] Lawyers say the officer committed a "constitutional tort." In the United States, a federal statute known by its number—Section 1983 of Title 42 of the United States Code—empowers people to sue certain officials for constitutional torts. So if a police officer injures someone during a violent arrest, the victim can bring a Section 1983 action against the officer. To study adjudication, we imagine a suit like this.

A police officer injured James during a traffic stop, leading to a $10,000 loss (medical bills, emotional suffering). James would like to sue the officer and recover $10,000. However, litigation is costly. James must hire a lawyer, pay court fees, and devote time and attention to the case. After months or years of effort, he might lose. Should James sue? An economist might weigh the costs of suit against the expected value of the legal claim. If the expected value of the claim exceeds the costs, James should sue.

To determine the costs of suit, James must study court and lawyers' fees, and he must consider his mental state: Does he have the fortitude for litigation? To determine the expected value of his claim, James considers what will happen after he files a suit. In consultation with a lawyer, James sketches Figure 10.1. This decision tree shows the probabilities and payoffs of different events.

Beginning on the left, James makes a choice between filing suit, which costs $100, and not filing suit, in which case he neither gains nor loses anything (payoff of $0).[14] If he files suit, James anticipates that the police department will negotiate with him and his lawyer. There is a 60 percent chance the department will offer James $5,000 to drop the case (this is called a *settlement*). James's lawyer works for a contingency fee. Under this arrangement, the lawyer gets 30 percent of any award that James receives and nothing if he loses. So if James gets a settlement for $5,000, he will only keep 70 percent of the money, meaning he will get $3,500. There is a 40 percent chance the department will offer James nothing. Regardless of whether he receives a settlement offer, the negotiations will cost James $500 in time and attention. If the department does not offer a settlement, the case will proceed to trial, where James has a 50 percent chance of losing (payoff of $0) and a 50 percent chance of winning. If James wins, he will get $10,000 in damages (to simplify, we assume the defendant will not appeal). Because of the contingency fee, James will only keep 70 percent of the $10,000,

[12] U.S. Const. amend. IV.

[13] In fact, the law is more complicated than this. Qualified immunity could protect the officer. We address qualified immunity later.

[14] We assume that parties to litigation pay their own costs, including court fees and lawyers' fees. This is typical in the United States, though *not* in Section 1983 suits. In those suits, the defendant sometimes pays both sides' costs. We ignore this complication for the sake of example. Later we will say more about the allocation of costs and its effects on litigation.

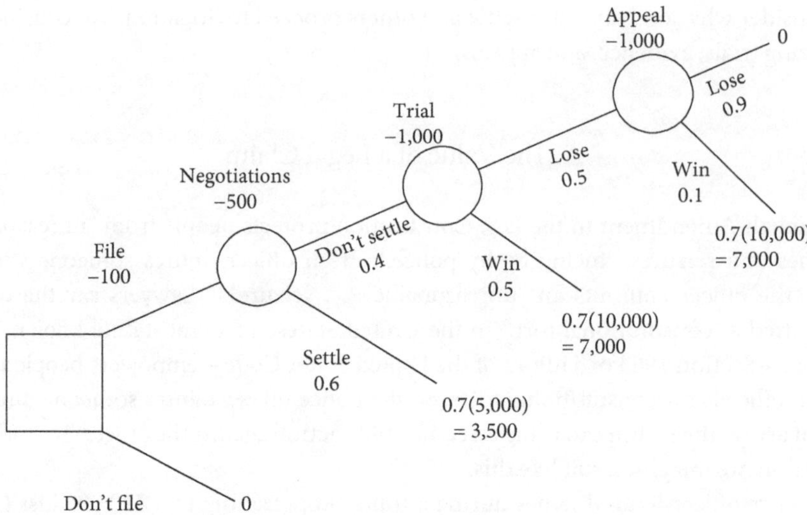

Figure 10.1. Expected Value of the Plaintiff's Claim

meaning he will get $7,000. Regardless of whether he wins or loses, going to trial will cost James $1,000 in time and attention. Finally, if James loses at trial, he can appeal. James has a 90 percent chance of losing an appeal (payoff of $0) and a 10 percent chance of winning, in which case he gets $7,000 (70 percent of the $10,000). Regardless, appealing will cost James $1,000.

Should James file suit against the officer? To answer, we use backward induction, meaning we start at the end. The expected value of the appeal equals 0.1($7,000) + 0.9($0) – $1,000 = –$300. Because the value is negative, James will not appeal. If he loses at trial, he will give up. Moving to the prior stage, the expected value of the trial equals 0.5($7,000) + 0.5($0) – $1,000 = $2,500. In that equation, the term "$0" represents the payoff from losing at trial (he will not appeal, so losing at trial concludes the case). Now we move to the prior stage, negotiations. The expected value of negotiations equals 0.6($3,500) + 0.4($2,500) – $500 = $2,600. In that equation, the term "$2,500" represents the expected value of the trial. There is a 40 percent chance the department does not offer a settlement, meaning the case proceeds to trial with an expected value of $2,500. Having analyzed every stage of litigation, we can state the expected value of James's claim: $2,600. Because the expected value of his claim exceeds the filing fee of $100, James should file suit.

In this example, James knows his probabilities and payoffs. In reality, people usually lack this information. Still, decision trees can help. Suppose that James does not know his odds of winning on appeal. Instead of specific percentages, James can use variables. Figure 10.2.a reimagines the appeals stage of James's case. If he appeals a loss at trial, he has a probability p of winning and a probability $(1 - p)$ of losing. Regardless, an appeal costs James $1,000 in time and attention. His expected value of appeal equals p($7,000) + $(1 - p)$($0) – $1,000 = $7,000$p$ – $1,000. The value of not appealing equals $0. So James should appeal if $7,000$p$ – $1,000 > $0. This equation holds when $p > 1/7$ (about 14 percent). If James's probability of winning on appeal is 1/7 or greater, he should appeal, even if he does not know his exact odds.

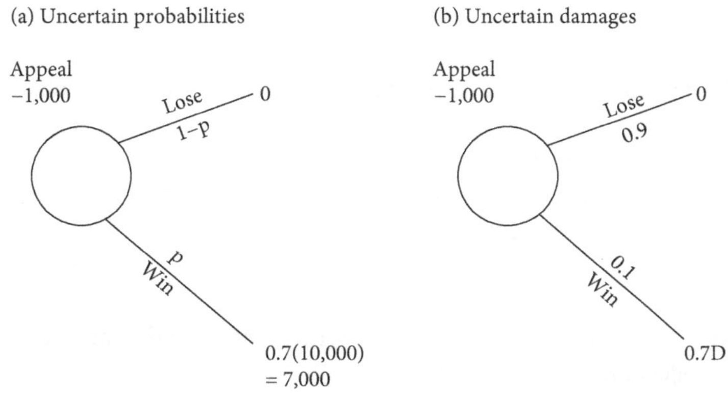

Figure 10.2. Variables in the Decision Tree

We can also use variables to represent damages. James suffered \$10,000 in harm, but the court might award him a different amount on appeal. The court might discount his emotional harm and award only \$6,000 for his medical bills. Or the court might award punitive damages (punitive damages aim to punish the offender, in this case the officer), bringing his total award to, say, \$12,000. Figure 10.2.b depicts uncertainty over damages with the variable *D*. If James appeals a loss at trial, he has a 90 percent chance of losing and getting nothing and a 10 percent chance of winning damages of *D*, of which he will keep 70 percent (remember the contingency fee). Regardless, an appeal costs James \$1,000 in time and attention. His expected value of appeal equals $0.1(0.7(D)) + 0.9(\$0) - \$1{,}000 = 0.07D - \$1{,}000$. The value of not appealing equals \$0. So James should appeal if $0.07D - \$1{,}000 > \$0$. This equation holds when $D > \$1{,}000/0.07$, or about \$14,286. If James expects damages on appeal of \$14,286 or more, he should appeal, otherwise he should not appeal.

To summarize, the decision to sue depends on the cost of filing suit and the expected value of the legal claim. To determine the expected value of the legal claim, litigants must work backward, first calculating the expected payoff from appeal and then considering each prior stage of litigation. With perfect information, litigants can determine the expected value of their claim with precision. Without perfect information, litigants must estimate the expected value.

Good lawyers help their clients estimate the expected value of their claims. However, even the best lawyers make mistakes. They face uncertainty from many sources. Judges make errors, witnesses lose credibility, and jurors fall asleep. In addition, lawyers must consider their opponent's strategy. In our example, we concentrated on James's strategic choices: whether to file suit, and whether to appeal. In reality, the defendant also makes strategic choices, like whether to offer a settlement and how much.[15] As in chess, the best strategy for one player depends on the other's moves, which can be difficult to predict.

[15] On strategy in litigation, see, for example, Lucian Arye Bebchuk, *Litigation and Settlement Under Imperfect Information*, 15 RAND J. ECON. 404 (1984).

Questions

10.1. The defendant offers the plaintiff $1,000 to settle the case. The plaintiff can accept the settlement or proceed to trial, where she has a 50 percent chance of winning $2,000 and a 50 percent chance of losing and getting nothing. The case involves no other costs, fees, or damages. Would a risk-averse plaintiff go to trial? Would a risk-neutral plaintiff accept the settlement?

10.2. Use the amounts and probabilities in Figure 10.1 to answer the following questions.

(a) If the police offer James a $5,000 settlement, should he accept, or should he reject the offer and go to trial?

(b) What is the smallest settlement that James would accept? In answering, assume that James is risk neutral.

(c) Assume that James's probability of winning on appeal rises to 20 percent. Everything else in Figure 10.1 remains the same. What is the expected value of James's claim?

10.3. A client asks a lawyer to take Case *X*. If the lawyer takes Case *X* and wins, the lawyer will receive 35 percent of the judgment. If the lawyer takes Case *X* and loses, he will receive nothing. The lawyer has a 70 percent chance of winning Case *X* and a 30 percent chance of losing Case *X*. If the lawyer does not take Case *X*, he can work on Case *Y* and earn $5,000. Should the lawyer take Case *X*?

Who Pays the Lawyers?

In the United States, parties to litigation usually pay their own costs, including attorney's fees.[16] In much of Europe and elsewhere, the losing party pays some or all of the winner's costs. To simplify, the "American" rule is "each pays her own," and the "European" rule is "the loser pays all." To illustrate the difference, consider our example involving James. Under the American rule, he would pay $100 to file his lawsuit, and he would pay his lawyer 30 percent of any winnings. Under the European rule, James would pay nothing if he won, but he would pay both sides' court costs and attorney's fees if he lost.

The difference in rules can affect litigation.[17] To illustrate, suppose that a plaintiff has a high probability of winning her case. If she sues under the American rule, she will probably recover damages but pay her costs. If she sues under the European rule, she will probably recover damages and pay no costs. *In general, the European rule encourages high-probability suits.* Now suppose the plaintiff has a low probability of winning her case. If she sues under the American rule, she will probably win nothing

[16] For lawyers, the word "costs" has a special meaning in litigation. It includes payments for things like court fees and expert witnesses but not for lawyers. Payments to lawyers are called attorney's fees. We ignore these distinctions. For us, "costs" is a general term.

[17] The following draws on Steven Shavell, *Suit, Settlement, and Trial: A Theoretical Analysis under Alternative Methods for the Allocation of Legal Costs*, 11 J. LEGAL STUD. 55 (1982).

and pay her costs. If she sues under the European rule, she will probably win nothing and pay double costs. *In general, the European rule discourages low-probability suits.*[18]

By discouraging low probability suits, the European rule has cross-cutting effects on society. It discourages meritorious suits with weak evidence, as when a person suffered harm but struggles to provide proof. However, the European rule benefits society by discouraging frivolous litigation.

The American and European rules can affect litigation in another way. Instead of money, suppose a plaintiff seeks an *injunction*, meaning an order requiring the defendant to take a certain action. For example, a plaintiff might seek an injunction requiring a mining company to stop dumping waste in the river. Injunctions are valuable and important, but you cannot use them to pay a lawyer. If a poor plaintiff seeks an injunction, she might struggle to find a lawyer under the American rule, even if her case is strong. Lawyers might doubt the plaintiff's ability to pay. In contrast, the European rule encourages a lawyer to take the case. The defendant might have more resources than the plaintiff, and if the lawyer wins the defendant will have to pay.

To make these ideas concrete, consider *Newman v. Piggie Park Enterprises, Inc.*[19] The defendant operated a restaurant chain that refused service to African Americans. Title II of the Civil Rights Act of 1964 forbade racial discrimination in public accommodations like restaurants. However, Title II did not allow for damages. Instead of money, a successful plaintiff could get an injunction. Anne Newman won an injunction requiring the restaurant to stop discriminating. But what about the attorney's fees? Title II gave courts discretion to shift attorney's fees to the losing party. The Court held that the defendant had to pay Newman's fees:

> If successful plaintiffs were routinely forced to bear their own attorney's fees, few aggrieved parties would be in a position to advance the public interest by invoking the injunctive powers of the federal courts. Congress therefore enacted the provision for counsel fees—not simply to penalize litigants who deliberately advance arguments they know to be untenable but, more broadly, to encourage individuals injured by racial discrimination to seek judicial relief under Title II.[20]

In *Piggie Park*, the Court applied the European rule. Since then, Congress has authorized the shifting of attorney's fees to the losing party in many civil rights cases (including Section 1983 cases like our example involving James). Shifting fees discourages defendants from making frivolous claims. In *Piggie Park*, the restaurant's discrimination clearly violated the law, but the owner litigated anyway. The Court punished it by increasing its attorney's fees. Furthermore, shifting fees makes it easier for poor plaintiffs to find lawyers.

[18] To be precise, the European rule discourages the filing of low-probability suits. Once filed, low-probability suits might proceed to trial more often under the European rule than under the American rule. *See* A. Mitchell Polinsky & Daniel L. Rubinfeld, *Does the English Rule Discourage Low-Probability-of-Prevailing Plaintiffs?*, 27 J. LEGAL STUD. 141 (1998).

[19] 390 U.S. 400 (1968).

[20] *Id.* at 402.

B. Settlement Bargaining

In our example involving James, the police had the option to offer a settlement before trial. In reality, a defendant can offer a settlement at just about any time—before the plaintiff files his lawsuit, during jury selection, while judges deliberate on appeal, and so on. Many cases settle, sometimes just minutes before the court issues a decision. Economics shows why many parties favor settlement.

In general, the parties to a case can reach a settlement that exactly replicates the expected outcome of litigation.[21] They achieve that outcome without the expense and hassle of litigation. To illustrate, suppose that a plaintiff has a 60 percent chance of winning $10,000 at trial and a 40 percent chance of losing and getting nothing. Regardless, trial costs her $1000. For the plaintiff, the expected value of the trial equals 0.6($10,000) + 0.4($0) – $1,000 = $5,000. What about the defendant? We assume the defendant makes the mirror-image calculation. He has a 60 percent chance of losing and paying $10,000 and a 40 percent chance of winning and paying nothing. Regardless, trial costs the defendant $1,000. For the defendant, the expected value of trial equals 0.6(–$10,000) + 0.4($0) – $1,000 = –$7,000.

Let's apply bargaining theory to the case. The parties can either settle (cooperative solution) or go to trial (noncooperative solution). If the defendant goes to trial, he expects to pay $7,000, so –$7,000 is his threat point. In negotiations with the plaintiff, the defendant can credibly threaten to reject any settlement costing him more than $7,000. Meanwhile, the plaintiff expects to get $5,000 from trial. For the plaintiff, $5,000 is her threat point in negotiations. She will reject any settlement paying her less than $5,000.

The noncooperative value of the bargaining game equals the sum of the parties' threat points: –$7,000 + $5,000 = –$2,000. Instead of litigating, the parties can cooperate by settling. If they settle, the defendant pays the plaintiff some amount of money, which we will call *s*. Furthermore, we assume that settlement costs each party $100 in time and attention. So settlement costs the defendant –*s* – $100, and the plaintiff receives *s* – $100. The cooperative value of the bargaining game equals the sum of payoffs if the parties cooperate: –*s* – $100 + *s* – $100 = –$200.

The cooperative surplus equals the difference between the cooperative and noncooperative values: –$200 – (–$2,000) = $1,800. Notice that this equals the difference between the parties' total costs of litigating ($2,000) and their total costs of settling ($200). Now you can see why settlement is the cooperative outcome. The parties cooperate to save themselves the expense of litigation.

The reasonable distribution in a bargaining game gives each party his or her threat value plus an equal share of the cooperative surplus. Applied to this case, the plaintiff should get $5,900, and the defendant should get –$6,100. To achieve these payoffs, the defendant should pay the plaintiff $6,000. After each party bears his or her settlement costs, the plaintiff will end up with $5,900 and the defendant will end up with –$6,100. *The reasonable settlement equals $6,000.*

[21] Our analysis in this section draws on Robert Cooter & Thomas Ulen, Law and Economics 399–401 (6th ed. 2016).

What happens if the parties litigate instead of settle? The plaintiff has a 60 percent chance of winning $10,000 and a 40 percent chance of winning nothing. *The expected judgment equals $6,000.*

In our example, the reasonable settlement exactly equals the expected judgment from litigation. However, the reasonable settlement only costs each party $100, whereas litigation costs each party $1,000. This difference explains why parties generally prefer settlement to trial. They can achieve the same outcome at lower cost.

Like the parties, settlement can benefit society. Running a court system costs money. It requires judges, clerks, records, courthouses, and jurors. In general, the parties who use the court system do not pay its full costs. When settlement replicates litigation, it can deliver the same outcomes as the court system but at lower cost.

The reasonable settlement matches the expected judgment from litigation when two conditions hold: *(1) the parties have the same expectations about the trial, and (2) they bear the same costs to resolve the dispute.*[22] The next section elaborates on these conditions.

C. No Settlement

An earlier chapter explained that optimism causes litigation. Here we explain why in greater detail.[23] We assumed earlier that the plaintiff and defendant had the same expectations about litigation: the plaintiff had a 60 percent chance of winning $10,000 and a 40 percent chance of winning nothing. Now suppose the plaintiff is relatively optimistic. She believes that she has a 70 percent chance of winning $10,000 and a 30 percent chance of winning nothing. Given these percentages, the expected value of the trial for the plaintiff equals 0.7($10,000) + 0.3($0) – $1,000 = $6,000. The defendant's expectations have not changed, so his expected value of trial equals 0.6(–$10,000) + 0.4($0) – $1,000 = –$7,000. We assume the defendant's belief is correct—the plaintiff actually has a 60 percent chance of winning.

As before, the noncooperative value of the bargaining game equals the sum of the parties' threat points: –$7,000 + $6,000 = –$1,000. If the defendant pays s to settle the case, and assuming again that settlement costs each party $100, then settlement yields $-s$ – $100 for the defendant and s – $100 for the plaintiff. The cooperative value of the game equals the sum of payoffs if the parties cooperate: $-s$ – $100 + s – $100 = –$200. The putative surplus equals the difference between the cooperative and noncooperative values: –$200 – (–$1,000) = $800. We call this the "putative" surplus because, though apparent, it is not real. The plaintiff cannot have a 70 percent chance of winning (her belief) and also a 60 percent chance of winning (the defendant's belief). The plaintiff has made an error. Her error yields a putative surplus of $800.

Now we can calculate the reasonable settlement. With a putative surplus of $800, the reasonable settlement gives each party his or her threat value plus $400. The plaintiff

[22] *Id.* at 401.

[23] For an early analysis of optimism, pessimism, and settlement, see John P. Gould, *The Economics of Legal Conflicts*, 2 J. LEGAL STUD. 279 (1973). Scholars have developed sophisticated models of settlement. For an overview, see Andrew F. Daughtery & Jennifer F. Reinganum, *Settlement and Trial*, *in* 3 THE OXFORD HANDBOOK OF LAW AND ECONOMICS (Francesco Parisi ed., 2017).

should get a payoff of \$6,400, and the defendant should get a payoff of –\$6,600. To achieve these payoffs, the defendant should pay the plaintiff \$6,500. The reasonable settlement equals \$6,500.

Remember that the plaintiff actually has a 60 percent of winning, not a 70 percent chance of winning. So the expected judgment if the case proceeds to trial equals 0.6(\$10,000) + 0.4(\$0) = \$6,000. (We define "expected judgment" objectively. It equals the expected award given accurate beliefs.) The reasonable settlement does not match the expected judgment. The mismatch results from the divergence in the parties' expectations about trial. The plaintiff is more optimistic than the defendant.

In our example, the plaintiff's optimism shrinks the cooperative surplus from \$1,800 to \$800. Though the surplus has shrunk, settlement remains possible. The defendant prefers paying \$6,500 than going to trial, where his expected payoff equals –\$7,000. Likewise, the plaintiff prefers receiving \$6,500 than going to trial, where her expected payoff equals \$6,000. The plaintiff's optimism has diminished but not eliminated the possibility of settlement.

Now consider a case where optimism makes settlement impossible. The plaintiff believes that she has a 90 percent chance of winning \$10,000 and a 10 percent chance of winning nothing. Her expected value of trial equals 0.9(\$10,000) + 0.1(\$0) – \$1,000 = \$8,000. The defendant's expectations, which are accurate, have not changed. His expected value of trial equals –\$7,000. The noncooperative value of the game equals the sum of the parties' threat points: –\$7,000 + \$8,000 = \$1,000. As before, the cooperative value of the game equals $-s$ – \$100 + s – \$100 = –\$200. The putative surplus equals the difference between the cooperative and noncooperative values: –\$200 – (\$1,000) = –\$1,200.

The negative sign implies that cooperation destroys value for the parties instead of creating it. Given the negative sign, we do not anticipate cooperation. Nevertheless, we can continue the analysis. The reasonable settlement gives each party his or her threat value and half of the surplus (in this example, –\$600). The plaintiff should get a payoff of \$7,400, and the defendant should get a payoff of –\$7,600. To achieve these payoffs, the defendant should pay the plaintiff \$7,500.

This settlement is impossible. The defendant will not pay \$7,500 to avoid a trial that he expects to cost only \$7,000. Likewise, the plaintiff would not accept \$7,500 to avoid a trial that she expects to yield \$8,000. The plaintiff's optimism has made cooperation impossible. *If optimism reduces the putative surplus below zero, settlement cannot occur.*[24]

Whereas optimism discourages settlement, pessimism promotes it. To illustrate, suppose that the defendant continues to believe, correctly, that the plaintiff has a 60 percent chance of winning \$10,000 and a 40 percent chance of losing and getting nothing. Litigation costs the defendant \$1000, so his expected value of trial equals 0.6(–\$10,000) + 0.4(\$0) – \$1,000 = –\$7,000. The plaintiff is relatively pessimistic. She believes that she has only a 30 percent chance of winning \$10,000 and a 70 percent chance of getting nothing. Litigation costs her \$1,000, so her expected value of trial equals 0.3(\$10,000) + 0.7(\$0) – \$1,000 = \$2,000. Now we can apply bargaining theory as before. The noncooperative value of the game equals –\$7,000 + \$2,000 = –\$5,000. The

[24] Robert Cooter & Thomas Ulen, Law and Economics 402 (6th ed. 2016).

cooperative value of the game equals: $-s - \$100 + s - \$100 = -\$200$. The putative surplus equals: $-\$200 - (-\$5{,}000) = \$4{,}800$. Finally, the reasonable settlement equals $4,500.[25]

The plaintiff's pessimism increases the putative surplus from cooperation. The chance of successful cooperation increases with its perceived benefit. To make this concrete, recall our first example in which the plaintiff and defendant had the same, accurate expectations about trial. The plaintiff's threat point was $5,000, and the defendant's threat point was –$7,000. Any settlement between $5,000 and $7,000 would make both parties better off. In the example with the pessimistic plaintiff, any settlement between $2,000 and $7,000 would make both parties better off. Pessimism grows the bargaining range, which can improve the chances of settlement.

To summarize, we have shown that optimism discourages settlement whereas pessimism encourages settlement. We have also shown how differing expectations among the parties to a case can drive a wedge between the expected judgment and the reasonable settlement. In our examples, the expected judgment always equals $6,000. Depending on the plaintiff's beliefs, the reasonable settlement equals $6,000, $6,500, $7,500, or $4,500.

Earlier we explained that the reasonable settlement matches the expected judgment when two conditions hold: (1) the parties have the same expectations about the trial, and (2) they bear the same costs to resolve the dispute. We have explored the first condition, and now we consider the second.

Recall our example of James suing the police. James has a 50 percent chance of winning and getting a judgment of $10,000, and he has a 50 percent chance of losing and getting nothing. If James wins, he can keep 70 percent of the judgment; the rest goes to his lawyer. Win or lose, trial costs James $1,000 in time and attention.[26] For James, the expected value of trial equals $0.5(0.7(\$10{,}000)) + 0.5(\$0) - \$1{,}000 = \$2{,}500$. The police have the same beliefs as James. They have a 50 percent chance of losing and paying $10,000 and a 50 percent chance of winning and paying nothing.[27] Regardless, trial costs the police $1,000. For the police, the expected value of trial equals $0.5(-\$10{,}000) + 0.5(\$0) - \$1{,}000 = -\$6{,}000$.

To calculate the reasonable settlement, we follow the steps as before. The noncooperative payoff equals $\$2{,}500 - \$6{,}000 = -\$3{,}500$. Assuming settlement costs each party $500, then the cooperative payoff equals $-s - \$500 + s - \$500 = -\$1{,}000$. The cooperative surplus equals $-\$1{,}000 - (-\$3{,}500) = \$2{,}500$. The reasonable settlement gives each party his (or its) threat value plus half the surplus. So James should get a payoff of $3,750, and the police should get a payoff of –$4,750. To achieve these payoffs, the police should pay James $4,250, and each side should bear its own settlement costs of $500. *The reasonable settlement equals $4,250.*

James has a 50 percent chance of winning $10,000 and a 50 percent chance of winning nothing. So *the expected judgment equals $5,000.* The reasonable settlement does

[25] Here is the calculation. The reasonable settlement gives each party his or her threat value plus half of the (putative) surplus. The plaintiff should get $\$2{,}000 + \$2{,}400 = \$4{,}400$, and the defendant should get $-\$7{,}000 + \$2{,}400 = -\$4{,}600$. The parties get these payoffs when the defendant pays the plaintiff $4,500 and each party bears his or her own settlement costs of $100.

[26] Recall that we assume James pays his own costs. In reality, courts often shift attorney's fees in successful Section 1983 suits.

[27] We assume the police will not appeal a loss.

not match the expected judgment. The difference results from the parties' varying costs. For the police, trial costs $1,000 whether they lose or win. For James, trial costs $1,000 if he loses (time and attention) and $4,000 if he wins (time and attention plus the lawyer's contingency fee). James has an even chance of losing and winning, so his expected trial costs equal 0.5($1,000) + 0.5($4,000) = $2,500. Compared to the police, James has high trial costs. The high costs encourage him to settle rather than litigate. This gives the police an advantage in bargaining. They can offer a settlement smaller than the expected judgment.

When the parties to a case bear different costs, the reasonable settlement differs from the expected judgment. In reality, parties often have different costs. In our example, the difference grows from lawyers: James pays a contingency fee that the police do not. But the difference can grow from many other sources. Take the police officer in our example. We assumed that a loss at trial costs the officer $10,000. Who pays the $10,000? Depending on the circumstances, the money could come from the officer or from taxpayers who fund the police budget. If the money comes from taxpayers, the police might pay $0 instead of $10,000. In this scenario, the police externalize costs. Externalities is our next topic.

Questions

10.4. In the last example involving James, the expected judgment equals $5,000 and the reasonable settlement equals $4,250. Would James accept the reasonable settlement, or would he reject it and proceed to trial? In answering, remember that James pays 30 percent of any award, including money from a settlement, to his lawyer.

10.5. A company has almost finished construction of a skyscraper when the neighbor files a lawsuit. According to the neighbor, the skyscraper crosses the property line and must be torn down. In fact, the claim is frivolous, and both parties know it. Consequently, both parties agree that the neighbor has a 0 percent chance of winning and a 100 percent chance of losing at trial. However, the company must stop construction for trial. For the company, stopping construction means missing a deadline, which is costly. Trial costs the company $20,000 in lawyers' fees and an additional $80,000 from missing the deadline. Trial costs the neighbor $2,000. Settlement costs each party $1,000.

(a) Suppose the parties cooperate by settling. What is the surplus from cooperation?

(b) What is the reasonable settlement?

(c) According to Judge Posner, parties can be "forced by fear of the risk of bankruptcy to settle even if they have no legal liability."[28] These are called "blackmail settlements."[29] Is the reasonable settlement in this problem a blackmail settlement?

[28] Matter of Rhone-Poulenc Rorer, Inc., 51 F.3d 1293, 1299 (7th Cir. 1995).

[29] *See, e.g.*, Henry J. Friendly, Federal Jurisdiction: A General View 120 (1973).

(d) Suppose that the court, upon concluding that the neighbor's suit had no merit, would make the neighbor pay for the company's lawyers (i.e., apply the European rule). Would this prevent a blackmail settlement?
(e) Suppose the company can ask the court to refuse to enforce any settlement. If settlements are unenforceable, would the neighbor file his lawsuit?[30]

Discovery

Parties to a case often share information with one another. In our running example involving James and the police, James might share his medical bills, and the police might share evidence that James was intoxicated at the time of his arrest. Sometimes parties share information voluntarily, but other times law forces them to share. *Discovery* allows parties to demand information from one another, including information that each side would prefer to keep private. Perhaps the officer who injured James wore a body camera. Discovery can help James access the video.

Our analysis of settlement can illuminate discovery. Left to their own devices, parties withhold information that would strengthen the other side's case. To illustrate, recall that James has a 50 percent chance of winning $7,000 (the other $3,000 go to his lawyer) and a 50 percent chance of getting nothing. Regardless, trial costs him $1,000, so his expected value of trial should equal $2,500. However, suppose James is pessimistic. He thinks he has only a 20 percent chance of winning and an 80 percent chance of losing. Consequently, he thinks his expected value of trial equals only $400. If James remains pessimistic, the police can settle with him for, say, $500. If James gets access to the body camera video, and assuming it shows police misconduct, then the video corrects his pessimism. With corrected beliefs, James expects trial to yield $2,500. Now the police will have to pay a lot more than $500 to settle the case. Thus, the police do not voluntarily share the video. *Discovery forces parties to share information that corrects the other side's pessimism.*

Next, we develop the opposite point. Parties tend to share information that would weaken the other side's case. The police believe they have a 50 percent chance of winning the case. But they are too optimistic. A passenger in James's car filmed the incident with her phone, and the video clearly shows police misconduct. In fact, the police have a 0 percent chance of winning the case. Rather than withhold the video, James has an incentive to share it. When the police realize their case is weak, they will settle for a larger amount. *Parties volunteer information that corrects the other side's optimism.*

To summarize, bad news for your case is usually free, meaning the other party will share it voluntarily. Good news for your case is usually costly. To get good news, you often must use discovery.

Does discovery cause litigation? By uncovering good news, discovery makes parties more confident in their cases. The expected value of trial increases, and parties demand more to settle. When parties demand more to settle, the probability

[30] *See* David Rosenberg & Steven Shavell, *A Solution to the Problem of Nuisance Suits: The Option to Have the Court Bar Settlement*, 26 INT'L REV. L. ECON. 42 (2006).

of settlement decreases.[31] (To illustrate, settlement is easier when James expects $400 from trial than when he expects $2,500 from trial.) However, discovery might have another effect. Without discovery, parties might lie, as when the police deny having video from a body camera. With discovery, dishonesty becomes harder. James can access the video, catching the police in a lie. When the costs of lying increase, parties are more likely to tell the truth. When parties tell the truth, bargaining between them gets easier.[32] So discovery has cross-cutting effects. *Discovery encourages litigation by correcting parties' pessimism, but discovery encourages settlement by lowering the transaction costs of bargaining.*

Of course, discovery can encourage settlement through another channel. Sometimes complying with a discovery order is costly—so costly that the defendant prefers to settle the case.

D. Litigation Externalities

Kelly slips at the grocery store and breaks her wrist. In the ensuing case, Kelly and the store have a stake. Does anyone else? The case seems simple, so you might think the answer is no. In fact, the answer could be yes. The case might cause the store to keep the floor dry, decreasing the risk to all shoppers, not just Kelly. A *litigation externality* arises when a case has effects beyond the parties. Litigation externalities are common in cases between private actors like Kelly and the grocer. However, litigation externalities are especially common in public law, where the government is often a party. As usual, externalities cause inefficiency.

To appreciate the scope of litigation externalities, consider different steps in adjudication. Courts (especially trial courts) make *findings of fact*: Who did what to whom, when, and why? Findings of fact can affect people outside of the case. To illustrate, suppose a patient sues the Department of Veterans Affairs for medical malpractice, and the court finds that a government doctor acted negligently. This finding might make people with similar claims more confident in their cases, encouraging them to file suits against the Department.

Courts also order *remedies*. Recall our example of James suing the police officer for a constitutional tort. If James wins, the court might award him damages (say, $10,000). James alone gets the money. But if the damages deter police misconduct in the future, then everyone in the jurisdiction benefits. Separate from damages, courts sometimes order injunctions. President Trump forbade people from some majority-Muslim countries from entering the United States (his order was called the "travel ban"). A judge issued a nationwide injunction halting enforcement of the travel ban.[33] The injunction benefited the parties to the case and every other person negatively affected by the order.

[31] *See* Robert D. Cooter & Daniel L. Rubinfeld, *An Economic Model of Legal Discovery*, 23 J. LEGAL STUD. 435, 440–41 (1994).

[32] *See* Amy Farmer & Paul Pecorino, *Civil Litigation with Mandatory Discovery and Voluntary Transmission of Private Information*, 34 J. LEGAL STUD. 137 (2005).

[33] Hawai'i v. Trump, 245 F. Supp. 3d 1227 (D. Haw. 2017). The injunction was vacated by the Supreme Court. *See* Trump v. Hawaii, 138 S. Ct. 2392 (2018).

Finally, courts provide a *rationale* for their decisions. The rationale explains the logic behind the disposition (who won and why). In appellate courts, the rationale becomes the rule or *precedent* that courts apply going forward. The precedent affects everyone subject to the court's jurisdiction, not just the parties to the case. In *Bostock v. Clayton County*, the Supreme Court held that the Civil Rights Act prohibits workplace discrimination on the basis of sexual orientation or gender identity.[34] That decision benefited Gerald Bostock, who was fired for being gay. But it also benefited every other gay and transgender person in the United States.

We have concentrated on positive externalities from litigation. Now consider some negative externalities, beginning with the first stage of a case. When a party files a lawsuit, she ordinarily pays a fee to the court. Usually the fee is much lower than the court's costs. In Virginia, a tenant filing a lawsuit against a landlord might pay only $54. The cost to the judicial system of processing the tenant's complaint surely exceeds $54. The plaintiff externalizes costs to taxpayers, who make up the difference through the state budget. Now consider the rationale in cases. The precedent set in *Bostock* harmed some employers outside of the case who would like to discriminate on the basis of sexual orientation. According to President Trump, the injunction on his travel ban harmed the safety of all Americans.

Externalities affect litigation. In general, *cases with positive externalities get litigated too rarely*. To illustrate, assume that James's injury resulted from police misconduct—say, unjustified use of a chokehold. Let's assume that if James litigates the case to judgment, (1) James will receive damages (i.e., money), (2) James will benefit from an injunction prohibiting unjustified use of the chokehold, (3) and other residents in the jurisdiction will benefit from the same injunction.[35] To make this concrete, assign some numbers (we assign numbers to simplify the analysis, not to equate police misconduct with dollars and cents). The damages are worth $10,000 to James; the injunction is worth $5,000 to James; and the injunction is worth $100,000 to everyone else. Expressed in money, James's case is worth $115,000. However, James only internalizes $15,000 in value. If his costs of litigation exceed $15,000, then he will not sue, even though the total benefits to society exceed the costs.

If positive externalities decrease litigation, negative externalities must increase it. In general, *cases with negative externalities get litigated too often*. The federal Clean Power Plan aimed to cut emissions from coal-fired power plants. Some energy companies sued to block the plan.[36] For the sake of example, assume that the companies had a 50 percent chance of winning (payoff of $1 billion for the companies, but payoff of –$10 billion for society) and a 50 percent chance of losing (payoff of $0 for everyone). Litigation would cost the companies $100 million. For the companies, the expected benefit exceeds the cost of litigation, so they sue. If the companies internalized all costs to society, they would not sue.

Public law and private institutions aim to mitigate litigation externalities. Fee-shifting encourages litigants to sue by reducing their expected costs. Nonprofit organizations

[34] Bostock v. Clayton County, Georgia, 140 S. Ct. 1731 (2020).

[35] In reality, a court probably would not order the injunction. *See* City of Los Angeles v. Lyons, 461 U.S. 95 (1983).

[36] *See* West Virginia v. Env't Prot. Agency, No. 15-1363 (D.C. Cir. Oct. 23, 2015). The case was dismissed.

like the American Civil Liberties Union and the Institute for Justice represent clients for free. Private attorneys volunteer their time (this is called "pro bono" service). These mechanisms allow clients to externalize costs. *Externalizing costs encourages litigation, offsetting external benefits that discourage litigation.* The government intervenes in some cases with a public stake. For example, the Equal Employment Opportunity Commission litigates on behalf of some private individuals, and the Department of Justice gets involved when someone challenges the constitutionality of a federal statute. The government is supposed to represent all citizens. In theory, *the government internalizes more costs and benefits from litigation than private parties.* In the case about the Clean Power Plan, cities, businesses, environmental groups, consumer unions, members of Congress, and others submitted *amicus briefs* to the court. These "friend-of-the-court" briefs allow actors outside of the case to supply facts and legal analysis to judges. With amicus briefs, fewer costs and benefits get externalized.

Class action suits also mitigate externalities. In a class action, many people with similar claims join a common case. More litigants internalize more benefits. Remember our example of James suing the police. The damages are worth $10,000 to James; the injunction is worth $5,000 to James; and the injunction is worth $100,000 to everyone else. If James acts alone, he internalizes only $15,000 in benefits, so he might not sue. If James joins others in a class, they collectively internalize a lot more than $15,000. The class might sue when an individual would not.[37]

Many mechanisms work to counteract externalities in litigation. However, the mechanisms are imperfect. Furthermore, litigants do not always conduct cost-benefit analyses when making decisions. Inevitably some people litigate when economists think they should not, and some people fail to litigate when economists think they should.[38]

Questions

10.6. Explain why precedents are public goods.[39]

10.7. Use the concept of litigation externalities to defend the following statement: "The court system should charge lower fees for appeals than for trials."

10.8. Courts have limited capacity. If I file a lawsuit today, I slow down your lawsuit tomorrow. Access-to-justice programs aim to improve poor people's access to courts. Do these programs help the poor? Or do they cause a "tragedy of the judiciary"?[40]

[37] Class actions suits can mitigate externalities in other ways. For example, suppose an asbestos manufacturer is liable for causing cancer. The manufacturer has limited resources for paying damages. Without a class action, the first plaintiff can impose a negative externality on others by collecting all of the money from the manufacturer and leaving nothing for other plaintiffs. With a class action, all plaintiffs' interests get considered simultaneously. *See* Ortiz v. Fibreboard Corp., 527 U.S. 815 (1999).

[38] *See generally* Steven Shavell, *The Fundamental Divergence Between the Private and the Social Motive to Use the Legal System*, 62 J. LEGAL STUD. 575 (1997).

[39] *See* William M. Landes & Richard A. Posner, *Adjudication as a Private Good*, 8 J. LEGAL STUD. 235 (1979).

[40] *See* Ivo Teixeira Gico, Jr., *The Tragedy of the Judiciary: An Inquiry into the Economic Nature of Law and Courts*, 21 GERMAN L.J. 644 (2020).

10.9. In the early 2000s, record companies sued people for illegally downloading music. The companies offered to settle with each defendant for $3,000. High litigation costs caused some defendants to settle even though they had valid defenses. What value did those defendants externalize? Would a "class action defense" help?[41]

Playing for the Rule

Some people use law rarely. These "one shotters" care about their individual cases. Other people use law often. "Repeat players" care about the run of cases. To succeed in the run of cases, repeat players want the law on their side. To get the law on their side, repeat players do not "play" to win each case. They play for the rule.[42]

Imagine a renter named Liam and his landlord, Mia. Liam will rent an apartment for a short period in his life before buying a home. Mia owns many apartments and lets them to earn a living. Liam expects to have few experiences with landlord-tenant law, whereas Mia expects to have many. Consequently, Mia cares more about landlord-tenant law. Now imagine two kinds of cases between Liam and Mia: tenant-favoring cases, meaning cases Liam will likely win, and landlord-favoring cases. Mia offers to settle tenant-favoring cases because she does not want a court to set a tenant-favoring precedent. Conversely, Mia litigates landlord-favoring cases because she wants a court to set a landlord-favoring precedent. A favorable precedent will benefit Mia in many rentals over many years, justifying the expense of litigation. Over time, the law tends to favor landlords like Mia who play for the rule.

This example involves private law, but the same phenomenon operates throughout public law. Prosecutors are repeat players, whereas most criminal defendants are not. The Department of Homeland Security is a repeat player with respect to immigration law, whereas most immigrants are one shotters. The Internal Revenue Service and Social Security Administration are repeat players, whereas most taxpayers and social security beneficiaries are not (many people pay taxes and receive entitlements, but few people litigate tax and entitlement cases every year). Over time, law tends to favor prosecutors over defendants, immigration authorities over immigrants, and the IRS over taxpayers, or so goes the prediction.

Our analysis of externalities unites these examples. Making a precedent ordinarily requires a judgment by an appellate court (trial court decisions do not set precedents). Repeat players internalize value from a favorable precedent, so they have an incentive to litigate for an appellate judgment. One shotters externalize most of the value of a favorable precedent. In our example, Liam will soon become

[41] *See* Assaf Hamdani & Alon Klement, *The Class Defense*, 93 CAL. L. REV. 685 (2005). The conceptual case for a "class defense" seems strong, but we are unaware of any class defense in practice.

[42] This discussion is based on Marc Galanter, *Why the "Haves" Come Out Ahead: Speculations on the Limits of Legal Change*, 9 LAW & SOC'Y REV. 95 (1974).

a homeowner, so he does not care about landlord-tenant law. One shotters have a weaker incentive to litigate for an appellate judgment. Instead, they settle, dropping their cases in exchange for money.

E. Trial

"The only real lawyers are trial lawyers."[43] If parties overcome externalities and sue, and if settlement fails, the case proceeds to trial. Lawyers make opening and closing statement, present evidence, examine witnesses, and persuade jurors. Trial culminates in a verdict, like "the defendant is guilty." To reach a verdict, the court makes findings of fact and conclusions of law. Did the defendant drive fast, fire the employee, mine without a permit, or tear down the statue? These are questions of fact. Did blocking the bridge constitute federal wire fraud? Did choking James violate the Fourth Amendment? These are questions of law.[44] Later we concentrate on law, but here we stick to facts.

To find the facts, courts hear evidence. In adversarial systems like the United States, the lawyers develop and present the evidence. The judge acts as referee, and (if relevant) the jury watches passively. In inquisitorial systems like France, the judge takes the lead in developing the evidentiary record. Which system is better? The adversarial system encourages competition among lawyers whose pay and reputation depend on success in court. Each side has an incentive to present the best evidence for their client. Without competitive pressure, inquisitorial judges might work less diligently than adversarial lawyers. However, judges might seek truth, whereas many lawyers seek only victory. To generalize, the adversarial system should tend to produce more evidence by biased lawyers, whereas the inquisitorial system should tend to produce less evidence by unbiased judges.[45]

Rules of evidence govern what the judge and jury see. In the United States, the federal rules of evidence permit "relevant" evidence and forbid "irrelevant" evidence.[46] Even relevant evidence gets excluded "if its probative value is substantially outweighed" by other factors like the "danger of . . . unfair prejudice, confusing the issues," or "undue delay."[47] Judges rule on many issues: amount of discovery, number of witnesses, length of trial, and so on. All of these decisions affect the production of evidence.

Scholars have applied economics to many steps in the fact-finding process.[48] Rather than review their analyses, we generalize across them. Evidence law aims to balance the benefit of facts against the cost of finding them. The costs are apparent: producing and reading documents, preparing witnesses, presenting exhibits, taking testimony from experts like scientists—these steps and others require time and effort. The benefit grows from increased accuracy in adjudication. Accuracy promotes justice and other

[43] This quote is often attributed to famous trial attorney Clarence Darrow.

[44] They might better be described as "mixed" questions of law and fact.

[45] For a discussion of the trade-off, see Richard A. Posner, *An Economic Approach to the Law of Evidence*, 51 Stan. L. Rev. 1477 (1999).

[46] Fed. R. Evid. 402.

[47] Fed. R. Evid. 403.

[48] For a review, see Chris William Sanchirico, *Law and Economics of Evidence*, *in* 3 The Oxford Handbook of Law and Economics (Francesco Parisi ed., 2017).

values like deterrence (people violate the law less often when they expect to be correctly identified and punished).

We will say more about accuracy in adjudication later. Here we concentrate on the mechanics of fact-finding. How does the presentation of evidence generate truth? Economists often model the process using *Bayes' Theorem*.[49] The theorem shows how a rational, truth-seeking person updates her beliefs given new evidence. We illustrate the theorem using another version of the case of James suing the police.

James claims that an officer punched him without justification during a traffic stop. The officer claims that James was already injured at the time of the stop, possibly from a fight earlier that day. At the outset of the case, the judge trusts the police. Translated into probabilities, the judge believes there is only a 5 percent chance that the officer punched James (equivalently, the judge believes there is a 95 percent chance that someone besides the officer punched James). This is the judge's prior or *a priori* belief. Now James presents evidence—specifically, he shows photos of his injuries. The photos show a bruise from a ring with an unusual shape. The officer James has accused wears a ring with that shape. Only 4 percent of the population wears that kind of ring.

Given the bruise, what is the probability that the officer punched James? Bayes' Theorem supplies a formula:

$$P(C|B)=\frac{P(B|C)*P(C)}{P(B|C)*P(C)+P(B|not\ C)*P(not\ C)}$$

"$P(B\,|\,C)$" refers to the probability of having the bruise (*B*) given a punch by the accused officer (*C* for "cop"). In other words, if this officer punched James, what are the chances of him developing the unusual bruise? The answer is 100 percent. "*P*(*C*)" is the judge's prior belief about the officer punching James (5 percent). "$P(B\,|\,not\ C)$" is the probability of having the bruise if the injurer were not this officer (4 percent). "$P(not\ C)$" is the judge's prior belief that the injurer was not the officer (95 percent). Substituting these figures yields:

$$P(C|B)=\frac{1*0.05}{1*0.05+0.04*0.95}$$

"$P(C\,|\,B)$" is the probability that James was punched by the officer given that he has the unusual bruise. It equals about 57 percent. This is the judge's posterior or *a posteriori* belief.

To begin, the judge thought there was a 5 percent chance that the officer punched James. After observing the evidence, the judge believes there is a 57 percent chance that the officer injured James. The judge has engaged in *Bayesian updating*. Rational people

[49] *See* Thomas Bayes, *An Essay towards Solving a Problem in the Doctrine of Chances*, 53 PHILOSOPHICAL TRANSACTIONS OF THE ROYAL SOCIETY OF LONDON 370 (1763). For other approaches to fact-finding, see Chris William Sanchirico, *Law and Economics of Evidence*, *in* 3 THE OXFORD HANDBOOK OF LAW AND ECONOMICS (Francesco Parisi ed., 2017); Sean Sullivan, *A Likelihood Story: The Theory of Legal Fact-Finding*, 90 U. COLO. L. REV. 1 (2019).

use Bayesian updating to assess evidence. In our example, we imagined only one piece of evidence, but the parties could present many pieces of evidence and the judge could update after each one.

Much depends on the fact-finder's prior belief. In our example, the judge had a prior belief of 5 percent (there was a 5 percent chance the officer punched James). This yielded a posterior probability of 57 percent. What if the judge had a prior belief of 30 percent? After seeing the evidence and updating, the judge's posterior belief would equal 91 percent (there is a 91 percent chance the officer punched James). If the judge had a prior belief of just 1 percent and saw the evidence, his posterior belief would equal 20 percent. Bayes' Theorem teaches how to update from a prior belief, but it does not specify the correct prior belief. Different people have different beliefs. Consequently, different fact-finders can use Bayes' Theorem and reach different conclusions.

In practice, do people reason according to Bayes' Theorem? Often the answer is no. Probabilities can be hard to compute. Psychologists have shown that people treat low-probability events as zero-probability events.[50] We treat salient events like earthquakes and plane crashes as high probability when in fact they are low probability. We treat identical probabilities differently. For example, a surgery might attract more patients when advertised with a "10 percent mortality rate" than a "90 percent survival rate." Bayes' Theorem shows how people *should* update their beliefs. It often fails to predict how people *do* update their beliefs.

Suppose that fact-finders could calculate probabilities correctly. Even so, they might draw erroneous conclusions of law.[51] Suppose that James claims the officer injured him twice, once during the traffic stop and again at the police station. The two events are independent, meaning whether James was injured during the stop does not affect the probability of him being injured at the station, and vice versa. After seeing evidence and updating, the judge concludes that there is only a 40 percent chance the officer hurt James during the stop and only a 40 percent chance the officer hurt James at the station. James has failed to prove either claim by a "preponderance of the evidence." (Preponderance of the evidence is usually interpreted to mean "more than 50 percent chance." We will discuss this standard and other burdens of proof in a later chapter.) James will lose the case.

This might seem right as a matter of law, but it seems puzzling as a matter of statistics. Figure 10.3 diagrams the situation. The top-most branch shows a 40 percent chance of an injury during the stop and a 40 percent chance of an injury at the station. According to the conjunction rule, the probability of two independent events both happening equals the product of their individual probabilities. So the probability of James being injured at both places equals $0.4 * 0.4 = 16$ percent. The second-from-top branch shows the probability of James being injured during the stop but not at the station: 24 percent. And so on.

[50] This observation and others in this paragraph trace to work by the psychologists Daniel Kahneman and Amos Tversky, who studied decision-making heuristics and biases. For an accessible discussion, see DANIEL KAHNEMAN, THINKING, FAST AND SLOW (2011). Recent research attempts to reconcile some of the findings from psychology and the logic of Bayesian updating. *See* Nick Chater et al., *Probabilistic Biases Meet the Bayesian Brain*, 29 CURRENT DIRECTIONS PSYCH. SCI. 506 (2020).

[51] The following draws on Ronald J. Allen, *A Reconceptualization of Civil Trials*, 66 B.U. L. REV. 401 (1986).

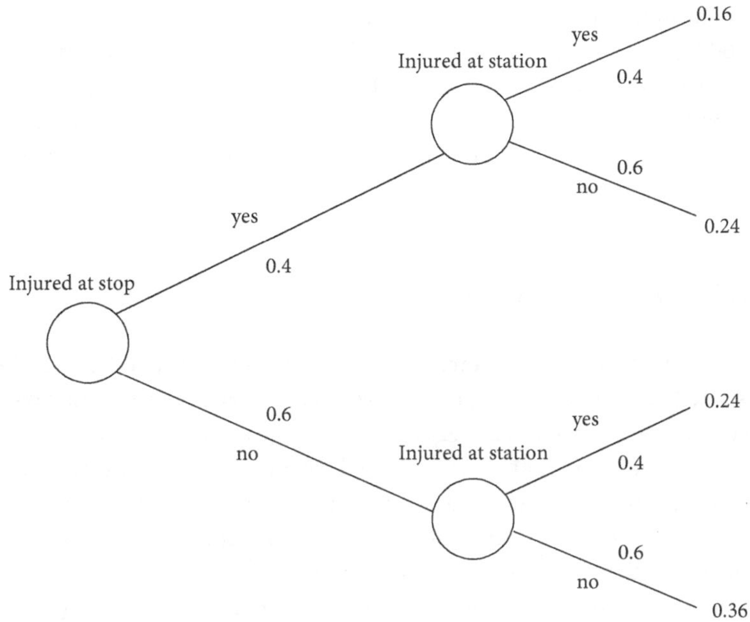

Figure 10.3. The Conjunction Rule

As the bottom branch shows, the probability that the officer *never* injured James equals only 36 percent. The probability that the officer injured James during the stop, at the station, or both equals the sum of the other branches: 64 percent. A Bayesian updater might conclude that James has proven by a preponderance of the evidence that the officer injured him at some point. However, this is probably insufficient. To win the case, James must prove that one of his *particular* claims has a greater than 50 percent chance of being true. The evidence does not support this.

To summarize, trials often concentrate on fact-finding. Judges find facts through the presentation of evidence. Rules structure the presentation of evidence. Many of the rules balance the benefit of facts against the cost of finding them. Economists often use Bayes' Theorem to model the translation of evidence into beliefs about facts. The theorem shows a truth seeker how to accurately update her beliefs. In reality, people make mistakes when updating. Even when people update correctly, Bayes' Theorem can lead to conclusions of fact that conflict with proper conclusions of law.

Questions

10.10. James sues the officer for an unconstitutional tort. The judge's prior belief is that there is a 2 percent chance the officer punched James. Then James provides evidence that his bruise matches the officer's ring. In the general population, 2 percent of people wear that particular ring. What is the judge's posterior belief? Has James proved by a preponderance of the evidence that the officer punched him?

10.11. Four hundred people buy tickets for a concert and occupy their seats. Then 600 other people "crash the gates" and occupy the remaining seats, even though they don't have tickets. The concert organizer takes a picture of a random person, Nate, in the crowd. Then he sues Nate for the value of the concert ticket. Has he proven by a preponderance of the evidence that Nate crashed the gate?[52]

Juries and the Wisdom of the Crowd

We have discussed fact-finding at trial by judges. In reality, juries often find the facts. Verdicts like "the defendant is guilty" have a factual element: the jury concludes that the defendant engaged in certain acts. Sometimes juries announce verdicts like "the defendant caused $45,000 in harm." Civil trials often feature juries, and the U.S. Constitution grants people accused of a crime the right to a jury. Thomas Jefferson considered trial by jury "the only anchor ever yet imagined . . . by which a government can be held to the principles of its constitution."[53]

Juries are supposed to be fair and impartial. They check the state and inject community norms into legal proceedings. They make law legitimate. Later we will return to some of these ideas. Here we concentrate on a different justification for juries: information. Juries can capture "the wisdom of the crowd."

To illustrate, imagine a factual allegation: "the officer punched James." Three jurors use majority rule to decide if the allegation is true. In fact, the allegation is true, but the jurors are not sure of this. Each juror has a 60 percent chance of drawing the correct conclusion (the officer punched James) and a 40 percent chance of drawing the wrong conclusion (the officer did not punch James). If all three jurors vote "true" we can represent the vote as *TTT*. If the first juror votes "true" and the others vote "false" we can represent the vote as *TFF*. Here are all possible votes and the probabilities of each:

Vote	Probability
TTT	0.6 * 0.6 * 0.6 = 0.216
TTF	0.6 * 0.6 * 0.4 = 0.144
TFT	0.6 * 0.4 * 0.6 = 0.144
TFF	0.6 * 0.4 * 0.4 = 0.096
FTT	0.4 * 0.6 * 0.6 = 0.144
FTF	0.4 * 0.6 * 0.4 = 0.096
FFT	0.4 * 0.4 * 0.6 = 0.096
FFF	0.4 * 0.4 * 0.4 = 0.064

52 This is the gatecrasher's paradox. *See* David Kaye, *The Paradox of the Gatecrasher and Other Stories*, 1979 ARIZ. ST. L.J. 101 (1979). People tend to disregard "naked statistical evidence" of the sort presented in the question when making decisions about liability. *See* Gary L. Wells, *Naked Statistical Evidence of Liability: Is Subjective Probability Enough?*, 62 J. PERSONALITY & SOC. PSYCH. 739 (1992).

53 Thomas Jefferson, *Letter to Thomas Paine*, *in* 2 MEMOIRS, CORRESPONDENCE, AND PRIVATE PAPERS 495 (Thomas Jefferson Randolph ed., 1829).

For the jury to conclude that the allegation is true requires a majority of *T* votes. The probability of the group concluding that the allegation is true equals 0.216 + 0.144 + 0.144 + 0.144 = 0.648. The group has a 65 percent chance of making the correct decision, whereas any individual member has only a 60 percent chance of making the correct decision.

The *Condorcet Jury Theorem* generalizes the logic of this example. When a group of people (1) use majority rule to (2) choose between two factual alternatives, and members of the group (3) vote independently and sincerely, and (4) are more likely to be right than wrong, the probability of reaching the correct decision approaches 100 percent as the group increases in size.[54]

This theorem appears to make a powerful case for fact-finding by juries rather than individual judges. However, the theorem makes strong assumptions that do not always hold. Juries often choose from more than two alternatives, as when they calculate damages. Jurors deliberate and might influence one another, in which case they do not vote independently.[55] Sometimes jurors are more likely to be wrong than right. If each of our three jurors has a 40 percent chance of making the correct decision and a 60 percent chance of making the incorrect decision, then the probability of the group reaching the correct decision equals only 35 percent.[56] The group has a worse chance of reaching the correct result than any individual member.

The Condorcet Jury Theorem assumes majority rule. In reality, juries often operate under unanimity rule. In *Ramos v. Louisiana*, the Supreme Court held that the Constitution requires juries to use unanimity rule in serious criminal cases.[57] Compared to majority rule, unanimity rule can increase the probability of the group making the correct decision.[58] However, unanimity rule provokes holdouts. A "hung jury" cannot agree on a verdict, which means the case starts over. Restarting a case wastes resources.[59] The Court's decision in *Ramos* promotes accurate convictions at the expense of more litigation.

54 *See* Nicolas de Condorcet, *Essay on the Application of Analysis to the Probability of Majority Decisions* (1785). For a formal statement of the theorem and extensions, see Shmuel Nitzan & Jacob Paroush, *Collective Decision-Making and Jury Theorems, in* 1 THE OXFORD HANDBOOK OF LAW AND ECONOMICS (Francesco Parisi ed., 2017).

55 On these and other relaxations of the conditions, see *id.*

56 Four configurations of votes would lead the jury under majority rule to conclude that the allegation is true: *TTT, TTF, TFT, FTT*. The probability of the first configuration equals 0.064, and the probability of each of the others equals 0.096. By addition, the probability of the group reaching the correct results equals 0.352.

57 140 S. Ct. 1390 (2020).

58 *See* Shmuel Nitzan & Jacob Paroush, *Are Qualified Majority Rules Special?*, 42 PUB. CHOICE 257 (1984); Ruth C. Ben-Yashar & Shmuel I. Nitzan, *The Optimal Decision Rule for Fixed-Size Committees in Dichotomous Choice Situations: The General Result*, 38 INT'L ECON. REV. 175 (1997).

59 To prevent this waste, states reduced the size of some juries. Fewer jurors, the argument went, should find it easier to agree. But apparently this argument was wrong. Juries "hung" at about the same rate whether larger or smaller. Why? Here is one theory. Jurors announce their views in succession ("I think the defendant is guilty"). As more jurors announce the same view, subsequent jurors are more likely to adopt that view, rejecting their own, independent view. The potential for this "information cascade" to cause a uniform view grows with the size of the group. So shrinking the jury has cross-cutting effects. Smaller groups find it easier to agree, preventing hung juries. But smaller groups are less subject to information cascades that cause uniformity. *See* Barbara Luppi & Francisco Parisi, *Jury Size and the Hung-Jury Paradox*, 42 J. LEGAL STUD. 399 (2013).

F. Appeal

The party who loses at trial usually has the option to appeal to a higher court. Sometimes the higher court must accept the appeal (*mandatory* review). Other times the higher court has the choice (*discretionary* review). To illustrate, U.S. federal courts are organized in a hierarchy with district (trial) courts on the bottom, circuit courts (also called courts of appeals) in the middle, and the Supreme Court on top. Circuit courts must accept appeals from final decisions of district courts. In general, the Supreme Court gets to choose whether to accept appeals from circuit courts.

Appellate courts review some or all of the trial court's decisions. With respect to findings of fact, appellate courts often defer. In the United States, appellate courts only reverse findings of fact when they find "clear error" by the trial court. With respect to conclusions of law, appellate courts usually do not defer. In the United States, appellate courts place no weight on the trial court's legal conclusions (this is called *de novo* review). Having analyzed fact-finding earlier, we focus here on conclusions of law.

In reviewing the trial court's conclusions of law, appellate courts do two things: correct errors and create precedents. We begin with error correction. Trial courts can make legal errors in at least two ways. First, they can make an error in the rationale, as when the judge misreads a statute or misses a step in the legal analysis. Second, trial courts can make an error in the disposition, as when the plaintiff should win but loses. To illustrate, the Administrative Procedure Act authorizes federal courts to invalidate agency rules that are "arbitrary and capricious."[60] Forgetting to apply the arbitrary and capricious test constitutes an error in rationale, whereas applying it but reaching the wrong conclusion can lead to an error in the disposition.[61]

Separate from correcting errors, appellate courts often make new precedents. Making precedent clarifies law and occasionally changes society. In *Gideon v. Wainwright*, the Supreme Court held that the Constitution grants criminal defendants the right to a lawyer.[62] *Craig v. Boren* made it harder for the government to discriminate on the basis of sex.[63] *Marbury v. Madison* held that federal courts have the power of judicial review, meaning the power to strike down statutes that do not comport with the Constitution.[64]

Whether correcting errors or making precedents, appellate courts often have discretion. "Discretion" comes in different forms. Here we focus on *legal discretion*. To explain, consider a famous example.[65] Suppose the law says, "no vehicles in the park." Surely the law forbids buses of schoolchildren from entering the park, and surely it does not forbid pedestrians from walking through the park. These cases fall in the "core" of the law's meaning. Cases in the core have clear, determinate answers, meaning judges have little discretion. Now suppose a person rides a bicycle or motorized wheelchair through the park. Or suppose the city mounts a military jeep (in working order) in the park to

60 *See* 5 U.S.C. 706(2)(A).

61 *See, e.g.*, Dep't of Homeland Sec. v. Regents of the Univ. of California, 140 S. Ct. 1891 (2020), where the Supreme Court held that the agency's decision was arbitrary and capricious.

62 372 U.S. 335 (1963).

63 429 U.S. 190 (1976).

64 5 U.S. 137 (1803).

65 The following discussion draws on the famous debate between Lon Fuller and H.L.A. Hart. *Compare* H.L.A. Hart, *Positivism and the Separation of Law and Morals*, 71 HARV. L. REV. 593 (1958), *with* Lon L. Fuller, *Positivism and Fidelity to Law—A Reply to Professor Hart*, 71 HARV. L. REV. 630 (1958).

commemorate war heroes. Do these activities violate the law? Are bikes, wheelchairs, or commemorative jeeps "vehicles"? These cases fall in the law's "penumbra." Cases in the penumbra do not have clear answers. To resolve them, judges must exercise discretion.

How should judges exercise discretion? One option is to find the law's purpose. If the law forbids vehicles in the park to reduce pollution, then the commemorative jeep can enter the park (like a statue, it will emit neither noise nor smoke). If the law aims to increase green space, then the jeep cannot enter the park. Of course, finding a law's purpose can be difficult. We will say more about this topic a little later.

Separate from purpose, another option is to apply moral principles. Would it be unjust to punish a disabled person from riding a wheelchair through the park? If so, the law does not forbid all wheelchairs. Ronald Dworkin argued that every case has a correct moral answer, though judges cannot always discern it.[66] He might say that law is always "determinate" (there is a right answer) but sometimes "inconclusive" (we cannot find it).

We will say more about how judges exercise discretion soon. Here we reframe some of the discussion in economic terms. Appeals create costs by adding a step to the adjudicative process. The parties to the case usually do not internalize all of these costs. Appeals create benefits by correcting errors and establishing precedents that clarify law. The parties to the case internalize benefits from error correction, but they usually externalize benefits from the creation of precedent. A clear precedent can save many people (whether they are in or out of court) time and effort when ascertaining the law's meaning.

Figure 10.4 visualizes error correction and precedent creation.[67] To explain the figure, recall some facts. The Supreme Court reviews statutes to determine if they comport with the Constitution. To make this determination, the Court often reviews the government's interests (i.e., its objectives, goals, or *ends*) and tailoring (how well the government's *means* promote its ends). The exact nature of judicial review depends on the circumstances. Race-based laws draw "strict scrutiny." In *Fisher v. University of Texas*, the state had to prove that its affirmative action policy for college admissions was "narrowly tailored" (the means) to achieve a "compelling" government interest (the end).[68] By contrast, most business regulations draw only "rational basis review." When Minnesota banned plastic milk containers but not paper milk containers, the plastic industry sued, claiming a violation of the Fourteenth Amendment. In *Minnesota v. Clover Leaf Creamery*, the state proved that its ban on plastic was "rationally related" (the means) to a "legitimate" state interest (the end).[69]

The horizontal axis in Figure 10.4 represents the strength of the government's interest. The left end of the axis corresponds to illegitimate government interests, like intentionally mistreating a minority group. The government's interest strengthens as we move rightward. The vertical axis represents tailoring. The bottom corresponds to especially poor tailoring, as when a state bans plastic milk jugs to promote driving safety

[66] *See generally* Ronald Dworkin, Taking Rights Seriously (1977).

[67] The figure relates to the "case space" model. *See* Jeffrey R. Lax, *The New Judicial Politics of Legal Doctrine*, 14 Ann. Rev. Pol. Sci. 131 (2011); Lewis A. Kornhauser, *Modeling Courts*, *in* Theoretical Foundations of Law and Economics (Mark D. White ed., 2008).

[68] 570 U.S. 297 (2013).

[69] 449 U.S. 456 (1981).

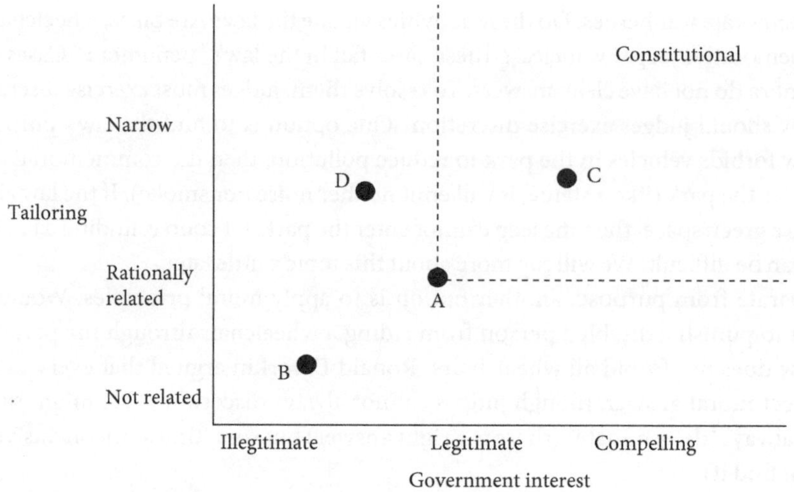

Figure 10.4. Graphing Judicial Review

or moon research. The means do not further the ends, so the tailoring is poor. Tailoring improves—the means better promote the ends—as we move upward.

Point *A* represents a case like *Clover Leaf Creamery*. The state had a legitimate (but not compelling) interest in resource conservation. Banning nonrefillable plastic containers was rationally related (but not narrowly tailored—why not ban all nonrefillable containers?) to that interest. Thus, the Supreme Court upheld the statute. In reaching this conclusion, the Court corrected an error by the lower court, which had invalidated the statute.[70] We can use the figure to visualize the error. Perhaps the lower court thought the statute corresponded to a point like *B*, which would not satisfy rational basis review. Or perhaps the lower court thought that rational basis review was more demanding and the statute had to correspond to a point like *C*.

Separate from error correction, we can use Figure 10.4 to analyze precedent. *Clover Leaf Creamery* set a precedent that we can state abstractly: in cases at point *A*, the law being challenged survives rational basis review. In fact, the precedent is broader than point *A*. Imagine a statute about containers and conservation that is situated to the right of point *A*. Compared to the statute in *Clover Leaf Creamery*, the new statute uses equally good tailoring (the means) to further an even stronger government interest (the end). Alternatively, imagine a statute situated above point *A*. Compared to the statute in *Clover Leaf Creamery*, this statute uses better tailoring to further an equally strong government interest. Generalizing, all statutes about containers and conservation in the area marked "constitutional" survive rational basis review under the precedent set in *Clover Leaf Creamery*.

What about a statute at point *D*? Compared to the statute in *Clover Leaf Creamery*, this one has better tailoring but a weaker government interest. Perhaps the Court in *Clover Leaf Creamery* did not mention this kind of statute. Or perhaps it mentioned this kind of statute but only in dicta. *Dicta* refers to arguments or conclusions in a judicial

[70] In this case, the "lower court" was the Supreme Court of Minnesota. *See* Clover Leaf Creamery Co. v. State, 304 N.W. 2d 915 (Minn. 1981).

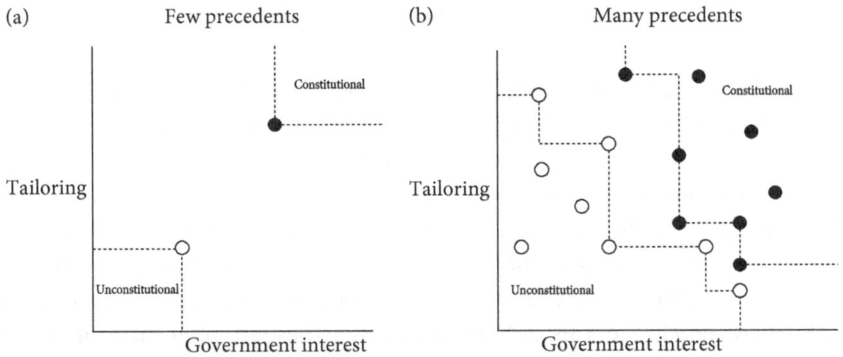

Figure 10.5. Precedent and Certainty

opinion unessential to the resolution of the case. Dicta do not bind future courts. Thus, *Clover Leaf Creamery* does not determine the result in case *D*. Rather than following precedent, a court would have to resolve case *D* by reviewing the law afresh.

Figure 10.5 illustrates how the accretion of precedent clarifies law. Concentrate on the left panel labeled Figure 10.5.a. The court invalidated the statute in the case with the hollow point. Following the preceding reasoning, that precedent renders "unconstitutional" every statute in the region with that label. The court upheld the statute in the case with the solid point, so every statute is "constitutional" in the region with that label. The constitutionality of statutes in the large, unlabeled space remains unclear. The law in this area is uncertain. Now concentrate on the right panel labeled Figure 10.5.b. Every hollow point represents a case in which the court invalidated the statute, and every solid point represents a case in which the court upheld the statute. Compared to the left panel, the right panel has more labeled space ("constitutional," "unconstitutional") and less unlabeled space. More precedents tend to increase certainty in law.

Questions

10.12. In *Craig v. Boren*, the Supreme Court held that laws discriminating on the basis of sex demand "intermediate scrutiny."[71] Such laws must "substantially relate" to the furtherance of an "important" government interest. In Figure 10.4, sketch a plausible region in which laws discriminating on the basis of sex are constitutional.

10.13. Three judges use majority rule to resolve cases. In Figure 10.4, the first judge believes that every statute above and/or right of point *B* satisfies rational basis review. The second judge believes that every statute above and/or right of point *D* satisfies rational basis review. The third judge believes that every statute above and/or right of point *A* satisfies rational basis review. In Figure 10.4, sketch the region in which a majority of the judges believe that the statute satisfies rational basis review.

10.14. We wrote, "more precedents tend to increase certainty in law." When will adding precedents *decrease* certainty in law?

[71] 429 U.S. 190 (1976).

II. Judicial Behavior

Judges make countless decisions—on discovery, witnesses, motions, facts, jury instructions, and law. How do judges make these decisions? Economists assume that people behave to satisfy their preferences. To understand judicial behavior, we must understand judges' preferences. Real preferences are complicated, so economists simplify. To illustrate, some CEOs care about employees and customers, but economists simplify by assuming CEOs care only about profits. Simple preferences make the analysis manageable. We concentrate on two simplifications about judicial preferences: judges care only about law, and judges care only about policy.[72] These simplifications are common and useful. However, simple preferences misrepresent real preferences, causing errors when making predictions about behavior.

A. The Legal Model

According to the *legal model*, judges apply rules, precedents, and logical operations to facts. Law works like a syllogism, with a question, major premise, minor premise, and conclusion:

Did Noah speed?
Driving faster than 65 mph constitutes speeding.
Noah drove 80 mph.
Noah sped.

The legal model is both an ideal (judges should behave this way) and a prediction (judges do behave this way). In general, lawyers have confidence in the prediction. When advising clients and arguing in court, they learn the facts, study the statutes, and master the precedents. They argue points of law. Lawyers perform this work, and clients pay for it, because law is often the best predictor of judicial decisions.

Why? What causes judges to "do law"? Economists assume that people satisfy their preferences subject to constraints. Noah prefers to drive 80 mph, but he faces a constraint: the fine for speeding. So Noah drives as fast as he can subject to that constraint. Constraints explain many behaviors, but they often cannot explain why judges adhere to the legal model. Judges face few constraints. In the United States, federal judges enjoy life tenure (they cannot be fired) and salary protections (no one can reduce their income). Independence empowers judges to decide cases as they please. Without constraints, judges can satisfy their preferences.

Perhaps judges have a preference for making decisions on the basis of law. Law school and legal norms might inculcate these preferences in judges. Alternatively, judges might seek the esteem of lawyers and other judges, which they achieve by adhering to law.[73]

[72] On other possible goals of judges, see Lawrence Baum, *What Judges Want: Judges' Goals and Judicial Behavior*, 47 Pol. Res. Q. 749 (1994).

[73] *See, e.g.*, Nuno Garoupa & Tom Ginsburg, Judicial Reputation: A Comparative Theory (2015).

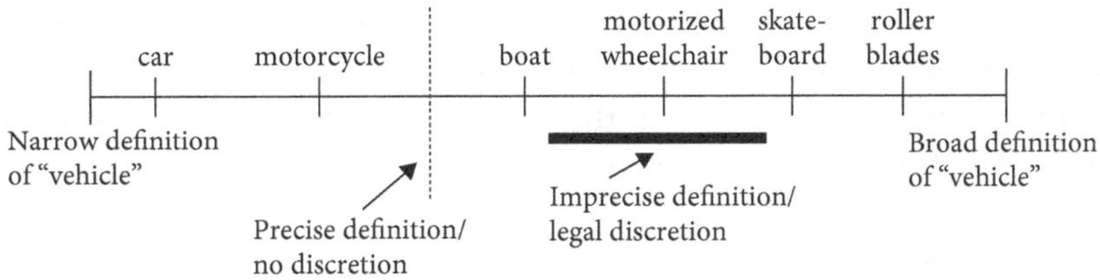

Figure 10.6. Legal Discretion

Scholars have shown that judges are intrinsically motivated to produce careful opinions,[74] and some judges enjoy the "game" of law.[75]

The legal model appears to explain many judicial decisions.[76] However, it cannot explain all. Earlier we discussed legal discretion, which arises when a case lacks a clear answer. Does a law prohibiting "vehicles" in the park forbid motorized wheelchairs? The text of the statute does not answer the question. Many judges would look beyond the text and consult the statute's legislative history. While debating the bill, the legislature might have produced a report defining "vehicle" or describing the law's purpose. But legislative history is often inconclusive. Some judges might consider justice. Would it be immoral to forbid motorized wheelchairs? Sometimes judges share moral intuitions about a case, but often they disagree.

Figure 10.6 visualizes legal discretion. The dimension captures the breadth of the term "vehicle." The left end corresponds to a very narrow definition. "Vehicle" encompasses only those means of transport that spring naturally to mind, like cars and trucks. Moving rightward, the meaning of "vehicle" broadens to include boats, skateboards, and so on. The dashed vertical line represents a precise definition of "vehicle." With the precise definition, the statute forbids items left of the dashed line from entering the park and permits items right of the dashed line. Judges have no discretion.[77] Now suppose the statute includes an imprecise definition of "vehicle," as indicated by the horizontal bar. The statute forbids items left of the bar like cars, and the statute permits items right of the bar like skateboards. However, the statute does not resolve items inside the bar. Judges decide for themselves whether items inside the bar constitute "vehicles." The bar represents judges' range of legal discretion.

Do judges usually have discretion? Is the bar wide or narrow? Beginning in the 1920s, a school of thought called *legal realism* debated these questions.[78] Some legal realists

[74] Elliott Ash & W. Bentley MacLeod, *Intrinsic Motivation in Public Service: Theory and Evidence from State Supreme Courts*, 58 J.L. Econ. 863 (2015). *Cf.* Matias Iaryczower & Matthew Shum, *The Value of Information in the Court: Get It Right, Keep It Tight*, 102 Am. Econ. Rev. 202 (2012) (providing evidence that Supreme Court Justices' decisions depend on the facts of cases).

[75] Richard A. Posner, *What Do Judges and Justices Maximize? (The Same Thing Everybody Else Does)*, 3 Sup. Ct. Econ. Rev. 1, 23–30 (1993).

[76] For evidence of the legal model, see, for example, Herbert M. Kritzer & Mark J. Richards, *Jurisprudential Regimes and Supreme Court Decisionmaking: The* Lemon *Regime and Establishment Clause Cases*, 37 Law & Soc'y Rev. 827 (2003); Michael D. Gilbert, *Does Law Matter? Theory and Evidence from Single-Subject Adjudication*, 40 J. Legal Stud. 333 (2011); Michael A. Bailey & Forrest Maltzman, The Constrained Court: Law, Politics, and the Decisions Justices Make (2011).

[77] We assume no disagreement over the ordering of conveyances from left to right. In reality, people will disagree on whether, say, a motorized wheelchair is more or less "vehicle like" than a bicycle.

[78] Legal realism began to flourish in the 1920s. However, the movement traces to 1881, when Oliver Wendell Holmes, a scholar and judge, wrote: "The life of the law has not been logic: it has been experience.

argued that appellate judges exercise some discretion.[79] Others argued that many judges exercise substantial discretion.[80] Beginning in the 1970s, scholars in *critical legal studies* pushed further, arguing that judges nearly always have discretion.[81] The debate goes on.

When judges have discretion, law cannot guide their choices. Discretion arises because law "runs out."[82] How do judges make decisions when law runs out? The next section has an answer.

What Sustains Judicial Independence?

"[T]here is no liberty, if the power of judging be not separated from the legislative and executive powers."[83] Montesquieu made a powerful case for independent courts. If the legislature and executive can influence the judiciary, then courts cannot restrain the state or vindicate rights. If the parties to a case can threaten the judge, then impartial justice fails. To promote the rule of law, judges must be independent. With independence, judges can ignore outside pressures and decide on the basis of law.

Many constitutions make judges independent by protecting their salaries and granting them long tenures. (In the United States, federal judges hold their offices for life.) However, constitutions do not enforce themselves. "Parchment barriers" cannot stop avaricious politicians.[84] Many states defy their constitutions. North Korea's constitution protects the freedom of speech, but the state silences its people.

Thus, we face a puzzle. Judges frustrate powerful actors like legislators and executives. Powerful actors could ignore their constitutions and punish the judges. But often they do not. Often politicians abide by judges' decisions, even when they oppose them. Why? Why do politicians respect judicial independence? "Why would people with money and guns ever submit to people armed only with gavels?"[85]

One answer involves bargaining.[86] Sometimes legislatures resemble markets. Politicians "sell" laws (tax cuts for oil companies, subsidies for coalminers) in

The felt necessities of the time, the prevalent moral and political theories, intuitions of public policy, avowed or unconscious, even the prejudices which judges share with their fellow-men, have had a good deal more to do than the syllogism in determining the rules[.]" OLIVER WENDELL HOLMES, JR., THE COMMON LAW 1 (1881).

[79] *See, e.g.*, KARL LLEWELYN, THE COMMON LAW TRADITION—DECIDING APPEALS (1960).

[80] *See, e.g.*, JEROME FRANK, LAW AND THE MODERN MIND (1930).

[81] *See* Mark V. Tushnet, *Critical Legal Studies: A Political History*, 100 YALE L.J. 1515, 1538 (1991) ("[Imagine] a measure of the determinacy of a set of legal rules, the 'determinile.' A completely determinate legal system would measure 100 determiniles, while a completely indeterminate one would measure zero. [Critical legal studies] adherents at present defend the position that the proper measure of legal systems is probably between five and fifteen; that is, no system is completely indeterminate, but the level of determinacy is relatively low.").

[82] Alternatively, law may be inconclusive, meaning there is a correct answer but judges cannot find it. Either way the point about discretion holds.

[83] CHARLES DE SECONDAT, BARON DE MONTESQUIEU, THE SPIRIT OF THE LAWS (1748).

[84] *See* THE FEDERALIST NO. 48, at 251 (James Madison) (Ian Shapiro ed., 2009).

[85] Matthew C. Stephenson, *"When the Devil Turns . . .": The Political Foundations of Independent Judicial Review*, 32 J. LEGAL STUD. 59, 60 (2003).

[86] *See* William M. Landes & Richard A. Posner, *The Independent Judiciary in an Interest-Group Perspective*, 18 J.L. ECON. (1975). For theories of judicial independence distinct from the two we review here, see, for example, MARTIN SHAPIRO, COURTS: A COMPARATIVE AND POLITICAL ANALYSIS 32–35 (1981); F. Andrew Hanssen, *Is There a Politically Optimal Level of Judicial Independence?*, 94 AM. ECON. REV. 712 (2004); Ran Hirschl, *The Political Origins of Judicial Empowerment Through Constitutionalization: Lessons from Four*

exchange for votes and campaign contributions. Like all salespeople, politicians want to sell at a high price. They can demand a higher price when their laws endure. Oil companies will pay more for a ten-year tax cut than a one-year tax cut. How can politicians make their laws endure? In other words, how can they make a credible commitment not to change the terms of the deal? By making judges independent. With independence, judges can enforce interest group deals as written. To change the deal, politicians will have to pass a new law. Passing a new law requires many politicians to agree, whereas influencing a judge requires only one politician to make a threat. By insulating judges from tomorrow's political pressure, independence raises the value of today's political deal.

Interest group theory supplies one explanation for judicial independence. The *insurance model* supplies another.[87] Independent judges can thwart the majority, as when the Supreme Court invalidates popular legislation. However, independent judges can protect the minority, as when courts block the state from seizing private property or suppressing political speech. Today's majority might reason as follows: "If we weaken the courts, we will enjoy more power. However, we will lose protection later when our opponents win and we become the minority. The benefits of protection tomorrow outweigh the costs of judicial obstruction today. We will respect courts' independence." Politicians who reason like this resemble consumers buying home or auto insurance. They pay a price today to avoid a grave loss in the future.

For the insurance model to work, power must rotate. The party in office today must expect to lose the office tomorrow. To generalize, political competition promotes the independence of courts, whereas political monopoly depresses the independence of courts. Where do judges enjoy greater independence: in democracies or dictatorships?

B. The Attitudinal Model

A long tradition in political science holds that judges vote ideologically.[88] According to the *attitudinal model*, conservative judges vote for conservative outcomes and liberal judges vote for liberal outcomes.[89] A conservative court will favor police, employers, business, and religion, whereas a liberal court will favor criminal defendants, employees,

Constitutional Revolutions, 25 LAW & SOC. INQ'Y 91, 100–01 (2000); James R. Rogers, *Information and Judicial Review: A Signaling Game of Legislative-Judicial Interaction*, 45 AM. J. POL. SCI. 84, 95 (2001); Eli M. Salzberger, *A Positive Analysis of the Doctrine of Separation of Powers, or: Why Do We Have an Independent Judiciary?*, 13 INT'L REV. L. ECON. 349 (1993); Georg Vanberg, *Legislative-Judicial Relations: A Game-Theoretic Approach to Constitutional Review*, 45 AM. J. POL. SCI. 346 (2001).

[87] *See* TOM GINSBURG, JUDICIAL REVIEW IN NEW DEMOCRACIES 25 (2003). *See also* J. Mark Ramseyer, *The Puzzling (In)dependence of Courts: A Comparative Approach*, 23 J. LEGAL STUD. 721 (1994); Matthew C. Stephenson, *"When the Devil Turns . . .": The Political Foundations of Independent Judicial Review*, 32 J. LEGAL STUD. 59 (2003).

[88] *See, e.g.*, GLENDON SCHUBERT, THE JUDICIAL MIND: THE ATTITUDES AND IDEOLOGIES OF SUPREME COURT JUSTICES 1994–1963 (1965); Stuart S. Nagel, *Political Party Affiliation and Judges' Decisions*, 55 AM. POL. SCI. REV. 843 (1961).

[89] JEFFREY A. SEGAL & HAROLD J. SPAETH, THE SUPREME COURT AND THE ATTITUDINAL MODEL REVISITED (2002).

and government regulations. The attitudinal model especially applies to courts of last resort, like the U.S. Supreme Court. The Justices enjoy independence and, in many cases, legal discretion. No higher court can overturn their decisions. The Justices can exploit their autonomy and vote ideologically.

Ideology is complicated. For some judges, partisan politics might drive them. The judges' political affiliation, Republican or Democrat, predicts their decisions. For other judges, personal characteristics and life experiences matter more than partisanship. In sex discrimination cases, female judges vote in favor of the party alleging discrimination more often than male judges.[90] Black judges find violations of the Voting Rights Act more often than white judges.[91] Other characteristics, like a judge's age or religion, can matter too.[92]

The attitudinal model is easier to discuss than to prove. Scholars cannot measure ideology directly. They cannot peer into judges' minds. Instead, they rely on rough proxies, like the political party of the President who appointed the judge.[93] Moreover, the outcome that judges personally prefer might match the outcome that law requires. In such cases, law, not ideology, might best explain judges' decisions. Notwithstanding these challenges, much scholarship supports the attitudinal model.

The attitudinal model seems convincing. If you were a member of the Supreme Court in a case without a clear answer, how would you resolve it? Wouldn't you rely on your intuitions and values? But perhaps the attitudinal model is incomplete. Suppose your values guide you to a decision that you know will not endure. The President will not enforce your decision, or legislators will override it by passing a new statute. Would you make the decision anyway? Or would you modify your decision in light of these constraints?[94]

C. The Strategic Model: Separation of Powers

Title VII of the Civil Rights Act prohibits discrimination on the basis of sex. Does an employer who discriminates on the basis of pregnancy violate the act? In *General Electric Co. v. Gilbert*, the Supreme Court said no.[95] Two years later, Congress overrode the Court by amending Title VII. One sponsor of the amendment said: "By concluding that pregnancy discrimination is not sex discrimination . . . the Supreme Court disregarded the intent of Congress in enacting title VII. That intent was to protect all individuals

[90] Christina L. Boyd, Lee Epstein, & Andrew D. Martin, *Untangling the Causal Effects of Sex on Judging*, 54 Am. J. Pol. Sci. 389 (2010).

[91] Adam Cox & Thomas Miles, *Judging the Voting Rights Act*, 108 Colum. L. Rev. 1 (2008).

[92] *See, e.g.*, Carol T. Kulik, Elissa L. Perry, & Molly B. Pepper, *Here Comes the Judge: The Influence of Judge Personal Characteristics on Federal Sexual Harassment Case Outcomes*, 27 Law & Hum. Behav. 69 (2003); Donald R. Songer & Susan J. Tabrizi, *The Religious Right in Court: The Decision Making of Christian Evangelicals in State Supreme Courts*, 61 J. Pol. 507 (1999).

[93] *See* Joshua B. Fischman & David S. Law, *What Is Judicial Ideology, and How Should We Measure It?*, 29 Wash. U. J.L. & Pol'y 133 (2009).

[94] Lee Epstein, Jack Knight, & Andrew D. Martin, *The Supreme Court as a Strategic National Policymaker*, 50 Emory L.J. 583, 591 (2001) ("Why would Justices who are policy-preference maximizers take a position they know Congress would overturn?").

[95] 429 U.S. 125 (1976).

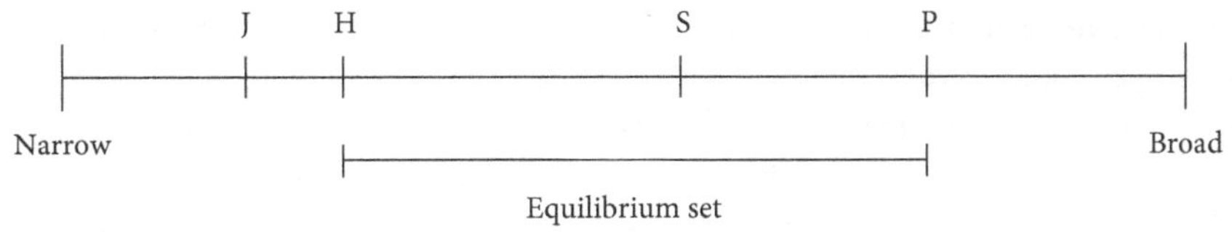

Figure 10.7. Interpretations of Title VII

from unjust employment discrimination, including pregnant women."[96] In other words, the Court erred, and Congress fixed its mistake.

Courts do not work in a vacuum. They face constraints, including from other branches of government. Constraints change behavior. Earlier we mentioned Noah, who would like to drive 80 miles per hour. The speed limit constrains Noah, causing him to slow down. Similarly, political actors constrain courts, tempering their decisions.

Figure 10.7 sharpens this idea with a spatial model.[97] The dimension represents possible interpretations of Title VII. Interpretations on the left are narrow, meaning the law forbids little discrimination. An interpretation on the far left might forbid only those policies that explicitly discriminate against women ("We pay women less than men"). Moving rightward, the interpretation broadens, meaning Title VII forbids more. An interpretation on the far right might forbid all explicit discrimination, including discrimination against men and transgendered persons, discrimination based on pregnancy, discrimination based on sexual orientation, and so on. The House of Representatives prefers interpretation *H*, the Senate prefers interpretation *S*, and the President prefers interpretation *P*. The actors have single-peaked, symmetrical preferences, meaning they always prefer interpretations closer to their ideal points.

Suppose the Supreme Court gets a case about the meaning of Title VII. Suppose the Justices review the relevant legal materials—the text of Title VII, precedents, possibly the statute's legislative history—and conclude that the law is indeterminate. Consequently, the Justices have legal discretion in resolving the case. Suppose the Justices prefer interpretation *J*. According to the attitudinal model, the Justices will select interpretation *J*. But this will prompt an override. The House, Senate, and President prefer interpretations right of *J*. They will pass a new statute that amends Title VII to achieve their preferred interpretation.

If the Justices foresee this override, will they select interpretation *J*? No. They can do better by selecting the interpretation at *H*. This interpretation gets the Justices as close as possible to their preferred outcome without provoking an override from the other branches. The *strategic model* predicts that the Justices will choose *H*.

[96] Discrimination on the Basis of Pregnancy, 1977: Hearings on S. 995 Before the Subcommittee on Labor of the Senate Commission on Human Resources, 95th Cong., 1st Sess. (1977) (opening statement of Sen. Williams).

[97] This kind of model originated in Brian Marks, *A Model of Judicial Influence on Congressional Policymaking: "Grove City College v. Bell"*, Working Paper in Political Science P-88-7 (1988). Important works expanded on it. *See, e.g.*, Rafael Gely & Pablo T. Spiller, *A Rational Choice Theory of Supreme Court Statutory Decisions with Applications to the* State Farm *and* Grove City *Cases*, 6 J.L. Econ. & Org. 263 (1990); John Ferejohn & Charles Shipan, *Congressional Influence on Bureaucracy*, 6 J.L. Econ. & Org. 1 (1990); William N. Eskridge, Jr., *Overriding Supreme Court Statutory Interpretation Decisions*, 101 Yale L.J. 331 (1991).

We can generalize from this example. If the Justices prefer any interpretation left of *H*, the strategic model predicts that they will select *H*. If the Justices prefer any interpretation right of *P*, the model predicts that they will choose *P*. *For ideal points outside the equilibrium set, the Court is constrained.* What if the Justices prefer an interpretation between *H* and *P*? The range between *H* and *P* is the equilibrium set. For any interpretation in this range, at least one actor will oppose any move rightward, and at least one actor will oppose any move leftward. All three actors must agree to pass a new statute that overrides the Court. Thus, the Justices can select their preferred interpretation without provoking an override. *For ideal points inside the equilibrium set, the Court is unconstrained.*

Lawyers often debate judicial discretion. Judges have *legal* discretion when the law they interpret is indeterminate, perhaps because its language is vague (what counts as a "vehicle"?). Judges exercise legal discretion when they select a precise meaning for the law. Judges have *policy* discretion when their decisions are not subject to override, irrespective of whether their decisions are right as a matter of law. The strategic model of adjudication illuminates judges' policy discretion. For the court of last resort, its policy discretion matches the equilibrium set. In Figure 10.7, the Supreme Court can select any interpretation of Title VII between *H* and *S*.

The strategic model makes sharp predictions about the relationship between judges' policy discretion and the other branches of government. Under unified government, one political party controls the House, Senate, and presidency. The ideal points of *H*, *S*, and *P* tend to cluster together under unified government, meaning the Supreme Court's policy discretion is narrow. Under divided government, different political parties control the other branches. For example, Democrats might control the House while Republicans control the Senate and the presidency. The ideal points *H*, *S*, and *P* tend to separate under divided government, widening the Supreme Court's policy discretion.

In theory, strategic judges should never get overridden. They should always select interpretations within the equilibrium set. In reality, the House, Senate, and President often cooperate to override the Supreme Court.[98] Does this mean the Justices do not behave as the strategic model predicts? Not necessarily. To act strategically, judges need good information. They need to know the ideal points of the political actors. For their interpretations to endure, judges need to know the ideal points of *future* political actors—legislators and executives who have not yet been elected (or even born). Judges do not possess this information. Thus, overrides do not disprove the strategic model. Politicians might override the Court because the Justices failed to act strategically, or because the Justices acted strategically but made a mistake.[99]

Questions

10.15. Use Figure 10.7 to explain this statement: "Sometimes the Supreme Court has policy discretion but not legal discretion."

[98] *See* William N. Eskridge, Jr. & Matthew R. Christiansen, *Congressional Overrides of Supreme Court Statutory Interpretation Decisions, 1967–2011*, 92 TEX. L. REV. 1317 (2014).

[99] For an empirical test of the strategic model, and a helpful discussion of the associated challenges, see Jeffrey A. Segal, Chad Westerland, & Stefanie A. Lindquist, *Congress, the Supreme Court, and Judicial Review: Testing a Constitutional Separation of Powers Model*, 55 AM. J. POL. SCI. 89 (2011).

10.16. In 2017, President Trump attempted to rescind the Deferred Action for Childhood Arrivals (DACA) program, which prevented the government from deporting certain noncitizens from the United States. Challengers argued that this decision violated the Administrative Procedure Act and the Fifth Amendment of the U.S. Constitution.[100] The Supreme Court could resolve the case on statutory grounds or on constitutional grounds. Which approach would give the Court more policy discretion? Given the choice, why do courts tend to resolve cases on statutory, not constitutional, grounds?[101]

10.17. Suppose the Justices choose interpretation *J* in Figure 10.7.
- (a) What set of interpretations does the House prefer to *J*? What about the Senate and the President?
- (b) The House, Senate, and President must agree to replace *J*. What is the broadest (that is, furthest to the right) law that they will agree to enact?

10.18. To override the Court, Congress must enact a statute. Statutes originate in committees, like the House Committee on the Judiciary. In general, the House cannot consider a bill unless the committee votes in favor of it first. Under a *closed* rule, the House can approve or reject the committee's bill, but it cannot amend the committee's bill. Under an *open* rule, the House can amend the committee's bill.[102]
- (a) In Figure 10.7, suppose the House committee most prefers an interpretation just left of *J*. What interpretation would strategic Justices select given a closed rule? What about an open rule?
- (b) In Figure 10.7, suppose the House committee most prefers an interpretation just right of *J*. What interpretation would strategic Justices select given a closed rule? What about an open rule?

Strategic Interpretation

The strategic model illuminates policy discretion. Can it illuminate legal discretion too? Consider the Religious Land Use and Institutionalized Persons Act (RLUIPA), which protects religious exercise. RLUIPA states that it "shall be construed in favor of a broad protection of religious exercise."[103] This language instructs judges and other interpreters to read the act broadly.

Figure 10.8 depicts possible interpretations of RLUIPA, with the narrowest interpretation (little protection of religion) on the left end and the broadest interpretation on the right end. *S*, *P*, and H_1 represent the ideal points of the Senate, President, and House that enacted RLUIPA (ignore H_2 for now). The spatial model helps

[100] *See* Dep't of Homeland Sec. v. Regents of the Univ. of California, 140 S. Ct. 1891 (2020).

[101] *See* Pablo Spiller & Matthew L. Spitzer, *Judicial Choice of Legal Doctrines*, 8 J.L. Econ. & Org. 8 (1992).

[102] On open and closed rules, see, for example, Kenneth A. Shepsle & Barry R. Weingast, *The Institutional Foundations of Committee Power*, 81 Am. Pol. Sci. Rev. 85 (1987); Michael Doran, *The Closed Rule*, 59 Emory L.J. 1363 (2010).

[103] 42 U.S.C. § 2000cc-3(g). Here is the full quote: "This chapter shall be construed in favor of a broad protection of religious exercise, to the maximum extent permitted by the terms of this chapter and the Constitution." To simplify, we ignore the second clause.

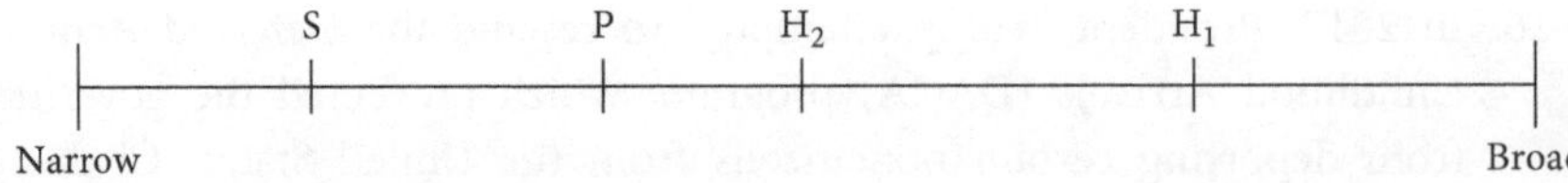

Figure 10.8. Interpretations of RLUIPA

visualize the interpretive instruction. When RLUIPA is subject to multiple, plausible interpretations, judges should select the interpretation furthest to the right.

Suppose a provision of RLUIPA has two plausible interpretations, one at H_1 and one right of H_1. Which one should a judge select? The literal language in the instruction—RLUIPA "shall be construed in favor of a broad protection"—suggests that the judge should select the interpretation right of H_1. But perhaps the judge should not read the instruction literally. The House, Senate, and President would not have enacted an interpretation right of H_1. All three actors prefer an interpretation at H_1 to any alternative on its right. A judge focused on the intentions of RLUIPA's drafters might read the instruction like this: "Construe the law broadly, but do not adopt a construction that the enacting House, Senate, and President would reject."

Suppose that an election changes the composition of the House, Senate, and President. The new House has ideal point H_2. To simplify, assume that the ideal points of the Senate and President have not changed, even though their membership has. A case about RLUIPA arises, and the provision in question has two plausible interpretations, one at H_1 and the other at H_2. The interpretation at H_1 offers the broadest protection, so perhaps the judge should select H_1. But what will happen if she does? The House, Senate, and President will pass a new statute that overrides the court. The new statute will implement protection left of H_2. If the judge foresees this, should she select the interpretation at H_1? Would it be more faithful to the intentions of RLUIPA's drafters to select H_2? If the judge selects H_2, is she acting in accordance with the strategic model or the legal model of judging?[104]

D. The Strategic Model: Judicial Hierarchy

Sometimes judges engage in strategic games with legislators and executives, as discussed earlier. Other times judges play games with other judges. Consider Stephen Reinhardt, who spent 37 years on the U.S. Court of Appeals for the Ninth Circuit. He was a liberal judge, and the conservative Supreme Court frequently overturned his decisions. A student asked Judge Reinhardt why he made decisions that he knew the Supreme Court would reject. The judge smiled and said, "They can't catch 'em all."[105] In this section we study games among judges, like the game Judge Reinhardt played with the Supreme Court.[106]

[104] *See* John A. Ferejohn & Barry Weingast, *A Positive Theory of Statutory Interpretation*, 12 INT'L REV. L. ECON. 263 (1992).

[105] Linda Greenhouse, *Dissenting Against the Supreme Court's Rightward Shift*, N.Y. TIMES, Apr. 12, 2018.

[106] For an overview of strategy in the judicial hierarchy, see Jonathan P. Kastellec, *The Judicial Hierarchy: A Review Essay*, *in* OXFORD RESEARCH ENCYCLOPEDIA OF POLITICS (2017).

Most judicial systems are organized in a hierarchy. In the United States, the federal system has district (trial) courts on bottom, appellate courts in the middle, and the Supreme Court on top. Like regular people, judges sometimes disagree with one another. Disagreement can lead lower courts to make decisions that higher courts oppose. Higher courts cannot discipline lower court judges in the usual ways. Appellate judges, for example, cannot fire trial judges for bad decisions or pay them for good decisions. But higher courts do have some tools at their disposal. They can review and overturn lower court decisions. They can remand cases, forcing lower court judges to adjudicate them again. A high court can adopt a lower court's reasoning, which grows the latter's reputation, and so on. Varying preferences and a limited capacity to punish supply the ingredients for a strategic game.

To begin, consider a game between appellate courts and the Supreme Court. To make the game concrete, we present it in the context of a case, *American Legion v. American Humanist Association*.[107] In 1925, a private organization used private funds to build a 40-foot-tall cross honoring soldiers killed in World War I. Ninety years later, the cross still stood, but the land beneath it belonged to the government, and the government paid to illuminate and maintain the cross. The question was whether this arrangement violated the Establishment Clause in the U.S. Constitution. That clause prohibits the state from making any law "respecting an establishment of religion."[108] The appellate court found a constitutional violation, but the Supreme Court reversed, holding that the cross could remain.

Figure 10.9 captures the case. The dimension indicates the breadth of the Establishment Clause. The point *A* represents the appellate court's ideal interpretation, which is relatively broad. This interpretation would require more separation of church and state and prohibit the cross. The point *S* represents the Supreme Court's ideal interpretation, which is narrower. The Court would require less separation of church and state and permit the cross.

If unconstrained, the appellate court would adopt interpretation *A*. However, the Supreme Court has the power to review the case and adopt a different interpretation, one that the appellate court might strongly oppose. During its review, the Supreme Court could even punish the appellate court, perhaps by criticizing its reasoning. Given these risks, what interpretation should the appellate court adopt? The answer depends on the Supreme Court's ability to review the lower court. If the Supreme Court can review at zero cost, then the appellate court should select interpretation *S*. Any other choice would trigger punishment that the lower court does not want. In reality, the Supreme Court cannot review at zero cost. Every year the Court reviews about 80 cases among the thousands decided by appellate courts. Thus, the Court has limited capacity. Furthermore, correcting an appellate court requires the Supreme Court to write an opinion, which takes valuable time. For the Supreme Court, review is not always worth the trouble.

Figure 10.9 visualizes this trade-off. As the interpretation drifts rightward from *S*, the Supreme Court's dissatisfaction grows. We can restate this idea using language from the chapter on delegation. As the interpretation moves rightward from *S*, the Supreme

[107] 139 S. Ct. 2067 (2019).
[108] U.S. CONST. amend. I.

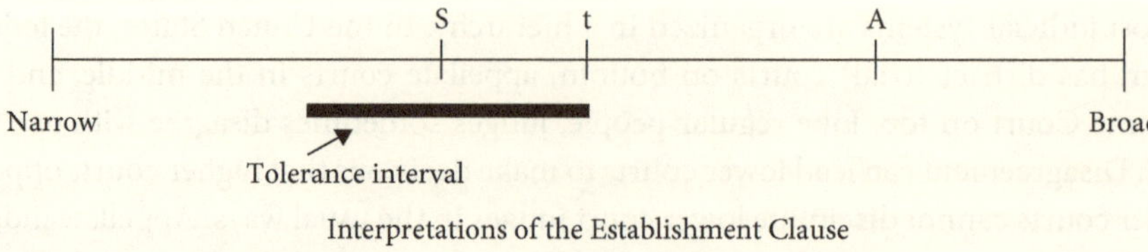

Figure 10.9. Strategy in the Judicial Hierarchy

Court's *diversion costs* grow. At some point the costs become so large that the Court is better off reviewing and correcting the appellate court. The point *t* marks the tipping point. For interpretations between *S* and *t*, the Supreme Court's review costs exceed its diversion costs, so the Court will not review. For interpretations right of *t*, the Court's diversion costs exceed its review costs, so the Court will review and adopt interpretation *S*.

Just as the appellate court cannot select an interpretation too far right of *S*, it cannot select one too far left of *S*. Figure 10.9 captures these limitations with the shaded tolerance interval. If the appellate court makes a decision inside the tolerance interval, the Supreme Court will not intervene, and the interpretation will stand. In Figure 10.9, a strategic appellate court will select interpretation *t*.

The tolerance interval represents the appellate court's discretionary power. As the Supreme Court's review costs increase, the appellate court's discretionary power grows. What factors affect the Court's review costs? To be specific, what are the costs to the Supreme Court of reviewing the appellate court's decision in *American Legion*? Here is a generalization. As the number of other cases to review increases, as the Court's interest in those other cases grows, and as the gap between the preferences of the Supreme Court and other appellate courts widens, the costs of reviewing *American Legion* increase.

We have analyzed a strategic game involving the *rule*, meaning the interpretation that becomes a precedent. Appellate court decisions also involve a *disposition*, meaning a determination of who won. We can fold the disposition into the game.[109] In *American Legion*, the Supreme Court wanted a narrow interpretation of the Establishment Clause (the rule) and a disposition in favor of the government (the cross can stay in place). If the appellate court chose a broad interpretation and a disposition against the government, the Supreme Court would surely review it. What if the appellate court chose a broad interpretation but a disposition in *favor* of the government? This would weaken the Supreme Court's incentive to review. To generalize, lower courts have more interpretive discretion when they issue dispositions favorable to the higher court, and they have more discretion over the disposition when they issue interpretations favorable to the higher court.

We have studied Supreme Court review of one appellate court. In reality, the Supreme Court reviews decisions by many appellate courts. The high court can manage this complexity by reviewing *outliers*, meaning those appellate decisions furthest from its ideal point. This strategy provokes competition among appellate courts. No appellate court wants to be the outlier, so all move closer to the Supreme Court's preferences.[110]

[109] *See, e.g.*, Clifford J. Carrubba & Tom S. Clark, *Rule Creation in a Political Hierarchy*, 106 AM. POL. SCI. REV. 622 (2012).

[110] *See, e.g.*, Matthew D. McCubbins, Roger G. Noll, & Barry R. Weingast, *Politics and the Courts: A Positive Theory of Judicial Doctrine and the Rule of Law*, 68 S. CAL. L. REV. 1631 (1995); Matt Spitzer & Eric Talley, *Judicial Auditing*, 29 J. LEGAL STUD. 649 (2000).

To identify outliers, the Supreme Court sometimes looks for dissenting opinions. To illustrate, suppose an appellate court gets a case with two possible outcomes, *A* and *B*. Two of the appellate judges prefer *A*, but the third judge and the Supreme Court believe that *B* is correct. If the first two appellate judges choose *A*, the third judge can write a dissent arguing that *B* is the proper outcome. Like a whistleblower, the dissenting judge can expose the appellate court's error to the Supreme Court.[111] The threat of whistleblowing discourages the appellate court from choosing *A* in the first instance.

We have studied strategy between the Supreme Court and appellate courts. Next, we discuss strategy between appellate courts and district courts. Unlike the U.S. Supreme Court, which hears only about 80 cases per year, appellate courts hear nearly every case that gets appealed (they have *mandatory* jurisdiction). However, automatic appeal does not mean automatic reversal. Appellate courts often juggle dozens of cases simultaneously. They cannot review every case completely and carefully. If the record is long or confusing, if the district court's opinion seems carefully reasoned, and if the district court's interpretation seems close (or close enough) to what the appellate court prefers, then the appellate court will not reverse.[112] The costs of reversal give district courts some discretion.

The extent of a lower court's discretion depends on the standard of review. Appellate courts review conclusions of law *de novo*, meaning from scratch. By contrast, appellate courts review findings of fact for clear error. To illustrate the difference, imagine a case about pollution. The district court concludes that the law permits mercury emissions up to 8 units (conclusion of law) and that the defendant emitted 10 units (finding of fact). The appellate court will reconsider the law afresh. If it concludes that the best interpretation of the law permits emissions up to 12 units, then the law permits emissions up to 12 units. However, the appellate court will defer on the facts. Unless the district court *clearly erred*, the appellate court will accept that the defendant emitted 10 units of mercury.

Different standards of review give district judges more discretion over facts than law. In the pollution example, suppose the appellate court thinks the law permits emissions up to 12 units, and suppose the district judge wants to find the defendant liable. The district judge might conclude that law permits emissions up to 12 units and the defendant emitted 14. This would be harder to reverse than a conclusion that law permits emissions up to 8 units and the defendant emitted 10.[113]

Questions

10.19. The district judge concludes that the law permits up to 12 units of pollution and that Opal emitted 14 units of pollution. The appellate court believes that

[111] *See* Frank B. Cross & Emerson H. Tiller, *Judicial Partisanship and Obedience to Legal Doctrine: Whistleblowing on the Federal Courts of Appeals*, 107 YALE L.J. 2155 (1998). *See also* Jonathan P. Kastellec, *Hierarchal and Collegial Politics on the U.S. Courts of Appeals*, 73 J. POL. 345 (2011).

[112] *See generally* Susan B. Haire, Stefanie A. Lindquist, & Donald R. Songer, *Appellate Court Supervision in the Federal Judiciary: A Hierarchical Perspective*, 37 LAW & SOC'Y REV. 143 (2003).

[113] On fact "shading" by district judges, see Nicola Gennaioli & Andrew Shleifer, *Judicial Fact Discretion*, 37 J. LEGAL STUD. 1 (2008). *See also* Joshua B. Fischman & Max M. Schanzenbach, *Do Standards of Review Matter? The Case of Federal Criminal Sentencing*, 40 J. LEGAL STUD. 405 (2011).

the district judge has intentionally overstated the pollution and that Opal should not be held liable. To counter the district court's manipulation of fact, the appellate court could manipulate law by holding that law permits up to 14 units of pollution. What are the costs and benefits of this strategy?[114]

10.20. Appellate judges can "blow the whistle" by writing dissents that criticize the reasoning and conclusions of their colleagues. The Supreme Court relies on whistleblowers to identify outlying cases for review.[115]
(a) If you were a Supreme Court Justice, would you prefer that dissenting opinions be common or rare? (Hint: would dissents be helpful if every opinion included one?)
(b) Suppose the Supreme Court is conservative. In general, which is more likely to attract the Court's attention, liberal whistleblowers or conservative whistleblowers?
(c) Suppose the appellate panel has two judges in the majority and one judge in dissent. Why might the Supreme Court pay more attention if the dissenting judge has moderate views rather than extreme views?

Panel Effects

Skeptics believe that adjudication is ideological. Judges simply vote their politics as the attitudinal model predicts. If judges vote their politics, we should see many dissenting opinions. But we don't. In the United States, three-judge panels hear appeals in federal cases. The three judges on a panel often have different political views. One judge might have been appointed by a conservative Republican President while the other two were appointed by liberal Democratic presidents. Yet three-judge panels usually reach unanimous decisions. Harry Edwards, the chief judge of the D.C. Circuit Court of Appeals, argued that low dissent rates disprove the skeptics. Rather than voting their politics, he argued that judges find "the correct judgment in a given case."[116]

Why do politically diverse judges agree so often? Scholars studying this question discovered something interesting. The propensity of a judge to decide a particular way depends on the other judges. To illustrate, suppose Pablo is a conservative judge on a three-judge panel. The odds of Pablo making a conservative decision are smallest when the other two judges are liberal, larger when one of the other judges is conservative, and largest when both other judges are conservative. To generalize, conservative judges behave more conservatively, and liberal judges behave more liberally, when surrounded by like-minded colleagues. Scholars call this *panel effects*.[117]

[114] *See* Sepehr Shahshahani, *The Fact-Law Distinction: Strategic Factfinding and Lawmaking in a Judicial Hierarchy*, 37 J.L. Econ. & Org. 440 (2021).

[115] The following questions grow from Deborah Beim, Alexander V. Hirsch, & Jonathan P. Kastellec, *Whistleblowing and Compliance in the Judicial Hierarchy*, 58 Am. J. Pol. Sci. 904 (2014).

[116] Harry T. Edwards, *Collegiality and Decision Making on the D.C. Circuit*, 84 Va. L. Rev. 1335, 1359 (1998).

[117] *See* Richard L. Revesz, *Environmental Regulation, Ideology, and the D.C. Circuit*, 83 Va. L. Rev. 1717 (1997); Cass R. Sunstein, David Schkade, Lisa M. Ellman, & Andres Sawicki, Are Judges Political? An Empirical Analysis of the Federal Judiciary (2006); Jonathan P. Kastellec, *Panel Composition and Voting on the U.S. Courts of Appeals over Time*, 64 Pol. Res. Q. 377 (2011); Lee Epstein, William M. Landes,

Panel effects operate beyond political ideology. Suppose a female plaintiff brings a sex discrimination case. The probability of a male judge ruling for the plaintiff increases when a female judge joins the panel.[118] Similarly, the probability of a white judge voting in favor of minority rights increases when a black judge joins the panel.[119]

What explains panel effects? Scholars have different theories.[120] Perhaps judges share information. To illustrate, a female judge might have perspective on sex discrimination that affects her male colleagues' votes.[121] Perhaps judges behave strategically. To prevent whistleblowing, conservative judges might moderate their views when a liberal judge joins the panel.[122] Perhaps judges simply "go along" with their colleagues, either because dissenting takes too much effort[123] or because judges follow a norm of consensus.[124]

Panel effects make it hard to assess judicial opinions. To illustrate, professional ethics usually discourage lawyers from bringing weak cases. Suppose you lose an appeal three votes to zero. Does this mean your case was weak? Appellate panels usually reach unanimous decisions, just like Judge Edwards said. Does unanimity imply that law is determinate and judges simply find correct answers?

III. Normative Theory of Adjudication

We have presented a positive theory of adjudication. The positive theory addresses questions like why litigants file lawsuits, when bargaining among them will succeed, and how judges decide cases. Now we turn to a normative theory of adjudication. We concentrate on a question of special interest to lawyers: How *should* judges decide cases? To resolve disputes, judges must find facts and interpret law. In an ideal world, judges would promptly find all facts and correctly interpret all laws. In the real world, fact-finding and law interpretation take time and effort. Economists take all costs into account. According to economic theory, judges should balance the benefits of accuracy in adjudication against its costs.

& RICHARD A. POSNER, THE BEHAVIOR OF FEDERAL JUDGES: A THEORETICAL AND EMPIRICAL STUDY OF RATIONAL CHOICE (2013).

118 *See* Christina L. Boyd, Lee Epstein, & Andrew D. Martin, *Untangling the Causal Effects of Sex on Judging*, 54 AM. J. POL. SCI. 389 (2010).

119 Adam B. Cox & Thomas J. Miles, *Judging the Voting Rights Act*, 108 COLUM. L. REV. 1 (2008); Jonathan P. Kastellec, *Racial Diversity and Judicial Influence on Appellate Courts*, 57 AM. J. POL. SCI. 167 (2013).

120 For summaries of the theories and citations to the original work, see Joshua B. Fischman, *Interpreting Circuit Court Voting Patterns: A Social Interactions Framework*, 31 J.L. ECON. & ORG. 808, 831–34 (2015); Emerson H. Tiller, *The Law and Positive Political Theory of Panel Effects*, 44 J. LEGAL STUD. S35 (2015).

121 Christina L. Boyd, Lee Epstein, & Andrew D. Martin, *Untangling the Causal Effects of Sex on Judging*, 54 AM. J. POL. SCI. 389 (2010). *See also* Matthew Spitzer & Eric Talley, *Left, Right, and Center: Strategic Information Acquisition and Diversity in Judicial Panels*, 29 J.L. ECON. & ORG. 638 (2013).

122 Frank B. Cross & Emerson H. Tiller, *Judicial Partisanship and Obedience to Legal Doctrine: Whistleblowing on the Federal Courts of Appeals*, 107 YALE L.J. 2155 (1998). *See also* Jonathan P. Kastellec, *Hierarchal and Collegial Politics on the U.S. Courts of Appeals*, 73 J. POL. 345 (2011).

123 Richard A. Posner, *What Do Judges and Justices Maximize? (The Same Thing Everybody Else Does)*, 3 SUP. CT. ECON. REV. 1, 20 (1993).

124 Joshua B. Fischman, *Interpreting Circuit Court Voting Patterns: A Social Interactions Framework*, 31 J.L. ECON. & ORG. 808, 831–34 (2015).

A. Accuracy in Fact-Finding

Did the nuclear plant leak? Did the employer discriminate? Did the cop punch the suspect? To resolve disputes, judges must find facts. Errors in fact-finding can cause injustice in the individual case. They can also cause broader social problems. Earlier we discussed a litigation externality, which arises when a case has effects beyond the parties. Errors in fact-finding can cause negative externalities, as we will explain.

Law punishes people for behaving badly. Punishment serves different purposes. One purpose involves retribution: lawbreakers "get what they deserve." Economists usually focus on a different purpose of punishment: deterrence. By punishing lawbreaking today, we can prevent more lawbreaking tomorrow. The mere threat of punishment can deter wrongdoing. The threat of imprisonment prevents people from stealing cars, corrupting officials, and selling state secrets.

Errors in fact-finding can weaken deterrence.[125] To take a simple example, suppose that Quita drove faster than the speed limit, and an officer gave her a ticket. Quita challenges the ticket in court, and the judge makes an error of fact. Quita sped, but the judge concludes that she did not, so Quita does not pay a fine. This error is a *false negative*. The judge concludes that something did not happen when in fact it did. If Quita expects the judge to make similar errors in the future, she will drive even faster than before. If other drivers expect similar errors, they will drive faster too, even though they were outside the case. False negatives reduce punishment, causing more lawbreaking.

Consider the opposite case. Quita did not speed, but an officer ticketed her anyway. Quita challenges the ticket in court, and the judge concludes that Quita sped, so she must pay a fine. This error is a *false positive*. The judge concludes that something happened when in fact it did not. False positives can lead to grave injustice, as when innocent people go to prison. False positives can also weaken deterrence. If Quita expects the judge to make similar errors in the future, she might reason as follows: "I will get fined whether I speed or not. I might as well speed." Drivers outside of the case might reason the same way. False positives punish people who obey the law, encouraging them to disobey the law.

We have explained that errors in fact-finding encourage unlawful behavior. They can also discourage lawful behavior. To demonstrate, suppose the fine for speeding is high. Quita would like to drive her car—to work, to shop, to see friends and family. But if she drives, she might have to pay a fine for speeding, even if she does not speed. If the fine is high enough, Quita will not drive, or she will drive so slowly that no judge could conclude she sped. At a minimum, the risk of a false positive wastes Quita's time by causing her to drive slowly. It could even prevent her from driving at all, even though she would drive lawfully. Other drivers face the same dilemma. False positives can waste many people's time and prevent many people from engaging in valuable activities.

In sum, errors in fact-finding can impose significant costs on society. Consequently, accuracy in fact-finding conveys significant benefits. But accuracy is not cheap. Consider

[125] The following discussion draws on Louis Kaplow & Steven Shavell, *Accuracy in the Determination of Liability*, 37 J.L. Econ. 1 (1994); Louis Kaplow, *The Value of Accuracy in Adjudication: An Economic Analysis*, 23 J. Legal Stud. 307 (1994); I.P.L. Png, *Optimal Subsidies and Damages in the Presence of Judicial Error*, 6 Int'l Rev. L. Econ. 101 (1986).

Quita's case. How can a judge determine if she sped? Quita will have to testify. If Quita had a passenger in the car, the passenger might have to testify too. The officer will testify, and he will have to explain how he measured Quita's speed. Did he use a radar? What did the radar say? Did wind or rain affect the reading? What about intervening vehicles? Time spent on these issues cannot be spent on others. Quita will miss work, and the officer will spend his day in court instead of on patrol. Other cases will languish on the court's docket. Fact-finding creates opportunity costs for litigants and society.

We have described the costs of fact-finding in a simple case about speeding. Imagine the costs in a complicated case. One class action lawsuit involving securities fraud lasted eight years.[126] Another lawsuit over discrimination in the workplace lasted nine years.[127] *Shelby County v. Holder* addressed the constitutionality of the Voting Rights Act, and the record in the case exceeded 15,000 pages.[128]

Economists take all costs into account. In adjudication, this means weighing the costs of inaccuracy against the costs of error correction. Judges should gather more information until the marginal benefit to society of increased accuracy just equals the marginal cost of fact-finding.

Questions

10.21. Before approving a new drug, the Food and Drug Administration (FDA) must find facts. Does the drug work? Does it cause side effects? The FDA can gather many facts (exhaustive studies, extensive review of data), or it can gather few facts. If you ran the FDA, how many facts would you gather? Would you gather more facts for a vaccine against COVID than you would for, say, a drug to prevent hair loss?

10.22. Some CEOs defraud investors. The investors can sue for damages. To illustrate, if Roger the CEO caused $1 million in harm to investors, the investors can demand that Roger pay them $1 million in damages.[129]

(a) Suppose courts usually underestimate damages. In Roger's case, the court orders him to pay only $800,000, even though he caused $1 million in harm. What effect does consistent underestimation of damages have on deterrence?

(b) Suppose courts usually overestimate damages. In Roger's case, the court orders him to pay $1.5 million, even though he caused only $1 million in harm. What effect does consistent overestimation of damages have on deterrence?

(c) Suppose courts make random errors when calculating damages. For every case in which they overestimate damages by $100,000, another case exists in which they underestimate damages by $100,000. What effect do random errors in damages have on deterrence?

[126] Carpenters Health & Welfare Fund v. Coca-Cola Co., 587 F. Supp. 2d 1266, 1271 (N.D. Ga. 2008).
[127] Stagi v. Nat'l R.R. Passenger Corp., 880 F. Supp. 2d 564, 570 (E.D. Pa. 2012).
[128] 570 U.S. 529, 565 (2013) (Ginsburg, J., dissenting). Many cases have much longer records than this!
[129] The following questions grow from Louis Kaplow & Steven Shavell, *Accuracy in the Assessment of Damages*, 39 J.L. Econ. 191 (1996).

Procedural Due Process

The Fifth Amendment of the U.S. Constitution forbids the federal government from depriving anyone of "life, liberty, or property, without due process of law."[130] This is the *Due Process Clause*. What counts as due process? The Supreme Court addressed this question in *Mathews v. Eldridge*.[131] George Eldridge suffered from anxiety and pain. In 1968, he began receiving disability benefits from the government. In 1972, the government concluded that Eldridge's health had improved, though Eldridge disagreed. The government terminated the benefits without holding a hearing, meaning Eldridge had no opportunity to present his case in person. Eldridge claimed that failing to hold a hearing violated the Due Process Clause.

Terminating the benefits deprived Eldridge of a "property" interest. What about the process? The government gathered information from Eldridge and his doctors. The government shared its report with Eldridge, and it gave him an opportunity to present evidence in writing. So the government followed a fact-finding process. Did it provide *due* process? The Supreme Court said yes. The government did not violate the Constitution.

In reaching this conclusion, the Court identified three factors for courts to consider when deciding if the Due Process Clause requires additional procedures. First, "the degree of potential deprivation that may be created by a particular decision." Second, "the probable value, if any, of additional procedural safeguards." And third, "the administrative burden and other societal costs that would be associated with requiring, as a matter of constitutional right, an evidentiary hearing."[132]

We can express these factors algebraically. Let H equal the harm of an erroneous deprivation. This is factor one. Let p equal the probability of an erroneous deprivation. This is factor two. Let B equal the burden (or "cost") to society of additional procedures. This is factor three. We can combine these factors into a familiar equation: $B < p * H$.[133] Understood in marginal terms, the left side of the equation represents the cost of additional procedures. The right side of the equation represents the benefit of additional procedures. Additional procedures create a benefit by reducing the probability of an error. If the benefit of additional procedures exceeds the cost, the Constitution requires the procedures.

Let's apply the equation to Eldridge's case. Losing disability benefits would impose a cost on him. Assume the cost would equal \$1,000, so H equals \$1,000. Eldridge sought a hearing prior to the termination of his benefits. Holding a hearing would require time and effort. In money, assume the hearing would cost \$100, so B equals \$100. A hearing would give Eldridge and the government another opportunity to present evidence about his health. More evidence would reduce the probability of an error. Let's assume that without a hearing, the probability of an error would equal 20 percent. With a hearing, the probability of an error would equal 15 percent. Thus,

[130] U.S. CONST. amend. V.
[131] 424 U.S. 319 (1976).
[132] *Id.* at 341–47.
[133] This matches the Hand Formula applied in tort law. Judge Hand expressed that formula in *United States v. Carroll Towing Co.*, 159 F.2d 169 (2d. Cir. 1947). We used the formula in our discussion of speech.

the hearing would reduce the probability of an error by five percentage points. Now we can solve the equation. The cost of the hearing ($B = \$100$) exceeds its expected benefit ($.05 * \$1{,}000 = \$50$). A rational government would not pay $100 to save $50.

According to the test in *Mathews v. Eldridge*, the Due Process Clause does not require a hearing in this numerical example. If the hearing would reduce the probability of an error by more than 10 percentage points, then the Constitution would require a hearing. The Court's test captures the economic approach to fact-finding.

Let's assume the Court made the right decision in *Mathews*. The benefits to society of an in-person hearing did not justify the costs. Why might Eldridge sue anyway? Would he internalize the benefits of a hearing? Would he internalize the costs?

B. Accuracy in Interpretation

Officials boarded the boat of John Yates, a fisherman in the Gulf of Mexico. The officials discovered dozens of grouper (a kind of fish) shorter than 20 inches in length. Law required grouper shorter than 20 inches to be released. The officials ordered Yates to keep the unlawful catch until he returned to port, at which time a fuller investigation would commence. While returning to port, Yates and his crew threw the fish overboard. A prosecutor charged Yates with violating the following statute:

> Whoever knowingly alters, destroys, mutilates, conceals, covers up, falsifies, or makes a false entry in any record, document, or tangible object with the intent to impede, obstruct, or influence the investigation or proper administration of any matter within the jurisdiction of any department or agency of the United States . . . shall be fined under this title, imprisoned not more than 20 years, or both.[134]

According to the prosecutor, Yates knowingly destroyed a "tangible object"—the grouper—with the intent to obstruct an investigation.

Yates's case reached the U.S. Supreme Court,[135] and it did not depend on facts. Everyone agreed that he threw the fish overboard. The case depended on law. Did Yates violate the statute? The question is harder than it seems. Focus on the statute's language. Yates "altered" the location of the fish by throwing them in the sea. But he did not "alter" the fish themselves, nor did he "destroy" or "mutilate" them. You might say he "concealed" or "covered up" the fish, but usually we don't use those words in that way. When you "conceal" something, you know where to find it. Yates could not find the fish again. One cannot "falsify" or make a "false entry" in a fish.

Moving down the statute, is a fish a "tangible object"? Yes, in the literal sense. You can see and touch a fish (as opposed to, say, a dream). But the statute does not say "tangible objects" in isolation. It forbids destruction of "any record, document, or tangible object." For lists like this, lawyers often apply a canon of construction called *noscitur a sociis*. According to that canon, each term in the list should mean

134 18 U.S.C. § 1519.
135 Yates v. United States, 574 U.S. 528 (2015).

something similar.[136] Thus, "tangible object" should mean something similar to "record" and "document." The term could include physical things that contain information, like chalkboards and hard drives, but exclude farmhouses, oil wells, and fish.[137]

Yates's case raised many other legal puzzles. To resolve the puzzles, judges applied different methods of interpretation. Later we will say more about those methods. Here we focus on a different issue: effort.

Like finding facts, interpreting law takes time and resources. One district judge, three appellate judges, and nine Supreme Court Justices considered Yates's case. Each spent hours (maybe days) studying statutes and writing opinions. Lawyers for Yates and the government did research, argued in court, and wrote motions and briefs. Everyone incurred opportunity costs. Does legal interpretation merit so much effort? Why work so hard to find the correct interpretation in one case, especially when the defendant is clearly blameworthy?

Like accuracy in fact-finding, accuracy in interpretation creates social benefits. To explain why, we return to a theme from an earlier chapter: institutional competence.

Consider the problem of speeding. Driving fast causes accidents. To prevent accidents, we should impose speed limits. But what should we choose as a maximum speed? The answer is not clear. Low speed limits reduce accidents, but they slow everyone down. Every commute and every delivery requires more time. High speed limits speed everyone up, but they cause more accidents. The optimal balance of safety and speed depends on facts like the condition of this road, the angle of that turn, and so on. It also depends on values. How much inconvenience should we bear to save a bumper? What about a life?

Making good law requires expertise and values. In a successful democracy, legislators and executives have both. They can hold hearings, hire engineers, commission reports, and conduct surveys. Elections should align their values with the public's values. In contrast, judges usually lack policy expertise. They usually cannot hire engineers, commission reports, or conduct surveys. Cases present them with particular facts about particular parties, not general phenomena. Independent judges lack accountability to the public. Consequently, their opinions and values can stray from the public's. For these reasons, legislators and executives usually make better law than judges.

Now we can return to interpretation. Through interpretation, judges find law's meaning. They find (or attempt to find) the meaning that legislators and executives agreed upon. Usually, the law that legislators and executives agreed upon is better than the law that judges would create.

Consider speed limits again. Suppose Quita sped while driving her sister to the hospital for a medical emergency. Does the speed limit contain an exception for medical emergencies? This question raises a difficult trade-off. Not speeding

[136] This canon aims in part to prevent superfluity. If "tangible object" takes its literal meaning, then it risks making the terms "record" and "document" superfluous. In general, lawyers assume that legislators do not use language superfluously.

[137] *See* Yates v. United States, 574 U.S. 528, 550 (2015) (Alito, J., concurring) ("the term 'tangible object' should refer to something similar to records or documents. A fish does not spring to mind—nor does an antelope, a colonial farmhouse, a hydrofoil, or an oil derrick. All are 'objects' that are 'tangible.' But who wouldn't raise an eyebrow if a neighbor, when asked to identify something similar to a 'record' or 'document,' said 'crocodile'?").

endangers the patient, but speeding endangers everyone. Suppose the correct interpretation of the law would punish Quita, but a court misinterprets the statute and does not punish her. This misinterpretation reduces punishment and weakens deterrence. Quita and other people in her situation can drive at speeds that legislators and executives wanted to forbid.

Suppose that the correct interpretation would *not* punish Quita, but the court misinterprets the statute and punishes her. This misinterpretation increases punishment beyond what legislators and executives agreed upon. False positives can discourage people from engaging in activities that they value and that legislators and executives agreed to support, like speeding to get sick people to the hospital.

We have explained that errors of law by judges tend to create social costs, whereas correct interpretations create social benefits. Seeking the correct interpretation uses the legal system's time and resources. Judges should continue interpreting until the marginal benefit from error correction just equals the marginal cost. The marginal benefit tends to be higher in certain circumstances: first, when the possible interpretations from which judges choose differ a lot; and second, when the interpretation will affect many people rather than few.

We can apply these ideas to *Yates*. Should the Supreme Court have taken the case? Remember the opportunity cost; the Court only hears about 80 cases each year. The fisherman was charged under the provision quoted earlier. Congress enacted the provision in the Sarbanes-Oxley Act of 2002, a statute designed to protect investors and restore trust in the economy after the collapse of the Enron Corporation. Remember the key question in the case: What counts as a "tangible object"? The term either means something narrow like "physical things that contain information," or something broad like "literally anything tangible." These two interpretations differ a lot. The broad interpretation would vastly expand the reach of the statute, subjecting thousands or millions of people to criminal penalties, including people like Yates who have nothing to do with corporations or bankruptcy. The Court held that "tangible object" has a narrow meaning. The fisherman did not violate this law.

Questions

10.23. The Supreme Court reviews lower court conclusions of law more carefully than lower court findings of fact. Why?

10.24. Why does the federal judiciary have three levels of courts (district, appellate, Supreme Court) instead of four or five?[138]

10.25. Recall the Condorcet Jury Theorem. To capture the wisdom of the crowd, the Supreme Court could have presented hundreds or even thousands of lawyers with the question in *Yates*. The lawyers could have voted independently on the proper interpretation of "tangible object" (narrow or broad). Why don't courts do this?

[138] *See* Charles M. Cameron & Lewis A. Kornhauser, *Decision Rules in a Judicial Hierarchy*, 161 J. Inst. Theoretical Econ. 264 (2005).

C. Indeterminacy and Default Rules

Sometimes law resembles a multiple-choice exam. Each legal question has a single, correct answer, and greater effort improves the odds of finding it. In such cases, law is determinate. In other cases, however, this analogy fails. Some legal issues do not have a single, correct answer. Perhaps the legal materials do not address the question at hand (is a commemorative jeep a "vehicle?"). Or perhaps the legal materials contradict one another. Consider the key phrase in *Yates*: "any record, document, or tangible object." Lawyers usually give words their ordinary meaning, and the ordinary meaning of "tangible object" encompasses fish. Furthermore, the word "any" suggests we should interpret the phrase broadly. But the canon *noscitur a sociis* suggests we should interpret the phrase narrowly.

In cases like *Yates*, law is indeterminate.[139] The legal question does not have a single, correct answer. Thus, judges have legal discretion, and different judges exercise that discretion differently. In *Yates*, five Justices interpreted "tangle object" narrowly, meaning the fisherman did not violate the law. The other four Justices dissented. They would have interpreted the phrase broadly and punished the fisherman.

Recall this prescription: judges should continue interpreting until the marginal benefit from error correction just equals the marginal cost. The prescription works for cases with determinate law. But it fails in cases with indeterminate law. Once a judge concludes the law is indeterminate, the marginal benefit of additional interpretation becomes zero, so the judge should stop interpreting. Yet the case is not finished. Someone must win, and someone must lose. The court might want to establish a precedent on the legal question. Because the law is indeterminate, the court does not know the answer.

To resolve cases with indeterminate law, judges need a default rule, meaning a rule to break the impasse. They could decide based on justice or liberty.[140] If justice demands a broad interpretation that would punish the fisherman, then the judge should interpret the law broadly. Often this approach will fail because the demands of justice and liberty are unclear. Different people have different conceptions of these values. Alternatively, judges could flip a coin. But this would make cases depend on luck rather than reason.

Early in the book we presented the median voter theorem. The positive version of the theorem makes a prediction: under certain conditions, majority rule causes law to gravitate toward the political center. The normative version of the theorem makes an assessment. If citizens have symmetrical preferences—the intensity of right-wing feeling offsets the intensity of left-wing feeling—setting law at the median maximizes social welfare. We can use the normative version of the theorem to generate a default rule for cases with indeterminate law: judges should select the interpretation closest to the preference of the median citizen. We call this the *median default*.

[139] Some scholars distinguish indeterminacy from underdeterminacy. Law is "indeterminate" when it fails to narrow the range of answers to the legal question, and law is "underdeterminate" when it narrows the range but not to one. We refer to both possibilities as "indeterminacy." Law is "metaphysically indeterminate" when no single, correct answer exists. Law is "epistemologically indeterminate" (or simply "inconclusive") when a single, correct answer exists, but judges lack the information necessary to find it.

[140] *See, e.g.*, RANDY E. BARNETT, RESTORING THE LOST CONSTITUTION (2004). Some jurists would include values like justice in the original determination of what law requires. This relates to an old debate on whether the "rule of law" requires substantive justice or simply fair notice, fair procedures, and the like.

To clarify the median default, consider an example involving five people from an earlier chapter: Kim, Larry, Mary, Ned, and Olivia. These five citizens have different opinions on the legalization of recreational drugs like heroin. Kim prefers to legalize most drugs, Olivia prefers not to legalize any drugs, and the others take positions in between. Suppose a court interprets a statute about legalizing drugs. To simplify, assume the statute only applies to these five citizens. The statute is indeterminate. One plausible interpretation aligns with Mary's preference, and the other plausible interpretation aligns with Ned's preference. According to the median default, the court should select the interpretation that aligns with Mary's preference because Mary is the median.

Having clarified the idea, we can apply the median default to a real case, *West Virginia University Hospitals, Inc. v. Casey*.[141] Residents of Pennsylvania received medical services from a hospital across the border in West Virginia. Some low-income patients used a government program to pay their hospital bills. When Pennsylvania reduced its payments to the hospital under that program, the hospital sued. To make its case, the hospital hired lawyers and experts in accounting. The hospital won the case. Afterward, the hospital wanted Pennsylvania to pay for its litigation expenses. The relevant statute authorized the court to award "a reasonable attorney's fee."[142] Thus, the court could make Pennsylvania pay for the hospital's lawyers. But what about the accountants? The hospital paid them over $100,000 to write reports and testify. Does "a reasonable attorney's fee" include fees paid to expert witnesses? This question reached the U.S. Supreme Court.

The Justices faced competing legal arguments. On the one hand, courts had long understood "attorney's fees" broadly. The term was understood to encompass not only fees paid to lawyers but also fees paid to lawyers' assistants and secretaries. Furthermore, the U.S. Senate produced a report about the statute in question. The report said, "[C]itizens must have the opportunity to recover *what it costs them*" to vindicate their rights.[143] All of this suggests that "attorney's fees" include expert witness fees. On the other hand, Congress had enacted other statutes about fee-shifting, and many of them distinguished between attorney and expert witness fees. For example, the Toxic Substances Control Act states that prevailing parties can recover "reasonable fees for attorneys *and expert witnesses*."[144] If members of Congress had wanted to shift expert fees in cases like the hospital's, they would have written "fees for attorneys *and expert witnesses*" in the statute, just like they did in the Toxic Substances Control Act.

The Supreme Court fractured, with the majority ruling against the hospital and three dissenting Justices taking the opposite view. To reach their conclusions, the Justices weighed the competing arguments and picked the one they found most convincing.

Suppose the Justices concluded that the statute was indeterminate and applied the median default. They would ask, "Which of the two competing interpretations would the median citizen prefer?" This might be a hard question to answer. But is it harder

141 499 U.S. 83 (1991).

142 42 U.S.C. § 1988 provides: "In any action or proceedings to enforce a provision of [various statutes], the court, in its discretion, may allow the prevailing party, other than the United States, a reasonable attorney's fee as part of the costs, except that in any action brought against a judicial officer for an act or omission taken in such officer's judicial capacity such officer shall not be held liable for any costs, including attorney's fees, unless such action was clearly in excess of such officer's jurisdiction."

143 West Virginia Univ. Hosps., Inc. v. Casey, 499 U.S. 83, 108 (1991) (Stevens, J., dissenting).

144 15 U.S.C. § 2618(d) (emphasis added).

than deciding which competing legal argument is strongest? Probably the median citizen would think that the state of Pennsylvania, having violated the law, should have to pay for the hospital's expert witnesses.[145]

The median default raises a question of timing: Should judges seek the median citizen at the time of enactment, or the median citizen at the time of interpretation? Sometimes judges interpret laws decades after enactment, so the two medians could differ a lot. To find law's meaning, judges might consider the preference of the median at the time of enactment. In an earlier chapter we presented the *median theory of interpretation*, which directs courts to do exactly that when interpreting ballot initiatives. However, in cases with indeterminate law, judges cannot find law's meaning. They must invent meaning themselves. They should invent a good meaning, and the preferences of the median citizen at the time of interpretation provide a basis for determining good meaning.

Usually, judges do not know the exact preference of the median citizen. But the median default does not require such precision. The question is: Among the plausible interpretations, which lies closest to the median? If a law has two plausible interpretations, one moderate and one extreme, the moderate one lies closer to the median. Economics supplies a target for judges in cases with indeterminate law. It cannot ensure that judges hit the bullseye every time.

The median default offers one method for breaking ties. However, the method is not universal. It fits some situations better than others. To illustrate, imagine two cases, one simple and one complex. The simple case asks whether the government should have to pay the legal fees of people whose rights the government has violated. The complex case asks whether the administrator of a company's pension plan violated law when calculating the benefits of employees who left the company, accepted pension payments, and then rejoined the company.[146] Citizens probably have confident opinions about the simple case but not the complex case. Generalizing, the median default works best in cases where citizens have well-formed preferences over the possible outcomes. This is more likely in cases that raise simple, nontechnical questions.

An earlier chapter presented a default rule for resolving rights conflicts, as when the gay couple sought a wedding cake from the religious baker. According to the *conflict avoidance principle*, the judge should rule against the party who could have avoided the conflict more easily. That default rule works best for conflicts among individual rights. It does not work so well for cases like *West Virginia University Hospitals*. In that case, the government did not act on behalf of an individual, so the dispute did not involve rights on both sides. In contrast, the government in *Masterpiece Cakeshop* acted on behalf of the gay couple in their suit against the baker.

In sum, when judges cannot determine the correct answer to a legal question, they need a default rule to resolve the impasse. The best default rule depends on the type of case. The median default is a good tiebreaker for cases in which the law is uncertain but people have clear preferences on the underlying issue.

[145] One might argue that *justice* requires Pennsylvania to pay. The median default and justice might often lead to the same result. But they won't always do so, and in any case the demands of justice are often unclear.

[146] *Cf.* Conkright v. Frommert, 599 U.S. 506 (2010).

Questions

10.26. The median default is normative, whereas the median theory of interpretation is interpretive. Explain the difference.

10.27. Use your intuition: Would the median citizen want an exception to the speed limit for medical emergencies? Would the median citizen want to punish the fisherman for discarding illegal fish in violation of a law on corporate bankruptcy?

10.28. Margaret McIntyre made and distributed political flyers without her name. She violated a law prohibiting anonymous political pamphleteering. She argued that the freedom of speech in the First Amendment protected her right to speak anonymously, and thus the law was unconstitutional. Both sides had good arguments. After reviewing them, Justice Scalia called this a "most difficult case" that "involves not just history but judgment."[147] He then announced a default rule:

> Where the meaning of a constitutional text (such as "the freedom of speech") is unclear, the widespread and long accepted practices of the American people are the best indication of what fundamental beliefs it was intended to enshrine.[148]

Many states had prohibited anonymous political pamphleteering for many years. Thus, Justice Scalia concluded that the law was constitutional. Is Justice Scalia's default rule the same as the median default?

Optimal Independence

The Framers of the Constitution debated judicial independence. Alexander Hamilton argued that an independent judiciary offers "the best expedient which can be devised in any government, to secure a steady, upright, and impartial administration of the laws."[149] But others feared making judges too powerful. Brutus, an Anti-Federalist who opposed the Constitution, wrote: when "power is lodged in the hands of men independent of the people, and of their representatives, . . . no way is left to controul them."[150]

Social scientists ask positive questions, like how independent are judges, and what sustains their independence? The Framers debated a normative question: How independent *should judges be*? Lawyers and constitution drafters continue to debate this question today. We supply a framework for answering.[151]

Judges get two kinds of cases: those with determinate law, and those with indeterminate law. In cases with determinate law, we expect judges to find the correct answer to the legal question. We do not want judges to ignore law and exercise policy discretion. Let's call the probability of judges seeking correct answers the *propensity*

[147] McIntyre v. Ohio Elections Comm'n, 514 U.S. 334 (1995).
[148] *Id.* at 378 (Scalia, J., dissenting).
[149] THE FEDERALIST NO. 78, at 392 (Alexander Hamilton) (Ian Shapiro ed., 2009).
[150] *Essay XV of Brutus, in* 2 THE COMPLETE ANTI-FEDERALIST 442 (Herbert Storing ed., 1981).
[151] *See* Michael D. Gilbert, *Judicial Independence and Social Welfare*, 112 MICH. L. REV. 575 (2014).

for legalism. In cases with indeterminate law, we expect judges to exercise discretion for society's benefit. We have shown that judges tend to promote social welfare by exercising discretion consistent with the preferences of the median citizen. Let's call the alignment between judges and the median citizen *median congruence*.

Increasing judicial independence insulates judges from outside pressure. Without pressure, judges can do what law requires without fear of payback. Thus, greater independence should tend to increase judges' propensity for legalism. However, more independence implies less accountability to the public. Rather than answering to politicians or voters, independent judges answer to themselves. Without accountability, judges can stray far from the median. Thus, greater independence should tend to decrease judges' median congruence.

Now we can state the trade-off. More independence increases judges' propensity for legalism, meaning more cases get decided according to law. That's good. But in the relatively few cases where judges exercise discretion, they tend to make relatively poor decisions because of their distance from the median. That's bad. We should increase judicial independence until the marginal benefit from a greater propensity for legalism just equals the marginal cost to median congruence.[152]

We can use these ideas to evaluate some legal institutions. In the United States, federal judges enjoy high levels of independence, but most state and local judges compete in elections. Elections make judges dependent on voters, and this should increase their median congruence. But elections subject judges to pressure. Rather than deciding according to law, judges facing elections might decide according to popular opinion.[153] Thus, judicial elections increase median congruence but decrease propensity for legalism.

Now consider the U.S. Supreme Court. Compared to lower courts, the Supreme Court decides many cases with indeterminate law. Consequently, the Justices exercise discretion relatively often. This makes median congruence important. Does the Supreme Court track the median American? In summer 2022, the Court had three liberal Justices (Jackson, Kagan, Sotomayor), and six conservative Justices (Alito, Barrett, Gorsuch, Kavanaugh, Roberts, Thomas). The United States is not two-thirds conservative. Thus, this does not sound like a group likely to track the median. Perhaps the Supreme Court should be more politically accountable. But that would decrease the Court's propensity for legalism. Where is the propensity for legalism most important: in trial courts, appellate courts, or the Supreme Court?

IV. Interpretive Theory of Adjudication

We presented the median default as a tiebreaker. In some cases where judges cannot ascertain the correct answer to the legal question, they can apply the median default.

[152] Note that the trade-off might not arise. If greater independence increases the propensity for legalism and median congruence, then maximum independence is best.

[153] For empirical evidence of this, see, for example, Gregory A. Huber & Sanford C. Gordon, *Accountability and Coercion: Is Justice Blind When It Runs for Office?*, 48 Am. J. Pol. Sci. 247 (2004).

Tiebreakers might benefit the legal system and society. However, most lawyers don't spend time on tiebreakers. They don't ask, "What should we do if the case is too hard?" They ask questions like, "Does the phrase 'attorney's fees' encompass expert witness fees?" These are questions of interpretation, and lawyers resolve most cases by answering them. Throughout the book we have used economics to address some questions of interpretation. Here we present a general theory of interpretation that applies in many settings. To develop the theory, we start by returning to the idea of legislative intent.

A. Purposivism

Many U.S. states elect their judges. A dispute over electing judges in one state, Louisiana, ended up in the U.S. Supreme Court. Here are the facts. Louisiana's highest court had seven members. However, the state was divided into only six judicial districts. Five of these were "single-member" districts, meaning that voters in each elected one judge to the court. The remaining district, which had about twice as many people as the others, was a "multimember" district. Voters there elected two judges to the court.

The multimember district had a sizable African American population. Dividing that district into two single-member districts would give African American voters a majority in one of them. In the multimember district, they constituted a minority. These voters claimed that the multimember district diluted their voting strength in violation of the Voting Rights Act of 1965. To win, they had to show that they had "less opportunity than other members of the electorate to participate in the political process and to elect *representatives* of their choice."[154] The case turned on that italicized word, which was added to the act in 1982. Were elected judges "representatives"? If not, the Voting Rights Act did not apply, and the African American voters would lose their case.

In *Chisom v. Roemer*, the Supreme Court held that elected judges qualify as "representatives."[155] To reach this conclusion, the Justices examined the text and history of the law. They also wrote the following:

> Congress enacted the Voting Rights Act of 1965 for the broad remedial purpose of "rid[ding] the country of racial discrimination in voting." *South Carolina v. Katzenbach*, 383 U.S. 301, 383 U.S. 315 (1966). In *Allen v. State Board of Elections*, 393 U.S. 544, 393 U.S. 567 (1969), we said that the Act should be interpreted in a manner that provides "the broadest possible scope" in combatting racial discrimination.[156]

This method of interpretation is called *purposivism* because it inquires into the law's purpose.

To clarify purposivism, let's return to a broader concept, legislative intent. When interpreting a statute, judges often ask what the legislators who enacted it "intended." In

[154] 96 Stat. 134, Pub. L. 97-205 (1982) (emphasis added).
[155] 501 U.S. 380 (1991).
[156] *Id.* at 403.

Chisom, the Justices might have asked, "Did Congress intend 'representatives' to include elected judges?" This question is more complicated than it seems. We can understand "intent" in different ways.[157]

To begin, suppose that Congress made a decision on whether to apply the Voting Rights Act to judicial elections. For whatever reason, the text of the act didn't make that decision clear. In this scenario, the legislators had a *specific* intention, and courts try to find it. Given a specific intention, asking "what did Congress intend?" is equivalent to asking "what decision did Congress actually make?"

Suppose Congress never considered whether the law should apply to judicial elections. The issue didn't arise, so Congress did not have any specific intention on it. Thus, the question changes. It becomes "what decision *would Congress have made* on judicial elections had the issue come up?" To answer, courts engage in "imaginative reconstruction." They seek legislators' *reconstructed* intent.

Specific and reconstructed intent usually involve particular questions. "What did Congress decide, or what would Congress have decided, on the particular issue of elected judges?" Now consider a version of intent that involves an abstract question. When judges seek *general* intent, they ask, "What did the legislature aim to achieve with this law?" This is equivalent to asking, "What is the *purpose* of this law?" Thus, the search for general intent is synonymous with purposivism. According to purposivism, judges should identify the purpose of the law and use that purpose to answer the specific questions before them.

Chisom illustrates purposivism. The Supreme Court had to decide if the term "representatives" in the Voting Rights Act includes elected judges. To make this decision, the Court found the law's purpose: to rid the United States of racial discrimination in voting. Interpreting "representatives" to include elected judges would further this purpose by applying the law to more elections. So the Court made this interpretation, broadening the reach of the law.

Earlier in the book we saw another example of purposivism. A church in New York signed a contract with a noncitizen named Warren. Under the terms of the contract, Warren moved from England to New York and worked as a pastor. Did the church break the law prohibiting importation of a noncitizen "under contract or agreement . . . to perform labor or service"? In *Church of the Holy Trinity v. United States*, the Supreme Court said no.[158] The Court wrote, "A guide to the meaning of a statute is found in the evil which it is designed to remedy."[159] The Court continued:

> The motives and history of the act are matters of common knowledge. It had become the practice for large capitalists in this country to contract with their agents abroad for the shipment of great numbers of an ignorant and servile class of foreign laborers. . . . The effect of this was to break down the labor market, and to reduce [American] laborers engaged in like occupations.[160]

[157] For an especially lucid discussion, see William N. Eskridge, Jr., Philip P. Frickey, & Elizabeth Garrett, Legislation and Statutory Interpretation 221–30 (2d ed. 2006).
[158] 143 U.S. 457 (1892).
[159] *Id.* at 463.
[160] *Id.*

According to the Court, the law aimed to protect U.S. citizens who did manual labor from foreign competition. Pastors do not perform manual labor; they are, in the Court's words, "brain toilers."[161] Therefore, excluding foreign pastors would not further the law's purpose. The church did not violate the law.

Purposivism has a long history in U.S. law. The Supreme Court decided *Holy Trinity* in 1892 and *Chisom* in 1991. The Court uses purposivism today.[162] Yet purposivism sparks controversy for at least two reasons. First, identifying a law's purpose can be difficult. Consider three possible purposes of the Voting Rights Act: (1) to eliminate racial discrimination in voting; (2) to eliminate racial discrimination in voting for legislators and executives;[163] (3) to eliminate racial discrimination in voting without infringing on the sovereignty of individual states. If (1) is the correct purpose, then the Voting Rights Act should apply to judicial elections, just like the Court held in *Chisom*. However, if (2) is the correct purpose, then the act should not apply to judicial elections. If (3) is the correct purpose, then we can't tell. The answer depends on whether applying the act to judicial elections would infringe on Louisiana's sovereignty. Uncertainty over purpose diminishes the value of purposivism. It also increases judicial discretion. Given a menu of purposes, judges can select the one that will achieve their preferred outcome.

Purposivism suffers from a second drawback that we can illustrate with *Holy Trinity*. According to the Court, the statute aimed to protect U.S. manual laborers from foreign competition. Let's assume the Court got the purpose right. Now we must ask about the means Congress chose to achieve its purpose. Here are two possibilities: (1) Congress chose to exclude noncitizens who do manual labor; (2) Congress chose to exclude all noncitizens because distinguishing manual laborers from "brain toilers" is too difficult. If Congress chose (1), then the Court in *Holy Trinity* made the right decision. However, if Congress chose (2), then the church broke the law. To generalize, resolving a case often requires knowing more than a law's purpose. Judges need information on purpose and the means chosen to achieve it.

In sum, purposivism is a common method of interpretation with flaws. Courts nevertheless rely on purposivism, in part because alternative methods of interpretation also have flaws. Sometimes words are unclear, so judges cannot simply follow the text. Specific and reconstructed intent are hard to identify (if they even exist). Purposivism is useful in certain cases, just as a hammer is useful for certain jobs. Purposivism works best when law has a single, clear purpose.

B. The Incentive Principle of Interpretation

Can I burn leaves on Saturday? How many votes does the bill need to become law? Can I deduct this expense from my taxes? How do I comment on the proposed airline

161 *Id.* at 464.

162 Richard M. Re, *The New Holy Trinity*, 18 Green Bag 2d 407 (2015); Student Note, *The Rise of Purposivism and the Fall of* Chevron: *Major Statutory Cases in the Supreme Court*, 130 Harv. L. Rev. 1227 (2017).

163 One might say that a reasonable legislator would never seek to prevent racial discrimination in voting for some officials but not others, like judges. This would be the position of the scholars Henry Hart and Albert Sacks, who directed judges to place themselves in the position of reasonable legislators enacting reasonable laws. *See* Henry M. Hart, Jr. & Albert M. Sacks, The Legal Process: Basic Problems in the Making and Application of Law (William N. Eskridge, Jr. & Phillip P. Frickey eds., 1995). Of course, real legislators are not always reasonable.

regulation? A lawyer is supposed to know the law so that she can answer questions about what it requires or enables people to do. In an easy case, a law's language and the facts leave no doubt about what it requires or enables people to do. In a hard case, however, the proper application of law to the facts is uncertain. Assigning definite meaning to an ambiguous law requires reasoning about the law's purpose, history, the intentions of lawmakers, and so on. Legal reasoning is the fundamental skill acquired by legal education.

Lawmakers enact laws to achieve certain consequences. The achievement of a desirable consequence is a law's purpose. Different laws have different purposes such as developing vaccines, disseminating information, subsidizing farmers, empowering voters, and protecting workers from competition, to name just a few.

Finding a law's correct interpretation often requires knowing its purpose and predicting the consequences of alternative interpretations. To predict the consequences of alternative interpretations, lawyers should use the best evidence available to them, including social scientific studies. The best evidence from social science can come from any of its branches—political science, sociology, psychology, anthropology—but this book emphasizes economics. Economics differs from other social sciences in its steadfast commitment to analyzing incentives, especially the incentives of rational actors.

Analyzing incentives often provides the best-available predictions of consequences for two reasons. First, predicting the effects of alternative interpretations ideally draws on rigorous empirical research. When available, courts should draw on such research. High-quality empirical research often comes from combining incentive models and statistics. Second, most legal decisions are made without empirical research because cases outpace scholars. Absent empirical research, lawyers and judges rely heavily on practical reasoning and common sense. Their arguments about the consequences of a rule's interpretation usually refer to incentives created by it. An incentive model can usually improve on practical reasoning and common sense by correcting inconsistencies and pursuing reasons to their logical conclusions. In this way, incentive models raise practical reasoning and common sense to a higher level of rigor and precision.

These ideas lead to the *incentive principle of interpretation*: a law's correct interpretation in hard cases creates incentives that best fulfill its purpose. In economic language, a law's correct interpretation provides incentives to maximize the fulfillment of its actual purposes. Sometimes efficiency is the actual purpose of law, as when a statute mandates the use of cost-benefit analysis. However, most laws have purposes other than efficiency.[164] Efficiency is not decisive for interpreting a law whose main purpose is something else—nondiscrimination, affirmative action, redistribution, or the protection of workers from foreign competition.

To apply the incentive principle, use legal reasoning to find the purpose of a law, and then use economic reasoning to predict the fulfillment of the purpose by alternative

[164] A common approach to interpretation in economics might be called the *efficiency principle of interpretation*: the correct interpretation of an ambiguous law has the most efficient consequences. Thus, Richard Posner famously wrote, "economics is the deep structure of the common law and the doctrines of that law are the surface structure." RICHARD A. POSNER, ECONOMIC ANALYSIS OF LAW 297 (9th ed. 2014). Louis Kaplow and Steven Shavell claim that all laws ought to maximize social welfare. LOUIS KAPLOW & STEVEN SHAVELL, FAIRNESS VERSUS WELFARE (2006). These theories present efficiency in one form or another as the ultimate purpose of the law. Propositions about ultimate purposes belong to philosophy or religion, not to social science.

interpretations. In this ideal sequence, legal reasoning leads and economic reasoning follows. In reality, however, the two forms of reasoning mix. Instead of proceeding in order, they circle back on each other, like this: first, describe a law's possible purpose; second, predict its fulfillment by alternative interpretations; third, reconsider the law's purpose in light of the predictions; fourth, predict the fulfillment of reconsidered purpose; and so on. The end of this process is a "reflective equilibrium," which settles on the law's correct interpretation.[165]

Like purposivism, the incentive principle works best when the law has a clear purpose. Likewise, the principle works when the law has multiple purposes that converge, so that one course of action advances all of them. Sometimes law has multiple purposes that diverge, as with a statute that aims to promote voting and respect state sovereignty. With divergent purposes, the course of action that advances one of them the most does not advance the other the most. With divergent purposes, courts need a theory of value that encompasses heterogeneous purposes. Encompassing values could include welfare, well-being, utility, or justice. Whatever the encompassing value, the best course of action creates more of it. Of course, deciding on an encompassing value can be controversial.

The incentive principle begins with purposive reasoning. Thus, it faces the challenges of purposive reasoning, and it cannot overcome all of them. However, it can improve interpretation in those cases where purposivism applies.

We have used the incentive principle throughout this book. Recall our discussion of federalism. Article I, Section 8 of the U.S. Constitution divides power between the national government and the states. The national government has the power to provide for the "general welfare." What constitutes "general welfare"? To answer, we explained that the purpose of federalism is to enjoy the advantages resulting from the largeness and smallness of governments. To secure those advantages, we can interpret the General Welfare Clause to empower the national government to act on interstate externalities when the states cannot bargain among themselves. This interpretation incentivizes national lawmakers to act only when the federal government has the advantage. We began with the purpose of Article I, Section 8 and developed an interpretation that provides incentives to fulfill its purpose.

Consider another example from an earlier chapter. The single subject rule limits ballot initiatives to one "subject." What constitutes a "subject"? To answer, we began with the rule's purpose, which is to prevent logrolling. We explained that voters can logroll only when they have separable preferences over the parts of an initiative. Thus, courts should strike down initiatives that combine issues on which voters have separable preferences (such initiatives have more than one subject). Drafters do not want courts to strike down their initiatives, so our approach would encourage drafters to separate proposals over which voters have separable preferences. We began with the purpose of the single subject rule and developed an interpretation that incentivizes drafters to fulfill its purpose.

In sum, the incentive principle of interpretation unites the humanistic discipline of law and the social science of economics. We use law to find the purpose and economics to find the best incentives for achieving it. The incentive principle sharpens purposive

[165] *See* John Rawls, A Theory of Justice (1971).

reasoning that many judges already use, and it can unravel hard problems in law like federalism and the single subject rule.

Questions

10.29. Did the legislature delegate this power to the agency? To help answer, an earlier chapter developed the delegation canon, which asks: "Would the legislature's administrative savings from this delegation exceed its diversion costs?" Is the delegation canon consistent with the incentive principle of interpretation?

10.30. The law in *Holy Trinity* aimed to protect manual laborers from foreign competition. Here are two ways to achieve that purpose: (1) exclude noncitizens who do manual labor; (2) exclude all noncitizens because distinguishing manual laborers from others is difficult. Purposivism might allow a judge to choose at will between these two possibilities. Would the incentive principle? In answering, consider whether a judge using the incentive principle would ask lawyers different kinds of questions than a judge using purposivism.

Conclusion

Adjudication sits at the heart of public law. Litigants file claims, present facts, settle, or go to trial. Courts weigh evidence, interpret law, and make precedents. Ambiguous or vague law gives judges legal discretion. Even with clear law, judges often have policy discretion, so they can make their preferred decisions without threat of override or punishment. In deciding cases, judges should seek correct answers to the legal questions. But economists take all costs into account. Thus, judges should weigh the marginal costs of more fact-finding and interpretation against the marginal benefits of accuracy. Indeterminate law calls for a good tiebreaker, like the median default. These are positive and normative aspects of adjudication. We concluded by presenting an interpretive theory of adjudication, the incentive principle. Together these ideas illuminate the process of adjudication. In the next chapter we apply them to a variety of legal issues.

11
Adjudication Applications

Charles Evans Hughes was an acclaimed American jurist. He said, "[T]he Constitution is what the judges say it is, and the judiciary is the safeguard of our liberty."[1] All laws, including constitutions, require interpretation. Judges decide what the law means. Judges interpret law in the course of resolving cases. Thus, the contents of public law, including rights, freedoms, and the powers of government, emerge through adjudication. The prior chapter analyzed positive, normative, and interpretive aspects of adjudication. Here we apply those ideas to enduring problems in law. We address questions like these:

Example 1: Chief Justice Marshall said that judges follow "the will of the law."[2] The philosopher Friedrich Nietzsche said that "[a]ll things are subject to interpretation" and "whichever interpretation prevails is a function of power and not truth."[3] Does interpretation by judges produce truth or reflect power?

Example 2: The Louisiana legislature passed a law allowing litigants to impeach (i.e., challenge) the testimony of their opponents "in any *un*lawful way."[4] Did the legislators make a mistake? Can judges correct it?

Example 3: In *US Airways v. Barnett*, the Supreme Court considered whether a company's seniority system trumped a disabled worker's right to transfer to a less physically demanding job. Writing for a majority, Justice Breyer said the answer is ordinarily yes, but a circumstance could arise in which the answer is no. Writing in dissent, Justice Scalia criticized the majority for "eschewing clear rules" and turning the law into a "standardless grab bag."[5] What's more important: making the law on disability responsive to different circumstances, or making it clear?

Example 4: "The judiciary should make the best interpretation of the constitution, not the best constitution by interpretation." What's the difference?

To address these questions, we begin by studying interpretive methods. Judges can emphasize the text of law, consult the lawmakers' intentions, or seek law's purpose. Economics illuminates these methods by connecting them to some important values,

[1] Charles Evans Hughes, *Speech before the Elmira Chamber of Commerce, May 3, 1907*, *in* Addresses and Papers of Charles Evans Hughes 133, 139 (1908).

[2] Osborn v. Bank of United States, 22 U.S. 738, 866 (1824).

[3] Versions of this phrase are attributed to Nietzsche, but we could not find a definitive source. However, the quote resembles something he wrote. *See* Friedrich Nietzsche, The Will to Power 267 (Walter Kaufmann & R.J. Hollingdale eds., 1968) ("Against positivism, which halts at phenomena—'There are only facts'—I would say: No, facts is precisely what there is not, only interpretations. . . . It is our needs that interpret the world; our drives and their For and Against. Every drive is a kind of lust to rule; each one has its perspective that it would like to compel all the other drives to accept as a norm.").

[4] Scurto v. LeBlanc, 184 So. 567, 574 (La. 1938).

[5] US Airways, Inc. v. Barnett, 545 U.S. 391, 412–14 (2002) (Scalia, J., dissenting).

Public Law and Economics. Robert D. Cooter and Michael D. Gilbert, Oxford University Press. © Oxford University Press 2022.
DOI: 10.1093/oso/9780197655870.003.0011

like communication and transition costs. After interpretation, we analyze legal doctrine. Judges choose between writing rule-like and standard-like opinions, and they choose between following their precedents and making new ones. Economics can inform these choices. Finally, we study decisions by multimember courts. Many judges work in groups with other judges. The Supreme Court, for example, has nine Justices. Groups of logical judges can make illogical decisions, as we will show.

I. Methods of Interpretation

Does the President have authority to declare war? Does the steel tariff violate international law? Is a fish a "tangible object" under the Sarbanes-Oxley Act? To answer questions like these, lawyers interpret law. In public law, most interpretation involves the text of a regulation, statute, treaty, or constitution. How should judges interpret legal texts? This question burns in the hearts of lawyers. Politicians care too. President Trump wanted judges who are "textualists who believe the words of the statute."[6] President Obama wanted judges "who understand[ ] that justice isn't about some abstract legal theory . . . [but] about how our laws affect the daily realities of people's lives."[7] In the United States, your theory of interpretation often says a lot about your politics.

We apply economics to theories of interpretation. We begin by describing some challenges in interpretation, including conflicts between a law's text and purpose. Next, we use coordination games to study communication between lawmakers and citizens. Coordination games illuminate important questions, like when courts should correct errors in statutes. Finally, we relate interpretation to transition costs and justice.

A. Text versus Intent

Public law begins with words, and words require interpretation. Recall this statute: "Anyone possessing arms in a public library shall be punished." Does the law forbid you from entering the library with a pistol? What about the limbs attached to your shoulders? We cannot tell because the word "arms" is ambiguous. It could mean weapons or appendages. Here's another question: Does the law forbid you from possessing arms on the street? You might say no, it only forbids arms "in a public library." But read closely. Perhaps the law forbids possessing arms anywhere, and if you violate the law, then "in a public library" you shall be punished.

How do lawyers make sense of laws like this? Usually they keep reading and use common sense. Common sense tells you that "arms" refers to weapons. If the rest of the statute addresses guns and public safety, that strengthens the conclusion: "arms" includes pistols but not limbs. If the government never punishes people "in a public library," then that phrase must refer to where "arms" are possessed, not to the punishment. To generalize, lawyers make sense of words by giving them their ordinary meaning in

6 *See* Tessa Berenson, *Hoping to Bring Out Conservative Voters, Donald Trump Releases New Supreme Court Shortlist*, TIME, Sept. 9, 2020.

7 *See* Janet Hook & Christi Parsons, *Obama Says Empathy Key to Court Pick*, L.A. TIMES, May 2, 2009.

context. To help find ordinary meaning, judges often use canons of construction. We discussed some canons like *noscitur a sociis* in earlier chapters.

Ordinary meaning and the canons of construction often succeed in making sense of legal texts. But not always. A Virginia law punished any driver "who fails to stop, when approaching from any direction, any school bus which is stopped . . . for the purpose of taking on or discharging children."[8] Read closely and you will see the problem. The law does not tell drivers to stop "at" or "for" any school bus. It just directs drivers to "stop . . . any school bus which is stopped." Apparently, drivers don't have to stop their own cars. They have to stop the bus! Of course, this is impossible because the bus is already stopped (the law only applies when approaching a bus "which is stopped"). The language doesn't make sense.

This law contains a *scrivener's error*, meaning a mistake in the language. The lawmakers left out a word.[9] Scrivener's errors can put pressure on the ordinary meaning principle. Surely the law's purpose is to protect children by making drivers stop. Yet the ordinary meaning of the language does not require drivers to stop. The law's ordinary meaning conflicts with its purpose. A court might correct the error by "reading in" the word "at."

In this example, common sense shows us the error. Sometimes errors are harder to diagnose. A statute required miners to file annual paperwork with the government "prior to December 31" or lose their mining claims. Some miners filed their paperwork on December 31. According to the ordinary meaning of the statute, they filed one day late and forfeited their claims. But why would the government need the documents the day *before* the last day of the year? According to Justice Stevens, "no one . . . suggested any rational basis for omitting just one day" from the calendar.[10] He concluded that the law contained a scrivener's error. Congress meant to write "on or before December 31," or "prior to the close of business on December 31." Justice Stevens failed to persuade his colleagues. In *United States v. Locke*, the Supreme Court stripped the miners of their claims, stating, "[T]he legislative purpose is expressed by the ordinary meaning of the words used."[11] Justice Stevens perceived a scrivener's error, but the other Justices did not.

Scrivener's errors relate to a perplexing problem in interpretation: conflicts between the text of law and its makers' intentions (or apparent intentions). We have discussed such conflicts throughout the book. Here we consider them again using a famous case. Francis Palmer wrote a will that would, upon his death, bequeath property to his grandson Elmer. Later Francis got angry at Elmer and threatened to remove him from the will. Elmer responded by murdering Francis. The law punished Elmer for his crime, but what about the will? Francis hadn't changed it before his death. The statute said, "No will in writing, except in the cases hereinafter mentioned, nor any part thereof, shall be revoked or altered otherwise."[12] The statute made no exceptions for murder.

[8] *See* Tom Jackman, *2 Little Letters Acquit Man Who Passed Stopped School Bus*, WASH. POST, Dec. 1, 2010.

[9] Instead of forgetting a word, perhaps they forgot a comma after "approaching." Or perhaps they erroneously included a comma after "direction." There is more than one way to understand the error.

[10] United Sates v. Locke, 471 U.S. 84, 123 (1985) (Stevens, J., dissenting).

[11] *Id.* at 95.

[12] Riggs v. Palmer, 22 N.E. 188, 192 (N.Y. 1889) (Gray, J., dissenting) (internal quotations marks omitted).

So according to the ordinary meaning of the words in the statute, Elmer should get the inheritance.

In *Riggs v. Palmer*, the court denied Elmer the inheritance. The majority of the court wrote:

> It was the intention of the law-makers that the donees in a will should have the property given to them. But it never could have been their intention that a donee who murdered the testator to make the will operative should have any benefit under it. If such a case had been present to their minds, and it had been supposed necessary to make some provision of law to meet it, it cannot be doubted that they would have provided for it.[13]

The court relied on a concept discussed in the previous chapter, reconstructed intent. Had the lawmakers considered it, they would have forbidden murderous heirs like Elmer from inheriting, or so the court concluded. The court also relied on a canon of construction called the *absurdity doctrine*.[14] That doctrine authorizes judges to avoid outcomes that "all mankind would, without hesitation, unite in rejecting."[15]

Letting Elmer inherit certainly seems absurd, so the decision not to seems justified. But consider exactly what the court did. The text of the statute supported Elmer. The court effectively amended the text by adding a new (but unwritten) sentence, something like, "Murderous heirs shall not inherit." Should judges have the power to amend statutes? How can they distinguish "absurd" results they can correct from other results—bad, silly, wasteful—that they cannot? Don't legislatures usually make better laws than judges? What other statutes might judges decide to amend? Concerns like these led Judge Gray to dissent in *Riggs*. He wrote:

> [T]he matter does not lie within the domain of conscience. We are bound by the rigid rules of law, which have been established by the legislature, and within the limits of which the determination of this question is confined. The question we are dealing with is, whether a testamentary disposition can be altered, or a will revoked, after the testator's death, through an appeal to the courts, when the legislature has, by its enactments, prescribed exactly when and how wills may be made, altered and revoked.[16]

According to Judge Gray, the statute "left no room for the exercise of an equitable jurisdiction by courts."[17]

Judge Gray's opinion represents a method of statutory interpretation called *textualism*.[18] Textualism emphasizes the language of the law, not the intent or purpose behind

[13] *Id.* at 189.

[14] *Id.* ("If there arise out of [an interpretation of a statute] collaterally any absurd consequences manifestly contradictory to common reason, they are with regard to those collateral consequences void.") (internal quotation marks and citation omitted).

[15] Sturges v. Crowninshield, 17 U.S. 122, 203 (1819). *See also* John Manning, *The Absurdity Doctrine*, 116 Harv. L. Rev. 2387 (2003).

[16] Riggs v. Palmer, 22 N.E. 188, 191 (N.Y. 1889) (Gray, J., dissenting).

[17] *Id.*

[18] Textualism comes in different forms. The "new" textualism emphasized by U.S. judges today may differ from Judge Gray's textualism in *Riggs*. All forms of textualism emphasize the words of the statute.

it. The language of the law in *Riggs* let Elmer inherit, so most textualists would grant Elmer the property under the will, even though he committed murder. Similarly, the words of the law in *Locke* indicated that the miners filed late, so most textualists would strip the miners of their claims. Textualism contrasts with *intentionalism*. Intentionalists emphasize the intentions of the law's makers. Intentionalists might search the legislative history for evidence of specific intent (what the lawmakers actually agreed to), or they might rely on fairness and common sense to reconstruct intent (what the lawmakers would have agreed to had they considered the specific case). Intentionalists might try to identify the purpose of the law and let that purpose guide their interpretation. Compared to textualists, intentionalists feel freer to depart from the law's text. The court's decision in *Riggs* represents intentionalism. The statute's words let Elmer inherit, but surely the legislators who drafted the statute would not have wanted that absurd result. The court forbade the inheritance.

Judges and scholars debate the merits of textualism and intentionalism. Sometimes the debate feels like a brawl. Here's a brief summary of some main arguments. Supporters of textualism argue that it promotes predictability. Given textualist judges, you can learn what law requires by reading it. You don't have to read the law *and* read the legislative history *and* consider the legislators' intentions (assuming such intentions exist). Furthermore, textualism limits judicial discretion. Judges do what the law says, not what they wish the law said, or what they imagine legislators wanted the law to say. Finally, textualism encourages careful drafting. If legislators want to prohibit murderers from inheriting, they must say so in the statute.

Supporters of intentionalism reject these arguments. They say that text is often ambiguous or vague, and the canons of constructions (on which textualists rely heavily) often point to different answers. So textualism is often unpredictable and does not limit judicial discretion. Supporters of intentionalism say their method promotes justice, as when the court in *Riggs* forbade Elmer from inheriting. They argue that written law cannot address every situation adequately. Law's true meaning depends on circumstances, intentions, and deep principles like equality and fairness, not simply words on a page. A good judge does more than read. Thus, they argue that intentionalism is more faithful to law than textualism. And so on.

This debate is as old as law itself. Aristotle pondered laws and their exceptions over 2,000 years ago.[19] Economics cannot resolve the debate, but the following pages show how it can help.

Questions

11.1. Are textualism and intentionalism opposites? How would you describe a judge who thinks that a law's meaning depends on its makers' intentions and that the law's text is the best evidence of those intentions?[20]

11.2. The statute says, "Anyone possessing arms in a public library shall be punished." In world one, the legislative history addresses safety in public buildings and

[19] *See generally* W. von Leyden, *Aristotle and the Concept of Law*, 42 PHIL. 1 (1967).
[20] *See* Caleb Nelson, *What Is Textualism?*, 91 VA. L. REV. 347 (2005).

nothing else. In world two, the legislative history addresses safety in public buildings, safety on the streets, punishments, physical disabilities, and many other topics. Judges must interpret the statute. Do textualists have more or less discretion than intentionalists in world one? What about in world two?

11.3. Consider two cases from earlier chapters. The law forbade anyone from obstructing the mail. In *United States v. Kirby*, the Court held that the law did not apply to a sheriff who arrested a mailman wanted for murder.[21] The law forbade anyone from bringing a foreigner to the United States to work. In *Church of the Holy Trinity v. United States*, the Court held that the law did not apply to a church that hired a pastor from England.[22] In both cases the Court invoked the absurdity doctrine. Does the absurdity doctrine promote or undermine the rule of law?

B. Law and Coordination

Law involves language, and language involves communication. Listeners want to understand, and speakers want to be understood. The same goes for writing. Most authors want to send a message, and most readers want to receive it. A common language lowers the cost of communication among people. Easy communication promotes cooperation that benefits all. In Lewis Carroll's novel *Through the Looking-Glass*, Humpty Dumpty says, "When *I* use a word it means just what I choose it to mean—neither more nor less."[23] This sentence is amusing and silly. If speakers choose the meanings of their words, listeners won't understand them. So why listen? If no one listens, why speak?

These ideas apply in law. Law prohibits driving fast, colluding on prices, and polluting the oceans. Lawmakers express these prohibitions in writing that they want citizens to understand. Citizens want to understand these prohibitions before acting, lest they violate law and face penalties. Lawyers are central to legal communication. Like good speechwriters, they help lawmakers draft clear laws. Like good translators, they help citizens understand them.

Early in the book we introduced coordination games. In coordination games, the interests of all players converge. Driving offers a good example. We do not care if we drive on the left or right side of the road as long as everyone makes the same choice. The driving game has two equilibria: everyone drives on the left, and everyone drives on the right.

We can use coordination games to understand communication in law.[24] Figure 11.1 illustrates a communication between a lawmaker and a citizen. The question is whether the citizen can take a certain action, like digging a mine on public land. If the lawmaker answers "yes" and the citizen understands "yes," then the parties coordinate on meaning and receive high payoffs. The same holds if the lawmaker answers "no" and the citizens understands "no." However, if the lawmaker says "no" and the citizen understands

21 74 U.S. 482 (1868).
22 143 U.S. 457 (1892).
23 Lewis Carroll, Through the Looking-Glass 106–07 (1896).
24 On language and coordination, see David Lewis, Convention: A Philosophical Study (1969).

		Citizen: Yes	Citizen: No
Lawmaker	Yes	5, 5	0, 0
	No	0, 0	5, 5

Figure 11.1. Coordinating on Meaning

"yes," or vice versa, then the parties are out of equilibrium. They fail to coordinate on meaning. The citizen either does something illegal or refrains from doing something legal (and valuable, at least to her). The parties receive low payoffs.

In general, coordination is easier for small groups. Two people can coordinate their driving, especially if they can communicate ("Let's drive on the right"). Likewise, one lawmaker and one citizen can coordinate on the meaning of law. If the citizen gets confused, she can probably ask the lawmaker for clarification. In reality, groups are often large, and this makes coordination hard. Thousands of drivers struggle to coordinate, as anyone driving in Mumbai knows. Likewise, lawmakers and millions of citizens struggle to coordinate. No matter how carefully lawmakers write and citizens read, someone will misunderstand. With large groups, misunderstandings are inevitable.

To begin, let's consider a minor misunderstanding. This occurs when lawmakers and citizens mostly coordinate on the meaning of law but fail in some cases. To illustrate, suppose the question is whether Stella can dig a new mine on public land. Through the statute, lawmakers sent the answer "no," and most citizens received the answer "no," but Stella received the answer "yes." Stella dug the mine, and now she finds herself in court. Depending on the facts, deciding in favor of Stella might promote justice in her case. We will say more about justice later. But deciding in favor of Stella would scramble communications. Lawmakers sent a "no" signal, and most citizens understood it. If the court decides that "no" means "yes," then lawmakers and citizens must change how they communicate or suffer from more miscommunications in the future. This would create *communication costs*. Deciding that "no" means "no" would minimize communication costs by supporting most people's expectations.

We can relate these ideas to Figure 11.1. Stella is in the bottom-left box, but everyone else is in the bottom-right box. Stella is out of equilibrium. The court can facilitate coordination on the meaning of law by ruling against Stella. Stella will not want to repeat her mistake, so an adverse ruling will push her to change how she understands law going forward. Stella, but no one else, will bear communication costs. To generalize, *given a minor misunderstanding, courts minimize communication costs by finding and enforcing the equilibrium.*

We can apply this analysis to real cases. Recall the law punishing drivers who fail to "stop . . . any school bus which is stopped" to load or unload children. Did John Mendez violate this law when he passed a bus discharging kids?[25] According to the literal language, no. Mendez only had to stop the bus (which was already stopped); he did not have to stop himself. Many judges would reject this literal approach and correct the scrivener's error. Why? Because in this case the meaning is clear. Surely the lawmakers who wrote the statute agreed on its purpose (to protect children), and surely they agreed on the means for achieving it (make drivers stop their cars). Surely most citizens who read the statute understood this. The scrivener's error in this statute resembles the minor misunderstanding we studied above, with Mendez and his car replacing Stella and her mine. Nearly everyone has coordinated on the law's meaning (drivers must stop their own cars). To minimize communication costs, judges should find and enforce that equilibrium. Mendez broke the law.

Questions

11.4. The law on school buses was 40 years old when Mendez's case arose. Does this affect your assessment of whether people had coordinated on its meaning?

11.5. In the real case, the judge *refused* to correct the scrivener's error, stating, "[Mendez] can only be guilty if he failed to stop any school bus," and "there's no evidence he did."[26] Did the judge's decision create communication costs? For whom?

11.6. When interpreting statutes, intentionalists look for what drafters intended, whereas most textualists look for what readers (or a "reasonable" reader[27]) understood. This difference might seem stark. But Justice Scalia, a leading textualist, wrote, "what the text would reasonably be understood to mean" and "what it was intended to mean" are inquiries that "chase one another back and forth to some extent."[28] Use coordination games to explain Justice Scalia's statement.

11.7. Critics say the absurdity doctrine is unprincipled. Why draw the line at "absurd?" Why not reject "bad" or "unreasonable" results too? Use our analysis of coordination and communication costs to respond to the critics.

A High Bar for Scrivener's Errors

In *United States v. Locke*, Justice Stevens concluded that the law contained a scrivener's error. He thought lawmakers intended to write, "prior to *the close of business on* December 31."[29] But a majority of the Justices rejected his argument. They took a position like Justice Scalia, who wrote, "[T]he *sine qua non* of any 'scrivener's error' doctrine . . . is that the meaning genuinely intended but inadequately expressed must

[25] *See* Tom Jackman, *2 Little Letters Acquit Man Who Passed Stopped School Bus*, Wash. Post, Dec. 1, 2010.
[26] *Id.*
[27] *See* Frank H. Easterbrook, *The Role of Original Intent in Statutory Construction*, 11 Harv. J.L. Pub. Pol'y 59, 65 (1988).
[28] Antonin Scalia, *Response*, *in* A Matter of Interpretation: Federal Courts and the Law 144 (1997).
[29] United States v. Locke, 471 U.S. 84, 119 (1985) (Stevens, J., dissenting).

be absolutely clear."[30] In other words, the error must be obvious, otherwise courts won't correct it. This is a common approach to scrivener's errors.

Why do judges set the bar so high? According to Justice Scalia, correcting a less clear error might amount to "rewriting the statute rather than correcting a technical mistake."[31] Let's assume "rewriting the statute" means "introducing a mistake into the statute." Does setting a high bar prevent judges from introducing mistakes into statutes? Not necessarily.[32] To see why, suppose a statute contains a mistake that is clear (say, 70 percent likely to be a mistake) but not *absolutely* clear (say, 95 percent likely to be a mistake). Justice Scalia would not correct the statute because the mistake is not absolutely clear. But there is a 70 percent chance the statute has a mistake. In this example, lowering the bar is more likely to prevent a mistake than to cause one.

Minimizing mistakes does not seem to justify the high bar for diagnosing scrivener's errors. Can communication costs justify the high bar? An error is "absolutely clear" when nearly everyone recognizes it. The law requiring drivers to "stop . . . any school bus which is stopped" provides an example. Nearly everyone recognizes the error in that law and knows what the language means (drivers must stop their own vehicles). In cases like this, correcting the error amounts to finding the equilibrium. Courts minimize communication costs when they find the existing equilibrium. An equilibrium is most likely to exist—people are most likely to have coordinated on meaning—when the error is absolutely clear.

These ideas support the high bar for scrivener's errors. They also refine the scrivener's error doctrine. The case for correcting an error in a statute gets stronger as the error *and its correction* become clear to more people.

Finding the Common Law

Most public law is imposed from the top down, as when legislators enact statutes regulating people's behavior. In contrast, some private law develops from the bottom up. In medieval England, merchants bought and sold goods at trade fairs.[33] The merchants developed their own norms about contracts, property, payments, defective goods, and so on. As the legal system developed, English judges assumed jurisdiction over disputes among merchants. The judges did not know enough about the specialized business transactions to design sensible rules. So the judges allegedly tried to discover the norms that the merchants had developed themselves. The judges

[30] United States v. X-Citement Video, Inc., 513 U.S. 64, 82 (1994) (Scalia, J., dissenting).

[31] *Id.*

[32] *See* Ryan D. Doerfler, *The Scrivener's Error*, 110 Nw. U.L. Rev. 811 (2016).

[33] This discussion is based on Robert D. Cooter, *Decentralized Law for a Complex Economy: The Structural Approach to Adjudicating the New Law Merchant*, 144 U. Pa. L. Rev. 1643, 1644–54 (1996) and the sources cited therein. For criticism of this historical account, see Emily Kadens, *The Medieval Law Merchant: The Tyranny of a Construct*, 7 J. Legal Analysis 251 (2015).

required merchants to follow old norms found below, not new norms imposed from above.

This account is consistent with common law adjudication. In common law systems like England and the United States, judges usually resolve disputes by following old precedents, meaning past decisions about similar disputes. However, judges sometimes develop new precedents when they face a novel case or circumstances change. In developing new precedents, judges are not supposed to do as they please. They are not supposed to "make" law. They are supposed to "find" it.

Consider Lord Mansfield, a famous English judge. In the eighteenth century, merchants used complicated financial instruments to pay one another. The instruments raised difficult questions about the allocation of risk. To illustrate, suppose *A* delivers goods to *B*, and *B* gives a note to *A* promising to make payment at a later date. *A* sells the note to *C*. Then *B* discovers that the goods are defective. Must *B* pay *C* anyway? Must *C* seek redress from *A*? Lord Mansfield apparently found answers by scrutinizing existing business practices and incorporating the best ones into the common law.

Coordination games provide perspective on this history. In general, everyone subject to law wants to understand it, and everyone who makes law wants it to be understood. Everyone benefits from clear communication. Sometimes the communication is clear to most people though not all. In such cases, good judges find and enforce the existing equilibrium.

C. Communication in the Long Run

We have discussed minor misunderstandings, as when lawmakers send the message "yes" and Stella alone hears "no." Nearly everyone has coordinated on meaning. Here we consider major misunderstandings. Major misunderstanding occurs when lawmakers and citizens fail to coordinate on meaning. Through the statute, lawmakers might send the message "yes," but most citizens receive the message "no." This corresponds to the top-right box in Figure 11.1. In this case, courts cannot find the equilibrium because it does not exist. Court must make the equilibrium.

Making an equilibrium—announcing the meaning of a law—has many consequences. For now we focus on one consequence, communication costs. Lawmakers sent the message "yes" and citizens received "no." If the court holds that the law means "no," then lawmakers must change how they send messages. Lawmakers bear communication costs. If the court holds that the law means "yes," then citizens must change how they receive messages. Citizens bear communication costs. Fewer costs are better, and citizens vastly outnumber legislators, so perhaps judges should hold that the law means "no." This would place the onus on legislators.

To make these ideas concrete, let's return to *Locke*. The statute required miners to file paperwork "prior to December 31" or lose their claims. For the sake of example, let's assume a major misunderstanding. Lawmakers wanted a deadline of December 30 as the text says. However, the text is clumsy (why not say "by December 30"?), and the deadline is arbitrary (who wants paperwork the day before the year's end?). So miners understood the deadline to be December 31. If a court makes the deadline December 31, then lawmakers must change how they communicate. Next time they will have to write something like, "by December 30—and yes, we mean December 30!" If a court makes the deadline December 30, then miners must change how they communicate. They will have to learn to concentrate on text and ignore background considerations, like the arbitrariness of the deadline. Getting hundreds of legislators to change a few words seems easier than getting thousands of miners to change how they read. To minimize communication costs, the court should make the deadline December 31.

This conclusion seems right in the individual case. What about the run of cases? Lawmakers and miners do not communicate about one deadline only. Through statutes and regulations, lawmakers communicate many messages to miners, probably hundreds. Miners want to receive those messages. Both sides want to communicate accurately at low cost. Some methods of communication work better than others. We can convey details more accurately with words than with smoke signals. How can a court minimize communication costs in the run of cases?

Let's formulate the problem with a matrix showing long-run payoffs. Suppose the lawmakers are textualists (the law means what it says), whereas the miners are intentionalists (the law means what they think lawmakers intended). This difference explains the major miscommunication. In Figure 11.2, the parties are in the top-right box. Making the deadline December 31 would push the parties to the bottom-right box. Coordinating on intentionalism would yield a long-run payoff of 5 for each. Making the deadline December 30 would push the parties to the top-left box. Coordinating on textualism would yield a long-run payoff of *x* for each. The court should make the deadline December 30 if *x* exceeds 5, and it should make the deadline December 31 if 5 exceeds *x*. The best decision turns on whether textualism has lower or higher communication costs than intentionalism in the run of cases.

In our example, textualism surely has higher costs in the short term. Miners must change how they read mining statutes. That's costlier than getting relatively few legislators to change how they draft bills. But in the long term, textualism might make all communication easier. Miners need not read legislative history or contemplate lawmakers' mental states. They just need to read the words. If the long-term gains are large enough, then coordinating on text is best for communication.

		Miners: Text	Miners: Intent
Lawmakers	Text	x, x	0, 0
	Intent	0, 0	5, 5

Figure 11.2. Text or Intent?

This analysis provides an economic foundation for textualists who argue that concentrating on text makes law more predictable. In our language, "predictable" means "low communication costs." Textualists believe their preferred equilibrium will minimize those costs in the long term.

Are the textualists right? The short-term cost of getting people to change how they read and interpret could be significant. Remember that textualism relies heavily on the canons of construction. How many miners know, for example, *noscitur a sociis*? This short-term cost increases with the number of interpreters (in our example, the number of miners). On the benefit side, even if we assume that textualism comes with lower communication costs, this does not settle the question. We need to know how much lower. If intentionalism usually produces difficult and costly communication, with regulated parties wasting time and effort reading committee reports and contemplating intentions, then coordinating on text offers a substantial improvement. But if intentionalism usually produces easy and clear communication, with only occasional breakdowns as in *Locke*, then forcing people to coordinate on text offers only a small improvement, perhaps too small to justify the switch. In this case, x in Figure 11.2 is less than 5.

To generalize, *given a major misunderstanding, courts must make the equilibrium. A good equilibrium minimizes communication costs in the run of cases.* This prescription supplies judges with a target, but hitting it is difficult. Courts usually cannot determine the cost-minimizing equilibrium with certainty.

Questions

11.8. To facilitate coordination, a judge makes a textualist decision today and commits to making textualist decisions in the future. Is this commitment credible? Why, despite centuries of interpretation by courts, have lawmakers and citizens failed to coordinate on a method of interpretation?

11.9. Does the statute let Elmer inherit from Francis even though he murdered him? Assume a major misunderstanding. Lawmakers meant to answer "yes," but most people understood "no" because of morality: it would be unjust to let Elmer inherit through murder. In the long run, is it easier for lawmakers to write clearer text or for people to suspend morality when reading text?[34]

11.10. "Drop everything!" If you heard this command, you might drop your pencil, but you wouldn't drop your baby. Is it possible for people to coordinate on the meaning of words alone? Will we always understand written laws to have exceptions?[35]

[34] *Cf.* Andrew Gold, *Absurd Results, Scrivener's Errors, and Statutory Interpretation*, 75 U. Cin. L. Rev. 25 (2006) (arguing that sufficiently absurd results, or sufficiently clear errors, would be taken into account by competent readers, so applying the absurdity doctrine and fixing scrivener's errors should be acceptable to textualists).

[35] *See* Lon L. Fuller, *The Case of the Speluncean Explorers*, 62 Harv. L. Rev. 616, 625–26 (1949).

Who Reads the Law?

The Class Action Fairness Act of 2005 made it possible to remove (i.e., transfer) some big-dollar lawsuits in the United States from state courts to federal courts. Plaintiffs in those cases usually preferred to stay in state court. According to the statute, they could appeal an order to move to federal court "not less than 7 days after entry of the order."[36] This language is very peculiar. To prevent litigation from dragging on, statutes like this usually create deadlines ("You have one week to appeal"). But this statute creates a waiting period. It says you cannot appeal for at least one week. The statute almost certainly contains an error. Lawmakers wrote "less" but meant "more."

Many courts corrected the error, but not without controversy. Judge Bybee on the U.S. Court of Appeals for the Ninth Circuit thought "less" meant "less." Turning "less" into "more," he wrote, "strips citizens of the ability to rely on the laws as written."[37]

Our analysis illuminates and challenges Judge Bybee's argument. He believed that correcting the error would increase citizens' communication costs. Instead of reading the text alone, citizens must read the text and consider lawmakers' likely intentions. Stated this way, correcting the error sounds like it will increase costs. But let's state it another way. Correcting the error means that citizens can rely on common sense about law's meaning, whereas not correcting the error means that citizens must ignore common sense and read legal text carefully. Stated this way, *not* correcting the error sounds like it will increase costs.

If the citizens reading this law are ordinary people, then Judge Bybee might have it wrong. Ordinary people might find it difficult to ignore common sense and read text very carefully. Do you think ordinary people read this law? Probably not. The law addresses big-dollar class action lawsuits. Most people reading this law are lawyers, and lawyers are trained to read text carefully. Perhaps Judge Bybee got the argument right but stated it wrong (a scrivener's error?). Perhaps he should have argued that turning "less" into "more" would increase *lawyers'* communication costs.

D. Transition Costs

We have connected interpretation to communication, which is central to the rule of law. Law should be clear and accessible.[38] Next we connect interpretation to transition costs. When law changes, people incur transition costs. Transition costs come in many forms. Here are examples: a new prohibition on alcohol makes a distillery worthless; abolishment of an agency forces employees to find new jobs; a reduction in the military's budget requires planners to reassess priorities; an environmental law leads carmakers to change their manufacturing process; passage of the Sarbanes-Oxley Act causes banks to hire lawyers to advise them.

36 Class Action Fairness Act of 2005, Pub. L. 109-2, 119 Stat. 4 (2005) (codified at 28 U.S.C. § 1453(c)(1)).

37 Amalgamated Transit Union Local 1309, AFL-CIO v. Laidlaw Transit Services, Inc., 448 F.3d 1092, 1100 (9th Cir. 2006) (Bybee, J., dissenting from the denial of rehearing en banc).

38 *See, e.g.*, LON L. FULLER, THE MORALITY OF LAW 49–51 (1964).

In these examples, legislators change law by statute. However, judges can effectively change law through interpretation. Recall the example of Stella, who dug a mine on public land. The question is whether the law authorized her mine. Suppose the statute seems to say "yes," but a court interprets the statute and says the answer is "no." For Stella, the court's interpretation has effectively changed the law, wasting her investment in the mine. Interpretation by courts can create transition costs.

In the last section, we argued that good interpretation minimizes communication costs. In fact, a communication cost can be a type of transition cost. Thus, we can generalize and say that good interpretation minimizes all transition costs.

Coordination games help us connect interpretation to transition costs. Suppose we face a minor misunderstanding. Lawmakers and citizens mostly coordinate on the meaning of law but fail in some cases. In this situation, judges minimize transition costs by finding and enforcing the equilibrium. To illustrate, recall again the law punishing drivers who fail to "stop . . . any school bus which is stopped" to load or unload children. Surely the legislators wanted drivers to stop *at* school buses, and surely nearly everyone who read the statute understood this. Stopping *at* school buses is the existing equilibrium. Enforcing this equilibrium matches almost everyone's expectations, so almost no one must change behavior. Legislators need not pass a new law, and bus drivers need not develop new protections for their passengers. Finding the equilibrium minimizes transition costs.

What if we face a major misunderstanding, meaning lawmakers and citizens have failed to coordinate? In this case, the judge makes an equilibrium through interpretation. To minimize transition costs, we must estimate the costs associated with every possible equilibrium and compare them. Judges cannot do this with certainty because transition costs are difficult to measure. However, we can make progress with careful reasoning. To see how, consider *Riggs*. The court had to decide if murderous heirs could inherit. For the sake of example, assume lawmakers and citizens disagreed among themselves on the correct answer to this question. The court could resolve the disagreement by answering "yes" or "no." If the court answered "yes," then many people would rewrite their wills. They would add a sentence saying something like, "I leave my farm to Tucker, unless he murders me." This would require time and attention. If the court answered "no," then few people would rewrite their wills. Answering "no" might scramble the plans of some heirs planning a murder, but presumably there wouldn't be many of them. Answering "no" would minimize transition costs.

We drew this conclusion without attempting to measure transition costs. To minimize those costs, we don't need to know their absolute values. We don't need to know whether, translated into money, answering "yes" in *Riggs* would create \$100 million in costs and answering "no" would create \$5 million. We just need relative values. Answering "no" would create fewer costs than answering "yes."

Transition costs in *Riggs* seem easy to analyze. Other cases are harder. Recall *Locke* and the law requiring miners to file paperwork "prior to December 31." Let's assume a major misunderstanding. Lawmakers wanted a deadline of December 30, but miners understood the deadline to be December 31. If a court makes the deadline December 31, the government must change how it processes paperwork. This might require, for example, extra employees to work on New Year's Eve. If a court makes the deadline December 30, then some miners will lose their claims. Which decision has higher transition costs? The answer depends on how many miners would lose their claims, the value of those claims, how many government employees would have to work an extra day, and so on. We can only speculate about these relative costs.

Having discussed transition costs, we now relate them to the two methods of interpretation, textualism and intentionalism. Either method can cause surprise in a particular case, as when people coordinate on intent ("drivers must stop *at* the bus") but the court makes a textualist decision, or vice versa. Surprise creates transition costs. In the run of cases, textualism might minimize communication costs, and low communication costs mean fewer surprises. But as discussed earlier, the long-run relationship between textualism and communication costs is uncertain. Finally, intentionalism is usually thought to give judges more discretion. They might use that discretion to reduce transition costs or (inadvertently) to create them.

Questions

11.11. In *Locke*, making the deadline December 30 would cause a miner to lose his claim. Suppose the mine would close and transfer to the government, which would then transfer the mine to a new owner to reopen. The prior owner pays a cost. Does the new owner get a benefit? Is there an overall cost for society?

11.12. We wrote that "good interpretation minimizes all transition costs." This prescription masks difficult trade-offs. In *Locke*, suppose that making the deadline December 30 would minimize communication costs but create other transition costs because some valuable mines would close for a while. Does making the deadline December 30 minimize all transition costs?

11.13. The Class Action Fairness Act said that litigants could appeal an order "not less than 7 days after entry of the order."[39] The law contained a scrivener's error. Lawmakers meant to write "more," not "less." In an intentionalist opinion, the Ninth Circuit Court of Appeals held that "less" meant "more."[40] In a textualist opinion, Judge Bybee argued that "less" meant "less."[41] In another textualist opinion, Judge Easterbrook held that "less" meant "less" but that another provision capped the time to appeal at 30 days, alleviating any risk of "indefinite delay."[42] Which approach minimizes transition costs? Which creates the most transition costs?

E. Justice and Exceptions

When people read a gripping case, they don't think first of communication or transition costs. They think of justice. In *Riggs*, Elmer murdered his grandfather to secure the

[39] Class Action Fairness Act of 2005, Pub. L. 109-2, 119 Stat. 4 (2005) (codified at 28 U.S.C. § 1453(c)(1)). Congress later amended the law, replacing "not less than 7 days" with "not more than 10 days." Statutory Time-Periods Technical Amendments Act of 2009, Pub. L. 111-16, 123 Stat. 1607 (amending 28 U.S.C. § 1453(c)(1)).

[40] *See* Amalgamated Transit Union Local 1309, AFL-CIO v. Laidlaw Transit Services, Inc., 435 F.3d 1140 (9th Cir. 2006).

[41] *See id.* at 1095 (Bybee, J., dissenting from the denial of rehearing en banc).

[42] Spivey v. Vertrue, 528 F.3d 982, 985 (7th Cir. 2008).

inheritance. Most people reading the case don't think, "What decision about Elmer will clarify law?" They think, "What does justice require?" The text of the statute permitted Elmer to inherit. However, the court consulted "general principles of natural law and justice" to conclude that Elmer could not inherit "from an ancestor . . . whom he has murdered."[43]

Riggs exemplifies a general feature of law: it can produce injustice in some cases. Most laws appear to permit some behavior that justice forbids and forbid some behavior that justice permits. Cases like *Riggs* expose these errors. Judges must decide whether to allow an error by applying the law as written or to correct the error by making an exception.

To correct an error in the name of justice, judges must confront a hard question: What *is* justice? Plato and Aristotle debated the answer in ancient Greece, and philosophers and lawyers debate it today. Justice involves freedom, fairness, equality, distribution, impartiality, reason giving, and more. Different people understand and weigh these values differently. Thus, opinions about justice differ. Even cases like *Riggs* divide people. The court thought justice prohibited Elmer from inheriting. But Judge Gray dissented, arguing that "the demands of public policy are satisfied by the proper execution of the laws and the punishment of the crime."[44] In other words, justice demands doing what the law says and no more. The law said to let Elmer inherit.

Economists do not have a theory of justice. Often they equate justice with social welfare,[45] so whatever maximizes social welfare must maximize justice. This does not satisfy many lawyers or philosophers. Economics cannot assist public law by dictating commitments that lawyers reject. It must accommodate law's commitments. Thus, we accept justice as an end of law that can be distinct from social welfare. However, we do not attempt to define justice. Instead, we analyze who can identify what justice requires. That depends on information.

In general, legislators have better information than judges. They can hire experts, commission reports, and hold hearings. Good legislators know something about the preferences and priorities of the citizens they represent. Thus, legislators usually make better policy than judges. Similarly, we expect legislators to have a better (or at least equally good) sense of justice as judges. Suppose a lithium mine creates jobs for workers, profits for shareholders, and batteries for devices like cellphones and laptops. But the mine also pollutes groundwater in a nearby community. What does justice require? Closing the mine, restoring the groundwater, paying reparations to the community? What if closing the mine impoverishes the community and worsens climate change (electric cars use lithium-ion batteries)? The demands of justice seem complex. In general, we expect legislators to surpass judges in managing complex problems. This reasoning supports Judge Gray. Compared to judges, legislators have better information when writing laws. So judges promote justice by doing what the law says and no more.

Sometimes, however, judges have an information advantage. Legislators make law for the typical case, whereas judges see anomalous cases. In *Riggs*, the legislators had

[43] Riggs v. Palmer, 22 N.E. 188, 190 (N.Y. 1889).

[44] *Id.* at 192 (Gray, J., dissenting).

[45] *Cf.* Louis Kaplow & Steven Shavell, Fairness Versus Welfare (2002). Recall that for economists "social welfare" is an aggregation of individuals' utility.

enacted a statute for the usual inheritance, but the case involved a very unusual inheritance. Anomalous cases can reveal information that legislators did not consider.

To deepen our analysis, let's distinguish two kinds of facts. *Legislative facts* relate to lawmaking in general, whereas *adjudicative facts* relate to an individual case.[46] Do lithium mines create jobs, pollute groundwater, and promote clean cars? These are legislative facts. Did a specific mine discharge a specific quantity of pollution near Perth, Australia? This is an adjudicative fact.

Judges usually have good adjudicative facts because they review individual cases. To illustrate, the judges in *Riggs* knew that Elmer murdered Francis in cold blood (he poisoned him). What about legislative facts? Usually legislators have better legislative facts, but not always. If the legislators who drafted the statute in *Riggs* never considered the possibility of murderous heirs, then the judges had a better legislative fact. The case revealed something that the legislators didn't know (murderous heirs exist). But perhaps the legislators had considered murderous heirs. They might have reasoned as follows:

> We do not want cold-blooded murderers to inherit. But what if someone kills a testator to alleviate her suffering? What if forbidding the murderous heir from inheriting would cause the testator's property to go to someone she liked less? And what about false convictions? If *A* is erroneously convicted of murdering *B*, then *A* will go to prison unjustly. We should not compound the injustice by forbidding *A* from inheriting from *B*. Murderous heirs are complicated. We think it's best to let them inherit.

If legislators reasoned like this, then they had better legislative facts than the judges. The legislators considered the problem of murderous heir comprehensively, whereas the judges reviewed just one case.

To generalize, doing justice requires good information. When judges have more adjudicative and legislative facts, they can promote justice better than legislators. The case for making exceptions to written law is stronger. Conversely, when judges have fewer adjudicative and legislative facts, the case for making exceptions is weaker. In the typical case, judges have more adjudicative facts but fewer legislative facts. To make an exception to written law, the justice gained by responding to the facts of a specific case should exceed the justice lost from disrupting an all-things-considered good law. People disagree about this balance. People disagree on whether justice can be balanced at all.

We conclude by relating these ideas to textualism and intentionalism. Both methods of interpretation can cause injustice. With textualism, judges resist making exceptions to written law. This can cause injustice in egregious cases. With intentionalism, judges make more exceptions to written law. This can cause injustice when judges err, placing too much emphasis on the adjudicative facts they know and too little on the legislative facts they don't. *Riggs* demonstrates the problem. Who had justice on his side: Judge Earl, who wrote the court's opinion and invented an exception to the legislature's law? Or Judge Gray, who would let a murderer inherit?

[46] *See* Kenneth Culp Davis, *An Approach to Problems of Evidence in the Administrative Process*, 55 Harv. L. Rev. 364, 404–07 (1942).

Questions

11.14. Are transition costs relevant to justice?

11.15. According to an old case, a court should only disregard a statute's text if "the absurdity and injustice of applying the provision to the case, would be so monstrous, that all mankind would, without hesitation, unite in rejecting the application."[47] Who has better facts in such a case, the judge hearing it or the legislators who made the statute?

11.16. Justice Holmes, a famous American judge, wrote, "Great cases, like hard cases, make bad law. For great cases are called great, not by reason of their importance . . . but because of some accident of immediate overwhelming interest which appeals to the feelings and distorts the judgment."[48] Can you restate this idea using the concepts of adjudicative facts, legislative facts, and judicial error?

11.17. Earlier we connected justice to information. This question asks you to connect justice to two other factors, impartiality and capacity.

(a) Suppose the legislature is dominated by partisans who are not representative of society, whereas the judges are independent. To promote justice, should the judges make more exceptions to written law?

(b) Recall the case of John Mendez, who drove by the bus discharging children. The judge refused to correct the scrivener's error in the law, and he let Mendez go. The judge said, "I hope that this is addressed [by the legislature] so we don't have to keep dealing with this."[49] In fact, the legislature was not in session, so lawmakers could not correct the scrivener's error for at least a month. Does the legislature's limited capacity affect whether the judge should fix the error?

Minimizing Errors, Maximizing Justice

Should courts follow the law wherever it leads, or should they make exceptions to promote justice? This venerable question relates to a topic from the previous chapter: accuracy in adjudication. Recall Quita the driver. If Quita sped but the judge concludes she did not (false negative), Quita might speed next time because she knows she can get away with it. If Quita did not speed but the judge concludes she did (false positive), Quita might speed next time because she has nothing to lose, she'll get punished for speeding either way. To improve Quita's driving, law must make fewer errors, but this is hard. Improving one type of error often worsens the other. To illustrate, suppose the state requires less evidence to punish people for speeding. This will decrease false negatives but increase false positives. Good law minimizes the combination of errors.

[47] Sturges v. Crowninshield, 17 U.S. 122, 203 (1819).

[48] N. Sec. Co. v. United States, 193 U.S. 197, 364 (1904) (Holmes, J., dissenting).

[49] Tom Jackman, *2 Little Letters Acquit Man Who Passed Stopped School Bus*, WASH. POST, Dec. 1, 2010.

We can apply these ideas to interpretation.[50] Legislators lack information and face other constraints. Thus, they write imperfect laws that occasionally produce injustice. To correct injustice, judges must first identify it. They need a test to decide if the law produces a just outcome, meaning they should apply it, or an unjust outcome, meaning they should make an exception. Like radar guns for speeding, tests for injustice make mistakes because judges are not omniscient. Imagine a "liberal" test that is quick to identify injustice. The test will improve one kind of error (injustice in the law that warrants an exception). But it will introduce another kind of error (the law is just, but judges err and make an exception anyway). A "conservative" test runs the opposite risk. It will decrease one kind of error but increase another.

In general, intentionalists favor a liberal test for finding injustice, whereas textualists favor a conservative test. Sometimes their disagreement feels like a pitched battle between two grand legal traditions. But perhaps that overstates the matter. They might just disagree about the distribution of errors.

F. Epilogue on Interpretation

All words require interpretation. In law, much interpretation happens through the ordinary meaning principle. People read a law's words, consider the context, and isolate the meaning. Diverse lawyers and judges coordinate on the meaning of law in this way. But sometimes this fails. Some words are ambiguous, and different canons of construction yield different conclusions. Drafting errors put pressure on ordinary meaning. Our sense of justice drives our judgment. Thus, we do not always settle into an equilibrium. Divisions emerge over how best to interpret the law.

We have studied two methods of interpretation, textualism and intentionalism. Often these methods yield the same conclusion about a law's meaning, but not always. In *Riggs*, most textualists would conclude that Elmer could inherit because that's what the words said. Many intentionalists would reach the opposite conclusion. In general, intentionalists feel freer to depart from a law's text.

Which method is better?[51] We have analyzed three values that affect the answer: communication, transitions, and information. A good method of interpretation lowers communication costs among lawmakers and citizens. In general, coordinating on law's text (as opposed to the intentions or purposes behind it) would seem to simplify communication. This supports textualism in ordinary cases. But textualists and intentionalists usually agree about meaning in ordinary cases. They divide in controversial cases like

[50] This discussion draws on Frederick Schauer, *The Practice and Problems of Plain Meaning: A Response to Aleinikoff and Shaw*, 45 VAND. L. REV. 715, 729–32 (1992). *See also* Mario J. Rizzo & Frank S. Arnold, *An Economic Framework for Statutory Interpretation*, 50 LAW & CONTEMP. PROBS. 165 (1987).

[51] Lawyers might ask a different question: "Which method is permissible?" Some believe that intentionalism, regardless of its consequences, is impermissible because judges lack legal authority to depart from law's text or to consult extra-textual sources like legislative history. This must be right in extreme circumstances. Judges do not have authority to ignore or rewrite statutory text as they please, nor do they have authority to consult tea leaves or tarot cards to find meaning. We focus on typical circumstances, as when most judges mostly follow the text of law, but some judges depart from the text in unusual circumstances. Judges in many legal systems have done this for centuries.

Riggs. Would it help or hurt communication to reject the absurdity doctrine and adhere rigorously to text? The answer depends on things that are hard to observe and measure, like whether people can suspend their moral intuitions when reading laws.

A good method of interpretation minimizes transition costs. How does textualism affect transition costs? The answer depends on how regulated parties interpret law. If they are mostly intentionalists, a textualist decision might surprise them, driving up transition costs. We'd have fewer surprises if everyone—judges, lawyers, citizens—coordinated on one method of interpretation. Coordinating so many people is difficult. Among other problems, a judge using one method today cannot credibly commit to using the same method tomorrow.

Compared to textualism, intentionalism seems to offer flexibility in interpretation. Flexibility lets judges manage transition costs case by case. But judges make errors like everyone else. Whether they manage transition costs well depends in part on their information.

This gets us to justice. To do justice, judges need information. Often they have many adjudicative facts but few legislative facts. Do judges have enough information to justify making some exceptions to written law? Textualists usually assume the answer is "no." Sometimes this causes injustice because sometimes judges do have good information. Intentionalists are more willing to make exceptions. This promotes justice when their information is good but impedes it when their information is bad.

All things considered, which method is best? The answer depends on many factors that are difficult to assess. In Samuel Beckett's play, *Waiting for Godot*, Vladimir and Estragon debate religion and philosophy while waiting for the mysterious Godot.[52] Similarly, lawyers debate interpretation while waiting for the right answer to emerge. Godot never arrives.

II. Legal Doctrine

In deciding cases, judges rely on old precedents and make new ones. *Legal doctrine* refers to the body of precedents that judges produce. In public law, legal doctrine translates constitutions, statutes, and other laws into actionable procedures. To illustrate, the Equal Protection Clause in the U.S. Constitution prohibits states from denying "to any person within its jurisdiction the equal protection of the laws."[53] Recall Minnesota's law banning plastic milk containers but not paper milk containers. The law treats plastic and paper manufacturers unequally, but does it violate the Constitution? The language of the Equal Protection Clause does not supply the answer. Instead, lawyers consult the legal doctrine. According to the doctrine, the ban on plastic is constitutional if it "rationally relate[s]" to a "legitimate" state interest.[54]

In this section we analyze legal doctrine. We begin by studying the form of doctrine. Like legislators, judges choose between rules and standards. Then we analyze prophylactic rules, meaning rules that deliberately overprotect rights or interests. Next, we

52 Samuel Beckett, Waiting for Godot (Harold Bloom ed., 1987).
53 U.S. Const. amend. XIV.
54 Minnesota v. Clover Leaf Creamery Co., 449 U.S. 456 (1981).

consider why judges follow precedents that they oppose. Finally, we analyze acquiescence. Failure by legislators to override an interpretation does not mean the interpretation is correct.

A. Revisiting Rules versus Standards

An earlier chapter discussed rules and standards. Rules are precise, such as a speed limit of 55 miles per hour, whereas standards are imprecise, such as a limit of "reasonable speeds." Like legislators setting speed limits, judges choose between rules and standards when making legal doctrine. Consider *Caperton v. A.T. Massey Coal Co.*[55] A jury held that a coal company owed $50 million in damages. The company appealed to the Supreme Court of West Virginia. Before the appeal happened, the company's chairman spent millions of dollars getting Brent Benjamin elected to that court. Could the new judge Benjamin hear the company's appeal?[56] The U.S. Supreme Court said "no." The Court announced a standard: judges must recuse themselves from cases when there is "risk of actual bias."[57]

When analyzing delegation, we identified trade-offs between rules and standards. We wrote, "rules decrease diversion costs but increase inflexibility costs, whereas standards increase diversion costs but decrease inflexibility costs." Let's consider these trade-offs in legal doctrine. *Caperton* involved a judge who got political support from a litigant. Future cases could involve a judge who shares a friendship, hobby, or religion with a litigant. Must judges recuse themselves in such circumstances? The standard in *Caperton* lets lower courts gather adjudicative facts and decide case by case. Thus, the standard decreases inflexibility costs. However, the standard gives lower courts discretion. Judges might exploit that discretion and decide cases the way they want, not the way the Supreme Court wants. Thus, the standard increases diversion costs.

Four Justices dissented in *Caperton*. They thought judges should have to recuse in two circumstances: (1) cases where they have a direct financial interest, and (2) criminal contempt cases that result from the defendant's hostility toward the judge.[58] The dissent's test is relatively rule-like. It does not allow lower courts to respond to new circumstances that might warrant recusal, like a case where the judge and litigant are roommates.[59] The dissent's rule would increase inflexibility costs. However, the rule would limit lower court discretion, decreasing diversion costs.

Rules and standards raise another trade-off. In our chapter on delegation we wrote, "standards are cheaper to draft than rules" but "costlier to apply." In *Caperton*, a majority of the Justices thought Benjamin had to recuse himself. However, existing precedents did not require that outcome. So the Court had to make a new precedent. The Court could make the standard—"risk of actual bias"—or it could make a rule identifying

[55] 556 U.S. 868 (2009).

[56] In fact, Benjamin *did* hear the case, and he cast the decisive vote in favor of the coal company, meaning the company did not have to pay the $50 million. Afterward, the U.S. Supreme Court held that Benjamin should have recused himself, so the case had to be litigated again.

[57] Caperton v. A.T. Massey Coal Co., Inc., 556 U.S. 868, 883–84 (2009).

[58] *See id.* at 890–902 (Roberts, C.J., dissenting).

[59] In the United States, judicial codes of conduct, but not the Constitution, forbid a judge from deciding a case involving her roommate.

specific circumstances that require recusal. Formulating the standard is easier than formulating the rule. However, applying the standard is harder than applying a rule. With the standard, lower courts must assess risk case by case. With a rule, lower courts could follow a formula like this: Does the judge have a financial interest in the case, or does the case involve criminal contempt? If the answer to either question is yes, then the judge must recuse, but otherwise he need not.[60]

We have shown that the analysis of rules and standards presented earlier in this book applies to legal doctrine. Now we analyze something new. When lawyers debate rules and standards, they often focus on a value we haven't emphasized: predictability. Consider Chief Justice Roberts's dissenting opinion in *Caperton*. He argued that the Court's "risk of actual bias" standard "provides no guidance to judges and litigants."[61] To illustrate, imagine a judge getting a case involving his favorite high school teacher. Or suppose you sue the chef at the judge's favorite restaurant. Must the judge in either case recuse? The answer depends on whether there's "risk of actual bias." The answer is not obvious.

We can sharpen this idea using a familiar concept: standards create communication costs. People want to know what the law requires them to do. Standards make it harder to figure that out. People might need to hire a lawyer and consider case-specific facts.

Many judges place great weight on predictability. Consider Justice Scalia, an influential jurist who dissented in *Caperton*. He wrote that a "principal purpose" of the Supreme Court "is to clarify the law," and the new risk of bias test "create[s] vast uncertainty."[62] Translated into our language, vaguer legal doctrine increases communication costs.

Do these costs provide a decisive argument against standards? No. To see why, suppose the Court made the following rule: "[T]he Constitution never requires judges to recuse." The language is clear, so communication costs should be low. But the rule is inflexible. It does not respond to different facts. Sometimes the rule will produce results inconsistent with what the Constitution, properly interpreted, requires.

To generalize, standards are better when diversion and communication costs are low. Diversion costs are low when lower courts are faithful agents of the high court that adopts the standards. Communication costs are low when cases have extreme facts (they clearly do or do not violate the standard) and not borderline facts. Furthermore, communication costs are low when the law is rarely tested. Few cases about judicial recusals mean that few people must analyze and predict the vague standard from *Caperton*. Finally, standards are better when inflexibility costs are high. Inflexibility costs are high when the correct outcome of each case depends on facts that are hard to visualize and specify in advance.

To state the converse, rules are better when diversion and communication costs are high and inflexibility costs are low. Diversion costs are high when lower courts are not faithful agents of the high court. Inflexibility costs are low when we can imagine the facts necessary to craft the best rule. Communication costs are high when

[60] We compare a complex standard (many factors could affect the risk of bias) to a simple rule with only two parts. In reality, standards can be simple, and rules can be complex. A complex rule might be harder to apply than a simple standard. *See generally* Louis Kaplow, *A Model of the Optimal Complexity of Legal Rules*, 11 J.L. ECON. & ORG. 150 (1995).

[61] Caperton v. A.T. Massey Coal Co., Inc., 556 U.S. 868, 890–91 (2009) (Roberts, C.J., dissenting).

[62] *Id.* at 902 (Scalia, J., dissenting).

the law is frequently tested. Many cases about recusals mean that many people must analyze and predict the vague standard from *Caperton*. Justice Scalia worried about that problem. Recall that *Caperton* involved political support for an elected judge. In his dissenting opinion, Scalia wrote that the new standard creates uncertainty "with respect to a point of law that can be raised in all litigated cases in (at least) those 39 States that elect their judges."[63]

Questions

11.18. Do textualists tend to favor rules or standards? What about intentionalists?

11.19. *Rules* have their content determined ex ante, before anyone acts, whereas *standards* have their content determined ex post. *Simple* directives depend on few facts, whereas *complex* directives depend on many.[64] Here's an example of a simple standard: the speed limit is "reasonable speeds," where reasonableness depends only on the weather.
   (a) Give an example of a simple rule, a complex rule, and a complex standard.
   (b) Compare a complex rule and a simple standard. Which one has higher inflexibility costs? Which one is costlier to apply?
   (c) Commentators often compare simple rules to complex standards, as we did in the analysis above. Why?

B. Cycles in Doctrine

Scholars studying legal doctrine in the United States noticed something interesting. In many areas of law, the doctrine seems to oscillate, shifting from rules to standards, then back to rules, and so on. What explains this pattern?

One answer involves personnel. Some judges prefer rules, others prefer standards, and the doctrine shifts depending on who sits on courts.[65]

Another explanation involves *selection bias*. Selection bias arises when the population you observe does not represent the population generally. Here is a simple illustration. If you spend all of your time around weightlifters, you might think that everyone is strong. But this is wrong. The weightlifters you observe are a biased sample of the population. Here is a complicated illustration of selection bias. During World War II, British planes attacked the German army. Some planes suffered damage but returned safely to base. Other planes got shot down. The British asked Abraham Wald, a statistician, where they should add extra armor to their planes. Wald observed the damaged planes after their missions and gave this advice: add armor where the planes do *not* have damage. For example, if the planes only have damage on their wings, then add armor to the body. Why did he offer this advice? Wald did not see all damaged

[63] *Id.*

[64] *See* Louis Kaplow, *A Model of the Optimal Complexity of Legal Rules*, 11 J.L. Econ. & Org. 150 (1995); Louis Kaplow, *Rules Versus Standards: An Economic Analysis*, 42 Duke L.J. 557 (1992).

[65] Kathleen M. Sullivan, *The Supreme Court, 1991 Term—Foreword: The Justices of Rules and Standards*, 106 Harv. L. Rev. 22 (1992).

planes, only damaged planes that returned safely to base. If those planes had damage on their wings but not their bodies, that meant that planes hit in the body must crash. So add armor to the body.[66]

Judges face selection bias when the disputes they see do not represent disputes in general. This can affect the doctrine they make.[67] To explain the idea, let's imagine two cases. In Case 1, Uma drives through a red light because she has a medical emergency. In Case 2, Vince drives through a red light because he's late for a meeting. Suppose the doctrine begins as a rule: "No running red lights." Given this rule, the police give Uma and Vince tickets. Vince does not bother challenging his ticket because his violation is obvious. The judge does not see Case 2. However, Uma challenges her ticket because the rule seems unfair in her case. The judge sees Case 1 and decides that the rule is too inflexible. The judge replaces the rule with a standard: "No running red lights, unless you have a reasonable excuse." Now suppose Cases 1 and 2 happen again. Uma does not get a ticket because she has a reasonable excuse. The judge does not see Case 1. However, Vince gets a ticket because the police do not think his excuse is reasonable. Vince challenges his ticket, so the judge sees Case 2. The judge decides that the rule is too flexible. People like Vince challenge their tickets, wasting the court's time. So the judge replaces the standard with a rule: "No running red lights." And the process repeats.

Judges usually do not make doctrine on traffic lights. However, the idea applies in settings where they do make doctrine. For example, the Fifth Amendment to the U.S. Constitution protects people from self-incrimination.[68] Police cannot force you to confess to a crime. At first the doctrine prohibited "involuntary" confessions.[69] This standard led to difficult questions, like whether a 19-year-old drug addict described as a "near mental defective" had voluntarily confessed to a crime.[70] In *Miranda v. Arizona*, the Supreme Court replaced the standard with a rule. For a confession to be admissible in court, the police must advise the accused that he has a "right to remain silent, that any statement he makes can be used against him," and so on, and the accused must waive his right.[71] The rule led to difficult questions, like whether a cop must state the Miranda warning in urgent situations, as when a suspect is hiding a gun.[72] The Court relaxed the rule by adding a "public safety" exception.[73] Fifth Amendment doctrine oscillates between rules and standards.

[66] For a recent account of this famous story, see Peter Brannen, *Why Earth's History Appears So Miraculous*, The Atlantic, Mar. 15, 2018.

[67] The following discussion draws on Adrian Vermeule, *The Cycles of Statutory Interpretation*, 68 U. Chi. L. Rev. 149 (2001), and Scott Baker & Pauline Kim, *A Dynamic Model of Doctrinal Choice*, 4 J. Legal Analysis 329 (2012). *See also* Jason Scott Johnston, *Uncertainty Chaos and the Torts Process: An Economic Analysis of Legal Form*, 76 Cornell L. Rev. 341 (1991).

[68] U.S. Const. amend. V ("No person . . . shall be compelled in any criminal case to be a witness against himself.").

[69] *See* Miranda v. Arizona, 384 U.S. 436, 442–66 (1966).

[70] Townsend v. Sain, 372 U.S. 293, 307–09 (1963).

[71] Miranda v. Arizona, 384 U.S. 436, 469 (1966) ("At the outset, if a person in custody is to be subjected to interrogation, he must first be informed in clear and unequivocal terms that he has the right to remain silent . . . [which] must be accompanied by the explanation that anything said can and will be used against an individual in a court.") The exact language used by police varies by location.

[72] *See* New York v. Quarles, 467 U.S. 649 (1984).

[73] *Id.* at 657–58.

Cycles of Interpretation

We used selection bias to illuminate shifts between rules and standards. The same idea might explain shifts between methods of interpretation.[74] In Case 1, the statute has ambiguous text, but the legislature's intention seems clear given the legislative history. In Case 2, the statute has clear text, but the legislative history is ambiguous. If everyone knows the judge is a textualist, no one bothers bringing Case 2. They know how the judge will rule, so they settle out of court and save the expense of litigation. The judge does not see Case 2. However, the judge sees Case 1. Case 1 persuades the judge (or the court) to embrace intentionalism because intentionalism resolves the case. Now the cases repeat. No one brings Case 1 because they can predict how the judge will rule. However, the judge sees Case 2. Case 2 persuades the judge (or the court) to reject intentionalism and embrace textualism because textualism resolves the case. And so on.

For this kind of cycle to recur, judges must forget. In our example, the judge must forget about Case 1 when resolving Case 2. Forgetfulness leads to the *switcher's curse*.[75] The curse happens when a decision maker keeps switching to a new approach because he has forgotten the reasons for the old approach. If he remembered those reasons, he might keep the old approach, saving himself and everyone subject to his decisions a lot of transition costs.

The switcher's curse might be rare among individual judges. Many judges have keen memories for their cases. However, the curse might be common among multiple judges. In the United States, Chief Justice John Marshall emphasized text in the early 1800s.[76] The Supreme Court decided *Church of the Holy Trinity*, an intentionalist opinion relying on legislative history, in the late 1800s.[77] Justice Scalia began pushing the Supreme Court toward textualism a century later.[78] Of course, this sketch of history ignores many details. The Supreme Court has always mixed textualism and intentionalism.

C. Prophylactic Rules

Compared to standards, rules are inflexible. Inflexibility makes rules under- and overinclusive when assessed against their purposes. As a reminder, an underinclusive rule does not apply in situations where it should, and an overinclusive rule applies in situations where it should not. An earlier chapter demonstrated with voting. Suppose

[74] The following discussion draws on Adrian Vermeule, *The Cycles of Statutory Interpretation*, 68 U. Chi. L. Rev. 149 (2001).

[75] Aaron Edlin, *Conservatism and Switcher's Curse*, 19 Am. L. Econ. Rev. 49 (2017).

[76] *See* John F. Manning, *Textualism and the Equity of the Statute*, 101 Colum. L. Rev. 1 (2001). *But see* William N. Eskridge, Jr., *All About Words: Early Understandings of the "Judicial Power" in Statutory Interpretation, 1776–1806*, 101 Colum. L. Rev. 990 (2001) (arguing that Marshall was a strategic textualist who interpreted statutes equitably).

[77] 143 U.S. 457 (1892).

[78] *See* Jonathan R. Siegel, *The Legacy of Justice Scalia and His Textualist Ideal*, 85 Geo. Wash. L. Rev. 857 (2017).

the law forbids people younger than 18 from voting. The purpose of the law is to ensure that only mature people vote. The rule is underinclusive because it allows some immature adults to vote. The rule is overinclusive because it prevents some mature children from voting.

In general, good rules minimize under- and overinclusiveness. To illustrate with numbers, suppose that making the voting age 18 causes 100 immature adults to vote and stops 50 mature children from voting. The law causes 150 errors. Suppose that a voting age of 19 would cause 70 immature adults to vote and stop 55 mature children from voting. This would cause only 125 errors. Among these two voting ages, 19 minimizes under- and overinclusiveness. So make the voting age 19.

This discussion treats every instance of under- and overinclusiveness the same. Sometimes, however, they deserve different treatment because one is worse than the other. Criminal law supplies a classic example. An underinclusive criminal justice system fails to punish a person guilty of bad conduct. An overinclusive criminal justice system punishes an innocent person. Most people think that punishing an innocent person is worse than freeing a guilty person. According to William Blackstone, a famous English jurist, "better that ten guilty persons escape, than that one innocent suffer."[79]

Under- and overinclusiveness deserve different treatment when one imposes more costs on society than the other. In this case, good rules do not minimize under- and overinclusiveness. Good rules minimize the *costs* of under- and overinclusiveness.

Figure 11.3 represents these ideas. The vertical axis on the left represents errors, and the horizontal axis represents the harshness of the criminal justice system. A system on the left end of the horizontal axis lets many people go without punishment, including many criminals. A system on the right end of the axis punishes many people, including many innocents. Moving rightward from the origin, one solid curve shows the errors from overinclusiveness increasing, and another solid curve shows the errors from underinclusiveness decreasing. The solid u-shaped curve labeled "total errors" sums the two prior two curves, and it represents the total errors from over- and underinclusiveness. In other words, it represents the sum of punished innocents and unpunished criminals. The error-minimizing system of criminal justice has harshness e, where e stands for the number of errors. This corresponds to the low point on the "total errors" curve.

Like Blackstone, most people think that punishing innocents is worse than freeing criminals. Figure 11.3 depicts this idea. The vertical axis on the right represents social costs. As we move rightward from the origin, more innocent people get punished. The dashed, upward-sloping curve shows the social costs of overinclusiveness increasing rapidly. To simplify, we assume that the social costs and instances of underinclusiveness are equal, so that curve does not change. The dashed u-shaped curve labeled "total costs" represents the total social cost of over- and underinclusiveness. In other words, it represents the sum of the social harm from punishing innocents and the social harm from not punishing criminals. The cost-minimizing system of criminal justice has harshness c.

[79] William Blackstone, Commentaries on the Laws of England 1027 (1882).

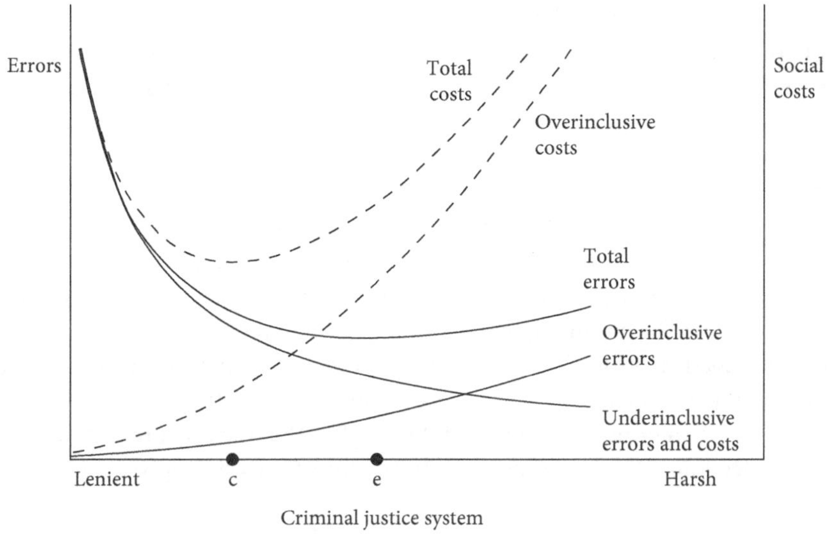

Figure 11.3. Under- and Overinclusiveness

The cost-minimizing system is less harsh than the error-minimizing system. The difference grows from the relatively high cost of punishing innocents and the relatively low cost of freeing criminals. Moving from *e* to *c* increases the number of errors but decreases costs.

This discussion is abstract. Let's make it concrete with a real example. Earlier we mentioned the Fifth Amendment to the U.S. Constitution, which states, "No person . . . shall be compelled in any criminal case to be a witness against himself."[80] This language is clear enough for some cases. Suppose a cop tells a suspect, "Confess to the crime or I'll burn you with a cigarette."[81] Most lawyers would agree that the suspect was "compelled" in violation of the Fifth Amendment. But consider some harder cases. A cop tells a suspect, "Confess to the crime and we'll let your accomplice go." Or, "Confess to crime *x* and we'll stop investigating crime *y*, which we think you also committed." Were the suspects "compelled"? The answer isn't clear. The Fifth Amendment is too vague to resolve these cases.

The Supreme Court has developed legal doctrine about the Fifth Amendment. Prior to the 1960s, the Court adopted a "voluntariness" test.[82] If a suspect confessed voluntarily, the government could use that confession while prosecuting him in court. Conversely, if a suspect confessed involuntarily, the government could not use the confession to make its case. Like the text of the Fifth Amendment, the voluntariness test is a vague standard. Lower courts struggled to apply the standard, and they did not always decide cases the way the Supreme Court wanted.

The Supreme Court sought to replace the voluntariness standard with a rule. A rule would decrease diversion costs but increase inflexibility costs. Inflexibility costs result from under- and overinclusiveness. How to minimize the costs of under- and overinclusiveness? To answer we must compare the two costs. Blackstone considered

[80] U.S. Const. amend. V.
[81] This example is based on a real case of police brutality. *See* Miranda v. Arizona, 384 U.S. 436, 446 (1966) (citing *People v. Portelli*, 15 N.Y. 2d 235 (1965)).
[82] *See, e.g.*, Chambers v. State of Florida, 309 U.S. 227, 238–40 (1940) (finding that a confession, given under prolonged interrogation and isolation, was compelled rather than voluntary).

it worse to punish an innocent person than to free someone guilty. Similarly, many people think it's worse to permit an involuntary confession than to block a voluntary confession. The costs of making Fifth Amendment doctrine underinclusive (allowing some involuntary confessions) exceed the costs of making it overinclusive (blocking some voluntary confessions). Thus, to minimize total costs the rule should be overinclusive.

In *Miranda v. Arizona*, the Supreme Court changed its doctrine on the Fifth Amendment by announcing a rule. Before interrogating a suspect, police must advise him that "he has the right to remain silent[,]" anything he says "can and will be used against" him, and "he has the right to consult with a lawyer and to have the lawyer with him during interrogation[.]"[83] This is the "*Miranda* warning." In general, the police cannot use any statements or confessions by a suspect unless they give him the *Miranda* warning first. By reminding suspects of their rights, the warning prevents some involuntary confessions. However, police sometimes forget the warning, blocking many voluntary confessions.

Compared to the voluntariness standard, the *Miranda* warning is a deliberately overinclusive rule. It deliberately overprotects the Fifth Amendment right. Lawyers have a special term for deliberately overprotective rules made by judges. They call them *prophylactic rules*.

Questions

11.20. Give an example, real or hypothetical, of a prophylactic standard and a deliberately underinclusive rule.

11.21. Some people accept "ordinary" legal doctrine but criticize prophylactic rules. Is there a difference? Evan Caminker says no. He wrote:

> [I]f the argument is that prophylactic rules are different because they rest on some institutional judgments concerning the capacity of courts to enforce constitutional norms, rather than merely on some "pure" interpretation of those norms, this is just wrong. . . . Almost all constitutional doctrine . . . represents a judicial judgment both about the content of the constitutional norm . . . *and also* about a court's institutional capacity to enforce that norm in various ways, taking into account both its own propensities and limitations and those of other relevant actors such as lower federal and state courts.[84]

(a) Suppose that "ordinary" rules aim to minimize *instances* of over- and underinclusiveness, whereas prophylactic rules aim to minimize the *costs* of over- and underinclusiveness. Is one target more objective and manageable than the other?

(b) Judges cannot determine the costs of over- and underinclusiveness with precision. Does this mean they should ignore those costs when making doctrine?

[83] Miranda v. Arizona, 384 U.S. 436, 467–71 (1966).

[84] Evan H. Caminker, Miranda *and Some Puzzles of "Prophylactic" Rules*, 70 U. Cin. L. Rev. 1, 25–26 (2001).

D. On Precedent and "Slippery Slopes"

Throughout this book we have discussed *stare decisis*. According to stare decisis, judges should decide today's case by following the precedents set in prior cases. This principle raises many questions, like what counts as a precedent, and when (if ever) should judges change precedent? Here we explore a different question: Why do judges follow precedent?

Let's begin with some distinctions. *Vertical* stare decisis means a lower court applies a precedent set by a higher court. When trial judges apply the standard set by the Supreme Court in *Caperton*, they engage in vertical stare decisis. The prior chapter analyzed discretion in the judicial hierarchy, and that discussion relates to vertical stare decisis. We do not study vertical precedent here.

Horizontal stare decisis means a court follows its own precedents. When the Supreme Court applies the test from *Caperton* to a new case, it engages in horizontal stare decisis. If the judge or judges do not change, then horizontal stare decisis is predictable. Judges set a precedent they liked, and they continue to apply it.[85] The phenomenon is more interesting when judges change. To illustrate, today's Supreme Court relies on precedents set decades ago by different Justices. The U.S. Court of Appeals for the Ninth Circuit has 29 judges who hear cases in panels of three. Why does the panel consisting of judges x, y, and z follow the precedent set by judges u, v, and w?

Scholars have many explanations for horizontal stare decisis. Judges might feel a duty to follow their court's precedents, or they might value stability in law. Judges might enjoy the "game" of identifying and applying precedents.[86] Here are two other possibilities rooted in economics. First, making a new precedent takes time and effort. If a judge can save herself time and effort by applying an existing precedent, then she might follow the existing precedent, even if she dislikes it. Relatedly, precedents contain information. Suppose Judge Willow got a case about a confusing statute. She resolved the case by making the precedent P.[87] Afterward, Judge Xu gets a similar case about the same statute. Judge Xu can apply the precedent P, or he can make a new precedent. If Judge Xu believes that Judge Willow is capable, then Judge Xu might conclude that he cannot improve upon P. Knowing this, Judge Xu follows the existing precedent, even if he does not fully understand it, rather than make a new precedent.

These ideas help explain horizontal stare decisis. But they cannot explain every instance. Suppose Judge Xu gets a case. The precedent made by Judge Willow supports outcome A, but Judge Xu prefers outcome B. Judge Xu feels some duty to apply his court's precedents, and he places some value on legal stability, but these commitments are not absolute. Judge Xu has time to spare, and he believes he understands the issue better than Judge Willow. None of the previous explanations for horizontal stare decisis apply. Nevertheless, might Judge Xu follow the precedent?

85 If a judge's values change, or if she learns new information, then she might reject her precedent. *See generally* Lewis A. Kornhauser, *An Economic Perspective on Stare Decisis*, 65 Chi.-Kent L. Rev. 63 (1989). This section draws on Kornhauser's work.

86 *See* Richard A. Posner, *What Do Judges and Justices Maximize? (The Same Things Everyone Else Does)*, 3 Sup. Ct. Econ. Rev. 1 (1993).

87 In the United States, individual trial judges do not formally set precedents. For the sake of example, this discussion assumes they do. The ideas apply to more complicated settings with panels of judges who do set precedents.

The answer is yes. To see why, let's return to a concept from early in the book: the prisoner's dilemma. Instead of prisoners, we'll play with judges. Xu can follow Willow's precedent, or he can "buck" precedent (i.e., ignore her precedent) and decide how he likes. Likewise, Willow can follow a precedent made by Xu, or she can buck precedent and decide how she likes. Figure 11.4 shows the possibilities. The top-left box shows the payoffs to the judges if both follow precedent. The bottom-right box shows the payoffs to the judges if both buck precedent. The other boxes show the payoffs if one judge follows precedent and the other bucks. For example, if Xu follows precedent and Willow bucks, he gets a payoff of −3 and she gets a payoff of 4, as the top-right box shows.

We have explained the boxes and payoffs. Now consider the intuitions behind them. Xu would like to buck Willow's precedent, and he would like Willow to follow his precedent. Thus, the highest payoff for Xu appears in the bottom-left box. Willow makes the mirror image calculation, so her highest payoff appears in the top-right box. As a second choice, both judges prefer everyone to follow precedent. As a third choice, both judges prefer no one to follow precedent.

The outcome "follow, follow" yields 6, the highest total payoff for the group. However, this is not the equilibrium. If Willow follows precedent, Xu can follow for a payoff of 3 or buck for a payoff of 4. If Willow bucks precedent, Xu can follow for a payoff of −3 or buck for a payoff of 2. Regardless of Willow's choice, Xu prefers to buck. Willow makes the same calculation, so both judges buck. "Buck, buck" is the equilibrium, yielding a group payoff of 4.

In this example, each judge makes one choice to apply or ignore the other judge's precedent. Usually judges make many such choices. The 29 judges on the Ninth Circuit Court of Appeals decide again and again whether to follow their colleagues' precedents. Instead of a "one-shot" prisoner's dilemma, their game resembles a "repeated" prisoner's dilemma. Cooperation is possible in the repeated game.

Assume Judge Xu reasons as follows. "I can follow Judge Willow's precedent in Case One, or I can buck her precedent. If I buck her precedent, I can decide Case One as I wish. However, Judge Willow will punish me by bucking my precedent when she decides Case Two." Given this reasoning, Judge Xu imagines a stream of payoffs for himself as indicated in Figure 11.5. He decides the odd-numbered cases, and Judge Willow decides the even-numbered cases. In Case One, Judge Xu gets 2 from bucking precedent

		Willow: Follow	Willow: Buck
Xu	Follow	3, 3	−3, 4
	Buck	4, −3	2, 2

Figure 11.4. Precedential Dilemma

		Case 1	Case 2	Case 3	Case 4	Case 5	...
Judge Xu's strategy	Buck	2	0	2	0	2	...
	Follow	1	2	1	2	1	...

Figure 11.5. Repeated Precedential Dilemma

and 1 from following precedent. If he bucks in Case One, he gets 0 in Case Two because Judge Willow retaliates and ignores his precedent. If he follows in Case One, he gets 2 in Case Two because Judge Willow follows his precedent. Bucking yields a payoff of 2 over the course of two cases, whereas following yields a payoff of 3 over two cases. Repeated interactions incentivize Judge Xu to follow precedent. If all judges reason like Judge Xu, all judges follow precedent. [88]

The repeated prisoner's dilemma helps explain why judges follow precedents, including precedents they oppose. It also illuminates *slippery slopes*. Sometimes a desirable action today can facilitate an undesirable action tomorrow. Lawyers and judges often worry about slippery slopes. Consider *Washington v. Glucksberg*.[89] Terminally ill patients wanted their doctors to help them commit suicide. The doctors could prescribe lethal drugs that the patients would ingest themselves. State law prohibited assisted suicide. The question was whether the patients had a liberty interest, protected by the Constitution, that overrode the state law. The Supreme Court said no. The Court reasoned that "the State may fear that permitting assisted suicide will start it down the path to voluntary and perhaps even involuntary euthanasia."[90] Justice Souter, in a concurring opinion, argued similarly:

> [A] physician who would provide a drug for a patient to administer might well go the further step of administering the drug himself; so, the barrier between assisted suicide and euthanasia could become porous, and the line between voluntary and involuntary euthanasia as well. The case for the slippery slope is fairly made out here . . . because there is a plausible case that the right claimed would not be readily containable.[91]

The metaphor captures this reasoning. If we permit assisted suicide, we step from the stable plateau onto the slippery slope. From there we might slide to the bottom, where doctors kill vulnerable patients in exchange for money.

Slippery slopes happen in different situations.[92] The repeated prisoner's dilemma illuminates one of them. If Judge Xu bucks precedent today (he steps on to the slope), then Judge Willow might respond by bucking precedent tomorrow. Soon every judge might ignore precedent, making law unstable (we slide to the bottom). If Judge Xu fears sliding to the bottom tomorrow, he might follow precedent today.

[88] For a sophisticated version of the analysis presented here, see Eric Rasmussen, *Judicial Legitimacy as a Repeated Game*, 10 J.L. ECON. & ORG. 63 (1994). For early work on the repeated prisoner's dilemma, see ROBERT AXELROD, THE EVOLUTION OF COOPERATION (1984).

[89] 521 U.S. 702 (1997).

[90] *Id.* at 732.

[91] *Id.* at 785 (Souter, J., concurring).

[92] *See* Eugene Volokh, *The Mechanisms of the Slippery Slope*, 116 HARV. L. REV. 1026 (2003).

Questions

11.22. In the one-shot game, both judges buck precedent. Could bargaining prevent this outcome? What impediments to bargaining do the judges face?

11.23. If Judge Xu bucked precedent, we assumed that Judge Willow retaliated by bucking precedent in one case. However, Judge Willow could have adopted a harsher strategy. She could have retaliated by bucking precedent in two cases, or she could have retaliated by bucking precedent in every future case (the "grim trigger" strategy). Would a harsher strategy affect Judge Xu's choice between following and bucking precedent? Why might Judge Willow prefer the lenient strategy?

11.24. Police have three choices: (1) no street cameras, (2) street cameras to solve crimes, or (3) street cameras to solve crimes and track citizens' movements. The status quo is (1). People oppose moving from (1) to (3) but would support moving from (2) to (3). Why? Is this a slippery slope?[93]

The End Game

We described a strategy according to which judges reward other judges who follow precedent and retaliate against other judges who buck precedent. This strategy has been called "tit for tat" (if you cooperate, I reward you; if you don't cooperate, I punish you). Tit for tat can sustain cooperation for long periods. Tit for tat is a common strategy in relationships of all kinds. However, most relationships eventually end. As the end approaches, cooperation often unravels and conflict begins, even among people who have cooperated successfully for a long time. Here we explain why.

Earlier we assumed that the back and forth between Judge Xu and Judge Willow continued indefinitely. Now suppose their game ends at a specific, predictable point. In Figure 11.5, the game ends after Case Five. Judge Xu decides the odd-numbered cases, so he will decide Case Five. He could buck precedent for a payoff of 2 or follow precedent for a payoff of 1. If the game continued, Judge Xu might follow precedent, accepting 1 in Case Five to secure 2 in the next case. But the game ends after Case Five. Without the promise of a future reward, the best strategy for Judge Xu is to buck precedent in Case Five. Now consider Judge Willow, who decides Case Four. Her strategy and payoff stream are the same as Judge Xu's. She could follow precedent in Case Four for a payoff of 1, but Judge Xu will not reward her for this in Case Five. He will buck precedent in Case Five no matter what she does. So Judge Willow's best choice is to buck precedent in Case Four for a payoff of 2. By the same logic, Judge Xu will buck precedent in Case Three, and the reasoning will repeat. Both judges buck precedent in every case. Knowing the end game causes all cooperation to unravel.

In business, people often overcome the end game problem with a contract. Imagine a buyer and seller of cotton. They initiate their relationship by signing a contract. After cooperating for a long period, each side trusts the other. The buyer does not bother

[93] *See id.* at 1043–44.

weighing each shipment of cotton because she trusts the seller to send the proper amount. During this period of cooperation, the parties do not rely on the contract. However, when the end of the relationship becomes apparent, cooperation could unravel. The seller might try to send a light shipment, and the buyer might delay payment. Now the contract matters. It forces the parties to fulfill their obligations in the end game.

Government officials usually cannot sign contracts like buyers and sellers of cotton. However, sometimes public law substitutes for a contract. The previous chapter explained that political competition can promote judicial independence. The logic resembles the repeated prisoner's dilemma. Today's strong party respects judicial independence, even though independent courts can thwart its agenda, because it expects to be tomorrow's weak party. Independent courts protect the weak party. Likewise, today's weak party will respect judicial independence tomorrow when it becomes the strong party. Repeated interactions among the parties can sustain cooperation without a formal agreement. However, when the end game becomes apparent—perhaps one party becomes dominant, so power stops rotating—cooperation might fail. The powerful party might like to weaken the courts. Now the constitution, which protects judicial independence, might matter. It might force the powerful party to respect judicial independence in the end game.

E. Acquiescence to Precedent

Cooperation and self-interest can cause judges to respect precedent, as we illustrated with Judges Willow and Xu. However, judges might not think in these terms. Rather than explicitly bargaining, judges might follow a social norm of deferring to precedent. Social norms relate to enforcement, a broad topic that we will address later. Here we address something different: acquiescence. In deciding whether to follow precedent, judges do not write about repeated games and tit for tat. They write about other issues, including this: Has the legislature objected to the precedent? If not, judges say the legislature "acquiesced." Acquiescence provides a reason to follow the precedent.

We introduced acquiescence in an earlier chapter. The U.S. Congress enacted the Sherman Antitrust Act to guard against monopolies in business. In *Flood v. Kuhn*, the Supreme Court had to decide if the act applied to professional baseball leagues.[94] The act applied to other professional sports like basketball and football. At the time of the case, television and radio carried baseball across the country, making it an interstate affair within the purview of Congress. Consequently, the Court had good reasons to apply the act to baseball. But *Flood* was not a case of first impression. In two earlier cases, *Federal Baseball* and *Toolson*, the Court held that the act does *not* apply to baseball.[95] In *Flood*, the Court followed its precedents, exempting baseball from antitrust law.

To explain its decision, the Court wrote:

[94] 407 U.S. 258 (1972).

[95] *See* Fed. Baseball Club v. Nat'l League, 259 U.S. 200 (1922); Toolson v. New York Yankees, Inc., 346 U.S. 356 (1953).

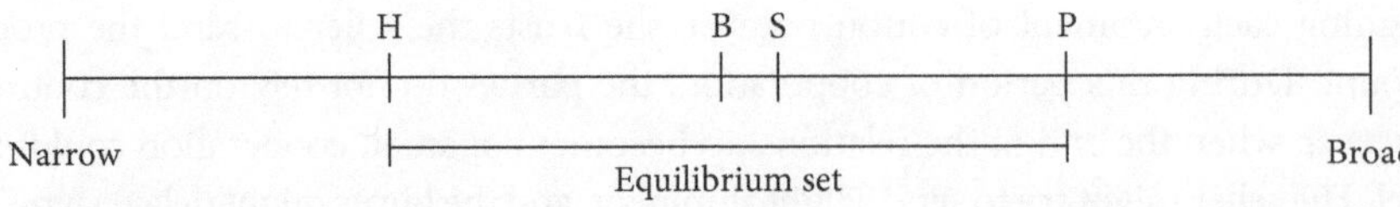

Figure 11.6. Acquiescence

> We continue to be loath, 50 years after *Federal Baseball* and almost two decades after *Toolson*, to overturn those cases judicially when Congress, by its positive inaction, has allowed those decisions to stand for so long and, far beyond mere inference and implication, has clearly evinced a desire not to disapprove them legislatively.[96]

This is an argument about acquiescence. Members of Congress knew about the Court's precedents. Several bills were introduced to override the precedents and extend the act to baseball, but none became law. Congress's "positive inaction" must have meant that legislators approved of the Court's precedents. So the Court continued to follow them.

Does acquiescence by legislators mean the precedent is correct? Spatial models from the previous chapter can help answer. Figure 11.6 depicts antitrust law. A statute on the left side of the dimension is narrow, meaning it regulates few businesses, whereas a statute on the right side regulates many businesses. The ideal points of the House of Representatives (*H*), Senate (*S*), and President (*P*) are pictured. Suppose those actors enact a statute at *B*, where *B* represents the legislative bargain on antitrust. Now suppose a court gets a case about the meaning of the statute. If the court interprets the statute to mean *B*, the legislature will not override it. The House will not approve a new statute to the left of *B*, and the Senate will not approve a new statute to the right of *B*. The court's interpretation is correct, and the legislature acquiesces.

Now suppose the court makes a different choice. It interprets the statute to mean something other than *B*, perhaps a point just right of *H* or left of *P*. Those interpretations are incorrect (*B* is the correct interpretation), yet the legislature does not override them. To generalize, the court can select any interpretation between *H* and *P* without prompting an override. Acquiescence by the legislature does not mean that the court made the correct interpretation. It just means that the interpretation lies in the equilibrium set.

This example assumes that the ideal points of the House, Senate, and President stay fixed over time. In fact, they change, but this does not affect the logic. The Supreme Court's decision on baseball endured for decades, even as ideal points moved from one election to the next. Congress always acquiesced, so apparently the precedent remained within the shifting equilibrium set.

We have shown that acquiescence by the legislature does not mean that the court got it right. Nevertheless, acquiescence might supply helpful information to courts. An earlier chapter introduced the transitions theory of interpretation. That theory applies when a court gets a case governed by erroneous precedent. Courts should weigh the benefits of bucking the precedent and correcting the error against the transition costs associated with changing law. Usually courts do not know those benefits and transition

[96] Flood v. Kuhn, 407 U.S. 258, 283–84 (1972).

costs. They must guess based on limited information. Acquiescence supplies some limited information. If a precedent remains stable for many years, even as legislators debate and attempt to override it, that suggests changing the law would create high transition costs. High transition costs probably help explain why the legislature has not changed the law itself. Thus, acquiescence supplies a reason to support an existing precedent. However, the reason involves transition costs, not the accuracy of the precedent.

III. Puzzles and Paradoxes

The philosopher Ronald Dworkin imagined Hercules, a judge of superhuman wisdom, learning, and skill.[97] Hercules resolves every case correctly. He also works alone. In reality, judges are fallible, and many of them work in teams. In the United States, appellate panels usually have three judges, and the Supreme Court has nine. Multiple judges work together to make a group decision. Sometimes group decision-making leads to surprising results. A court with wise judges can make unwise or even nonsensical decisions. This section shows why by applying economics to legal doctrine in multimember courts.

A. The *Marks* Rule

Juries in the state of Oregon convicted three men of committing crimes. In two of the cases, the jurors voted 11–1 in favor of conviction, and in the third case the jurors voted 10–2. The men appealed to the U.S. Supreme Court. They argued that the Sixth Amendment to the Constitution, which protects the right to trial by jury, requires unanimous jury verdicts. Since the jurors did not vote unanimously, the men claimed that they could not be convicted. In *Apodaca v. Oregon*, the Supreme Court rejected this claim.[98] Four Justices joined an opinion saying that the Sixth Amendment does not require unanimous jury verdicts. Justice Powell wrote an opinion saying that the Sixth Amendment *does* require unanimous jury verdicts, but only in federal trials (i.e., federal court trials involving violations of federal criminal laws). The men violated state criminal laws. Together those five Justices formed a majority, so their judgment—the men were lawfully convicted—decided the case. Four dissenting Justices argued that the Sixth Amendment requires unanimous verdicts in all criminal trials.[99]

What precedent did the Court set in *Apodaca*? Ordinarily, we find the precedent in the majority opinion. But cases like *Apodaca* do not have a majority opinion. No more than four Justices joined a single opinion, and it takes five Justices to form a majority. *Apodaca* is a *plurality opinion*.

[97] Ronald Dworkin, Law's Empire 239–75 (1986).

[98] Apodaca v. Oregon, 406 U.S. 404 (1972). This decision was abrogated by a later decision of the Court, which held that the Sixth Amendment requires a unanimous verdict to convict a defendant of a serious offense. *See* Ramos v. Louisiana, 140 S. Ct. 1390, 1394 (2020).

[99] *See* Apodaca v. Oregon, 464 U.S. 404, 414–15 (1972) (Stewart, J., dissenting). Justices Brennan, Marshall, and Douglas wrote dissenting opinions in the companion case to *Apodaca*, *Johnson v. Louisiana*, 406 U.S. 356, 395–403 (1972). This does not affect our analysis.

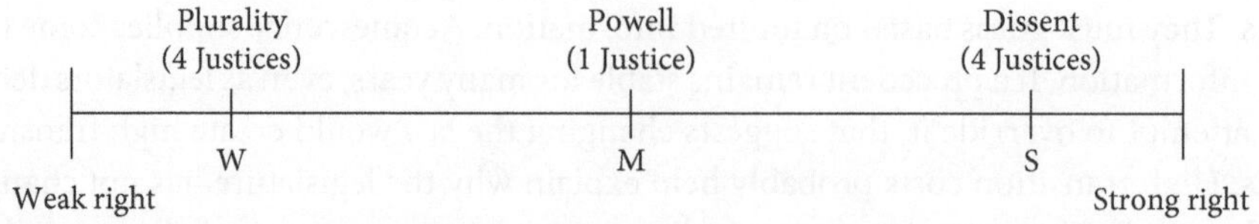

Figure 11.7. Applying *Marks* to *Apodaca*

Do plurality opinions make precedent? Yes. According to the Supreme Court, "When a fragmented Court decides a case and no single rationale explaining the result enjoys the assent of five Justices, the holding of the Court may be viewed as that position taken by those Members who concurred in the judgments on the narrowest grounds[.]"[100] This is called the *Marks* Rule after the name of the case in which the Court developed it.

In *Apodaca*, Justice Powell concurred in the judgment (i.e., he agreed with the Court's conclusion that the men had been lawfully convicted). His opinion represents the narrowest grounds for the holding in the sense that it takes the more moderate position. Whereas the four-Justice plurality would block all Sixth Amendment claims about unanimous jury verdicts, Justice Powell would only block some Sixth Amendment claims about unanimous verdicts (the claims involving state juries). According to the *Marks* Rule, Justice Powell's opinion controls the case.

This seems surprising. Eight of the nine Justices rejected Justice Powell's opinion. Yet his opinion apparently set the precedent for the Supreme Court and lower courts to follow.

We can rationalize the *Marks* Rule using tools from an earlier chapter.[101] In *Apodaca*, nine Justices took positions on the right to a jury trial. The four-Justice plurality interpreted the right weakly (it does not require unanimous juries). Call this interpretation *W*. The four Justices in dissent interpreted the right strongly (it requires unanimous juries). Call this interpretation *S*. Justice Powell took a moderate position (sometimes it requires unanimous juries). Call this interpretation *M*. Figure 11.7 locates the Justices on an interpretive dimension, with the left end corresponding to a weak right and the right end corresponding to a strong right. Suppose the Justices cast pairwise votes over the three competing interpretations. Powell and the four-Justice plurality prefer *M* to *S*. Powell and the four dissenting Justices prefer *M* to *W*. *M* defeats all alternatives.

Justice Powell wrote an opinion only for himself, but a majority of the Justices prefer it to every other opinion. Letting Justice Powell make the precedent no longer seems surprising.

This analysis relies on the median voter theorem, which we discussed in the chapters on voting. The median voter theorem can justify the *Marks* Rule. However, the theorem requires some assumptions. One assumption is that voters have single-peaked preferences. We assumed that the four-Justice plurality preferred interpretation *W* to *M* and *M* to *S*. Likewise, we assumed that the dissenting Justices preferred interpretation *S* to *M* and *M* to *W*. These are single-peaked preferences. Suppose the dissenting Justices

[100] Marks v. United States, 430 U.S. 188, 193 (1977) (internal quotation marks and citations omitted).

[101] This discussion is based on Maxwell Stearns, *Modeling Narrowest Grounds*, 89 GEO. WASH. L. REV. 101 (2021).

have double-peaked preferences instead. They prefer *S* to *W* and *W* to *M*. This changes the vote. A majority either prefers *W* to the alternatives, or the Justices spin in circles because their group preferences are intransitive.[102] For the median voter theorem to justify the *Marks* Rule, we must assume judges have single-peaked preferences.

The median voter theorem makes another assumption: one dimension of choice. Given single-peaked preferences, casting pairwise votes on a single dimension of choice selects the median. If we move to two or more dimensions of choice, and even if we hold the other assumptions fixed, voting usually leads to intransitivity.[103]

Let's apply this idea. In *Apodaca*, we can arrange the opinions on one dimension representing the strength of the jury right. This helps us apply the median voter theorem to the case. In some other cases, however, opinions cut across multiple dimensions. Consider *McDonald v. City of Chicago*.[104] The Second Amendment to the U.S. Constitution protects the right to "keep and bear Arms."[105] This limits the power of the federal government to regulate guns. The question in *McDonald* was whether the Second Amendment also applies to states, meaning that it limits the power of state and local governments to regulate guns. Five Justices answered yes. Four of them joined a plurality opinion saying that the Due Process Clause makes the Second Amendment applicable to states. The fifth, Justice Thomas, wrote an opinion saying that the Privileges and Immunities Clause makes the Second Amendment applicable to states. In dissent, four Justices said the Second Amendment does not apply to states. Table 11.1 summarizes the Justices' positions.[106]

McDonald is a plurality opinion. To find the precedent, we must apply the *Marks* Rule. Which decision represents the narrowest grounds for the holding? We cannot answer. Like apples and oranges, the plurality opinion and Justice Thomas's opinion are not comparable. Voting shows the problem. Let *P* signify the plurality's opinion, *T* signify Justice Thomas's opinion, and *D* signify the dissent's opinion. Which wins in a pairwise vote, *P* or *T*? We cannot tell. The dissenting Justices will cast the decisive votes, and we cannot infer which option they prefer. In *Apodaca*, the dissenting Justices most preferred a strong right, so it seems sensible to assume their second choice was a moderate right and their third choice was a weak right. In *McDonald*, the dissenting Justices most preferred not to apply the Second Amendment to the states. Their first choice supplies no basis for determining whether *P* or *T* is their second choice. The problem is multidimensionality. Knowing a preference on one dimension (whether to apply the Second Amendment to the states) conveys no information about preferences on the other dimension (Due Process versus Privileges or Immunities). Even if we knew the Justices' preferences on both dimensions, aggregating them might lead to intransitivity.

In sum, the *Marks* Rule tells lawyers how to identify the precedent in a plurality opinion. Commentators have criticized the rule, in part because it allows a minority of Justices, or even a single Justice, to make precedent. Economic analysis of voting can

[102] The four-Justice plurality prefers *W* to *M* and *M* to *S*. The four dissenting Justices prefer *S* to *W* and *W* to *M*. If Justice Powell prefers *M* to *W* and *W* to *S*, then *W* beats both *M* and *S*. If Justice Powell prefers *M* to *S* and *S* to *W*, then the group has intransitive preferences (*W* beats *M*, *M* beats *S*, and *S* beats *W*).

[103] See Chapter 4 for a refresher.

[104] 561 U.S. 742 (2010).

[105] U.S. CONST. amend. II.

[106] This is based on table 3 in Maxwell Stearns, *Modeling Narrowest Grounds*, 89 GEO. WASH. L. REV. 101, 134 (2021).

Table 11.1. Does the Second Amendment Apply to States?

	Yes, through Privileges or Immunities Clause	No, not through Privileges or Immunities Clause
Yes, through Due Process Clause		Plurality (4 Justices)
No, not through Due Process Clause	Thomas (1 Justice)	Dissent (4 Justices)

justify the *Marks* Rule, but only in some situations. When the assumptions of the median voter theorem hold, the *Marks* Rule tends to select the median opinion, meaning the opinion that a majority of Justices prefer to all others.

Questions

11.25. In *Vieth v. Jubelirer*, the Supreme Court had to decide if gerrymandered district lines violated the Constitution.[107] Four Justices held that gerrymandering claims are nonjusticiable, meaning the Court lacks jurisdiction to decide them. Writing for himself, Justice Kennedy issued a very unusual opinion, holding that gerrymandering claims are justiciable, the standard for identifying an unconstitutional gerrymander is unknown, and the challengers in the case did not satisfy that (unknown) standard. Four Justices—Breyer, Ginsburg, Souter, and Stevens—dissented. Justice Breyer wrote an opinion arguing that gerrymandering violates the Constitution when it gives a minority party a majority of seats. Justice Souter wrote an opinion, joined by Justice Ginsburg, presenting a multistep test for identifying unconstitutional gerrymanders. Justice Stevens wrote an opinion arguing that gerrymandering violates the Constitution when partisan motivations dominate.
(a) Did the gerrymander violate the Constitution?
(b) Which opinion decided the case on narrowest grounds?
(c) Which opinion is the median?

11.26. The government hires contractors to do things like build roads and bridges. Can the government reserve 15 percent of its contracts for minority-owned businesses? Six Justices say "yes." Of them, three conclude that affirmative action in contracting never violates the Constitution; two propose a lenient test, meaning affirmative action sometimes violates the Constitution but not in this case; and one proposes a strict test, meaning affirmative action usually violates the Constitution but not in this case. In dissent, three Justices conclude that affirmative action in contracting always violates the Constitution. Which opinion decided the case on narrowest grounds? Is this the median opinion?[108]

[107] 541 U.S. 267 (2004).

[108] This question is based loosely on *Fullilove v. Klutznick*, 448 U.S. 448 (1980). Professor Stearns uses *Fullilove* to identify an "imperfection" in the *Marks* Rule. *See* Maxwell Stearns, *Modeling Narrowest Grounds*, 89 Geo. Wash. L. Rev. 101, 158–61 (2021). Recall that in the text we wrote, "the *Marks* Rule *tends* to select the median opinion."

B. The Doctrinal Paradox

Sir Edward Coke, a famous English jurist, said, "[R]eason is the life of the Law."[109] Unlike executives and legislators, judges usually have an obligation to explain themselves. Judges make *and justify* their decisions. To see the difference, recall *Caperton*. The Supreme Court decided that Judge Benjamin had to recuse himself from the case involving his political benefactor. The Court ordered Benjamin to recuse and wrote a long opinion justifying its decision. Through opinions, judges supply reasons to justify outcomes.

When a single judge decides a case, her reasons support her decision. However, when multiple judges decide a case, reasons and decisions can separate.[110]

To explain, let's begin by imagining a single judge in a case about a contract. The buyer claims that the seller breached the contract and owes her damages. The seller claims that she never had a contract with the buyer, and in any event her actions did not constitute a breach. Given the arguments, the judge focuses on two questions: did the parties have an enforceable contract, and did the seller breach? Table 11.2 lists the two questions and three combinations of answers that the judge could give.

In combination 1, the parties had a contract and the seller breached. This reasoning supports the outcome of the case: the seller is liable and owes damages. In combination 3, the seller's actions would have constituted a breach if the parties had an enforceable contract, but they didn't. Without a contract, the seller cannot be held liable. Again, this reasoning supports the outcome: the seller is not liable and thus does not owe damages. In every scenario, the judge's reasons correspond to her final decision. If you know the answers to the questions, you know the outcome.

Now imagine the same case before a panel of three judges. Instead of one judge answering the two questions, three judges answer the two questions, and their answers may vary. Table 11.3 depicts one possible combination of answers.

Panels of judges often make decisions using majority rule. Judges 1 and 2, a majority, conclude that the buyer and seller had an enforceable contract, and Judges 1 and 3, a majority, conclude that the seller breached. This implies that the seller owes damages. But wait. If you ask the three judges whether the seller owes damages, only Judge 1 says yes. Judges 2 and 3, a majority, say no.

In this case, the answers to the questions do not explain the outcome. The court's reasons do not correspond to its decision. This is the *doctrinal paradox*.[111]

To appreciate the paradox, consider the parties to the contract dispute. If the court rejects the buyer's claim for damages, the buyer will demand an explanation. But the explanation probably will not satisfy him. After all, most of the judges think he had an enforceable contract with the seller, and most of the judges think the seller's action constituted a breach. Conversely, if the court orders the seller to pay damages, the seller

[109] Edward Coke, The Selected Writings and Speeches of Sir Edward Coke 701 (Steve Sheppard ed., 2003).

[110] This discussion is based on Lewis A. Kornhauser & Lawrence G. Sager, *Unpacking the Court*, 96 Yale L.J. 82 (1986); Lewis A. Kornhauser, *Modeling Collegial Courts. II. Legal Doctrine*, 8 J.L. Econ. & Org. 441 (1992); Lewis A. Kornhauser & Lawrence G. Sager, *The One and the Many: Adjudication in Collegial Courts*, 81 Cal. L. Rev. 1 (1993).

[111] This label comes from Lewis A. Kornhauser, *Modeling Collegial Courts. II. Legal Doctrine*, 8 J.L. Econ. & Org. 441 (1992).

Table 11.2. Reasons and Outcomes for One Judge

	Reasons		Outcome
	Was there a contract?	**Was there a breach?**	**Is the seller liable?**
Combination 1	Yes	Yes	Yes
Combination 2	Yes	No	No
Combination 3	No	Yes	No

Table 11.3. Doctrinal Paradox

	Reasons		Outcome
	Was there a contract?	**Was there a breach?**	**Is the seller liable?**
Judge 1	Yes	Yes	Yes
Judge 2	Yes	No	No
Judge 3	No	Yes	No
Court's decision	Yes	Yes	No

will demand an explanation. But the explanation probably will not satisfy her. After all, most of the judges think she does not owe damages.

We have introduced the doctrinal paradox in a hypothetical case about private law. Now consider a real case involving the U.S. Constitution. An insurance company in the District of Columbia filed a case in federal court against a company in Maryland. Maryland is a U.S. state. The District of Columbia is the U.S. capital, but it is not a state, nor is it part of a state. The question was whether the federal court had jurisdiction to hear the insurer's case. The insurer argued "yes" based on a federal statute that granted jurisdiction in cases like this. The defendant argued "no" based on Article III of the Constitution, which limits federal court jurisdiction to cases involving "citizens of different States."[112] The dispute turned on two questions: (1) Can Congress expand federal court jurisdiction in cases like this by statute? And (2) does the word "States" in Article III include the District of Columbia?

In *National Mutual Insurance Co. v. Tidewater Transfer Co.*, the Supreme Court decided in favor of the insurer.[113] Table 11.4 shows the names of the nine Justices and their answers to the two questions.[114]

Only three Justices concluded that Congress could expand federal court jurisdiction. Only two Justices concluded that the word "States" in Article III included the District.

[112] U.S. Const. art. III, § 2. Federal courts also have jurisdiction to hear cases implicating federal law, like disputes related to the U.S. Constitution, a federal statute, or a federal regulation.
[113] 337 U.S. 582 (1949).
[114] This is based on Lewis A. Kornhauser & Lawrence G. Sager, *The One and the Many: Adjudication in Collegial Courts*, 81 Cal. L. Rev. 1 (1993).

Table 11.4. *National Mutual Insurance v. Tidewater Transfer Co.*

Justice name	Can Congress expand federal court jurisdiction in cases like this by statute?	Does the word "States" in Article III include the District of Columbia?	Does the court have jurisdiction to hear the case?
Black	Yes	No	Yes
Burton	Yes	No	Yes
Jackson	Yes	No	Yes
Murphy	No	Yes	Yes
Rutledge	No	Yes	Yes
Douglas	No	No	No
Frankfurter	No	No	No
Reed	No	No	No
Vinson	No	No	No
Court's decision	No (6 to 3)	No (7 to 2)	Yes (5 to 4)

Together they constituted a majority for the position that the federal court had jurisdiction. The insurer won the case, but the Court could not explain why. Like a table without legs, the decision lacked support. No reason got a majority of the votes.

To resolve cases with multiple questions, courts can decide by issue or decide by case. In *Tidewater*, deciding by issue would mean voting on the questions. A majority of the Justices voted "no" on both questions. Thus, deciding by issue would cause the insurer to lose. Deciding by case would mean voting on whether the federal court had jurisdiction. A majority of the Justices concluded that the court had jurisdiction. Thus, deciding by case would cause the insurer to win. The doctrinal paradox occurs when issue voting and case voting produce different results.

The insurer won in *Tidewater*, so the Court must have decided by case. Was this the best approach? Perhaps not. Deciding by case led to an unreasoned outcome. The insurer won, but the Court could not explain why.

Deciding by issue would prevent this problem by aligning reasons and outcomes. However, deciding by issue has drawbacks too. To illustrate, imagine a case of police brutality. The cops detain and beat a suspect, coerce him to confess, and discard evidence that could exonerate him. The suspect claims the cops violated his Fourth Amendment (unreasonable search and seizure), Fifth Amendment (self-incrimination), and Fourteenth Amendment (due process) rights. Three Justices vote in favor of the suspect on the Fourth Amendment only, three other Justices vote in his favor on the Fifth Amendment only, and the final three Justices vote in his favor on the Fourteenth Amendment only. Under issue voting, the suspect would lose on every claim by a 6 to 3 vote. But all nine Justices believe the cops violated the suspect's rights. Does issue voting promote justice?

Scholars disagree on whether deciding by issue or deciding by case works best. More generally, the doctrinal paradox raises difficult questions about courts and legal doctrine. Puzzling over those questions deepens our understanding of law. It also helps us think strategically. Suppose you were the lawyer for the seller in the contract dispute. Suppose you argue before the three judges with the opinions shown in Table 11.3. How would you frame your argument? Would you say, "Your honors, this case involves two questions, one about the contract and one about breach?" Or would you say, "This case involves one question: Does my client owe damages?"

Questions

11.27. Explain this sentence: "Any plurality opinion case is a paradoxical case lurking in disguise."[115]

11.28. Suppose that after deciding *Tidewater*, the Supreme Court got a case about a new statute. The statute grants federal courts jurisdiction to hear cases between citizens of Guam, a U.S. territory, and citizens of U.S. states. Guam is not a "State" under Article III of the Constitution, so the case turns on whether Congress has power to expand federal court jurisdiction. Does the precedent from *Tidewater* require the Court to uphold the new statute?[116]

11.29. High courts make precedents for lower courts to apply. Why might deciding by issue make more sense for high courts than for lower courts?

C. Intransitivity in Court

Courts should make consistent decisions. Consistency promotes equal treatment, predictability, and other legal values. In reality, courts sometimes make inconsistent decisions. A court might prioritize the right to a jury trial today but minimize the right tomorrow. Inconsistency opens courts to criticism.

Why do courts make inconsistent decisions? One explanation involves people. New judges with new ideas replace old judges who retire. Another explanation involves error. Like the rest of us, judges sometimes make mistakes.

These explanations do not tell the whole story. Even if the composition of courts never changed, and even if judges never erred, courts would struggle to behave consistently. The problem lies in their structure. Like a legislature, a court is a single entity made up of many individuals. Different individuals have different opinions. Aggregating those opinions leads to a familiar and confounding problem: intransitivity.[117]

To illustrate, suppose the legislature enacts statutes that provide support to religion. One statute provides funds to schools, including religious schools, for textbooks. Another statute pays for crosses on government buildings. The constitution requires separation between religion and the government. Do the statutes violate the

[115] *Id.* at 29.
[116] *See id.* at 26–27.
[117] This discussion draws on Frank H. Easterbrook, *Ways of Criticizing the Court*, 95 Harv. L. Rev. 802 (1982). *See also* Maxwell L. Stearns, *Standing Back from the Forest: Justiciability and Social Choice*, 83 Cal. L. Rev. 1309 (1995).

constitution? The answer depends on what exactly the constitution means. This is a question of interpretation. The constitution might forbid any government support for religion, in which case both statutes violate the constitution. Call this interpretation *A* for "absolutist." The constitution might permit "neutral" government support that treats religious and secular institutions the same. Under this view, the statute providing funds for crosses violates the constitution, but the statute providing funds for textbooks does not because it provides the same money for religious and nonreligious schools. Call this interpretation *N* for "neutrality." Finally, the constitution might require a case-by-case balancing test that considers the extent of support for religion, the purpose of the law, and other factors. Call this interpretation *B* for "balancing."

Litigants challenge the statutes before a court of three judges. The first judge thinks *B* represents the best interpretation, *A* is second best, and *N* is worst. The second judge thinks *N* represents the best interpretation, *B* comes second, and *A* comes third. The remaining judge prefers *A* to *N* and *N* to *B*. We can summarize the judge's preferences as follows:[118]

Judge 1: $B > A > N$
Judge 2: $N > B > A$
Judge 3: $A > N > B$

The litigants in Case One challenge the textbook statute, and they argue about two interpretations, *N* and *B*. Ordinarily, courts do not consider arguments that litigants do not raise. So the court in Case One limits itself to two choices, *N* and *B*. Judges 2 and 3, a majority, prefer *N* to *B*, so the court selects *N*. The litigants in Case Two challenge the crosses statute, and they argue about interpretations *A* and *N*. Judges 1 and 3, a majority, prefer *A* to *N*, so the court selects *A*. The litigants in Case Three challenge another statute and present the judges with a choice of *B* and *A*. Judges 1 and 2, a majority, prefer *B* to *A*, so the court selects *B*. The court's preferences are $B > A > N > B$.

The doctrine turns circles over the sequence of cases. The court makes inconsistent decisions, even though its members have consistent preferences. The honorable judges chase their tails. Increasing the number of judges (the U.S. Supreme Court has nine Justices) and increasing the number of interpretations (*C*, *D*, etc.) increases the probability of this circular result.

Suppose the court follows a rule against reintroduction. Once a majority votes against an interpretation, the court cannot reconsider it. This prevents intransitivity. After our second imaginary case, the court has selected *A* and rejected *B* and *N*. With a rule against reintroduction, the court cannot reconsider the defeated alternatives, so the doctrine remains stable at *A*.

In general, judges do not follow detailed voting procedures. They do not adopt Robert's Rules of Order. Consequently, formal rules do not prevent judges from reintroducing defeated alternatives. But a powerful norm does: stare decisis. In our sequence of cases, we imagine the judges choosing first between interpretations *N* and *B*. They choose *N*. The second case pits *N* against a new interpretation *A*. Stare decisis does not necessarily require the court to select *N* over *A*. After all, the court has never

[118] *See* Frank H. Easterbrook, *Ways of Criticizing the Court*, 95 Harv. L. Rev. 802, 816 (1982).

considered *A*. The decision in the first case does not necessarily control all future cases, especially cases raising novel arguments. So the court can (and does) choose *A*. Only one case remains, and it pits *A* against *B*. But *B* does not necessarily raise a novel argument. The court already considered and rejected *B* in the first case. So stare decisis leads the court to reject *B*. *A* becomes the stable precedent.

Stare decisis stops cycling by acting like a rule against reintroduction. Where does the cycle stop? Which interpretation prevails? The answer depends on the order of voting. Earlier we imagined this sequence: *N* versus *B* in Case One (*N* wins), and *A* versus *N* in Case Two (*A* wins). The court has rejected *B* and *N*, so *A* becomes the stable precedent. Suppose we change the order: *A* versus *B* in Case One (*B* wins), and *N* versus *B* in Case Two (*N* wins). The court has rejected *A* and *B*, so *N* prevails. The prevailing precedent depends on the order of the vote.

Who decides the order of the vote? In the legislature, a powerful official decides, like the Speaker of the House in the U.S. Congress. The Speaker chooses the order strategically to produce her preferred outcome. Things work differently in court. In general, litigants set the court's agenda. They decide what cases to bring, what arguments to make, and when to make them. In many jurisdictions, litigants are too numerous to coordinate. Thousands or even millions of people can sue at any time. The order of voting, and thus the prevailing precedent, depends on who sues when. Precedent depends on chance. Legal doctrine is random.

Questions

11.30. A strategic litigant wants *B* to become the stable precedent, and he knows the preferences of the three judges as previously described. What case would he bring—in other words, what competing interpretations would he raise—first?

11.31. Intransitivity presents two problems for legal doctrine. First, it can make doctrine random. Second, it can make doctrine manipulable, as when a strategic litigant orders the cases to produce a particular outcome.

(a) Litigants need "standing" to sue. A liberal approach to standing lets many people sue. A conservative approach to standing lets few people sue. Which approach to standing worsens the problem of randomness?

(b) Which approach to standing worsens the problem of manipulation?[119]

11.32. Does our analysis imply that all legal doctrine is random? Or just legal doctrine in areas where judges substantially disagree?

[119] These questions are based on a discussion in Maxwell L. Stearns, *Standing Back from the Forest: Justiciability and Social Choice*, 83 CAL. L. REV. 1309, 1401–12 (1995).

Bargaining among Judges

Should judges trade votes to decide cases? As we explained in a chapter on voting, bargaining can prevent intransitivity. To see how, return to the three judges previously described. Judge 1 prefer *B* to *N*, whereas Judge 2 prefers *N* to *B*. Judge 1 might make the following offer to Judge 2: "Vote for interpretation *B* in the cases on religion, and in exchange I will vote for your preferred interpretation in other cases that you prioritize." If Judge 2 accepts the offer, the court will not cycle. A majority will vote for *B* over both alternatives, making *B* the stable precedent in the cases on religion.

Bargaining can do more than prevent cycling. It can promote the welfare of judges. In an early chapter we imagined Adam and Blair bargaining over jail cells. Each had something (money, empty cells) that the other valued more, making a trade mutually beneficial. The same logic applies in court. Suppose Judge 1 cares more about religion and Judge 2 cares more about speech. Each has something (a vote on religion doctrine, a vote on speech doctrine) that the other values more. Trading votes can make both parties better off.

Do judges bargain in practice? This question is difficult to answer because judges often work in secret. However, some observations suggest the answer is "yes." Many judges work together for many years. This can breed a spirit of cooperation, where judges defer when other judges have strong convictions (recall our discussion of panel effects). Cooperation and deference can substitute for explicit bargaining. Other mechanisms can produce a similar result. In the United States, Supreme Court Justices trade drafts of opinions. One Justice might offer to join an opinion if the author adds or removes certain language. The author might accept the offer to secure a majority (majority opinions set a stronger precedent than plurality opinions). The Justices trade words for votes in particular opinions.[120]

Codes of ethics usually forbid judges from trading votes, especially across cases. One explanation involves representation. In private life, bargaining often affects the parties to the bargain only, as when you pay a farmer for blueberries. In public law, bargaining often affects third parties. The trade between Judges 1 and 2 might help them but hurt society. To generalize, bargaining by representative judges should tend to benefit society, whereas bargaining by unrepresentative judges tends to harm society. Independence from politics can make judges unrepresentative. Perhaps elected judges should trade votes but independent judges should not.

Many people have a strong conviction that judges should not trade votes. However, failing to trade votes can lead to intransitivity or randomness in legal doctrine. Perhaps judges should trade votes over doctrine but not over dispositions. Under this view, Judges 1 and 2 could bargain over whether the constitution requires interpretation *B* or *N*, but they could not bargain over whether the defendant goes to prison or the statute gets struck down. Would this distinction work in practice?

[120] For studies on judicial bargaining, see, for example, Jeffrey R. Lax & Charles M. Cameron, *Bargaining and Opinion Assignment on the US Supreme Court*, 23 J.L. Econ. & Org. 276 (2007); James F. Spriggs II, Forrest Maltzman, & Paul J. Wahlbeck, *Bargaining on the U.S. Supreme Court: Justices' Responses to Majority Opinion Drafts*, 61 J. Pol. 485 (1999).

Conclusion

Every constitution, statute, and treaty requires interpretation. Judges make interpretations with the force of law when deciding cases. Thus, adjudication is fundamental to public law. The previous chapter studied adjudication in general, and this chapter applied some of those ideas to important issues. We began by studying methods of interpretation, including textualism and intentionalism. Then we studied the formation of precedent. We concluded by uncovering some puzzles in adjudication. Sometimes courts make decisions without justifications (the doctrinal paradox). Other times legal doctrine runs in circles or exhibits randomness instead of reason.

Whether reasoned or not, judicial interpretations sit at the heart of law. They translate legal texts and traditions into actionable guides for litigants and society. But interpretations do not execute themselves. Nor do statutes or regulations. Simply announcing the law, even in a well-reasoned opinion, does not necessarily change behavior. Changing behavior usually requires enforcement. Enforcing law involves threats, detection, and social norms. It involves information, moral suasion, and standards of proof. And it involves punishments handed down by courts. Much of the state's machinery concentrates on enforcement, and much law seems pointless without it. Enforcement is our next topic.

12
Theory of Enforcement

People steal jewelry, poison the air, defraud investors, bribe judges, and sell state secrets. Law aims to prevent harmful activities like these by influencing people's behavior. Sometimes law can influence behavior by harnessing character. If people feel a duty to obey the law, then enacting and publicizing a new law will change their actions. To illustrate, suppose a sign warns drivers not to change lanes in the tunnel. Reading the sign might cause a dutiful driver to stay in her lane, regardless of whether she sees cops or other cars nearby.[1] Duty motivates some people some of the time, but often it cannot secure compliance. The jurist Oliver Wendell Holmes imagined a "bad man" who "cares nothing for an ethical rule" and only for "material consequences."[2] Appealing to the "bad man's" conscience will not change his behavior. We must punish him.

Punishment is a key ingredient in a fundamental legal process: enforcement. Everywhere we look we see people enforcing law. Officials inspect bridges, monitor smokestacks, check passports, search ships, scrutinize tax forms, and measure a fisherman's catch. Judges review schools and prisons for compliance with the Constitution. The state arrests suspects, fines businesses, and occasionally sentences people to die. To secure compliance, governments everywhere devote substantial resources to enforcement. Enforcement is so fundamental that some scholars consider it part of law's essence, meaning you can't have law without it.[3] According to a proverb, "Better no law than laws not enforced."[4]

This chapter applies economics to the enforcement of law. It illuminates questions like these:

Example 1: The speed limit equals 55, but drivers go 60 with impunity. The legal scholar Roscoe Pound blamed slippage like this on "our machinery of justice." He argued that lawyers must "make the law in action conform to the law in the books."[5] Do you agree? Should we ticket drivers for traveling one mile per hour above the limit?

Example 2: President Nixon recorded himself covering up a burglary. A prosecutor demanded the tapes, and Nixon refused, citing executive privilege. Nixon's attorney said, "The President wants me to argue that he is as powerful a monarch

[1] Philosophers might say the driver has "internalized" the law, meaning she lets law guide her conduct regardless of any sanctions. *See* H.L.A. Hart, The Concept of Law (1961). Economists use the term "internalized" in a different way.

[2] Oliver Wendell Holmes, Jr., *The Path of the Law*, 10 Harv. L. Rev. 457, 459 (1897).

[3] John Austin, for example, understood law as an obligation backed by a sanction. John Austin, The Province of Jurisprudence Defined (Wilfrid E. Rumble ed., 1995) (1st ed. 1832).

[4] Henry George Bohn, A Polyglot of Foreign Proverbs, Comprising French, Italian, German, Dutch, Spanish, Portuguese, and Danish, with English translations and a General Index 350 (1857).

[5] Roscoe Pound, *Law in Books and Law in Action*, 44 Am. U.L. Rev. 12, 35–36 (1910).

Public Law and Economics. Robert D. Cooter and Michael D. Gilbert, Oxford University Press. © Oxford University Press 2022.
DOI: 10.1093/oso/9780197655870.003.0012

as Louis XIV . . . and is not subject to the processes of any court in the land except the court of impeachment."[6] The Supreme Court ordered Nixon to turn over the tapes, which he did. Did the Court make the right decision? What would have happened if the President had not complied?

Example 3: A thief breaks a museum door and steals a sculpture. Repairing the door costs $1,000, and the sculpture is worth $100,000. The thief is an art dealer, and when apprehended he suffers a loss to his reputation worth $50,000. The court makes him return the sculpture. Should the court make him pay a fine too? If so, how much?

To answer these questions, we begin with a positive analysis of enforcement that concentrates on deterrence. Deterrence is an important goal of enforcement, and economists have studied it extensively. Next, we present a normative analysis of enforcement, addressing topics such as when the state should enforce law and what punishment it should impose. Finally, we present an interpretive theory of enforcement. Our theory addresses the judicial power to hold people in contempt for refusing to obey court orders. The legal doctrine on contempt is vague, and we use economics to sharpen it.

I. Positive Theory of Enforcement

Governments enforce their laws for different reasons. Economists focus on one reason in particular: deterrence. Enforcing the law today discourages violations tomorrow. The mere threat of enforcement can deter lawbreaking, as when a thief considers robbing a bank but, upon seeing an officer, changes his mind. Enforcement often targets private individuals, as when a cop walks the beat or the tax authority conducts an audit. In public law, some enforcement targets government officials, as when investigators uncovered widespread corruption among state prison guards.[7] We begin with a general analysis of deterrence that applies to both situations. Later we will consider some special issues that arise when enforcing against the government.

A. The Costs and Benefits of Lawbreaking

Breaking the law comes with costs and benefits. The costs might include a guilty conscience and, if you get caught, embarrassment, damage to your reputation, the loss of your job, and even criminal punishment. The benefits might include money, power, convenience (as when you skip applying for a required permit), and even the pleasure of punishing an enemy or exacting revenge. To analyze enforcement, economists begin by imagining a rational person weighing those costs and benefits when deciding how to behave. This person resembles Holmes's "bad man." If the costs of violating the law

[6] Michael G. Trachtman, The Supremes' Greatest Hits: The 37 Supreme Court Cases that Most Directly Affect Your Life 138–39 (2d. ed. 2009).

[7] Yanan Wang, *"Staggering Corruption": 46 Georgia Prison Officers Indicted in FBI Drug and Contraband Sting*, Wash. Post, Feb. 12, 2016.

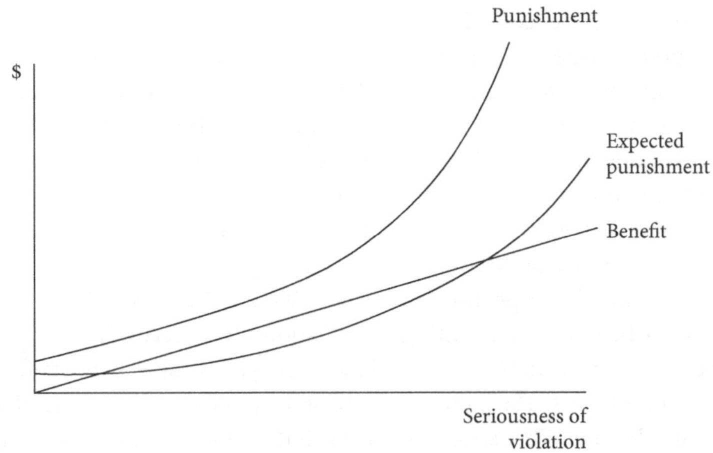

Figure 12.1. Costs and Benefits of Lawbreaking

exceed the benefits, the "bad man" is deterred. If the benefits exceed the costs, he violates the law.

To illustrate, suppose a company runs oil rigs in the Gulf of Mexico. To promote safety and prevent leaks, law requires the company to inspect and maintain its facilities. Skipping an inspection violates the law, and if the company gets caught, it will pay a fine. However, skipping an inspection saves the company time and effort. It will not have to pay engineers to travel to the facilities, examine the pipes, make repairs, and so on.

Figure 12.1 captures the costs and benefits to the company of violating the law.[8] The horizontal axis is labeled "seriousness of violation." As we move rightward on the axis, the company conducts laxer inspections, or it skips inspections entirely. The vertical axis is money. The benefit line represents the benefit to the company of violating the law. Moving rightward from the origin, the company devotes fewer resources to inspections and saves more money, hence the benefit line's upward slope.[9]

Focus on the curve labeled "punishment." This represents the cost to the company of violating the law in a world with perfect enforcement. If the company does not inspect properly, the government will find out, and the company will pay a fine. The more serious the company's violation, the greater the fine, hence the upward slope. The punishment curve always lies above the benefit line, meaning that the cost of violating the law always exceeds the benefit. A rational company will always comply with the law by inspecting and maintaining the facilities.

We have imagined a scenario with perfect enforcement. The government always discovers violations and always assesses fines. In reality, enforcement is usually uncertain. If the company skips an inspection, the government might not find out, or it might find out but botch the investigation, perhaps by failing to preserve evidence. The curve labeled "expected punishment" accounts for this possibility. It represents the punishment for violating law discounted by the probability of enforcement.

[8] This figure resembles one in Robert Cooter & Thomas Ulen, Law and Economics 465 (6th ed. 2014).

[9] We depict the benefit from violating law with a straight line. This simplifies our analysis without affecting its conclusions.

To make this concrete, consider Figure 12.2, which adds some details to the prior figure. The point labeled v_1 on the horizontal axis corresponds to the company committing a somewhat serious violation of law by skipping some inspections. Skipping the inspections saves the company $50,000 as the benefit line shows. The fine for skipping the inspections equals $75,000 as indicated by the punishment curve. With perfect enforcement, the company would not skip the inspections because the cost of $75,000 exceeds the benefit of $50,000. However, enforcement is imperfect. The government has only a 50 percent chance of discovering the company's violation, so the *expected* punishment for skipping the inspections equals $37,500 (0.5 * $75,000).[10] Given imperfect enforcement, the benefit of committing the violation at v_1 exceeds the cost.

To generalize, every action in the "violation set" yields more benefits for the company than expected costs. Thus, the company prefers to make a choice in that set than to comply with the law. What specific choice will the company make? You might think the answer is v_2. That point represents the most serious violation for which the benefit exceeds (or at least equals) the expected cost. But that is incorrect. The company does not want the most serious violation; it wants the most profitable violation. Profit is the difference between the benefit and expected cost. A rational company will commit violation v^*, where the distance between the benefit line and expected cost curve is maximized.

We can deepen our understanding of Figure 12.2 with marginal reasoning. From v_1, suppose the company moves rightward to v_2, meaning it commits a more serious violation. That increases the company's benefit from $50,000 to $60,000, so the marginal benefit equals $10,000. However, it increases the company's expected cost from $37,500 to $60,000, so the marginal cost equals $22,500. The marginal cost exceeds the marginal

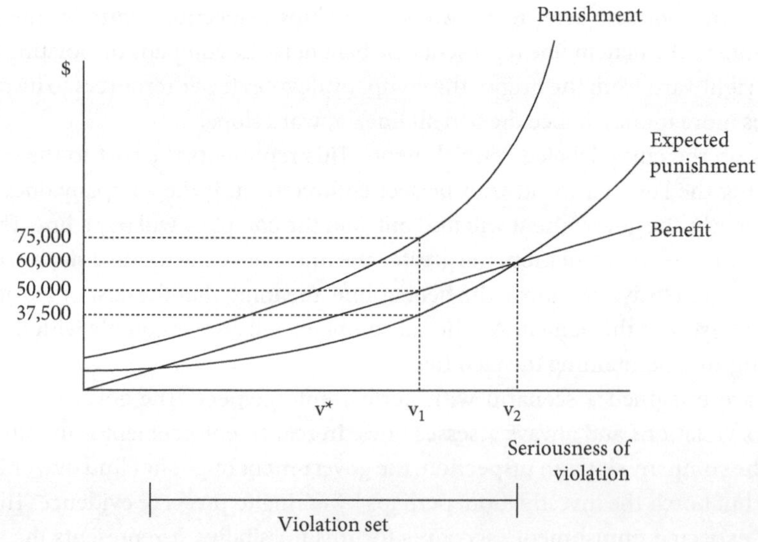

Figure 12.2. Rational Lawbreaking

[10] To simplify, we assume that the probability of discovering the violation equals the probability of enforcement. In fact, the two are not synonymous. Officers might observe many traffic violations (speeding, running red lights) but, because of limited time and resources, enforce the law only occasionally. The probability of enforcement is usually smaller than the probability of detection.

benefit, so a rational company would not move from v_1 to v_2. To analyze this from the other side, suppose the company starts at v_2 and moves leftward to v_1. That decreases the company's benefit from $60,000 to $50,000, so the marginal benefit equals –$10,000. However, it decreases the company's expected cost from $60,000 to $37,500, so the marginal cost equals –$22,500. The marginal benefit of –$10,000 exceeds the marginal cost of –$22,500, so a rational company would move from v_2 to v_1. From any starting point on the horizontal axis, a rational company would move leftward or rightward until the marginal cost of its move just equals the marginal benefit, and then it would stop. That occurs at v^*.

In sum, economists imagine people coldly weighing benefits and costs. If the benefits of violating the law exceed the costs, then people violate the law. Furthermore, they calibrate the seriousness of their violation to maximize their net benefit. This is a positive theory, meaning it makes predictions about how people behave.

Is the prediction accurate? Do real people behave like the company in our example? Here is one reason to say no: people do not always act rationally. Emotions like anger and jealousy can cause irrational behavior, as can drugs, alcohol, and many other factors.

This is a powerful but not fatal challenge to the economic theory of enforcement. The question is not whether economic models of enforcement (or anything else) are perfectly accurate. The question is whether they are sufficiently accurate to be useful when making law and policy. Later we will say more about irrationality.

Questions

12.1. The company in our example knows the exact benefit and expected cost of every possible violation of law. Do real people possess such information? If people have only rough estimates, are economists' predictions about their behavior useless?

12.2. The Wood Group was fined $7 million for falsely reporting that its employees had performed safety inspections on oil facilities. Apparently, the CEO did not cancel the inspections to save money. Instead, the company's employees were overwhelmed by other work and found it easier to falsify reports than to conduct the inspections.[11] Did the employees act as economic theory would predict?

12.3. Suppose the government adds $20 to every fine. If the fine for a minor violation was $100 before, now it equals $120, and if the fine for a serious violation was $1,000 before, now it equals $1,020. What effect does this have on the expected punishment curve in Figure 12.2? How serious of a violation will the company commit?

12.4. Suppose the government adds 20 percent to every fine. If the fine for a minor violation was $100 before, now it equals $120, and if the fine for a serious violation was $1,000 before, now it equals $1,200. What effect does this have on the expected punishment curve in Figure 12.2? How serious of a violation will the company commit?

[11] Company to Pay $9.5 Million for False Reporting of Safety Inspections and Clean Water Act Violations That Led to Explosion in Gulf of Mexico, Office of Public Affairs, Department of Justice (Feb. 23, 2017), available at https://www.justice.gov/opa/pr/company-pay-95-million-false-reporting-safety-inspections-and-clean-water-act-violations-led.

Why Punish?

Deterrence is an important but not exclusive goal of enforcement and punishment. Punishment can serve at least three other purposes: retribution, incapacitation, and rehabilitation. Retribution involves morals and vengeance. Wrongdoers "get what they deserve." Incapacitation involves imprisonment or similar restraints. We cannot deter an "incorrigible" person, but we can prevent some of his crimes by locking him up. Rehabilitation involves treatment and training that convert the offender into a law-abiding citizen.

Economists have studied some of these purposes. For example, they have argued that incapacitating a person is efficient when the benefit from preventing his crimes exceeds the cost of imprisoning him.[12] If prison rehabilitates, then we should be especially eager to imprison people because doing so yields a benefit beyond deterrence and incapacitation.[13]

Notwithstanding studies like these, most economists focus on deterrence. We focus on deterrence too, though we will occasionally gesture at these other purposes. To illustrate, the next chapter will consider preference change as a tool of enforcement. Should we improve people's behavior by altering their character? This question relates to rehabilitation. The answer is more complicated than you might think.

B. The "Law" of Deterrence

We have shown that deterring people requires making their expected cost from violating law exceed their benefit. In the figures, the expected punishment curve must lie above the benefit line. Behind this analysis lies a fundamental concept from economics: the law of demand. According to the law of demand, higher prices cause consumers to demand lower quantities. If you raise the price of bananas, people buy fewer bananas. Likewise, if you raise the "price" of lawbreaking by increasing expected punishments, people engage in less lawbreaking.

Applied to enforcement, the law of demand becomes the *law of deterrence*. According to the law of deterrence, increasing expected punishments decreases the total amount of lawbreaking in society. Figure 12.3 provides an illustration.[14] The horizontal axis represents the total amount of lawbreaking, and the vertical axis represents expected punishments. The solid, downward-sloping line captures the relationship between them. High expected punishments correspond to relatively little lawbreaking, whereas low expected punishments correspond to more lawbreaking.

Economists have confidence in the law of deterrence. In general, higher expected punishments must deter lawbreaking, assuming people are more or less

[12] Steven Shavell, *A Model of Optimal Incapacitation*, 77 Am. Econ. Assoc. Papers & Proc. 107 (1987). Note that the benefit of incapacitation diminishes if the prisoner commits crimes in prison.

[13] *See id.*

[14] This figure resembles one in Robert Cooter & Thomas Ulen, Law and Economics 468 (6th ed. 2014).

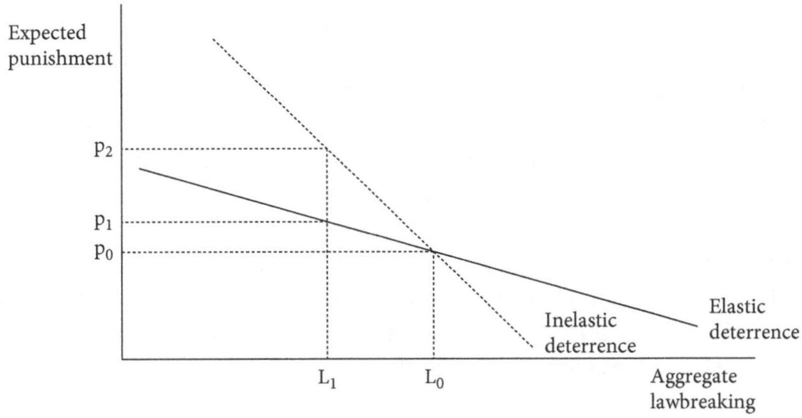

Figure 12.3. The Law of Deterrence

rational. But by how much? Does increasing the sanction deter a little or a lot? This question implicates another concept from economics, the elasticity of demand. Demand is *elastic* when a change in price has a relatively large effect on people's purchases, whereas demand is *inelastic* when a change in price has a relatively small effect on people's purchases. To illustrate, suppose the prices of bananas and cigarettes double. If the price increase causes many people to stop buying bananas (perhaps they buy apples instead), then demand for bananas is elastic. If the price increase has little effect on cigarette purchases, then demand for cigarettes is inelastic. Consumers do not respond much to changes in the price of cigarettes, perhaps because of addiction.

Figure 12.3 shows the importance of elasticity in enforcement. The solid, downward-sloping line depicts elastic deterrence. Relatively small changes in expected punishment have relatively large effects on aggregate lawbreaking. The dashed, downward-sloping line depicts inelastic deterrence. To appreciate the difference, suppose society experiences aggregate lawbreaking equivalent to L_0. Lawmakers promise to reduce lawbreaking to L_1. Given elastic deterrence, they can accomplish this by increasing expected punishment from p_0 to p_1. Given inelastic deterrence, they must increase expected punishment much more, from p_0 to p_2.

Determining the elasticity of deterrence is challenging because lawbreaking has many causes. Different people derive different benefits from violating the law. Likewise, different people experience sanctions differently. Fines cause more hardship for the poor more than for the rich. Different people have different tolerances for risk. A cautious person might never use illegal drugs, whereas a risk-welcoming person might seek them out. Some people have good information about expected punishments, whereas others are ignorant of law. Crime correlates with education. Of course, people sometimes act irrationally.

These complications do not negate the law of deterrence. However, they obscure the exact relationship between sanctions and lawbreaking. Increasing punishment tends to decrease the total amount of lawbreaking, sometimes by a little and other times by a lot. Not everyone can be deterred, and some lawbreaking seems inevitable.

C. Law in Books and Law in Action

Enforcing law involves many actors. The state must hire and train agents like police officers, forest rangers, environmental inspectors, and bank examiners. The targets of enforcement often end up in court, where lawyers present evidence, jurors make decisions, and judges write opinions. Finally, the state assesses penalties, which requires collectors for fines and wardens for prisons. Every step in the process costs a lot. For every actor in the system, the costs sometimes outweigh the benefits.

To take a simple example, consider street vending. In New York City, thousands of people sell books, t-shirts, and other items from sidewalk displays. The city code regulates the size and location of those displays:

> No general vendor display may exceed five feet in height from ground level. The display may not be less than twenty-four inches above the sidewalk where the display surface is parallel to the sidewalk, and may not be less than twelve inches above the sidewalk where the display surface is vertical.[15]

Why regulate the height of vendors' displays? One answer involves safety. A tall display might fall and harm someone, especially in windy weather, and a short display might trip someone.

Consider the challenge of enforcing this regulation. Officers must measure the heights of displays on busy sidewalks, which takes time and effort. If they discover a violation—the table is 23 inches above the sidewalk, not 24—they must write a ticket. The vendor might pay the ticket, or the vendor might contest it. If the vendor contests the ticket, the police officer might have to testify in court, which means less time to police other violations of law. The total costs of enforcement seem high.

Meanwhile, the benefits of enforcement seem low. The table is one inch too short, and one inch cannot make much difference for safety. Furthermore, if the vendor contests the ticket, the judge might acquit her. The alleged infraction was trivial, and perhaps the officer made an error when measuring the height of the display. If the judge acquits her, the vendor will not pay a fine, and she might not be deterred. She will use the same, short table tomorrow, meaning the enforcement effort was wasted.

In sum, the costs of ticketing the vendor outweigh the benefits. An officer with limited time and resources will not enforce the law. Foreseeing no enforcement, the vendor will use her short table.

Our analysis generalizes to countless other settings. Law limits the weight of trains, the size of tuna, the hours of work, and the alcohol content in wine. It regulates transporting currency, packaging food, building skyscrapers, and approaching wildlife in national parks. Fundamental laws establish human rights, protect the environment, and limit the discretion of government agencies. Across every area of law, enforcement comes with costs. Sometimes the costs are so high relative to the benefits that enforcers do not enforce.

[15] N.Y.C., N.Y., Admin. Code § 20-465(n) (2021).

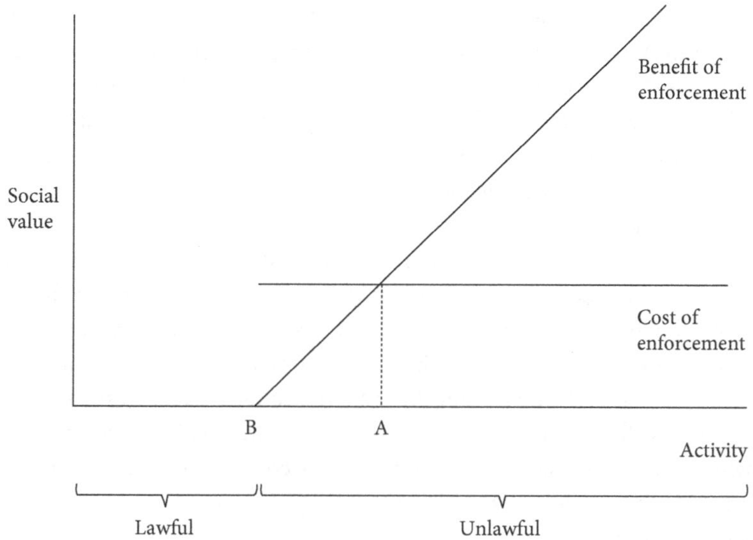

Figure 12.4. The Enforcement Gap

Figure 12.4 clarifies the relationship between costs and enforcement. The horizontal axis represents the extent or magnitude of a regulated activity. Moving rightward from the origin, the height of the vendor's display increases, soot emissions from a factory rise, the size of a fisherman's catch grows, or whatever else. The point *B* represents the legal limit on the activity, like a maximum catch of 100 lobsters. Points at or left of *B* represent legal acts, whereas points right of *B* represent illegal acts (e.g., catching more than 100 lobsters). The benefit line shows the gain from enforcing the law against a lawbreaker. The line slopes upward because punishing and deterring major violations has a greater benefit than punishing and deterring minor violations. The cost line shows the cost of enforcing the law.

For violations right of *A*, the benefit of enforcement exceeds the cost, so the state will enforce. For violations at or left of *A*, the cost exceeds the benefit, so the state will not enforce.[16] Given this, regulated parties who have the information in Figure 12.4 will choose the unlawful activity at *A*. They do as much as they can without triggering enforcement. The lobsterman, for example, might catch 110 lobsters, even though law limits him to 100 lobsters.

The cost of enforcement causes a gap to emerge between the "law in books" at point *B*, which indicates how people should act, and the "law in action" at point *A*, which indicates how people do act.[17] For a common example of the gap, consider driving. If the speed limit is 55 miles per hour, many drivers will go 60 miles per hour with impunity.

What happens to the gap when the benefit of enforcement increases? Suppose lobsters become a threatened species. Enforcing the catch limit is more beneficial than before, and we can represent this in Figure 12.4 by making the slope of the benefit line

[16] At point *A*, the cost of enforcement equals the benefit, so the state is indifferent about whether to enforce. We assume the state "breaks the tie" by not enforcing.

[17] Roscoe Pound, *Laws in Books and Law in Action*, 44 Am. U.L. Rev. 12, 14–15 (1910).

steeper. The new benefit line intersects the cost line at a point left of *A*, so regulated parties act left of *A*. Greater benefits from enforcement shrink the gap between the law in books and the law in action. Now suppose the cost of enforcement increases. The cost line shifts upward, which changes the point of intersection. Regulated parties can get away with worse behavior, so the gap grows. Different laws have different costs and benefits of enforcement, which helps explain why the state enforces some laws strictly and others leniently.

In our example, law limits the catch to 100 lobsters, but the lobsterman knows the state will not enforce minor violations, so he harvests 110. Can we deter the lobsterman with harsher penalties? The expected cost of lawbreaking equals the probability of enforcement *p* multiplied by the fine *f*. Suppose we triple the fine for violating the limit, so *f* increases. If the probability of enforcement exceeds zero, then tripling the fine increases the lobsterman's expected cost of lawbreaking, which might deter him. However, if the probability of enforcement equals zero, then tripling the fine has no effect on the expected cost of lawbreaking. If *p* equals zero, then $p * f$ equals zero, regardless of the value of *f*.

The root problem involves a familiar concept: credible commitments. If an enforcer could credibly commit to enforcing minor violations of law, then fewer people would commit such violations. But making a credible commitment is difficult. It requires the enforcer to commit to enforcing law even when doing so is irrational because her cost of enforcement outweighs the benefit. This is the *enforcer's dilemma*.[18] Without a credible commitment, the probability of enforcement for a sufficiently small violation equals zero. Given a zero probability of enforcement, harsher penalties cannot improve compliance. The gap between law in books and law in action is pervasive.

Questions

12.5. Governments can deter drivers from running red lights by posting officers at busy intersections, or they can install cameras that automatically photograph vehicles and their license plates. Cameras cost less than officers.

(a) Using Figure 12.4, explain the relationship between the invention of red light cameras, the cost of enforcement, and the size of the gap between the law in books and the law in action.

(b) Red light cameras have built-in "grace periods." They wait, say, one second after the light turns red to begin photographing vehicles in the intersection. Why?

12.6. Figure 12.4 assumes that enforcement costs the same whether the violation of law is minor or major. In reality, enforcing major violations might cost less because the evidence of wrongdoing is clearer. Alternatively, enforcing major violations might cost more because major violations carry heavier penalties, so defendants will fight harder by hiring better lawyers, not cooperating with investigators, and so on. Use Figure 12.4 to graph these possibilities. Do either of them affect the gap?

[18] *See, e.g.*, Scott Baker & Anup Malani, *Trial Court Budgets, the Enforcer's Dilemma, and the Rule of Law*, 2014 U. Ill. L. Rev. 1573 (2014).

12.7. Suppose the state commits to detecting and punishing every violation of law by investing heavily in enforcement. If the state's commitment is credible, will anybody violate the law? If nobody violates the law, can the state maintain its commitment?

D. Enforcement through Settlements

The high cost of enforcement prevents the state from fully applying its laws. Consequently, some unlawful acts are not deterred. People drive too fast, catch too many lobsters, and so on. Lowering the cost of enforcement mitigates the problem. One way to lower the cost of enforcement is to settle. Settlement saves the parties the time and effort of going to court: filing motions, preparing witnesses, presenting exhibits, testifying, paying court fees, and so on. An earlier chapter studied settlement in detail. Here we adapt that analysis to enforcement.

Suppose Yvette committed a crime, and a prosecutor brought charges against her. The evidence is imperfect, so even though Yvette is guilty, conviction is not certain. Both parties believe the probability of conviction equals 70 percent and the probability of acquittal equals 30 percent. If Yvette is convicted, she will pay a fine of $20,000, and the prosecutor will get a benefit. In the following box we address the motives of prosecutors and other enforcement agents. For now, let's make a simple assumption: the benefit to the prosecutor equals the cost to Yvette. If Yvette is convicted, she will pay $20,000, and the prosecutor will get a benefit (reputational, psychological) worth $20,000. Trial costs both parties $2,000.

As in prior chapters, we can apply bargaining theory to the case. Yvette's expected payoff from trial equals $.7(-20{,}000) + .3(0) - 2{,}000 = -\$16{,}000$. The prosecutor's expected payoff from trial equals $.7(20{,}000) + .3(0) - 2{,}000 = \$12{,}000$. The noncooperative value of the game equals the sum of these threat points, $-16{,}000 + 12{,}000 = -\$4{,}000$. Instead of trial, the parties could settle. Settlements in criminal law are called *plea bargains*. In exchange for a reduction in sanctions, the defendant pleads guilty, saving both sides the time and expense of trial.[19]

Let's consider a plea bargain between the prosecutor and Yvette. Assume settlement is free, meaning it would save the parties a total of $4,000 in trial costs. The reasonable settlement gives each party his or her threat value plus half the surplus, so the prosecutor should get $14,000, and Yvette should get –$14,000. Under the reasonable plea bargain, Yvette agrees to plead guilty in exchange for a reduction in the fine from $20,000 to $14,000. Both parties prefer the plea bargain to trial.

Plea bargaining saves both parties time and effort. This "mutuality of advantage" promotes the efficient use of resources.[20] For the prosecutor, spending less time on Yvette's case leaves more time for other, perhaps more serious cases. Plea bargaining reduces uncertainty, which the defendant in particular might value. Yvette gets the certainty of a smaller punishment rather than the uncertainty of trial. (To appreciate

[19] The economic analysis of plea bargaining began with an influential paper: William Landes, *An Economic Analysis of the Courts*, 14 J.L. Econ. 61 (1971).

[20] Brady v. United States, 397 U.S. 742, 752 (1970).

the value of certainty, just imagine going to trial when acquittal means freedom and conviction means life in prison.) Plea bargains can act like a screen, with guilty defendants mostly accepting the deal and innocent defendants mostly going to trial and winning.[21]

Of course, plea bargaining has downsides. Trials have procedural protections for defendants—rules of evidence, the high burden of proof—that plea bargaining lacks. Defendants might misunderstand their choices or feel coerced. The screen never works perfectly. Some innocent defendants plead guilty to a crime they did not commit. They prefer the plea bargain to trial, where they run the risk of a false conviction and large penalty.

These are important objections to plea bargaining, but we set them aside to focus on a different problem: deterrence. Suppose a thief considers stealing a painting. We could deter the thief by making him pay a fine of, say, $10,000. If the probability of enforcement equals 50 percent, then the fine should equal $20,000, as this makes the expected fine $10,000—if the thief goes to trial. But the thief will not go to trial. If he commits the crime and gets caught, the prosecutor will offer him a plea deal. To induce the thief to accept, the prosecutor will have to make the penalty less than $10,000, perhaps $8,000. If the thief knows this, then his expected cost of committing the crime equals $8,000, which is too low to deter him. Plea bargaining can weaken deterrence.[22]

The state can offset this problem by increasing penalties.[23] To illustrate, suppose the penalty for stealing the painting increases from $20,000 to $24,000. Given a 50 percent chance of enforcement, the expected penalty at trial becomes $12,000. To induce the thief to accept a plea deal, the prosecutor could offer a fine of $10,000, exactly the amount needed for deterrence.

In theory, increasing penalties offers a simple solution to underdeterrence. In practice, it causes problems. People object to severe sanctions, especially when they do not trust the motives of enforcers. One way to increase sanctions is to multiply offenses. "Charge stacking" occurs when a prosecutor charges someone with multiple crimes for one act, as when carrying a handgun constitutes possession of a firearm by a felon, possession of a firearm near a school, and possession of a pistol without a permit. To charge stack, prosecutors need a large menu of crimes. William Stuntz characterized American criminal law as a "world in which the law on the books makes everyone a felon."[24]

Whether good or bad, plea bargaining is widespread. In the United States, over 90 percent of criminal cases result in a plea bargain.

We have discussed enforcing some criminal laws through plea bargaining. The government enforces many other laws through *consent decrees*. Consent decrees are judicial orders that settle a dispute according to an agreement among the parties. For example, when the government sued the company AT&T for employment

[21] *See, e.g.*, Gene Grossman & Michael Katz, *Plea Bargaining and Social Welfare*, 73 Am. Econ. Rev. 749–57 (1983); Scott Baker & Claudio Mezzetti, *Prosecutorial Resources, Plea Bargaining, and the Decision to Go to Trial*, 17 J.L. Econ. & Org. 149 (2001).

[22] A. Mitchell Polinsky & Daniel L. Rubinfeld, *The Deterrent Effects of Settlements and Trials*, 8 Int'l Rev. L. Econ. 109 (1988).

[23] *See id.*

[24] William J. Stuntz, *The Pathological Politics of Criminal Law*, 100 Mich. L. Rev. 505, 511 (2001).

discrimination, AT&T settled. The company agreed to change its employment practices and to pay compensation to women and minority workers, and in exchange the government dropped its lawsuit and stopped threatening to revoke AT&T's government contracts.[25] In the United States, many regulations get enforced through consent decrees. In 2018, federal courts entered 109 consent decrees in civil environmental lawsuits alone.[26]

Consent decrees and plea bargains share some fundamental features. In both cases, settlement saves resources and reduces the parties' uncertainty. However, settlement can weaken deterrence. AT&T agreed to give $15 million in back pay to certain workers, less than its critics wanted or the government might have secured through trial.[27] To maintain deterrence, the state can increase penalties. As in criminal law, however, harsh penalties can generate controversy.

Questions

12.8. Hayes already had two felony convictions when he was caught forging a check for $88.30. The prosecutor made him an offer: plead guilty and spend five years in prison, or plead not guilty, go to trial, and risk life in prison. Hayes rejected the offer, went to trial, and was sentenced to life in prison. Was the prosecutor's offer a "legitimate use of available leverage in the plea-bargaining process"?[28]

12.9. A prosecutor charges you with a crime carrying a fine of $50,000. He makes you an offer: plead guilty and pay a fine of $5,000. Does this offer signal anything about the strength of the prosecutor's case?[29] If so, would the prosecutor make such an offer?

12.10. Some criminal defendants cannot afford to pay bail, meaning they remain detained in jail until trial. Explain why pretrial detention encourages innocent defendants to accept plea deals.[30]

12.11. Prosecutors do not have the resources to bring everyone charged with a crime to trial. If all defendants refused to accept plea bargains, prosecutors would have to drop the charges against most of them. Why don't defendants coordinate and refuse to accept plea bargains.[31]

[25] *See* Eileen Shanahan, *A.T.&T. to Grant 15,000 Back Pay in Job Inequities*, N.Y. Times, Jan. 19, 1973.

[26] Tracy Hester, *Consent Decrees as Emergent Environmental Law*, 85 Mo. L. Rev. 687, 691 (2020). Between 2012 and 2017, the U.S. Department of Interior entered into over 460 consent decrees and other settlements generating over $4 billion in monetary payments. *See id.* at 690–91.

[27] Eileen Shanahan, *A.T.&T. to Grant 15,000 Back Pay in Job Inequities*, N.Y. Times, Jan. 19, 1973 ("The National Organization for Women issued a statement calling the $15-million in back pay 'chickenfeed' compared to the $4-billion that it said was really owed to the company's women employees.").

[28] Bordenkircher v. Hayes, 434 U.S. 357, 359 (1978). The Supreme Court upheld Hayes's sentence.

[29] *See* Jennifer Reinganum, *Plea Bargaining and Prosecutorial Discretion*, 78 Am. Econ. Rev. 713–28 (1988).

[30] *See* Megan T. Stevenson, *Distortion of Justice: How the Inability to Pay Bail Affects Case Outcomes*, 34 J.L. Econ. & Org. 511 (2018).

[31] *See* Oren Bar-Gill & Omri Ben-Shahar, *The Prisoners' (Plea Bargain) Dilemma*, 1 J. Legal Analysis 737 (2009).

Agency Costs in Enforcement

Economists make simple assumptions to study complex phenomena. Ideally, the assumptions make the analysis manageable while remaining approximately accurate. When studying enforcement, many economists assume that the enforcer is a social welfare–maximizing monolith. This assumption is not very accurate. Enforcement involves coordination by multiple actors including legislators, cops, prosecutors, judges, and jurors, each with their own interests and objectives. We can conceptualize the problem in familiar terms. Citizens are the principal, and they want welfare-maximizing enforcement. Enforcers are the agents, and they exercise discretion to pursue their own goals. Enforcement suffers from agency costs.[32]

Consider some examples. Legislators pass tough-on-crime laws to generate political support, not to optimize deterrence. Prosecutors bring serious charges to please the President who appointed them (and who might reward them with judgeships). Officers do not bother checking vendor displays because they don't care about the height regulation. Jurors hand down a long sentence because they do not pay the costs of imprisonment. The common theme in these examples is externalities. Enforcers externalize various costs and benefits, causing their choices to deviate from the social optimum.

Overlooking agency costs causes errors in prediction. To demonstrate, focus on fines. According to most economic models of enforcement, the government does not care whether it collects fines or not. This is because fines do not alter the amount of money in society, they just transfer it from the target of enforcement to the state. Total value does not change, so the welfare-maximizing enforcer does not care. The enforcer collects fines only to deter lawbreaking, never to earn a profit.

In reality, some enforcers do care about profit. In the United States, hundreds of local governments rely on fine revenues to finance their budgets.[33] Police departments enforce minor traffic violations because they treat the collection of fines as a benefit, not a transfer. The social cost of enforcement exceeds the benefit, so economic models predict no enforcement, but in fact enforcement is widespread.[34] Failing to account for agency costs does not undermine economists' basic analysis of deterrence, but it weakens the accuracy of their predictions.

[32] For criticisms of the failure of economics to account for agency problems in enforcement, see, for example, Thomas J. Miceli, *Plea Bargaining and Deterrence: An Institutional Approach*, 3 Eur. J.L. & Econ. 249 (1996); Nuno Garoupa & Frank H. Stephen, *Why Plea-Bargaining Fails to Achieve Results in So Many Criminal Justice Systems: A New Framework for Assessment*, 15 Maastricht J. Eur. & Comp. L. 319 (2008); Richard H. McAdams, *Bill Stuntz and the Principal-Agent Problem in Criminal Law*, *in* The Political Heart of Criminal Procedure: Essays on Themes of William J. Stuntz 47 (Michael Klarman, David Skeel, & Carol Steiker eds., 2012).

[33] *See* Mike Maciag, *Addicted to Fines*, Governing Magazine, Aug. 19, 2019.

[34] "Rent-seeking" governments enforce minor violations of law more aggressively than welfare-maximizing governments. *See* Nuno Garoupa & Daniel Klerman, *Optimal Law Enforcement with a Rent-Seeking Government*, 4 Am. L. Econ. Rev. 116 (2002).

E. Irrationality and Discounting

We began our discussion of deterrence by imagining a rational criminal weighing the costs and benefits of lawbreaking. We continued by imagining a rational enforcer weighing the social costs and social benefits of enforcement. These thought experiments simplify analysis, but they strike many people as unreasonable. Enforcers do not always act in society's best interest. Some people weigh the costs and benefits of lawbreaking, as when an oil executive decides whether to inspect the facilities, but many other people do not. Many criminals are irrational.

In economics, the word "irrational" has a particular meaning. A rational person makes the choice that best satisfies her preferences given her beliefs and constraints. Making any other choice is irrational. To illustrate, suppose Zeke the college student chooses among three courses, *A*, *B*, and *C*. Course *C* sounds especially interesting, but it has a prerequisite that Zeke has not satisfied, so he cannot take it. The prerequisite is a constraint. Of the remaining choices, Zeke prefers *A*, so he takes *A*. Choosing *A* is rational, whereas choosing *B* or attempting to choose *C* would be irrational.

Stated this way, rationality seems certain, almost tautological. But this is not right. Scholars have shown that people appear to behave irrationally in a range of circumstances. For example, consider *anchoring bias*.[35] In scenario one, a salesman tells you the car costs $30,000. In scenario two, the salesman tells you the car ordinarily costs $40,000 but is on sale for $30,000. Both scenarios involve the same buyer, car, price, and salesman, so economists expect buyers to behave the same. In fact, people are more likely to buy the car in scenario two. Announcing the $40,000 price "anchors" people's thinking about the value of the car.

In addition to anchoring, scholars have identified other patterns of behavior that seem to contradict rational choice. These patterns underpin an important field of research called behavioral economics.[36] Behavioral economics might help explain lawbreaking,[37] but here we focus on a different explanation that fits within traditional economics: discounting.

Many choices yield costs and benefits over time. Purchasing a stock means paying today and earning a profit later (you hope), whereas downhill skiing means pleasure today and soreness tomorrow (you hope not). Discounting is the process through which people compare the immediate gains from a choice to the longer-term losses, or vice versa.

To illustrate, suppose a student receives an invitation to a party today, but he has an important exam tomorrow. The party would be fun, yielding a benefit today of 6 utils. However, attending the party would cause the student to fail the exam, yielding a cost tomorrow of 10 utils. If the student places the same weight on tomorrow as today—if he does not discount the future—then he compares the benefit of 6 to the cost of 10 and skips the party. If the student places half as much weight on tomorrow as today, then he

[35] *See* Amos Tversky & Daniel Kahneman, *Judgment under Uncertainty: Heuristics and Biases*, 185 SCIENCE 1124 (1974).

[36] For an accessible introduction by one of the field's pioneers, see DANIEL KAHNEMAN, THINKING, FAST AND SLOW (2011).

[37] *See, e.g.*, EYAL ZAMIR & DORON TEICHMAN, BEHAVIORAL LAW AND ECONOMICS (2018); Richard H. McAdams & Thomas S. Ulen, *Behavioral Criminal Law and Economics*, *in* CRIMINAL LAW AND ECONOMICS (Nuno Garoupa ed., 2009).

compares the benefit of 6 to a cost of 5 and attends the party. In the second case, the student has a high *discount rate*. He places much more weight on the present than on the future, causing him to make choices today that he regrets tomorrow.

We can relate choices to discount rates with a simple formula:[38]

If $b_1 - {}^{c_2}\!/_{r} > 0$, then take the action, otherwise do not take the action.

The term b_1 represents the present benefit (6 in the previous example), c_2 represents the future cost (10 in the previous example), and r represents the discount rate. The student who does not discount the future has a discount rate of $r = 1$, so he does not attend the party. The student in the second case has a higher discount rate of $r = 2$, so he attends the party.[39] Rearranging terms in the equation generates the tipping point:

$$r^* = \frac{c_2}{b_1}$$

People with discount rates greater than ${}^{c_2}\!/_{b_1}$ will take the action, whereas people with discount rates below ${}^{c_2}\!/_{b_1}$ will not. In our example, the student will attend the party if his discount rate exceeds 1.67.

Discounting is rational. We place less weight on the future because we cannot be sure the future will arrive. Even high discount rates are rational in the economic sense.[40] However, high discount rates are often imprudent. A prudent student would not attend the party today knowing that it will cause him to fail an important exam tomorrow. Tomorrow may never arrive, but probably it will.

Discount rates provide the foundation for a model of lawbreaking. When contemplating a violation of law, people weigh the immediate benefit against the future punishment. As discount rates increase, people place less weight on the punishment, encouraging them to take the illegal action. To illustrate, recall again our example of the thief and the painting. The expected punishment for stealing the painting equals 10,000. Let's assume the benefit to the thief of the crime equals $8,000 (perhaps he can sell the painting for that amount). The benefit is immediate, whereas the punishment will come later. As the thief's discount rate grows, the punishment weighs less heavily on his decision. If his discount rate exceeds 1.25, he will steal the painting.

Our discussion imagines two time periods, today and the future, but this is too simple. The future could be one week, one month, or one year away. The further away the consequence, the greater the discount. If the thief expects to pay a fine in one month, it weighs

[38] This formula appears in Robert Cooter & Thomas Ulen, Law and Economics 471 n.9 (6th ed. 2014).

[39] Note that a discount rate of $r = 2$ is equivalent to multiplying the cost term by ½.

[40] Economists treat discount rates as a preference, a "taste" for time comparable to tastes for parties, good grades, and chocolate ice cream. Preferences are not irrational so long as they are consistent (more formally, so long as they are complete and transitive). Note that *hyperbolic* discounting is irrational because it implies an inconsistency in preferences for time. Here is an example of hyperbolic discounting: you prefer $1 today to $3 tomorrow, but you prefer $3 in 366 days to $1 in 365 days. *See, e.g.*, Richard H. Thaler, *Some Empirical Evidence on Dynamic Inconsistency*, 8 Econ. Letters 201 (1981).

relatively heavily on his choice. If the thief expects to pay a fine in 10 years, he mostly ignores it. A person with a high discount rate who faces punishment soon might behave the same as a person with a lower discount rate who faces punishment much later.

We have treated discount rates as fixed. In fact, discount rates might vary in the same way that people's moods vary.[41] A prudent, stable person might usually have a discount rate of, say, 1.03 but occasionally have a rate of 1.02 or 1.04 depending on her mood. An imprudent, volatile person might have a discount rate of 1.5 on average but often have a rate of 1.3 or 1.7. Variable discount rates might explain occasional offenders, people who mostly follow the law but occasionally act rashly and break it.

The theory of discounting illuminates lawbreaking and enforcement. People with especially high or especially variable discount rates violate more laws. Delays in punishment, as when court proceedings take years, exacerbate the problem by pushing punishment further into the future. In theory, we can deter high discounters with harsher punishments. In the previous formula, we can offset increases in r with increases in c_2. In practice, discounting limits the effectiveness of punishment. For a person with a high discount rate, a prison sentence of 20 years and a prison sentence of 25 years might have nearly the same deterrent effect because the last five years, which are decades away, get almost no weight in his decision-making. (Meanwhile, those last five years of imprisonment cost society a lot.)

This discussion leads to two hypotheses. First, given high discounting, swifter and surer punishment works better.[42] The intuition is simple: if people heavily discount the future, then the possibility of punishment later does not deter as well as certain punishment today. We can illustrate with an example. If the thief steals the painting, he faces a 50 percent chance of going to prison for two years. Translated into utility, the first year in prison will cost him 100 but, because of discounting, the second year will cost him only 50. The expected punishment for stealing the painting is .5(100 + 50) = 75. Instead, suppose the thief faces an 80 percent chance of going to prison for one year. His expected punishment is higher, .8(100) = 80.

Here is the second hypothesis: the government can prevent lawbreaking by reducing the size and variability of discount rates. Less discounting effectively increases punishment, deterring more violations of law. Discount rates relate to moods, self-control, and volatility. We might reduce discount rates through education, therapy, mental health programs, and treatment for addiction. The theory of discounting connects two features of modern government, social services and the justice system. They offer alternative mechanisms for deterring wrongdoing.

Questions

12.12. A criminal is sentenced to 10 years in prison. The state could incarcerate the criminal immediately, or the state could wait a few years until the prison is

[41] *See, e.g.*, Robert Cooter, *Models of Morality in Law and Economics: Self-Control and Self-Improvement for the Bad Man of Holmes*, 78 B.U. L. REV. 903 (1998).

[42] *See* A. Mitchell Polinsky & Steven Shavell, *On the Disutility and Discounting of Imprisonment and the Theory of Deterrence*, 28 J. LEGAL STUD. 1 (1999).

less crowded or the state budget is balanced. Why do we incarcerate people immediately?[43]

12.13. Defend this sentence: "To prevent crimes by youths we should offer social services, but to prevent crimes by corporations we should increase punishments."

12.14. Are rehabilitation and deterrence distinct justifications for punishment?

II. Normative Theory of Enforcement

We have concentrated on the positive theory of deterrence. According to that theory, the state can deter violations of law by making the expected punishment greater than the lawbreaker's benefit. Given high discount rates, the state must impose especially severe punishments or attempt to lower discount rates, perhaps through social services. This theory is simple and elegant, and it can explain some real enforcement practices, though of course not perfectly.

Here we turn to normative analysis. We begin by identifying the economic purpose of enforcement, which is to minimize social costs. Often the state minimizes social costs by deterring lawbreaking, but sometimes it minimizes costs by permitting lawbreaking. Next, we consider the mechanisms of deterrence. To prevent lawbreaking, the state can hire many cops, train many prosecutors, impose harsh punishments, and so on. Which mechanism is optimal? Finally, we consider the choice between fines and imprisonment.

A. Enforcement and Social Welfare

What is the purpose of law enforcement? For some retributivists, the answer is to punish all wrongdoing. For others, the purpose is to deter all lawbreaking. We offer a different answer. For economists, the purpose of enforcement is to minimize social costs, where social costs equal the sum of the costs of lawbreaking and the costs of prevention.

Start with lawbreaking. Violating law usually comes with costs. Sometimes the costs are large, as when lax inspections cause oil rigs to explode and harm workers. Other times the costs are small, as when a vendor uses a table that's slightly too short, thus imposing a small risk of someone tripping. Occasionally violating law creates social benefits. In *Les Misérables*, the peasant Jean Valjean steals bread to feed his impoverished family. His crime harmed the baker, but it benefited his sister and her seven children. All things considered, did his crime harm society? This example comes from a novel, but art imitates life.

Now consider the costs of prevention. Enforcing law requires many resources: detectives, squad cars, cameras, evidence labs, jury rooms, prosecutors, bank examiners, handcuffs, jail cells, defense attorneys, clerks, radar guns, and the list goes on. Enforcing one law leaves less time and fewer resources to enforce other laws.

[43] *See* A. Mitchell Polinsky & Paul N. Riskind, *Deterrence and the Optimal Use of Prison, Parole, and Probation*, 62 J.L. Econ. 347 (2019).

This leads to a prescription: *the government should enforce the law when the marginal social benefit of enforcement exceeds the marginal social cost.* To illustrate, suppose the state inspects nuclear plants for compliance with safety regulations once per year. Should the state inspect them twice per year? A second inspection requires time and effort by engineers, so the cost of a second inspection is not trivial. Suppose, however, that a second inspection reduces the probability of a nuclear meltdown. If the marginal benefit (less risk of a catastrophe) exceeds the marginal cost, the government should inspect twice per year. Perhaps the state should inspect more than twice per year. We can use marginal reasoning to find the optimal number of inspections.

Consider one more example. To prevent jaywalking, the city could position a jaywalking enforcer on every street corner. The marginal cost of moving from the status quo to such aggressive enforcement would be very high. The city would need many such enforcers, and spending more money on enforcers would leave less money for schools, roads, and other priorities. Meanwhile, the marginal benefit would be small because the social costs of jaywalking are usually insignificant. The city should not assign a jaywalking enforcer to every corner. Perhaps the city should never enforce the law against jaywalking because the marginal cost is too high. Policing jaywalkers takes time away from policing more serious violations.

Once we understand enforcement in terms of social costs and benefits, we see why economists emphasize deterrence as a goal of punishment. Reasoning about deterrence—society should spend *x* today to prevent harm greater than *x* tomorrow—fits naturally in a cost-benefit framework. Two other goals of punishment, incapacitation and rehabilitation, also fit this framework. Society should spend *y* incapacitating or rehabilitating an offender if this prevents harm greater than *y* in the future. The remaining goal of punishment, retribution, does not fit the cost-benefit framework. Retributivists punish people who deserve it. Rather than incentivizing good behavior before people act, retributivism concentrates on punishing bad behavior after people act. This seems like a double loss. Society incurs one harm from the bad behavior and another harm from the punishment (the cost of police, courts, jails, and so on).

Understanding enforcement in terms of social costs and benefits illuminates our discussion of the gap. For officials, the cost of enforcement sometimes exceeds the benefit, as when a cop is too busy to measure a vendor's table. When enforcers do not enforce, some regulated parties do not obey. Knowing the cop will not measure, the vendor uses the short table. A gap opens between the law in books (how people should behave) and the law in action (how people do behave).

You might think the gap reflects an agency problem. If officials considered society's costs and benefits rather than their own, they would enforce the law rigorously and the gap would disappear. But this is incorrect. If officials represented society perfectly, they would not enforce the law if the social cost of doing so exceeded the social benefit. For minor infractions like jaywalking, using a short table, and driving five miles per hour over the speed limit, the social cost of enforcement usually exceeds the social benefit. Even when enforcers maximize social welfare, a gap between the law in books and the law in action persists. It *should* persist.[44]

[44] A. Mitchell Polinsky & Steven Shavell, *The Economic Theory of Public Enforcement of Law*, 38 J. Econ. Lit. 45, 70 (2000) ("Optimal enforcement tends to be characterized by some degree of underdeterrence . . . because allowing some underdeterrence conserves enforcement resources.").

Questions

12.15. Suppose the state punishes a criminal secretly, without anyone else finding out. Explain why this punishment might satisfy a retributivist but not an economist.

12.16. Arresting an arsonist does not incentivize someone else to become an arsonist. In contrast, arresting a drug dealer does incentivize someone else to become a drug dealer by freeing up a profitable corner. Explain why an economist might recommend incapacitation for an arsonist but not for a drug dealer.

12.17. For retributivists, punishment gives offenders "what they deserve." Suppose that giving an offender what he deserves makes the public happy. Does this mean the punishment comes with more social benefits than costs? Can we measure the psychological benefit to the public of punishment?

Enforcement and the Rule of Law

People everywhere celebrate the rule of law. The United Nations considers it an "indispensable foundation[ ] for a more peaceful, prosperous and just world."[45] How can society establish the rule of law? Policymakers struggle to answer. One issue involves definitions; people disagree on what exactly the "rule of law" means. We focus on a different issue: enforcement. The rule of law requires substantial compliance. Rule-of-law states like Japan and Australia can secure substantial compliance with their laws through enforcement, but states like El Salvador and Sierra Leone cannot. Societies that most need the rule of law lack enforcement capacity.

The root problem involves more than resources. It involves externalities. Imagine an undeveloped society trying to establish the rule of law. Leaders make laws, but they lack professional enforcers. Mostly they rely on private citizens to enforce the laws against each other. A citizen who observes a violation of law might reason as follows: "If I punish the wrongdoer, he will behave better tomorrow, benefiting me and everyone else. However, punishing the wrongdoer exposes me to danger. He might become violent or seek revenge, and the state cannot protect me. I will not enforce." The enforcer internalizes the full cost of enforcement but not the full benefit. When people externalize benefits from an activity, they do too little of it. In this case, they underenforce.

An earlier chapter explained that security suffers from free riding. Everyone waits for someone else to build the stone wall around the village. With everyone waiting, no one builds. A similar problem arises with enforcement. Everyone waits for

[45] Declaration of the High-level Meeting of the General Assembly on the Rule of Law at the National and International Levels, United Nations, Nov. 30, 2012.

someone else to enforce, so no one enforces. To build the rule of law, society must overcome free riding in enforcement.[46]

B. Social Welfare and Deterrence

The state should deter an act of lawbreaking whenever the marginal social benefit exceeds the marginal social cost. We have analyzed the social costs of enforcement, which include paying police, training regulators, buying equipment, and so on. Here we concentrate on the social benefit. When the state deters a violation of law, the social benefit equals the difference between the payoff to society with and without the violation. Calculating that payoff raises tricky issues about distribution and preferences.

Start with distribution. A thief breaks an art gallery window and steals a painting. Replacing the window costs $500, and the painting has a market value of $8,000. What did the crime cost society? You might say $8,500, but this is not quite right. The gallery lost $8,500, but society encompasses everyone, including the thief, and the thief gained $8,000. The crime redistributed $8,000 in value and destroyed $500 in value. The state should spend up to $500 to deter this crime, but no more. Similarly, a company saves itself $200,000 by failing to maintain an oil facility. Consequently, the facility explodes, causing harm totaling $1 million. The social cost of the company's violation equals $800,000, so the state should spend up to $800,000 to deter it.[47]

In both examples, we count the lawbreaker's benefit when determining the cost of the act (and therefore the benefit of deterring it). The theft costs society $500 because the criminal's gain offsets the gallery's loss. If we did not count the lawbreaker's benefit, the social costs of the violations described earlier would be higher, $8,500 and $1 million, and society should spend more to deter them.

Why count the lawbreakers' benefit? Economists aim to satisfy preferences. Social welfare aggregates the preference satisfaction of all people, including lawbreakers. Excluding lawbreakers from the social welfare calculation would raise very difficult questions. Should we exclude lawbreakers even if their action was just, as when Jean Valjean stole bread? Should we include law followers even if the law they follow is unjust? Who else should we include or exclude, and why? Answering these questions requires a moral theory separate from preference satisfaction, but economics does not have such a theory (and moral philosophers do not agree on one). Economists tend to avoid these complications by counting all people and all preferences in social welfare, whoever those people and whatever those preferences happen to be.[48]

[46] On overcoming the collective action problem, see Gillian K. Hadfield & Barry R. Weingast, *Microfoundations of the Rule of Law*, 17 ANN. REV. POL. SCI. 21 (2014).

[47] To be clear, the violation leads to a benefit to the company of $200,000 and a cost to others of $1 million for a net cost of $800,000. Not violating the law would have meant no benefit for the company and no cost to others for a net cost of $0.

[48] For dissenting views by Nobel Prize–winning economists, see John C. Harsanyi, *Rule Utilitarianism and Decision Theory*, 11 ERKENNTNIS 25, 30 (1977) (arguing that scholars should "define social utility in terms of the various individuals' 'true' preferences," thus disregarding "not only preferences distorted by factual or logical errors, but also preferences based on clearly antisocial attitudes, such as sadism, resentment, or malice"); George J. Stigler, *The Optimum Enforcement of Laws*, 78 J. POL. ECON. 526, 527 (1974) ("what evidence is there that society sets a positive value upon the utility derived from a murder, rape, or arson?").

Counting the lawbreaker's benefit has a surprising implication: sometimes we should permit violations of law, even if enforcement is costless. Suppose that violating a particular law usually yields a payoff of 5 for the lawbreaker and a cost of 8 for everyone else. The act usually causes a net loss of 3, which justifies the law prohibiting it. However, in a special case the act yields a payoff of 8 for the lawbreaker and a cost of 5 for everyone else, meaning it causes a net gain of 3. In the special case, the state promotes social welfare by *not* enforcing the law.

If the state could sort every violation of law into "net loss" and "net gain," then it could selectively enforce the former but not the latter. However, sorting requires information that the state usually lacks. Often the state cannot determine the benefit to the lawbreaker of the violation, so it cannot assess whether his gains outweigh others' losses.

In general, people with the most information should make the decision. The economic theory of enforcement embraces this idea. For economists, *the optimal expected punishment equals the harm caused to others.*[49] Punishment attaches a cost to lawbreaking, and it lets the lawbreaker decide whether to pay it. The lawbreaker alone knows if his benefit exceeds the cost. Setting the expected cost equal to the harm incentivizes only those violations of law that yield net benefits. To illustrate, consider our thief. Breaking the window and stealing the painting causes $8,500 in harm to the gallery, so the optimal expected punishment equals $8,500. A rational thief will commit the crime only if his benefit exceeds $8,500—in other words, only if the total benefits of the crime exceed the total costs.

The theory of optimal punishment aligns with concepts from earlier in the book. People behave efficiently when they internalize the costs and benefits of their actions. The optimal punishment forces lawbreakers to internalize the costs of their lawbreaking.

The optimal punishment does not match the optimal enforcement effort. Breaking the window and stealing the painting causes a loss of $8,500 to the gallery, a gain of $8,000 to the thief, and a loss of $500 to society (the window). The social loss equals $500, so the state should spend no more than $500 trying to prevent it. However, the state should make the expected penalty $8,500.

Punishments work like prices. You can have a banana if you pay a dollar, and you can steal a painting if you pay a fine. However, law does not describe them like prices. Law does not say, "Crimes on sale for $8,500." Law says, "Do not commit the crime, and if you do, you must pay." Why? One answer involves morality. Some acts are inherently wrong, and people should never engage in them. We give a different answer rooted in economics. Optimal punishment requires precise information about the costs of lawbreaking. Sometimes we can estimate those costs in individual cases, as with the stolen painting, but other times we cannot. What does it cost society when a school discriminates based on race, an arsonist burns an old-growth forest, or an attacker assaults a victim? Lawmakers cannot price such harms accurately. For many violations of law, the concept of "price" makes little sense. We can compare money to bananas but not to dignity, freedom, or bodily integrity.

[49] *See* A. Mitchell Polinsky & Steven Shavell, *The Economic Theory of Public Enforcement of Law*, 38 J. ECON. LIT. 45, 50 (2000). We assume that lawbreakers are risk neutral and internalize their own costs and benefits from lawbreaking.

When harms seem especially severe or especially nebulous, law does not price them. It forbids them. The law makes a command ("Do not burn the forest") backed by a sanction. This is good economics. If you cannot quantify the costs and benefits of an act but feel confident that the costs are greater, then prohibit the act.[50]

Why do we limit sanctions? Burning a forest for pleasure surely does more harm than good. Why don't we forbid burning forests *and* attach a severe penalty, like life in prison? The next section has answers.

Questions

12.18. To prevent the painting from being stolen, police can patrol the neighborhood, or the gallery can install security cameras. Which approach costs more? Does either approach have a positive externality?

12.19. A politician defames her opponent, a CEO defrauds investors, and a worker stabs his boss. Do the perpetrators benefit from their illegal acts? Should we count those benefits in social welfare?

12.20. Through plea bargaining and consent decrees, different people face different punishments for the same violation of law. Is this consistent with optimal punishment?

12.21. A restaurant has a bottle of wine with a market value of $1,000. A thief with fine tastes values drinking the wine at $1,500. He could buy the wine from the restaurant, or he could steal it. Either way, transferring the wine to the thief promotes social welfare by moving a good from someone who values it less to someone who values it more. Why is buying better than stealing?

C. Optimal Deterrence

To prevent disease, law regulates the cleanliness of meat packing plants. A company could save money by not cleaning its plants. Suppose this act of lawbreaking would cause $1 million in harm to consumers. Thus, the optimal expected fine equals $1 million. How can the state set the punishment at that level? The expected punishment equals the probability of punishment multiplied by its magnitude. The formula has two inputs, probability and magnitude, meaning the state has two tools for achieving its objective.

To elaborate, suppose you regulate the meat packing industry, and you have the aforementioned information. You could set the expected punishment at $1 million by making the probability of punishment 100 percent and the fine $1 million. Alternatively, you could make the probability of punishment 50 percent and the fine $2 million. You have many other options as shown in Table 12.1. As you move down the table, increases in the size of the fine offset decreases in the probability of punishment. Consequently, the expected punishment stays at the optimal level.

Many combinations of probability and magnitude will yield the optimal expected punishment. Which combination should you choose? Economists answer by

[50] *See* Robert Cooter, *Prices and Sanctions*, 84 COLUM. L. REV. 1523 (1984).

Table 12.1. Expected Punishment

Probability of punishment (p)	Magnitude of fine (f)	Expected punishment (p*f)
1	$1,000,000	$1,000,000
0.5	$2,000,000	$1,000,000
0.2	$5,000,000	$1,000,000
0.1	$10,000,000	$1,000,000
0.01	$100,000,000	$1,000,000

comparing costs. Increasing the fine seems to impose few costs on society. Yes, larger fines mean more costs for offenders, but they also mean more benefits for the recipients of those fines like victims, citizens, and state agencies. Those costs and benefits seem to cancel out (we will say more about this later). We need the same procedure for assessing and collecting fines, depositing payments, and so on whether the fine equals $1 million or $100 million. So increasing fines does not seem costly. In contrast, increasing the probability of punishment seems very costly. To increase the probability of punishing the meat packing plant, we need more inspectors with better training, superior testing equipment, good lawyers, and so on.

As another example, recall our discussion of jaywalking. To increase the fine for jaywalking, the city council must pass a new ordinance. To increase the probability of punishing jaywalkers, the city council must hire more officers, and that costs a lot.

This analysis yields a prescription: *to achieve the optimal expected punishment, combine severe penalties with a low probability of enforcement*. We call this *Beckerian enforcement* after the economist Gary Becker, who developed the idea.[51] In Table 12.1, the regulator should choose the combination at the bottom. If the regulator could go lower—probability of 0.001 and fine of $1 billion—she should.

Many people oppose Beckerian enforcement. Harsh punishments often seem unfair, especially for minor violations of law. Of course, if harsh punishments deterred all lawbreaking, then the state would never impose them, and no unfairness would result. According to Montesquieu, the severity of the laws prevents their execution.[52] But perfect deterrence is impossible. For retributivists, the punishment must fit the crime. No one deserves a severe fine for jaywalking, regardless of their probability of punishment.

Even if we set fairness aside, Beckerian enforcement still has important limitations. Consider an extreme version of Becker's approach. A large city like London or Shanghai might have a single police officer, and the punishment for every crime might be execution. The probability of punishment would be so close to zero that many people would (irrationally) treat it as zero. The threat of death would not deter lawbreaking.

Consider another problem related to agency costs. Suppose the probability of punishment for jaywalking is close to zero, and accordingly the fine for jaywalking is very

[51] *See* Gary S. Becker, *Crime and Punishment: An Economic Approach*, 76 J. Pol. Econ. 169 (1968).

[52] *See* Charles De Secondat, Barron de Montesquieu, Spirit of Laws 64 (Thomas Nugent trans., 6th ed. 1793) ("The excessive severity of the laws hinders, therefore, their execution: when the punishment surpasses all measure, they are frequently obliged to prefer impunity to it.").

high, say, $50,000. If a cop catches someone jaywalking, will he write the ticket? Or will he think the fine is too high and pretend he didn't see?[53] If the cop writes the ticket, the jaywalker will probably contest it in court. Will a judge or jury convict a person for jaywalking knowing that the penalty is so high? [54] Perhaps not. If severe penalties discourage officials from enforcing the law or finding guilt, deterrence fails.

Consider a final problem related to deterrence. Suppose the penalty for bank robbery is execution. An armed criminal takes his chances and robs a bank. During the robbery, cops surround the exit, leaving the robber with two choices: surrender or shoot his way out. Surrender is better for society, as no one gets hurt. But think about the problem from the robber's point of view. If he surrenders, he faces death. If he shoots, he might face death, or he might escape. Shooting gives him a chance, whereas surrendering does not, so he will shoot. The severity of the punishment for the first act encourages him to do the second, more harmful act. To correct the robber's incentives, we must lower the punishment for bank robbery. To generalize, we discourage major violations of law by reducing the punishment for minor violations of law. This is the theory of *marginal deterrence*.[55]

Beckerian enforcement does not achieve marginal deterrence, and it faces other shortcomings too. It can inform but not determine the optimal system of punishment.

Questions

12.22. A vendor in New York City sold cellphone cases from a sidewalk display. His display was one inch too tall and two inches too close to a store entrance. The city fined him over $2,000.[56]
  (a) Is this consistent with Beckerian enforcement?
  (b) Suppose the high fine generated protests, and in response the city said, "This isn't oppressive, it's the optimal fine because the probability of punishment is very low." How would citizens know if this were true?

12.23. The International Criminal Court tries and punishes people for crimes against humanity, including war and genocide. The Court can sentence offenders to life in prison.
  (a) Does the existence of the Court deter crimes against humanity?
  (b) Suppose a dictator commits a crime against humanity. Does the existence of the Court encourage or discourage him from peacefully transferring power?[57]

[53] *See* Dan M. Kahan, *Gentle Nudges vs. Hard Shoves: Solving the Sticky Norms Problem*, 67 U. Chi. L. Rev. 607 (2000).

[54] *See* James Andreoni, *Reasonable Doubt and the Optimal Magnitude of Fines: Should the Penalty Fit the Crime?*, 22 RAND J. Econ. 385 (1991).

[55] George Stigler, *The Optimum Enforcement of Laws*, 78 J. Pol. Econ. 526 (1970). *See also* Jeremy Bentham, *An Introduction to the Principles of Morals and Legislation*, *in* The Utilitarians 171 (1973) (punishment should "induce a man to choose always the least mischievous of two offenses; therefore [w]here two offenses come in competition, the punishment for the greater offense must be sufficient to induce a man to prefer the less.") (emphasis removed).

[56] Sally Goldenberg, *Street Vendor Selling Cellphone Cases Fined 2G Fine for Inches*, N.Y. Post, Oct. 8, 2012.

[57] *See* Michael P. Scharf, *The Amnesty Exception to the Jurisdiction of the International Criminal Court*, 32 Cornell Int'l L.J. 507 (1999).

12.24. Corrupt enforcers charge people with violating law and then offer to drop the charges in exchange for money. Do severe penalties improve or worsen corruption in enforcement?[58]

The Excessive Fines Clause

The Eighth Amendment to the U.S. Constitution limits the government's power to punish: "Excessive bail shall not be required, nor excessive fines imposed, nor cruel and unusual punishments inflicted." Focus on the language in the middle. What constitutes an "excessive fine"? The Supreme Court answered in a case called *United States v. Bajakajian.*[59] The defendant tried to leave the country with $357,144 in cash. Law requires people transporting $10,000 or more in cash abroad to file a report, which the defendant failed to do. The government sought forfeiture of all the money, but the Court said no: "Comparing the gravity of respondent's crime with the $357,144 forfeiture the Government seeks, we conclude that such a forfeiture would be grossly disproportional[.]"[60] The Court held that "grossly disproportional" fines violate the Eighth Amendment.

The decision in *Bajakajian* limited the size of fines and therefore limited Beckerian enforcement. However, it also limited abuse. The Eighth Amendment was enacted in 1791, when England's rule and the Revolutionary War remained salient. The Kings of England assessed unpayable fines, not to deter lawbreaking but to raise money and keep their political enemies in debtor's prison.[61] The Eighth Amendment aimed to prevent unjust and self-serving practices by the state.[62]

Should we worry about such practices today? Consider a recent case. Tyson Timbs was arrested for selling about $400 of heroin from his vehicle.[63] He pled guilty in state court and was sentenced to house arrest and probation. The court also ordered him to pay about $1,200. At the time of his arrest, police seized Timbs's vehicle, a Land Rover worth $42,000. Timbs had purchased the vehicle with an inheritance after his father's death. The state of Indiana wanted to keep the vehicle.

In *Timbs v. Indiana*, the Supreme Court had to decide whether the Eighth Amendment's prohibition on excessive fines applied only to the federal government or also to states like Indiana.[64] The Court held that it applied to states, meaning Indiana could not fine Timbs a "grossly disproportional" amount. The Court wrote, "Protection against excessive punitive economic sanctions secured by the Clause is . . . fundamental to our scheme of ordered liberty and deeply rooted in this Nation's history

[58] *See* David Friedman, *Why Not Hang Them All: The Virtues of Inefficient Punishment*, 107 J. Pol. Econ. S259 (1999).
[59] 524 U.S. 321 (1998).
[60] *Id.* at 339–40.
[61] *See id.* at 345–55 (Kennedy, J., dissenting); Timbs v. Indiana, 139 S. Ct. 682, 688 (2019).
[62] *Cf.* Murat C. Mungan & Thomas J. Miceli, *Legislating for Profit and Optimal Eighth-Amendment Review*, 59 Econ. Inq'y 1403 (2021).
[63] *See* State v. Timbs, 84 N.E. 3d 1179, 1181 (Ind. 2017).
[64] 139 S. Ct. 682 (2019).

and tradition."[65] Why did Indiana want to seize Timbs's vehicle? Do you think this seizure would deter people from selling $400 worth of heroin?

D. Fines versus Imprisonment

We have referred to different forms of punishment, and here we consider their details. To deter lawbreaking, the government can make lawbreakers pay money. Law uses different labels for the payment, depending on the circumstance: fine, fee, restitution, forfeiture, and so on. Sometimes enforcement involves the seizure of assets, as when the government takes possession of a printer used to make counterfeit documents or a vehicle used to transport drugs. For the targets of enforcement, the effect in all cases is generally the same. Value travels from them to someone else, usually the government.

Separate from charging money, the government can deter lawbreaking by restricting people's liberty. Law can restrict liberty by jailing people before trial, imprisoning them after trial, or both. Law can restrict liberty in other ways too. The government might limit a person's movements by seizing her driver's license or passport. Release from prison sometimes comes with conditions, like a prohibition on consuming alcohol or returning to the site of the crime.

Economists usually cut through these distinctions and reduce punishment to two basic types, fines and imprisonment. We will compare them.[66]

Fines have an important advantage over imprisonment: they are relatively cheap. To explain this idea, let's start by considering administrative costs. To enforce the law with fines, the government needs a system for assessing and collecting them. This might involve little more than a fine schedule, an official to send letters, and an account to receive payments. Of course, the government must track down people who don't pay, and it must keep records. Administering fines is not costless, but it need not be expensive.

In contrast, imprisonment costs a lot. The state needs to build and maintain the prisons. It must hire guards and pay their salaries and benefits. Prisons need computers, printers, desks, telephones, filing cabinets, vehicles, parking lots, and lightbulbs. They need beds for inmates, kitchens for cooking, tables for eating, and spaces for exercise. Prisons cost much more to administer than a system of fines.

Fines are cheap for the government in another way: they can sidestep the criminal process. In general, people do not go to prison without being convicted of a crime. Convicting someone of a crime is costly. In the United States, criminal defendants have a right to a jury trial, and trials involve time and effort by government officials, including judges and clerks. The prosecutor must prove guilt beyond a reasonable doubt, a high threshold that requires hard work to surpass.[67] In contrast, many fines do not

[65] *Id.* at 689 (internal quotation marks and citations omitted).

[66] This discussion draws on Gary S. Becker, *Crime and Punishment: An Economic Approach*, 76 J. Pol. Econ. 169 (1968) and A. Mitchell Polinsky & Steven Shavell, *The Optimal Use of Fines and Imprisonment*, 24 J. Pub. Econ. 89 (1984).

[67] The high cost of trials helps explain why most criminal cases in the United States settle through plea agreements.

require criminal convictions. A *civil fine* is a "remedial" payment owed to the state, as when a company spills oil and pays a fine to cover the state's cleanup costs.[68] Civil fines do not require criminal convictions, so the state can assess them without spending so many resources.

Fines have one more advantage. When a lawbreaker pays a fine, money travels from his pocket to the state's treasury. The lawbreaker suffers and the state benefits (or citizens benefit, as when the state spends the money on cleaning the environment). The total amount of money is the same before and after. The utility gains to citizens might more or less offset the utility losses to the lawbreaker paying the fine. Imprisonment works differently. When a person goes to prison, he suffers in many ways, including financially. Most prisoners lose their jobs and incomes. However, the losses to the prisoner do not translate into gains for society. The state's treasury does not grow when a prisoner loses his job. We do not usually think that a prisoner's lost utility (isolation, loneliness, shame) gets transferred to non-prisoners, like money moving between accounts. *Fines redistribute value, whereas imprisonment destroys value.*

If imprisonment costs so much, why does the state imprison people? One answer relates to a concept from an earlier chapter: judgment proofness. Recall the thief who considers stealing a painting. Suppose we could deter the thief by making him pay a fine of $10,000. The thief only has $6,000. Thus, he internalizes $6,000 of the fine and externalizes $4,000 of the fine. The thief's limited budget diminishes the state's threat, causing underdeterrence. He will steal the painting unless the state finds a way to increase his punishment. Imprisonment would increase his punishment.

These ideas lead to some prescriptions. *The government should use fines first because fines deter lawbreaking at relatively low cost. The government should use imprisonment only when fines are insufficient for deterrence.*

Do these prescriptions match reality? In the United States, many violations of law lead to fines only, and many others lead to fines and the possibility of imprisonment. Few violations lead to imprisonment only. To illustrate, a class 3 misdemeanor in Virginia results in a fine of not more than $500, whereas a more serious class 2 misdemeanor results in jail for not more than six months and/or a fine of not more than $1,000. This pattern is broadly consistent with the economic theory. However, it does not match the economic theory. Punishment has objectives other than deterrence, and it depends on factors like morality and politics, not just economic costs.

Questions

12.25. The fine for littering equals $50. Billionaires and homeless people might litter anyway. Why? Should we imprison people for littering?

12.26. Some countries in Europe punish people with "day fines." The size of a day fine depends on the offender's wealth, so rich people pay more than poor people

[68] In U.S. law, whether a fine is "criminal" or "civil" depends on whether it aims to punish the offender (criminal) or serve some other purpose, like compensation (civil). Despite this legal distinction, we treat civil fines as a form of punishment. Paying a fine costs the offender regardless of where the money goes and why.

for the same violation of law. Could a day fine deter billionaires and homeless people from littering?[69]

12.27. GPS bracelets allow the government to monitor offenders from afar. Scanners and X-rays allow the government to search prisoners quickly, without using so many guards. Did the invention of GPS encourage or discourage the use of imprisonment? What about the invention of scanners and X-rays?

Economics and Animus

In 2011, a group of white teenagers attacked a black man in a parking lot. They beat him, robbed him, and ran him over with a truck. The victim died. The investigation revealed that some of the teenagers had participated in other, similar attacks. When sentencing the attackers, Judge Carlton Reeves delivered a powerful address:

> [W]hat could transform these young adults into the violent creatures their victims saw? It was nothing the victims did . . . There is absolutely no doubt that . . . the victims were targeted because of their race. The simple fact is that what turned these children into criminal defendants was their joint decision to act on racial hatred.[70]

This case illustrates a very disturbing motive: animus. Some people take pleasure in harming members of a group, often a racial or religious minority.

How can we deter crimes motivated by animus? Few questions are more important than this. A complete answer might involve education, training, and exposure to difference. Here we focus on one part of the answer, deterrence. According to economic theory, the expected cost of committing a crime of animus must exceed the criminal's benefit. In the United States, statutes on "hate crimes" increase the punishment for violent acts motivated by racism, sexism, or other prejudices.

Can we make punishments for hate crimes more effective? A scholar named Andrew Hayashi has an idea.[71] A person motivated by animus experiences pleasure or satisfaction when the targeted group suffers. Conversely, a person motivated by animus experiences negative emotions when the targeted group prospers. Instead of paying the state, we could make criminals motivated by animus pay their targets.

To make this concrete, imagine a criminal motivated by animus burning a Jewish synagogue. This hate crime carries a fine of $10,000, so the criminal's financial cost equals $10,000. Instead of adding the money to the state treasury, suppose the law transfers the $10,000 to the synagogue. This effectively increases the punishment by

[69] *See* Elena Kantorowicz-Reznichenko, *Day Fines: Reviving the Idea and Reversing the (Costly) Punitive Trend*, 55 Am. Crim. L. Rev. 333 (2018). Day fines increase administrative costs by requiring the state to gather information on offenders' wealth. *See* Elena Kantorowicz-Reznichenko & Maximilian Kerk, *Day Fines: Asymmetric Information and the Secondary Enforcement System*, 49 Eur. J.L. & Econ. 339 (2020). In Finland, a wealthy driver received a day fine of over $100,000 for exceeding the speed limit by 15 miles per hour. *See* Joe Pinsker, *Finland, Home of the $103,000 Speeding Ticket*, The Atlantic, Mar. 12, 2015.

[70] The full text of this remarkable speech appears in NPR Staff, *A Black Mississippi Judge's Breathtaking Speech to 3 White Murderers*, NPR Code Switch, Feb. 13, 2015, available at https://www.npr.org/sections/codeswitch/2015/02/12/385777366/a-black-mississippi-judges-breathtaking-speech-to-three-white-murderers.

[71] *See* Andrew T. Hayashi, *The Law and Economics of Animus*, U. Chi. L. Rev. (Forthcoming 2022).

creating a psychological cost. The criminal pays the fine *and* supports the group he hates. Redirecting the money makes the fine costlier to the criminal. Because the fine amount does not change, the problem of judgment proofness does not worsen.

This ingenious solution might not deter all hate crimes, but it could help. It shows the power of economics to address pressing problems in law.

III. Interpretive Theory of Enforcement

We have presented a positive and normative analysis of enforcement. According to the positive analysis, the state deters lawbreaking by making the expected cost greater than the benefit. According to the normative analysis, the state should enforce only when the marginal social benefit exceeds the marginal social cost. In general, the state can lower the social cost of enforcement by combining a low probability of enforcement with high penalties. These ideas anchor sophisticated research by scholars in economics, criminology, and other disciplines. They inform the drafting of statutes and the design of enforcement systems. Can they help lawyers and judges too? We think the answer is yes. In the following pages, we use economic theory to address an important topic for lawyers: the power of contempt.

A. On Remedies

Enforcement often concludes in a courthouse. At the end of an enforcement action, a judge issues an order. The nature of the order depends on the circumstances. In criminal law, the order might mandate jail time, require community service, assess a fee, or even demand an apology. Earlier we analyzed two possibilities in depth, fines and imprisonment. Outside of criminal law, a judicial order can again take many forms. We concentrate on two common forms, damages and injunctions. To begin, we will discuss these remedies in a famous case from private law, *Boomer v. Atlantic Cement Co.*[72] Afterward, we will address public law.

Dust, noise, and vibrations from a cement plant diminished the value of Oscar Boomer's land. He sued, claiming the plant constituted a public nuisance that violated his property rights. This is a common scenario in private law: one actor imposes a negative externality on another, causing the latter to file a lawsuit. The court found that the plant constituted a nuisance, and the question turned to remedies. The court could order damages, meaning payments from the cement company to its neighbors for their harm. Alternatively, the court could order an injunction, meaning a command to stop polluting. Of course, the court could order both: damages to remediate past harms, and an injunction to prevent future harms.

These choices appear throughout private law. When a soda bottle injures a consumer, the court can award damages for the harm, an injunction ("you cannot sell this kind of bottle"), or both. When a promisor breaches his contract, the court can award damages

[72] 257 N.E. 2d 870 (N.Y. 1970).

to the promisee for her harm, or it can issue an injunction requiring the promisor to fulfill his obligation (lawyers calls this "specific performance").

The choice between damages and injunctions raises many trade-offs that economists have studied intensively.[73] We will summarize three of them. First, damages are costly to calculate. To award damages in a case like *Boomer*, the court must determine the harm from pollution. This means testimony from the neighbors, information on their lost restaurant sales and damaged equipment, counterarguments from the cement plant, and guesses about the hurt caused by noise and vibrations. This is time consuming and difficult. Sometimes damages seem unmeasurable or even incoherent. Recall our example of racial discrimination in schools. Could any amount of money right that wrong? In contrast to damages, injunctions are cheap and easy.[74] In *Boomer*, the court could simply order the plant to stop polluting, with no need to estimate the neighbors' harm.

Second, damages promote efficiency, at least when they are accurate, whereas injunctions might not. In *Boomer*, the harm to the neighbors totaled $185,000. Meanwhile, the Atlantic Cement Company had invested over $45 million in the plant. With damages, the plant could remediate the neighbor's harm and continue to operate. With an injunction, the plant might shut down, wasting a large investment to save small ones. Efficiency required the plant to operate, and damages made that possible. The court in *Boomer* reasoned exactly this way, requiring the plant to shut down *unless* it paid the neighbors for their harm.

This discussion might make injunctions sound undesirable, but they have advantages. We have already explained that injunctions save courts and litigants the trouble of calculating damages. Moreover, injunctions clarify rights, and clarifying rights tends to lower the transaction costs of bargaining. Before going to court, Boomer could have complained to the cement plant about its pollution. If his rights were unclear—maybe the plant wasn't a nuisance, meaning he had no claim—the plant might have ignored him. After going to court and getting an injunction, his rights would be clear. The plant could not operate without Boomer's permission. The injunction would incentivize the plant to strike a deal according to which it paid Boomer in exchange for Boomer waiving the injunction. Successful bargaining promotes efficiency among parties.

We have discussed damages and injunctions in private law. Courts award the same or similar remedies in public law. For example, an earlier chapter described 42 U.S.C. § 1983, a federal statute that authorizes lawsuits against anyone acting under color of law who deprives someone of their constitutional rights. After officers stopped Adolph Lyons for driving with a broken taillight, they placed him in a stranglehold, apparently without provocation. Lyons was rendered unconscious and bloody. He sued under Section 1983, seeking damages for his harm and an injunction limiting the use of strangleholds by police.[75]

[73] For the germinal work, see Guido Calabresi & A. Douglas Melamed, *Property Rules, Liability Rules and Inalienability: One View of the Cathedral*, 85 Harv. L. Rev. 1089 (1972). *See also* Lucian A. Bebchuk, *Property Rights and Liability Rules: The Ex Ante View of the Cathedral*, 100 Mich. L. Rev. 601 (2001); Louis Kaplow & Steven Shavell, *Property Rules versus Liability Rules: An Economic Analysis*, 109 Harv. L. Rev. 713 (1996).

[74] This is the conventional view among economists, but it has not always been the conventional view among lawyers. For illuminating discussion, see Douglas Laycock, The Death of the Irreparable Injury Rule (1991).

[75] *See* City of Los Angeles v. Lyons, 461 U.S. 95 (1983).

Under Section 1983, courts have broad discretion over remedies. Other statutes limit them. The Federal Insecticide, Fungicide, and Rodenticide Act regulates the use of certain chemicals in the United States. The statute caps the civil penalty for some violations at about $20,000.[76] (Unlike damages, which go to victims, civil penalties go to the government.) Or consider *Tennessee Valley Authority v. Hill*.[77] After Congress spent $100 million constructing the Tellico Dam, scientists discovered an endangered fish nearby. Completing the dam would kill the fish in violation of the Endangered Species Act. The Supreme Court concluded that the statute offered only one remedy: an injunction. The Court halted construction of the dam.

Later we will return to judicial discretion and remedies in public law. Here we concentrate on a different question. What happens when someone ignores a court's order?

B. Introduction to Contempt

Suppose the court in *Boomer* awarded the neighbors a judgment for damages. Or suppose a judge ordered Allen to make child support payments to his former spouse. What would happen if the cement plant or Allen refused? Law addresses this problem. A sheriff might seize some of the plant's assets, auction them, and give the money to the neighbors. Or law might force Allen's employer to deduct money from his paycheck. These procedures can help satisfy the defendant's debts, even if the defendant does not cooperate.

What if the remedy is an injunction? Suppose Allen hid his child by moving her to a relative's home. A court orders Allen to produce the child so the mother can exercise her visitation rights. Or suppose a treasure hunter hid the gold he recovered from a shipwreck. A court orders him to produce the gold for investors who funded the expedition.[78] What happens if the parties refuse to comply?

Courts do not have soldiers or guns to enforce their orders. Judges cannot wave a magic wand and make people comply like puppets on a string. However, judges do have an important power: *contempt*. If a party disrupts the courtroom or disobeys an order, a judge can hold the party in contempt.[79]

The contempt power comes in different forms. Criminal contempt involves criminal punishment for an offense. If a defendant obstructs the trial by interrupting the lawyers, or if a witness violates a gag order and talks publicly about a case, the judge might hold them in criminal contempt.[80] The purpose of criminal contempt is to punish someone for undermining the administration of justice. Criminal contempt does not aim to help the other party in litigation. In contrast, civil contempt does aim to help the other party. *Compensatory* civil contempt compensates one side for the other side's disobedience.

[76] *See* Environmental Protection Agency; Civil Monetary Penalty Inflation Adjustment, 85 Fed. Reg. 83818 (Dec. 23, 2020).

[77] 437 U.S. 153 (1978).

[78] *See* Williamson v. Recovery Ltd. P'ship, 731 F.3d 608, 611 (6th Cir. 2013).

[79] For a lucid discussion of contempt and many examples, see Douglas Laycock & Richard L. Hasen, Modern American Remedies 787–863 (5th ed. 2019).

[80] Our description omits many details. For criminal contempt, the judge must get a prosecutor to bring a case, and many of the protections of criminal procedure apply.

Suppose, for example, that the court orders the cement plant to stop polluting, but the plant operates anyway. The court might require the plant to pay the neighbors damages for operating in violation of the injunction.

We will focus on a final category, *coercive* civil contempt. This form of contempt aims to force parties to comply—to "coerc[e] the defendant to do what he had refused to do."[81]

Suppose the court ordered Allen to reveal the location of his daughter, but he refused. The judge might fine Allen, say, $100 per day or even jail him until he produces the child. Coercive contempt does not aim to punish bad behavior in the past. Rather, it aims to encourage good behavior in the future. The defendant has "the keys to the jail in hand." Allen can end his punishment—no more fines, no more confinement—by choosing to comply with the court's order.

In the United States, "courts have inherent power to enforce compliance with their lawful orders through civil contempt."[82] However, the contempt power does have limits. For coercive civil contempt, the "contemnor"—that is, the noncomplying party—must have the ability to "purge." The contemnor purges by complying with the court's order. If the contemnor cannot comply with the order, then the court cannot hold the contemnor in coercive contempt. To illustrate, suppose a witness agrees to testify against a co-conspirator as part of a plea bargain. When his co-conspirator's trial begins, the witness reneges and refuses to testify. A court might jail him during the trial, with the promise of release if he testifies. However, when the trial ends, the court must release him from coercive contempt because testifying is no longer possible. Similarly, suppose Allen's daughter ran away. If Allen cannot find his daughter, then he cannot comply with the court's order to reveal her location. If Allen proves that he cannot comply, then the court cannot hold him in coercive contempt.[83]

Coercive contempt has other limits. Courts must "consider the character and magnitude of the harm threatened by continued contumacy [i.e., noncompliance], and the probable effectiveness of any suggested sanction in bringing about the result desired."[84] Furthermore, "in fixing the amount of a fine to be imposed," courts must "consider the amount of defendant's financial resources and the consequent seriousness of the burden to that particular defendant."[85] "[I]n selecting contempt sanctions, a court is obliged to use the least possible power adequate to the end proposed."[86] Appellate courts review contempt sanctions for abuse of discretion.[87]

Notwithstanding these limits, the contempt power is expansive. Consider the case of Beatty Chadwick, who transferred $2.5 million to offshore accounts beyond the reach of a state court. The court ordered Chadwick to return the money, some of which he owed

[81] Gompers v. Buck's Stove & Range Co., 221 U.S. 418, 442 (1911).

[82] Shillitani v. United States, 384 U.S. 364, 370 (1966). Separate from any inherent power, statutes and codes in the United States grant and attempt to structure the power of contempt. *See, e.g.*, 18 U.S.C.A. § 401 (West).

[83] Separate from showing that compliance is impossible, the contemnor sometimes can escape coercive contempt by showing that compliance is impracticable, meaning very difficult.

[84] United States v. United Mine Workers of Am., 330 U.S. 258, 304 (1947).

[85] *Id.*

[86] Spallone v. United States, 493 U.S. 265, 276 (1990) (internal quotation marks and citations omitted).

[87] *See* Green v. United States, 356 U.S. 165, 188 (1958). Coercive contempt has other limitations. Coercive contempt amounts to criminal contempt, and thus requires more procedural safeguards, when the penalties are severe and the facts complicated. *See* United Mine Workers v. Bagwell, 512 U.S. 821 (1994).

to his ex-wife. Chadwick refused, so the court sent him to jail in coercive contempt—where he remained for 14 years.[88]

C. Economic Theory of Contempt

Coercive contempt is a powerful and dangerous tool. Jailing a person for years seems oppressive, even tyrannical. Yet courts need a mechanism to enforce their orders. What balance does law require? What does it mean to "use the least possible power adequate to the end proposed," and when does a court abuse its discretion? These are legal questions. We use economics to sketch some answers.

Coercive contempt resembles deterrence. Through deterrence, the state discourages people from violating law. Through coercive contempt, the judge discourages the contemnor from flouting an order. Given the similarity, we can borrow from the preceding analysis, but we cannot copy it exactly. Coercive contempt differs from ordinary deterrence in some important ways.

To begin, recall this prescription: the state should deter an act of lawbreaking whenever the marginal social benefit exceeds the marginal social cost. Flouting a court's order often creates a special cost, which is weaker deterrence.

To explain this idea, let's consider an example about enforcement and learning. Driver 1 cannot tell if the police officer is monitoring the intersection. She runs the red light and doesn't get a ticket. Has she learned much about enforcement? No. Probably the officer was not monitoring the intersection, meaning she got lucky. She does not change her beliefs about the probability of enforcement. In contrast, driver 2 sees the officer watching the intersection. She runs the red light anyway, perhaps because her brakes fail. She does not get a ticket. Why? The likely explanation is that the officer does not ticket people for running the red light. Thus, driver 2 has learned something. The probability of a ticket is lower than she thought, making her more likely to run the red light.

To clarify this example, let's distinguish two concepts, detection and enforcement. If you do not know whether the state detected your violation of law, then non-enforcement sends a noisy signal. You cannot determine if you got lucky (no detection) or the state is weak (detection but no enforcement). If you *do* know that the state detected your violation—"the cop saw me do it"—then non-enforcement sends a clearer signal: the state is weak. The clearer signal weakens deterrence.

Let's relate these ideas to contempt. The court orders Allen to reveal the location of his daughter. If Allen does not comply, the judge will find out because the child's mother will tell. Likewise, if the cement plant does not stop polluting, the neighbors will promptly alert the court. In many situations, courts are certain to detect violations of their orders. When detection is certain, enforcement is especially important. Non-enforcement signals weakness that dilutes deterrence.

This analysis does not imply that courts should always use coercive contempt. However, it suggests that courts should enforce their orders vigilantly, perhaps more vigilantly than the state should enforce many ordinary laws.

[88] *See* United States v. Harris, 582 F.3d 512 (3d Cir. 2009).

We have explained why enforcing court orders is especially beneficial. Next, we consider how to do it. To begin, focus on money only, and recall this prescription from before: the optimal expected punishment equals the harm caused to others. This prescription seems to provide guidance for contempt. Suppose the cement plant violates the injunction and continues to operate. Pollution from the plant causes harm of $1,000 per day to the neighbors. Addressing the violation imposes costs of $50 per day on the court (neighbors file motions, complain to the clerk, etc.). According to the prescription, the court should hold the plant in contempt and charge it $1,050 for every day that it violates the injunction. Of this amount, $1,000 should go to the neighbors as compensation and $50 should go to the state.[89] The plant will continue to violate the injunction only if its benefit from doing so exceeds the total cost. Thus, the contempt sanction promotes efficiency.

This might sound like an appealing approach, but it has some shortcomings. The sanction we have described changes the remedy from an injunction ("do not pollute") to damages ("you can pollute if you pay $1,050 per day"). As described previously, injunctions sometimes promote efficiency better than damages, as when damages are very costly to calculate. Thus, converting the remedy to damages might cause inefficiency. Furthermore, we cannot calculate damages in a sensible way when money and harm are incommensurable. The cement plant does not present this dilemma, but remember Allen. He hides his daughter in violation of a court order, causing emotional harm to the child and the child's mother. Can you express their emotional harm in dollars? What's the amount per day?

These problems involve economics. Consider a different problem: the law. The purpose of coercive contempt is *not* to promote efficiency. Rather, the purpose is to induce the contemnor to comply with the court's order. Consequently, the court does not have authority to fine the cement plant $1,050 per day, at least not using coercive contempt.[90] That remedy induces efficiency, not compliance. To use coercive contempt, the court must design a sanction to induce compliance.

To induce compliance, the court should make the penalty exceed the contemnor's benefit. Specifically, "to use the least possible power adequate to the end proposed," the court should set the penalty for violating the injunction just above the contemnor's benefit from violating the injunction. If the cost of noncompliance exceeds the benefit, the contemnor will comply (assuming, of course, that the contemnor is rational).

Sometimes the court knows the contemnor's benefit. If litigation reveals that the cement plant earns $2,000 per day, the court can fine the plant $2,001 per day. Often, however, the court cannot determine the contemnor's benefit with confidence. The court must guess. How? In answering, let's distinguish between three kinds of benefit streams. A fixed stream accrues in the same amount, as when operating earns the cement plant $2,000 per day. An increasing stream grows over time (increasing marginal benefits), and a decreasing stream shrinks over time (decreasing marginal benefits).

89 The sanction we have described simplifies for the sake of clarity. In reality, compensatory and coercive contempt involve separate proceedings, and compensatory damages are only available for the contemnor's conduct to date.

90 The court probably does have authority to sanction the cement plant as described previously using criminal contempt or compensatory civil contempt, perhaps in combination with coercive contempt. In practice these categories sometimes overlap.

To induce compliance, suppose the court fines the cement plant $1,000 per day. If the plant gets a fixed benefit stream from noncompliance, and if the plant does not comply, then the plant's benefit must exceed $1,000 per day. The plant will never comply. To induce compliance, the court must increase the daily fine, and it should do so immediately. The logic applies more forcefully if the plant gets an increasing benefit stream from noncompliance. Suppose that every day the plant operates it generates new business. Its benefit from noncompliance equals $2,000 the first day, $2,100 the second, $2,200 the third, and so on. If the plant does not comply on the first day, the court should immediately increase the fine. What if the plant gets a decreasing benefit stream? Business is drying up, so the benefit from noncompliance equals $2,000 the first day, $1,900 the second, and so on. With a decreasing benefit stream, the court can (eventually) secure compliance without increasing the fine.

Recall some of the legal doctrine on coercive contempt. The court must "consider the character and magnitude of the harm" from noncompliance and assess the "probable effectiveness" of any sanction.[91] The court must "use the least possible power adequate to the end proposed."[92] We have sharpened this doctrine. The court uses the "least possible power" when it sets the penalty for noncompliance just above the contemnor's benefit. The court assesses the "probable effectiveness" of a sanction by estimating the contemnor's benefit, setting the sanction just above it, and then observing if the contemnor complies. If the contemnor does not comply, the court should reassess and, unless the contemnor has a decreasing stream of benefits, increase the sanction.[93] The greater the "character and magnitude of the harm" from non-compliance, the more the court should increase it.

Let's refine the analysis by focusing on the increasing stream of benefits. Recall the witness who agreed to testify against a co-conspirator but then reneged. The co-conspirator is a crime boss, and the witness fears that testifying will cost him his life. The trial lasts 10 days. If the witness testifies at any point during those 10 days, he will pay a cost. For the sake of example, let's translate that cost into money: $100,000.

We can reformulate this cost as a benefit. If the witness testifies at any point during the trial, he will get a benefit of zero. If he refuses to testify, he will get a benefit at the end of the trial equal to $100,000. As reformulated, the witness has an increasing stream of benefits from contempt. His payoff from refusing to testify equals zero after each of the first nine days and $100,000 after the tenth day.

To induce the witness to testify, the court must fine him more than $100,000. The court could do this in different ways. For example, it could fine him $100,001 at the conclusion of the trial, or it could fine him $10,001 per day for 10 days. Does the method matter? Maybe. Suppose the court tries the second method, threatening to fine the witness $10,001 per day. The witness should immediately testify because he would rather testify and face risk from the crime boss (payoff of zero) than not testify and pay 10 days of fines (payoff of –$10).[94] But suppose the witness *doesn't* testify. Perhaps he makes a math error or acts irrationally. Or perhaps the judge has not specified the fine schedule, so the witness does not understand the stakes. Whatever the explanation, the witness

[91] United States v. United Mine Workers of Am., 330 U.S. 258, 304 (1947).

[92] Spallone v. United States, 493 U.S. 265, 276 (1990) (internal quotation marks and citations omitted).

[93] Even if the defendant has a decreasing stream of benefits, the court might want to increase the sanction to secure compliance sooner.

[94] If the witness testifies, he gets no benefit but pays no fines, so his net payoff equals zero. If he does not testify, he gets a benefit worth $100,000 but pays fines of $100,010, for a net payoff of $–10.

does not testify. On the second day, the judge explains the fine schedule and threatens to charge him another $10,001. The witness reasons as follows: "I owe $10,001 from yesterday whether I testify or not. My best choices now are to testify today and get zero, or not testify during the next nine days, pay fines totaling $90,009, and get a benefit of $100,000, for a net payoff of $9,991. I will not testify."

As this example shows, past fines are *sunk costs*. Sunk costs do not affect the choices of rational people. To induce the contemnor to comply, the judge must increase the sanction. If the contemnor refuses to testify on the first day, the judge must set the sanction for refusing to testify during the remaining nine days greater than $100,000. Likewise, if the contemnor refuses to testify during the first nine days, the judge must set the sanction for refusing to testify on the final day greater than $100,000.

This conclusion is counterintuitive. One can imagine a judge reasoning as follows: "The witness failed to testify on day one, so I fined him $10,001. If he fails to testify on day two, I will keep up the pressure by fining him another $10,001. Eventually he will crack." The judge's reasoning might seem sound, but it's not. The judge imagines the pressure increasing every day. In fact, the pressure on the witness decreases every day. To increase pressure, the court must increase the sanction.

This discussion refines our analysis of coercive contempt in two ways. First, in assessing the "probable effectiveness" of a sanction, the court should consider its size *and* its clarity. Simple, clear sanctions should cause fewer miscalculations and reduce sunk costs. Second, past fines do not induce compliance. The threat of future fines induces compliance. Even if the court has already fined the contemnor a significant amount, increasing future sanctions is consistent with using the "least possible power" to secure compliance. In fact, failing to increase sanctions might constitute an abuse of discretion by harming the contemnor without any possibility of changing his behavior.

If the witness has lots of money, the court can increase the sanction indefinitely. What if he does not have lots of money? Suppose the witness has $10,000. After the first day's fine, he becomes judgment proof. If the witness cannot pay additional fines, then more fines will not change his behavior. Their "probable effectiveness" equals zero. Thus, the court should not impose coercive contempt fines on a judgment-proof contemnor.

Notice the connection between sunk costs and judgment proofness. If the court sets the fine too low, the contemnor will not comply. The contemnor will, however, have to pay the fine, and paying the fine brings him closer to judgment proofness. Thus, when assessing the initial fine, the court must balance. Setting the fine too high might abuse the court's power, but it likely induces compliance. Setting the fine too low does not abuse the court's power, but it might not induce compliance, and it brings the contemnor closer to judgment proofness.

If the contemnor is judgment proof, the court retains one form of leverage: send the contemnor to jail. Earlier we explained that the government should use imprisonment to deter only when fines are insufficient. This is because imprisonment imposes more costs on society. The same idea applies to coercive contempt. Using the "least possible power" implies that courts should jail people only when fines are ineffective.

Jail can help with judgment proofness. The contemnor has no money, but he has time, and the court can make that time miserable by placing him behind bars. But jail cannot solve the problem of sunk costs. Instead of a fine, suppose the court threatens to jail the witness if he refuses to testify. On the first day of trial, the witness asks himself: "Would

I rather testify and get zero, or not testify, get a benefit worth $100,000, but spend ten days in jail?" He prefers not to testify, so the court jails him for the first day. On the morning of the second day, the witness asks himself: "Would I rather testify and get zero, or not testify, get a benefit worth $100,000, but spend *nine* days in jail?" The cost of refusing to testify has decreased because the first day in jail is a sunk cost. Meanwhile, the benefit of refusing to testify remains the same.

If the witness does not testify immediately, then he will probably never testify.[95] Specifically, if the witness experiences fixed or decreasing costs from incarceration, then a witness who refuses to testify immediately will refuse to testify ever. If the witness experiences increasing costs from incarceration, then he might refuse to testify at first but crack eventually. The witness experiences increasing costs when the tenth day in jail is worse than the ninth, the ninth day is worse than the eighth, and so on. The court could ensure that the witness faces increasing costs by worsening his treatment. For example, on the first day of jail he might have a cell to himself with access to the cafeteria and the yard. On the second day he might have a cellmate, and by the end of trial he might face solitary confinement. In practice, courts in the United States do not appear to worsen treatment in this way.

We can summarize our analysis. To induce compliance with its order, the court should assess a daily fine just above its estimate of the contemnor's daily benefit. If the contemnor does not comply immediately and does not have a decreasing stream of benefits, then the court should immediately increase the fine and continue to do so until the contemnor complies or becomes judgment proof. If the contemnor becomes judgment proof, the court should attempt to induce compliance through imprisonment. Past punishments are sunk costs. To induce compliance, the court must make future punishments exceed the contemnor's benefit from noncompliance.

Our approach to contempt represents an application of the incentive principle of interpretation. According to that principle, a law's correct interpretation in hard cases provides incentives to maximize the fulfillment of its purposes. Coercive contempt represents a hard case in the sense that the legal doctrine is vague and subject to multiple interpretations. The purpose of coercive contempt is clear—to induce the contemnor to comply. A court applying our analysis incentivizes the contemnor to comply with its order. Furthermore, a court applying our analysis "consider[s] the . . . probable effectiveness of any suggested sanction" in securing compliance,[96] considers the "defendant's financial resources and the consequent seriousness of the burden to that particular defendant,"[97] and uses "the least possible power adequate to the end proposed."[98]

Questions

12.28. The court wants the witness in our running example to testify. The court believes that the witness's benefit from not testifying equals $100,000, but

[95] Recall that our example assumes a definite period in jail: 10 days. If the period is unpredictable, the witness might not testify at first but testify later as he updates his beliefs about the length of confinement.

[96] United States v. United Mine Workers of Am., 330 U.S. 258, 304 (1947).

[97] *Id.*

[98] Spallone v. United States, 493 U.S. 265, 276 (1990) (internal quotation marks and citations omitted).

his actual benefit could be higher or lower. The court could fine the witness $10,001 the first day and, if the witness refuses to testify, increase the fine the second day. Or the court could fine him $100,001 after 10 days.

(a) Which approach allows the court to learn more about the witness's benefit of noncompliance?

(b) Which approach is more likely to make the witness judgment proof?

12.29. The defendant refuses to comply with the court's order. The court fines him $1,000 and says, "If you fail to comply tomorrow, I will fine you $2,000. If you comply tomorrow, I will not fine you, and I will cancel today's fine."

(a) Explain why the promise to cancel today's fine encourages the defendant to comply tomorrow.

(b) The defendant is more likely to comply if the court's threat to punish noncompliance is credible. Does canceling fines make the court's threat more or less credible?

A License for Crime?

A court ordered Gerardo Catena, a suspected criminal, to testify about organized crime activities. He refused, so the court sent him to jail until he cooperated. Four years later, Catena remained in jail. He was 72 years old and in poor health when a court reconsidered his case. The court wrote, "Once it appears that the commitment has lost its coercive power, the legal justification for it ends and further confinement cannot be tolerated."[99] This is the doctrine of *exhausted coercion*. If the contemnor will never obey the court's order, regardless of the sanctions, then the court cannot hold him in coercive contempt.

Exhausted coercion is consistent with the economic theory of enforcement. According to that theory, the state should enforce the law only if the social benefit from doing so exceeds the social cost. Sanctioning a contemnor imposes many costs. In Catena's case, he lost his freedom, presumably his family suffered, and taxpayers spent thousands of dollars to confine him. If Catena testified, society would benefit. Presumably the benefit of less organized crime would outweigh the costs of holding him in contempt. However, if Catena never testified, society would receive nothing. If a contemnor will never cooperate, the costs of coercive contempt necessarily outweigh the benefits, and the court should stop sanctioning him.

This logic reaches beyond contempt. A defendant had over 30 convictions for "theft of services." Each case had the same facts: he hopped the turnstile and rode New York City's subway without paying the fare. After his latest conviction, he accepted a plea deal that included nine months in jail.[100] Jailing the defendant for nine months imposed many costs on society. Do you think it had a social benefit? Does this person seem deterrable?

[99] Catena v. Seidl, 321 A.2d 225, 228 (N.J. 1974).

[100] *See* Josh Bowers, *What If Nothing Works? On Crime Licenses, Recidivism, and Quality of Life*, 107 Va. L. Rev. 959, 965–66 (2021).

A scholar named Josh Bowers has a proposal for cases like this.[101] He would give incorrigible defendants a "crime license," meaning permission to commit certain petty crimes without punishment. The license could take different forms. In the subway case, the state could buy the defendant a lifetime pass to ride the trains. Buying him a subway pass would cost much less than sending him to jail.

In theory, crime licenses and exhausted coercion might work well. They offer ways to avoid imposing costly sanctions that will not yield a social benefit. In practice, they face challenges involving incentives and information. Regarding incentives, would the availability of crime licenses encourage people to sneak onto subways? Regarding information, was holding Gerardo Catena in contempt pointless because he would never testify? After he spent four years in jail, the court wrote: "Catena has not demonstrated that the order of commitment no longer has any coercive impact. . . . [H]e has the burden of showing that there is no reasonable likelihood that continued incarceration will cause him to break his silence. He has not done so on the present record."[102]

D. Contempt in Public Law

We have analyzed coercive contempt in cases involving the cement plant and Allen's family. In both cases, one private actor sues another, so we call them private law cases. Public law cases involve the state, as when prosecutors charge people with crimes, regulators fine companies, and individuals sue the government for violating their constitutional rights. How does coercive contempt work in public law?

If the contemnor is a private actor, then it works the same way. Consider our reluctant witness. Prosecutors seek his testimony in a criminal matter, making it a public law case. The court could fine or jail the witness like it could fine or jail Allen.

Our witness case is hypothetical.[103] Now consider some real cases. The U.S. Department of Justice sued the company IBM for violating antitrust law. When IBM failed to comply with a discovery order, the court held the company in coercive contempt and fined it $150,000 per day.[104] The National Labor Relations Board brought an action against a private company for interfering with union activities. When the company refused to comply with an injunction, the court threatened to jail the owners.[105]

What happens when the contemnor is the government? In *Brown v. Board of Education*, the U.S. Supreme Court held that racial segregation in public schools violates the Constitution. The Court ordered schools to desegregate, but many did not. By violating the Court's order, public schools—that is, government actors—became contemnors. Eventually the President ordered federal troops to provide security around schools and facilitate integration. Few cases of government contempt

[101] *See generally id.*
[102] Catena v. Seidl, 321 A.2d 225, 229 (N.J. 1974).
[103] However, it resembles real cases like the one involving Gerardo Catena.
[104] Int'l Bus. Machines Corp. v. United States, 493 F.2d 112, 113–14 (2d Cir. 1973).
[105] Aguayo v. S. Coast Refuse Corp., No. CV 99-3053 AHM, 2000 WL 1280926, at *4 (C.D. Cal. Feb. 29, 2000).

proceed so dramatically. Short of military action, how can courts force governments to comply?

Before answering, consider some other cases of government contempt. A federal court ordered local authorities to stop detaining people whom they believed to be in the country illegally. In general, federal officials, not local officials, enforce immigration law. Sheriff Joe Arpaio did not comply.[106] The Supreme Court held that states must recognize same-sex marriages. Afterward, a government clerk with strong religious views refused to issue marriage licenses to anyone.[107] A court ordered the City of Yonkers to support construction of public housing in a predominantly white neighborhood. The city council refused.[108]

Sometimes courts hold government actors in coercive contempt. When the city council in Yonkers voted against public housing, the court ordered the council members to pay fines and report to jail until they changed their votes.[109] In one case, a court fined a federal agency $500 per day until it paid an employment discrimination award.[110] Similarly, a court ordered a federal agency to pay a Social Security benefit or face a daily fine.[111] In those two cases, the agency complied before any fines accrued. Cases like these are unusual. In general, federal courts do not hold government actors, especially federal agencies, in contempt.[112]

Suppose a court did fine an agency for contempt. Would fines cause the agency to comply? Perhaps not. Individual officials decide whether to comply with a court order, but those officials do not pay the fines. The agency pays, or perhaps a separate government fund pays.[113] If officials do not internalize fines, then fines might not coerce them. If courts fined officials as individuals, they would more likely comply, but this raises difficult legal questions. In the Yonkers litigation, the Supreme Court held that sanctions should have run against the city itself, not individual members of the city council.[114]

Instead of fines, courts could send officials to jail. When the county clerk refused to issue marriage licenses in violation of law, a federal court jailed her for six days. Confinement might cause compliance. However, confinement of officials is exceedingly rare. Perhaps judges think they lack the power. Or perhaps judges do not know whom to sanction. The Social Security Administration has 60,000 employees. A political appointee with limited power and information runs the agency. If the agency fails to pay a Social Security benefit, who should go to jail?

Here is a final possibility: courts do not attempt to jail officials because officials might not comply. The President appoints the Commissioner of the Social Security

[106] Melendres v. Maricopa Cnty., 897 F.3d 1217 (9th Cir. 2018).

[107] Miller v. Davis, 123 F. Supp. 3d 929 (E.D. Ky. 2015).

[108] *See* Douglas Laycock & Richard L. Hasen, Modern American Remedies 801–03 (5th ed. 2019).

[109] *See id.* The Supreme Court later relaxed the penalties. *See* Spallone v. United States, 493 U.S. 265 (1990). Local governments do not have sovereign immunity in the United States, whereas states and the federal government do. With sovereign immunity, contempt must run against officers, not the government itself.

[110] Henderson v. Orr, No. CIV.A. C-3-81-554, 1987 WL 19715, at *2 (S.D. Ohio May 5,1987).

[111] *See* Nicholas R. Parrillo, *The Endgame of Administrative Law: Governmental Disobedience and the Judicial Contempt Power*, 131 Harv. L. Rev. 685, 713 (2018).

[112] *See generally id.*

[113] In the United States, federal agencies' judicially determined debts usually get paid from a general government judgment fund. *See id.* at 738.

[114] *See* Spallone v. United States, 493 U.S. 265 (1990).

Administration. Suppose a federal court holds the Commissioner in coercive contempt for failing to make a required payment and orders her to jail. If the Commissioner refuses, the court can order the U.S. Marshals Service to arrest her. The President appoints the Attorney General, who oversees the Marshals Service. If the President supports the Commissioner, he might order the Attorney General to order the marshals not to arrest the Commissioner. What will the marshals do?

In a famous passage, James Madison wrote, "In framing a government . . . the great difficulty lies in this: you must first enable the government to control the governed; and in the next place oblige it to control itself."[115] Forcing the government to obey its own laws presents a difficult challenge. It requires more than coercive contempt. We will return to this topic in the next chapter.

Questions

12.30. To induce compliance by the City of Yonkers, the judge threatened to fine the city $100 the first day and then double it daily, so the second day's fine would equal $200, the third day's fine would equal $400, and so on. What would the fine equal on the thirtieth day? Can a city become judgment proof?

12.31. A court ordered a journalist to name her confidential sources. The journalist refused, so the court imposed fines using coercive contempt. The court ordered the journalist to pay the fines from her personal assets, without accepting any financial support from others. Why?[116]

Conclusion

Laws usually do not enforce themselves. To secure compliance, governments everywhere devote substantial resources to enforcement. We have provided a positive, normative, and interpretive analysis of enforcement. According to the positive analysis, the government deters lawbreaking by setting the expected punishment greater than the benefit. According to the normative analysis, the government should only enforce when the social benefit exceeds the social cost, and it should combine relatively severe penalties with a low probability of enforcement. In practice, enforcement often concludes in a courthouse. How can courts secure compliance with their orders? By using the power of coercive contempt. We applied the incentive principle of interpretation to coercive contempt, showing how courts can use it effectively and in compliance with law. These ideas lay the foundation of enforcement. The next chapter builds on top.

[115] THE FEDERALIST NO. 51, 264 (James Madison) (Ian Shapiro ed., 2009).
[116] *See* Hatfill v. Mukasey, 539 F. Supp. 2d 96 (D.D.C. 2008).

13
Enforcement Applications

In the *Federalist Papers*, Hamilton wrote about enforcement: "It is essential to the idea of a law, that it be attended with . . . a penalty or punishment for disobedience. If there be no penalty . . . , the resolutions or commands which pretend to be laws will, in fact, amount to nothing more than advice or recommendation."[1] Hamilton put deterrence at the center of enforcement, as we did in the prior chapter. Deterrence plays a central role in securing compliance with law worldwide. But deterrence raises many complications. We cannot punish lawbreaking without searching for evidence, apprehending perpetrators, and proving guilt. Every step requires policy choices. We need laws about enforcing laws. Furthermore, deterrence is incomplete. Sometimes people comply with laws even when breaking them would not lead to fines or imprisonment.

This chapter broadens our analysis. We discuss the law of law enforcement, and we consider enforcement mechanisms beyond deterrence. We also return to the issue of government compliance. The chapter addresses questions like these:

Example 1: According to the U.S. Supreme Court, "[a] police officer may arrest a person if he has probable cause to believe that person committed a crime."[2] Making an arrest can impose substantial costs. Arrestees—some of whom are innocent—might lose their freedom, owe booking fees, feel humiliation, and suffer injury. Do officers internalize these costs? Should they have less authority to make arrests?[3]

Example 2: The state of Oregon adopted the initiative power, meaning citizens could make laws without the legislature. The Supreme Court had to decide if the initiative power violated the Constitution's Guarantee Clause, which promises every state "a republican form of government."[4] The initiative power was popular among citizens, and the Guarantee Clause is vague. The Court avoided the case, stating, "[T]he issues presented, in their very essence, are . . . determined to be political . . . [I]t follows that the case presented is not within our jurisdiction[.]"[5] Should courts avoid political cases?

Example 3: Suppose the standard of proof for speeding is low, meaning police can charge any driver with speeding and win in court. To raise money, police randomly charge people with speeding. Speed has no relationship to enforcement, so nearly everyone speeds. Thus, nearly everyone the police charge is guilty and gets

[1] The Federalist No. 15, at 76 (Alexander Hamilton) (Ian Shapiro ed., 2009).
[2] Tennessee v. Garner, 471 U.S. 1, 7 (1985).
[3] *Cf.* Rachel A. Harmon, *Why Arrest?*, 115 Mich. L. Rev. 307 (2016).
[4] U.S. Const. art. 4, § 4. Here is the full clause: "The United States shall guarantee to every State in this Union a Republican Form of Government."
[5] Pac. States Tel. & Tel. Co. v. State of Oregon, 223 U.S. 118, 151 (1912).

Public Law and Economics. Robert D. Cooter and Michael D. Gilbert, Oxford University Press. © Oxford University Press 2022.
DOI: 10.1093/oso/9780197655870.003.0013

convicted. Does the standard of proof for speeding produce a high ratio of correct to incorrect decisions in court? Is this a good standard of proof?[6]

To answer these questions, we begin by discussing the law of enforcement in the United States, concentrating on the Constitution's Fourth Amendment. Next, we analyze forms of law. To simplify enforcement, the state can make laws precise or lower the standard of proof. The state can even adopt "insincere" rules, meaning artificially strict rules. We consider mechanisms of compliance distinct from deterrence. Sometimes law improves people's behavior by supplying information, coordinating action, or (possibly) changing preferences. We conclude by discussing judicial power: When will powerful actors comply with court orders? Throughout the chapter, we combine positive, normative, and interpretive reasoning.

I. The Law of Enforcement

Enforcement requires many steps. Officials must gather DNA, measure fish, review tax records, monitor traffic, write briefs, collect fines, store evidence, inspect banks, and take eyewitness testimony. This work requires auditors, detectives, sheriffs, lawyers, accountants, judges, and others. Many officials contribute to enforcement. Importantly, no official has total discretion. Law structures the choices of every official, from parking attendants to prosecutors. Law regulates the enforcement of law. This section introduces the law of enforcement by concentrating on an important provision in the U.S. Constitution: the Fourth Amendment.

A. Introduction to the Fourth Amendment

"Writs of assistance" let British officials search for smuggled goods in the American colonies. They barged into homes and seized people's property and papers. The lawyer James Otis called writs "the worst instrument of arbitrary power" because they placed "the liberty of every [person] in the hands of every petty officer."[7] After the Revolution, the Framers of the Constitution responded by adopting the Fourth Amendment, which states:

> The right of the people to be secure in their persons, houses, papers, and effects, against unreasonable searches and seizures, shall not be violated, and no Warrants shall issue, but upon probable cause, supported by Oath or affirmation, and particularly describing the place to be searched, and the persons or things to be seized.[8]

In principle, the Amendment restrains arbitrary power. In practice, it raises difficult questions.

[6] *See* Louis Kaplow, *Burden of Proof*, 121 Yale L.J. 738, 801–03 (2012).
[7] Boyd v. United States, 116 U.S. 616, 625 (1886) (internal citations omitted).
[8] U.S. Const. amend. IV.

The Amendment protects against "searches and seizures." If the government's action does not qualify as either, the Fourth Amendment does not apply. Let's concentrate on the first term. What counts as a search? Federal agents attached a listening device to a public telephone booth. When Charles Katz used the phone, they recorded his conversation and charged him with crimes. In *Katz v. United States*, the Supreme Court held that a search occurs when the government invades a person's "reasonable expectation of privacy."[9] Katz was alone in the booth, and he closed the door. Reasonable people in that situation do not expect others to hear their conversations. Thus, listening constituted a search, and the Fourth Amendment protected Katz.

Separate from phone booths, a search occurs when officers physically enter a person's home, open a person's mail, or check someone's pockets. A search does not occur when officers observe someone in public, rifle through roadside garbage, or photograph a backyard from an airplane.[10] Changing technology has led to interesting cases. In *Kyllo* v. *United States*, the Supreme Court held that measuring heat emanating from a home amounted to a search (the government sought a marijuana "grow room"). In *Carpenter v. United States*, the Court held that collecting some cellphone location records constituted a search, in part because cellphones are "such a pervasive and insistent part of daily life that carrying one is indispensable."[11]

In general, cases about "searches" seem guided by privacy. According to the Supreme Court, the Fourth Amendment "seeks to secure the privacies of life against arbitrary power."[12] The more private the space, the more likely an intrusion counts as a search.

Suppose the government wants to enter Birdie's home without her consent. This constitutes a search, so the Fourth Amendment applies. The Amendment requires the search to be reasonable. In general, a search authorized by a warrant is reasonable. To get a search warrant, officers usually must show "probable cause," meaning proof of "a fair probability that contraband or evidence of a crime will be found in a particular place."[13] If a reliable informant provides information about wrongdoing in Birdie's basement, then the police have probable cause. If the informant is not reliable or offers few details, then the police do not have probable cause.

Separate from showing probable cause, officers must limit their search to a particular place, and they must specify the targets of their search. If they seek a large stolen painting, they cannot search a small jewelry box. This "ensures that the search will be carefully tailored to its justifications" and prevents the "wide-ranging exploratory searches the Framers intended to prohibit."[14] A judge must issue the warrant.

Suppose Birdie uses a gun to rob a bank, and the cops chase her home. She runs inside and locks the door. Do the cops need a warrant to enter? No. Officers in hot pursuit of a suspect can search a home without a warrant.[15] Failing to search could lead to destruction of evidence (what if she burns the money?) or violence (what if she takes a

[9] 389 U.S. 347, 360 (1967) (Harlan, J., concurring).

[10] For a concise summary of what counts as a "search," see CHRISTOPHER SLOBOGIN, ADVANCED INTRODUCTION TO U.S. CRIMINAL PROCEDURE 22–28 (2020).

[11] Carpenter v. United States, 138 S. Ct. 2206, 2220 (2018) (internal quotation marks and citation omitted).

[12] *Id.* at 2214 (internal quotations marks and citation omitted). Earlier in history, Fourth Amendment jurisprudence focused less on privacy and more on property and trespass.

[13] Illinois v. Gates, 462 U.S. 213, 238 (1983).

[14] Maryland v. Garrison, 480 U.S. 79, 84 (1987).

[15] *But see* Lange v. California, 141 S. Ct. 2011 (2021) (holding that officers in hot pursuit cannot conduct a warrantless search of a home if the suspect committed only a minor offense).

hostage?). "Exigent" circumstances like this make the search reasonable, even without a warrant.[16] Law permits warrantless searches in other situations. For example, if the police arrest a criminal on the street, they can search his backpack. Under *Terry v. Ohio*, police can "frisk" someone—pat down clothing in search of weapons—if they have a "reasonable suspicion" that the person is armed and dangerous.[17]

Suppose officers find evidence through an unreasonable search. For example, suppose they find stolen gems in Birdie's house, but they did not have a warrant for the search or any other authorization. The *exclusionary rule* might prohibit the government from using the evidence against Birdie. In general, officers need evidence gathered through constitutional means. The Supreme Court has justified the exclusionary rule on different grounds over time. Today, the dominant (perhaps sole) justification involves deterrence. In *United States v. Calandra*, the Court wrote, "[T]he rule's prime purpose is to deter future unlawful police conduct and thereby effectuate the guarantee of the Fourth Amendment against unreasonable searches and seizures."[18] According to this reasoning, if police cannot use the evidence, they are less likely to conduct the unconstitutional search.

Suppose the police conduct an unreasonable search of Birdie's house. Thus, they violate her Fourth Amendment rights. If the government plans to charge Birdie with a crime, the exclusionary rule might provide a kind of remedy. If the government's case depends on evidence recovered through the unreasonable search, the exclusionary rule makes it harder (perhaps impossible) to convict her. What if the government does not plan to charge Birdie with a crime? Perhaps officers did not find any evidence, so there is nothing to exclude. Perhaps Birdie is not a criminal. Can she get a remedy for the unconstitutional search?

Maybe. Earlier chapters introduced a statute known by its number, 42 U.S.C.§ 1983. The statute allows civil suits (i.e., suits for money) against officers for violations of constitutional rights.[19] However, winning a Section 1983 suit against an officer is difficult. The plaintiff must establish a constitutional violation and overcome *qualified immunity*. An officer has qualified immunity—and wins the case—unless the plaintiff can show a violation of a "clearly established" right of which "a reasonable person would have known."[20]

To demonstrate, consider a case. An officer pulled over Clarence Jamison, apparently because of a faulty tag on Jamison's car. The officer checked Jamison's license and insurance card and ran a background check (the check came back clean). The officer placed his arm through Jamison's window and asked for permission to search his car. According

[16] *See, e.g.*, Warden, Md. Penitentiary v. Hayden, 387 U.S. 294 (1967).

[17] 392 U.S. 1 (1968).

[18] 414 U.S. 338, 347 (1974).

[19] The statute states: "Every person who, under color of any statute, ordinance, regulation, custom, or usage, of any State or Territory or the District of Columbia, subjects, or causes to be subjected, any citizen of the United States or other person within the jurisdiction thereof to the deprivation of any rights, privileges, or immunities secured by the Constitution and laws, shall be liable to the party injured in an action at law." People can sue some federal officials for violations of their constitutional rights under *Bivens v. Six Unknown Named Agents*, 403 U.S. 388 (1971).

[20] Harlow v. Fitzgerald, 457 U.S. 800, 818 (1982). Qualified immunity doctrine has other details that we do not address.

to the officer, Jamison agreed. According to Jamison, he refused, but then the officer lied ("someone reported cocaine in your car") and coerced him. Jamison consented under pressure, and the officer searched his car exhaustively. The officer found nothing. The stop lasted almost two hours and, according to Jamison, caused $4,000 in damage to his car's seats and convertible top.

Jamison sued the officer for damages under Section 1983. In *Jamison v. McClendon*, the court found that the "physical intrusion into Jamison's car was an unreasonable search in violation of the Fourth Amendment."[21] Then the court turned to qualified immunity:

> [T]he question . . . is whether it was clearly established that an officer who has made five sequential requests for consent to search a car, lied, promised leniency, and placed his arm inside of a person's car during a traffic stop while awaiting background check results has violated the Fourth Amendment. It is not.[22]

We can clarify the court's reasoning. At the time of the stop, existing precedent allowed the officer to ask for permission to search the car. Existing precedent forbade the officer from threatening Jamison's life, destroying his car, or detaining him for 12 hours.[23] The actual case fell between theses extremes. The officer asked for permission repeatedly and applied pressure, but he did not threaten Jamison's life. The officer damaged the car but did not destroy it. He detained Jamison for two hours, not 12. Existing precedents did not "clearly establish" that the officer's conduct violated the Constitution, so he had qualified immunity.

Why do we have qualified immunity? The Supreme Court offers different justifications. Without the immunity, officers (including innocent officers who get sued wrongly) would spend money and effort on litigation, distracting them from fighting crime. Without the immunity, people might refuse to become officers. Finally, the "fear of being sued" will "dampen the ardor" of officers "in the unflinching discharge of their duties."[24] Without qualified immunity, officers will not do their jobs.

We have provided a brief sketch of some Fourth Amendment doctrine. We could fill many pages (books, actually[25]) with more details. Instead, we will fill some pages with economics.

"Shoot First and Think Later"

Qualified immunity has generated intense controversy in the United States. Some of the controversy involves law, with people (including Clarence Thomas, a Supreme Court Justice) questioning its legal foundations.[26] However, most of the controversy

21 476 F. Supp. 3d 386, 411 (S.D. Miss. 2020).
22 *Id.* at 416.
23 This is a hypothetical precedent invented for the sake of clarity. The actual precedent on vehicle stops is voluminous and complicated.
24 Harlow v. Fitzgerald, 457 U.S. 800, 814 (1982) (internal quotation marks and citations omitted).
25 *See, e.g.*, RACHEL HARMON, THE LAW OF THE POLICE (2021).
26 *See, e.g.*, Baxter v. Bracey, 140 S. Ct. 1862 (2020) (Thomas, J., dissenting from the denial of cert.); Joanna C. Schwartz, *The Case Against Qualified Immunity*, 93 NOTRE DAME L. REV. 1797 (2018).

involves policy. The doctrine shields officers in many situations. Thus, critics argue that it empowers officers to violate many rights, especially the rights of racial minorities. In *Jamison v. McClendon*, for example, the driver was black, and the officer was white. The judge in that case wrote the following:

> Our courts have shielded a police officer who shot a child while the officer was attempting to shoot the family dog; prison guards who forced a prisoner to sleep in cells "covered in feces" for days; police officers who stole over $225,000 worth of property; a deputy who body-slammed a woman after she simply "ignored [the deputy's] command and walked away"; an officer who seriously burned a woman after detonating a "flashbang" device in the bedroom where she was sleeping; an officer who deployed a dog against a suspect who "claim[ed] that he surrendered by raising his hands in the air"; and an officer who shot an unarmed woman eight times after she threw a knife and glass at a police dog that was attacking her brother.[27]

Justice Sotomayor summarized the problem: qualified immunity "tells officers that they can shoot first and think later."[28]

The story has another side. Officers make many split-second decisions. When a suspect brandishes a gun, officers have only a moment to respond. They don't have time to determine if the gun is real or fake. When officers get called to a fight, they must intervene fast. They don't have time to sort aggressors from innocent bystanders. To prevent harm, officers act quickly under pressure, and they inevitably make errors. Some people get arrested, injured, or even killed by mistake. Holding officers accountable for every mistake seems unjust to many people, especially to officers doing a difficult job. Qualified immunity protects them.

On balance, does qualified immunity do more harm than good? Should we eliminate the doctrine or reform it? Who should reform the doctrine, courts or legislators? Few questions seem more important today. We cannot answer these critical questions, but we can use economics to illuminate the debate.

B. Economic Analysis of Search

Economics can illuminate and sharpen some Fourth Amendment doctrine, beginning with its purpose. The doctrine on searches protects privacy. Recall the Supreme Court's language: the Fourth Amendment "seeks to secure the privacies of life."[29] Privacy has intrinsic value. Like freedom, it gives people a zone of autonomy to enjoy. Privacy represents an end akin to happiness or health, making it an input in people's utility.

We offer an additional account of privacy. Suppose law did *not* protect it. Cops could search a home, car, jacket, or laptop at will. They could tap a phone or hack email.

[27] Jamison v. McClendon, 476 F. Supp. 3d 386, 403–04 (S.D. Miss. 2020) (internal quotation marks and citations omitted).

[28] Kisela v. Hughes, 138 S. Ct. 1148, 1162 (2018) (Sotomayor, J., dissenting).

[29] Carpenter v. United States, 138 S. Ct. 2206, 2214 (2018) (internal quotation marks and citation omitted).

Without law to protect them, people would seek privacy protections on their own. They might add bolts to their doors, secret compartments to their cars, and secret pockets to their clothes. They might invest in software that locks their devices. In response, the state might buy codebreaking programs and invest in technology that sees through walls. To counter, people might hide their devices in tunnels or line their walls with lead. Like an arms race, each side would invest more in response to the other. Both sides burn resources, and the chance of uncovering crime might not improve. By protecting privacy, the Fourth Amendment dampens the arms race. Citizens do not invest in unnecessary protections, and police do not invest in forbidden techniques.

Consider individual searches. The police think Birdie robbed a jewelry story. To prove it, they need evidence. Should they search Birdie's home? The search would impose many costs. Officers would spend time and resources driving to her home, rifling through boxes, and checking her clothing and furniture. They might damage property. Birdie and her family would feel exposed and humiliated (they pay a "privacy cost"). However, searching the basement might uncover evidence of a crime.

Imagine a benevolent social planner making the decision. She will allow the search only if it does more good for society than harm. In making this decision, she might compare the marginal cost of the search and its marginal benefit. The police have already incurred costs investigating the crime, but those costs are sunk, meaning the police cannot recoup them. The marginal cost of the search captures only those costs associated with the search itself. We summarized those costs earlier, and we represent them with the variable c. The marginal benefit captures the benefit of the search. It depends on the probability p that the search uncovers something and the value v of the thing it uncovers. The planner will allow the police to conduct the search only if $c < p * v$. We have seen this formula in other chapters.[30]

This formula is simple and illuminating. Increasing the marginal cost of the search makes the planner less likely to approve. Increasing the probability of uncovering evidence makes the planner more likely to approve. If the evidence will have little value—"this does not solve the crime"—the planner is unlikely to approve.

If police reasoned like the benevolent social planner, they would only conduct socially beneficial searches. But they do not. Enforcement presents a delegation game, with citizens, mayors, and legislators acting as the principal (i.e., the social planner) and officers acting as their agents. Agents should do what's best for the principal. In enforcement, doing what's best for the principal means following the law and accounting for all costs and benefits. In reality, agents might do what's best for themselves. They might violate law and ignore some costs and benefits. In our example, police might search Birdie's home even if the marginal cost is very high. They externalize her privacy cost, so it does not affect their decision-making.

An earlier chapter introduced Hobbesian rights. Hobbesian rights prevent the state from taking action that would probably do more harm than good and that bargaining cannot prevent. The players in enforcement—citizens, officers, suspects—cannot bargain on the spot. Cops and suspects struggle to bargain, especially during robberies and

[30] For example, we discussed this formula in connection with Judge Hand's decision in *Dennis v. United States*, 183 F.2d 201 (2d Cir. 1950). For an application of Hand's formula to the Fourth Amendment, see Craig S. Lerner, *The Reasonableness of Probable Cause*, 81 Tex. L. Rev. 951, 1019–22 (2003).

gunfights. Even when they can bargain, the principal (citizens, mayors, legislators) are usually absent, making the optimal deal elusive.[31] Thus, bargaining often cannot prevent harmful enforcement. Ideally, the Fourth Amendment acts as a Hobbesian right to prevent harmful enforcement.

Let's apply these ideas to some doctrine.[32] Police could take a variety of actions to gather evidence. They could break into Birdie's home, read her mail, follow her car, or photograph her footprints on a public sidewalk. Some of these actions, like breaking into her home and reading her mail, seem especially intrusive. These actions create substantial privacy costs. Left to their own devices, police might take the actions anyway because they externalize costs. The Fourth Amendment offers a corrective by protecting against unreasonable "searches." A "search" occurs when officers do something especially intrusive, like enter a person's home, read her mail, or track her movements with cellphone data. The amendment offers protection against actions with substantial privacy costs that officers externalize. Our formula captures the idea. As the marginal cost c of an action increases, the action more likely becomes a "search," meaning the Fourth Amendment applies.

The Fourth Amendment does not prohibit officers from conducting a search. Rather, it requires them to get a warrant.[33] To get a search warrant, police must show probable cause, meaning "a fair probability that contraband or evidence of a crime will be found in a particular place."[34] The phrase "fair probability" matches p in our formula, and the phrase "contraband or evidence of a crime" matches v in our formula. To get the warrant, police must convince a judge that the probability of finding something is high and that its value is significant. If $p * v$ seems sufficiently large, the judge will issue the warrant. Though intrusive, the expected benefit of the search outweighs its cost.

Recall the particularity requirement. To get a warrant, officers must limit their search to a particular place and particular things. According to the Supreme Court, this prevents the "wide-ranging exploratory searches the Framers intended to prohibit."[35] By forcing police to narrow their search, the amendment forces them to reduce costs. In our formula, particularity decreases c.

The warrant requirement does more than discourage harmful searches. It encourages low-cost evidence gathering. To illustrate, suppose police have two ways to investigate a drug deal: eavesdrop on a conversation in public, or tap a cellphone. Either approach would provide equally strong evidence. However, tapping the cellphone would impose an especially high privacy cost. Under Fourth Amendment doctrine, tapping the phone constitutes a search requiring a warrant, which can be difficult to acquire. The warrant requirement encourages police to eavesdrop in the park, the lower-cost approach.

Not every search requires a warrant. Suppose Birdie robs a jewelry store with a gun and hides in her home. Police in hot pursuit can enter without a warrant. We can

[31] Recall this statement of the Public Coase Theorem: "As the transaction costs of political bargaining among representative lawmakers approach zero, laws will become socially efficient." Even if the cost of bargaining between police and suspects equaled zero, those actors would not represent citizens, mayors, and legislators, precluding the optimal deal.

[32] This discussion draws on Orin S. Kerr, *An Economic Understanding of Search and Seizure Law*, 164 U. Pa. L. Rev. 591 (2016).

[33] Or otherwise have authorization, as with exigent circumstances.

[34] Illinois v. Gates, 462 U.S. 213, 238 (1983).

[35] Maryland v. Garrison, 480 U.S. 79, 84 (1987).

understand this with our formula. Searching a home imposes a large privacy cost *c*. However, the search has a large expected benefit. The material inside the home (the perpetrator, her gun, stolen jewelry) has substantial value, and apprehending Birdie might prevent violence. The variable *v* is large. Since the police followed Birdie home, they know her location with certainty. Thus, the probability *p* of realizing benefits by searching is high. The search clearly seems to create more benefits than costs, so the Fourth Amendment does not require a warrant.

Contrast this with another example.[36] Edward Welsh drove his car while intoxicated. He drove erratically, parked in a field, and wandered home. Minutes later, police arrived, entered the home without a warrant, and arrested him. In *Welsh v. Wisconsin*, the Supreme Court held that the hot pursuit exception did not apply, making the search of Welsh's home unconstitutional.[37] Yes, the probability *p* of apprehending Welsh was high. However, Welsh "had already arrived home" and "abandoned his car," so there was "little remaining threat to the public safety."[38] Furthermore, state law made driving while intoxicated a minor crime. Finding evidence of a minor crime (in this case, Welsh's blood alcohol level) is not especially valuable. In our formula, the value *v* of the search seemed small, so $p * v$ did not exceed the privacy cost of searching the home. The search violated the Fourth Amendment.[39]

To summarize, we can understand the Fourth Amendment as a response to agency problems in policing. Courts regulate investigative practices in ways that loosely track cost-benefit analysis used in economics. For lawyers familiar with Fourth Amendment doctrine—which often requires "reasonableness" and "balancing"—the connection might seem apparent.

We have used economics to reframe some Fourth Amendment doctrine. Next, we use it to sharpen some doctrine. Sometimes people confuse marginal costs and benefits with total costs and benefits. We provided an example early in the book. By studying for 20 hours at a cost of 20 utility, a student will get an A on the exam worth 50 utility. Foreseeing a net gain of 30, the student studies for 20 hours. However, he could have gotten an A by studying for 10 hours. After 10 hours, the marginal benefit of additional studying equaled zero, but the marginal cost exceeded zero. The student reasoned in total rather than marginal terms, causing him to study too much.

Sometimes judges make the same mistake.[40] The U.S. government tapped the telephone of Wadih El-Hage, a U.S. citizen suspected of terrorism. The government monitored and recorded many of his conversations, including conversations about business and family that had no connection to crime. El-Hage claimed an unreasonable search in violation of the Fourth Amendment. The court agreed that he suffered "a significant invasion of privacy by virtue of the government's year-long surveillance of his telephonic communications."[41] The court weighed that cost against "the self-evident

[36] This example is discussed in Orin S. Kerr, *An Economic Understanding of Search and Seizure Law*, 164 U. Pa. L. Rev. 591, 621–22 (2016).

[37] 466 U.S. 740 (1984).

[38] *Id.* at 753.

[39] For a related case, see Lange v. California, 141 S. Ct. 2011 (2021).

[40] This example is discussed in Orin S. Kerr, *An Economic Understanding of Search and Seizure Law*, 164 U. Pa. L. Rev. 591, 639–40 (2016).

[41] In re Terrorist Bombings of U.S. Embassies in E. Afr., 552 F.3d 157, 175 (2d Cir. 2008).

need to investigate threats to national security presented by foreign terrorist organizations."[42] The court permitted the search.

Perhaps the court reached the right conclusion. However, it erred in reasoning. The court weighed the *marginal* cost to El-Hage against the *total* benefit of investigating terrorism. Total benefits exceed marginal benefits, so the court tilted the balance erroneously in the government's favor. Instead, the court should have focused on the margin: What benefit was the phone surveillance likely to produce? If the answer was valuable information that the government could not gather through other means, then the marginal benefit was large. If the answer was valueless information or information that the government could gather in a less-intrusive way, then the marginal benefit was small. The government searched El-Hage's property and seized physical evidence. If that evidence secured the case against him, then other surveillance had little value. Perhaps the marginal benefit of the phone surveillance became trivial after the physical search.

Lawyers and judges cannot determine marginal costs and benefits with precision. Economics cannot supply answers in all Fourth Amendment cases. But it supplies a useful framework for analyzing many questions.

Questions

13.1. Law prohibits police from using "excessive force." To determine whether force is excessive, courts balance "the intrusion on the individual's Fourth Amendment interests against the countervailing governmental interests at stake."[43] Courts must pay "careful attention to the facts and circumstances of each particular case, including the severity of the crime at issue, whether the suspect poses an immediate threat to the safety of the officers or others, and whether he is actively resisting arrest or attempting to evade arrest by flight."[44] Does this doctrinal test instruct courts to balance marginal costs and benefits? If not, what does it instruct?

13.2. The Fourth Amendment makes policing private spaces (homes, garages, cellphones, laptops) relatively difficult. Officers might concentrate on policing public spaces like streets and parks instead. Who spends more time in public spaces, rich people or poor people? Who has more access to private spaces? Who does the Fourth Amendment protect?[45]

C. Exclusion and Immunity Revisited

Our introduction to the Fourth Amendment discussed two remedies for violations, the exclusionary rule and Section 1983 suits. We briefly revisit both.

In general, the exclusionary rule prohibits the government from using evidence gathered in an unconstitutional manner. The rule's "prime purpose," the Supreme Court

42 *Id.* at 175.
43 Graham v. Connor, 490 U.S. 386, 396 (1989) (internal quotation marks and citations omitted).
44 *Id.* (internal quotation marks and citations omitted).
45 *See* William J. Stuntz, *Distribution of Fourth Amendment Privacy*, 67 GEO. WASH. L. REV. 1265 (1999).

wrote, "is to deter future unlawful police conduct."[46] If officers cannot use the evidence, they are less likely to engage in the unlawful search.

Does the rule deter like the Court imagines? Many critics say no. Economics clarifies some of their arguments. When courts exclude evidence, law may go unenforced and criminals may walk free, weakening deterrence.[47] Thus, excluding evidence creates costs. Officers do not bear all of those costs. They externalize some of them. When people externalize costs of an activity, they usually do too much of it. Thus, officers conduct too many unconstitutional searches, even with the exclusionary rule in place.

The exclusionary rule cannot deter all illegal searches, but it can deter some. Probably the rule has *some* deterrent effect. However, that benefit comes at a cost. The exclusionary rule often requires courts to "ignore reliable, trustworthy evidence."[48] Exclusion can "set the criminal loose in the community without punishment."[49] These concerns require balancing. According to the Supreme Court, the exclusionary rule only applies if "the deterrence benefits . . . outweigh its heavy costs."[50]

As this language shows, the doctrine on the exclusionary rule resembles cost-benefit analysis.[51] In our formula, excluding evidence obscures the truth and frees criminals, creating a cost c. However, excluding evidence has a probability p of improving police conduct, which has value v. Courts should exclude evidence if $c < p * v$, otherwise they should permit the evidence.

This reasoning seems consistent with several cases, even if courts do not use the formula. Consider *United States v. Leon*.[52] Officers conducted a search pursuant to a warrant and discovered illegal drugs. Afterward, a court concluded that the warrant was invalid, making the search illegal. The warrant was invalid because the judge who issued it made a mistake. The Supreme Court did not apply the exclusionary rule, meaning officers could use the drugs as evidence. The Court reasoned that excluding the drugs would not improve officers' incentives. The risk of a warrant being declared invalid ex post due to judicial error would not change officers' behavior ex ante.[53] In our formula, $p * v$ equaled zero.

Courts have applied this kind of reasoning in many other Fourth Amendment cases.[54] Some cases have generated controversy.[55] Our formula captures the roots of the controversies: people disagree about the values of c, p, and v.

[46] United States v. Calandra, 414 U.S. 338, 347 (1974).

[47] *See* Hugo M. Mialon & Sue H. Mialon, *The Effects of the Fourth Amendment: An Economic Analysis*, 24 J.L. ECON. & ORG. 22 (2008) (showing how the rule increases crime).

[48] Davis v. United States, 564 U.S. 229, 237 (2011).

[49] *Id.*

[50] *Id.*

[51] Orin S. Kerr, *An Economic Understanding of Search and Seizure Law*, 164 U. PA. L. REV. 591, 629 (2016) ("[T]he Supreme Court's exclusionary rule jurisprudence is expressly economic in orientation.").

[52] 468 U.S. 897 (1984).

[53] *Id.* at 918, 921 ("If exclusion of evidence obtained pursuant to a subsequently invalidated warrant is to have any deterrent effect . . . it must alter the behavior of individual law enforcement officers. . . . Penalizing the officer for the magistrate's error [in issuing the warrant] . . . cannot logically contribute to the deterrence of Fourth Amendment violations.").

[54] In one case, officers conducted a search that was lawful under binding precedents. Later the Supreme Court overruled those precedents, making the search unlawful. The Court did not exclude the evidence, in part for reasons akin to those in *Leon*. The risk of a judicial precedent changing ex post would not alter officers' behavior ex ante. *See* Davis v. United States, 564 U.S. 229 (2011).

[55] In one case, officers had a warrant to search a home. Upon arriving they entered almost immediately. Usually officers must knock, announce their presence, and wait, at least briefly. A divided Court held that failure to knock and announce does not trigger the exclusionary rule. *See* Hudson v. Michigan, 547 U.S. 586 (2006).

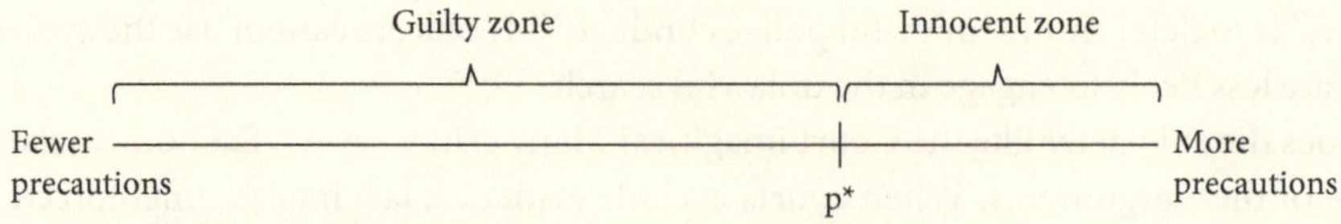

Figure 13.1. Precautions in a Perfect World

Now let's return to qualified immunity. Recall the law: when a plaintiff sues an officer for damages, she must show, among other things, that the officer violated a "clearly established" right of which "a reasonable person would have known."[56] Qualified immunity makes it difficult to sue officers successfully. Knowing they have immunity, officers can sometimes violate law (or at least "stretch" law) with impunity. Remember Clarence Jamison. An officer pressured him, searched his car for two hours, and damaged his seats in violation of the Fourth Amendment, yet the officer was immune from suit. This makes qualified immunity sound bad. On the other hand, qualified immunity makes it easier for officers to do their jobs. They need not worry that every search or arrest could lead to a costly lawsuit. This makes qualified immunity sound good.

We can illuminate qualified immunity with some graphs. The line in Figure 13.1 represents precautions by officers to avoid violating rights. As we move rightward, officers take more precautions. For example, as officers learn more about law—"what actions violate rights?"—they move rightward on the graph. As officers exercise greater restraint—"I will not injure the suspect, break into Birdie's home, or damage Mr. Jamison's car"—they move rightward on the graph. Conversely, as officers take fewer precautions, they move leftward on the graph. If a police department condones violence, mistreats arrestees, and ignores the courts, it lies on the left end of the spectrum.

Precautions decrease Fourth Amendment violations. When officers learn the law and refrain from violence, fewer rights get violated, and fewer harms accrue. Thus, precautions decrease the "social costs" of rights violations. However, precautions increase social costs in two other ways. First, precautions raise the costs of training and police action. Officers must learn the law and remember to obey it. They must find creative and potentially costly ways to do their jobs. Rather than tackling a suspect, they must find a nonviolent way to restrain him. Rather than bursting into Birdie's home immediately, they must stake the house, talk to informants, and apply for a warrant. Second, more precautions increase crime. To see why, consider the extreme case. To ensure they don't harm anyone, police can refrain from enforcement. If they never search people, collect evidence, or make arrests—if they simply play card games at the station—they cannot violate anyone's Fourth Amendment rights. Of course, if police don't enforce the law, more people will commit crimes.

In sum, more precautions decrease the costs of rights violations and increase the costs of training and crime. Society must balance these competing costs.

For the sake of example, let's assume that p^* in Figure 13.1 represents the optimal level of precautions. Taking fewer precautions than p^* would increase the costs of rights violations by more than it would decrease the costs of training and crime. Likewise, taking more precautions than p^* would increase the costs of training and crime by more

[56] Harlow v. Fitzgerald, 457 U.S. 800, 818 (1982).

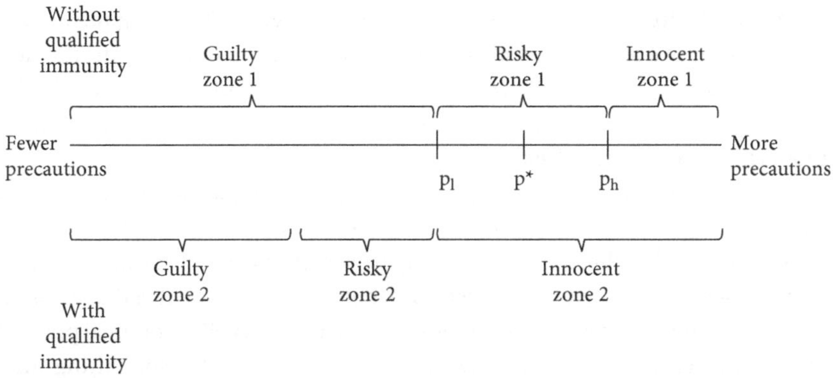

Figure 13.2. Precautions in the Real World

than it would decrease the costs of rights violations. The point p^* might correspond to the following: officers make serious efforts to learn law and do not use force, make arrests, or damage property without a very good reason.

Imagine a world with a costless and accurate legal system. Defending against a frivolous lawsuit costs nothing, and only guilty defendants get punished (and punished every time). Suppose the law in this world requires officers to take optimal precautions at p^*. If officers took fewer precautions—in Figure 13.1, any point left of p^* in the "guilty zone"—plaintiffs would sue and win. Given the threat of lawsuits, officers would not take precautions left of p^*. Likewise, officers would not take precautions right of p^*. Taking greater precautions would impose costs on them (more training, more restraint) that law does not require and that they would not choose to bear. Thus, officers would choose p^*, the left end of the "innocent zone." This represents the fewest precautions necessary to avoid liability. In a perfect world, officers take optimal precautions at p^* without qualified immunity.

Now imagine the real world. Defending against frivolous suits takes time and money. Sometimes courts make mistakes, finding innocent defendants guilty and guilty defendants innocent. In this world, law could require officers to take optimal precautions at p^*, but officers would not comply. Figure 13.2 shows the problem. If officers take precautions of p_h or more ("innocent zone 1"), they do not violate any rights. No court would find an officer taking so many precautions guilty, so no plaintiff would sue. If officers take precautions of p_l or less ("guilty zone 1"), they violate some rights. Someone will sue and win. If officers take precautions between p_l and p_h ("risky zone 1"), they might violate rights, and they might get sued and lose. It depends on the facts of the case, the beliefs of the judge, the persuasiveness of the plaintiff, and so on.

To avoid risk, officers will take precautions at p_h. This choice is individually rational but suboptimal. The point p_h lies to the right of p^*, meaning officers take too many precautions. The "fear of being sued . . . dampen[s] the ardor" of officers "in the unflinching discharge of their duties."[57]

To correct the problem, judges create the doctrine of qualified immunity. Now officers will win in court unless they violate a "clearly established" right. Some precaution levels

[57] *Id.* at 814 (internal quotation marks and citations omitted).

that were perilous for officers before become safe. In Figure 13.2, the guilty, risky, and innocent zones move leftward, as illustrated by the zones on bottom with the number "2." With qualified immunity, officers can select precautions of p^* without risk of being sued. That's good. However, officers can also do less. They can take precautions as low as p_l without risk of being sued. That's bad.

Critics of qualified immunity imagine something like "innocent zone 2." With qualified immunity, officers take suboptimal precautions at p_l. They behave recklessly and harm people. Supporters of qualified immunity imagine something else. They imagine qualified immunity stretching "innocent zone 1" leftward, but not so far. The left end of the innocent zone they imagine terminates at p^*, meaning qualified immunity elicits optimal precautions.

Suppose the critics have it right. Qualified immunity creates something like "innocent zone 2," with officers taking too few precautions. Figure 13.2 uncovers some solutions to the problem. First, courts could change qualified immunity. Instead of protecting officers unless they violate a "clearly established" right, qualified immunity could protect them unless they violate an "established" right. By removing "clearly" from the legal test, the doctrine would protect officers less. In Figure 13.2, the new doctrine would create a new innocent zone whose left end lies between p_l and p_h. The left end might match p^*, eliciting optimal precautions.

Figure 13.2 hints at another solution: increase the required precautions. We have assumed that constitutional law requires officers to take optimal precautions at p^*. The challenge lies in compliance. Without qualified immunity, officers will choose p_h, and with qualified immunity they will choose p_l. Instead of tinkering with qualified immunity, suppose courts interpret the Constitution to require precautions at p_h. Without qualified immunity, officers would choose precautions above p_h, and with qualified immunity they would choose precautions below p_h—perhaps at p^*. Would making the constitutional rule "insincerely" strict solve the problem?[58] The next section has an answer.

Questions

13.3. Law attempts to discourage unlawful searches by excluding the evidence. Instead, law could permit the evidence but allow the defendants to sue officers for damages. "Your unlawful search sent me to jail, so you owe me money." Would civil suits discourage unlawful searches better than the exclusionary rule? Would juries award money to criminals?[59]

13.4. The court excludes evidence because of an unlawful search. The prosecutor could drop the case, or the prosecutor could proceed with "holes" in his case. Jurors will make assumptions about those holes. Suppose they assume the holes in the prosecutor's case result from the exclusion of evidence. Does the exclusionary rule still protect criminal defendants?[60]

[58] *See* Michael D. Gilbert & Sean P. Sullivan, *Insincere Evidence*, 105 Va. L. Rev. 1115 (2019).

[59] *See* Richard A. Posner, *Rethinking the Fourth Amendment*, 1981 Sup. Ct. Rev. 49 (1981).

[60] *See* Tonja Jacobi, *The Law and Economics of the Exclusionary Rule*, 87 Notre Dame L. Rev. 585 (2013).

13.5. In *Kisela v. Hughes*, the Supreme Court expanded qualified immunity.[61] Now the doctrine protects officers unless the violation of a clearly established right is "beyond debate."[62] In Figure 13.2, sketch the effect of *Kisela* on the guilty, risky, and innocent zones.

13.6. Instead of protecting officers unless they violate a "clearly established" right, qualified immunity could protect them unless they violate an "established" right. Would this change widen the risky zone in Figure 13.2?

II. Enforcement and Legal Design

The previous chapter explained that the costs of enforcing law sometimes exceed the benefits. In this circumstance, a rational state refrains from enforcement. Consequently, a gap opens between the law in books and the law in action. Law mandates one behavior, but regulated parties do something else, as when police officers frisk more people than law allows, or street vendors use a table that's an inch too tall.

To shrink the gap and improve enforcement, lower its costs. Technology offers one way to lower enforcement costs. Cameras at red lights cost less than posting an officer at the intersection. GPS bracelets monitor criminals for less than the cost of imprisonment. "Body cams" make it easier to monitor police. These methods treat law as *exogenous*. Law is fixed, and officials seek low-cost ways to enforce it.

In this section, we make law *endogenous*. We imagine lawmakers looking to the future before adopting a law. Anticipating the high costs of enforcing Law One, they adopt Law Two instead. The challenges of enforcement ex post influence the design of law ex ante.

A. Enforcing Rules and Standards

Rules provide precise directives, whereas standards provide imprecise directives. To illustrate, imagine soot emissions from a factory. A law prohibiting emissions "above 10 units" represents a rule, whereas a law prohibiting "unreasonably dense smoke" represents a standard.[63]

We have compared rules and standards throughout the book. Among other tradeoffs, we explained that standards are cheaper to draft than rules but costlier to apply. Take the factory example. Legislators want to clean the air without forcing every factory to close. Drafting a good rule takes time and effort. They must study the costs of pollution and the costs of abatement to strike the right balance. Drafting a good standard is easier. Legislators can simply prohibit unreasonably dense smoke. The standard decreases the effort required to draft the law, but it increases the effort required to apply

[61] 138 S. Ct. 1148 (2018).

[62] *Id.* at 1152 (internal quotation marks and citation omitted).

[63] An 1881 ordinance in Chicago made "dense smoke . . . from any chimney" a public nuisance. *See* Cale Jaffe, *Environmental Federalism as Forum Shopping*, 44 Wm. & Mary Envtl. L. & Pol'y Rev. 669, 677 (2020).

it. Every time a factory emits dark smoke, enforcers must decide if the emission is unreasonable. Enforcers must strike the balance that legislators avoided.

This has an important implication: rules are cheaper to enforce than standards.[64] If the law prohibits unreasonably dense smoke, enforcers must determine the costs and benefits of every emission in every case. This might include studying the risks from the pollution ("Does anyone live nearby?"). This might include studying the layout of the factory ("Could you install scrubbers on the smokestacks?"). This might include studying the factory's product ("Does it make medicine or knickknacks?"). Fining the factory could lead to litigation. In that case, enforcers must prove their case. They must convince a judge that the pollution caused harm, the factory could install scrubbers, and so on. Each step requires time and effort. Enforcing standards is costly.

In contrast, enforcing rules is cheap. If the law prohibits emissions of soot above 10 units, enforcers can simply measure emissions of soot. If their tests reveal emissions greater than 10, the factory violated the law. Enforcers need not study risk, inspect the factory, or contemplate the social value of its product. If the factory files a lawsuit, enforcers can make their case simply by presenting the tests.

In sum, enforcing rules costs less than enforcing standards. Consequently, the gap between the law and books and the law in action should tend to shrink under rules and grow under standards.

Does this provide a decisive argument for rules? No. As we have shown throughout the book, the choice between rules and standards depends on more than enforcement. Even with respect to enforcement, rules have a disadvantage.[65]

Suppose legislators enact a rule: no emissions of soot above 10 units. Suppose Carlos's factory emits dark smoke with impunity. Darcy owns the factory across the river. She can tell by looking at the smoke that Carlos has violated the law. She knows the enforcers see the smoke too, and she knows they have not enforced. What does she infer? The state has high enforcement costs. Enforcement would create more costs for the state than benefits. Thus, Darcy knows she can violate the law too.

Instead of a rule, suppose legislators enact a standard: no unreasonably dense smoke. Now let's reconsider our scenario. Carlos's factory emits dark smoke with impunity. Darcy observes the smoke from her factory across the river, she knows the enforcers see it too, and she knows they have not enforced. What does she conclude? She might infer that the state has high enforcement costs. *Or* she might infer that Carlos has an extenuating circumstance. Perhaps wind from the river carries away his soot, whereas hers harms the neighbors. Perhaps he makes medicine, whereas she makes plastic baubles. Carlos's dark smoke might be reasonable, whereas hers would be unreasonable. Darcy does not violate the law.

We can generalize from these examples. Failing to enforce a rule sends a relatively clear signal to regulated parties. Because rules depend less on context, failing to

[64] *See, e.g.*, Isaac Ehrlich & Richard A. Posner, *An Economic Analysis of Legal Rulemaking*, 3 J. LEGAL STUD. 257 (1974). To be clear, rules are cheaper to enforce than standards of similar complexity. A rule with many exceptions may cost more to apply than a simple standard dependent on only one factor. *See* Louis Kaplow, *Rules Versus Standards: An Economic Analysis*, 42 DUKE L.J. 557 (1992).

[65] This discussion draws on Nicholas Almendares, Michael D. Gilbert, & Rebecca Kerley, Enforcing Rules Versus Enforcing Standards, Virginia Law and Economics Research Paper No. 2021-07 (2021).

enforce them probably does not reflect special or idiosyncratic circumstances. Non-enforcement of a rule probably means the government has high enforcement costs. In contrast, failing to enforce a standard sends a relatively noisy signal to regulated parties. The proper enforcement of a standard depends on context, like whether the wind carries away the soot from Carlos's factory. Observers like Darcy often do not know the context, so they learn less. For observers, non-enforcement of a standard might mean the government has high enforcement costs, or it might mean others have special circumstances that they lack.

To summarize, enforcing rules costs less than enforcing standards. However, *failing* to enforce rules costs more than *failing* to enforce standards. This is because failing to enforce a rule reveals information about the state's enforcement costs, causing some observers to violate law. Failing to enforce a standard reveals less information about enforcement costs, causing some observers to comply.

Questions

13.7. In *Brown v Board of Education*, the Supreme Court ordered states to end racial segregation in public schools with "all deliberate speed."[66] Could the Court force schools to comply? Should the Court have made the deadline, say, January 1, 1957?[67]

13.8. A "strong" enforcer wants everyone to know that it has low costs and will enforce law vigorously. Would the enforcer prefer rules or standards?

13.9. Non-enforcement sends a noisy signal about the state's capacity when these conditions hold: (1) regulated parties can observe enforcement or non-enforcement in others' cases; (2) extenuating circumstances excuse otherwise unlawful behavior; and (3) observers know less than the enforcer about other people's circumstances.[68]

(a) The law states, "no emissions of soot above 10 units unless the factory has a Model A burner." Is this a rule or a standard?

(b) The law from (a) applies. Darcy observes Carlos's factory emit dark smoke with impunity. Does the failure to enforce send a clear or noisy signal to Darcy about the state's enforcement capacity?

(c) Why might standards tend to satisfy the three previous conditions more often than rules?

B. Insincere Rules

A legislator in New Jersey worried about the safety of pedestrians and bicyclists. He proposed a bill that would double the fines for speeding and decrease speed limits. The

[66] Brown v. Board of Educ. of Topeka, Kan., 349 U.S. 294, 301 (1955).

[67] *Cf.* Jeffrey K. Staton & Georg Vanberg, *The Value of Vagueness: Delegation, Defiance, and Judicial Opinions*, 52 AM. J. POL. SCI. 504 (2008).

[68] *See* Nicholas Almendares, Michael D. Gilbert, & Rebecca Kerley, Enforcing Rules Versus Enforcing Standards, Virginia Law and Economics Research Paper No. 2021-07 (2021).

committee rejected the higher fines but approved the lower speed limits.[69] Why did the committee support one provision but not the other? We explore an interesting possibility: the provisions were substitutes. Stricter laws can substitute for harsher penalties.[70]

According to deterrence theory, we can prevent violations of law by setting the expected punishment above the benefit of lawbreaking. The expected punishment equals the probability of enforcement multiplied by the punishment. The punishment often depends on the severity of the violation. Exceeding the speed limit by 25 miles per hour usually comes with a larger fine than exceeding the speed limit by five miles per hour. To keep the math simple, we make the fine one dollar for every mile per hour that a driver exceeds the limit. So if a driver gets ticketed for driving 70 in a 55-mile-per-hour zone, the fine equals $15.

Suppose the speed limit in a residential area equals 35 miles per hour. Many drivers violate the law by going 45 miles per hour. Apparently the $10 fine for this violation is too small. To deter speeding, lawmakers must increase the punishment. Let's assume that increasing the punishment to $20 would achieve the lawmakers' goal. To make the punishment $20, they could double the fine. If the fine equaled two dollars for every mile per hour above the limit, the punishment for driving 45 in the 35-mile-per-hour zone would equal $20.

Doubling the fine seems like a natural solution. However, it's not the only solution. Instead of increasing the fine, lawmakers could reduce the speed limit from 35 to 25 miles per hour. Under the new speed limit, driving 45 exceeds the limit by 20 miles per hour instead of 10. Thus, the fine for driving 45 increases from $10 to $20—exactly the punishment the lawmakers sought. The stricter speed limit substitutes for a higher fine.

We can generalize from this example. *Sincere rules* mandate the behavior that lawmakers most prefer, whereas *insincere rules* mandate some other behavior. If lawmakers prefer drivers to go 35 miles per hour, then a speed limit of 35 represents a sincere rule and a speed limit of 25 represents an insincere rule. Insincere rules can improve compliance by magnifying the seriousness of violations. Insincere rules convert what would be a minor violation (in our example, driving 45 in a 35-mile-per-hour zone) into a major violation (driving 45 in a 25-mile-per-hour zone). If major violations carry larger fines, then insincere rules enhance punishments.

We have shown that the state can achieve the same deterrent by increasing the fine (make it $2 for every mile per hour above the limit) or by adopting an insincere rule. When would lawmakers prefer the insincere rule? Sometimes punishment must "fit the crime." Constitutional law might prohibit the state from charging large fines for small violations. Voters might punish officials for charging unfair amounts. A street vendor in New York got fined over $2,000 for using a table one inch too tall and two inches too close to a store, prompting calls for reform.[71] Agency problems might prevent enforcement when fines seem disproportionate to the offense. Knowing the fine, an officer might ignore the street vendor's minor violation. Given these constraints, increasing the fine schedule might not work. Lawmakers might prefer insincere rules instead. Insincere rules have two simultaneous effects: they make violations of law

[69] David Levinsky, *Asking Motorists to Slow It Down*, BURLINGTON COUNTY TIMES, May 16, 2013.
[70] This discussion draws on Michael D. Gilbert, *Insincere Rules*, 101 VA. L. REV. 2185 (2015).
[71] Sally Goldenberg, *Street Vendor Selling Cellphone Cases Fined 2G Fine for Inches*, N.Y. POST, Oct. 8, 2012.

more severe, and therefore they increase punishments. In our example, the insincere speed limit converts a 10-mile-per-hour violation into a 20-mile-per-hour violation, which increases the fine from $10 to $20. When violations become more severe, harsher punishments "fit the crime."

We have shown that insincere rules can improve compliance by increasing penalties. Now we consider a second effect: insincere rules simplify proof.[72] Enforcing law requires many steps. Enforcers must (1) observe or gather evidence about lawbreaking, (2) apprehend the perpetrator, (3) prove the violation, and (4) punish the perpetrator. Other parts of the book have discussed factors (1), (2), and (4). Here we focus on (3).

Proving a violation of law requires effort. Suppose an officer's radar detects Enzo driving 50 miles per hour in a 45-mile-per-hour zone. The officer writes him a ticket. If Enzo pays the ticket, the enforcement action ends. However, if Enzo contests the ticket, he goes to court. Going to court requires judges, prosecutors, clerks, and possibly jurors. The ticketing officer will have to testify, which has an opportunity cost. Spending time on Enzo's case leaves the officer with less time for other, more serious cases. During his testimony, the officer will have to explain the reading on his radar. Radars make errors, so the officer will have to explain why his reading was accurate. He might have to testify about the weather, intervening vehicles, the detection angle, and his own experience. In the end, the court might find in Enzo's favor, wasting much of the enforcement effort. Foreseeing these difficulties, the officer might not ticket Enzo in the first place.

We can relate this discussion to enforcement costs. As proving a violation of law becomes more difficult, enforcement costs increase.

The difficulty of proving a violation depends in part on its severity. Proving major violations is often easy. If the officer tickets Enzo for driving 75 in a 45-mile-per-hour zone, the case is simple. Radars make small errors, not large ones. Enzo will lose in court. Foreseeing this, he will not contest the ticket. Conversely, proving minor violations of law is often hard. Suppose the officer tickets Enzo for driving 46 in a 45-mile-per-hour zone. Radars frequently make one-mile-per-hour errors. Wind, rain, reflective surfaces, or the officer's shaky hands could explain the radar's reading. Enzo has a good chance of winning in court, making him more likely to contest the ticket.

Figure 13.3 illustrates these ideas.[73] The horizontal axis represents drivers' speed, and the vertical axis represents the social payoff from enforcement. The speed limit equals 45. The upward-sloping line captures the benefit of enforcement. As drivers go faster (55, 65, etc.), the social benefit of enforcing the speed limit against them grows. The downward-sloping curve represents the cost of enforcement. It incorporates the difficulties of proof. Proving a one-mile-per-hour violation is harder than proving a 30-mile-per-hour violation. Thus, the cost of enforcement at 46 exceeds the cost of enforcement at 75.

A rational state will not enforce unless the benefit outweighs the cost. In Figure 13.3, 55 miles per hour represents the break-even point. Officers should enforce the speed limit against people who drive faster than 55, and they should not enforce the speed

[72] This discussion draws on Michael D. Gilbert & Sean P. Sullivan, *Insincere Evidence*, 105 Va. L. Rev. 1115 (2019). Insincere rules can improve compliance through a third pathway that involves deceiving regulated parties. *See* Michael D. Gilbert, *Insincere Rules*, 101 Va. L. Rev. 2185, 2201–06 (2015).

[73] *See* Michael D. Gilbert & Sean P. Sullivan, *Insincere Evidence*, 105 Va. L. Rev. 1115, 1132, 1137 (2019).

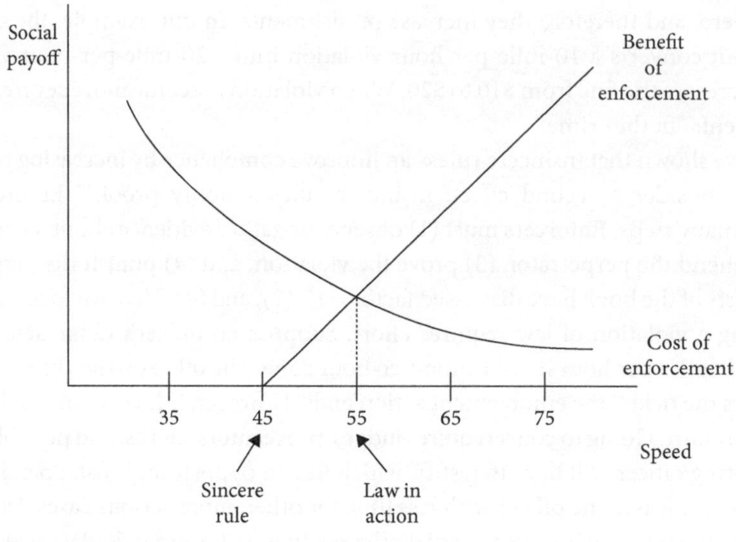

Figure 13.3. Proof and Enforcement

limit against people who drive 55 or slower.[74] If regulated parties understand the state's costs and benefits, they will drive 55. Enforcement costs open a gap between the law in books (45) and the law in action (55).

We have assumed a sincere rule. Lawmakers want drivers to go 45, so they make the speed limit 45. Now suppose lawmakers adopt an insincere rule by reducing the speed limit to 35. Figure 13.4 shows this change. The optimal speed remains 45, so the benefit line stays the same. No benefit accrues unless the state enforces against people going faster than 45. However, the costs change. The stricter speed limit makes every violation of law more serious and therefore easier to prove. To illustrate, driving 46 transforms from a one-mile-per-hour violation under the sincere rule to an 11-mile-per-hour violation under the insincere rule. Proving an 11-mile-per-hour violation is easier than proving a one-mile-per-hour violation, so the cost of proof decreases. Figure 13.4. captures this by shifting the cost curve leftward.

The insincere rule moves the break-even point from 55 to 50 miles per hour. The gap between the law in books and the law in action does not shrink (in the figure, it actually grows). However, the gap between drivers' optimal speed (45) and their actual speed (50) narrows. Insincere rules improve behavior by lowering the cost of enforcement.

Insincere rules have this effect when a few conditions hold.[75] First, the cost of proof decreases with the seriousness of the violation. In other words, proving major violations of law is easier than proving minor violations.[76] Second, lawmakers

[74] At the break-even point the state is indifferent between enforcement and non-enforcement, and we assume it does not enforce.
[75] *See id.* at 1141.
[76] A person charged with a major violation of law might invest more in his defense than a person charged with a minor violation of law. Thus proving major violations will not always be easier than proving minor violations.

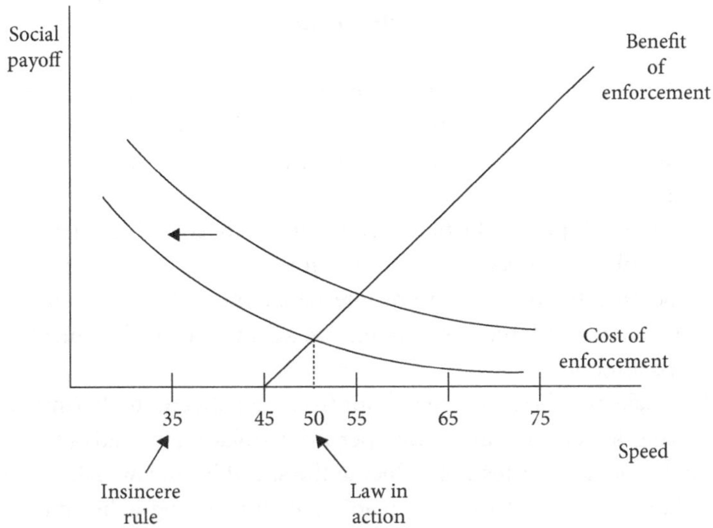

Figure 13.4. Insincere Rules and Enforcement

can adjust the content of law to convert minor violations into major ones. Third, enforcers and adjudicators apply the law as written. In our example, if the court treats the 35-mile-per-hour speed limit as authoritative, and if Enzo drives 50, then proving his violation will be easy, even if everyone knows the "best" speed limit is 45.

These conditions do not always hold. If the speed limit is absurd—say, one mile per hour—no one will enforce, so the third condition fails. However, these conditions sometimes hold, and when they do, insincere rules can improve behavior. Lawmakers might adopt insincere rules on subjects like these: emissions of mercury, soot, or other pollutants; the size and weight of fish; decibels at airports and music venues; milligrams of ingredients in food and medicine; distances between guns and schools and protesters and abortion clinics.

So far, our analysis concentrates on "bad men." We assume drivers like Enzo go as fast as possible without triggering punishment. An insincere speed limit causes "bad men" to slow down. But not everyone behaves like Enzo. Some people comply with law because they have a sense of duty or perceive law as legitimate. Imagine Fay, a "law follower" who always obeys the speed limit. In the preceding analysis, reducing the speed limit from 45 (sincere) to 35 (insincere) slows down Enzo. However, it also slows down Fay, who goes 35 instead of 45. By assumption, the optimal speed is 45, meaning Fay drives too slowly.

To generalize, insincere rules deter harmful activity, which is good, but they also chill beneficial activity, which is bad. For lawmakers, this complicates the choice of law. As the percentage of rule followers in society increases, insincere rules become less attractive, and vice versa.

The trade-off between deterring harmful activity and chilling beneficial activity is not unique to insincere rules. This trade-off occurs throughout law, as we will show.

Questions

13.10. Facilities storing prescription drugs must have "adequate lighting."[77] Suppose lawmakers change the law to require "excellent lighting." Does this make it easier to enforce the law against dimly lit facilities? Is the new law an insincere standard?

13.11. The optimal speed is 45, but given enforcement costs, the state should not enforce unless drivers go 56 or faster. However, officers ticket people for going 46 because the officers do not internalize the full costs of enforcement. To restrain over-enforcement, should we adopt insincerely lenient rules, like a speed limit of 55?

13.12. Lawmakers reduce the speed limit from 45 (sincere) to 35 (insincere). Thus, driving 46 becomes an 11-mile-per-hour violation instead of a one-mile-per-hour violation. Instead of reducing the speed limit, lawmakers could rig the radars so they add 10 to every reading. Again, driving 46 becomes an 11-mile-per-hour violation (the radar says 56) instead of a one-mile-per-hour violation. What distinguishes insincere rules from rigged radars?[78]

Proxy Crimes

Possessing burglar's tools does not cause harm. However, people who possess such tools tend to commit burglary, which does cause harm. Likewise, driving with an open container of alcohol does not cause harm, but it correlates with drunk driving, which causes accidents. Because of these correlations, law prohibits possessing burglar's tools and driving with open containers of alcohol. These are called *proxy crimes*.[79]

Our analysis illuminates proxy crimes. Lawmakers might desire strict adherence to such laws—no driving with an open container—because of the risk of harm. In that case, proxy crimes are sincere rules. Alternatively, lawmakers might *not* desire strict adherence to such laws. They might reason like this:

> We do not want to stop people from driving with open containers. We want to stop drunk driving. However, proving drunk driving is hard. Officers must measure blood alcohol content, which requires a test that makes errors. Proving that someone drove with an open container of alcohol is easier. Let's prohibit driving with an open container to lower the costs of enforcement against drunk drivers.

If lawmakers reason like this, proxy crimes are insincere rules. They do not mandate the behavior lawmakers prefer (no drunk driving). However, they promote the behavior lawmakers prefer by lowering the cost of proof.

[77] 21 C.F.R. § 205.50 (2019).
[78] *See* Michael D. Gilbert & Sean P. Sullivan, *Insincere Evidence*, 105 VA. L. REV. 1115, 1138–39 (2019).
[79] *See, e.g.*, LARRY ALEXANDER & KIMBERLY KESSLER FERZAN, REFLECTIONS ON CRIME AND CULPABILITY: PROBLEMS AND PUZZLES 83–92 (2018).

Proxy crimes change the elements of an offense.[80] In our example, lawmakers remove the requirement of drunkenness (hard to prove) and add the requirement of an open container of alcohol (easier to prove). Changing the elements of an offense leads to mistakes. Officers might ticket a sober driver with a half-empty bottle of wine in her car. In our discussion of insincere rules, we did not change the elements of an offense, we just changed the threshold, as when reducing the speed limit from 45 to 35. Does changing the threshold lead to fewer mistakes? To make drunk driving easier to prove, could lawmakers change a threshold?

C. Standards of Proof

Is the moon made of cheese? The answer must be no, but can you prove it? Have you traveled to the moon, tasted its rocks, or smelled its soil? Proving facts is difficult, even when the facts seem obvious. Consider an example in law. Did Gary steal the watch? Three witnesses saw him do it, but witnesses make mistakes. Gary's watch matches the stolen one, but perhaps that's coincidental. He might have bought the same watch at another store. Security footage seems to show Gary stealing the watch, but perhaps he has a twin brother. Given the evidence, the probability that Gary stole the watch is very high, perhaps 99.9 percent. But it's not 100 percent.

Supplying absolute proof of a fact is usually impossible. Thus, law does not require it. You can prove something in court by satisfying a lower standard. The standard depends on the type of case. In the United States, civil cases require proof by a "preponderance of the evidence." To illustrate, suppose you sue a builder for breaching his contract. This is a civil (not criminal) case. You must prove the breach by a preponderance of the evidence, meaning you must show that the probability the builder did what you claim exceeds 50 percent. Criminal cases require proof "beyond a reasonable doubt." To convict Gary of theft, prosecutors must prove his guilt beyond a reasonable doubt, meaning they must show that the probability he committed the crime exceeds, say, 95 percent. Some cases require "clear and convincing evidence," an intermediate standard of proof.

Proving a fact beyond a reasonable doubt requires more effort and information than proving a fact by a preponderance of the evidence. The higher the standard of proof, the higher the cost of enforcement. Thus, the government can assess civil penalties, like a fine for violating a regulation, more easily than it can send criminals to prison. The gap between the law in books and the law in action should tend to widen in criminal law and shrink in civil law.

Why not lower the standard of proof? The U.S. Constitution does not specify "beyond a reasonable doubt" for criminal cases. Perhaps courts could lower the standard

[80] *Cf.* William J. Stuntz, *The Pathological Politics of Criminal Law*, 100 MICH. L. REV. 505, 519 (2001) ("Suppose a given criminal statute contains elements ABC; suppose further that C is hard to prove, but prosecutors believe they know when it exists. Legislatures can make it easier to convict offenders by adding new crime AB, leaving it to prosecutors to decide when C is present and when it is not."). On the connection between Stuntz's argument and insincere rules, see Michael D. Gilbert & Sean P. Sullivan, *Insincere Evidence*, 105 VA. L. REV. 1115, 1158–61 (2019).

through interpretation, or perhaps lawmakers could amend the Constitution and entrench a lower standard.

If prosecutors only charged guilty people with crimes, then we should lower the standard of proof. Doing so would deter illegal acts by reducing enforcement costs. Likewise, if people only sued guilty defendants, then we should lower the standard of proof in civil cases. Conversely, if prosecutors only charged innocent people with crimes and private actors only sued innocent defendants, then we should raise all standards of proof to 100 percent.

Reality falls between these extremes. Prosecutors inevitably charge some innocent people with crimes, even if they mostly charge guilty people. Civil suits involve some innocent defendants and some guilty defendants. Different standards of proof balance the costs of these errors. Convicting an innocent person of a crime seems especially costly, so law sets the standard high. "Proof beyond a reasonable doubt" lets some criminals go free, but it protects innocent defendants. The benefit of protecting innocents plausibly exceeds the cost of releasing some criminals. Convicting an innocent person in a civil case seems less costly, so law sets the standard lower. "Preponderance of the evidence" provides less protection for innocent defendants, but it provides less security for guilty defendants. We discussed these ideas in our chapters on adjudication.

Standards of proof affect the choices of enforcers. Higher standards make judges and jurors less likely to find a person guilty. Consequently, higher standards make the government and private actors less likely to initiate legal actions (why bother?). Lower standards would encourage more criminal and civil cases.

Just as standards of proof affect the choices of enforcers, they can affect the choices of regulated parties.[81] Assume the speed limit equals 45, and recall our drivers Enzo and Fay. Lowering the standard of proof would make it easier to convict someone of speeding. This would discourage Enzo from breaking the law. However, it would also discourage Fay from following the law. She wants to drive 45, but she knows that radars make errors. If she goes 45, the officer's radar might show 48. Lowering the standard of proof makes it more likely that a court would erroneously convict her of speeding. To avoid this outcome, she goes 42. To generalize, *lowering the standard of proof deters some unlawful behavior but also chills some lawful behavior.*

Consider the problem from the other side. Raising the burden of proof would make it harder to convict someone of speeding. This would encourage Enzo to break the law; he will go even faster. However, raising the standard would free Fay to follow the law. If she goes 45, and even if the officer's radar shows 48, she will not get punished. The higher standard of proof protects her from an erroneous conviction. So she goes 45. To generalize, *raising the standard of proof encourages some unlawful behavior but also some lawful behavior.*

These ideas apply in many settings, not just speeding. Take our earlier example on soot emissions. Raising the standard of proof lets lawbreakers pollute even further above the limit. However, it also lets law followers reach the limit without fear of punishment. Earlier we listed areas of law where lawmakers might adopt insincere rules: the size and weight of fish; decibels at airports and music venues; milligrams of ingredients

[81] This discussion draws on Louis Kaplow, *Burden of Proof*, 121 YALE L.J. 738 (2012).

in food and medicine; distances between guns and schools and protesters and abortion clinics. In these areas and many others, lowering the standard of proof should tend to deter some unlawful behavior but also chill some lawful behavior, and vice versa.

The ideal standard of proof accounts for these effects. If lowering the standard of proof for speeding would deter speeders without chilling law followers, then we should lower the standard of proof. If raising the standard of proof would encourage people to exercise their First Amendment rights without encouraging lawbreaking, then we should raise the standard of proof.

In reality, we cannot measure the exact deterrent and chilling effects of the standard of proof. We often cannot observe how people act in the shadow of the law. Even if we could, we probably could not fine-tune the standard of proof. To illustrate, suppose that lowering the standard of proof in criminal cases would deter unlawful activities without chilling lawful activities. So we should lower the standard of proof. How should we phrase the new standard? Proof "beyond an almost-reasonable doubt?" Instead, we could express the standard with percentages. Under the old standard, jurors needed, say, "95 percent certainty" to convict, but under the new standard they need "91 percent certainty." Would that modification change jurors' behavior?

Standards of proof have important incentive effects on regulated parties that are difficult to measure. In fact, many aspects of enforcement have these features. We began this chapter by discussing the Fourth Amendment, which protects people from unreasonable searches. Loosening the Fourth Amendment would make it easier for police to conduct searches. This could deter crime. However, it could also chill lawful activity. ("The meeting is legal, but police will barge in anyway, so let's cancel the meeting.") Hiring more officers could deter crime by increasing the probability of punishment. However, it could also chill lawful activity. If police stand on every corner, people might stay in their homes, cancel their parties, and refrain from driving because they fear an erroneous search or arrest. An insincere speed limit deters Enzo from speeding. However, it chills Fay's activity. She drives 35 when the optimal speed is actually 45.

In sum, standards of proof affect enforcement. A good standard of proof balances the costs of errors, as when courts find innocent people guilty and guilty people innocent. Ideally, a good standard of proof deters unlawful activity without chilling lawful activity. Identifying the best standard of proof is easier in theory than in practice.

Questions

13.13. Lawmakers want to decrease the cost of enforcing the speed limit. They could lower the standard of proof, or they could adopt an insincerely low speed limit. Which change seems more likely to affect drivers' behavior?

13.14. Figure 13.4 showed how insincere rules could improve behavior by lowering the cost of proof. Suppose the standard of proof in the figure is preponderance of the evidence.

(a) What would happen to the cost curve and the equilibrium if the standard switched to beyond a reasonable doubt?

(b) Would making the rule even stricter offset the higher standard of proof?

(c) William Stuntz criticized criminal law in the United States, saying "the law on the books makes everyone a felon."[82] Does your answer to the prior question illuminate his quote?

III. Beyond Deterrence

Why do people comply with law? Deterrence, which we have analyzed in detail, provides one important answer. But deterrence cannot provide a complete answer. Sometimes people comply even without the threat of fines or imprisonment because law works through other mechanisms. Many scholars concentrate on two mechanisms, duty and legitimacy. If people feel an obligation to law, or if they perceive law as "legitimate," then they comply, regardless of any sanctions.[83] We will address these ideas, but first we concentrate on different mechanisms. Law can influence behavior by providing information, coordinating action, and even changing preferences. The following pages show how.

A. Law as Information

A tourist finds herself on a pristine beach with sunny skies, palm trees, and blue waves. A sign in the sand interrupts her view:

Swimming Prohibited
Rip Tides
City code § 602

Does she swim? If she swims and gets caught, she might pay a fine. But the beach is deserted, so she will not get caught, meaning the expected punishment for a violation equals zero. Nevertheless, she probably will not swim. She will comply because the law taught her something important: the water is dangerous.[84]

According to economics, people make choices to satisfy their preferences given their beliefs and constraints. Law can influence behavior by imposing constraints, as with punishments. Deterrence works by creating constraints. In the beach example, law works through a different mechanism: it changes beliefs. By changing people's beliefs, law can change behavior, even without the threat of punishment.

To change beliefs, law must satisfy some conditions.[85] First, people must know about the law. The tourist does not read the city code, but she sees the sign on the beach.

[82] William J. Stuntz, *The Pathological Politics of Criminal Law*, 100 Mich. L. Rev. 505, 511 (2001).

[83] *See, e.g.*, H.L.A. Hart, The Concept of Law (2d ed. 1994) (on internalization); Tom R. Tyler, Why People Obey the Law (1990) (on "procedural" legitimacy); Paul H. Robinson & John M. Darley, *The Utility of Desert*, 91 Nw. U.L. Rev. 453 (1997) (on "substantive" or moral legitimacy); Elizabeth Mullen & Janice Nadler, *Moral Spillovers: The Effect of Moral Violations on Deviant Behavior*, 44 J. Exper. Soc. Psych. 1239 (2008) (on moral legitimacy).

[84] This discussion draws on Richard H. McAdams, The Expressive Powers of Law 136–68 (2015).

[85] We reformulate some of McAdams' conditions. *See id.* These conditions are necessary but not sufficient. People must be willing to learn, they must update their beliefs correctly, and so on.

Second, people must assume that lawmakers have relevant, private information. In our example, the tourist assumes the city council knows something about the water that she does not. Third, people must assume that the law reveals that private information. If the tourist assumes the sign reflects lawmakers' superior knowledge of risk, then she learns something. If she assumes swimming is prohibited for some other reason, then she might not learn anything, even though lawmakers know more about the water.

Focus on the third condition. Suppose the tourist sees the sign, and she assumes the lawmakers have private information. They know if the water is safe or not. However, she reasons like this:

> If I can't swim here, I'll have to pay the rich hotel next door for access to its private beach. The rich hotel probably controls the city council. The city council probably made this law to drive tourists to the hotel. This law doesn't promote safety, it enriches a special interest.

If the tourist reasons this way, she might ignore the law and swim. Yes, she saw the sign, and yes, lawmakers have private information. But she does not think the law conveys that information. She thinks the city council regulates swimming to help the hotel, not to promote safety, so she can't learn anything about safety from the law on swimming. The sign does not change the tourist's beliefs because the third condition fails.

We have shown how and when the sign on the beach can inform a tourist. Consider some other settings where law can provide information, starting with driving. A solid yellow line means "changing lanes is prohibited." A sign on the freeway says, "Curve ahead, speed limit 45." Most drivers do not cross solid yellow lines, and most drivers seeing the sign slow down, at least a little. Drivers do not necessarily comply with these traffic laws because they fear punishment. They comply because the law teaches them something about safety. Consider one more example. The pesticide bottle says, "Applying this product near water is strictly prohibited by law." Does the farmer spray the pesticide near the stream? Does he throw the empty bottle in the ditch? No one can see him, making the threat of punishment nil. Nevertheless, he might keep the product away from water because the law taught him something about its dangerousness.

Our examples so far involve harms from currents, accidents, or chemicals. The law teaches people about physical risks. Law might also teach people about emotional or social risks.[86] Suppose the legislature enacts a law that forbids smoking in the park. Will Helen the smoker comply? Cops do not have time to ticket people for smoking in the park, so there is little risk of a fine. Nevertheless, Helen might comply because the law teaches her something: smoking in the park is unpopular. If she smokes there, people will dislike it. They might shun or insult her. Her reputation will suffer. To avoid emotional harms and social sanctions, Helen does not smoke in the park.

Earlier we identified three conditions that law must satisfy to change beliefs about physical risks. The same conditions apply here. Smokers must learn about the law, perhaps from a sign that says, "Smoking in the park is prohibited." They must assume that lawmakers have relevant, private information (in this case, they know more about public attitudes on smoking). Finally, they must assume that law reveals the private

[86] McAdams refers to these categories as risk and attitude signaling. *See id.* at 137–39.

information: the ban on smoking reflects public attitudes. These conditions are not always satisfied. Even in a democracy, laws do not always reflect public attitudes, meaning the third condition fails. But when the conditions hold, law can supply information.

This chapter began with a quote from Alexander Hamilton, who thought punishment essential. Without punishment, he wrote, a law would "amount to nothing more than advice or recommendation." Hamilton missed something important. In the right circumstances, a law that merely provides "advice" can change behavior.

Questions

13.15. In our beach example, lawmakers posted a sign that said, "Swimming prohibited, rip tides, city code § 602." What if there were no law, and a private citizen posted a sign that said, "Swimming prohibited, rip tides." Would the tourist update her beliefs? Why might the lawmakers' sign work better?

13.16. A new law forbids all vaping, but the government does not enforce it. The law might reduce vaping in restaurants but not in private homes. Explain why.

13.17. The legislature could ban single-use plastic bags by statute, or citizens could ban them by passing a ballot initiative. Explain why a ballot initiative might cause more compliance.

Enforcement as Information

We have explained that the content of law can change people's beliefs. Enforcement can change beliefs too. If you think cops do not enforce the ban on smoking in public, and if you see someone ticketed for lighting up in the park, then you might revise upward your risk of getting punished for smoking in public. Likewise, if you think cops *do* enforce the ban on fireworks, and if you see cops ignore someone lighting bottle rockets, then you might revise downward your risk of getting punished for fireworks.

For enforcement to supply accurate information, observers must know the law and the facts. But knowing the law and the facts is often difficult.[87] To illustrate, suppose the sign says, "No alcohol in the park," but you see people drinking wine with impunity. You think you can drink wine too, so you open a bottle and promptly get a ticket. The wine drinkers are not in the park; they are on the property of an adjacent restaurant. Or suppose you see someone in street clothes scalping tickets outside of a concert. You have an extra ticket, so you try to sell it, but the police promptly give you a citation. The scalper has a license to resell tickets, whereas you do not. Finally, suppose you thought the cops did not enforce the ban on fireworks, but then you saw someone get a ticket for lighting a Roman candle. You revised your beliefs and put away your sparklers. This was unnecessary because the law makes an exception for sparklers. In all three cases, the observer misunderstands the law, the facts, or both, and this causes errors in beliefs. Enforcement sends "shallow signals."[88]

[87] The following discussion draws on Bert I. Huang, *Shallow Signals*, 126 Harv. L. Rev. 2227 (2013).
[88] *See id.*

To learn more from enforcement, people must learn the law and the facts. The state could help. It could make ticket scalpers wear a badge that says, "Licensed reseller." If you saw the badge, you might not try to scalp your ticket. Instead of "No alcohol in the park," the sign could say, "Alcohol on private property only." If you saw this sign, you might investigate the boundary of the restaurant before opening your wine. In these examples, law makes us aware of our ignorance.

Imagine the official in charge of enforcing the ban on alcohol in the park. She has very limited enforcement capacity, so inevitably some people will drink wine in the park, and others will see them drinking wine without getting a ticket. The official does not want anyone to know that her enforcement capacity is so limited. Would she prefer a sign saying "Alcohol on private property only" or a sign saying "No alcohol in the park"?

B. Law and Reputation

Helen refrains from smoking in the park, not because she fears a ticket but because she fears social stigma. When we presented this example earlier, we focused on information. The law teaches Helen something about public attitudes. Here we focus on Helen's objective: she wants a good reputation.

Most people seem to care about their reputations. We want people to like us, respect us, and trust us. We seek the esteem of others.[89] The desire for a good reputation can motivate many behaviors like honesty and kindness. It can also motivate compliance with social norms. Why do people tip waiters, shake hands, hold open doors, wear ties to weddings, remove hats in church, and refrain from burping in public? These are examples of social norms. Law does not mandate these behaviors. Violating a norm does not invite fines or imprisonment. Nevertheless, many people comply with social norms much of the time. One explanation involves reputation. Violating a norm can lead to social stigma, so people comply with norms to protect their reputations.[90]

Why value a good reputation? Perhaps we have a "taste" for good reputations in the same way that we have tastes for health, comfort, and happiness. According to this view, a good reputation is an end in itself—an input in people's utility functions. This explanation probably has some merit. However, we do not focus on it. We focus on a different explanation: cooperation.

We benefit from cooperating with others when buying products, selling services, hiring employees, playing sports, and engaging in other activities. In general, cooperation gets easier with a good reputation. To demonstrate, which mechanic would you hire: the one people compliment, or the one nobody knows? The one who shakes your hand, or the one who burps in your face? An earlier chapter explained that reputation matters a lot in the market for lawyers. Most people do not know the law, so they cannot

[89] *See* GEOFFREY BRENNAN & PHILIP PETTIT, THE ECONOMY OF ESTEEM (2004).

[90] *See, e.g.*, Richard H. McAdams, *The Origin, Development, and Regulation of Norms*, 96 MICH. L. REV. 338 (1997).

assess lawyers' expertise. Instead, they assess lawyers' reputations. Lawyers cultivate good reputations to attract clients.

Violating law often leads to a bad reputation.[91] What will happen to a priest's reputation if he parks his car in spaces reserved for people with disabilities? Imagine a human resources manager at a company. What will happen if she flouts the rules on age discrimination or employer-sponsored health plans? These people value good reputations. The priest seeks parishioners, and the manager wants promotions and raises. To build good reputations, they comply with law. They might comply even if a violation would not lead to fines or imprisonment. The priest, for example, will not park in the reserved space even if the probability of getting a ticket equals zero.

We invented these examples for clarity. Now consider some real examples. In the United States, government actors nearly always comply with court orders. The explanation apparently involves reputation.[92] Officials comply because noncompliance causes shame and embarrassment. To illustrate, in the 1970s, a federal court held the U.S. Attorney General in contempt for failing to reveal certain information. The contempt did not involve any sanctions like fines or jail time. According to the court, "the status of civil contempt would, in and of itself, be a severe sanction."[93] In 2002, a federal court held the Secretary of Interior Gale Norton in contempt for noncompliance with an order. The Secretary appealed in her professional capacity, *and* she appealed in her personal capacity, meaning she hired and paid for her own lawyer. She argued that she had a personal stake because the contempt involved "disparagement of her reputation . . . that could affect her professional life in the future."[94]

We argued that people seek good reputations to facilitate cooperation. This idea applies to public officials. A bad reputation could make it difficult for the Attorney General—the chief law enforcement officer in the United States—to manage his subordinates in the Department of Justice.[95] A bad reputation could make it difficult for Gale Norton, a lawyer, to find another job after leaving the Department of Interior. If you ran a law firm, would you hire a former government official who got in trouble for making a mistake of law or ignoring a judge?

In sum, violating law can worsen a person's reputation. A bad reputation can foreclose opportunities by making cooperation with others difficult. To foster good reputations, many people, including officials, comply with law. They comply even if they would not face formal penalties like fines or imprisonment for a violation.

Reputational concerns promote compliance under certain conditions.[96] First, people must observe compliance or noncompliance. If no one learns about the priest parking illegally, then it cannot harm his reputation. Thus, reputations influence public behavior, meaning behavior others likely will see, more than private behavior. Second, the actor and observers must interact repeatedly. Secretary Norton worried about her reputation

[91] *See, e.g.*, Bruno Deffains & Claude Fluet, *Social Norms and Legal Design*, 36 J.L. Econ. & Org. 139 (2020).

[92] *See* Nicholas R. Parrillo, *The Endgame of Administrative Law: Governmental Disobedience and the Judicial Contempt Power*, 131 Harv. L. Rev. 685, 777–89 (2018), and citations therein.

[93] Socialist Workers Party v. Att'y Gen. of U.S., 458 F. Supp. 895, 903 (S.D.N.Y. 1978).

[94] *See* Nicholas R. Parrillo, *The Endgame of Administrative Law: Governmental Disobedience and the Judicial Contempt Power*, 131 Harv. L. Rev. 685, 784 (2018) (internal citation omitted).

[95] The Attorney General himself argued that the contempt finding "will adversely affect my ability to function as attorney general." *Id.* at 783 (internal citation omitted).

[96] We concentrate on some intuitive conditions. Our list is not exhaustive.

among people she expected to deal with again. Third, observers must reward compliance. In Washington, voters, journalists, and others respect officials for complying with law. In contrast, gang members do not respect their peers for complying with law. In some communities, people get good reputations by *breaking* law. Finally, the benefit of lawbreaking must be sufficiently small. Reputational harm works like a punishment. If the benefit of lawbreaking exceeds the punishment, people will break the law.

Our discussion treats a good reputation as a reward that people intentionally seek. Officials might consciously decide to comply with law to protect their reputations. People might obey social norms—holding doors, wearing black to funerals, waving flags on Independence Day—in the conscious pursuit of a good reputation.[97] However, intentions are not always necessary. Some people seem to "internalize" norms, including the norm of complying with law. When people internalize norms, they obey because of guilt or a sense of duty, not because of social sanctions. Perhaps we internalize norms that are especially valuable to us, like norms that build good reputations.[98]

Enforcing International Law

International law governs relations between sovereign states.[99] Much international law originates in treaties, like the Geneva Conventions addressing war and the General Agreement on Tariffs and Trade addressing cross-border exchange. Other international law originates in custom, like the custom of granting immunity to visiting heads of state. "Soft law" refers to declarations, principles, or other statements that might influence states but do not formally bind them. Consent sits at the heart of international law. In general, states have obligations under international law only if they consent to them.

International law raises a vexing problem of compliance. The world does not have a global police force that can monitor states' behavior. Some international law lacks any kind of formal enforcement. Other international law gets enforced by special tribunals, but they have limited power. For example, the Appellate Body of the World Trade Organization (WTO) hears trade disputes among states, and the Inter-American Court of Human Rights reviews human rights claims against certain countries. Tribunals like these can rule against states, but they lack an executive to enforce their orders. How can a handful of judges make Brazil or Mexico pay damages? How can they make China or the United States lower tariffs?

In practice, nations often seem to comply with international law.[100] Why? Some people think states comply because of commitments to law and justice. Economists

[97] *See* Eric A. Posner, Law and Social Norms (2000).

[98] On the internalization of norms, see Robert Cooter, *Expressive Law and Economics*, 27 J. Legal Stud. 585 (1998).

[99] We refer to "public" international law. We do not address "private" international law, which addresses some interactions and conflicts among people from different countries.

[100] *See, e.g.*, Tom Ginsburg & Richard H. McAdams, *Adjudicating in Anarchy: An Expressive Theory of International Dispute Resolution*, 45 Wm. & Mary L. Rev. 1229 (2004). Note that observing compliance is harder than it sounds. If a state wants to do *X*, international law requires *Y*, and consequently the state does *Y*, then the state complies with international law. If a state wants to do *X*, international law requires *X*, and the state does *X*, then the state acts consistently with international law, but it does not comply with

usually look for different explanations. One explanation involves reciprocity. If State *A* does not raise tariffs on State *B*, then State *B* will not raise tariffs on State *A*. Conversely, if *A* violates the trade agreement by raising tariffs on *B*, then *B* will respond by raising tariffs on *A*. The WTO Appellate Body might authorize *B* to raise tariffs against *A* in this circumstance. We have seen the logic of reciprocity in prior chapters. Judges Willow and Xu follow one another's precedents, even though they would prefer to make their own precedents. The long-term benefits of cooperation exceed the short-term benefits of defection.

Reciprocity can explain some but not all compliance with international law. Reputation provides another explanation.[101] States benefit from cooperating on topics like trade, security, tax, the environment, and cross-border crime. Cooperation requires bargaining, and bargaining gets easier when transaction costs are low. Transaction costs decrease when parties can make credible commitments to one another. Without a global enforcement mechanism, states cannot make credible commitments simply by signing a treaty. They can renege on treaties, sometimes with impunity. Instead of signatures, states rely on reputations to make their promises credible. State *A* trusts State *B*'s promise, not because *B* can be punished for reneging but because *B* has a good reputation. *B*'s good reputation facilitates cooperation with *A*.

How can State *B* develop this good reputation? By complying with international law. Recall that international law depends on consent. By consenting, State *B* has effectively promised to comply. By complying, *B* develops a reputation for keeping its promises.

C. Law and Coordination

Ian and Jess do not know each other, but they receive orders to meet in New York City. They don't know when or where. They cannot communicate, and neither knows where the other lives or works. Will they ever find each other? You might think the answer is no. Finding a common location seems impossible in a large city without some means of communication. In fact, they might find each other. When presented with a challenge like this, most people say they would go to the clock at Grand Central Station at noon.[102]

Let's analyze this example in detail. Ian and Jess play a game of coordination. They benefit if they coordinate on a location, otherwise they pay a cost. In general, coordination games have multiple equilibria. Equilibrium occurs when Ian and Jess go

international law. Compliance implies influence, and in the second example international law does not exert influence. If international law mostly requires states to do things they would have done anyway, then it mostly does not influence states. *See* JACK L. GOLDSMITH & ERIC A. POSNER, THE LIMITS OF INTERNATIONAL LAW (2005).

[101] *See, e.g.*, Andrew T. Guzman, *A Compliance-Based Theory of International Law*, 90 CAL. L. REV. 1823 (2002); Beth Simmons, *Treaty Compliance and Violation*, 13 ANN. REV. POL. SCI. 273 (2010).

[102] *See* THOMAS C. SCHELLING, THE STRATEGY OF CONFLICT 57 (1960). This book is a landmark in game theory by a Nobel Prize–winning economist. Whether Grand Central Station remains salient 60 years later is debatable.

		Driver 2	
		Left	Right
Driver 1	Left	0, 0	−10, −10
	Right	−10, −10	0, 0

Figure 13.5. Coordination on Driving

to the same place, New York City has many places, so the game has many equilibria. Communication facilitates coordination. If Ian and Jess could talk, they could easily agree on a place to meet. Without communication, players need a focal point. A *focal point* is a common solution to a coordination problem that arises without communication. If Ian thinks Jess will go to the clock at noon, and if Jess thinks Ian will go to the clock at noon, then they will find each other, even though they can't communicate. The clock at noon is a focal point.

To deepen our analysis, consider a classic coordination problem: driving. We introduced a version of this problem early in the book. Two drivers approach each other on a road. If both drive on the left side of the road, or if both drive on the right side, they will pass safely. If they drive on opposite sides they will collide. The drivers play a coordination game, just like Ian and Jess. Figure 13.5 captures their game. If the drivers choose the same side, they will get payoffs of zero apiece, as the top-left box and the bottom-right box show. However, if they choose opposite sides, they will collide for payoffs of negative 10 apiece.

Without communication, how can the drivers coordinate? Ian and Jess used a focal point. Each had an expectation about where the other would go. Perhaps the drivers have a focal point. If the custom is to drive on the left, then both will drive on the left and avoid a collision. Suppose, however, that they don't have a focal point. No custom tells them what to do. In circumstances like this, law can help. Suppose the state installs a sign that says, "Drive on the right." If the drivers see the sign, probably they will drive on the right and avoid a collision.

In this example, law improves behavior. It causes the drivers to drive on the same side and avoid a costly collision. *Law provides a focal point that facilitates coordination.*[103]

Punishing people for driving on the left would strengthen the focal point. If the expected fine for driving on the left is high, each driver prefers to drive on the right, and each driver expects the other to do the same. But punishment probably isn't necessary.

[103] McAdams has developed this idea in several papers. For an overview, see RICHARD H. MCADAMS, THE EXPRESSIVE POWERS OF LAW 57–135 (2015).

		Lana	
		Don't stop	Stop
Kai	Don't stop	−10, −10	0, −1
	Stop	−1, 0	−2, −2

Figure 13.6. Coordination on Stopping

Even if the expected punishment for driving on the left equals zero, drivers seeing the sign probably will drive on the right. Once they do, they will not change behavior. To see why, return to Figure 13.5. The sign pushes the drivers to the bottom-right box, which represents an equilibrium. Once both drive on the right, neither will switch to the left. Switching never increases the payoff.

To summarize, law can coordinate people's actions by providing a focal point. Once people coordinate, they tend to remain coordinated, producing value for all. Sometimes law can achieve coordination without any threat of punishment.

Figure 13.5 represents a "pure" coordination game. It has two equilibria (drive on the right, drive on the left), and both yield the same payoffs, making the drivers indifferent between them. Pure coordination games are probably rare. In reality, people often have preferences over equilibria. To illustrate, imagine a different scenario. Kai drives north, Lana drives west, and they will meet at the intersection. If one driver stops for the other, they will pass safely, but if neither stops they will collide. Figure 13.6 shows the possible outcomes and payoffs. If one driver stops, that person gets negative one and the other gets zero. To illustrate, if Kai stops and Lana does not, the drivers are in the bottom-left box, and Kai gets negative one and Lana gets zero. If neither driver stops, both get negative 10. If both drivers stop, they waste time, and they cannot tell when to go, so both get negative two.

Suppose Kai stops and Lana does not, placing them in the bottom-left box. Kai gets a payoff of negative one and Lana gets zero. If Kai switches to "don't stop," his payoff will decrease to negative 10, so he will not switch. If Lana switches to "stop," her payoff will decrease to negative two, so she will not switch. Neither party has an incentive to switch, so the bottom-left box represents an equilibrium. Likewise, the top-right box represents an equilibrium. The other two boxes do not represent equilibria.[104]

Like the prior game, this one has two equilibria. However, the players are not indifferent among them. Kai prefers the top-right box, and Lana prefers the bottom-left box. This does not affect the logic. To avoid an accident, both drivers want to coordinate, and

[104] If the drivers find themselves in the top-left box, each has an incentive to switch to "stop." If the drivers find themselves in the bottom-right box, each has an incentive to switch to "don't stop."

this is difficult without a focal point. The state can supply a focal point by placing a stop sign. If the state places the sign on Kai's road, he will stop and Lana will not.[105] If the state places the sign on Lana's road, she will stop and he will not.

To generalize, law can supply a focal point that coordinates people even when they disagree on the best equilibrium. This works when the benefit of coordination is sufficiently large. In our example, the benefit of avoiding a collision is large enough that one driver will stop to let the other pass, even though stopping imposes a cost.

Focal points help explain the purpose of and compliance with many traffic laws. Why do we see so many traffic lights, yield signs, and double-yellow lines, and why do people often comply with them? One answer involves coordination. Drivers want to avoid collisions, traffic laws help them coordinate, and once they coordinate, they remain coordinated. The law mostly enforces itself.

The focal point theory of law applies beyond traffic. Consider some topics in international law. Countries benefit from common protocols for air travel, the right of way among ships at sea, international mail, and agreement on weights on measures.[106] International law addresses these topics in the Chicago Convention on International Civil Aviation, the United Nations Convention on the Law of the Sea, the Treaty of the Metre, and so on. Surely different nations prefer different equilibria. Argentina and Greece might prefer different rules on air traffic control, but the benefits of coordination outweigh those differences, making agreement possible. When international law solves coordination problems, nations mostly comply without enforcement.

Consider constitutional law.[107] When designing a constitution, negotiators disagree about details—how many seats in the legislature, how many judges on the high court, the degree of judicial independence, and so on. However, the negotiators benefit from coordination. Everyone benefits from common expectations about the structure of government.

To clarify this idea, focus on sports. Basketball players disagree about the best rules for basketball. Some would allow "hand checking," which occurs when a defender places a hand on the dribbler, and others would forbid hand checking. However, all players benefit from coordination on the rules. Without a common set of rules, they cannot play basketball. Every game would bog down in conflict over permissible and impermissible behavior.

Sometimes constitutions work like sports. Constitutional designers disagree about the best constitution, but they benefit greatly from coordination. Without coordination, government cannot function, and conflict results. Conflict over government is much more destructive than conflict over basketball. Constitutions coordinate behavior, including the behavior of powerful actors. Once those actors coordinate, they tend to stay coordinated, just like basketball players tend to play by the rules and drivers tend to stop at stop signs.

[105] To be precise, if the state places the sign only on Kai's road, he will not expect Lana to stop, so he will stop. Knowing that Kai will stop, Lana will not stop.

[106] *See* Richard H. McAdams, The Expressive Powers of Law 69 (2015).

[107] Hardin pioneered the study of constitutions as coordination devices. *See* Russell Hardin, *Why a Constitution?*, *in* The Federalist Papers and the New Institutionalism (Bernard Grofman & Donald Wittman eds., 1989).

To summarize, life presents many coordination games. The failure to coordinate harms everyone involved. Sometimes law can facilitate coordination by providing a focal point. Focal points can change behavior and improve outcomes, even without the threat of punishment. Again, Hamilton missed something important. In the right circumstance, a law that merely provides a "recommendation" can change behavior.

Questions

13.18. We imagined the state posting a sign that says, "Drive on the right." If a private citizen with no legal authority posted the sign instead, would drivers drive on the right? Is law necessary for coordination?

13.19. The streets of Cairo have traffic signs, but drivers mostly ignore them. Is law sufficient for coordination? In answering, consider this statement: law can coordinate when "there are no stronger, competing focal points."[108]

13.20. Who "owns" Greenland? Denmark and Norway litigated the question in the Permanent Court of International Justice. The court resolved ambiguities in the international conventions on sovereignty and sided with Denmark. Norway complied with the court's judgment, without armed conflict. Did Denmark and Norway play a pure coordination game? Can judicial decisions provide a focal point?[109]

13.21. Buying things with money like U.S. dollars is easier than trading things through barter. Does money present buyers and sellers with a coordination problem? Why does money say things like, "This note is legal tender for all debts"?

Coordinating against the State

Recall Madison's quote: "In framing a government . . . the great difficulty lies in this: you must first enable the government to control the governed; and in the next place oblige it to control itself."[110] We have explored mechanisms by which states control the governed. How do states control themselves? Often they don't. Many governments repress their citizens to gain money and power. But some governments do control themselves. Some governments respect their citizens, even when doing so frustrates their plans. Why?

Coordination supplies an answer.[111] If citizens act alone, they cannot punish the government, so they cannot deter its oppressions. If citizens act together, they can. Consider the Arab Spring, a social movement featuring massive street protests.

[108] *See* Richard H. McAdams, The Expressive Powers of Law 62 (2015) (citing Richard H. McAdams & Janice Nadler, *Coordinating in the Shadow of the Law: Two Contextualized Tests of the Focal Point Theory of Legal Compliance*, 42 Law & Soc'y Rev. 865 (2008)).

[109] *See* Tom Ginsburg & Richard H. McAdams, *Adjudicating in Anarchy: An Expressive Theory of International Dispute Resolution*, 45 Wm. & Mary L. Rev. 1229, 1292–97 (2004).

[110] The Federalist No. 51, 264 (James Madison) (Ian Shapiro ed., 2009).

[111] *See* Barry R. Weingast, *The Political Foundations of Democracy and the Rule of Law*, 91 Am. Pol. Sci. Rev. 245 (1997).

Citizens marching together toppled governments across the Middle East.[112] For citizens to act together, they must coordinate. In particular, they must coordinate on a triggering event: What merits an uprising?

Law can help. Sometimes the constitution acts as a coordinating device—a focal point. If you observe a constitutional violation (the triggering event), you protest because you know others will do the same. The logic matches the example of Ian and Jess. When they get instructions to meet (the triggering event), he goes to Grand Central Station because he knows she will too, and vice versa. When the constitution becomes a focal point, it enforces itself. The state does not violate the constitution because doing so will trigger an uprising.

For the constitution to become a focal point, citizens must agree on what counts as a violation. To illustrate, consider two provisions in the U.S. Constitution, one limiting the President to two terms in office, and another forbidding the government from denying anyone "the equal protection of the laws."[113] If a President runs for a third term, everyone will agree this constitutes a violation. In contrast, people disagree on what violates equal protection. The provision on term limits can provide a focal point, whereas the Equal Protection Clause might not.

This reasoning might encourage vague drafting. A constitutional designer bent on seizing power might think, "I will make the constitution vague, like the U.S. Equal Protection Clause. With vague language, citizens will disagree on whether I have violated the constitution, so they will not coordinate against me." Alternatively, this reasoning might encourage precise drafting. A designer might think, "I will make the constitution precise. With a precise constitution, citizens can coordinate against me for violating law, which commits me to following law."

To illustrate the second possibility, suppose a nation seeks foreign investors, but investors worry that the state will steal their money. To reassure them, the state can amend its constitution to protect private property. Will the state make the amendment vague or precise? With a precise amendment, citizens will recognize a violation, making them more likely to coordinate and punish the state. A precise amendment makes the state's commitment to private property more credible, which is necessary to attract investors. The state makes the amendment precise.

What prevents the state from amending the constitution again? It could eliminate the property protection suddenly and expropriate the money legally, before investors have a chance to withdraw.[114] To reassure investors, the state needs an amendment rule (1) that prevents sudden changes to the constitution and (2) violations of which are apparent. The state can adopt a constitutional lock.[115] *Constitutional locks* are forced waiting periods for constitutional amendments, like South Africa's requirement that one month pass between publication of a proposed amendment and its

[112] Citizens coordinated successfully to bring down repressive governments. However, the new governments have not necessarily been better.

[113] U.S. Const. amend. XXII ("No person shall be elected to the office of the President more than twice."); U.S. Const. amend. XIV ("No state shall make or enforce any law which shall abridge the privileges or immunities of citizens . . . nor deny to any person within its jurisdiction the equal protection of the laws.").

[114] After the amendment, the expropriation would be legal under domestic law but not necessarily under international law.

[115] *See* Michael D. Gilbert, Mauricio Guim, & Michael Weisbuch, *Constitutional Locks*, 19 Int'l J. Const. L. 865 (2021).

submission to Parliament.[116] If the state violates the lock, citizens will know. They can tell if the state waited 30 days between publishing and adopting the amendment. If citizens can agree on violations of the lock, they can coordinate against the state, discouraging violations. The state will comply with the lock, meaning it will not surprise investors by changing the constitution suddenly.

Constitutions do not always provide focal points. If they did, fewer governments would violate their own laws. But constitutions provide focal points in some circumstances, and when they do, they enforce themselves.

D. Re-Coordination and Corner Equilibria

The last section imagined people in states of disequilibrium. They drove on different sides of the road, disagreed on which ship should yield, used different measures like pounds and kilograms, and so on. Disequilibrium harms everyone. Law coordinated people by providing focal points like road signs and the Treaty of the Metre. Sometimes law works like this, replacing chaos with coordination. Other times, however, law works differently. Sometimes people coordinate on their own but in harmful ways, and law aims to replace a bad equilibrium with a good one.

To illustrate, consider the problem of corruption. Mel works as a clerk for the city government, and he grants businesses permits to operate. Mel has many opportunities for corruption. For example, he could extort businesses by demanding money in exchange for permits. Will Mel act corruptly? He might reason as follows:

> If the other clerks extort businesses, I should extort them. I'll make extra money, and the other clerks will not report me to the police. However, if the other clerks are lawful, then I should be lawful, otherwise the other clerks will report me.

Mel wants to do what the other clerks do. If the other clerks feel the same, then they play a coordination game. They might coordinate on "lawful," meaning no clerk extorts, or they might coordinate on "corrupt," meaning all clerks extort. If they coordinate on "corrupt," the clerks are in a bad equilibrium. Good law moves them to the good equilibrium.

We can deepen our analysis with some graphs.[117] In Figure 13.7, the vertical axis represents payoffs, and the horizontal axis represents the percentage of clerks engaged in corruption. Moving rightward from the origin means a higher percentage of clerks extort businesses. Every individual clerk makes a choice between wrongdoing (extortion) and "rightdoing" (no extortion). Wrongdoing means the clerk makes extra money. Rightdoing means the clerk enjoys a better reputation among businesses and feels no guilt. The curves show the payoffs of making one choice or the other.

[116] *See id.* at 873.

[117] Our analysis draws on Robert Cooter, *Expressive Law and Economics*, 27 J. LEGAL STUD. 585, 589–92 (1998).

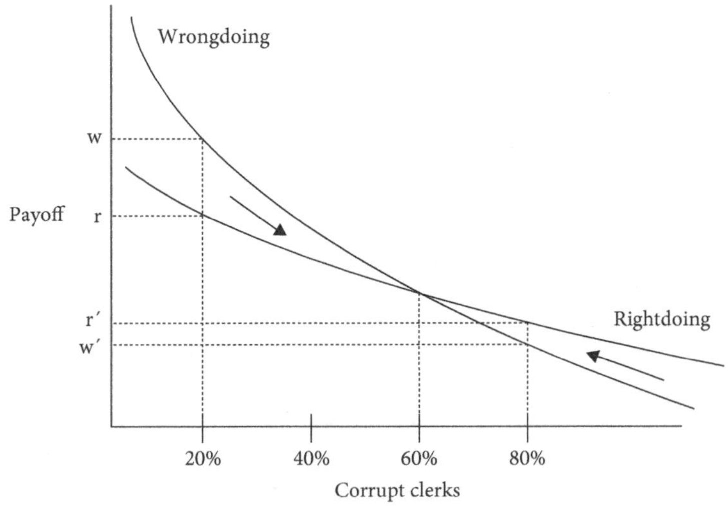

Figure 13.7. Corruption: Interior Equilibrium

Both curves slope downward. Whether an individual chooses wrongdoing or rightdoing, his payoff decreases as the percentage of corrupt clerks increases. To see why, consider the right end of the graph. With so much corruption, few businesses apply for permits. Wrongdoers cannot extort much money and rightdoers cannot develop good reputations if few businesses apply for permits. Without permits, most businesses operate outside of law, limiting their growth and the government's tax revenues for producing public goods like roads and schools. Everyone suffers from a weaker economy.

Mel gets hired as a clerk, and he must choose between wrongdoing and rightdoing. His choice depends on the other clerks, as Figure 13.7 shows. If 20 percent of clerks are corrupt, Mel can choose wrongdoing for a payoff of w or rightdoing for a payoff of r. Since w exceeds r, he will choose wrongdoing. If 80 percent of clerks are corrupt, Mel can choose wrongdoing for a payoff of w' or rightdoing for a payoff of r'. Since r' exceeds w', he will choose rightdoing. To generalize, if less than 60 percent of clerks choose wrongdoing, Mel will choose wrongdoing. His choice increases the percentage of clerks who act corruptly. If more than 60 percent of clerks choose wrongdoing, Mel will choose rightdoing, decreasing the percentage of clerks who act corruptly. The other clerks reason the same way. They settle into an *interior equilibrium* where the curves cross, with 60 percent of clerks doing wrong and the other 40 percent doing right.

In this equilibrium, 60 percent of the city's clerks extort businesses. To improve matters, the city cracks down on extortion by threatening larger punishments. This decreases the payoff from wrongdoing. In Figure 13.8, the wrongdoing curve shifts downward, changing the equilibrium. Now less than 60 percent of clerks extort.

Our analysis assumes a particular set of payoffs. The wrongdoing curve lies above the rightdoing curve to start and, as we move rightward from the origin, eventually falls below the rightdoing curve. This configuration is possible but not certain. One curve could always lie above or below the other at every point. Or, the wrongdoing curve could lie below the rightdoing curve to start and, as we move rightward, eventually move above the rightdoing curve. Figure 13.9 shows this configuration.

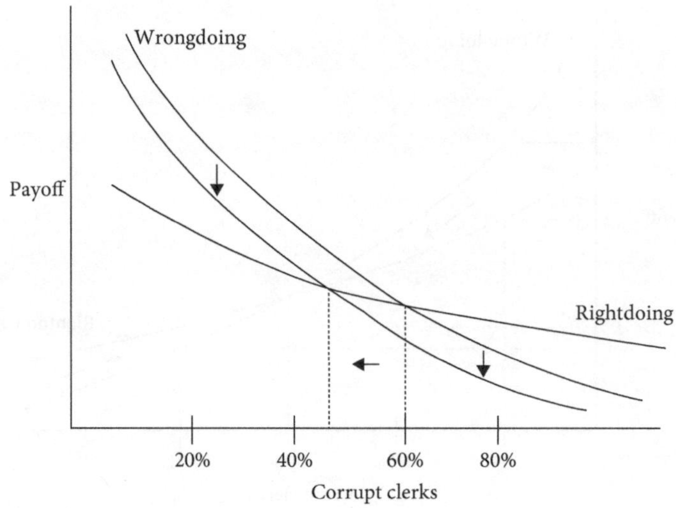

Figure 13.8. Deterring Corruption

Let's reconsider Mel's choices given Figure 13.9. If 20 percent of clerks are corrupt, Mel can choose wrongdoing for a payoff of *w* or rightdoing for a payoff of *r*. He will choose rightdoing. If 80 percent of clerks are corrupt, Mel can choose wrongdoing for a payoff of *w'* or rightdoing for a payoff of *r'*. He will choose wrongdoing. Generalizing, if less than 60 percent of clerks choose wrongdoing, Mel will choose rightdoing, and if more than 60 percent of clerks choose wrongdoing, he will choose wrongdoing. The other clerks reason the same way.

The new payoffs do not push clerks to an interior equilibrium at 60 percent. Rather, the new payoffs push the clerks to *corner equilibria*. They will settle into the "lawful" equilibrium at 0 percent, meaning no one extorts, or the "corrupt" equilibrium at 100 percent, meaning everyone extorts.

Which equilibrium will prevail? Imagine many clerks beginning work simultaneously. No one knows what percentage of clerks will extort businesses because everyone is new. Every clerk makes a guess and decides whether to do right or wrong. If the initial percentage of wrongdoers is less than 60 percent, then every clerk benefits from doing right, and they slide to the "lawful" equilibrium. However, if the initial percentage of wrongdoers exceeds 60 percent, then every clerk benefits from wrongdoing, and they slide to the "corrupt" equilibrium. The clerks' initial choices determine the equilibrium. Their initial choices might depend on character, trust, deterrence, or luck.

Suppose the "corrupt" equilibrium prevails. Every clerk extorts, few businesses apply for permits, and everyone suffers from a weak economy. To improve matters, the city could crack down on extortion by threatening larger punishments. This would shift down the wrongdoing curve. In the previous example, shifting down the wrongdoing curve reduced corruption (see Figure 13.8). However, in Figure 13.9, shifting down the wrongdoing curve by a little would have *no effect* on corruption. Every clerk would continue to extort.

This is a surprising result. Deterrence theory holds that even small increases in expected punishment should decrease wrongdoing, at least by small amounts. However,

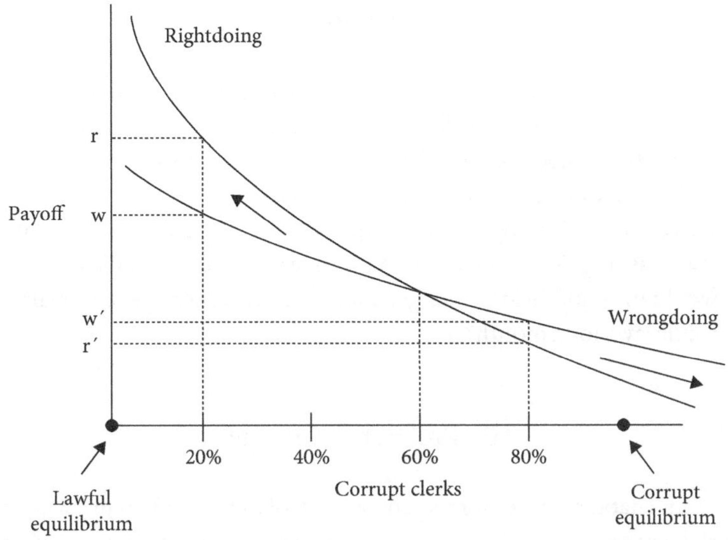

Figure 13.9. Corruption: Corner Equilibria

in a coordination game like the one we study, even large increases in expected punishment do not necessarily change behavior.

To reduce corruption in Figure 13.9, the city must "shock" the system. It must find a way to get more than 40 percent of clerks to switch from acting corruptly to acting lawfully. If the city can achieve this switch, even briefly, the clerks will re-coordinate and slide to the "lawful" equilibrium. Perhaps the city can shock the system with a high-profile prosecution or an aggressive enforcement campaign. Or perhaps the city can shock the system simply by announcing a new anti-extortion law.

In sum, people can coordinate on a bad equilibrium, meaning an equilibrium that makes everyone worse off compared to an alternative equilibrium. Increasing the expected punishment for wrongdoing will not necessarily help (though it will cost the state money). To change equilibria, we must shock the system and induce a critical mass of people to change their behavior together.

Our analysis relies on simple graphs and assumptions, and it yields extreme results: every clerk extorts, or no clerk extorts. Of course, the real world is more complicated. Nevertheless, our analysis captures important features of reality. Many scholars think models like the one we present help explain why corruption is rare in some places and widespread in others.[118] Once you understand corner equilibria and "shocks," you can see why corruption persists. This kind of analysis can illuminate many behaviors beyond corruption, including racial discrimination, segregation in housing, fashion, teenage smoking, and so on.[119]

[118] *See, e.g.*, Ray Fisman & Miriam A. Golden, Corruption: What Everyone Needs to Know (2017); Pranab Bardhan, *Corruption and Development: A Review of Issues*, 35 J. Econ. Lit. 1320 (1997).

[119] *See, e.g.*, Sushil Bikhchandani, David Hirshleifer, & Ivo Welch, *A Theory of Fads, Fashion, Custom, and Cultural Change as Informational Cascades*, 100 J. Pol. Econ. 992 (1992); Thomas C. Schelling, *Dynamic Models of Segregation*, 1 J. Math. Soc. 143 (1971).

Questions

13.22. Assume clerks are in the corrupt equilibrium as depicted in Figure 13.9. The city runs a campaign to eliminate corruption, with cops patrolling the clerks' office. This "shock" causes 30 percent of clerks to stop extorting businesses. Will this reduce corruption in the long term?

13.23. Drivers in Cairo are in a bad equilibrium. Mostly they disobey the traffic laws, causing delays for all. If every driver obeyed the traffic laws for a month, would the equilibrium change? Can the government get every driver to obey traffic laws for a month?

E. Preference Change

We began our chapters on enforcement with Holmes's "bad man" who cares only for "material consequences."[120] Law aims to deter the bad man by changing the consequences of his acts. What if law could change his character instead? Good people do not steal jewelry, poison the air, or extort businesses. If we could make the bad man good, we would not need so much enforcement. Perhaps we could dispense with law altogether. In a famous passage, James Madison wrote, "If men were angels, no government would be necessary."[121]

Let's adapt this idea to the rational actor model of economics. Economists assume that people make choices to satisfy their preferences given their beliefs and constraints. Law can improve behavior by imposing constraints (as with punishments) or changing beliefs (as with road signs). Here we concentrate on the third element of the model, preferences. If law could replace people's selfish preferences with sympathetic or compassionate preferences, fewer bad acts should take place. Good character makes enforcement unnecessary, or so goes the theory.

Can law change people's preferences? According to Aristotle, successful laws "make the citizen good by inculcating habits in them."[122] We can interpret this as a statement about law's capacity to shape preferences. Many scholars have made this kind of argument.[123] In the United States, the Civil Rights Act may have improved attitudes toward women and racial minorities.

Let's assume for the sake of argument that law can change people's preferences. *Should* law change preferences? The answer is more complicated than it seems.[124]

Manipulating preferences seems dangerous, a bit like brainwashing. We should not do it unless we have confidence that the new preferences will be better. To make this determination, we need a method for comparing preferences, but economics does not

[120] Oliver Wendell Holmes, Jr., *The Path of the Law*, 10 Harv. L. Rev. 457, 459 (1897).

[121] The Federalist No. 51, 264 (James Madison) (Ian Shapiro ed., 2009).

[122] Aristotle, Nicomachean Ethics 34 (Martin Ostwald trans., 1962) ("Lawgivers make the citizen good by inculcating habits in them, and this is the aim of every lawgiver; if he does not succeed in doing that, his legislation is a failure.").

[123] *See, e.g.*, Guido Calabresi, Ideals, Beliefs, Attitudes, and the Law: Private Law Perspectives on a Public Law Problem 84 (1985) ("Law . . . is fundamentally concerned with shaping tastes.").

[124] The following discussion draws on Michael D. Gilbert & Andrew T. Hayashi, *Do Good Citizens Need Good Laws? Economics and the Expressive Function*, 22 Theor. Inq. Law 153 (2021).

have one. In general, economics takes preferences as given and tries to satisfy them.[125] It does not assess preferences. Assessing preferences requires a moral theory separate from preference satisfaction. We discussed this problem in the prior chapter. Should a criminal's satisfaction from breaking law count toward social welfare? Answering "yes" seems immoral, but answering "no" implies that we can distinguish good and bad preferences. Economics does not have a way to make the distinction, and philosophers do not agree on one.[126]

This problem might trouble scholars more than lawmakers. Lawmakers might say, "I don't care about your theories, just make people nicer so I can spend less money on enforcement!" Would this work? Again, the answer is complicated.

Reconsider *Boomer*, a case from the prior chapter.[127] Dust from a cement plant harmed the neighbors. The root problem involved a negative externality: the plant's owners did not consider the neighbors' interests when operating. The court made the owners compensate the neighbors for their harm, thus forcing them to internalize their externality. Law corrected the owners' bad incentives, but at a high cost. The case required courthouses, judges, lawyers, evidence, a law on nuisance, and so on.

Law made the owners pay. Suppose instead that law made the owners nice. To make it concrete, suppose law made the owners "harm averse." Harm-averse owners feel bad if they harm the neighbors, even if they pay compensation.

This change in preferences would not solve the problem. To see why, imagine the owners before the preference change. By making them pay compensation, law *transfers* the harm from the neighbors to the owners. Now imagine the owners after the preference change. By making them harm averse, law *creates* harm. Harm aversion makes the owners feel bad, creating a new psychological cost. The owners internalize that psychological cost. However, to get incentives right, they must internalize all harm they cause, including the harm to the neighbors. To internalize the neighbors' harm, the owners must pay compensation.

To clarify, let's describe the parties' costs. The neighbors' costs depend on the harm they suffer and the compensation they receive. The worse the dust, the higher their costs, and the more compensation they receive, the lower their costs. We can express this as follows:

$$\text{Neighbors' costs} = \text{harm} - \text{compensation}$$

The selfish owners' costs depend on the compensation they pay and abatement. Paying compensation increases their costs, and abating dust increases their costs (cutting production, installing filters, etc.).

$$\text{Selfish owners' costs} = \text{compensation} + \text{abatement}$$

[125] Recall that economists usually aim to maximize social welfare, where social welfare is an aggregation of individuals' utility. Individuals' utility depends on the satisfaction of their preferences. Thus, preference satisfaction forms the bedrock of social welfare.

[126] To be clear, many people agree that certain preferences are good and others are bad. However, they disagree on why. Thus we lack consensus on the criteria for sorting good and bad preferences.

[127] Boomer v. Atlantic Cement Co., 257 N.E. 2d 870 (N.Y. 1970).

We can sum the individual costs to get social costs:

Social costs = harm − compensation + compensation + abatement

Compensation just transfers money from one pocket to another, so it cancels out, leaving us with:

Social costs = harm + abatement

To get the owners' incentives right, we want their costs (compensation + abatement) to match social costs (harm + abatement). Law achieves this when the compensation they pay equals the harm they cause.

Let's redo the analysis with harm aversion. The neighbors' costs do not change. Recall that harm-averse owners feel bad if they cause harm, even if they pay compensation.[128] Thus, the harm-averse owners' costs become:

Harm-averse owners' costs = compensation + abatement + psychological cost

Social costs sum the two, yielding:

Social costs = harm − compensation + compensation + abatement + psychological cost

As before, compensation cancels out, leaving:

Social costs = harm + abatement + psychological cost

To get the owners' incentives right, we want their costs (compensation + abatement + psychological cost) to match social costs (harm + abatement + psychological cost). Law achieves this when the compensation they pay equals the harm they cause—the same conclusion as before.

Making the owners harm averse does not solve the enforcement problem. Left to their own devices, nice owners still pollute too much. To create efficient incentives, law must make them pay for the harm they cause. We still need courthouses, judges, lawyers, evidence, a law on nuisance, and so on.

We have considered only one possible change to people's preferences, harm aversion. Many other changes are possible. Will any change solve the problem? To get the owners' incentives right, won't they always have to pay compensation, even if they feel sympathy, guilt, regret, remorse, or whatever else?

[128] Unlike harm-averse owners, "sympathetic" owners feel bad if they cause harm but feel good if they pay compensation. Making the owners sympathetic would not change our central point. *See* Michael D. Gilbert & Andrew T. Hayashi, *Do Good Citizens Need Good Laws? Economics and the Expressive Function*, 22 Theor. Inq. Law 153 (2021).

Questions

13.24. Harm-averse plant owners externalize costs, so they pollute too much. However, they pollute less than selfish plant owners. Explain why. (Hint: look at the cost formulas in the text.)

13.25. By making the owners harm averse, law decreases pollution costs and increases psychological costs. Does this increase or decrease overall social costs? Does economics have an answer?[129]

13.26. Instead of making the owners harm averse, suppose law made the neighbors selfless. Selfless neighbors do not care about pollution. Would selflessness eliminate the negative externality? Should law make people who suffer from pollution, discrimination, coercion, or other wrongs selfless?

IV. Judicial Legitimacy

Judges make decisions on fundamental matters like abortion, religion, national security, and the separation of powers. Sometimes their decisions anger powerful officials. During an election controversy in 2020, President Trump told supporters, "I'm not happy with the Supreme Court," and the Justices seem to "hurt our country."[130] Two centuries earlier in a case called *Worcester v. Georgia*, the Supreme Court held that states cannot regulate Native American lands.[131] The decision angered President Andrew Jackson, who said, "Chief Justice John Marshall has made his decision; now let him enforce it."[132]

We conclude our chapters on enforcement by returning to a perpetual challenge in public law: government compliance. The government must follow the law, including the constitution. When officials violate the law, courts rule against them (or should). How can courts make powerful officials respect their decisions? Courts have pens, not swords or guns. Hamilton called the judiciary the "least dangerous" branch of government because judges have "neither force nor will, but merely judgment."[133]

We have explored this challenge throughout the book. We have shown that low-level officials might comply because courts can (in theory) jail them. We have argued that officials might comply to protect their reputations (remember Secretary Norton). In competitive democracies, governments might comply because of reciprocity. Today's government follows the law in the expectation that tomorrow's competing government will reciprocate. Everyone benefits from the rule of law in the long term, even if it causes frustration in the short term.

Here we study another mechanism of compliance that impassions many lawyers: *judicial legitimacy*.

[129] *See id.*

[130] Natalie Colarossi, *Trump Suggests Supreme Court Is "Going Out of Their Way to Hurt Us" Amid Election Setbacks at D.C. Rally*, Newsweek, Jan. 6, 2021.

[131] 31 U.S. 515 (1832).

[132] This quote is widely attributed to Jackson, but it's unclear if he said it. *See* Edwin A. Miles, *After John Marshall's Decision:* Worcester v. Georgia *and the Nullification Crisis*, 39 J. So. Hist. 519, 519 n.1 (1973).

[133] The Federalist No. 78, at 392 (Alexander Hamilton) (Ian Shapiro ed., 2009).

A. Defining Legitimacy

According to Justice O'Connor, the Supreme Court's power lies "in its legitimacy, a product of substance and perception that shows itself in the people's acceptance of the Judiciary."[134] Her argument puts legitimacy at the center of compliance. What is legitimacy? Scholars use the term in different ways. "Legal" legitimacy means a court makes legally correct decisions, while "moral" legitimacy means a court makes morally correct decisions.[135] These forms of legitimacy might promote compliance, perhaps by fostering a duty to obey.[136]

We concentrate on another form of legitimacy, "sociological." Sociological legitimacy relates to public support.[137] When people disapprove of the court's performance, its sociological legitimacy suffers, and vice versa.[138] Apparently individual cases can affect the court's sociological legitimacy. To illustrate, in *National Federation of Independent Business v. Sebelius*, the Supreme Court upheld a controversial part of the Affordable Care Act (a "liberal" statute).[139] The Court's sociological legitimacy grew among liberals but suffered among conservatives.[140]

Sociological legitimacy can promote compliance by government actors, especially elected officials. If a court enjoys popular support, defying it comes at a political price. When the Supreme Court ordered President Nixon to release his tapes, Nixon had to comply. When the Court resolved the 2000 presidential election in favor of Bush, Gore could not resist. In both cases, public pressure acted as an enforcement mechanism.[141] Flouting the Supreme Court can become a focal point that generates a political cost.

Some judges worry about legitimacy, perhaps because they worry about enforcement. Justice Stevens wrote that *Bush v. Gore* would undercut "the Nation's confidence in the judge as an impartial guardian of the rule of law."[142] Justice Breyer worried that

[134] Planned Parenthood of Se. Pa. v. Casey, 505 U.S. 833, 865 (1992).

[135] *See generally* RICHARD H. FALLON, JR., LAW AND LEGITIMACY IN THE SUPREME COURT (2018).

[136] *See, e.g.*, MAX WEBER, ECONOMY AND SOCIETY: AN OUTLINE OF INTERPRETIVE SOCIOLOGY, VOL. 1 31 (Guenther Roth & Claus Wittich eds., 1978) (arguing that "belief in the existence of a legitimate order" can guide behavior and the "belief in legality" is the "most common form of legitimacy").

[137] Scholars divide sociological legitimacy into "diffuse" and "specific" categories. Diffuse legitimacy grows from commitments to democracy and the rule of law, whereas specific legitimacy grows from satisfaction with a court's performance. *See* James L. Gibson & Michael J. Nelson, *The Legitimacy of the US Supreme Court: Conventional Wisdoms and Recent Challenges Thereto*, 10 ANN. REV. L. SOC. SCI. 201, 204–05 (2014). We concentrate on specific legitimacy.

[138] Our brief discussion masks some complications. Some research suggests that diffuse and specific legitimacy are independent, while other research shows that decreases in specific legitimacy reduce diffuse legitimacy, either gradually or immediately. *See generally id.*; Gregory A. Caldeira & James L. Gibson, *The Etiology of Public Support for the Supreme Court*, 36 AM. J. POL. SCI. 635 (1992); Vanessa A. Baird, *Building Institutional Legitimacy: The Role of Procedural Justice*, 54 POL. RES. Q. 333 (2001); Brandon L. Bartels & Christopher D. Johnston, *On the Ideological Foundations of Supreme Court Legitimacy in the American Public*, 57 AM. J. POL. SCI. 184 (2013).

[139] 567 U.S. 519 (2012).

[140] *See* Dino P. Christenson & David M. Glick, *Chief Justice Roberts's Health Care Decision Disrobed: The Microfoundations of the Supreme Court's Legitimacy*, 59 AM. J. POL. SCI. 403, 415–16 (2015).

[141] *See* Diana Kapiszewski, Gordon Silverstein, & Robert A. Kagan, *Conclusion*, *in* CONSEQUENTIAL COURTS: JUDICIAL ROLES IN GLOBAL PERSPECTIVE 398, 402–03 (Diana Kapiszewski, Gordon Silverstein, & Robert A. Kagan eds., 2013). *See also* Clifford James Carrubba, *A Model of the Endogenous Development of Judicial Institutions in Federal and International Systems*, 71 J. POL. 55 (2009); Tom S. Clark, *The Separation of Powers, Court Curbing, and Judicial Legitimacy*, 53 AM. J. POL. SCI. 971 (2009).

[142] Bush v. Gore, 531 U.S. 98, 129 (2000) (Stevens, J., dissenting).

the case could undermine "the public's confidence in the Court."[143] In the case about the Affordable Care Act mentioned earlier, Chief Justice Roberts allegedly switched his vote to protect the Court's reputation.[144]

In sum, sociological legitimacy implies public support, and public support improves compliance with court orders. How can judges gain public support? Making popular decisions seems like a natural method. Sometimes, however, judges do not have this choice. Sometimes the popular decision and the lawful decision conflict.

Questions

13.27. Can a court without moral legitimacy have legal legitimacy? Can a court without legal legitimacy have sociological legitimacy?

13.28. The Supreme Court has nine Justices. Individual Justices can make choices to increase the Court's legitimacy. Does any individual Justice internalize the full benefit of such choices? Is judicial legitimacy a public good?

B. The Passive Virtues

In the 1950s, Ruby Elaine, a white woman, married Han Say Naim, an Asian man. They wed in North Carolina but settled in Virginia. When Ruby sought to annul the marriage a year later, state law supported her. Virginia's law prohibited interracial marriage. Her husband opposed the annulment, and federal law supported him. The Supreme Court had just decided *Brown v. Board of Education*, invalidating laws that segregated public schools by race.[145] If states could not discriminate by race in school, presumably they could not discriminate by race in marriage. In *Naim v. Naim*, the Supreme Court faced competing pressures.[146] Laws prohibiting interracial marriage were probably unconstitutional under *Brown*. However, they were widespread and popular.[147]

When law and politics collide, judges face a dilemma. They can make a principled decision that provokes powerful actors, or they can make an unprincipled decision that appeases them. Neither option is attractive. The first weakens the courts by inviting backlash. In *Naim*, the Supreme Court could invalidate the racial marriage law—and enrage governors, legislators, state courts, and possibly millions of voters. This could threaten the Court's sociological legitimacy. The second option, making an unprincipled decision, weakens the law. Upholding Virginia's racist statute would undermine *Brown* and threaten the Court's legal and moral legitimacy.

[143] *Id.* at 157 (Breyer, J., dissenting).

[144] *See* Tara Leigh Grove, *The Supreme Court's Legitimacy Dilemma*, 132 HARV. L. REV. 2240, 2243 (2019) (book review).

[145] 347 U.S. 483 (1954).

[146] 350 U.S. 891 (1955). *See also* Naim v. Naim, 87 S.E. 2d 749 (Va. 1955).

[147] MICHAEL J. KLARMAN, FROM JIM CROW TO CIVIL RIGHTS 321 (2004) ("[O]pinion polls in the 1950s revealed that over 90 percent of whites, even outside the South, opposed interracial marriage.").

A scholar named Alexander Bickel concentrated on a third option: avoid the dispute.[148] Judges can use legal maneuvers to sidestep cases like *Naim*. For example, federal courts in the United States might decide that a plaintiff does not have "standing" or the issue is not "ripe" for consideration. If the case presents a "political question," then the legislature and executive must resolve it, not the courts. Standing, ripeness, and political questions involve jurisdiction. If these requirements are not satisfied, federal courts lack jurisdiction and cannot hear the case.

When judges avoid controversial cases, they exercise *passive virtues*.[149] According to Bickel, passive virtues offer an escape from some difficult cases. Judges can stand on principle—"we lack jurisdiction"—without taking a position on polarizing issues. The Supreme Court exercised passive virtues in *Naim*. The Justices dismissed the case with a single paragraph, writing:

> The inadequacy of the record . . . and the failure of the parties to bring here all questions relevant to the disposition of the case, prevents the constitutional issue of the validity of the Virginia statute on miscegenation tendered here being considered in clean cut and concrete form, unclouded by such problems.[150]

In addition to miscegenation, the Court has avoided controversial cases on abortion, LGBTQ discrimination, English-only laws, the Vietnam War, and so on.[151]

Some scholars favor the passive virtues, while others do not.[152] Critics argue that judges lack legal authority to avoid cases for strategic reasons. They argue that avoidance causes injustice, as when the Supreme Court refused to strike down Virginia's racist statute.[153] They argue that avoiding cases might decrease sociological legitimacy, not increase it. In *Naim*, the question was whether people can marry whomever they love, regardless of race. How can avoiding a question so fundamental make courts *more* legitimate?

For better or for worse, courts worldwide exercise passive virtues.[154] Bickel identified an important phenomenon. In the next section, we use tools from this book to analyze it.

[148] Alexander Bickel, The Least Dangerous Branch (2d ed. 1986). Bickel did not use the term "judicial legitimacy" often, but we can understand him in these terms. *See id.* at 30; Alexander M. Bickel, The Supreme Court and the Idea of Progress 90 (1978) ("The Supreme Court's judgments may be put forth as universally prescriptive; but they actually become so only when they gain widespread assent. . . . [T]he Court's judgments need the assent and the cooperation first of the political institutions, and ultimately of the people.").

[149] Alexander Bickel, The Least Dangerous Branch 111–98 (2d ed. 1986).

[150] Naim v. Naim, 350 U.S. 891 (1955) (internal quotation marks and citations omitted). *See also* Doris Marie Provine, Case Selection in the United States Supreme Court 59–60 (1980) (reporting that Justice Burton's clerk hesitated to recommend taking *Naim* because of "the feeling that we ought to give the present fire a chance to burn down").

[151] *See* Stenehjem v. MKB Mgmt. Corp., 136 S. Ct. 981 (2016) (abortion); Baker v. Nelson, 409 U.S. 810 (1972) (discrimination); Lisa A. Kloppenberg, Playing It Safe: How the Supreme Court Sidesteps Hard Cases and Stunts the Development of Law 17–33 (2001) (English-only law); Rodric B. Schoen, *A Strange Silence: Vietnam and the Supreme Court*, 33 Washburn L.J. 275, 278–303 (1994) (war).

[152] *See, e.g.*, Jan G. Deutsch, *Neutrality, Legitimacy and the Supreme Court: Some Interactions Between Law and Political Science*, 20 Stan. L. Rev. 169 (1968).

[153] The Supreme Court struck down bans on interracial marriage in *Loving v. Virginia*, 388 U.S. 1 (1967).

[154] *See* Erin F. Delaney, *Analyzing Avoidance: Judicial Strategy in Comparative Perspective*, 66 Duke L.J. 1 (2016).

Questions

13.29. California law required public school students to recite the pledge of allegiance, which includes the phrase "under God." Michael Newdow claimed that the pledge amounted to religious indoctrination of his daughter by the state. The Supreme Court held that Newdow lacked standing because his ex-wife had legal custody of their daughter.[155] Since Newdow lacked standing, the Court dismissed his case. The Justices did not decide if the pledge violates the freedom of religion. Did the court exercise passive virtues?

13.30. In *Texas v. Johnson*, the Supreme Court held that people have a constitutional right to burn the American flag in protest.[156] The decision generated controversy that lasted for years. Should the Court have exercised passive virtues and avoided the issue? In answering, consider what Justice Kennedy wrote about the case: "[W]e are presented with a clear and simple statute to be judged against a pure command of the Constitution. The outcome can be laid at no door but ours."[157]

13.31. Bickel worried about the "countermajoritarian difficulty," which arises when unelected judges strike down laws enacted by democratic majorities. Do you think judges routinely frustrate majority will?[158]

C. Modeling Compliance

Let's summarize the discussion so far. We began by asking how courts can get powerful officials to comply with their decisions. Public support offers one answer. Disobeying a popular court can impose a political cost on legislators and executives, especially in a democracy. How can a court generate public support? Among lawyers, a court might generate support by making legally correct decisions. However, most citizens are not lawyers, and nonlawyers often cannot distinguish between legally correct and erroneous decisions. To generate support among the general public, a court might make popular decisions, or at least decisions that most citizens consider reasonable. This strategy might work in many cases, but not all. Cases like *Naim* pit law against politics. A court can make a legally correct decision or a popular decision, but not both. Bickel encouraged courts to avoid such cases.

We can sharpen these ideas using tools from earlier chapters. Figure 13.10 depicts a spectrum of legal doctrines, with the left side corresponding to politically liberal doctrines and the right side corresponding to politically conservative doctrines. For example, in a case about separation between church and state, the court might set doctrine on the left (liberal) end permitting almost no government support for religion, or the court might set doctrine on the right (conservative) end permitting substantial government support for religion. The point *L* indicates the legislature's preferred doctrine, and *E* indicates the

[155] Elk Grove Unified Sch. Dist. v. Newdow, 542 U.S. 1 (2004).
[156] 491 U.S. 397 (1989).
[157] *Id.* at 420 (Kennedy, J., concurring).
[158] *See, e.g.*, Jonathan P. Kastellec, *Empirically Evaluating the Countermajoritarian Difficulty: Public Opinion, State Policy, and Judicial Review before* Roe v. Wade, 4 J.L. & COURTS 1 (2016).

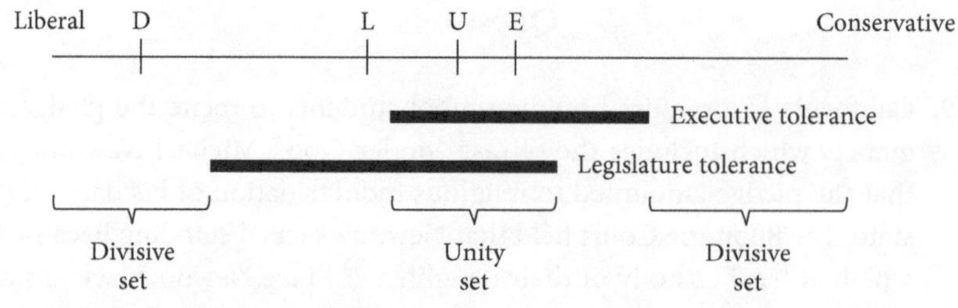

Figure 13.10. Cases and Compliance

executive's preferred doctrine. (Ignore *D* and *U* for now.) All actors prefer doctrine closer to their ideal points.

If the court decided the case at *E* or *L*, the corresponding actor would surely comply. However, the court is not so constrained. The legislature and executive have tolerance intervals indicated with horizontal bars. If the court decides in a tolerance interval, the corresponding actor will comply. To illustrate, suppose the court sets the doctrine at a point just left of *E*. This outcome does not match the executive's ideal point, but it lies within the executive's tolerance interval, so the executive will comply. The executive will not attempt to provide more support for religion than the court's doctrine allows.

The width of the tolerance intervals depends in part on public support—in other words, on the court's sociological legitimacy. If the court enjoys a high level of legitimacy, then disobedience would be especially costly for the executive and legislature. Those actors will tolerate large deviations from their preferred outcomes to avoid paying the political cost. Thus, the tolerance intervals are wide. If the court has little legitimacy, the tolerance intervals are narrow.

Suppose the court gets a case about religion. In Figure 13.10, *U* represents the legally correct answer. *U* lies within both actors' tolerance intervals. So the court can decide the case at *U*, and the executive and legislature will comply. This represents a *unity case*.[159] In a unity case, law and politics align. The court can make the legally correct decision and ensure compliance. To generalize, any case whose correct resolution lies in the "unity set" is a unity case.

To deepen the analysis, suppose the case does not have a single, correct outcome at *U*. The legal materials give judges discretion to set the doctrine anywhere between *U* and *E*. Again, this presents a unity case. If the court selects an outcome in that range, it will ensure compliance and make a legally permissible decision.

Now change the scenario. The court gets a case about religion, and *D* represents the legally correct answer. In Figure 13.10, *D* lies outside the tolerance intervals. If the court decides the case at *D*, the executive and legislature will not comply. For example, they might continue to subsidize religious schools, even though the doctrine *D* prohibits it. This represents a *divisive* case. To generalize, any case whose legally correct resolution lies in the "divisive set" is a divisive case.

We have translated some of the debate about legitimacy and the passive virtues into a spatial model. In Figure 13.10, the court should decide unity cases and avoid divisive cases.

[159] *See* Michael D. Gilbert & Mauricio A. Guim, *Active Virtues*, 98 WASH. U.L. REV. 857, 860 (2021).

Now let's extend the analysis.[160] The tolerance intervals incorporate the political costs to government actors of defying the court. The political costs depend in part on the court's sociological legitimacy, meaning the public's satisfaction with the court's performance. The political costs might also depend on the history of compliance. Suppose the executive and legislature routinely disobey the court. One more act of disobedience probably will not cost them much. It probably will not cause significant harm to their reputations, and importantly, it probably cannot serve as a focal point for public resistance. If citizens did not coordinate against the state's disobedience before, why would they coordinate now? Conversely, suppose the government has a long history of compliance. The court makes decisions, and the government complies. A sudden act of noncompliance could cost the government a lot. Officials' reputations would suffer. Defying the court could become a focal point, causing citizens to coordinate against the state.

We can apply this idea to Figure 13.10. If the court decides a case in the unity set, the government will comply. By complying today, the government increases the cost to itself of noncompliance tomorrow. Thus, the tolerance intervals grow slightly wider. Wider tolerance intervals imply a wider unity set, giving the court more flexibility. If the court makes more decisions in the unity set, the government will comply, and the unity set will widen further. Eventually the unity set will become so wide that the government will obey nearly any decision.

Imagine the opposite case. If the court decides in the divisive set, the government will not comply. By disobeying today, the government decreases the cost to itself of disobeying tomorrow. The tolerance intervals shrink, and the unity set narrows. The court has less flexibility. Eventually the unity set will disappear, meaning the court cannot secure full compliance with any decision.

We can relate these ideas to the passive virtues. Deciding a divisive case today weakens the court tomorrow by shrinking the unity set. Instead of deciding the case, the court could avoid it. Avoiding the case might decrease the court's sociological legitimacy (as well as its legal and moral legitimacy). Thus, avoiding the case might shrink the unity set. If deciding a divisive case would shrink the unity set by more than avoiding it, then the court should exercise passive virtues, and vice versa.

These ideas can help explain judicial power.[161] Established in 1991, the First Russian Constitutional Court formally enjoyed independence and jurisdiction over many matters. However, the court lacked sociological legitimacy. In a 1993 survey, only 10 percent of Russians trusted the court.[162] The court immediately made controversial decisions on executive power and federalism. Two years after the court's creation, and after the government ignored some of its decisions, President Boris Yeltsin suspended it. The Second Russian Constitutional Court has had more success. Rather than "itching for a political fight," the court focused on "safer" issues.[163] As one Justice put it, the court had to "find a stable niche in the state machinery" by developing its "prestige

[160] This discussion draws on Lee Epstein, Jack Knight, & Olga Shvetsova, *The Role of Constitutional Courts in the Establishment and Maintenance of Democratic Systems of Government*, 35 Law & Soc'y Rev. 117 (2001).

[161] *See id.* at 135–53 (describing the history of the Russian Constitutional Court).

[162] *See id.* at 144.

[163] *Id.* at 152–54.

and status."[164] The court has functioned since 1995. The story of Russia's Constitutional Court is consistent with the ideas developed here.

In sum, powerful officials comply with judicial decisions when the political costs of noncompliance are high. Courts can increase the political costs of noncompliance by making "safe" decisions that governments will obey—in the figure, decisions in the unity set. By generating a history of compliance, courts make noncompliance costlier. As the costs of noncompliance increase, the court has more discretion. Eventually the court can make the legally correct decision in all or nearly all cases.

According to this account, courts build power over time. To accomplish this, they might avoid important issues for a while, like limits on executive authority. Some people might reject this approach. They might say that courts should apply law correctly, not strategize about power. Applying law faithfully, regardless of whether the government will comply, might build a court's legal legitimacy (and perhaps its moral legitimacy). But applying law faithfully cannot by itself cause compliance, not when the law strikes at the core of state power or conflicts with popular will. What good is law without compliance? Who wants a court that cannot constrain the state?

Questions

13.32. A court gets a case whose legally correct resolution lies in the executive's tolerance interval but not the legislature's tolerance interval. Should the court decide the case?

13.33. A court could ensure compliance by the government in every case by ignoring the law and making decisions that please the executive and legislature. Would this increase the court's legitimacy?

13.34. The U.S. Supreme Court makes important decisions about constitutional law and government power. Unlike other federal courts, the Supreme Court has almost complete control over its docket, meaning it can refuse to hear cases. If you were a judge trying to build your court's legitimacy, would you want docket control? Should constitutional designers give the high court docket control?

13.35. We imagine a court deciding cases in the unity set and avoiding cases in the divisive set. In reality, judges have imperfect information. They do not know the exact boundaries of the sets, so they might make errors. Does the risk of error mean courts should not exercise passive virtues? Does docket control decrease the risk of error?

Active Virtues

In the United States, judges wait passively for cases to arrive at their doors. In an interview, Justice Scalia blamed *Bush v. Gore* on the candidate Al Gore, who initiated the litigation. The Supreme Court, Scalia said, "didn't go looking for trouble."[165]

[164] *Id.* at 153.

[165] Lesley Stahl, *Justice Scalia on the Record*, CBS News, Apr. 27, 2008, https://www.cbsnews.com/news/justice-scalia-on-the-record/. Gore initiated the litigation in state court. Bush appealed to the U.S. Supreme Court.

This passive stance is deeply ingrained in American jurisprudence. Elsewhere in the world, however, judges behave differently.

Consider some examples. In Colombia, an employee sued his employer over an injury at work. Neither party appealed the trial court's decision, meaning no one asked a higher court to intervene. Nevertheless, Colombia's Constitutional Court seized the case and made an important decision on the right to health.[166] In Pakistan, "suo moto" jurisdiction allows courts to initiate cases. When oil stoves killed people in their homes, a Pakistani judge initiated a case against the manufacturer.[167] The Supreme Court of India converts postcards and even newspaper articles into cases. The Court has made important precedents on prison conditions, due process, and other matters through this process.[168]

Why do these courts initiate cases? Why do they "go looking for trouble"? Here is a hypothesis. To build and sustain their legitimacy, courts exercise passive virtues and avoid some divisive cases. But they do not stop there. Courts also seek unity cases. When courts initiate unity cases to enhance their power, they exercise *active virtues*.[169] In Figure 13.10, courts find disputes in the unity set, convert them into cases, and make decisions that generate compliance.

New or developing courts might exercise active virtues as they struggle to build public support.[170] Once they have support and a record of compliance, they can become passive. Perhaps the U.S. Supreme Court fits this model. Today the Justices wait passively for cases, but they didn't always. In the Court's early years, the Justices "rode circuit." They served on the high court in Washington and traveled to hear cases as members of circuit courts. Under the Judiciary Act of 1802, circuit courts had only two judges, a local judge and the traveling Justice. When the two judges disagreed about a case, they "certified their division," which sent the case to the Supreme Court. Thus, Justices could manufacture ties on circuit courts to create cases for themselves on the Supreme Court. According to the legal historian G. Edward White, the Justices did exactly this.[171] They used the certificate of division to "expand their docket" and raise their Court's "stature" by seeking "numerous and important questions."[172]

166 *See* Corte Constitucional [C.C.] [Constitutional Court], junio 12, 2017, M.P: Carlos Bernal Pulido, Sentencia T-380/17, Gaceta de la Corte Constitucional (G.C.C.) T-6.033.140 (Colom.).

167 Mansoor Hassan Khan, Public Interest Litigation: Growth of the Concept and Its Meaning in Pakistan 72–74 (1993).

168 *See* Jamie Cassels, *Judicial Activism and Public Interest Litigation in India: Attempting the Impossible*, 37 Am. J. Comp. L. 495 (1989).

169 *See* Michael D. Gilbert & Mauricio A. Guim, *Active Virtues*, 98 Wash. U.L. Rev. 857, 860 (2021).

170 According to scholars, the activist litigation in India represents an "attempt to seek . . . legitimation of judicial power." Upendra Baxi, *Taking Suffering Seriously: Social Action Litigation in the Supreme Court of India*, 1 Third World Stud. 107, 113 (1985). *See also* Shyam Divan, *Public Interest Litigation*, *in* The Oxford Handbook of The Indian Constitution 662, 678 (Sujit Choudhry et al. eds., 2016) ("Indian courts have set apart judicial resources to foster [public interest litigation] to a point where this jurisdiction defines public perception of the higher judiciary . . . Their decisions generally add to the prestige of the judiciary[.]").

171 G. Edward White, Law in American History, Volume I 220–22 (2012).

172 *Id.* at 222.

Conclusion

To deter lawbreaking, increase the expected punishment. The formula seems simple, but it involves many details. The probability of punishment depends on whether officers can search homes and cellphones. It depends on whether prosecutors can use evidence in court and overcome the standard of proof. Every lever can offset another. If courts raise the standard of proof, which increases the cost of enforcement, legislators can adopt insincerely strict laws, lowering the cost of enforcement. We studied these topics in the first half of the chapter. In the second half we looked beyond deterrence. Law operates through many channels. It can improve behavior by providing information and coordinating action. It can trigger informal sanctions, as when violating law harms a person's reputation. Sometimes courts secure compliance through informal sanctions. The Supreme Court cannot "punish" the President or Congress for flouting its decisions, but voters can. Powerful courts have sociological legitimacy. Courts do not always develop such legitimacy by happenstance. Recall Chief Justice Marshall's statement: "It is emphatically the province and duty of the judicial department to say what the law is."[173] To "say what the law is," judges might think strategically about when to speak.

[173] Marbury v. Madison, 5 U.S. 137, 177 (1803).

Index

For the benefit of digital users, indexed terms that span two pages (e.g., 52–53) may, on occasion, appear on only one of those pages.

Tables and figures are indicated by *t* and *f* following the page number

Printed in the USA/Agawam, MA
February 13, 2023

805646.030